A Text Book on

Industrial Engineering, Robotics and Mechatronics

Useful for IAS / GATE / ESE / PSUs and other competitive examinations

Dr. Swadesh Kumar Singh
B.Tech. AMU Aligarh, Gold Medalist
M. Tech. and Ph.D. from IIT Delhi
Ex. IES officer, Govt. of India
Professor, GRIET, Hyderabad

Dr. Rajesh Purohit
M. Tech. and Ph.D. from IIT Delhi
Associate Professor, MANIT, Bhopal

MADE EASY Publications
Corporate Office: 44-A/4, Kalu Sarai (Near Hauz Khas Metro Station), New Delhi-110016
E-mail: infomep@madeeasy.in
Contact: 011-45124660, 8860378007
Visit us at: www.madeeasypublications.org

A text book on Industrial Engineering, Robotics and Mechatronics

© Copyright, by MADE EASY Publications
All rights reserved. No part of this publication may be reproduced, stored in or introduced into a retrieval system, or transmitted in any form or by any means (electronic, mechanical, photocopying, recording or otherwise), without the prior permission of the above mentioned publisher of this book.

First Edition: 2016

Reprint: 2019

MADE EASY PUBLICATIONS has taken due care in collecting the data and providing the solutions, before publishing this book. Inspite of this, if any inaccuracy or printing error occurs then MADE EASY PUBLICATIONS owes no responsibility. We will be grateful if you could point out any such error. Your suggestions will be appreciated.

FOREWORD

In my long teaching career I have come across many other fellow teachers but Dr. Swadesh Singh is unique. He has the rare combination of being Ex-IES officer in Govt. of India, a Ph.D from reputed Indian Institute of Technology Delhi, a Young Scientist award winner and a Career Award winner for teaching. As a teacher, he is one of those who really tries to understand the students from their perspective and helps them. He has a penchant for guiding and counseling students in choosing their careers and preparing them for their competitive exams. Many students have benefited from him and holds regard for him even years after graduating. Dr. Singh's book on Production Technology has become popular and is a standard among the students who are top rankers in competitive exams like GATE, CIVIL SERVICES etc. and the present book on Industrial engineering should stand testimony to the expertise of Dr. Singh's in presenting in a compact book what is just appropriate for preparing for such exams.

This book is a must-have for those who are serious in finding success in competitive exams.

Prof. P. S. Raju
Director
GRIET, Hyderabad, India

PREFACE

After the overwhelming response of my first book on Production Engineering, I thought of writing another book on the core subject of Industrial Engineering. After teaching for various competitive examinations for about 16 years, I found that although there are so many books available on the fundamentals of Industrial Engineering but there is no book available for competitive examinations. The book which student can have and crack any question that appears in examination like GATE, IES and other public sector examination. So in the present book my effort is to teach fundamentals by problem solving so that students can understand well. Apart from the solved example-problems, numerous objective-type practice problems from various competitive examinations are given, along with the answer keys. The first edition of this book I released in 2011. Since most of the work including the typesetting, editing and so on was carried out by me, there were many grammatical mistakes in that edition. While teaching and students solving the problem we have corrected the text thoroughly and I have also added some more relevant text in each topic making it more suitable for the competitive examinations. Along with Dr. Rajesh Purohit of MANIT Bhopal, I have added Robotics and Mechatronics to make the book suitable for IES and other competitive examinations.

I express my gratitude to my spiritual teacher who has given me inspiration to write this book. Every subject matter can be learned through the medium of a teacher only. He thought me both his precept and by his personal example how to be sincere at work and what is good for me and how can I help others in a genuine way.

The authors are thankful to Sunil Kumar, Deepen Banoriya, Utkarsh Pandey, Bhrant Kumar, Harish, Limbadri, Prudvi, Gangadhar and Srinivasu for taking pain in correcting the manuscript many times. We also thank MADE EASY proof editing staff and CMD Sri B. Singh for their full support in publishing this book.

We hope that aspirants of scoring high in GATE, ESE, IAS, PSU and any competitive exams find this book as a helpful aid in their preparations.

Dr. Swadesh Kumar Singh

Dr. Rajesh Purohit

CONTENTS

CHAPTER 1

Graphical Method

1.1 INTRODUCTION

Optimization is a process of either maximizing or minimizing a specific quantity called objective which depends upon a finite number of variables. These variables can be altogether independent or related to each other. Depending upon the availability of facilities in the department or plant, constraints will be formed. Graphical Method of solving these problems is limited to two dimensions only and the method can be understood by the following examples

Example: 1.1

Assume that the following specify a generalized linear programming problem:

$$\text{Max } Z = 45x + 40y$$

Subject to $2x + y \le 90$

$x + 2y \le 80$

$x + y \le 50$

$x, y \ge 0$

Solve it by using Graphical Method and slope method.

Solution:

(a) The equation of lines can be changed into this form

$$2x + y \le 90 \Rightarrow \frac{x}{45} + \frac{y}{90} \le 1$$

$$x + 2y \le 80 \Rightarrow \frac{x}{80} + \frac{y}{40} \le 1$$

$$x + y \le 50 \Rightarrow \frac{x}{50} + \frac{y}{50} \le 1$$

(b) Now plot these lines on the graph

(c) Mark the feasible region as shown in above graph

(d) Locate the end points of feasible region as *O*, *A*, *B*, *C*, *D*

(e) Find 'x' and 'y' coordinates of those points as shown below:

Fig. 1.1

$$Z = 45x + 40y$$

'O' $\to$ (0, 0) $\quad Z_{\text{at 'O'}} = 45(0) + 40(0) = 0$

'A' $\to$ (0, 40) $\quad Z_{\text{at 'A'}} = 45(0) + 40(40) = 1600$

'B' $\to$ (20, 30) $\quad Z_{\text{at 'B'}} = 45(20) + 40(30) = 2100$

'C' $\to$ (40, 10) $\quad Z_{\text{at 'C'}} = 45(40) + 40(10) = 2200 \to$ optimum point

'D' $\to$ (45, 0) $\quad Z_{\text{at 'D'}} = 45(45) + 40(10) = 2025$

(f) To find point of maxima directly we need to understand the following theory:
- Initially the objective function line is drawn passing through the origin, the moment the objective function line first touches the feasible region or feasible point that is the point of minima.
- The farthest point at which objective function line is touching the feasible region is the point of maxima.

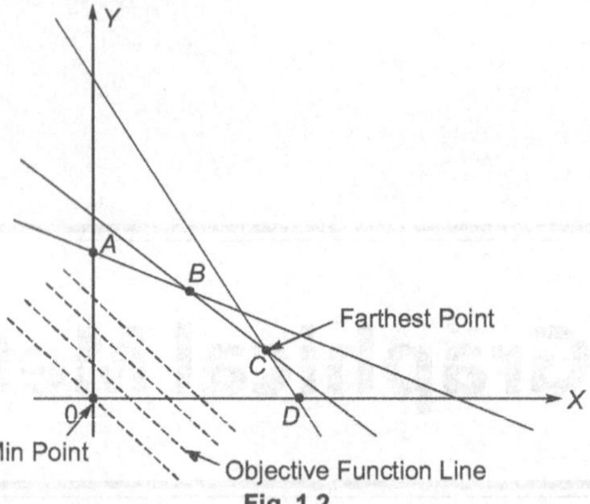

Fig. 1.2

(g) % Utilization of machines at the optimum point:
Now optimum point is (40,10) so,
Utilization of machine 1 is

$$2x + y = 2(40) + 10 = 90 \leq 90$$

$\therefore$ % Utilization of machine 1 is $\frac{90}{90} \times 100 = 100\%$

Utilization of machine 2 is $x + 2y = (40) + 2(10) = 60 \leq 80$

$\therefore$ % Utilization of machine 2 is $\frac{60}{80} \times 100 = 75\%$

Utilization of machine 3 is $x + y = 40 + 10 = 50 \leq 50$

$\therefore$ % Utilization of machine 3 is $\frac{50}{50} \times 100 = 100\%$

Slope Method:

Slope of the objective function $(m) = -\frac{45}{40}$

Slope of first constraint $(m_1) = -2$

Slope of second constraint $(m_2) = -\frac{1}{2}$

Slope of third constraint $(m_3) = -1$

As m lies between m_3 and m_1 the optimum point will be the intersection of line (1) and (3).

Note: If $m_3 < m_2 < m_1$ and
If $m \in (m_1, \infty)$ then optimum point will be the intersection of line (1) with y axis.
But if $m \in (0, m_3)$ then optimum point will be the intersection of line (3) with x axis.
(It should be noted that in certain cases this method may not give the right answer because in certain cases the point may not appear in the feasible region).

Example: 1.2

A certain company produces tea trays and ash trays out of sheet metal. Following data is given on capacity availability and economics of each product:

Department	Time Taken for		Total time
	Ash Tray	Tea Tray	
Stamping	10 sec	20 sec	30000 sec
Forming	15 sec	5 sec	30000 sec

Determine the optimum production schedule. Each ash tray contributes ₹ 20 to the gross profit and each tea tray contributes ₹ 30 to the gross profit. Total daily fixed costs amount to ₹ 45,000. Solve this problem graphically what is the maximum net profit per day at the optimum production level, including the effect of fixed cost.

Solution:

Let number of ash trays = $x \rightarrow$ Profit (₹ 20)
Number of tea trays = $y \rightarrow$ Profit (₹ 30)
Fixed cost = 45,000
$\therefore$ Objective function (max. Z) = $20x + 30y - 45{,}000$

For stamping machine $\Rightarrow 10x + 20y \le 30{,}000 \Rightarrow \frac{x}{3000} + \frac{y}{1500} \le 1$

For forming machine $\Rightarrow 15x + 5y \le 30{,}000 \Rightarrow \frac{x}{2000} + \frac{y}{6000} \le 1$

$$O\,(0, 0) \Rightarrow Z_{\text{at } O} = -45{,}000$$

$$A(2000,0) \Rightarrow Z_{\text{at } A} = 5{,}000$$

$$B(1800,600) \Rightarrow Z_{\text{at } B} = 9{,}000$$

$$C(0,1500) \Rightarrow Z_{\text{at } C} = 0$$

$\therefore$ ₹ 9000 is the net profit per day

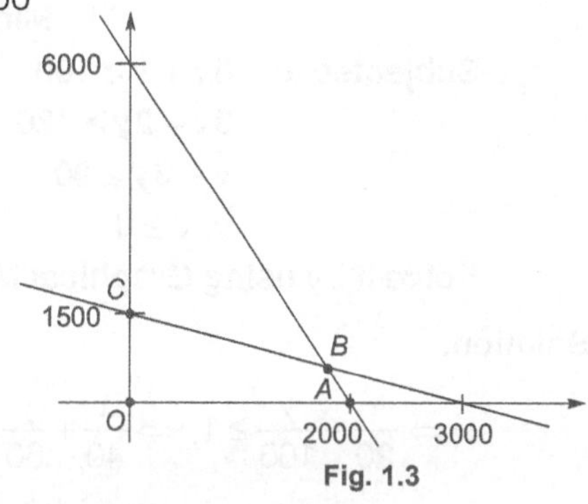

Fig. 1.3

Example: 1.3

Assume that the following specify a generalized linear programming problem:

$$\text{Max } f(x) = 2x_1 + x_2$$

Subject to $x_1 + x_2 \le 6$
$x_1 \le 3$
$2x_1 + x_2 \ge 4$
$x_1, x_2 \ge 0$

Graph this problem, identifying the three constraint equation lines and the feasible zone common to all of them. Plot dotted lines for values of 3, 6, 9 and 12 for the objective function $f(x)$. What appears to be the highest feasible value of $f(x)$ and for what values of x_1 and x_2 does it occurs?

Solution:

$$x_1 + x_2 \le 6 \Rightarrow \frac{x_1}{6} + \frac{x_2}{6} \le 1$$

$$x_1 \le 3 \Rightarrow \frac{x_1}{3} \le 1$$

$$2x_1 + x_2 \ge 4 \Rightarrow \frac{x_1}{2} + \frac{x_2}{4} \ge 1$$

$$x_1, x_2 \ge 0$$

Corresponding to Z = 12, there is over utilization of all facilities

Corresponding to Z = 9, since it is an optimum value there is 100% utilization of all facilities.
At Z = 6, there is under utilization of all facilities.
Corresponding to Z = 3, it is not a feasible solution.
By slope method

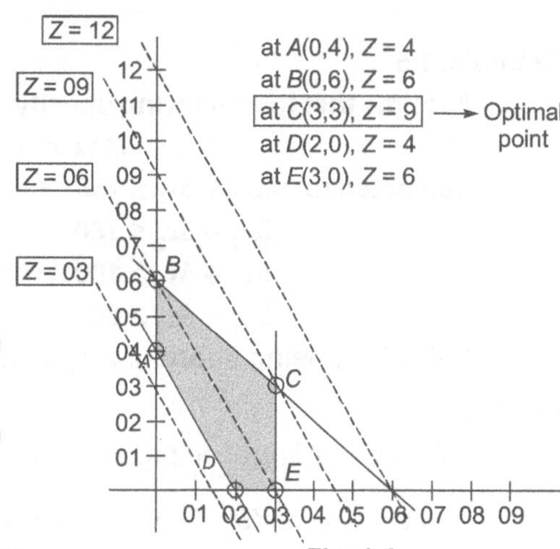

Fig. 1.4

$$Z = 2x_1 + x_2 \qquad m = -2$$

$$x_1 + x_2 \le 6 \qquad m_1 = -1$$
$$x_1 \le 3 \qquad m_2 = \infty$$
$$2x_1 + x_2 \ge 4 \qquad m_3 = -2$$

Here m and m_3 are equal but it is important to note that,in maximization of Z value, we will consider the equations which always have less than or equal to "≤ " sign, and not consider the equation having "≥" sign. In minimization, the converse is true.

Example: 1.4

Assume that the following specify a generalized linear programming problem:

$$\text{Min } Z = 2x + 3y$$

Subjected to $5x + y \ge 100$

$3x + 2y \ge 120$

$x + 3y \ge 90$

$x, y \ge 0$

Solve it by using Graphical Method.

Solution:

$$\Rightarrow \frac{x}{20} + \frac{y}{100} \ge 1, \quad \Rightarrow \frac{x}{40} + \frac{y}{60} \ge 1, \quad \Rightarrow \frac{x}{90} + \frac{y}{30} \ge 1$$

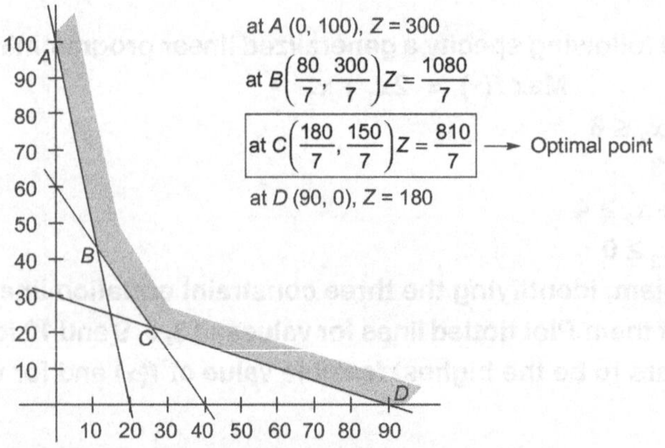

Fig. 1.5

Example: 1.5

Assume that the following specify a generalized linear programming problem:

$$\text{Max } z = 300x_1 + 400x_2$$

Subjected to $3x_1 + 6x_2 \le 150$

$5x_1 + 3x_2 \le 180$

$5x_1 + 4x_2 \ge 100$

$2x_1 + 4x_2 \ge 80$

Solve it by using shortcut slope method.

Solution:

As it is maximization problem, do not consider equations having '≥' sign.

$$m = -\frac{3}{4} = -0.75; \qquad m_1 = -\frac{3}{6} = -0.5; \qquad m_2 = -\frac{5}{3} = -1.33$$

$m \in (m_1, m_2)$ ∴ Optimum point is the intersection of line (1) and (2) i.e. (30, 10)

$$\Rightarrow \qquad \text{max } Z = 13000$$

Example 1.6

Assume that the following specify a generalized linear programming problem:

$$\text{Max } Z = 6x_1 + 4x_2$$

Subjected to $2x_1 + 3x_2 \le 30$

$3x_1 + 2x_2 \le 24$

$x_1 + x_2 \ge 3$

$x_1, x_2 \ge 0$

Solve it by using Graphical Method & slope methods.

Solution:

By graphical method:

$$\frac{x_1}{15} + \frac{x_2}{10} \le 1$$

$$\frac{x_1}{8} + \frac{x_2}{12} \le 1$$

$$\frac{x_1}{3} + \frac{x_2}{3} \ge 1$$

$$x_1, x_2 \ge 0$$

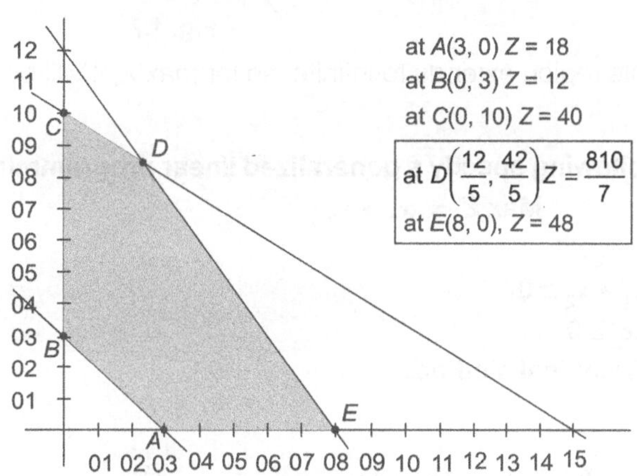

Fig 1.6

- In these situations at the farthest point, objective function line superimposes over one of the constraint lines, so all the points falling on '*DE*' line will be optimum.
- This is the case of **alternate solution** because the slope of objective function line is same as that of one of the constraints and objective function line is superimposing over the constraint line at the outermost point.

By slope method:

$$m = -\frac{6}{4} = -1.5$$

$$m_1 = -\frac{2}{3} = -0.66, \quad m_2 = -\frac{3}{2} = -1.5$$

$\because \quad m = m_2$

It has alternative solutions.

Example: 1.7

Assume that the following specify a generalized linear programming problem:

$$\text{Max } Z = 3x_1 + 2x_2$$

Subject to $x_1 - x_2 \leq 1$

$x_1 + x_2 \geq 3$

$x_1, x_2 \geq 0$

Solve it by using Graphical Method.

Solution:

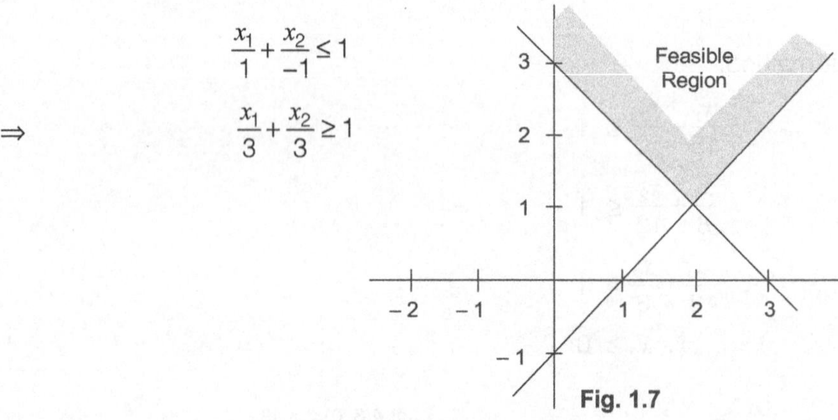

Fig. 1.7

In problem feasible region extends to infinite, so for max Z, it will be **unbounded** solution.

Example: 1.8

Assume that the following specify a generalized linear programming problem:

$$\text{Max } Z = x_1 + x_2$$

Subjected to $x_1 + x_2 \leq 1$

$-3x_1 + x_2 \geq 3$

$x_1, x_2 \geq 0$

Solve it by using Graphical Method.

Solution:

$$\frac{x_1}{1} + \frac{x_2}{1} \leq 1 \qquad \frac{x_1}{-1} + \frac{x_2}{3} \geq 1$$

(2)

3

2

1

(1)

−2 −1 1 2 3

−1

Fig 1.8

Regions (1) and (2) are not having any intersection region so there **is no feasible region,** so no solution.

○○○○

PRACTICE QUESTIONS

1. Consider the following linear programming problem:
Max. $Z = 2A + 3B$, subject to $A + B \leq 10$, $4A + 6B \leq 30$, $2A + B \leq 17$, $A, B \geq 0$ what can one say about the solution?
(a) It may contain alternative optima (b) The solution will be unbounded
(c) The solution will be degenerate (d) It cannot be solved by simplex method

2. In case of solution of a two variable linear programming problem by graphical method one constraint line comes parallel to the objective function line. Which one of the following is correct? The problem will have:
(a) Infeasible solution (b) Unbounded solution
(c) Degenerate solution (d) Infinite number of optimal solutions

3. Which of the followng are correct in respect of graphically solved linear programming problems?
1. The region of feasible solution has concavity property.
2. The boundaries of the region are lines or planes.
3. There are corners or extreme points on the boundary.
Select the correct answer using the codes given below:
(a) 1 and 3 (b) 2 and 3
(c) 1 and 3 (d) 1, 2 and 3

4. If m is the number of constraints in a linear programming with two variables x and y and non-negativity constraints $x > 0$, $Y > 0$; the feasible region in the graphical solution will be surrounded by how many lines?
(a) m (b) $m + 1$
(c) $m + 2$ (d) $m + 4$

5. Which one of the following is true in case of simplex method of linear programming?
(a) The constants of constraints equation may be positive or negative.
(b) Inequalities are not converted into equations.
(c) It cannot be used for two-variable problems.
(d) The simplex algorithm is an iterative procedure.

6. The linear programming is used for optimization problems which satisfy the following conditions:
1. Objective function expressed as a linear function of variables.
2. Resources are unlimited.
3. The decision variables are interrelated and non-negative.
Which of these statements is/are correct?
(a) 1, 2 and 3 (b) 2 and 3 only
(c) 1 only (d) 1 and 3 only

7. Consider the following statements:
1. Resources limitations must be known.
2. Relationship of variables must be known.
Which of these statements must be satisfied to deal with the graphical techniques of linear programming effectively?
(a) 1 only (b) 2 only
(c) both 1 and 2 (d) neither 1 nor 2

8. The first algorithm for Linear Programming was given by:
(a) Bellman (b) Dantzig
(c) Kulm (d) Van Neumann

9. Let y_1 and y_2 be the decision variables of the dual and v_1 and v_2 be the slack variables of the dual of the given linear programming problem. The optimum dual variables are:
(a) y_1 and y_2 (b) y_1 and v_1
(c) y_1 and v_2 (d) v_1 and v_2

10. If at the optimum in a linear programming problem, a dual variable corresponding to particular primal constraint is zero, then it means that
(a) Right hand side of the primal constraint can be altered without affecting the optimum solution.
(b) Changing the right hand side of the primal constraint will disturb the optimum.
(c) The objective function is unbounded.
(d) The problem is degenerate.

11. Consider an objective function $z(x_1, x_2) = 3x_1 + 9x_2$ and constraints:

$$x_1 + x_2 \leq 8$$
$$x_1 + 2x_2 \leq 4$$
$$x_1 \geq 0 \text{ and } x_2 \geq 0$$

The maximum value of the objective function is
(a) 16 (b) 12
(c) 18 (d) 72

12. A manufacturer produces two types of products, 1 and 2, at production levels of x_1 and x_2 respectively. The profit is given is $2x_1 + 5x_2$. The production constraints are:

$$x_1 + 3x_2 \leq 40, \qquad 3x_1 + x_2 \leq 24,$$
$$x_1 + x_2 \leq 10, \qquad x_1 > 0,\ x_2 > 0$$

The maximum profit which can meet the constraints is
(a) 29 (b) 38
(c) 44 (d) 75

13. Consider the following Linear Programming Problem (LPP):
Maximize: $z = 3x_1 + 2x_2$
Subject to $x_1 \leq 4$
$x_2 \leq 6$
$3x_1 + 3x_2 \leq 18$
$x_1 \geq 0,\ x_2 \geq 0$
(a) The LPP has a unique optimal solution.
(b) The LPP is infeasible.
(c) The LPP is unbounded.
(d) The LPP has multiple optimal solution.

14. Match **List-I** with **List-II** and select the correct answer using the codes given below the lists:

List-I	**List-II**
A. Linear programming	1. Ritchie
B. Dynamic programming	2. Dantzig
C. 'C' programming	3. Bell
D. Integer programming	4. Gomory

Codes:

	A	B	C	D
(a)	2	1	4	3
(b)	1	2	3	4
(c)	2	3	1	4
(d)	2	3	4	1

15. Linear programming model can be applied to:
1. Line balancing problem
2. Transportation problem
3. Project management

Of these statements:
(a) 1, 2 and 3 are correct
(b) 1 and 2 are correct
(c) 2 and 3 are correct
(d) 1 and 3 are correct

16. The primal of a LP problem is maximization of objective function with 6 variables and 2 constraints Which of the following correspond to the dual of the problem stated?
1. It has 2 variables and 6 constraints.
2. It has 6 variables and 2 constraints.
3. Maximization of objective function.
4. Minimization of objective function.

Select the correct answer using the codes given below:
(a) 1 and 3
(b) 1 and 4
(c) 2 and 3
(d) 2 and 4

17. Maximize: $P = x + 12y$

Subjected to $20x + 10y \leq 200$

$10x + 20y \leq 120$

$10x + 30y \leq 150$

$x \geq 0$ and $y \geq 0$

(a) 50
(b) 66
(c) 60
(d) 120

18. A feasible solution to the linear programming problem should
(a) satisfy the problem constraints.
(b) optimize the objective function.
(c) satisfy the problem constraints and non-negativity restrictions.
(d) satisfy the non-negativity restrictions.

19. Solution to max $z = 4x_1 + 6x_2$

$x_1 + x_2 \leq 4$

$3x_1 + x_2 \leq 12$

$x_1, x_2 \geq 0$

is
(a) unique
(b) unbounded
(c) degenerate
(d) infinite

20. Assumptions of linear programming include:
1. Linearity
2. Additivity
3. Divisibility
4. Certainty

Select the correct option
(a) 1 and 2 (b) 1 and 4
(c) 1, 3 and 4 (d) 1, 2, 3 and 4

21. Divisibility assumption in linear programming employs
(a) resources can be divided among product.
(b) product can be divided among the customers.
(c) decision variable may take an integer value.
(d) decision variable may take a fraction value.

22. Which of the following conditions are necessary of applying linear programming?
1. There must be a well-defined objective function.
2. The decision variables should be interrelated and non-negative.
3. The resources must be in limited supply.
(a) 1 and 2 only (b) 1 and 3 only
(c) 2 and 3 only (d) 1, 2 and 3

23. A variable which has no physical meaning, but is used to obtain an initial basic feasible solution to the linear programming problem is referred to as
(a) Basic variable (b) Non-basic variable
(c) Artificial variable (d) Basis

24. Consider the following statements regarding the characteristics ofthe standard form of a linear programming problem:
1. All the constraints are expressed in the form of equations.
2. The right-hand side of each constraint equation is non-negative.
3. All the decision variables are non-negative.
Which of these statements are correct?
(a) 1, 2 and 3 (b) 1 and 2
(c) 2 and 3 (d) 1 and 3

25. Which one of the following statements is NOT correct?
(a) Assignment model is a special ease of a linear programming problem.
(b) In queuing models, Poisson arrivals and exponential services areassumed.
(c) In transportation problems, the non-square matrix is made square byadding a dummy row or a dummy column.
(d) In linear programming problems, dual of a dual is a primal.

26. Which of the following are correct in respect of graphically solved linear programming problems?
1. The region of feasible solution has concavity property.
2. The boundaries of the region are lines or planes.
3. There are corners or extreme points on the boundary.
Select the correct answer using the code given below:
(a) 1 and 2 (b) 2 and 3
(c) 1 and 3 (d) 1, 2 and 3

27. In case of solution of linear programming problem using graphical method, if the constraint line of one of the non-redundant constraints is parallel to the objective function line, then it indicates
(a) an infeasible solution (b) a degenerate solution
(c) an unbound solution (d) a multiple number of optimal solutions

28. A company produces two types of paper towels, called regular and super soakers. Marketing has imposed a constraint that the total monthly production of regular should not be more than twice the production of super soakers. Letting x be the number of units of regular produced per month and y represents number of super soakers produced per month, appropriate constraints will be
(a) $x \leq 2y$
(b) $2x \leq y$
(c) $x + 0.5y \leq 0$
(d) $x - 0.5y \geq 0$

○○○○

ANSWERS

GRAPHICAL METHOD

1. (a)	**2.** (d)	**3.** (b)	**4.** (c)	**5.** (d)	**6.** (d)	**7.** (c)
8. (b)	**9.** (d)	**10.** (c)	**11.** (c)	**12.** (a)	**13.** (a)	**14.** (c)
15. (b)	**16.** (b)	**17.** (d)	**18.** (c)	**19.** (a)	**20.** (d)	**21.** (c)
22. (d)	**23.** (c)	**24.** (a)	**25.** (c)	**26.** (b)	**27.** (d)	**28.** (b)

CHAPTER 2

Simplex Method

2.1 INTRODUCTION

When there are more than two variables, graphical method cannot be used to solve optimization problems. As it was explained in the previous chapter that optimal solution exists always at the corner point at the feasible region, the simplex method is a systematic procedure at finding corner point solution and taking them for optimality. Simplex procedures are meant for profit maximization and if our objective is loss minimization then the problems has to be converted into profit maximization by multiplying the objective function by '–' sign before starting the simplex procedures.

While solving problems using simplex methods, we take slack variables, surplus variables and artificial variables. After solving the simplex problem, we can do the verification test of the result to make sure that the answer is correct. In many practical problems we want to find not only an optimal solution but also want to determine what happens to this optimal solution when certain changes are made in the system. For this we do the sensitivity. While doing sensitivity analysis if negative value appears in solution matrix, the matrix is not an optimum one and we move towards optimality by dual simplex procedure.

While solving problems using simplex methods if many artificial variables are to be used we will write a dual problem for the given problem and then solve it by simplex procedure. The intermediate steps and fundamentals involved in simplex procedure are given in the following problems.

Slack variables are those which are added to the constraint equations to get equal to sign ('=')

Example: 2.1

Assume that the following specify a generalized linear programming problem:

Maximize: $Z = x_1 - x_2 + 3x_3$

Subjected to $2x_1 - x_3 \leq 2$

$x_1 + x_2 - x_3 \leq 10$

$2x_1 - 2x_2 + 3x_3 \leq 0$

$x_1, x_2, x_3 \geq 0$

Solve it by using Simplex Method.

Solution:

Let s_1, s_2, s_3 be slack variables then the constraints become

$$2x_1 - x_3 + s_1 = 2; \qquad x_1 + x_2 - x_3 + s_2 = 10$$

$$2x_1 - 2x_2 + 3x_3 + s_3 = 0; \qquad x_1, x_2, x_3, s_1, s_2, s_3 \geq 0$$

$$\Rightarrow \qquad \text{Max } Z = x_1 - x_2 + 3x_3 + 0s_1 + 0s_2 + 0s_3$$

Table 1:

- The coefficients of all the variables in the objective function are written in the first row against "C_j".
- The coefficients of the slack variables in the objective function are written in the first column under "Basis".
- The coefficients of all the variables in the constraints are written in the corresponding rows as shown below.
- The constants in the constraints are written under "b"
- The E_j values of the variables are the sum of the products of the coefficients in the respective columns and the corresponding basis.
- e.g., $2 x 0 + 1 x 0 + 2 x 0 = 0$

Basis ↓ / C_j →	1 x_1	–1 x_2	3 x_3	0 s_1	0 s_2	0 s_3	b	$\theta = \frac{b}{C_i}$
0 s_1	2	0	–1	1	0	0	2	
0 s_2	1	1	–1	0	1	0	10	
0 s_3	2	–2	3	0	0	1	0	
E_j	0	0	0	0	0	0		
$E_j - C_j$	–1	1	–3	0	0	0		

- In $E_j - C_j$ row the value represents the corresponding profit on each machine.
- Select the maximum negative value in the pivot row, so that we select the max profit or min loss. The column corresponding to that value is called as entering column (C_i). This row is called pivot or key column.
- The θ values are calculated by dividing the values under b with corresponding elements in the entering column.
- Select the minimum positive value (including '0')in the $\left(\theta = \frac{b}{C_i}\right)$ column,
- This represents idleness of the machine as shown in above table. The corresponding row is called the leaving row. This row is called pivot or key row.

Basis ↓ / C_j →	1 x_1	–1 x_2	3 x_3	0 s_1	0 s_2	0 s_3	b	$\theta = \frac{b}{C_i}$	
0 s_1	2	0	–1	1	0	0	2	–2	
0 s_2	1	1	–1	0	1	0	10	–10	
0 s_3	2	–2	[3] *	0	0	1	0	0	← Min +ve Value including zero (Idleness)
E_j	0	0	0	0	0	0			
$E_j - C_j$	–1	1	–3	0	0	0			

↑

Max –ve value [means 3 units of profit] $\frac{d^2x}{dt^2} = -\text{ve(max)}$

- The element common in the entering column and leaving row is called pivotal value.
- The basis variable in the leaving row is replaced by the variable in entering column. i.e., s_3 leaves the basis, x_3 enters the basis ($s_3 \Leftrightarrow x_3$).

Basis ↓ C_j →	1 x_1	−1 x_2	3 x_3	0 s_1	0 s_2	0 s_3	b	$\theta = \frac{b}{C_i}$
0 s_1	2	0	−1	1	0	0	2	−2
0 s_2	1	1	−1	0	1	0	10	−10
0 s_3 ←	2	−2	[3]*	0	0	1	0	0
E_j	0	0	0	0	0	0		
$E_j - C_j$	−1	1	−3	0	0	0		

Table 2:

- Pivotal value in row is made '1' by applying only row operations and all other values in the column are made zero and only by following row operations.

$$R_{3\,new} = R_{3\,old} \div 3$$
$$R_{1\,new} = R_{1\,old} + R_{3\,new}$$
$$R_{2\,new} = R_{2\,old} + R_{3\,new}$$

- The E_j and $E_j - C_j$ values are calculated as explained earlier.

Basis ↓ C_j →	1 x_1	−1 x_2	3 x_3	0 s_1	0 s_2	0 s_3	b	$\theta = \frac{b}{C_i}$	
0 s_1	8/3	−2/3	0	1	0	1/3	2	−3	
0 s_2	5/3	[1/3]*	0	0	1	1/3	10	30	← Leaving row
3 x_3	2/3	−2/3	1	0	0	1/3	0	0	
E_j	2	−2	3	0	0	1			
$E_j - C_j$	1	−1	0	0	0	1			
		↑ Entering column							

- The entering column is identified and the θ values are calculated, then the leaving row are identified as explained earlier.

Note: The pivotal element should not be a negative number. So instead of "0" the next minimum positive number (here "30") is taken for the leaving row.

Basis ↓ C_j →	1 x_1	−1 x_2	3 x_3	0 s_1	0 s_2	0 s_3	b	$\theta = \frac{b}{C_i}$
0 s_1	8/3	−2/3	0	1	0	1/3	2	−3
0 s_2 ←	5/3	[1/3]*	0	0	1	1/3	10	30
3 x_3	2/3	−2/3	1	0	0	1/3	0	0
E_j	2	−2	3	0	0	1		
$E_j - C_j$	1	−1	0	0	0	1		

- For the new simplex table, the pivotal element is selected according to previous procedure.
- s_2 leaves the basis, x_2 enters the basis.

Table 3:

- Pivotal value in row is made '1' by applying only row operations and all other values in the column are made zero and only by following row operations.

$$R_{2\,new} = R_{2\,old} \div (1/3)$$
$$R_{1\,new} = R_{1\,old} + (2/3)\,R_{2\,new}$$
$$R_{3\,new} = R_{3\,old} + (2/3)\,R_{2\,new}$$

- The E_j and $E_j - C_j$ values are calculated as explained earlier.

Basis \ C_j	1 x_1	–1 x_2	3 x_3	0 s_1	0 s_2	0 s_3	b	$\theta = \frac{b}{C_i}$
0 s_1	6	0	0	1	2	1	22	
0 x_2	5	1	0	0	3	1	30	
3 x_3	4	0	1	0	2	1	20	
E_j	7	–1	3	0	3	2		
$E_j - C_j$	6	0	0	0	3	2		

- As all the elements of $E_j - C_j$ row are positive, it means it is an optimum matrix.
- The variable present in the basis are called basic variables.
- The variables which are not in the basis but are in the objective function are called non basic variables. (The non-basic variables are assigned zero solution.)
- So solution can be read it out from matrix i.e.,

$$\left.\begin{aligned} s_1 &= 22 \\ x_2 &= 30 \\ x_3 &= 20 \end{aligned}\right\} \text{Basic variables} \qquad \left.\begin{aligned} s_2 &= 0 \\ s_3 &= 0 \\ x_1 &= 0 \end{aligned}\right\} \text{Non-basic variables}$$

$\therefore$ by putting $(x_1, x_2, x_3) = (0, 30, 20)$ in the objective function the maximum value of

$Z = x_1 - x_2 + 3x_3 = 0 - 30 + 60 = 30$

Example: 2.2

Assume that the following specify a generalized linear programming problem:

Maximize: $Z = 45x + 40y$

Subjected to $2x + y \le 90$

$x + 2y \le 80$

$x + y \le 50$

$x, y \ge 0$

Solve it by using Simplex Method.

Solution:

Let s_1, s_2, s_3 be slack variables then the constraints become

$$2x + y + s_1 = 90$$
$$x + 2y + s_2 = 80$$
$$x + y + s_3 = 50$$
$$x, y, s_1, s_2, s_3 \ge 0$$

$$\Rightarrow \qquad Z = 45x + 40y + 0s_1 + 0s_2 + 0s_3$$

- The above information is tabulated.
- E_j and $E_j - C_j$ are calculated.
- The entering column is identified and the θ values are calculated, then the leaving row are identified.
- The pivotal element/value is identified from the table.

Basis \ C_j	45 x	40 y	0 s_1	0 s_2	0 s_3	b	$\theta = \frac{b}{C_i}$
← 0 s_1	[2]*	1	1	0	0	90	45 ←
0 s_2	1	2	0	1	0	80	80
0 s_3	1	1	0	0	1	50	50
E_j	0	0	0	0	0		
$E_j - C_j$	– 45 ↑	– 40	0	0	0		

Table-1

s_1 leaves the basis and x enters into the basis.

- The following row operations are performed:

$$R_{1\,new} = R_{1\,old}/2$$
$$R_{2\,new} = R_{2\,old} - R_{1\,new}$$
$$R_{3\,new} = R_{3\,old} - R_{1\,new}$$

- Then the table 1 becomes table 2.
- E_j and $E_j - C_j$ are calculated.
- The entering column is identified and the θ values are calculated, then the leaving row are identified.
- The pivotal element/value is identified from the table.
- s_3 leaves the basis, and y enters the basis.

Basis \ C_j	45 x	40 y	0 s_1	0 s_2	0 s_3	b	$\theta = \frac{b}{C_i}$
45 x	1	½	1/2	0	0	45	90
0 s_2	0	3/2	–1/2	1	0	35	70/3
← 0 s_3	0	*1/2	–1/2	0	1	5	10 ←
E_j	45	45/2	45/2	0	0		
$E_j - C_j$	0	–35/2 ↑	45/2	0	0		

Table-2

- The following row operations are performed:

$$R_{1\,new} = R_{1\,old}(R_{3\,new})/2$$
$$R_{2\,new} = R_{2\,old} - 3\,(R_{3\,new})/2$$
$$R_{3\,new} = 2R_{3\,old}$$

- Then the table 2 becomes

Basis \ C_j	45 x	40 y	0 s_1	0 s_2	0 s_3	b
45 x	1	0	1	0	– 1	40
0 s_2	0	0	1	1	– 3	20
40 y	0	1	– 1	0	2	10
E_j	45	40	5	0	35	
$E_j - C_j$	0	0	5	0	35	

Table-3

- E_j and $E_j - C_j$ are calculated.
- '$E_j - C_j$' Values present in the matrix are positive. So it is an optimum matrix.
- So solution can be read it out from matrix i.e.,

$$\left.\begin{array}{l} x = 40 \\ y = 10 \\ s_2 = 20 \end{array}\right\} \text{Basic variables} \qquad \left.\begin{array}{l} s_1 = 0 \\ s_3 = 0 \end{array}\right\} \text{Non-basic variables}$$

∴ by putting $(x, y) = (40, 10)$ in the objective function the maximum value of $Z = 45x + 40y = 2200$

- **Surplus variables** are those which are subtracted from the constraint equation to get equal to sign ('=')
- **Artificial variables** are those which are added to the constraint equations whenever we introduce a surplus variable in order to get the initial feasible solution, which incurs a heavy loss in the above function. And so we assign a large penalty "$-M$" to these variables in the objective function.

Example: 2.3

Assume that the following specify a generalized linear programming problem:

Minimize: $Z = 4x_1 + x_2$

Subjected to $3x_1 + 4x_2 \geq 20$

$x_1 + 5x_2 \leq 15$

$x_1, x_2 \geq 0$

Solve it by using Big M Method or artificial variable Method.

Solution:

By introducing surplus variable s_1 artificial variable a_1 and slack variable s_2 the problem may be written as follows:

Maximize: $Z = -4x_1 - x_2 + 0s_1 - Ma_1 + 0s_2$

Subject to: $3x_1 + 4x_2 - s_1 + a_1 = 20$

$x_1 + 5x_2 + s_2 = 15$

$x_1, x_2, s_1, s_2, a_1 \geq 0$

- The above information is tabulated.
- In any constraint if artificial variable is present that should enter first in the basis. (Once the artificial variable leaves the basis it will never enter again, so from the next simplex table onwards that variable can be deleted permanently.)
- E_j and $E_j - C_j$ are calculated.
- The entering column is identified and the θ values are calculated, then the leaving row are identified.
- The pivotal element/value is identified from the table.

Basis ↓ / C_j →	-4 x_1	-1 x_2	0 s_1	0 s_2	$-M$ a_1	b	$\theta = \frac{b}{C_i}$
$-Ma_1$	3	4	-1	0	1	20	5
← $0\ s_2$	1	[5]*	0	1	0	15	3 ←
E_j	$-3M$	$-4M$	M	0	$-M$		
$E_j - C_j$	$-3M+4$	$-4M+1$ ↑	M	0	0		

Table-1

- S_2 leaves the basis and X_2 enters the basis.
- The following row operations are performed:

$$R_{2\text{ new}} = (R_{2\text{ old}})/5; \quad R_{1\text{ new}} = R_{1\text{ old}} - 4\,(R_{2\text{ new}})$$

- Then the table 1 becomes

Basis ↓ / C_j →	-4 x_1	-1 x_2	0 s_1	0 s_2	$-M$ a_1	b	$\theta = \frac{b}{C_i}$
$-Ma_1$	11/5 *	0	-1	$-4/5$	1	8	40/11 ←
$-1\,x_2$	1/5	1	0	1/5	0	3	15
E_j	$\frac{-11M-1}{5}$	-1	M	$\frac{4M-1}{5}$	M		
$E_j - C_j$	$\frac{-11M+19}{5}$ ↑	0	M	$\frac{4M-1}{5}$	0		

Table-2

- E_j and $E_j - C_j$ are calculated.
- The entering column is identified and the θ values are calculated, then the leaving row are identified.
- The pivotal element/value is identified from the table.
- a_1 leaves the basis and x_1 enters the basis.
- As a_1 leaves the basis, it will never come back to the basis again, so that particular column is removed from matrix.
- The following row operations are performed:

$$R_{1\text{ new}} = 5\,(R_{1\text{ old}})/11; \quad R_{2\text{ new}} = R_{2\text{ old}} - (R_{1\text{ new}})/5$$

- Then the table 2 becomes table 3.
- E_j and $E_j - C_j$ are calculated.
- It is an optimum matrix since all the values obtained in '$E_j - C_j$' row are positive

Basis ↓ / C_j →	-4 x_1	-1 x_2	0 s_1	0 s_2	b
$-4\ x_1$		0	$-5/11$	$-4/11$	40/11
$-1\ x_2$	0	1	1/11	3/11	25/11
E_j	-4	-1	19/11	13/11	
$E_j - C_j$	0	0	19/11	13/11	

Table-3

- So solution can be read it out from matrix i.e.,

$$\left.\begin{aligned} x_1 &= \frac{40}{11} \\ x_2 &= \frac{25}{11} \end{aligned}\right\}\text{Basic variables} \qquad \left.\begin{aligned} s_1 &= 0 \\ s_2 &= 0 \\ a_1 &= 0 \end{aligned}\right\}\text{Non-basic variables}$$

∴ by putting $(x_1, x_2) = \left(\frac{40}{11}, \frac{25}{11}\right)$ in the objective function the maximum value of

$$Z = -4x_1 - x_2 = \frac{185}{11}$$

Example: 2.4

Assume that the following specify a generalized linear programming problem:

Minimum: $Z = 3x_1 + 2x_2$

Subject to: $2x_1 + x_2 \leq 2$

$3x_1 + 4x_2 \geq 12$

$x_2, x_2 \geq 0,$

Solve it by using Big *M* Method.

Solution:

By introducing slack variable s_1 surplusvariable s_2 and artificial variable a_2 the problem may be written as follows:

Maximize: $Z = -3x_1 - 2x_2 + 0s_1 + 0s_2 - Ma_2$

Subject to: $2x_1 + x_2 + s_1 = 2$

$3x_1 + 4x_2 - s_2 + a_2 = 12$

$x_1, x_2, s_1, s_2, a_2 \geq 0$

- The above information is tabulated.
- In any constraint if artificial variable is present that should enter first in the basis. (Once the artificial variable leaves the basis it will never enter again, so from the next simplex table onwards that variable can be deleted permanently.)

Basis ↓ C_j →	-3 x_1	-2 x_2	0 s_1	0 s_2	$-M$ a_2	b	$\theta = \frac{b}{C_i}$
$0\ s_1$	2	1*	1	0	0	2	2 ←
$-Ma_2$	3	4	0	-1	1	12	3
E_j	$-3M$	$-4M$	0	M	$-M$		
$E_j - C_j$	$-3M+3$	$-4M+2$ ↑	0	M	0		

Table-1

- E_j and $E_j - C_j$ are calculated.
- The entering column is identified andthe θ values are calculated, then the leaving row are identified.
- The pivotal element/value is identified from the table.
- s_1 leaves the basis, x_2 enters the basis.
- The following row operations are performed

$$R_{2\text{ new}} \rightarrow R_{2\text{ old}} - 4R_{1\text{ new}}$$

- Then the table 1 becomes

Basis ↓ C_j →	-3 x_1	-2 x_2	0 s_1	0 s_2	$-M$ a_1	b
$-2x_2$	2	1	1	0	0	2
$-Ma_2$	-5	0	-4	-1	1	4
E_j	$5M-4$	-2	$4M-2$	M	$-M$	
$E_j - C_j$	$5M-1$	0	$4M-2$	M	0	

Table-2

- It is an optimum matrix since all the values obtained in '$E_j - C_j$' row are positive.
- **But the optimum matrix contains artificial variable, this indicates infeasible solution i.e., (there is no feasible region).**

- If we do the same problem by graphical method we get

$\frac{x_1}{1}+\frac{x_2}{2}\le 1 \qquad \frac{x_1}{4}+\frac{x_2}{3}\ge 1$

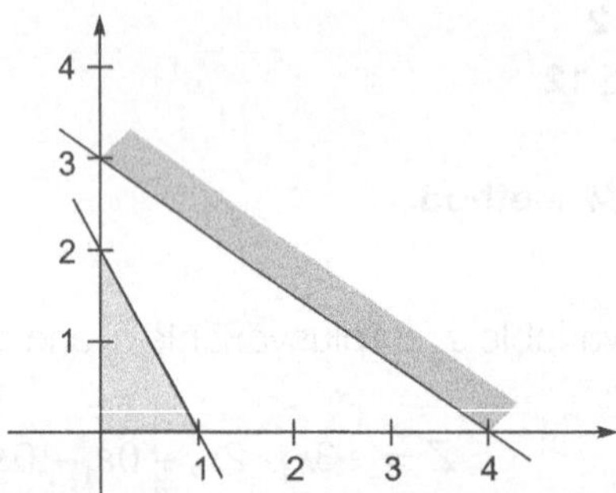

Note: After selecting the entering column, if all the values appear to be negative, it indicates that the solution is unbounded.

Example: 2.5

Assume that the following specify a generalized linear programming problem:

Maximize: $Z = 6x_1 + 4x_2$

Subject to $2x_1 + 3x_2 \le 30$

$3x_1 + 2x_2 \le 24$

$x_1 + x_2 \ge 3$

$x_1, x_2 \ge 0$

Solve it by using Big *M* Method.

Solution:

By introducing slack variables s_1, s_2 surplus variable s_3 and artificial variable a_1 the problem may be written as follows:

Maximize: $Z = 6x_1 + 4x_2 + 0.s_1 + 0.s_2 + 0.s_3 - Ma_1$

Subject to

$$2x_1 + 3x_2 + s_1 = 30$$
$$3x_1 + 2x_2 + s_2 = 24$$
$$x_1 + x_2 - s_3 + a_1 = 3$$
$$x_1, x_2, s_1, s_2, s_3, a_1 \ge 0$$

- The above information is tabulated.
- In any constraint if artificial variable is present that should enter first in the basis.
- E_j and $E_j - C_j$ are calculated.
- The entering column is identified and the θ values are calculated, then the leaving row are identified.
- The pivotal element/value is identified from the table

Basis \ C_j	6 x_1	4 x_2	0 s_1	0 s_2	0 s_3	−M a_1	b	$\theta = \frac{b}{C_i}$
0 s_1	2	3	1	0	0	0	30	15
0 s_2	3	2	0	1	0	0	24	8
M a_1	[1]*	1	0	0	−1	1	3	3 ←
E_j	−M	−M	0	0	M	−M		
$E_j - C_j$	−M−6 ↑	−M−4	0	0	M	0		

Table-1

- s_1 leaves the basis, x_2 enters the basis.
- The following row operations are performed:

$$R_{1\,new} = R_{1\,old} - 2\,R_{3\,new}$$
$$R_{2\,new} = R_{2\,old} - 3\,R_{3\,new}$$

- Then the table 1 becomes.
- E_j and $E_j - C_j$ are calculated.
- The entering column is identified and the θ values are calculated, then the leaving row are identified.
- The pivotal element/value is identified from the table.
- s_2 leaves the basis, s_3 enters the basis.

Basis ↓ C_j →	6 x_1	4 x_2	0 s_1	0 s_2	0 s_3	b	$\theta = \frac{b}{C_i}$
0 s_1	0	1	1	0	2	24	12
← 0 s_2	0	−1	0	1	[3]*	15	5 ←
6 x_1	1	1	0	0	−1	3	−3
E_j	6	6	0	0	−6		
$E_j - C_j$	0	2	0	0	−6 ↑		

Table-2

- The following row operations are performed:

$$R_{2\,new} = (R_{2old})/3$$
$$R_{2\,new} = R_{2\,old} - 2R_{2\,new}$$
$$R_{3\,new} = R_{3\,old} + R_{2\,new}$$

- Then the table 2 becomes.

Basis ↓ C_j →	6 x_1	4 x_2	0 s_1	0 s_2	0 s_3	b	$\theta = \frac{b}{C_i}$
← 0 s_1	0	[5/3]*	1	−2/3	0	14	42/5 ←
0 s_3	0	−1/3	0	1/3	1	5	−15
6 x_1	1	2/3	0	1/3	0	8	12
E_j	6	4	0	2	0		
$E_j - C_j$	0	(0) ↑	0	2	0		

Table-3

- E_j and $E_j - C_j$ are calculated.
- It is an optimum matrix since all the values obtained in '$E_j - C_j$' row are positive.
- So solution can be read it out from matrix i.e.,

$$\begin{matrix} s_1 = 14 & x_2 = 0 \\ s_3 = 5 & s_2 = 0 \\ x_1 = 8 & a_1 = 0 \end{matrix} \Rightarrow X_1 = \begin{pmatrix} x_1 \\ x_2 \\ s_1 \\ s_2 \\ s_3 \end{pmatrix} = \begin{pmatrix} 8 \\ 0 \\ 14 \\ 0 \\ 5 \end{pmatrix}$$

- **Normally in simplex, zero will appear in $E_j - C_j$ row corresponding to every basic variable. If it so happens that zero appears below a non basic variables it means there are alternate solutions.**
- Here x_2 is a non basic variable and is having '0' in row. So, this is the case of alternate solution.
- To get the alternative solution the entering column is identified as x_2 is having 0' in and is not in the basis and the θ values are calculated, then the leaving row are identified.
- The pivotal element/value is identified from the table.
- The following row operations are performed:

$$R_{1\,new} = 3(R_{1old})/5$$
$$R_{2\,new} = R_{2\,old} + (R_{1\,new})/3$$
$$R_{3\,new} = R_{3\,old} - (R_{1\,new})/3$$

- Then the table 3 becomes.

Basis ↓ / C_j →	6 x_1	4 x_2	0 s_1	0 s_2	0 s_3	b
4 x_2	0	1	3/5	–2/5	0	4275
0 s_3	0	0	1/5	1/5	1	39/5
6 x_1	1	0	–2/5	3/5	0	12/5
E_j	6	4	0	2	0	
$E_j - C_j$	0	0	0	2	0	

Table-4

- E_j and $E_j - C_j$ are calculated.
- It is an alternative optimum matrix since all the values obtained in '$E_j - C_j$' row are positive.
- So solution can be read it out from matrix i.e.,

$$X_2 = \begin{pmatrix} x_1 \\ x_2 \\ s_1 \\ s_2 \\ s_3 \end{pmatrix} = \begin{pmatrix} 12/5 \\ 45/2 \\ 0 \\ 0 \\ 39/5 \end{pmatrix}$$

- Here alternate solution means infinitely many solutions may be there because the objective function line is coinciding with the constraint line at the farthest point. The infinite number of solutions is represented as

$$x = (\lambda)x_2 + (1 - \lambda)x_2$$
$$y \in (0, 1)$$

Example: 2.6

Assume that the following specify a generalized linear programming problem:

Maximum: $Z = 2x_1 + x_2$

Subject to: $4x_1 + 3x_2 \leq 12$

$4x_1 + x_2 \leq 8$

$4x_1 - x_2 \leq 8$

$x_1, x_2 \geq 0$

Solve it by using Simplex Method.

Solution:

By introducing slack variables s_1, s_2 and s_3 the problem may be written as follows:

Maximum: $Z = 2x_1 + x_2 + 0s_1 + 0s_2 + 0s_3$

Subjected to:
$$4x_1 + 3x_2 + s_1 = 12$$
$$4x_1 + x_2 + s_2 = 8,$$
$$4x_1 - x_2 + s_3 = 8,$$
$$x_1, x_2, s_1, s_2, s_3 \geq 0$$

The above information is tabulated.

Basis \ C_j	2 x_1	1 x_2	0 s_1	0 s_2	0 s_3	b	$\theta = \frac{b}{C_i}$
0 s_1	4	3	1	0	0	12	3
0 s_2	4	1	0	1	1	8	2
← 0 s_3	[4]*	−1	0	0	0	8	2 ←
E_j	0	0	0	0	0		
$E_j - C_j$	−2 ↑	−1	0	0	0		

Table-1

- E_j and $E_j - C_j$ are calculated.
- The entering column is identified and the θ values are calculated.
- **In the 'θ' column when two minimum positive values are same and we are not able to decide which row to enter it is called degeneracy in simplex.**
- To find degenerate solution of simplex we have to find minimum $\left(\frac{s_i}{C_i}\right)$.

  Here in s_1 column both $\left(\frac{s_i}{C_i}\right)$ are same. But in s_2 column Min $\left(\frac{1}{4}, \frac{0}{4}\right)$ is '0'. So s_3 is identified as leaving row.
- The pivotal element/value is identified from the table.
- s_3 leaves the basis, x_1 enters the basis.
- The following row operations are performed:

$$R_{3\text{ new}} = (R_{3\text{ old}})/4$$
$$R_{1\text{ new}} = R_{1\text{ old}} - 4(R_{3\text{ new}})$$
$$R_{2\text{ new}} = R_{2\text{ old}} - 4(R_{3\text{ new}})$$

- Then the table 1 becomes.

Basis \ C_j	2 x_1	1 x_2	0 s_1	0 s_2	0 s_3	b	$\theta = \frac{b}{C_i}$
0 s_1	0	4	1	0	−1	4	1
← 0 s_2	0	[2]*	0	1	−1	0	0 ←
2 x_1	1	−1/4	0	0	1/4	2	−8
E_j	2	−1/2	0	0	1/2	4	−16
$E_j - C_j$	0	−3/2 ↑	0	0	1/2		

Table-2

- E_j and $E_j - C_j$ are calculated.
- The entering column is identified and the θ values are calculated, then the leaving row are identified.
- The pivotal element/value is identified from the table.
- s_2 leaves the basis, x_2 enters the basis.
- The following row operations are performed:

$$R_{2\,new} = (R_{2\,old})/2$$
$$R_{1\,new} = R_{1\,old} - 4(R_{2\,new})$$
$$R_{3\,new} = R_{3old} + (R_{2\,new})/4$$

- Then the table 1 becomes.

Basis ↓ C_j →	2 x_1	1 x_2	0 s_1	0 s_2	0 s_3	b	$\theta = \frac{b}{C_i}$
← 0 s_1	0	0	1	−2	[1]*	4	4 ←
1 x_2	0	1	0	1/2	−1/2	0	0
2 x_1	1	0	0	1/8	1/8	2	16
E_j	2	1	0	3/4	−1/4		
$E_j - C_j$	0	0	0	3/4	−1/4 ↑		

Table-3

- E_j and $E_j - C_j$ are calculated.
- The entering column is identified and the θ values are calculated, then the leaving row are identified.
- The pivotal element/value is identified from the table.
- s_1 leaves the basis, s_3 enters the basis.
- The following row operations are performed:

$$R_{2\,new} = R_{2\,old} + (R_{1\,new})/2$$
$$R_{3\,new} = R_{3\,old} - (R_{1\,new})/8$$

- Then the table 3 becomes.

Basis ↓ C_j →	2 x_1	1 x_2	0 s_1	0 s_2	0 s_3	b
0 s_3	0	0	1	−2	1	4
1 x_2	0	1	1/2	−1/2	0	2
2 x_1	1	0	−1/8	3/8	0	3/2
E_j	2	1	1/4	1/4	0	
$E_j - C_j$	0	0	1/4	1/4	0	

Table-4

- E_j and $E_j - C_j$ are calculated.
- It is an optimum matrix since all the values obtained in '$E_j - C_j$' row are positive.

- So solution can be read it out from matrix i.e.,

$$\begin{Bmatrix} x_1 \\ x_2 \\ s_1 \\ s_2 \\ s_3 \end{Bmatrix} = \begin{Bmatrix} 3/2 \\ 2 \\ 0 \\ 0 \\ 4 \end{Bmatrix}$$

- By putting $(x_1, x_2) = \left(\frac{3}{2}, 2\right)$ in the objective function the maximum value of $Z = 2x_1 + x_2 = 5$

2.2 VERIFICATION OF SIMPLEX RESULTS

If the product of the matrix under the slack or surplus variables in the final optimal table and the matrix of constants in the given constraints is equal to the solution matrix then the solution is correct.

Example 2.7

Assume that the following specify a generalized linear programming problem:

Maximum: $Z = 3x_1 + 2x_2$

Subject to: $x_1 + x_2 \leq 6$

$2x_1 + x_2 \leq 8$

$-x_1 + x_2 \leq 1, x_2 \leq 2$

Solve it by using Simplex Method and verify the result.

Solution:

By introducing slack variable s_1, s_2, s_3 and s_4 the problem may be written as follows:

Maximum: $Z = 3x_1 + 2x_2 + 0s_1 + 0s_2 + 0s_3 + 0s_4$

$$x_1 + x_2 + s_1 = 6$$
$$2x_1 + x_2 + s_2 = 8$$
$$-x_1 + x_2 + s_3 = 1$$
$$x_2 + s_4 = 2$$
$$x_1, x_2, s_1, s_2, s_3, s_4 \geq 0$$

- The above information is tabulated.

Basis ↓ C_j →	3 x_1	2 x_2	0 s_1	0 s_2	0 s_3	0 s_4	b	$\theta = \frac{b}{C_i}$
0 s_1	1	1	1	0	0	0	6	6
← 0 s_2	[2]	1	0	1	0	0	8	4 ←
0 s_3	−1	1	0	0	1	0	1	−1
0 s_4	0	1	0	0	0	1	2	∞
E_j	0	0	0	0	0	0		
$E_j - C_j$	−3 ↑	−2	0	0	0	0		

Table-1

- E_j and $E_j - C_j$ are calculated.
- The entering column is identified and the θ values are calculated, then the leaving row are identified.
- The pivotal element/value is identified from the table.
- S_2 leaves the basis, x_1 enters the basis.
- The following row operations are performed:

$$R_{2\text{ new}} = (R_{2\text{ old}})/2$$
$$R_{1\text{ new}} = R_{1\text{ old}} - R_{2\text{ new}},$$
$$R_{3\text{ new}} = R_{3\text{ old}} + R_{2\text{ new}}$$

- Then the table 1 becomes.
- E_j and $E_j - C_j$ are calculated.
- The entering column is identified and the θ values are calculated, then the leaving row are identified.
- The pivotal element/value is identified from the table.
- s_4 leaves the basis, x_2 enters the basis.

Basis ↓ / C_j →	3 x_1	2 x_2	0 s_1	0 s_2	0 s_3	0 s_4	b	$\theta = \frac{b}{C_i}$
0 s_1	0	1/2	1	– 1/2	0	0	2	4
3 x_1	1	1/2	0	1/2	0	0	4	8
0 s_3	0	3/2	0	1/2	1	0	5	10/3
← 0 s_4	0	[1] *	0	0	0	1	2	2 ←
E_j	3	3/2	0	3/2	0	0		
$E_j - C_j$	0	– 1/2 ↑	0	3/2	0	0		

Table-2

- The following row operations are performed:

$$R_{1\text{ new}} = R_{1\text{ old}} - (R_{4\text{ new}})/2,$$
$$R_{2\text{ new}} = R_{2\text{ old}} - (R_{4\text{ new}})/2,$$
$$R_{3\text{ new}} = R_{3\text{ old}} - 3(R_{4\text{ new}})/2$$

- Then the table 2 becomes table 3.
- E_j and $E_j - C_j$ are calculated.

Basis ↓ / C_j →	3 x_1	2 x_2	0 s_1	0 s_2	0 s_3	0 s_4	b
0 s_1	0	0	1	– 1/2	0	– 1/2	1
3 x_1	1	0	0	1/2	0	– 1/2	3
0 s_3	0	0	0	1/2	1	– 3/2	2
2 x_2	0	1	0	0	0	1	2
E_j	3	2	0	3/2	0	1/2	
$E_j - C_j$	0	0	0	3/2	0	1/2	

Table-3

- It is an optimum matrix since all the values obtained in '$E_j - C_j$' row are positive.

From table, $x = \begin{bmatrix} s_1 \\ x_1 \\ s_3 \\ x_2 \end{bmatrix}$ and $A = \begin{bmatrix} 1 & -1/2 & 0 & -1/2 \\ 0 & 1/2 & 0 & -1/2 \\ 0 & 1/2 & 1 & -3/2 \\ 0 & 0 & 0 & 1 \end{bmatrix}$,

From table, $B = \begin{bmatrix} 6 \\ 8 \\ 1 \\ 2 \end{bmatrix}$

- Here as $A \times B = X$ the solution is correct.

2.3 SENSITIVITY ANALYSIS OF SIMPLEX

The process of determining the effects of these changes without solving the problem from the very beginning is known as sensitivity analysis.

Example: 2.8

In (Q.No. 2.7) determine the effectin solution if the constant '6' in first constraint is changed to '7'.

Solution:

The simplex problem can be expressed in the form of matrices as follows:

$$Z = \overset{C}{(3\ 2)}\begin{pmatrix} x_1 \\ x_2 \end{pmatrix}$$

$$\begin{aligned} x_1 + 2x_2 &\le 6 \\ 2x_1 + x_2 &\le 8 \\ -x_1 + x_2 &\le 1 \\ x_2 &\le 2 \end{aligned} \Rightarrow \overset{D}{\begin{pmatrix} 1 & 2 \\ 2 & 1 \\ -1 & 1 \\ 0 & 1 \end{pmatrix}} \begin{pmatrix} x_1 \\ x_2 \end{pmatrix} \le \overset{B}{\begin{pmatrix} 6 \\ 8 \\ 1 \\ 2 \end{pmatrix}}$$

Its optimum simplex matrix is

Basis ↓ C_j →	3 x_1	2 x_2	0 s_1	0 s_2	0 s_3	0 s_4	b
0 s_1	0	0	1	– 1/2	0	– 1/2	1
3 x_1	1	0	0	1/2	0	– 1/2	3
0 s_3	0	0	0	1/2	1	– 3/2	2
2 x_2	0	1	0	0	0	1	2
E_j	3	2	0	3/2	0	1/2	
$E_j - C_j$	0	0	0	3/2	0	1/2	

$$A = \begin{bmatrix} 1 & -1/2 & 0 & -1/2 \\ 0 & 1/2 & 0 & -1/2 \\ 0 & 1/2 & 1 & -3/2 \\ 0 & 0 & 0 & 1 \end{bmatrix}; \quad X = \begin{bmatrix} x_2 = 1 \\ x_1 = 3 \\ s_3 = 2 \\ s_4 = 2 \end{bmatrix}$$

If we change constant value in problem the matrices will be become

$$\begin{matrix} x_1+2x_2 \le 7 \\ 2x_1+x_2 \le 8 \\ -x_1+x_2 \le 1 \\ x_2 \le 2 \end{matrix} \Rightarrow \overset{D}{\begin{pmatrix} 1 & 2 \\ 2 & 1 \\ -1 & 1 \\ 0 & 1 \end{pmatrix}} \begin{pmatrix} x_1 \\ x_2 \end{pmatrix} \le \overset{B}{\begin{pmatrix} 7 \\ 8 \\ 1 \\ 2 \end{pmatrix}}$$

Note: By changing the constants as negative values appeared in $A \times B$ matrix, the matrix is not an optimum one and sowe move towards optimality by dual simplex procedure.

$$A \times B = \begin{bmatrix} 1 & -1/2 & 0 & -1/2 \\ 0 & 1/2 & 0 & -1/2 \\ 0 & 1/2 & 1 & -3/2 \\ 0 & 0 & 0 & 1 \end{bmatrix} \begin{bmatrix} 7 \\ 8 \\ 1 \\ 2 \end{bmatrix} = \begin{bmatrix} 2 \\ 3 \\ 2 \\ 2 \end{bmatrix}$$

$\therefore \quad x_2 = 2, x_1 = 3, s_3 = 2, s_4 = 2$

Example: 2.9

In (Q.No. 2.7) determine the effect in solution if the constant '6 and 8' in constraints are changed to '5 and 10'.

Solution:

The simplex problem can be expressed in the form of matrices as follows:

$$Z = \overset{C}{(3\ 2)} \begin{pmatrix} x_1 \\ x_2 \end{pmatrix}$$

$$\begin{matrix} x_1+2x_2 \le 6 \\ 2x_1+x_2 \le 8 \\ -x_1+x_2 \le 1 \\ x_2 \le 2 \end{matrix} \Rightarrow \overset{D}{\begin{pmatrix} 1 & 2 \\ 2 & 1 \\ -1 & 1 \\ 0 & 1 \end{pmatrix}} \begin{pmatrix} x_1 \\ x_2 \end{pmatrix} \le \overset{B}{\begin{pmatrix} 6 \\ 8 \\ 1 \\ 2 \end{pmatrix}}$$

Its optimum simplex matrix is;

Basis ↓ C_j →	3 x_1	2 x_2	0 s_1	0 s_2	0 s_3	0 s_4	b
0 s_1	0	0	1	– 1/2	0	– 1/2	– 1
3 x_1	1	0	0	1/2	0	– 1/2	4
0 x_3	0	1	0	1/2	1	– 3/2	3
2 x_2	0	1	0	0	0	1	2
$E_j - C_j$	0	0	0	3/2	0	1/2	

If we change constant value in problem the matrices will be become

$$\begin{matrix} x_1+2x_2 \le 5 \\ 2x_1+x_2 \le 10 \\ -x_1+x_2 \le 1 \\ x_2 \le 2 \end{matrix} \Rightarrow \overset{D}{\begin{pmatrix} 1 & 2 \\ 2 & 1 \\ -1 & 1 \\ 0 & 1 \end{pmatrix}} \begin{pmatrix} x_1 \\ x_2 \end{pmatrix} \le \overset{B}{\begin{pmatrix} 5 \\ 10 \\ 1 \\ 2 \end{pmatrix}}$$

Note: By any change in the constant, if all the values of $A \times B$ appears to be "+ve" then, matrix is still an optimum one but the solution will change as below.

$$A \times B = \begin{bmatrix} 1 & -\frac{1}{2} & 0 & \frac{-1}{2} \\ 0 & \frac{1}{2} & 0 & \frac{-1}{2} \\ 0 & \frac{1}{2} & 1 & \frac{-3}{2} \\ 0 & 0 & 0 & 1 \end{bmatrix} \begin{bmatrix} 5 \\ 10 \\ 1 \\ 2 \end{bmatrix} = \begin{bmatrix} -1 \\ 4 \\ 3 \\ 2 \end{bmatrix}$$

2.4 DUAL SIMPLEX PROCEDURE

- The above matrices is tabulated as table 1.
- We will not calculate 'θ' column instead we will select max negative value from 'b' column as leaving row.

Basis ↓ / C_j →	3 x_1	2 x_2	0 s_1	0 s_2	0 s_3	0 s_4	b
0 s_1	0	0	1	− 1/2	0	− 1/2	− 1 ←
3 x_1	1	0	0	1/2	0	− 1/2	4
0 s_3	0	1	6	1/2	1	− 3/2	3
2 x_2	0	1	0	0	0	1	2
E_j	3	2	0	3/2	0	1/2	
$E_j - C_j$	0	0	0	3/2	0	1/2 ↑	

Table-2.1

- Select the min positive value excluding zero in $E_j - C_j$ row as entering column.
- Get the pivotal element (whichmay be negative also).
- s_3 leaves the basis, s_1 enters the basis
- The following row operations are performed:

$$R_{1\text{ new}} = R_{1\text{ old}} - 2(R_{3\text{ new}})/3,$$
$$R_{2\text{ new}} = R_{2\text{ old}} + (R_{3\text{ new}})/3\,,$$
$$R_{4\text{ new}} = R_{4\text{ new}} + 2(R_{3\text{ new}})/3$$

- Then the table 1 becomes

Basis ↓ / C_j →	3 x_1	2 x_2	0 s_1	0 s_2	0 s_3	0 s_4	b
0 s_4	0	0	− 2	1	0	1	2
3 x_1	1	0	− 1	1	0	0	5
0 s_3	0	0	− 3	2	−1/2	0	6
2 x_2	0	1	2	− 1	0	0	0
E_j	3	2	1	1	0	0	
$E_j - C_j$	0	0	1	1	0	0	

Table-2.2

- Thus the optimum solution will change as: $x_1 = 5$, $x_2 = 0$, $x_3 = 6$, $s_4 = 2$.

Example: 2.10

Convert the following simplex problem into a dual problem

Minimum: $Z = 5x_1 + 2x_2 + x_3$

Subjected to $2x_1 + 3x_2 + x_3 \geq 20$

$6x_1 + 8x_2 + 5x_3 \geq 30$

$7x_1 + x_2 + 3x_3 \geq 40$

$x_1 + 2x_2 + 4x_3 \geq 50$

$x_1, x_2, x_3 \geq 0$

Solution:

The simplex problem can be expressed in the form of matrices as follows:

Minimum, $$Z = A(5\ \ 2\ \ 1)\begin{pmatrix} x_1 \\ x_2 \\ x_3 \end{pmatrix};\quad B\begin{pmatrix} 2 & 3 & 1 \\ 6 & 8 & 5 \\ 7 & 1 & 3 \\ 1 & 2 & 4 \end{pmatrix}\begin{pmatrix} x_1 \\ x_2 \\ x_3 \end{pmatrix} \geq \begin{pmatrix} 20 \\ 30 \\ 40 \\ 50 \end{pmatrix} C$$

Note: If primal problem is $\begin{pmatrix} \min Z = AX \\ BX \geq C \end{pmatrix}$ then Dual Problem is $\begin{pmatrix} \max Z = C^T y \\ B^T Y \leq A^T \end{pmatrix}$

So the dual for the given problem becomes:

Maximum, $$Z = (20\ 30\ 40\ 50)\begin{pmatrix} y_1 \\ y_2 \\ y_3 \\ y_4 \end{pmatrix};\quad \begin{pmatrix} 2 & 6 & 7 & 1 \\ 3 & 8 & 1 & 2 \\ 1 & 5 & 3 & 4 \end{pmatrix}\begin{pmatrix} y_1 \\ y_2 \\ y_3 \\ y_4 \end{pmatrix} \leq \begin{pmatrix} 5 \\ 2 \\ 1 \end{pmatrix}$$

Note-1:

1. For every simplex there exists another problem which gives exactly same solution called dual.
2. Dual of dual will again be primal problem.
3. Before starting the normal simplex makes sure that constants of the constraintsare positive.When the negative sign appears multiplythe constraint by –ve sign.

Note-2:

1. Suppose there are "n" number of equations, if number of variables are more than number of equations (Rank of the matrix is less than "n"), then there will be infinite number of solutions.
2. If number of variables are equal to the number of equations (Rank is equal to "n"), then it will be a unique solution.
3. If numbers of equations are more than variables, then there will be no solution.

PRACTICE QUESTIONS

1. Which one of the following subroutines does a computer implementations linear programming by the Simplex method use?
(a) Finding a root of a polynomial
(b) Finding the determinant of a matrix
(c) Finding the Eigen values of a matrix
(d) Solving a system of linear equations

2. A variable which has no physical meaning, but is used to obtain an initial basic feasible solution to the linear programming problem is referred to as:
(a) Basic variable
(b) Non-basic variable
(c) Artificial variable
(d) Basis

3. In the solution of a linear programming problem by simplex method, if during iteration, all ratios of right-hand side b_1 to the coefficients of entering variable a are found to be negative, it implies that the problem has:
(a) Infinite number of solutions
(b) Infeasible solution
(c) Degeneracy
(d) unbound solutions

4. Consider the following statements regarding the characteristics of the standard form of a linear programming problem:
   1. All the constraints are expressed in the form of equations.
   2. The right-hand .side of each constraint equation is non-negative.
   3. All the decision variables are non-negative.

   Which of these statements are correct?
(a) 1, 2 and 3
(b) 1 and 2
(c) 2 and 3
(d) 1 and 3

5. Consider the following statements:
   1. A linear programming problem with three variables and two constraints can be solved by graphical method.
   2. For solutions of a linear programming problem with mixed constraints, Big-M method can be employed.
   3. In the solution process of a linear programming problem using Big-M method, when an artificial variable leaves the basis, the column of the artificial variable can be removed from all subsequent tables.

   Which of these statements are correct?
(a) 1, 2 and 3
(b) 1 and 2
(c) 1 and 3
(d) 2 and 3

6. Consider the following statements regarding linear programming:
   1. Dual of a dual is the primal.
   2. When two minimum ratios of the right-hand side to the coefficient in the key column are equal, degeneracy may take place.
   3. When an artificial variable leaves the basis, its column can be deleted from the subsequent Simplex tables.

   Select the correct answer from the codes given below:
(a) 1, 2 and 3
(b) 1 and 2
(c) 2 and 3
(d) 1 and 3

7. The primal of a LP problem is maximization of objective function with 6 variables and 2 constraints. Which of the following correspond to the dual of the problem stated?
   1. It has 2 variables and 6 constraints.
   2. It has 6 variables and 2 constraints.
   3. Maximization of objective function.
   4. Minimization of objective function.

   Select the correct answer using the codes given below:
   (a) 1 and 3 (b) 1 and 4
   (c) 2 and 3 (d) 2 and 4

8. In the solution of linear programming problems by Simplex method, for deciding the leaving variable:
   (a) The maximum negative coefficient in the objective function row is selected.
   (b) The minimum positive ratio of the right-hand side to the first decision variable is selected.
   (c) The maximum positive ratio of the right-hand side to the coefficient in the key column is selected.
   (d) The minimum positive ratio of the right-hand side to the coefficient in the key column is selected.

9. A tie for leaving variables in simplex procedure implies:
   (a) Optimality (b) Cycling
   (c) No solution (d) Degeneracy

10. In a linear programming problem, if a basic solution has no more than m positive $x_j (j = 1, 2......n)$, it is called:
    (a) Basic feasible solution
    (b) Unbounded solution
    (c) Non-degenerate basic feasible solution
    (d) None of the above

11. Which one of the following is the correct statement?
    In the standard form of a linear programming problem, all constraints are
    (a) of less than or equal to, type
    (b) of greater than or equal to, type
    (c) in the form of equations
    (d) some constraints are of less than equal to, type and some of greater than equal to, type

12. Which one of the following statements is not correct?
    (a) A linear programming problem with 2 variables and 3 constraints can be solved by Graphical method.
    (b) In big-M method if the artificial variable cannot be driven out it depicts an optimal solution.
    (c) Dual of dual is the primal problem.
    (d) For mixed constraints either big-M method or two phase method can be employed.

13. A linear programming problem with mixed constraints (some constraints of ≤ type and some of ≥ type) can be solved by which of the following methods?
    (a) Big-M method (b) Hungarian method
    (c) Branch and bound technique (d) Least cost method

14. While solving a linear programming problem by simplex method, if all ratios of the right-hand side (b_i) to the coefficient, in the key row (a_{ij}) become negative, then the problem has which of the following types of solution?
(a) An unbound solution
(b) Multiple solutions
(c) A unique solution
(d) No solution

15. When solving the problem by Big-M method, if the objective functions row (evaluation row) shows optimality but one or more artificial variables are still in the basis, what type of solution does it show?
(a) Optimal solution
(b) Pseudo optimal solution
(c) Degenerate solution
(d) infeasible solution

16. The leading basic variable in simplex method is the basic variable that
(a) has the lowest value.
(b) has the largest coefficient in the key row.
(c) has the smallest coefficient in the key row.
(d) goes to zero first as the entering basic variable in increased.

17. A company produces two types of toys: *P* and *Q*. Production time of *Q* is twice that of *P* and the company has a maximum of 2000 time units per day. The supply of raw material is just sufficient to produce 1500 toys (or any type) per day. Toy type *Q* requires an electric switch which is available @ 600 pieces per day only. The company makes a profit of Rs. 3 and Rs. 5 on type *P* and *Q* respectively. For maximization of profits, the daily production quantities of *P* and *Q* toys should respectively be
(a) 1000, 500
(b) 500, 1000
(c) 800, 600
(d) 1000, 1000

Statement for Linked Answer Questions (18 and 19):

Consider a linear programming problem with two variable and two constraints. The objective function is maximize $x_1 + x_2$. The corner points of the feasible region are (0, 0) (0, 2) (2, 0) and (4/3, 4/3).

18. If an additional constraint $x_1 + x_2 \leq 5$ is added the optimal solution is
(a) (5/3, 5/3)
(b) (4/3, 4/3)
(c) (5/2, 5/2)
(d) (5, 0)

19. Let Y_1 and Y_2 be the decision variables of the dual and v_1 and v_2 be the slack variables of the dual of the given linear programming problem. The optimum dual variables are
(a) Y_1 and Y_2
(b) Y_1 and v_1
(c) Y_1 and v_2
(d) v_1 and v_2

Common Data for Questions (20 and 21):

Consider the linear programme (LP):

Maximum: $4x + 6y$

Subject to $3x + 2y \leq 6$

$2x + 3y \leq 6$

$x, y \geq 0$

20. After introducing slack variables *s* and *t*, the initial basic feasible solution is represented by the tableau below (basic variables are $s = 6$ and $t = 6$, and the objective function value is 0).

	−4	−6	0	0	0
s	3	2	1	0	6
t	2	3	0	1	6
	x	y	s	t	RHS

After some simplex iterations, the following table au is obtained

	0	0	0	2	12
s	5/3	0	1	−1/3	2
t	2/3	1	0	1/3	2
	x	y	s	t	RHS

From this, one can conclude that

(a) the LP has a unique optimal solution.
(b) the LP has on optimal solution that is not unique.
(c) the LP is infeasible.
(d) the LP is unbounded.

21. The dual for the LP in **(Q.20)** is

(a) Min $6u + 6v$
subject to
$3u + 2v \geq 4$
$2u + 3v \geq 6$
$u, v \geq 0$

(b) Max $6u + 6v$
subject to
$3u + 2v \leq 4$
$2u + 3v \leq 6$
$u, v \geq 0$

(c) Max $4u + 6v$
subject to
$3u + 2v \geq 6$
$2u + 3v \geq 6$
$u, v \geq 0$

(d) Min $4u + 6v$
subject to
$3u + 2v \leq 6$
$2u + 3v \leq 6$
$u, v \geq 0$

22. Consider the following linear programming problem (LPP):

Maximize: $z = 3x_1 + 2x_2$
Subject to $x_1 \leq 4$
$x_2 \leq 6$
$3x_1 + 2x_2 \leq 18$
$x_1 \geq 0, x_2 \geq 0$

(a) The LPP has a unique optimal solution.
(b) The LPP is infeasible.
(c) The LPP is unbounded.
(d) The LPP has multiple optimal solution.

23. Simplex method of solving linear programming problem uses

(a) all the points in the feasible region.
(b) only the corner points of the feasible region
(c) intermediate points within the infeasible region.
(d) only the interior points in the feasible region.

24. Which one of the following is true in case of simplex method oflinear programming?
(a) The constants of constraints equation may be positive or negative.
(b) Inequalities are not converted into equations.
(c) It cannot be used for two-variable problems.
(d) The simplex algorithm is an iterative procedure.

25. Match **List-I (Persons with whom the models are associated)** with **List-II (Models)** and select the correct answer:

List-I	List-II
A. J. Von Newmann	1. Waiting lines
B. G. Dantzig	2. Simulation
C. A.K. Erlang	3. Dynamic programming
D. Richard Bellman	4. Competitive strategies
	5. Allocation by simplex method

Codes:

	A	B	C	D
(a)	2	1	5	4
(b)	4	5	1	3
(c)	2	5	1	4
(d)	4	1	5	3

OOOO

ANSWERS

SIMPLEX METHOD

1. (d)	2. (c)	3. (d)	4. (a)	5. (d)	6. (a)	7. (b)
8. (d)	9. (d)	10. (a)	11. (d)	12. (b)	13. (a)	14. (a)
15. (d)	16. (d)	17. (a)	18. (b)	19. (d)	20. (b)	21. (a)
22. (d)	23. (b)	24. (d)	25. (b)			

CHAPTER 3

Transportation

3.1 INTRODUCTION

Transportation problems are meant to optimize loss or cost minimization. If the profit matrix is given, it has to be converted into a loss matrix by subtracting the each element from the maximum available number in the matrix. There are various methods to find out initial basic feasible solutions in the transportation problem.

Transportation problems are that of loss minimization and when the profit matrix is given to you, select the maximum value appearing in the matrix and subtract each and every value of the matrix from this maximum value. That is how we convert a profit matrix into a loss matrix. After identifying the allocations of the cell, using this loss matrix, transport the allocations to the profit matrix to find the maximum profit.

3.2 NORTH WEST CORNER METHOD

For every transportation problem first we have to check whether the shell is balanced (or) not i.e., the capacity in rows should be equal to that in columns. Then take the NW corner cell and start allocating; the maximum value till either row (or) column capacity is exhausted.

Example 3.1:

A company has three plants at *A*, *B*, *C* which supply to stores I, II, III and IV. Weekly plant capacities are 22, 15, 8 tons respectively. Weekly store requirements are 7, 12, 17and 9 respectively. Unit transportation cost matrix is given below:

From \ To	I	II	III	IV
A	5	2	4	3
B	4	8	1	6
C	4	6	7	5

Allocate the cost using North West Corner Method.

Solution:

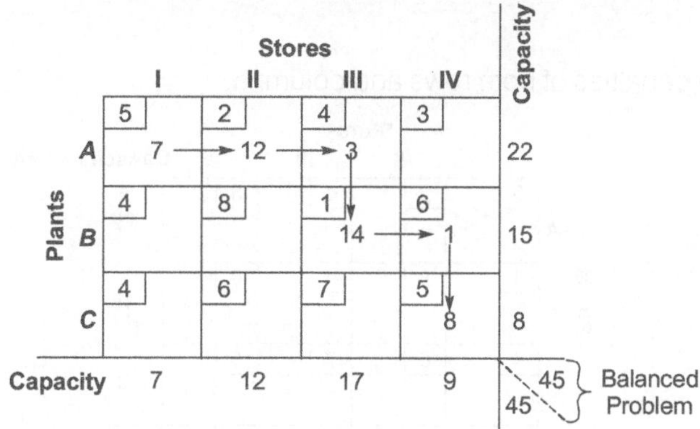

Total transportation, cost = $(5 \times 7) + (2 \times 12) + (4 \times 3) + (14 \times 1) + (6 \times 1) + (8 \times 5)$

$= 131$

3.3 LEAST COST METHOD

This method finds a better starting solution by concentrating on the cheapest routes. The method starts by assigning as much as possible to the cell with the smallest unit cost. Next, the non-exhausted cell with the smallest unit cost is allocated.

Example: 3.2

Take the data from the previous problem and allocate using least cost method.

Solution:

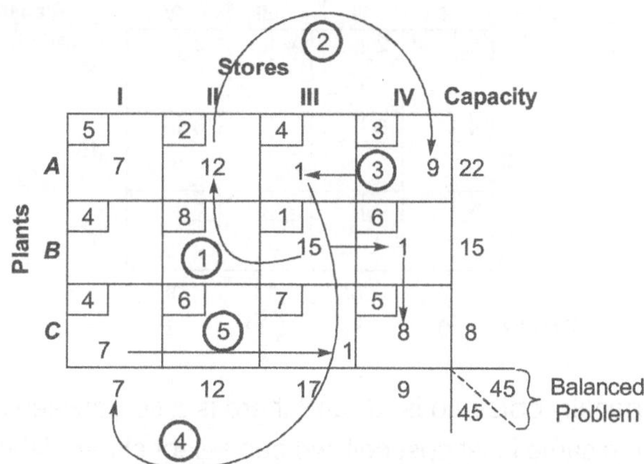

Total transportation, cost = $(2 \times 12) + (4 \times 1) + (9 \times 3) + (15 \times 1) + (7 \times 1) + (4 \times 7)$

$= 105$

3.4 VOGEL APPROXIMATION METHOD (VAM)

This method is the improved version of the least cost method. It produces better starting solutions. It is also called **Penalty Method.** In this method, we start allocating by calculating penalty. **Penalty** is the difference between the two minimum values of costs in rows or columns.

Example: 3.3

Take the data from the problem 3.1 and allocate using Vogel's approximation method.

Solution:

- Calculate the penalties of both rows and columns.

Plants \ Stores	I	II	III	IV	Capacity	Penalty
A	5	2	4	3	22	1
B	4	8	1	6	15	3
C	4	6	7	5	8	1
Capacity	7	12	17	9	45 / 45	
Penalty	0	(4) ↑	3	2		

- Select the maximum penalty column or row.In this maximum penalty is "4".
  Note: (If there is a tie in the maximum penalty we select that particular row or column, which has minimum transportation cost.)
- Select the minimum cost in that row or column and allocate the maximum possible value in that cell. Here in the selected column 2 is the minimum cost and '12' is allocated to it.
  Note: The maximum possible value that can be allocated in a cell is the minimum available of both in row and column.
- After allocation recalculate the penalties of rows and columns.
  Note: In these calculations, we will not consider the transportation costs of the cells, which are been allocated or exhausted.

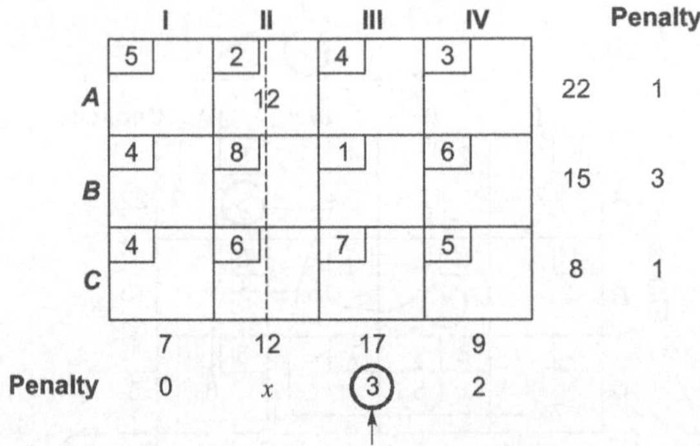

- The maximum penalty obtained is "3" and there is a tie between a row and column, but as both indicates the same least cost cell, we can select either of the two.

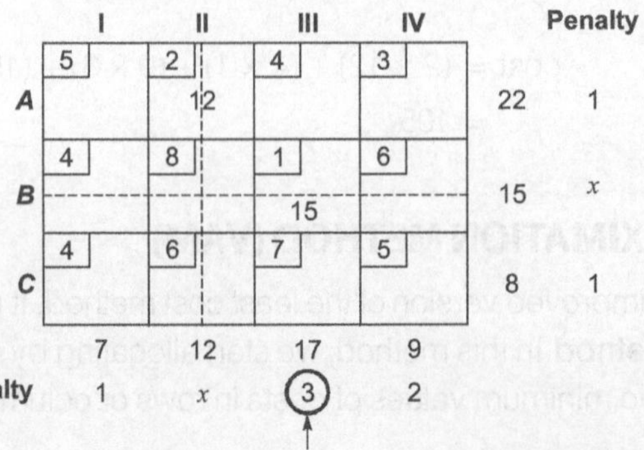

- After allocation recalculate the penalties of rows and columns.

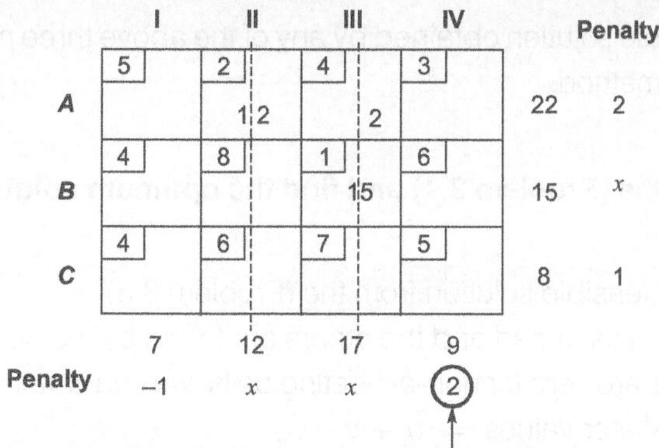

	I	II	III	IV		Penalty
A	5	2 / 12	4 / 2	3	22	2
B	4	8	1 / 15	6	15	x
C	4	6	7	5	8	1
	7	12	17	9		
Penalty	–1	x	x	(2)		

- Now the maximum penalty is "2"and there is a tie between a row and column, but as both indicates the same least cost cell, we can select either of the two because in that row or column least cost cell in sums.

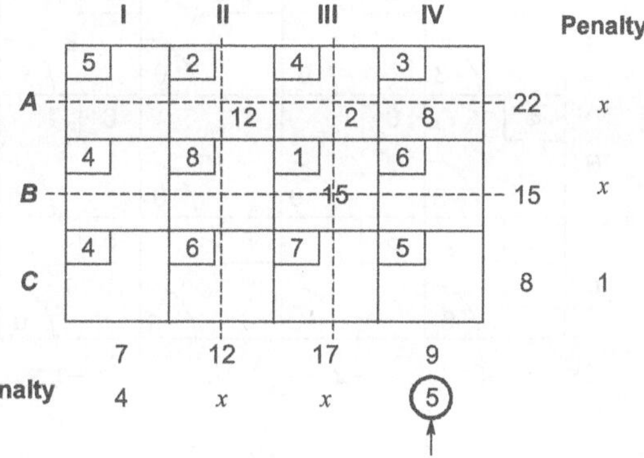

	I	II	III	IV		Penalty
A	5	2 / 12	4 / 2	3 / 8	22	x
B	4	8	1 / 15	6	15	x
C	4	6	7	5	8	1
	7	12	17	9		
Penalty	4	x	x	(5)		

- After allocation recalculate the penalties of rows and columns. The maximum penalty is "5" and so we allocate 8 in the least cost cell "3".

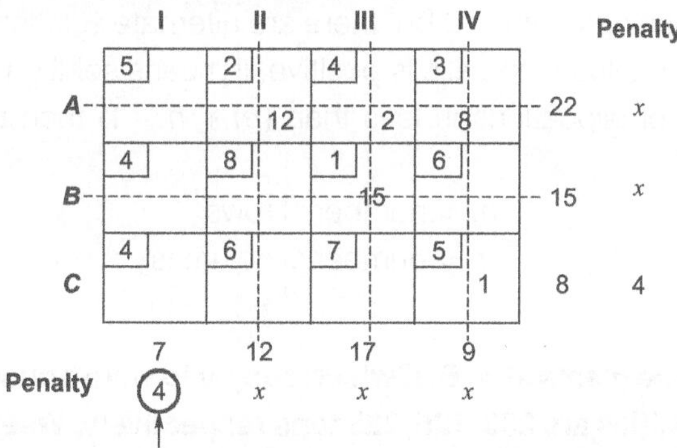

	I	II	III	IV		Penalty
A	5	2 / 12	4 / 2	3 / 8	22	x
B	4	8	1 / 15	6	15	x
C	4	6	7	5 / 1	8	4
	7	12	17	9		
Penalty	(4)	x	x	x		

- After allocation recalculate the penalties of rows and columns. The maximum penalty is '4" and so we allocate '7' in the least cost cell.

	I	II	III	IV	
A	5	2 / 12	4 / 2	3 / 8	22
B	4	8	1 / 15	6	15
C	4 / 7	6	7	5 / 1	8
	7	12	17	9	

- Thus total transportation cost is $(12 \times 2) + (4 \times 2) + (3 \times 8) + (15 \times 1) + (4 \times 7) + (5 \times 1) = 104$

3.5 MODI METHOD (MODIFIED DISTRIBUTION METHOD):

Using the initial feasible solution obtained by any of the above three methods,the optimum matrix is obtained by using MODI method.

Example: 3.4

Take the data from the (Problem 3.1) and find the optimum solution using MODI method.

Solution:

- Taking the initial feasible solution from the (Problem 3.3).
- Any one of u_i, v_j is assumed and the others are found by the condition that the water values of allocated cells are zero for non-allocating cells, we find water values by using the formula.

$$\text{Water Values} = u_i + v_j - c_{ij}$$

Where u_i and v_j are arbitrary constants and c_{ij} is transportation cost of that cell

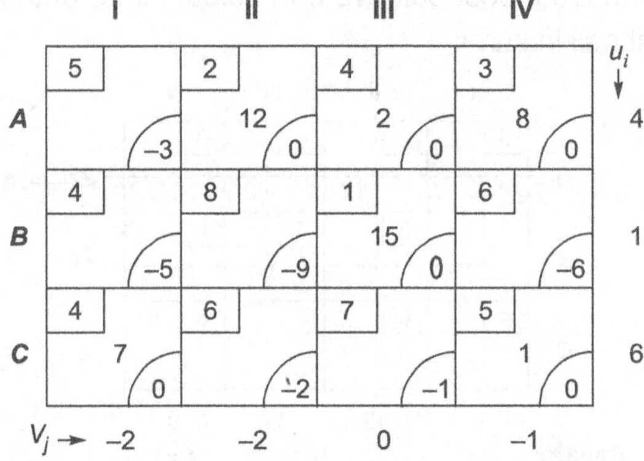

Note:

1. If the water values of all non-allocated cells are negative. It means it is optimum matrix.
2. If all the water values of non-allocating cells are negative but one value is zero it means solution is still an optimum one but there are alternate solutions.
3. If any of the non-allocating cells is positive, it means solution is not an optimum one.
4. If the number of allocations is less than $(m + n - 1)$ then the solution is considered as "Degenerated".

   Where, m = number of rows

   n = number of columns

Example: 3.5

A company has three plants at *A, B, C* which supply to ware houses located at *D, E, F, G* and *H*. Weekly plant capacities are 200, 125, 225 tons respectively. Weekly warehouse requirements are 75, 105, 130, 155 and 85 respectively. Unit transportation cost matrix is given below:

From \ To	D	E	F	G	H
A	50	82	65	60	35
B	45	70	70	65	50
C	80	45	75	60	40

Solution:

- Using penalty method the initial feasible solution.

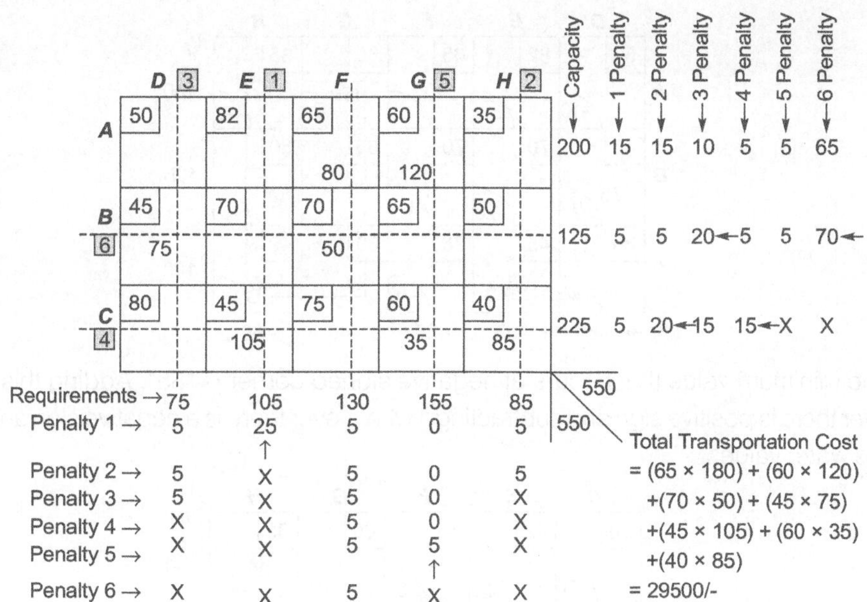

- The optimum matrix is obtained by using MODI method.

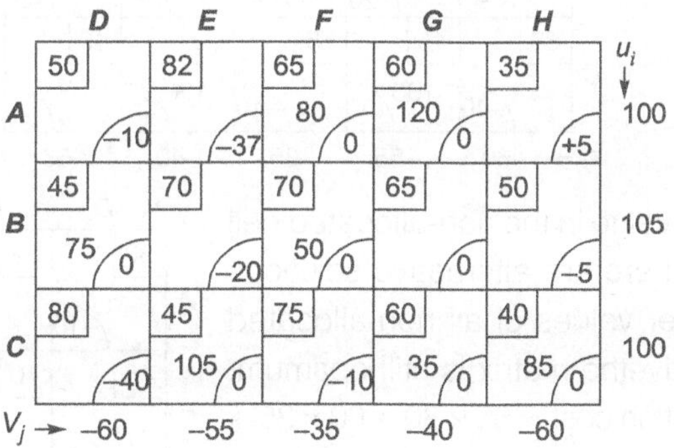

- The positive water value indicates that the matrix is not optimum.
- Now, select the unallocated cell which is having maximum positive water value.
- From this cell draw a unique loop by drawing horizontal and vertical lines in such a way that at each and every corner there are allocations as follows.

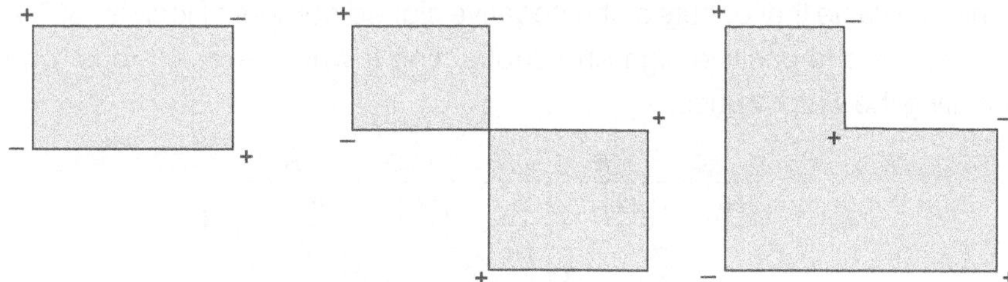

- Only a unique loop can be formed.
- Locate alternative positive and negative signs at corners of the loops starting with the positive at the corner in the (unallocated cell) i.e. maximum positive water value cell.
- On this loop, wherever negative sign is appearing, choose the minimum value out of those. Add the value where ever there is a positive sign and subtract this value where there is a negative sign.

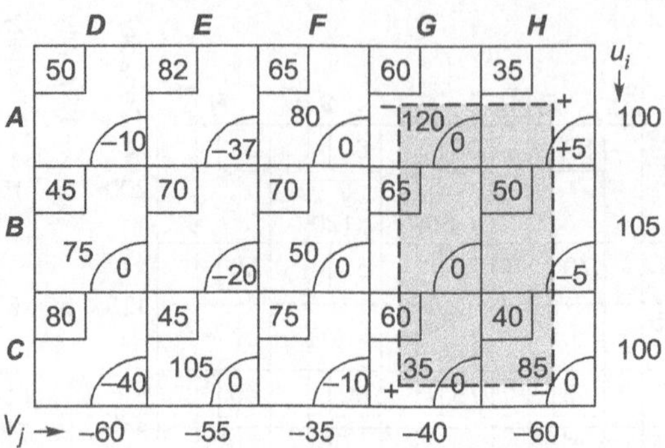

- The minimum value that occurs at negative signed corner is "85". Adding this value where ever there is positive sign and subtracting it where ever there is a negative sign and recalculate the water values.

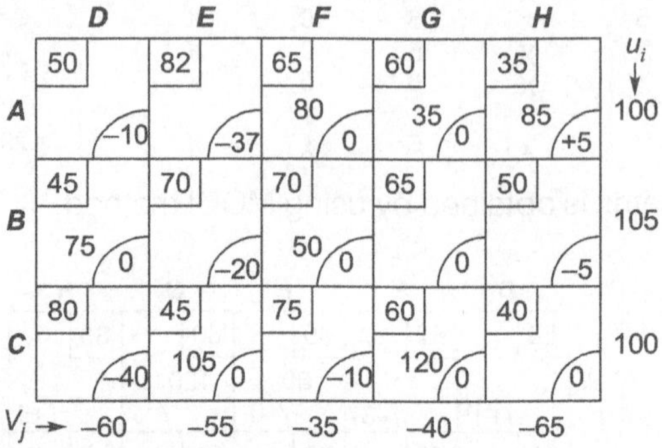

- The zero water value in the non-allocated cell indicates that there are alternative solutions but as the water values of all non-allocated cells are negativethe matrix is still optimum. Total transportation cost = 65 × 80 + 60 × 35 + 35 × 85 + 45 × 75 + 70 × 50 + 45 × 105 + 60 × 120 = 29075/-

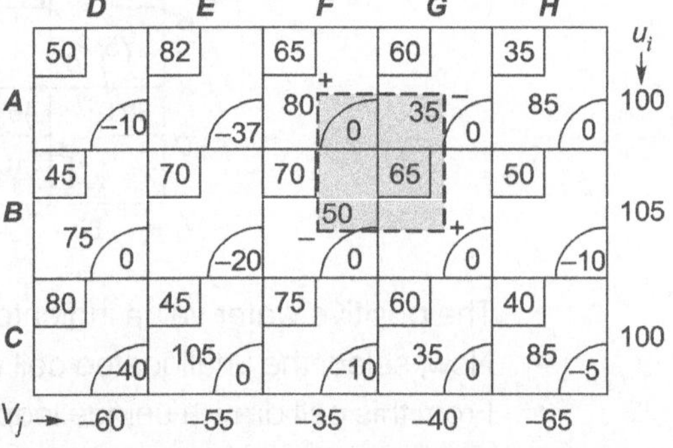

- **To find alternative solution** draw a loop starting with the non-allocated cell having zero water value.

The minimum value that occurs at the negative signed corners of loop is "35". Adding this value where ever there is positive sign and subtracting it where ever there is a negative sign and recalculating the water values.

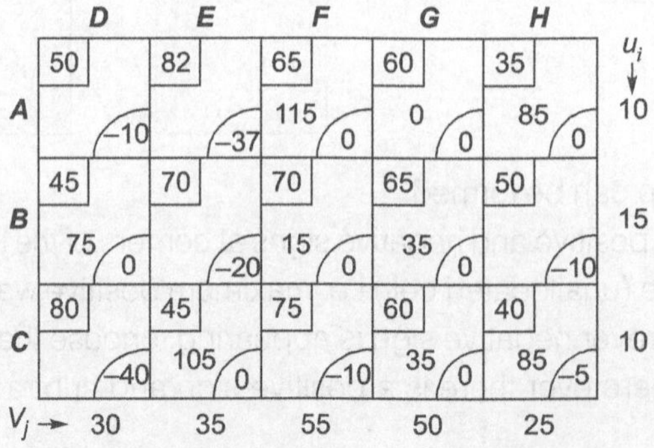

Total transportation cost = 65 × 115 + 35 × 85 + 45 × 75 + 70 × 15 + 65 × 35 + 45 × 105 + 60 × 120 = 29075

When we find the water values for this, we again get non-positive values with a zero. When we again try to find the alternate solution, we will result in the first solution (or) previous one.

Example: 3.6

A company has three plants at *A, B, C* which supply to ware houses located at I, II, III and IV. Weekly plant capacities are 15, 25, 10 tons respectively. Weekly warehouse requirements are 5, 15, 15 and 15 respectively. Unit transportation cost matrix is given below:

From \ To	I	II	III	IV
A	10	2	20	11
B	12	7	9	20
C	4	14	16	18

Solution:

- Using penalty method the initial feasible solution is

	I [1]	II [2]	III [3]	IV [5]	← Capacity	← 1 Penalty	← 2 Penalty	← 3 Penalty	← 4 Penalty	← 5 Penalty
A [2]	10	2 (15)	20	11	15	8	9 ←	X	X	X
B [4]	12	7	9 (15)	20 (10)	25	2	2	11 ←	20 ←	X
C	4 (5)	14	16	18 (5)	10	10 ←	2	2	18	18 ←
Requirements →	5	15	15	15						
Penalty 1 →	6	5	7	7						
Penalty 2 →	X	5	7	7						
Penalty 3 →	X	X	7	2						
Penalty 4 →	X	X	X	18						
Penalty 5 →	X	X	X	18						

- Here number of rows (m) = 4 and number of columns (n) = 3
  $m + n - 1 = 6$
- Number of allocations = 5
- Number of allocations < ($m + n - 1$) it means solution is degenerated.

Note: While allocating any cell in transportation, if both row and column gets cancelled simultaneously it means degeneracy has entered into the system.

- Before moving towards optimality, degeneracy has to be removed from the matrix, by allocating an insignificant number "∈" in any non-allocated cell, which has minimum transportation cost. Care should be taken that by this allocation, loop should not form in the matrix.
- The positive water value indicates that the matrix is not optimum.

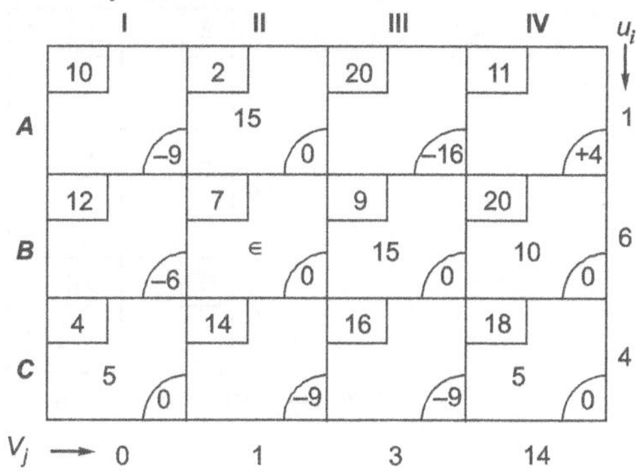

	I	II	III	IV	u_i
A	10 (−9)	2, 15 (0)	20 (−16)	11 (+4)	1
B	12 (−6)	7, ∈ (0)	9, 15 (0)	20, 10 (0)	6
C	4, 5 (0)	14 (−9)	16 (−9)	18, 5 (0)	4
V_j →	0	1	3	14	

- Now, select the unallocated cell which is having maximum positive water value.
- From this cell drawa unique loop by drawing horizontal and vertical lines in such a way that at each and every corner there are allocations.
- Locate alternative positive and negative signs at corners of the loops starting with the positive at the corner in the (nonallocated cell) i.e. maximum positive water value cell.

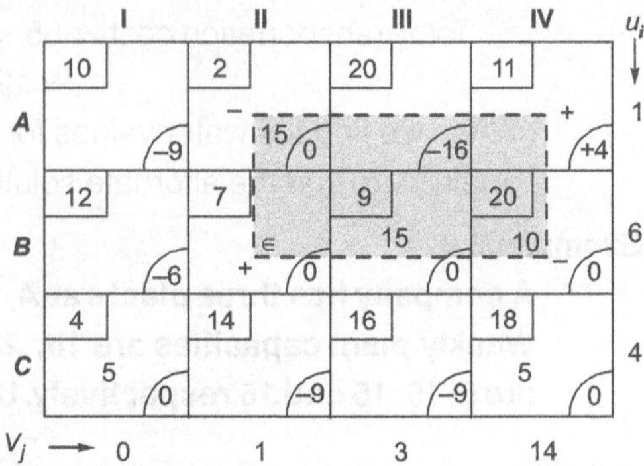

	I	II	III	IV	u_i
A	[10] (−9)	[2] 15 (−) (0)	[20] (−16)	[11] (+) (+4)	1
B	[12] (−6)	[7] ∈ (+) (0)	[9] 15 (0)	[20] 10 (−) (0)	6
C	[4] 5 (0)	[14] (−9)	[16] (−9)	[18] 5 (0)	4
V_j →	0	1	3	14	

- The minimum value that occurs at negative signed corner is "10", Adding this value where ever there is positive sign and subtracting it where ever there is a negative sign and recalculate the water values.

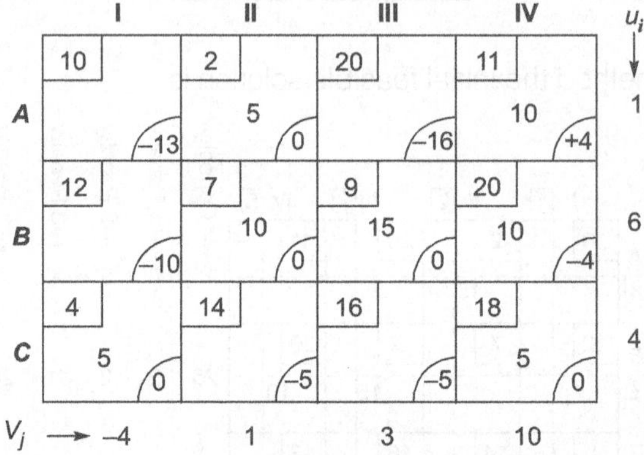

	I	II	III	IV	u_i
A	[10] (−13)	[2] 5 (0)	[20] (−16)	[11] 10 (+4)	1
B	[12] (−10)	[7] 10 (0)	[9] 15 (0)	[20] 10 (−4)	6
C	[4] 5 (0)	[14] (−5)	[16] (−5)	[18] 5 (0)	4
V_j →	−4	1	3	10	

- As the water values of all non-allocated cells are negative it is optimum matrix.

Total transportation cost = $(5 \times 2) + (7 \times 10) + (9 \times 15) + (11 \times 10) + (4 \times 5) + (18 \times 5)$

= 435

Example: 3.7

A company has three plants at *A*, *B*, *C* which supply to ware houses located at I, II, III, IV and V. Weekly plant capacities are 8, 12, 14 tons respectively. Weekly warehouse requirements are 4, 4, 6, 8 and 8 respectively. Unit transportation cost matrix is given below:

From \ To	I	II	III	IV	V
A	4	2	3	2	6
B	5	4	5	2	1
C	6	5	4	7	3

Solution:

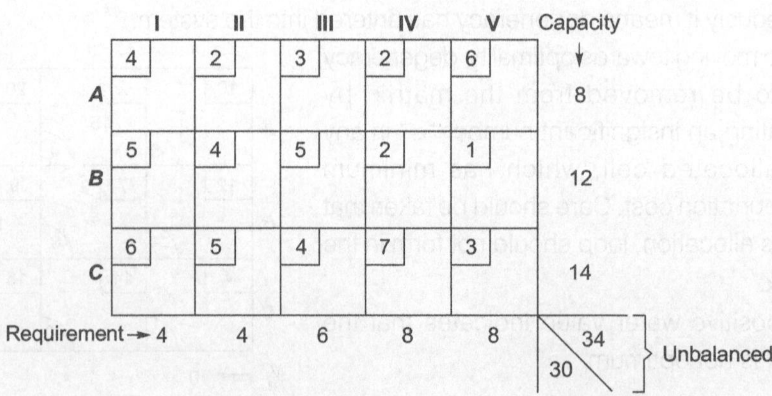

	I	II	III	IV	V	Capacity ↓
A	[4]	[2]	[3]	[2]	[6]	8
B	[5]	[4]	[5]	[2]	[1]	12
C	[6]	[5]	[4]	[7]	[3]	14
Requirement →	4	4	6	8	8	34 / 30 } Unbalanced

- If the matrix is unbalanced we need to add a dummy column or dummy row. Here by adding dummy column the matrix becomes.

	I	II	III	IV	V	Dummy	Capacity
A	4	2	3	2	6	0	8
B	5	4	5	2	1	0	12
C	6	5	4	7	3	0	14
Requirement →	4	4	6	8	8	4	34 / 34 Unbalanced

- Using penalty method the initial feasible solution is

	I	II [5]	III	IV [4]	V [2]	Dummy [1]	Capacity	1 Penalty	2 Penalty	3 Penalty	4 Penalty	5 Penalty
A [5]	4	2 (4)	3	2 (4)	6	0	8	2	0	0	0	1
B [3]	5	4	5	2 (4)	1 (8)	0	12	1	1	2	X ←	X
C	6 (4)	5	4 (6)	7	3	0 (4)	14	3 ←	1	1	1	1
Requirement →	4	4	6	8	8	4						
Penalty 1 →	1	2	1	0	2	0						
Penalty 2 →	1	2	1	0	2 ↑	X						
Penalty 3 →	1	2	1	0	X	X						
Penalty 4 →	2	3	1	5 ↑	X	X						
Penalty 5 →	2	3 ↑	1	X	X	X						

- Here number of rows (m) =3 and number of columns (n) = 6 so $m + n - 1 = 8$
- Number of allocations = 7
- Number of allocations < ($m + n - 1$) it means degeneracy has entered the cell.
- In such case, allocate "∈" in the cell of main matrix but not in the dummy cells.

	I	II	III	IV	V	Dummy	u_i
A	4 (+) [0]	2 (4)	3 [–1]	2 (4)	6 [–5]	0 [–2]	7
B	5 [–1]	4 [–2]	5 [–3]	2 (4) +	1 (8) –	0 [–2]	7
C	6 (4) –	5 [–1]	4 (6)	7 [–3]	3 (∈) +	0 (4)	9
V_j →	–3	–5	–5	–5	–6	–9	

- Since all the water values are non-positive it is an optimal solution.
- The optimal solution is = 2 × 4 + 2 × 4 + 2 × 4 + 1 × 8 + 4 × 6 + 6 × 4 = 80

Since one water value is zero there are alternate solutions available which can be found out by the loop given in the above table.

	I	II	III	IV	V	Dummy
A	4 (4)	2 (4)	3	2	6	0
B	5	4	5	2 (8)	1 (4)	0
C	6	5	4 (6)	7	3 (4)	0 (4)

- The alternative solution is = 4 × 4 + 2 × 4 + 2 × 8 + 1 × 4 + 4 × 6 + 3 × 4 = 80

Example: 3.8

A company has 3 plants at *A*, *B*, *C* which supply to ware houses located at I, II, III, IV and V. Weekly plant capacities are 8, 12, 14 tons respectively. Weekly warehouse requirements are 4, 4, 6, 8 and 8 respectively. Unit transportation cost matrix is given below.

From \ To	I	II	III	IV	V
A	10	2	20	11	6
B	12	7	9	20	1
C	5	14	16	18	3

Solution:

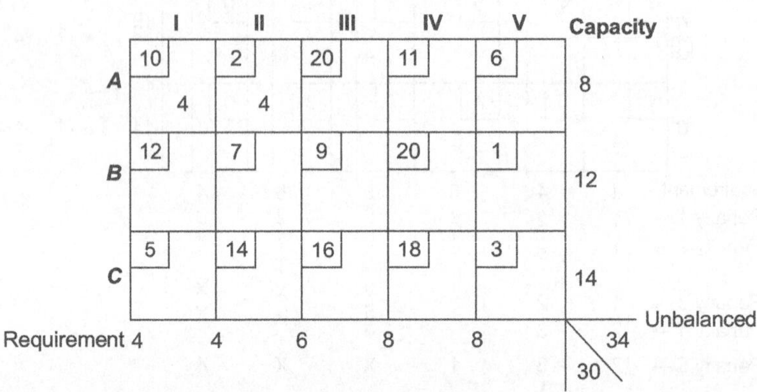

	I	II	III	IV	V	Capacity
A	10 (4)	2 (4)	20	11	6	8
B	12	7	9	20	1	12
C	5	14	16	18	3	14
Requirement	4	4	6	8	8	34 / 30 Unbalanced

- If the matrix is unbalanced we need to add a dummy column or row. Here by adding dummy column of capacity 4 the matrix becomes balanced.

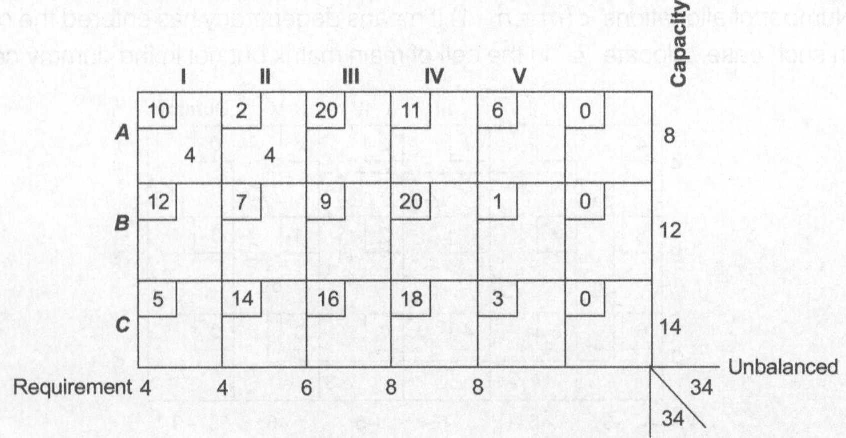

	I	II	III	IV	V		Capacity
A	10 (4)	2 (4)	20	11	6	0	8
B	12	7	9	20	1	0	12
C	5	14	16	18	3	0	14
Requirement	4	4	6	8	8		34 / 34 Unbalanced

- Using penalty method the initial feasible solution is

	I	II	III	IV	V	Dummy	Capacity	1 Penalty	2 Penalty	3 Penalty	4 Penalty
A	10	2	20	11 / 8	6	0	8	2	2	X	X
B	12	7 / 4	9 / 6	20	1 / 2	0	12	1	1	1	1
C	5 / 4	14	16	18	3 / 6	0 / 4	14	3	3	3	3
Requirement →	4	4	6	8	8	4					
Penalty 1 →	5	5	7	7	2	0					
Penalty 2 →											
Penalty 3 →	5	5	X	7	2	0					
Penalty 4 →	7	7	X	X	2	0					
Penalty 5 →	X	X	X	X	2	0					

- Here number of rows (m) = 3 and no. of columns (n) = 6 so $m + n - 1 = 8$
- Number of allocations = 7
- Number of allocations < ($m + n - 1$) it means degeneracy has entered the cell.
- In such cases, allocate "$\in$" in the cell of main matrix but not in the dummy cells.

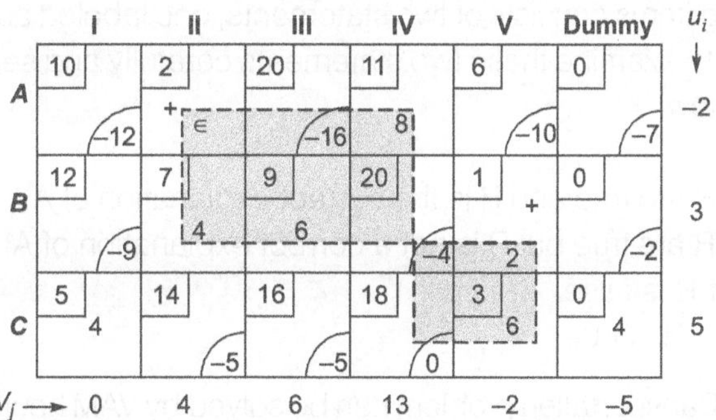

	I	II	III	IV	V	Dummy	u_i
A	10 / −12	2 / + $\in$	20 / −16	11 / 8	6 / −10	0 / −7	−2
B	12 / −9	7 / 4	9 / 6	20 / −4	1 / + 2	0 / −2	3
C	5 / 4	14 / −5	16 / −5	18 / 0	3 / 6	0 / 4	5
V_j →	0	4	6	13	−2	−5	

- Since all the water values are non-positive it is an optimal solution.
- The optimal solution is = 11 × 8 + 7 × 4 + 9 × 6 +1 × 2 + 5 × 4 + 3 × 6 + 0 × 4 = 210.
- Since one water value is zero there are alternate solutions available which can be found out by the loop given in the above table.

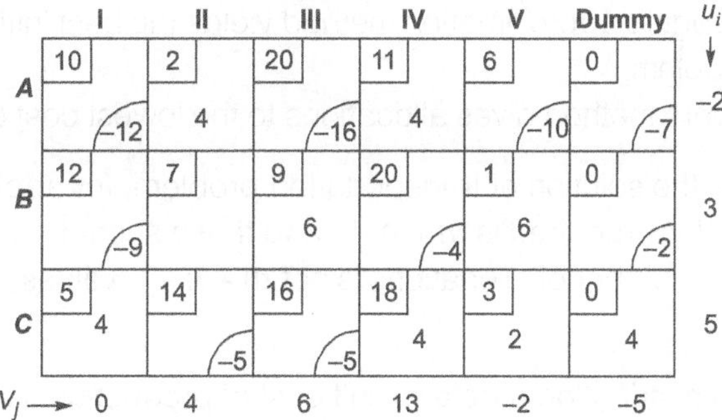

	I	II	III	IV	V	Dummy	u_i
A	10 / −12	2 / 4	20 / −16	11 / 4	6 / −10	0 / −7	−2
B	12 / −9	7	9 / 6	20 / −4	1 / 6	0 / −2	3
C	5 / 4	14 / −5	16 / −5	18 / 4	3 / 2	0 / 4	5
V_j →	0	4	6	13	−2	−5	

- The alternate solution is = 2 × 4 + 11 × 4 + 9 × 6 + 5 × 4 + 1 × 6 +18 × 4 + 3 × 2 = 210

○○○○

PRACTICE QUESTIONS

1. The solution in a transportation model (of dimension $m \times n$) is said to be degenerate if it has
   (a) exactly $(m + n - 1)$ allocations
   (b) fewer than $(m + n - 1)$ allocations
   (c) more than $(m + n - 1)$ allocations
   (d) $(m \times n)$ allocations

2. A solution is not a basic feasible solution in a transportation problem if after allocations:
   (a) There is no closed loop.
   (b) There is a closed loop.
   (c) Total number of allocations is one less than the sum of number of sources and destinations.
   (d) There is degeneracy.

3. In a transportation problem North-West corner rule would yield:
   (a) An optimum solution
   (b) An initial feasible solution
   (c) A Vogel's approximate solution
   (d) A minimum cost solution

4. In a transportation problem, the materials are transported from 3 plants to 5 warehouses. The basic feasible solution must contain exactly, which one of the following allocated cells?
   (a) 3
   (b) 5
   (c) 7
   (d) 8

Directions: The following items consists of two statements; one labeled as **'Assertion (A)'** and the other as **'Reason(R)'**. You are to examine these two statements carefully and select the answer to these items using the code given below:

Codes:
(a) Both A and R are true and R is the correct explanation of A.
(b) Both A and R are true but R is not a correct explanation of A.
(c) A is true but R is false.
(d) A is false but R is true.

5. **Assertion ((A):** Transportation problem can be solved by VAM heuristic much faster as compared to the solution through liner programming method.
   Reason (R): VAM heuristic gives an approximate solution. It is checked for optimality test. If it is optimal, the algorithm stops there. If it is not an optimal solution, then improved solutions are found out through very little iteration till optimality is reached.

6. **Assertion ((A):** Vogel's approximation method yields the best initial basic feasible solution of a transportation problem.
   Reason (R): Vogel's method gives allocations to the lowest cost elements of the whole matrix.

7. **Assertion (A):** In the solution of transportation problem, for application of optimality test, the number of allocations required is $m + n - 1$ and these should be in independent positions.
   Reason (A): If the number of allocations is not $m + n - 1$, values of all oddments, i.e., U_i and V_j cannot be found.

8. **Assertion (A):** In distribution problem, unit cost of production as well as transportation cost is considered.
   Reason (R): The Vogel approximation method can reduce the number of iterations to move from the initial assignment to the optimal solution.

9. Consider the following statements on transportation problem:
   1. In Vogel's approximation method, priority allotment is made in the cell with lowest cost in the column or row with least penalty.
   2. The North-West corner method ensures faster optimal solution.
   3. If the total demand is higher than supply, transportation problem cannot be solved.
   4. A feasible solution may not be an optimal solution.

   Which of these statements are correct?

   (a) 1 and 4 (b) 1 and 3
   (c) 2 and 3 (d) 3 and 4

10. Match **List-I (Techniques/Methods)** with **List-II (Models)** and select the correct answer using the codes given below the lists:

List-I	**List-II**
A. Vogel's approximation method	**1.** Assignment model
B. Floods technique	**2.** Transportation model
C. Two phase method	**3.** PERT and CPM
D. Crashing	**4.** Linear Programming

Codes:

	A	B	C	D
(a)	3	4	1	2
(b)	2	1	4	3
(c)	3	1	4	2
(d)	2	4	1	3

11. Which one of the following is not the solution method of transportation problems?

    (a) Hungarian method (b) Northwest corner method
    (c) Least cost method (d) Vogel's approximation method

12. Consider the following statements:
    The assignment problem is seen to be the special case of the transportation problem in which
    1. $m = n$ 2. all $a_i = 1$ 3. $x_{ij} = 1$
    (The symbols have the usual meaning)
    Which of these statements are correct?

    (a) 1, 2 and 3 (b) 1 and 2 only
    (c) 2 and 3 only (d) 1 and 3 only

13. In order for a transportation matrix which has six rows and four columns not to degenerate, what is the number of occupied cells in the matrix?

    (a) 6 (b) 9
    (c) 15 (d) 24

14. Consider the following statements:
    1. For the application of optimality test in case of transportation model, the number of allocations should be equal to $m + n$, where m is the number of rows and n is the number of columns of the matrix.
    2. Transportation problem is a special case of a linear programming problem.
    3. In case of assignment problem the first step is to make a square matrix by adding a dummy row or a dummy column.

    Which of these statements is/are correct?

    (a) 1, 2 and 3 (b) 1 and 2 only
    (c) 2 and 3 only (d) 2 only

15. In a transportation problem, how is an unacceptable transportation route handled?
(a) By giving it at a cost of zero (b) By carrying an extremely high cost
(c) By introducing a dummy destination (d) By introducing a dummy origin

16. A company has two factories S_1, S_2 and two warehouses D_1, D_2. The supplies from S_1 and S_2 are 50 and 40 units respectively. Warehouse D_1 requires a minimum of 40 units. Warehouse D_2 requires a minimum of 20 units. Over and above, it can take as much as it can be supplied. A balanced transportation problem is to be formulated for the above situation. The number of supply points and the number of demand points and the total supply or total demand in the balanced transportation problem respectively are:
(a) 2, 4, 90 (b) 2, 4, 110
(c) 3, 4, 90 (d) 3, 4, 110

17. Which one of the following conditions should be satisfied for the application of optimality test on an initial solution of transportation model?
(a) Number of allocations should be less than $m + n - 1$
(b) Number of allocations should be equal to $m + n - 1$
(c) Number of allocations should be equal to $m + n$
(d) Number of allocations should be more than $m + n$

18. When there are 'm' rows and 'n' columns in a transportation problem, degeneracy is said to occur when the number of allocations is:
(a) Less than $(m + n - 1)$ (b) Greater than $(m + n - 1)$
(c) Equal to $(m - n - 1)$ (d) Less than $(m - n - 1)$

19. Match **List-I (O.R. Techniques)** with **List-II (Application)** and select the correct answer using the codes given below the lists:

List-I	List-II
A. Linear programming	1. Warehouse location decision
B. Transportation	2. Machine allocation decision
C. Assignment	3. Product mix decision
D. Queuing theory	4. Project management decision
	5. Number of servers decision

Codes:

	A	B	C	D
(a)	1	2	3	5
(b)	3	1	2	5
(c)	1	3	4	5
(d)	3	2	1	4

20. In a 6 × 6 transportation problem, degeneracy would arise if the if the number of filled slots were
(a) Equal to thirty six (b) More than twelve
(c) Equal to twelve (d) Less than eleven

OOOO

ANSWERS

TRANSPORTATION

1. (b)	2. (b)	3. (b)	4. (c)	5. (a)	6. (c)	7. (a)
8. (a)	9. (d)	10. (b)	11. (a)	12. (a)	13. (b)	14. (c)
15. (d)	16. (c)	17. (b)	18. (a)	19. (b)	20. (d)	

CHAPTER 4

Assignment and Sequencing

4.1 ASSIGNMENT

Assignment problems are solved for cost minimization.

Example: 4.1

Five jobs I, II, III, IV & V and five machines *A, B, C, D, E*, time taken for each machine to do a particular job is given in minutes.

	I	II	III	IV	V
A	6	5	8	11	16
B	1	13	16	1	10
C	16	11	8	8	8
D	9	14	12	10	16
E	10	13	11	8	16

Assign the jobs to machines to minimize the total processing time. And find the minimum time taken.

Solution:

	I	II	III	IV	V
A	1	0	3	6	11
B	0	12	15	0	9
C	8	3	0	0	0
D	0	5	3	1	7
E	2	5	3	0	8

Steps-IV : If the number of lines is equal to the order of matrix then it is the optimal table. If the number of lines is less than the order of matrix, then select the minimum number which is not covered by the lines. Subtract this value from each and every element which is uncovered and add this value at the intersection point of lines. Here adding "3" minimum uncovered value at intersection and subtracting at non-covered values.

	I	II	III	IV	V
A	4	0	3	9	11
B	0	9	12	0	6
C	11	3	0	3	0
D	0	2	0	1	4
E	2	2	0	0	5

We will continue to repeat step IV, till number of lines are equal to the order of the matrix.Now number of lines are equal to the order of the matrix, so select zeros such that every column and row consists of one zero i.e., one allocation for one machine.

	I	II	III	IV	V
A	4	0	3	9	11
B	0	9	13	0	6
C	11	3	0	3	0
D	0	2	0	1	4
E	2	2	0	0	5

Assignment is *A*-II, *B*-IV, *C*-V, *D*-I, *E*-III

4.2 TRANSFERRING THE SOLUTIONS TO THE MAIN MATRIX

	I	II	III	IV	V
A	6	5	8	11	16
B	1	13	6	1	10
C	16	11	8	8	8
D	9	14	12	10	16
E	10	13	11	8	16

The total processing time is 34.

The matrix also has another solution: by observation it is *A*-II, *B*-I, *C*-V, *D*-III, *E*-IV.

I solution represented by circles and II solution is represented by boxes.

Example: 4.2

Following is the profit matrix. Find the allocations to maximize the profit.

	I	II	III	IV	V
A	30	40	40	25	29
B	37	24	32	38	62
C	40	27	33	49	41
D	28	21	30	36	34
E	40	36	35	36	39

Solution:

The profit matrix is converted into relative loss matrix by subtracting all the entries from the highest entry 62. Thus we have

	I	II	III	IV	V
A	32	22	22	37	33
B	25	38	30	24	0
C	22	35	29	13	21
D	34	41	32	26	28
E	22	26	27	26	23

Steps-I:
Select the minimum value of each row and subtract this value from each and every element from that particular row.

Steps-II:
Check whether at least one zero is available in each and every column if not do the first step for columns.

Steps-III: Cover all the zeros with minimum number of lines.

	I	II	III	IV	V
A	10	0	0	15	11
B	25	38	30	24	0
C	9	22	16	0	8
D	8	15	6	0	2
E	0	4	5	4	1

As number of lines is less than order of matrix. Here adding "6" minimum uncovered value at intersection and subtracting at non covered values.

	I	II	III	IV	V
A	10	0	0	21	17
B	19	32	24	29	0
C	3	16	10	0	8
D	2	9	0	0	2
E	0	4	5	10	7

As number of lines are equal to the order of the matrix, hence the matrix optimum one.

	I	II	III	IV	V
A	10	[0]	~~0~~	21	17
B	19	32	24	29	[0]
C	3	16	10	[0]	8
D	2	9	[0]	~~0~~	2
E	[0]	4	5	10	7

Hence solution is $A \rightarrow$ II, $B \rightarrow V$, $C \rightarrow$ IV, $D \rightarrow$ III, $E \rightarrow$ I

Transferring to the main matrix:

	I	II	III	IV	V
A	30	$\boxed{40}$	40	25	29
B	37	24	32	38	$\boxed{62}$
C	40	27	33	$\boxed{49}$	4
D	28	21	$\boxed{30}$	36	34
E	$\boxed{40}$	36	35	36	49

The maximum profit than can be obtained is Rs.221/-

Example: 4.3

Five jobs I, II, III, IV & V and five machines M_1, M_2, M_3, M_4, time taken for each machine to do a particular job is given in minutes.

Assign the jobs to machines to minimize the total processing time. And find the minimum time taken.

	I	II	III	IV	V
M_1	9	11	15	10	11
M_2	12	9	-	10	9
M_3	-	11	14	11	7
M_4	14	8	12	7	8

Solution:

As number of columns are not equal to number of rows. So, we add a dummy row to make it balanced.

	I	II	III	IV	V
M_1	9	11	15	10	11
M_2	12	9	-	10	9
M_3	-	11	14	11	7
M_4	14	8	12	7	8
M_5 (Dummy)	0	0	0	0	0

By following the procedure explained in the previous examples we get the optimal matrix as

	I	II	III	IV	V
M_1	$\boxed{0}$	2	6	1	2
M_2	3	$\boxed{0}$	-	1	~~0~~
M_3	-	4	7	4	$\boxed{0}$
M_4	7	1	5	$\boxed{0}$	1
M_5 (Dummy)	0	0	$\boxed{0}$	0	0

The solution is $M_1 \rightarrow$, I, $M_2 \rightarrow$ II, $M_3 \rightarrow V$, $M_4 \rightarrow$ IV, $M_5 \rightarrow$ III the total processing time is 32.

4.3 SEQUENCING

4.3.1 Partentry Control Strategies

1. First come, first served (FCFS)
2. Earlier due date (EDD)
3. Shortest processing time (SPT)
4. Red tag

Generally while sequencing the product we would like to arrange in increasing order of processing time but when earlier due date (EDD) is given, we process that product which has to be delivered at the earliest. Once any job gets Tardy (Delayed), we don't give it priority.

Example 4.4:

(a) Find the proper sequence of jobs for the given processing times.

Job	Processing Time
P	5
Q	2
R	3
S	2
T	1

(b) Find the proper sequence of jobs for the given due dates by EDD method.

Job	Processing Time	Due date (Days)
P	5	6
Q	2	4
R	3	5
S	2	6
T	1	5

Solution:

(a) Arranging the sequence according to SPT
As Job *T*, is having lowest processing time it is processed first.
Next Job *Q*, is processed as it is having next lowest processing time.
Next Job *S*, is processed.
Next R & P is processed.
Order is $T-Q-S-R-P$

Job	Processing Time	Total Days
T	1	1
Q	2	3
S	3	5
R	4	8
P	5	13

(b) By EDD method:

Job	Processing Time	EDD (Days)
Q	2	4
T	1	5
R	3	5
S	2	6
P	5	6

As Job *Q*, is having least *EDD* it is processed first.

Next *EDD* is for *R* and *T* but if we select *R* then 3 jobs will be delayed but if we select *T* only 2 jobswill get delayed so we will select *T*.

Now *R* and *P* will get delayed so we will not give priority to them so we will select *S*.

Next of *R* and *P*, *R* will be delayed least so we select *R*.

The order is *Q* – *T* – *S* – *R* – *P*

Shortest Processing Time (SPT): In multiple job 2 machines

Example 4.5:

The table below shows processing times of different jobs on different machines.

Jobs	*A*	*B*	*C*	*D*	*E*	*F*	*G*	*H*	*I*
Machine - I	2	5	4	9	6	8	7	5	4
Machine - II	6	8	7	4	3	9	3	8	11

Determine optimum cycle time, % idle time and % utilization time for each machine.

Solution:

Step-I: Select the minimum time of the matrix and if it appears for the first machine, process it first and if it appears for the second machine, process it last.

	1	7	4					8	5
Jobs	*A*	*B*	*C*	*D*	*E*	*F*	*G*	*H*	*I*
Machine - I	2	5	4	9	6	8	7	5	4
Machine - II	6	8	7	4	3	9	3	8	11
				6	2		3		

Step-II: If there is a tie, see the processing time of other machine and whichever product has got minimum processing time then take the decision on that job first.

The order comes to be

A – *C* – *I* – *B* – *H* – *F* – *D* – *G* – *E* (or) *A* – *C* – *I* – *H* – *B* – *F* – *D* – *G* – *E*

	M/C I		M/C II	
	IN	OUT	IN	OUT
A	0	2	2	8
C	2	6	8	15
I	6	10	15	26
B	10	15	26	34
H	15	20	34	42
F	20	28	42	51
D	28	37	51	55
G	37	44	55	58
E	44	50	58	61
				(Cycle time)

Gantt Charts: Charts used to represent the idle time of a machine

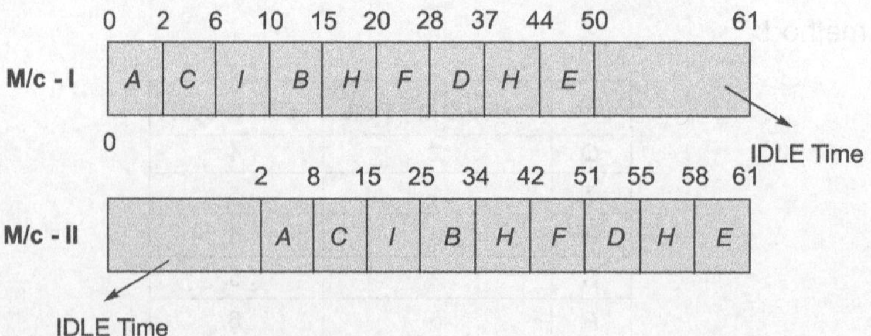

$$\text{Idleness of M/c I} = \frac{11}{61} \times 100 = 18.04\%$$

$$\text{Utilization of M/c I} = \frac{50}{61} \times 100 = 81.96\%$$

$$\text{Idleness of M/c II} = \frac{2}{61} \times 100 = 3.28\%$$

$$\text{Utilization of M/c II} = \frac{59}{61} \times 100 = 96.72\%$$

Example: 4.6

The table below shows processing times of different jobs on different machines.

Job	M_1	M_2	M_3
A	13	5	9
B	5	3	7
C	6	4	5
D	7	2	6

Determine optimum cycle time, % idle time for each machine.

Solution:

In this case, we solve the problem, by converting 3 machine problem into 2 machine problem by following method,

max $(m_i) \le$ min (m_j), then we will add m_i to the other machines

Since max (M_2) = 5 = min (M_1)

So, we add M_2 to M_1

Also, max (M_2) = 5 = min (M_3)

Therefore, we add M_2 and M_3

Now by solving the problem by normal procedure,

Jobs	$X = (M_1 + M_2)$	$Y = (M_2 + M_3)$
A	18	14
B	8	10
C	10	9
D	9	8

We get the order as, *B* – *A* – *C* – *D*. This sequence has to be projected on the original machines.

	M_1		M_2		M_3	
	IN	OUT	IN	OUT	IN	OUT
B	0	5	5	8	8	15
A	5	18	18	23	23	32
C	18	24	24	28	32	37
D	24	31	31	33	37	43 (Cycle Time)

Gantt Charts:

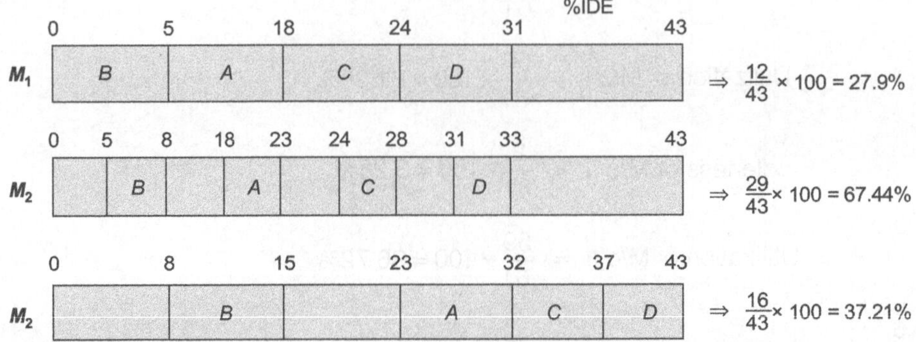

Example: 4.7

The table below shows processing times of different jobs on different machines.

Job	*X*	*W*	*M*
N	8	5	3
A	4	6	4
O	7	7	3
L	5	8	4
E	6	4	4

Determine optimum cycle time, % idle time and % utilization time for each machine.

Solution:

Min $(x) = 4 = \max(M)$

Add '*M*' to the other

	A = (*X* + *M*)	*B* = (*W* + *M*)
N	11	8
A	8	10
O	10	10
L	9	12
E	10	8

The order comes out to be, *A* – *L* – *O* – *N* – *E*

	M_1		M_2		M_3	
	IN	OUT	IN	OUT	IN	OUT
A	0	4	4	10	10	14
L	4	9	10	18	18	22
O	9	16	18	25	25	28
N	16	24	25	30	30	33
E	24	30	30	34	34	38 Cycle Time

Gantt Charts:

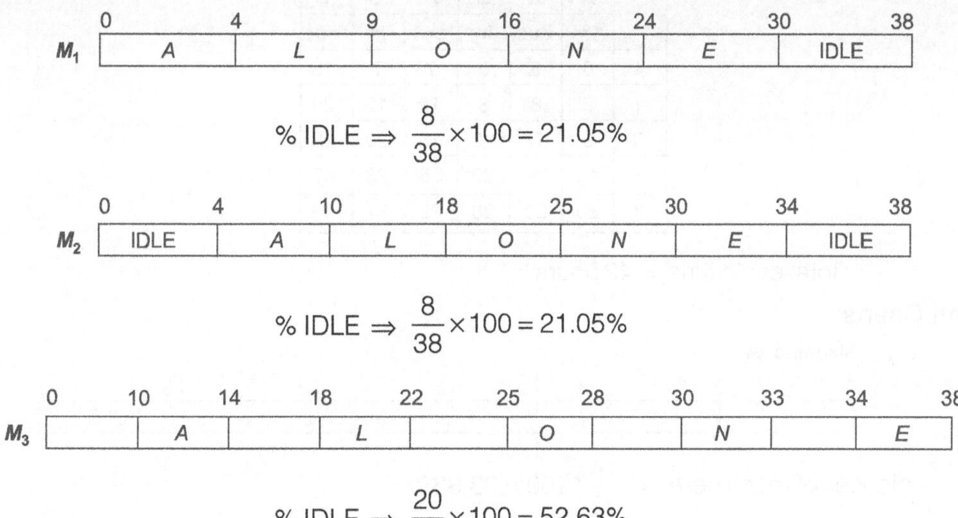

$$\% \text{ IDLE} \Rightarrow \frac{8}{38} \times 100 = 21.05\%$$

$$\% \text{ IDLE} \Rightarrow \frac{8}{38} \times 100 = 21.05\%$$

0 10 14 18 22 25 28 30 33 34 38

M_3 | | A | | L | | O | | N | | E |

$$\% \text{ IDLE} \Rightarrow \frac{20}{38} \times 100 = 52.63\%$$

Example 4.8

There are five jobs, each of which is to be processed through three machines *A, B, C* in the order *ABC*. Processing times in hours are:

Job	*A*	*B*	*C*
1	3	4	7
2	8	5	9
3	8	1	5
4	5	2	6
5	4	3	8

How should the jobs be loaded in order to minimize the total elapsed time?

Solution:

$$\text{Max}(M_i) \leq \text{Min}(M_j)$$
$$\text{Max}(B) = 5 = \text{Min}(C)$$

	$X = (A + B)$	$Y = (B + C)$
1	7	11
2	13	14
3	9	6
4	7	8
5	7	11

4-1-5-2-3 (or) 4-5-1-2-3

	A	A	B	B	C	C
	in	out	in	out	in	out
4	0	5	5	7	7	13
1	5	8	8	12	12	20
5	8	12	12	15	20	28
2	12	20	20	25	28	37
3	20	28	28	29	37	42

Total cycle time = 42 hours

Gantt Charts:

Machine -A

0	5	8	12	20	28	42
1	1	5	2	3	IDLE	

$$\text{Idleness of machine-A} = \frac{14}{42} * 100 = 33.33\%$$

$$\text{Utilization of Machine-A} = \frac{28}{42} * 100 = 66.67\%$$

Machine -B

0	5	7	8	12	15	20	25	28	29	42
IDLE	4	IDLE	1	5	IDLE	2	IDLE	3	IDLE	

$$\text{Idleness of Machine-B} = \frac{27}{42} * 100 = 64.29\%$$

$$\text{Utilization of Machine-B} = \frac{15}{42} * 100 = 35.71\%$$

Machine -C

0	7	13	20	28	37	42
IDLE	1	1	5	2	3	

$$\text{Idleness of machine-C} = \frac{7}{42} * 100 = 16.67\%$$

$$\text{Utilization Of Machine-C} = \frac{35}{42} * 100 = 83.33\%$$

PRACTICE QUESTIONS

1. There are two machines M_1 and M_2 which process jobs *A*, *B*, *C*, *D*, *E* and *F*. The processing sequence for these jobs is M_1 followed by M_2. Consider the following data in this regard: Process time required in minutes.

Jobs	A	B	C	D	E	F
M_1	4	7	3	12	11	13
M_2	11	7	10	8	10	9

The processing sequence of jobs that would minimize the make span is:
(a) C-A-B-F-E-D
(b) C-A-B-D-E-F
(c) C-A-D-B-F-E
(d) E-F-D-B-A-C

2. The assignment algorithm is applicable to which of the following combined situations for the purpose of improving productivity?
   1. Identification of the sales force-market.
   2. Scheduling of operator-machine.
   3. Fixing machine-location.

   Select the correct answer using the codes given below:
   (a) 1, 2 and 3
   (b) 1 and 3
   (c) 2 and 3
   (d) 1 and 2

3. Which one of the following statement is NOT correct?
   (a) Assignment model is a special case of a linear programming problem.
   (b) In queuing models, Poisson arrivals and exponential services are assumed.
   (c) In transportation problems, the non-square matrix is made square by adding a dummy row or dummy column.
   (d) In linear programming problems, dual of a dual is a primal.

4. Consider the following statements in respect of assignment method of optimization:
   1. The matrix format of the method must be a square matrix.
   2. Some type of rating has to be given to the performance of each pairing.

   Which of these above is/are correct?
   (a) only 1
   (b) only 2
   (c) only 1 and 2
   (d) neither 1 nor 2

5. In project scheduling, networks have an advantage over Gantt charts since networks
   (a) show start and finish of an activity clearly.
   (b) show activity and activity clearly.
   (c) show interrelation ship among activities clearly.
   (d) are easy to draw.

6. In assignment problem for variable x_{ij}.

   1. $x_{ij} = 1$ or 0
   2. $\sum_{j=1}^{n} X_{ij} = 1$
   3. $\sum_{i=1}^{n} X_{ij} = 1$

Which of these statements are correct?

(a) 1, 2 and 3 (b) 2 and 3 only
(c) 1 and 2 only (d) 1 and 3 only

7. A manufacturing shop processes sheet metal jobs, wherein each job must pass though two machines (M_1 and M_2, in that order). The processing time (in hours) for these jobs is.

Machine	Jobs					
	P	*Q*	*R*	*S*	*T*	*U*
M_1	15	32	8	27	11	16
M_2	6	19	13	20	14	7

The optimal make-span (in hours) of the shop is

(a) 120 (b) 115
(c) 109 (d) 79

8. A firm is required to procure three items (*P*, *Q* and *R*). The prices quoted for these items (in Rs.) by suppliers S_1, S_2 and S_3 are given in table. The management policy requires that each item has to be supplied by only one supplier and one supplier supply only one item. The minimum total cost (in Rs.) of procurement to the firm is

Items	Supplier		
	S_1	S_2	S_3
P	110	120	130
Q	115	140	140
R	125	145	165

(a) 350 (b) 360
(c) 385 (d) 400

9. A set of 5 jobs is to be processed on a single machine. The processing time (in days) is given in the table below. The holding cost for each job is ₹ K per day.
A schedule that minimizes the total inventory cost is

Job	P	Q	R	S	T
Processing Time	5	2	3	2	1

(a) T-S-Q-R-P (b) P-R-S-Q-T
(c) T-R-S-Q-P (d) P-Q-R-S-T

10. Six jobs arrived in a sequence as given below:

Job	I	II	III	IV	V	VI
Processing Time	4	9	5	10	6	8

Average flow time (in days) for the above jobs using shortest processing time rule is

(a) 20.83 (b) 23.16
(c) 125.00 (d) 139.00

OOOO

ANSWERS

ASSIGNMENT AND SEQUENCING

1. (a) **2.** (c) **3.** (c) **4.** (a) **5.** (c) **6.** (a) **7.** (b)
8. (d) **9.** (a) **10.** (a)

CHAPTER 5

Queuing Theory

5.1 INTRODUCTION

A Queuing process consists in customers arriving at a service facility, then waiting in a line (queue) if all servers are busy, eventually receiving service and finally departing from the facility. A queuing system is a set of customers, set of servers, and an order whereby customers arrive and are processed.

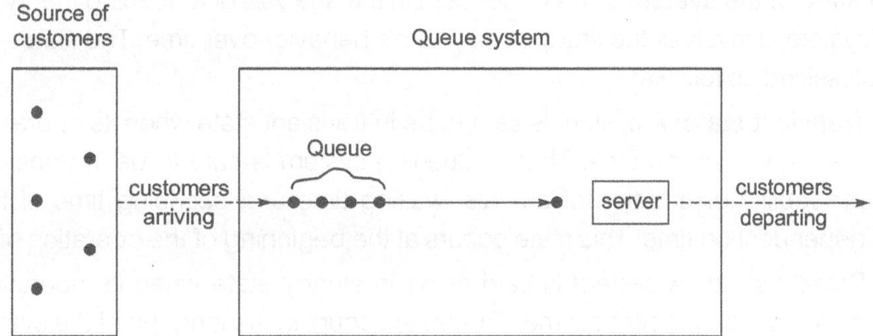

Fig: 5.1

Following are the definitions of important terms used in the queuing:

1. **Queue length (L_q)**: Queue length is defined by the number of customers waiting in the line at any time.

$$L_q = \sum_{n=c}^{\infty} (n-c)P_n$$

Where, c = number of servers

P_n = Probability that there are 'n' people in system

2. **System length (L_s)**: the average number of customers in the system.

$$L_s = \sum_{n=0}^{\infty} nP_n$$

$L_s - L_q \neq 1$. Since there is idle of time in service.

3. **Idle Period:** When all the units in the queue are served, the idle period of the server begins and it continues up to the time of arrival of the unit. This period of a server is the time during which he remains free because there is no customer present in the system.

4. **Average length of line:** It is defined by the no. of customers in the queue per unit time.
5. **Waiting time:** It is the time up to which a unit has to wait in the queue before it is taken into service.
6. **Service time:** The time taken for servicing of a unit is called as service time.
7. **Busy period:** Busy period of a server is the time during which he remains busy in servicing. Thus it is the time between the start of service of the first unit to the end of service of the last unit in the queue.
8. **Mean arrival rate (λ):** The mean arrival rate in a waiting line is defined as the expected no. of arrivals/unit time. Arrival rate follows *Poisson distribution.*
9. **Mean servicing rate (μ):** The mean servicing rate for a particular servicing station is defined as the expected no. of services completed in a time of length unity, given that the servicing is going on throughout the entire time limit. Service rate follows *Exponential distribution.*
10. **Percentage utilization (or) Traffic-intensity (ρ):** It is the ratio of its mean arrival rate and mean servicing rate: i.e.,

$$\rho = \frac{\text{Mean arrival rate}}{\text{Mean service rate}} = \frac{\lambda}{\mu}$$

if $\rho < 1$ converging queues
if $\rho > 1$ explosive queues

The state of the system: A basic concept in the analysis of a queuing theory is that of a state of the system. It involves the study of a system's behavior over time. The states of the system may be classified as follows:

1. **Transient state:** A system is said to be in transient state when its operating characteristics are dependent on time. Thus a Queuing system is said to be in transient state when the probability distribution of arrivals, waiting time and servicing time of the customers are dependent on time. This state occurs at the beginning of the operation of the system.
2. **Steady state:** A system is said to be in steady state when its operating characteristics become independent of time. This state occurs in the long run of the system.
   Let $P_n(t)$ denote the probability that there are n units in the system at time (t) then the system acquires steady state as $t \to \infty$ if $\lim_{t\to\infty} P_n(t) = P_n$ (independent of t).
3. **Explosive state:** If the arrival rate of the system is more than its servicing rate, the length of the queue will go on increasing with time and will tend to ∞ at $t \to \infty$. This state of the system is said to be explosive state.

- $P_n = \rho^n P_0$
- $\sum_{n=0}^{\infty} P_n = 1$

$$P_0 + P_1 + P_2 + \ldots\ldots\ldots\ldots + \infty = 1$$

$$P_0 + P_0\rho + P_0\rho^2 + \ldots\ldots\ldots + \infty = 1$$

$$P_0 (1 + \rho + \rho^2 + \ldots\ldots\ldots + \infty) = 1$$

$$P_0\left[\frac{1}{1-\rho}\right] = 1 \qquad (\because \rho < 1)$$

$$P_0 = 1 - \rho$$

- $$L_s = \sum_{n=0}^{\infty} nP_n = P_1 + 2P_2 + 3P_3 + ...+\infty$$

$$L_s = \rho P_0 + 2\rho^2 P_0 + 3\rho^3 P_0 + ...$$

$$L_s\rho = \rho^2 P_0 + 2\rho^3 P_0 + ...$$

$$L_s(1-\rho) = \rho P_0 + \rho^2 P_0 + \rho^3 P_0 + ...$$

$$= P_o\left(\frac{\rho}{1-\rho}\right) \qquad [\because P_0 = 1-\rho]$$

$$L_s = \frac{\rho}{1-\rho}$$

- $$L_q = \sum_{n=c}^{\infty}(n-c)P_n$$

Let, $C = 1$

$$L_q = \sum_{n=1}^{\infty}(n-1)P_n = \sum_{n=1}^{\infty} nP_n - \sum_{n=1}^{\infty} P_n$$

$$= \left(\frac{\rho}{1-\rho}\right) - [1-(1-\rho)] = \frac{\rho}{1-\rho} - \rho = \frac{\rho^2}{1-\rho}$$

$$L_q = \frac{\rho^2}{1-\rho}$$

$$L_s - L_q = \rho$$

- Waiting time in system = $W_s = \dfrac{L_s}{\lambda}$
- Waiting time in queue = $W_q = \dfrac{L_q}{\lambda}$
- The probability that the arrival has wait in the system for service more than 't' unit time = $e^{\frac{-t}{W_s}}$
- Probability that arrival has to wait in the queue for more than time (t) = $\rho e^{-\frac{t}{W_s}}$.

  Note: In examination when it is not clear, that whether we have to operate queue or system, if the word **mean** is given it refers to **queue** and if the word **average** it refers to **system**.
- Average length of non empty queues: It is the system length by neglecting the probability when there is nobody in the system = $\dfrac{L_s}{1-P_0}$

$$\because \qquad L_s = \frac{0P_0 + 1P_1 + ...+\infty}{\sum_{n=0}^{\infty} P_n = 1}$$

Example: 5.1

A job arrives in a machine shop following a Poisson distribution with a mean rate of 1 per hour. If average time to complete the job is 30min,what is probability that at leasttwo jobs will be waiting always?

Solution:

$$\lambda = 1 \text{ per hr}$$
$$\mu = 2 \text{ per hr}$$
$$\rho = \frac{\lambda}{\mu} = 0.5$$

From the diagram $n \geq 3$

$$P(n \leq 3) = 1 - P(n < 3) = 1 - (P_0 + P_1 + P_2)$$
$$= 1 - P_0(1 + \rho + \rho^2) = 1 - (1 - \rho)(1 + \rho + \rho^2)$$
$$= 1 - 0.875 = 0.125$$

Example: 5.2

Arrival to system follows Poisson distribution with mean rate 6 per hr and mean service time is 3 m in then

(a) what is expected queue length?

(b) what is expected no. of units in the system?

(c) what is probability that an arrival has to wait in queue for more than 10 min?

Solution:

$$\mu = \frac{1}{3} \text{min} = \frac{60}{3} = 20 \text{ per hr}$$
$$\lambda = \frac{6}{\text{hr}}$$
$$\rho = \frac{\lambda}{\mu} = \frac{6}{20} = 0.3$$

(a)
$$L_q = \frac{\rho^2}{1-\rho} = \frac{\frac{36}{400}}{\frac{14}{20}} = \frac{9}{70} = 0.128$$

(b)
$$L_s = \frac{\rho}{1-\rho} = 0.428$$

(c) Probability that an arrival has to wait in queue for more than 10 min.

$$= \rho e^{-\frac{t}{W_s}} = 0.3e^{-\frac{(10/60)}{(\rho/\lambda(1-\rho))}} = 0.3e^{-\frac{140}{60}} = 0.03 \quad \because \left(W_s = \frac{L_s}{\lambda}\right)$$

Example: 5.3

A computer terminal receives job for processing at a mean rate of 120 per hr. Processing time is exponentially distributed with a mean rate 150 per hr. Determine:

(i) Mean idle time per hr of computer terminal

(ii) Mean no.of jobs waiting for processing

(iii) Mean waiting time per job

(iv) Percentage utilization of terminal

Solution:

$$\rho = \frac{\lambda}{\mu} = \frac{120}{150} = 0.8$$

(i) $P_0 = 1 - \rho = 0.2$ and Time $60 \times 0.2 = 12$ min

(ii) $$L_q = \frac{\rho^2}{1-\rho} = 3.2$$

(iii) $$W_q = \frac{L_q}{\lambda} = 1.6$$

(iv) $\rho = 0.8 \times 100 = 80\%$

Example: 5.4

In a machine shop certain types of machines break down at an average of 6 per hr. The estimated cost of idle machine is Rs.15 per hr. To repair when *A* and *B* with different skills are being considered to be hired as repairmen. '*A*' takes 6 minutes on an average to repair a machine and his wages Rs. 8 per hr whereas the repairman '*B*' takes 5 minutes to repair the machine and his wages are Rs.10 per hr. Which repair man's service should be used and why? Assume 8 hrs work shift.

Solution:

A	*B*
μ = 10/hr	μ = 12/hr
Wages = 8/hr	Wages = 10/hr

$\lambda = 6$ per hr

idle m/c cost = 15 per hr

If (*A*) is selected:

$$\rho = \frac{\lambda}{\mu} = \frac{6}{10} = 0.6$$

$$L_s = \frac{\rho}{1-\rho} = \frac{0.6}{0.4} = 1.5$$

(i.e., on an average 1.5 machines are idle)

$$\text{Cost Involved} = 1.5 \times 15 \times 8 + 8 \times 8 = 244$$

If (*B*) is selected:

$$\rho = \frac{\lambda}{\mu} = \frac{6}{12} = 0.5$$

$$L_s = \frac{\rho}{1-\rho} = 1$$

(i.e., on an average 1 machine is idle)

Cost involved $1 \times 15 \times 8 + 10 \times 8 = 200$

As cost Involved when *B* is hired is less than that of *A*, *B* is selected.

Example: 5.5

A motor mechanic has a specialized garage for servicing Maruti cars. The repair time is exponentially distributed with a mean of 30 minutes. Cars arrive for repair according to Poisson distribution with a mean time of 45 minutes between arrivals. Garage has a waiting space that can accommodate two cars excluding the one being repaired. If the waiting area is full, car waits outside on the road.

(a) What is expected percentage of cars that has to wait outside due to inadequate waiting space?

(b) If the waiting area in the garage is full, Instead of waiting outside the garage, if any car that comes for repair goes back not to return again. Find the expected percentage of customers loss due to inadequate waiting space.

(c)

x x x Road

Workshop

Solution:

$$\lambda = \frac{1}{45}\text{min} = \frac{60}{45} = \frac{4}{3\text{hr}}$$

$$\mu \frac{2}{\text{hr}}$$

$$\rho = \frac{\lambda}{\mu} = \frac{2}{3}$$

(a)

$$P(n > 3) = 1 - P(n \leq 3)$$
$$= 1 - (P_0 + P_1 + P_2 + P_3)$$
$$= 1 - P_0(1 + \rho + \rho + \rho^3)$$
$$= 1 - (1 - \rho)(1 + \rho + \rho^2 + \rho^3)$$
$$= 0.1975 \Rightarrow 19.75\%$$

(b) This is the problem of restricted queue length so the formulas are modified as

$$\sum_{n=0}^{N} P_n = 1$$

$$L_s = \sum_{n=0}^{N} nP_n$$

$$L_q = \sum_{n=0}^{N} (n-c)P_n$$

$$\sum_{n=0}^{N} P_n = 1 \Rightarrow P_0 + P_1 + P_2 + ...P_n = 1 \quad ...(1)$$

$$P_0 + P_\rho P_0 + \rho^2 P_0 + ...\rho^N P_0 = 1$$

$$P_0\left(\frac{1-\rho^{N+1}}{1-\rho}\right) = 1$$

$$P_0 = \frac{1-\rho}{1-\rho^{N+1}}$$

if ($\rho = 1$), then from equation (1),

$$P_0 = \frac{1}{N+1}$$

$$L_s = \sum_{n=0}^{N} nP_n = 0P_0 + P_1 + 2P_2 + ...+nP_n$$

$$L_s = P_1 + 2P_2 + 3P_3$$
$$= \rho P_0 + 2\rho^2 P_0 + 3\rho^3 P_0$$

$$P_0 = \frac{1-\frac{2}{3}}{1-\left(\frac{2}{3}\right)^4} = \frac{27}{65}$$

$$(L_s)_{finite} = P_0(\rho + 2\rho^2 + 3\rho^3)$$

$$= \frac{27}{65}\left(\frac{2}{3}+2\frac{4}{9}+3\frac{8}{27}\right) = 1.015$$

$$(L_s)_{finite} = \frac{\rho}{1-\rho} = 2$$

$$\%\text{ customers lost} = \frac{2-1.015}{2}\times 100 = 49.25\%$$

Service Level : In a system of queues of finite length it is average number of customers we have served who approach towards the facility of service (In the above problem it is 50.8%).

Example: 5.6

A train reservation facility has 5 counters each capable of handling 20 requests per hour. The persons coming for reservation arrive at a mean rate of 90 per hour. Assume that each person comes with one request only calculate:

(a) (i) The mean number of persons at any time at this facility.

(ii) The mean time a person spends at the facility.

(iii) The average lengths of queue at each counter.

(b) What would happen to the queue if the arrival rate to reach 105 per hour?

Solution:

Multiple counter-Multiple queue

x	x	x	x	x	x 1
x	x	x	x	x	x 2
x	x	x	x	x	x 3
x	x	x	x	x	x 4
x	x	x	x	x	x 5

Each counter = μ = 20 per hr

Over all λ = 90 per hr

$$(\lambda)\text{ each counter} = \frac{90}{5} = 15\text{ per hr}$$

$$\rho = \frac{\lambda}{\mu} = \frac{18}{20} = 0.9$$

(a) (i) $L_s = 5 \times 9 = 45$

(ii) $W_s = \frac{(L_s)_{one\,queue}}{\lambda} = \frac{9}{18} = 0.5\text{ hr} = 30\text{ min}$

(iii) $(Lq)\text{ one queue} = \frac{\rho^2}{1-\rho} = \frac{0.81}{0.1} = 8.1$

(b)

$$\lambda = 105 \text{ per hr}$$

$$(\lambda) \text{ one counter } = 21 \text{ per hr}\left[\frac{105}{5}\right]$$

$$\rho = \frac{\lambda}{\mu} = \frac{21}{20} > 1 \qquad \text{(Explosive queue)}$$

5.2 MULTIPLE SERVICES SINGLE QUEUE

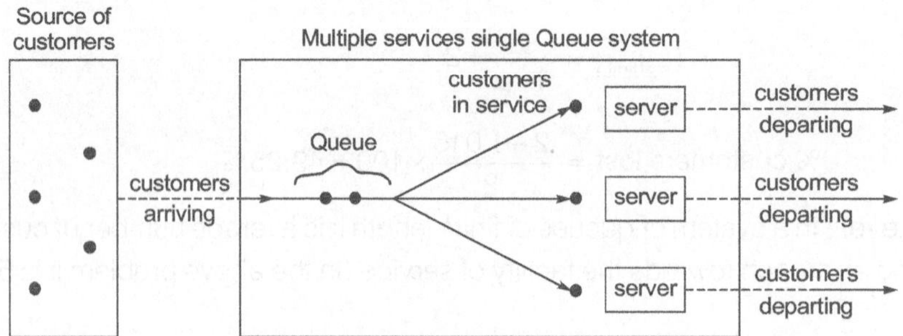

Fig: 5.2

1. $P_n = \begin{cases} \dfrac{\rho^n}{\lfloor n} P_0 \text{.........if } (0 \le n < C) \\ \dfrac{\rho^n}{C^{n-C}\lfloor C} P_0 \text{.....if } (n \ge C) \end{cases}$ 2. $L_s = \sum_{n=0}^{\infty} nP_n$

3. $L_q = \sum_{n=C}^{\infty} (n-C)P_n$ 4. $W_s = \dfrac{L_s}{\lambda}$ 5. $W_q = \dfrac{L_s}{\lambda}$

Example: 5.7

Workers come to tool store room to enquire about special tools needed in a particular project. The average time between two arrivals is 40 secs and the arrivals are assumed to be in Poisson distribution. The average time of the tool room attendant is 30 sec. Determine:

(a) (i) Average queue length

(ii) Average length of non-empty queues

(iii) Average number of workers in system including worker being attended

(iv) Mean waiting time of an arrival

(v) Average waiting time of an arrival

(b) Whether additional tool store room attendant is needed to minimize the combined cost of attendant's idle time and cost of the worker's time. Assume the charges of a skilled worker Rs. 15 per hours and that of a tool store room attendant Rs. 4 per hour and also 8 working hours a day.

Solution:

$$\lambda = \frac{60}{40} \text{ per min} = 1.5 \text{ per min}$$

$$\mu = 2 \text{ per min}$$

$$\rho = \frac{\lambda}{\mu} = \frac{1.5}{2} = 0.75$$

(a) (i) $L_q = \dfrac{\rho^2}{1-\rho} = \dfrac{0.75^2}{0.25} = 3\times0.75 = 2.25$

(ii) $\dfrac{L_s}{1-P_0} = \dfrac{L_s}{\rho} = \dfrac{1}{1-\rho} = 4$

(iii) $L_s = 3$

(iv) $W_q = \dfrac{L_q}{\lambda} = 1.5\text{ min}$

(v) $W_s = \dfrac{L_s}{\lambda} = 2\text{ min}$

(b) Total cost at present = $L_s \times 15 \times 8 + 4 \times 8 =$ ₹ 392

After employing second worker ($C = 2$)

$$\sum_{n=0}^{\infty} P_n = 1$$

$$\Rightarrow \frac{\rho^0}{\lfloor 0}P_0 + \frac{\rho}{\lfloor 1}P_0 + \frac{\rho^2 P_0}{2^{2-2}\lfloor 2} + \frac{\rho^3 P_0}{2^{3-2}\lfloor 2} + ...+\infty = 1$$

$$\Rightarrow P_0 + \rho P_0 + \frac{P_0}{\lfloor 2}\left[\frac{\rho^2}{1} + \frac{\rho^3}{2} + \frac{\rho^4}{4} + ...\right] = 1$$

$$\Rightarrow P_0 + \rho P_0 + \frac{P_0}{\lfloor 2}\left[\frac{\rho^2}{1-\frac{\rho}{2}}\right] = 1$$

$$\Rightarrow P_0 + \rho P_0 + \frac{\rho^2 P_0}{2-\rho} = 1 \qquad ...(1)$$

$$\Rightarrow P_0\left[1 + 0.75 + \frac{0.75^2}{2-0.75}\right] = 1$$

$$\Rightarrow P_0 = 0.455$$

$$L_s = \sum_{n=0}^{\infty} nP_n = P_1 + 2P_2 + 3P_3 + ...+\infty$$

$$= \frac{\rho}{\lfloor 1}P_0 + 2\frac{\rho^2}{1.\lfloor 2}P_0 + 3\frac{\rho^3 P_0}{2.\lfloor 2} + 4\frac{\rho^4 P_0}{4.\lfloor 2} + ...+\infty$$

$$L_s = \rho P_0 + \rho^2 P_0 + \frac{3}{4}\rho^3 P_0 + \frac{4}{8}\rho^4 P_0 + \frac{5}{16}\rho^5 P_0 + ...$$

$$\frac{\rho}{2}L_s = \frac{\rho^2}{2}P_0 + \frac{1}{2}\rho^3 P_0 + \frac{3}{8}\rho^4 P_0 + \frac{4}{16}\rho^5 P_0 + ...$$

$$\left(1-\frac{\rho}{2}\right)L_s = \rho P_0 + \frac{1}{2}\rho^2 P_0 + \frac{1}{4}\rho^3 P_0 + \frac{1}{8}\rho^4 P_0 + ...$$

$$= \rho P_0\left(1 + \frac{\rho}{2} + \frac{\rho^2}{4} + \frac{\rho^3}{8} + ...\right) = \frac{\rho P_0}{\left(1-\frac{\rho}{2}\right)}$$

$$L_s = \frac{\rho P_0}{\left(1-\frac{\rho}{2}\right)^2}$$

But from equation (1) we know that,

$$1 = P_0 + \rho P_0 + \frac{\rho^2 P_0}{2-\rho}$$

$$P_0 = \frac{2-\rho}{2+\rho}$$

$$\therefore \quad L_s = \frac{4\rho}{(2-\rho)^2}\left(\frac{2-\rho}{2+\rho}\right) = \frac{4\rho}{4-\rho^2} = 0.87$$

Total cost = 0.87 × 15 × 8 + 2 × 4 × 8 = 168

Here with one attendant the total cost is 392 whereas with two attendants the total cost is 168, therefore additional tool store room attendant is needed to minimize the total cost.

Kendall Notation

a/b/c : d/e/f

Where: a = arrival probability distribution, b = service probability, c = number of servers d = queue discipline, e = queue length, f = calling source population

e.g., M/M2: FCFS / ∞ / 2000

M = Marcovian (mean poison arrival exponential service)

Note: Formulae that can be asked in exams.

	Exponential	Poisson
Prob. density function	$f(t) = \lambda e^{-\lambda t}$	$\frac{(\lambda T)^n e^{-\lambda T}}{\lfloor n}$
Mean value	$\frac{1}{\lambda}$	λT (during T)
P (No arrivals during period A)	$e^{-\lambda A}$	$e^{-\lambda A}$

PRACTICE QUESTIONS

1. Match **List-I (OR technique)** with **List-II (Application)**:

List-I	**List-II**
A. Linear programming	**1.** Warehouse location decision
B. Transportation	**2.** Machine allocation decision
C. Assignment	**3.** Product mix decision
D. Queuing	**4.** Project management decision
	5. Number of servers decision

Codes:

	A	B	C	D
(a)	1	2	3	5
(b)	3	1	2	5
(c)	1	3	4	5
(d)	3	2	4	4

2. Match **List-I** with **List-II** and select the correct answer using the codes given below the lists:

A. Linear programming	**1.** Ritchie
B. Dynamic programming	**2.** Dantzing
C. 'C' programming	**3.** Bell
D. Integer programming	**4.** Gomory

Codes:

	A	B	C	D
(a)	2	1	4	3
(b)	1	2	3	4
(c)	2	3	1	4
(d)	2	3	4	1

3. If the arrival rate of units is λ and the service rate is μ for a waiting line system having '*m*' number of service stations, then the probability of a services unit being turned out in the time interval (t; $t + \Delta t$) (given that there are '*n*' units in the system at time '*t*' and '*n*' being less than '*m*' is equal to:
   (a) Zero
   (b) $\mu.\Delta t$
   (c) $m.\mu.\Delta t$
   (d) $n.\mu.\Delta t$

4. Consider two queuing disciplines in a single server queue. Case 1 has a first come first served discipline and case 2 has a last come first served discipline. If the average waiting times in the two cases are W_1 and W_2 respectively, then which one of the following inferences would be true?
   (a) $W_1 > W_2$
   (b) $W_1 < W_2$
   (c) $W_1 = W_2$
   (d) Data insufficient

5. Single server queue customers are served at a rate of μ. If W and W_q represent the mean waiting time in the system and mean waiting time in the queue respectively, then W will be equal to
   (a) $W_q - \mu$
   (b) $W_q + \mu$
   (c) $W_q + \dfrac{1}{\mu}$
   (d) $W_q - \dfrac{1}{\mu}$

6. For a M/M/1: FCFS/∞/∞ queue, the mean arrival rate is equal to 10 per hour and the mean service rate is 15 per hour. The expected queue length is
   (a) 1.33 (b) 1.53
   (c) 2.75 (d) 3.20

7. Weekly production requirements of a product are 1000 items. The cycle time of producing one product on a machine is 10 minutes. The factory works on two shift basis in which total available time is16 hours. Out of the available time about 25% is expected to be wasted on break downs, material unavailability and quality related problems. The factory works for 5 days in a week. How many machines are required to fulfil the production requirements?
   (a) 2 (b) 3
   (c) 4 (d) 6

8. The average time between two arrivals of customers at a counter in a ready-made garment store is 4 min. The average time of the counter clerk to serve the customer is 3 min. The arrivals are distributed as per Poisson distribution and the services are as per the exponential distribution. The probability that a customer arriving at the counter will have to wait, is
   (a) Zero (b) 0.25
   (c) 0.50 (d) 0.75

9. Arrivals at a telephone booth are considered to be Poisson with an average time of 10 minutes between one arrival and the next. The length of a phone call is assumed to be distributed exponentially with a mean of 3 minutes. The probability that a person arriving at the booth will have to wait, is
   (a) 0.043 (b) 0.3
   (c) 0.429 (d) 0.700

10. **Assertion (A):** In waiting line model, it is assumed that arrival rate is described by a Poisson probability distribution.
    Reason (R): The arrival rate is a probabilistic variable and queue discipline is first come firstserved.
    (a) Both A and R are true and R is the correct explanation of A.
    (b) Both A and R are true but R is not a correct explanation of A.
    (c) A is true but R is false.
    (d) A is false but R is true.

11. The span of control refers to be
    (a) total amount of control which can be exercised by the supervisor.
    (b) total number of persons which report to anyone supervisor.
    (c) delegation of authority by the supervisor to his subordinates.
    (d) delegation of responsibility by the supervisor to his subordinates.

12. At a self-service store. a cashier can serve 10 customers in 5 minutes. On an average 15 customers arrive every 10 minutes. If the arrivals are as per Poisson distribution and services as per exponential distribution, the probability that the cashier would be idle is
    (a) 0.5 (b) 0.75
    (c) 0.25 (d) 0

13. Customers arrive at a counter randomly at the rate of 6 customers per hour. The service is provided at the counter by a server. The mean time of the service is 4 minutes per customer. The services are exponentially distributed. What is the probability that a newly arrived customer has to wait?

(a) 0.4
(b) 0.6
(c) 0.66
(d) 0.8

14. Which one of the following statements is correct? Queuing theory is applied best in situations where

(a) Arrival rate of customers equal to service rate
(b) Average service. time is greater than average arrival time
(c) There is only one channel of arrival at random and the service time is constant
(d) The arrival and service rate cannot be analyzed through any standard statistical distribution

15. If the arrivals are completely random, then what is the probability distribution of number of arrivals in a given time?

(a) Negative exponential
(b) Binomial
(c) Normal
(d) Poisson

16. In single server queuing model if arrival rate is *A*. and service rate is μ, then what is the probability of the system being idle?

(a) $\frac{\lambda}{\mu}$
(b) $\frac{\mu}{\lambda}$
(c) $1-\frac{\lambda}{\mu}$
(d) $\left(\frac{1-\lambda}{\mu}\right)$

17. If average arrival rate in a queue is 6 per hr and the average service rate is 10 per hr, which one of the following is the average number of customers in the line, including the customer being served?

(a) 0.3
(b) 0.6
(c) 1.2
(d) 1.5

18. If the number of arrival in a queue follows the Poisson distribution, then the inter arrival time obeys which one of the following distributions?

(a) Poisson's distribution
(b) Negative exponential law
(c) Normal distribution
(d) Binomial

19. In a single server queuing system with arrival rate of λ and mean service time of μ the expected number of customers in the system is $\left(\frac{\lambda}{\mu-\lambda}\right)$.

What is the expected waiting time per customer in the systems?

(a) $\frac{\lambda^2}{(\mu-\lambda)}$
(b) $\mu-\lambda$
(c) $\frac{1}{\mu-\lambda}$
(d) $\frac{(\mu-\lambda)}{\lambda}$

20. The inter-arrival times at a tool crib are Poisson with an average time of 10 minutes and the length of the service time 6 minutes assumed to be exponential. The probability that a person arriving at the booth will have to wait is equal to:
(a) 0.15 (b) 0.40
(c) 0.42 (d) 0.6

21. Which of the following distributions is followed by the project completion time in PERT?
(a) Negative exponential distribution (b) Poisson distribution
(c) Normal distribution (d) beta distribution

22. If the arrivals at a service facility are distributed as per the Poisson distribution with a mean rate of 10 per hour and the services are exponentially distributed with a mean service time of 4 minutes, what is the probability that a customer may have to wait to be served?
(a) 0.40 (b) 0.50
(c) 0.67 (d) 1.00

23. A single-bay car wash with a Poisson arrival rate and exponential service time has cars arriving at an average rate of 10 minutes apart and an average service time of 4 minutes. What is the system utilization?
(a) 1.00 (b) 0.67
(c) 0.40 (d) 0.24

24. In the Kendall's notation for representing queuing models the first position represents.
(a) Probability law for the arrival (b) Probability law for the service
(c) Number of channels (d) Capacity of the system

25. A maintenance service facility has Poisson arrival rates, negative exponential service time and operates on a 'first come first served' queue discipline. Break-downs occur on an average of 3 per day with a range of zero to eight. The maintenance crew can service an average of 6 machines per day with a range of zero to seven.
The mean waiting time for an item to be serviced would be
(a) 1/6 day (b) 1/3 day
(c) 1 day (d) 3 day

26. Consider a single server queuing model with Poisson arrivals ($\lambda = 4$ per hour) and exponential service ($\mu = 4$ per hour). The number in the system is restricted to a maximum of 10. The probability that a person who comes in leaves without joining the queue is
(a) $\frac{1}{11}$ (b) $\frac{1}{10}$
(c) $\frac{1}{9}$ (d) $\frac{1}{2}$

27. The number of customers arriving at a railway reservation counter is Poisson distributed with an arrival rate of eight customers per hour. The reservation clerk at this counter takes six minutes per customer on an average with an exponentially distributed service time. The average number of the customers in the queue will be
(a) 3 (b) 3.2
(c) 4 (d) 4.2

28. In an M/M/1 queuing system, the number of arrivals in an interval of length T is a Poisson random variable (i,e. the probability of there being n arrivals in an interval of length T is $\frac{e^{-\lambda T}(\lambda T)^n}{n!}$. The probability density function $f(t)$ of the inter-arrival time is given by

(a) $\lambda^2(e^{-\lambda^2 t})$
(b) $\frac{e^{-\lambda^2 t}}{\lambda^2}$
(c) $\lambda e^{-\lambda t}$
(d) $\frac{e^{-\lambda t}}{\lambda}$

29. Little's law is a relationship between:
(a) Stock level and lead time in an inventory system.
(b) Waiting time and length of the queue in a queuing system.
(c) Number of machines and job due dates in a scheduling problem.
(d) Uncertainty in the activity time and project completion time.

30. At a production machine, parts arrive according to a Poisson process at the rate of 0.35 parts per minute. Processing time for parts have exponential distribution with mean of 2 minutes. What is the probability that a random part arrival finds that there are already 8 parts in the system (in machine in queue)?
(a) 0.0247
(b) 0.0576
(c) 0.0173
(d) 0.082

31. The cost of providing service in a queuing system increases with
(a) Increased mean time in the queue
(b) Increased arrival rate
(c) Decreased mean time in the queue
(d) Decreased arrival rate

32. In a single serve infinite population queuing model, arrivals follow a Poisson distribution with mean $\lambda = 4$ per hour. The service times are exponential with mean service time equal to 12 minutes. The expected length of the queue will be:
(a) 4
(b) 3.2
(c) 1.25
(d) 5

DIRECTIONS:

The following items consists of two statements; one labeled as 'Assertion (A)' and the other as 'Reason (R)' You are to examine these two statements carefully and select the answers to these items using the code below:

Codes:
(a) Both A and R are true and R is the correct explanation of A.
(b) Both A and R are true but R is not a correct explanation of A.
(c) A is true but R is false.
(d) A is false but R is true.

33. **Assertion (A):** The number of vehicles arriving per unit time at a vehicle maintenance shop at any instant of time can be assessed if the probability of that number and the average rate of arrivals is known:

Reason (R): The vehicles, '*k*' arriving at a vehicle maintenance shop with probability $p(k)$ is given by: $p(k) = \dfrac{\lambda^k e^{-\lambda}}{k!}$.

34. **Assertion (A):** In a queuing model, the assumption of exponential distribution with only one parameter family for service times is found to be unduly restrictive.
Reason (R): This is partly because the exponential distribution has the property that smaller service times are inherently less probable than large service time.

OOOO

ANSWERS

QUEUING THEORY

1. (b)	**2.** (c)	**3.** (b)	**4.** (c)	**5.** (c)	**6.** (a)	**7.** (b)
8. (d)	**9.** (b)	**10.** (a)	**11.** (d)	**12.** (c)	**13.** (a)	**14.** (b)
15. (d)	**16.** (c)	**17.** (d)	**18.** (b)	**19.** (c)	**20.** (d)	**21.** (c)
22. (c)	**23.** (c)	**24.** (a)	**25.** (b)	**26.** (a)	**27.** (b)	**28.** (c)
29. (b)	**30.** (c)	**31.** (d)	**32.** (b)	**33.** (a)	**34.** (c)	

CHAPTER 6

Inventory

6.1 INTRODUCTION

Inventory is stock on hand and it is kept to meet unforeseen demand or unexpected demands.Inventory can be in the form of raw material, semi-finished goods or in the form of final product. Following are the problems in maintaining the inventory in the plant:

- Some money has to be spent in maintaining the inventory.
- It blocks up the working capital.
- There are risks of the design getting obsolete.

Inventory is an American concept and opposite to inventory is Just in time (JIT) system. In this system, a product will be assembled only when the demand is placed by the customer. In JIT system, there are Kanban cards which is request of the material and these cards move from one workshop to another workshop.Kanban is a system of visual tools (usually signal cards) that synchronize and provide instruction to suppliers and customers both inside and outside the plant. A Kanban is an authorization to produce or withdraw and may also contain related information such as, the supplier of the part or product, the customer where to store it and how to transport it. Team members and the supervisors must have a deep understanding of Kanban rules as well as good problem solving skills. These rules are the following:

1. Never ship defective items
2. The customer withdraws only what is needed
3. Produce only the quantity with drawn by the customer
4. Level production
5. Use Kanban to fine-tune production
   (a) The Kanban system cannot respond to major changes in production. These must be added to the production plan. Kanban is a means for fine-tuning.
   (b) If the customer withdraws the pieces at a unstable rate – say, 100 pieces in the first hour, 200 pieces the second hour, 75 pieces the third hour – we are start supplies and inventory and invest in excess capacity (people and machinery) just in case, resulting in the collapse of the Kanban system.
6. Stabilize and strengthen the process

6.2 PRODUCTION LEVELING AND HEIJUNKA

This support standardized work and kaizen. The goal is to produce at the same pace everyday so as to minimize the peaks and valleys in the workload. Paradoxically, heijunka also supports quick adaptation to fluctuating demand. Just in time (JIT) production means producing the right item at the right time in the right quantity. Anything else entails waste . JIT was introduced in 1950s in response to following items:

1. Fragmented markets demanding many products in low volumes.
2. Tough competition.
3. Fixed or falling prices.
4. Rapidly changing technology.
5. High cost of capital.
6. Capable of workers demanding higher level of involvement.

Conventional mass manufacturers push the product through the system irrespective of actual demand. To understand the power of JIT we need basic Production physics. Little's law is the fundamental equation which is equivalent of Force = Mass × Acceleration in general physics. Little's law is applied in both manufacturing and the service industries

Cycle Time = Work in Process (WIP) ÷ Throughput, or

Throughput = Work in Process (WIP) ÷ Cycle Time

Where throughput is average output of a production process (e.g. machine, workstation, plant, line) per unit time (e.g. units per hour, patients per day, and insurance policies per week). Cycle time (also called average cycle time, flow time and throughput time) for a given routing is the average time from release of the part or unit of work to arrival at the end of the routing (e.g. the time it takes for a patient to go through admitting triage, general assessment, specialist assessment, treatment and release). Work in process is the inventory accumulated between the start and end points of a routing (e.g. the number of patients between admitting and release).

In the 1970s manual scheduling methods were replaced by computerized material requirements planning (MRP) systems. A good MRP system could keep track of inventory (more or less), order instructions to each department on what to make next. But there were still major problems. If all parts were not logged in to the system as they proceeded one production step to the next, errors began to accumulate. Defects equipment, down time, unscheduled changeovers, and other random events wreaked havoc with the reorder triggers. JIT production follows a few simple rules:

- Don't produce something unless the customer has ordered it.
- Level demand so that work may proceed smoothly throughout the plant.
- Link all the process to customer demand through simple visual tools (Kanbans).
- Maximize the flexibility of people and machinery.

Example: 6.1

A dual-card Kanban system needs to be designed for a manufacturing process that has a demand rate of 200 per hour of a certain item. The standard containers designed for the components can hold 25 items. The conveyance time and production time for the components are 30 minutes and one hour respectively. Assume a safety factor of 10%:

(i) Identify the number of C-kanbans and P-kanbans required in the system.

(ii) If there is a rounding off involved in arriving at the number of kanbans in the above case, compare the performance of the system when the when the number is rounded off to the immediate lower and next higher integer.

Solution:

A general expression for the number of Kanbans required is given as follows:

$$K = \frac{D(P+C)\,X(1+\alpha)}{Q}$$

This expression represents the ratio of (expected demand + safety stock) and size of the container. Where D is demand rate: P is production or process lead time; C is conveyance lead time; α is efficiency factor or safety factor; Q is container size. In the case of dual card Kanban systems the general expression mentioned above gets transformed for computing number of p-kanbans (k_P) and C-kanbans (K_c) is shown below.

$$K_p = \frac{DP(1+\alpha)}{Q}; \qquad K_C = \frac{DC(1+\alpha)}{Q}$$

In the problem it is given that,

Demand rate (D) = 200 per hour
Production time (P) = 1 hour
Conveyance time (C) = 0.5 hour
Container size (Q) = 25
Safety factor = 10% = 0.1 = α

Substituting the above values, we get

$$K_p = 8.8 \sim 9; K_C = 4.4 \sim 4$$

In the second part of the question it is asked to compare the performance of the system when the kanbans are rounded off to next immediate lower and next higher integer. So in the case of K_P next immediate lower and next higher integer are 8 and 9 while for K_C are 4 and 5. Here when K_P is 9, α comes out to be 0.125 and when it is 8, and, α is 0.

In the case of K_C, comes out to be 0 for K_C = 4 and 0.25 when K_C = 0.5

6.3 TYPES OF INVENTORY COSTS

1. **Set-up Cost:** This is the cost associated with the setting up of machinery before starting production. Set up cost is independent of quantity ordered for or produced.
2. **Ordering Cost (O.C.):** This is a cost associated with ordering of raw material for production purposes. Advertisements, consumption of stationery and postage, telephone charges, telegrams, rent for space used by the purchasing department, traveling expenditures incurred etc., constitute the ordering cost.
3. **Carrying Cost (C.C):** The carrying cost is associated with carrying inventory. This cost generally includes the costs such as rent for space used for storage, interest on the money locked-up, insurance of stored equipment, production, taxes, depreciation of equipment and furniture used etc.
4. **Total inventory cost** = O.C + C.C
5. **Shortage Cost:** The penalty cost for running out of stock (i.e., when as item cannot be supplied on the customer's demand) is known as shortage cost. This cost includes the loss of potential profit through sales of items and loss of good will, in terms of permanent loss of customers and its associated lost profit in future sales.
6. **Purchase or Production Cost:** The cost of purchasing (or producing) a unit of an item is known as purchase cost. The purchase price will become important when quantity discounts are allowed for purchases above a certain quantity or when economics of scale suggest that the per unit production cost can be reduced by a larger production.
7. **Salvage (or Selling Cost):** When the demand for certain commodity is affected by the quantity stocked, decision problem is based on profit maximization criterion that includes the revenue from selling.
   (i) Ordering cost / order= C_o Rs.
   (ii) Carrying cost (or) Holding cost/ Unit / Time= C_c Rs.

When a very small order is being placed, ordering cost will be very high because more number of orders has to be placed per unit time but the carrying cost will be very low. When the order quantity is very large although the number of orders per unit time will decrease but maintenance cost or carrying cost of inventory will go up.

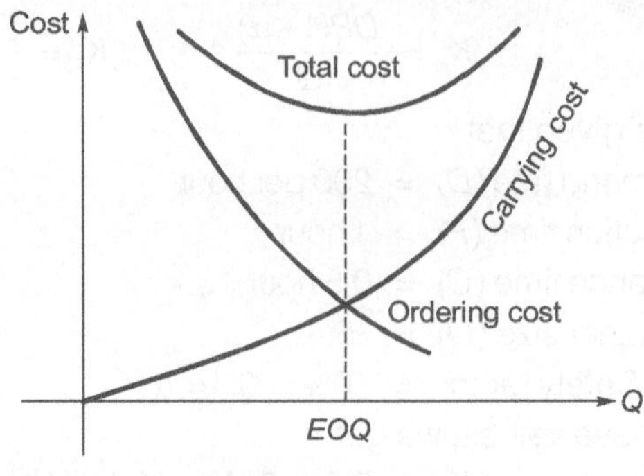

Fig: 6.1

There exists an optimum order level at which the total cost of inventory will be minimum, this is called Economic order quantity (EOQ).

6.4 TYPES OF INVENTORIES

Following are 5 types of inventories that enterprises can use for serving their purposes:

1. **Transportation Inventories:**These, also called transit or pipeline inventories, arise due to transportation of inventory items to distribution centers and customer from various production centers. The amounts of transportation inventory depend on the time consumed in transportation and the nature of demand.
2. **Buffer Inventories:** These are maintained to meet uncertainties of demand and supply. Such 'buffer' inventories which are in excess of those necessary to just meet the average demand during the lead time, held for protecting against the fluctuations in demand and lead time are also termed as safety stocks.
3. **Anticipation Inventories:** These are built up in advance for a big selling season, a promotion programme, or a plant shut-down period.Production of specialized items like electric fans and coolers while summers are approaching are some examples of anticipation inventories.
4. **Decoupling Inventories:** If various production stages operate successively then in the event of breakdown of one or any disturbance at some stage can affect the entire system. This kind of inter dependence is not only costly but also disruptive for the entire system. The inventories used to reduce the inter dependence of various stages of production system are known as decoupling inventories. Decoupling inventories are not only in the form of in process inventories to 'decouple' successive production stages but also is the form of raw material which are used to decouple the producers from the suppliers, and finished goods to decouple the consumer from producer. Inventories may also be carried to take advantage of quantity discounts of raw material price in the event of an expected rise in price.
5. **Lot-Size Inventories:** These are held for the reason that purchases areusually made in lots rather than for the exact amounts which may be needed at a point of time Lot-sizes inventories are also called cycle inventories.

6.5 INVENTORY MODELS

There are 3 models of maintaining the inventories:

1. Uncertain demands (*P*-system, *Q*-system)
2. Deterministic model
3. Probabilistic models

6.5.1 Uncertain demands

There are two types of uncertain models:

(i) **P-System or Fixed period system:** The moment we place an order, the time period after which the order reaches to our hand is called ***lead time.*** In this time period amount of inventory consumed by the workshop is called ***lead time consumption or reorder point.*** In P-system a fresh order has to be placed after a fixed period of time but the quantity of order will vary. At the time of placing the order, inventory manager looks at the store and according to the quantity of material available in the store, size of order is varied.

(ii) **Q-System or fixed quantity system:** In this system, a fixed quantity of order is placed every time but period is not fixed. A fresh order is placed by the company when the quantity of material reaches the re-order point.

Note: Re-order level: The level between maximum and minimum stock, which purchasing (or manufacturing) activities must start replenishment and known as re-ordered level.

Re-order Quantity: This is the quantity of replacement order. In certain cases it is the 'Economic order quantity'.

6.5.2 Deterministic Model

1. **Wilson Harris Model:** In this inventory model orders of equal size are placed at periodical intervals. The items against an order are replenished instantaneously and the items are consumed at a constant rate.

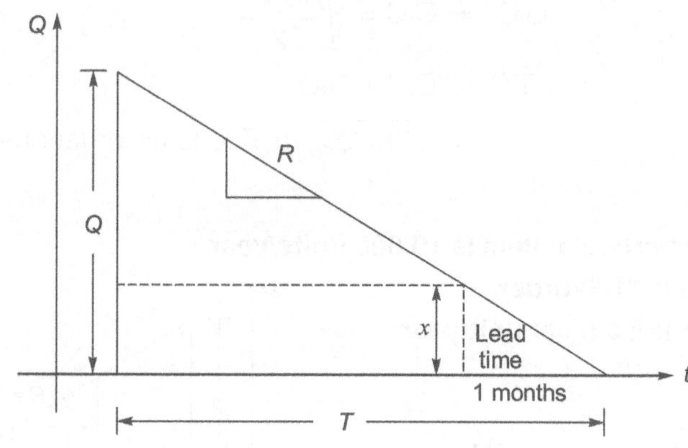

Fig: 6.2

R = rate of consumption (Units / time)
Q = amount of stored items
T = Cycle time

$$\text{Carrying cost} = \text{Avg. Inventory} \times C_c$$

$$= \left[\frac{\text{Total area}}{T}\right] \times C_c$$

$$\text{Total inventory cost (TIC)} = \text{Carrying cost} + \text{ordering cost}$$

$$= \left(\frac{0.5QT}{T}\right)C_c + N \times C_o = \frac{1}{2}QC_c + \frac{1}{T}C_o$$

Where, N = Number of order per unit time

1 order in time 'T' hence, orders in unit time

$$\Rightarrow \quad N = \frac{1}{T}$$

From triangle,
$$R = \frac{Q}{T}$$

$$\Rightarrow \quad \frac{1}{T} = \frac{R}{Q}$$

$$\text{TIC} = \frac{1}{2}QC_c + \frac{R}{Q}C_o$$

$$\frac{d(\text{TIC})}{dQ} = \frac{1}{2}C_c - \frac{R}{Q^2}C_o = 0$$

$$Q = \sqrt{\frac{2RC_o}{C_c}} = EOQ$$

So,
$$\text{carrying cost} = \frac{1}{2}QC_c = \sqrt{\frac{RC_oC_c}{2}}$$

And
$$\text{ordering cost} = \frac{1}{T}C_o = \sqrt{\frac{R^2C_cC_0^2}{2RC_o}} = \sqrt{\frac{R_cC_cC_o}{2}}$$

At EOQ,
$$\text{O.C.} = \text{C.C} = \sqrt{\frac{RC_oC_o}{2}}$$

$$\therefore \quad \text{TIC} = \text{C.C} + \text{O.C.}$$
$$= \sqrt{2RC_oC_c} \text{ at Economic order quantity}$$

Example: 6.2

The demand for a particular item is 10,000 units/year.
The ordering cost is ₹100/order.
The carrying cost is ₹ 0.5 per unit/year.
Determine:
(i) EOQ
(ii) Number of orders per year (N)
(iii) Time between orders (T)
(iv) Reorder point if lead time is 1 month
(v) Total cost when the unit cost is ₹ 2

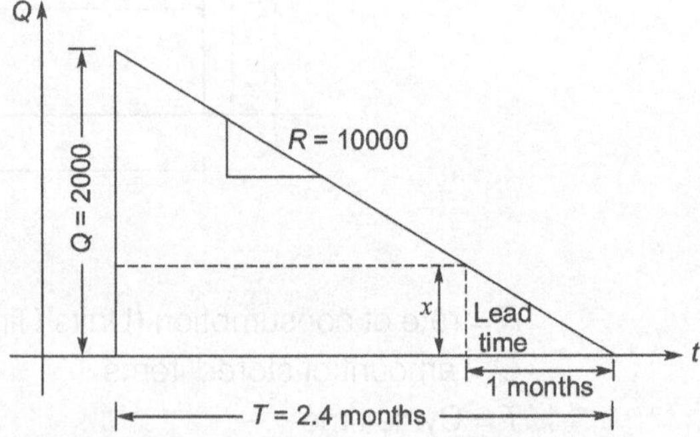

Solution:

R = 10,000 units/year; Order cost (C_o) = ₹ 100/order; Carrying cost (C_c) = ₹ 0.5/unit/year

(i)
$$EOQ = \sqrt{\frac{2RC_o}{C_C}} = \sqrt{\frac{20000 \times 100}{0.5}} = 2000 \text{ units}$$

(ii)
$$N = \frac{R}{Q} = \frac{10000}{2000} = 5$$

(iii)
$$T = \frac{Q}{R} = 0.2 \times 12 = 2.4 \text{ months}$$

(iv) $$\frac{x}{2000} = \frac{1}{2.4} \Rightarrow x = 833$$

(v) $$\text{Total cost} = \text{material cost} + \text{TIC}$$

$$= 10000 \times 2 + \sqrt{2RC_oC_c} = 21000$$

Note: If EOQ is in Rs Carrying cost per item $C_c = I\%$ of C_u then unit price = C_u

$$(\text{EOQ})_{Rs} = (EOQ \times C_u) = C_u\sqrt{\frac{2RC_o}{C_c}} = \sqrt{\frac{2RC_oC_u^2}{C_c}} = \sqrt{\frac{2RC_oC_u^2}{IC_u}}$$

$$= \sqrt{\frac{2(RC_u)C_0}{I}} = \sqrt{\frac{2AC_o}{I}}$$

Where 'A' is Rate of consumption in $Rs = RC_u$

Example: 6.3

The annual demand of items is Rs.10, 000. The ordering cost for placing a fresh order is Rs.25 per order. The carrying cost is 12.5% unit cost. Determine:

(i) $(EOQ)_{Rs}$

(ii) Number of orders per year

(iii) Carrying cost per year

(iv) Ordering cost per year and

(v) Total annual cost

Solution:

$A =$ ₹100000, $C_o =$ ₹ 25 per order, $C_c = 12.5\% \, (Cu)$, $I = 12.5\%$

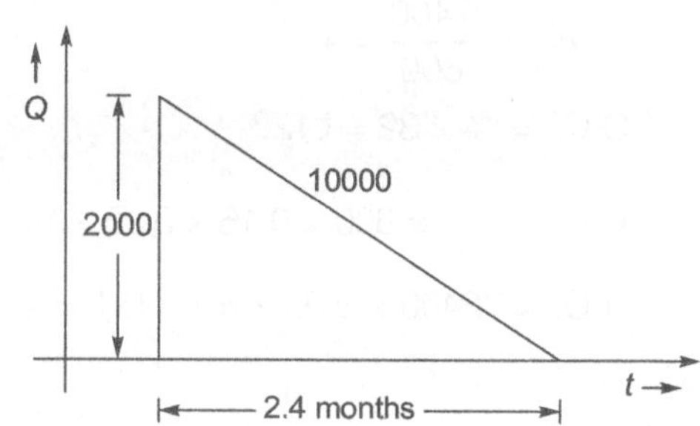

(i) $$(EOQ)_{Rs} = \sqrt{\frac{2AC_o}{I}} = \sqrt{\frac{2(10{,}000)(25)}{0.125}} = 2000$$

(ii) $$T = \frac{Q_{Rs}}{A} = \frac{2000}{10{,}000} = \frac{1}{5} = 2.4 \text{ months}$$

$$N = \frac{1}{T} = 5$$

(iii) $$\text{C.C} = \sqrt{\frac{RC_oC_c}{2}} = \sqrt{\frac{RC_oIC_u}{2}} = \sqrt{\frac{AC_oI}{2}}$$

$$= \sqrt{\frac{10000 \times 25 \times 12.5}{200}} = 125$$

(iv) At EOQ, C.C. = O.C. = 125

(v) Total cost, 10,000 + 125 + 125 = 10250

Example: 6.4

For *xyz* company, the annual requirement of an item is 2400 units. Each item costs the company ₹ 6. The supplier offers a discount of 5% if 500 or more quantities are purchased. The ordering cost is ₹ 32 per order and the average inventory cost is 16%.

(i) Is it advisable to accept the discount? Comment on the result?

(ii) How much will be the total cost? When the size of order is 600 units?

(iii) Demand of 2400 is being satisfied by placing 4 orders of 500 and one order of 400 annually. What is total cost?

Solution:

$R = 2400$ per year; $C_u = ₹\,6$; $C_o = ₹\,32$ per order; $I = 16\%$

(i)

$$EOQ = \sqrt{\frac{2RC_o}{IC_u}} = \sqrt{\frac{2(2400)(32)}{0.16 \times 6}} = 400$$

$$\text{TIC} = \sqrt{2RC_oC_c} = \sqrt{2 \times 2400 \times 32 \times 0.16 \times 6} = 384$$

$$\text{Total cost} = 2400 \times 6 + \text{TIC} = 14784$$

$$\text{If discount is accepted, } N = \frac{2400}{500} = 4.8$$

$$\text{O.C.} = N \times C_o = 4.8 \times 32 = 153.6$$

$$\text{C.C.} = \frac{1}{2} \times 500 \times 0.16 \times \{0.95 \times 6\} = 228$$

$$\text{T.C.} = 2400\,\{0.95 \times 6\} + \text{O.C.} + \text{C.C.} = 14061.6$$

Yes it is advisable to accept discount as the T.C is less when the discount is accepted.

(ii)

$$N = \frac{2400}{600} = 4$$

$$\text{O.C.} = 4 \times 32 = ₹128$$

$$\text{C.C.} = \frac{1}{2} \times 600 \times 0.16 \times 0.95 \times 6 = ₹\,273.6$$

$$\text{T.C.} = 2400 \times 0.95 \times 6 + \text{T.I.C.} = ₹14081.6$$

(iii)

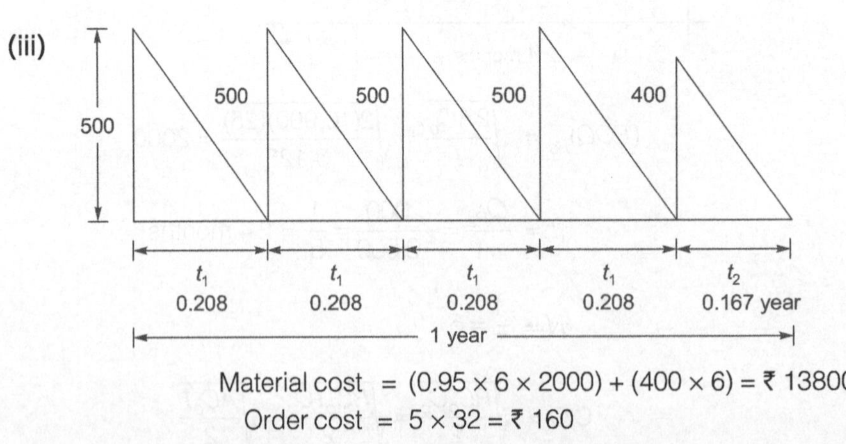

$$\text{Material cost} = (0.95 \times 6 \times 2000) + (400 \times 6) = ₹\,13800$$

$$\text{Order cost} = 5 \times 32 = ₹\,160$$

$$\text{Carrying cost} = \frac{\frac{1}{2} \times 500 \times t_1 \times 4 \times 0.95 \times 0.16 \times 6 + \frac{1}{2} \times 400 \times t_2 \times 0.16 \times 6}{1\text{ year}}$$

$$= ₹\,221.76$$

$$\text{T.C.} = ₹\,14181.76$$

2. **Production Model:**

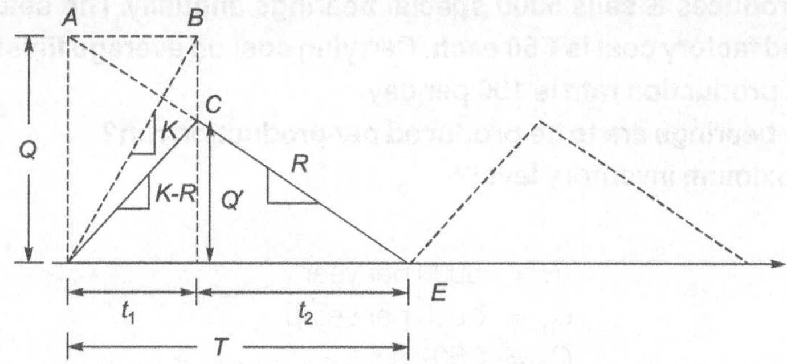

Fig: 6.3

Let the production and consumption units are integral with an economy.

K = Production rate; R = Consumption rate; C_o = Set up cost; C_c = Holding or carrying cost

From Δ^{le} OBD, $\dfrac{Q}{t_1} = K$ ...(1)

From Δ^{le} OCD, $\dfrac{Q^1}{t_1} = K - R$ ...(2)

From Δ^{le} OAE, $R = \dfrac{Q}{T}$

From Δ^{le} CDE $= \dfrac{Q^1}{t_2} = R$

$$\text{TIC} = \text{Holding cost} + \text{Setup cost} = \frac{1/2Q' \times T}{T} \times C_c + N \times C_o$$

From equations 1 and 2, $\dfrac{Q}{Q'} = \dfrac{K}{K-R}$

$$\text{TIC} = \frac{1}{2} \times \left(\frac{K-R}{K}\right) QC_c + \frac{R}{Q} C_o \qquad \left(\because N = \frac{1}{T} = \frac{R}{Q}\right)$$

At EOQ TIC is minimum hence,

$$\frac{d(TIC)}{dQ} = 0 \Rightarrow \frac{1}{2}\left(\frac{K-R}{K}\right)C_c = \frac{R}{Q^2}C_o$$

$$Q^2 = \frac{2KRC_o}{(K-R)C_c}$$

$$Q = \sqrt{\frac{2KRC_o}{(K-R)C_c}}$$

$$(\text{Holding cost})_{EOQ} = \frac{1}{2}\left(\frac{K-R}{K}\right)\left(\sqrt{\frac{2RC_o}{C_c}\frac{(K)}{K-R}}\right)C_c = \frac{1}{2}\sqrt{2RC_oC_c\left(\frac{K-R}{K}\right)}$$

$$(\text{Set up cost})_{EOQ} = R\left(\sqrt{\frac{(K-R)C_c}{2KRC_o}}\right)C_o = \frac{1}{2}\sqrt{2RC_oC_c\left(\frac{K-R}{K}\right)}$$

$$\Rightarrow \qquad \text{TIC} = \sqrt{2RC_oC_c\left(\frac{K-R}{K}\right)}$$

Example: 6.5

A company produces & sells 5000 special bearings annually. The setup cost per order is ₹ 900 setup and factory cost is ₹ 50 each. Carrying cost on average finished goods is 20% of unit price and production rate is 100 per day.

(i) How many bearings are to be produced per production run?

(ii) What is maximum inventory level?

Solution:

$$R = 5000 \text{ per year}$$
$$C_o = ₹\,900 \text{ per setup}$$
$$C_u = ₹\,50$$
$$I = 0.2$$
$$K = 100 \text{ per day} = 36500 \text{ per years}$$

(i) $$EOQ = \sqrt{\frac{2KR\,C_o}{(K-R)C_c}} = \sqrt{\frac{2\times 36500\times 5000\times 900}{31500\times 0.2\times 50}} = 1021.20$$

(ii) $$\frac{Q'}{Q} = \frac{K-R}{K}$$

$$Q' = \frac{31500}{36500}\times 1021.20 = 881.313$$

Example: 6.6

Following data refers to the production and demand for a certain product for three consecutive months,

	I	II	III
Regular	100	100	80
Overtime	20	20	40
Demand	90	130	110

C_u Regular Time = ₹ 20

Over time = ₹ 24

C_c = ₹ 2 per month/unit

For minimum cost, what should be production on machine 3 in the third month?

Solution:

$1 \to 100 \to 90, 10I \to 100\times 20 + 10\times 2$

$2 \to 100 + 20 \to 130, \text{OI} \to 100\times 20 + 20\times 24$

$3 \to 80 + 30 \to 110, \quad \text{OI} \to 8\times 20 + 30\times 24$

Minimum cost = $100\times 20 + 10\times 2 + 100\times 20 + 20\times 24 + 80\times 20 + 30\times 24 = 6820$

Example: 6.7

Max level of inventory in any system is 100 and the cycle time is 1.5 month if the ordering cost is (C_o =) ₹ 100 per order and carrying cost (C_c =) ₹ 10 per item/month, calculate annual cost in ₹ of plant neglecting the material cost?

Solution:

$$A = \frac{1}{2}\times 100\times 10\times 12 + \frac{12}{1.5}\times 100 = 6800$$

Example: 6.8

In Machine shop, pins of 15 mm dia are produced at a rate at 1000 per month and the same is consumed at a rate of 500 per month. The production and consumption continue simultaneously till the maximum inventory is reached. Then inventory is allowed to reduce to zero due to consumption. The lot size of production is 1000. If backlog is not allowed what is the maximum inventory level?

Solution:

K = 1000 per month (Refer figure 6.6)

R = 500 per month, Q = 1000

$$\frac{Q'}{Q} = \frac{K-R}{K} = \frac{500}{1000}$$

$$Q' = 500$$

Example: 6.9

The net requirements of an item over 5 consecutive weeks are 50-0-15-20-20. The inventory carrying cost and ordering cost are ₹ 1 per item per week and ₹ 100 per order respectively. Starting inventory is zero. Find minimum cost plan using least unit cost technique.

Solution:

C_c = ₹ 1 per item/week

C_o = ₹ 100 per order

Total demand = 105

Plan-1: If only one order s placed then $C_o = 100$

But only 50 is consumed in the first week so the carrying cost of the later weeks is

$$C_c = (55)1 + (55-0)1 + (55-15)1 + (40-20)1 = 170$$

$$TIC = 270$$

Plan-2: If two orders are placed in 50 in I week and 55 in III week then $C_o = 200$

Here 50 is consumed in I week but only 15 is consumed in III week so carrying cost for later weeks is $C_c = (55-15)1\ (40-20)1 = 60$

$$TIC = 260$$

Plan-3: If two orders are placed in 65 in I week and 40 in IV week then $C_o = 200$

Here only 50 is consumed in I week but only 20 is consumed in IV week so carrying cost for later weeks is $C_c = (65-50)1 + (15-0)1 + (40-20)1 = 50$

$$TIC = 250$$

3. **Shortage Model:**

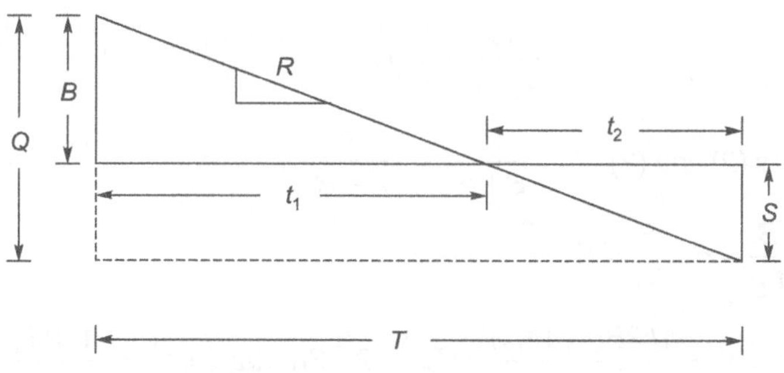

Fig: 6.4

$Q = B + S$

C_c = Carrying cost/unit/unit time

C_o = Ordering cost/order

C_s = Shortage cost/unit/unit time

1. Carrying cost = $\dfrac{\frac{1}{2}\times B\times t_1}{T}\times C_c$

2. Ordering cost = $N\times C_o = \dfrac{R}{Q}\times C_o$

3. Shortage cost = $\dfrac{\frac{1}{2}\times S\times t_2}{T}\times C_s$

4. $EOQ=\sqrt{\dfrac{2RC_o}{C_c}\times\dfrac{C_c+C_s}{C_s}}$

5. TIC = $\sqrt{2RC_oC_c\times\dfrac{C_s}{C_s+C_c}}$

6. At $EOQ\ B\times C_c=S\times C_s$

7. Service level = $\dfrac{t_1}{T}\times 100$

4. Production with Shortage Model

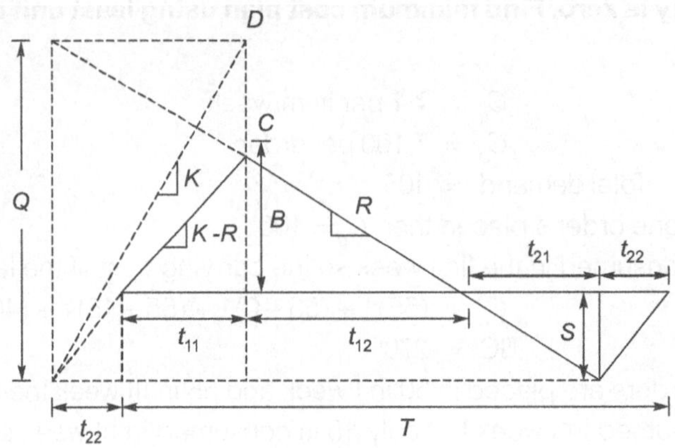

Fig: 6.5

From the above triangle, $EOQ = B+S+CD$

Production time $= t_{11}+t_{22}$

$$\frac{Q}{T}=R \quad \text{...(1)}$$

$$\frac{B+S}{t_{11}+t_{22}}=K-R \quad \text{...(2)}$$

$$\frac{Q}{t_{11}+t_2}=K \quad \text{...(3)}$$

From equations (2) and (3), $\dfrac{Q}{B+S}=\dfrac{K}{K-R}$

$$\frac{B}{t_{11}}=K-R;\ \frac{B}{t_{12}}=R;\ \frac{S}{t_{21}}=R;\ \frac{S}{t_{22}}=K-R$$

1. Carrying cost = $\dfrac{1/2B(t_{11}+t_{12})}{T}\times C_c$

2. Shortage cost = $\dfrac{1/2S(t_{21}+t_{22})}{T}\times C_s$

3. Ordering cost = $\dfrac{R}{Q}C_o$

4. At EOQ $B\times C_c=S\times C_s$

$$EOQ=\sqrt{\frac{2RC_o}{C_c}\times\frac{K}{K-R}\times\frac{C_s+C_c}{C_s}}$$

$$\text{TIC}=\sqrt{2RC_oC_c\times\frac{K-R}{K}\times\frac{C_s}{C_s+C_c}}$$

Example: 6.10

The demand for an item in a company is 18000 units per year. The company can produce these items at a rate of 3000 per month. The cost for one setup is ₹ 500. The holding cost is ₹ 0.15 per unit /month. The shortage cost per unit per year is ₹ 20. Determine:

(i) EOQ
(ii) Maximum inventory level
(iii) Maximum shortage
(iv) Production time
(v) Time between setup and max inventory level

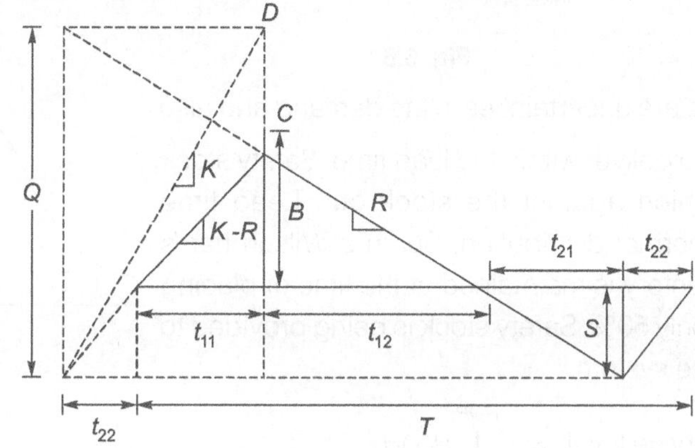

Solution:

$$R = 18000 \text{ per yr}$$
$$K = 3000 \text{ per month} = 36000 \text{ per yr}$$
$$Co = 500 \text{ per setup}$$
$$C_c = 0.15 \text{ per unit/month} = 1.8 \text{ per unit/yr}$$
$$C_s = \text{Rs.}20 \text{ per unit/yr}$$

(i)
$$EOQ = \sqrt{\frac{2RC_o}{C_c} \times \frac{K}{K-R} \times \frac{C_s + C_c}{C_s}}$$

$$= \left(\frac{2 \times 18000 \times 500}{1.8} \times \frac{36000}{18000} \times \frac{21.8}{20}\right)^{1/2} = 4669.05$$

(ii)
$$B \times C_c = S \times C_s$$
$$B(1.8) = S(20)$$
$$\frac{Q}{B+S} = \frac{K}{K-R}$$
$$\Rightarrow \quad B + S = \frac{1}{2}Q = 2334.52$$
$$\Rightarrow \quad S = 192.758; \quad B = 2141.764$$

(iii)
$$\frac{B+S}{t_{11}+t_{22}} = 1800$$
$$\Rightarrow \quad t_{11} + t_{22} = 0.1296 \text{ yrs}$$

(iv)
$$t_{12} = \frac{B}{R} \qquad t_{21} = \frac{S}{R}$$
$$t_{12} + t_{21} = \frac{B+S}{R} = 0.1296 \text{ yrs}$$

Safety stock:

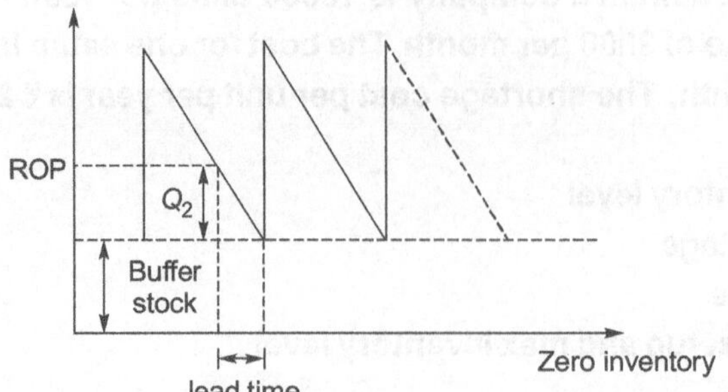

Fig: 6.6

During lead times, there are uncertainties in the demand and also order may not be able to deliver within the lead time. Safety stock is being provided as a cushion against the stock out. Lead time consumption always follows normal distribution. So, in a Wilson harr's model when reorder point inventory is maintained at the time of placing the order service level will be only 50%. Safety stock is being provided to increase the service level of the system.

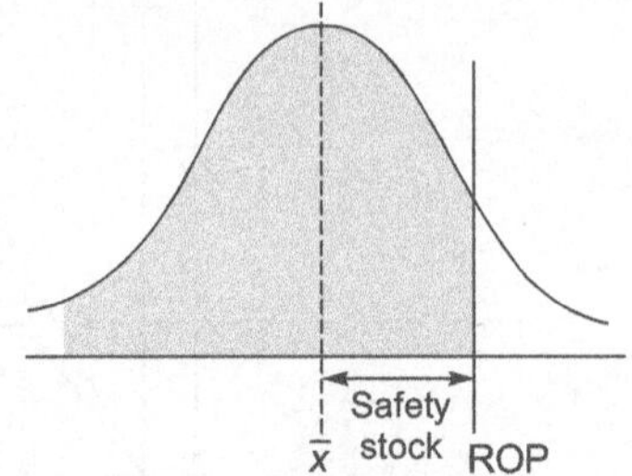

Fig: 6.7

$$\text{service level} = \int_{-\infty}^{ROP} P(x)dx$$

Note: By increasing the buffer stock will also increase.

Example: 6.11

A company requires 10,000 products per year. Whenever the order being placed 3,000 products are brought to stores. Ordering cost is ₹ 500 per order and carrying cost is ₹ 25 per unit/yr. According to management policy a safety stock of 100 is maintained all the time. What is TIC?

Solution:

R = 1000 units/year; Q = 3000; C_o = ₹ 500 per order; C_c = 25 per unit/year

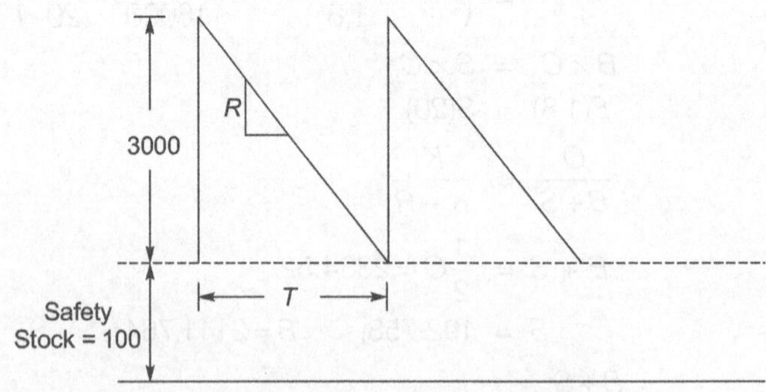

$$\text{Safety stock} = 100$$

$$N = \frac{R}{Q} = \frac{10000}{3000} = 3.34$$

$$\text{TIC} = 3.34 \times 500 + \left(\frac{1}{2} \times \frac{3000 \times T}{T} + 100\right) \times 25 = ₹\ 41{,}666$$

6.5.3 Probabilistic Model

If continuous function $f(x)$ is given then cumulative probability $= \int_{-\infty}^{x_1} f(x)dx$

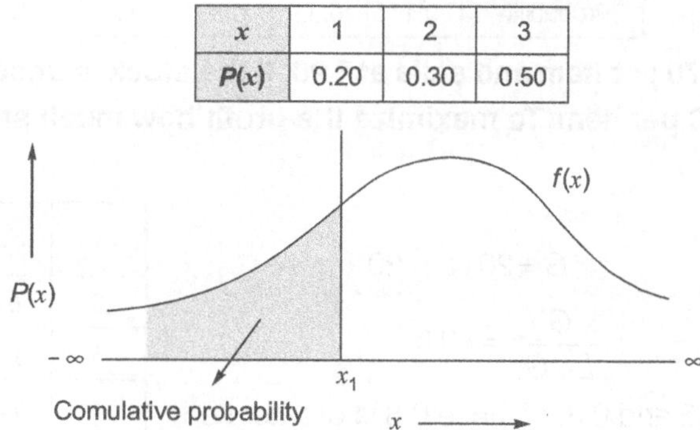

x	1	2	3
P(x)	0.20	0.30	0.50

Fig: 6.8

If discrete data is given we find optimum value of Q using

$$P(x-1) < \frac{G}{L+G} \le P(x) \text{ or } P(x-1) < \frac{C_s}{C_s + C_c} \le P(x)$$

Where, G = Gain = Profit and L = Loss

Example: 6.12

A newspaper boy buys the paper of ₹ 2 and sells it in ₹ 2.4. If the daily demand of newspaper follows according to the distribution given below. How many papers newspaper boy should purchase to maximize his profit?

x	30	31	32	33	34
P(y)	0.05	0.15	0.4	0.25	0.15

Solution:

$$L = 2$$
$$G = 0.4$$

$$\Rightarrow \quad \frac{G}{L+G} = \frac{0.4}{2.4} = 0.167$$

x	$P(x)$	Comulative Probability
30	0.05	0.05
31	0.15	0.20
32	0.40	0.60
33	0.25	0.85
34	0.15	1.00

} 0.167 (between 0.05 and 0.20)

0.167 lies between 0.05 and 0.2, of these 0.2 is greater so he should purchase 31 papers daily to get maximum profit.

Example 6.13

A stockist wishes to optimize the number of perishable items. He needs to maintain stock in every month in his store. The demand distribution for this perishable item is:

Demand	2	3	4	5
Probability	0.1	0.35	0.35	0.2

The stockist pay ₹ 70 per item and sells at ₹ 90. If the stock is unsold in any month, he can sell the item at ₹ 50 per item. To maximize the profit how much stock he must keep at his store?

Solution:

x	$P(x)$	Cumulative Probability
2	0.1	0.1
3	0.35	0.45
4	0.35	0.80
5	0.2	1.0

(0.5 lies between 0.45 and 0.80)

$$G = 20 \,;\, L = 20$$

$$\frac{G}{L+G} = 0.5$$

0.5 lies between 0.45 and 0.8, of these 0.8 is greater so he should keep in the store a stock of 4 every month to get maximum profit.

Example 6.14

The mean and standard deviation of the demand during lead time are 100 and 5 respectively. Determine the Re-order point and safely stock for 95% service level.

Solution:

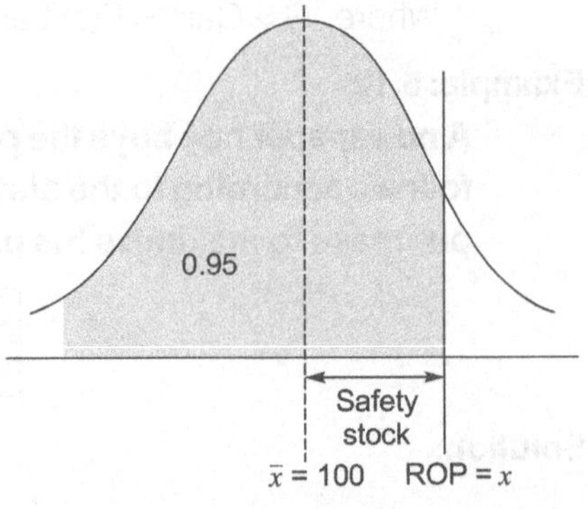

$$\bar{x} = 100$$

$$\sigma = 5$$

From normal distribution tables corresponding to 95% service level

$$z = 1.65$$

$$z = \frac{x-\bar{x}}{\sigma} = \frac{x-100}{5} = 1.65$$

$\Rightarrow$ $x = 108$

$\Rightarrow$ Buffer stock $= x - \bar{x} = 8$

Example: 6.15

The lead time demand and its probability are given in the following table. If ROP of the demand = 1.25 times the mean demand, what is the service level?

Lead time Demand	80	100	120	140
Probability	0.2	0.25	0.3	0.25

Solution:

$$\bar{x} = \frac{80\times0.2+100\times0.25+120\times0.3+140\times0.25}{1.00} = 112$$

$$\text{ROP} = 1.25\,\bar{x} = 1.25\times(112) = 140$$

$\therefore$ Service level $= P(X \le 140) = 0.2 + 0.25 + 0.3 + 0.25$
$= 1$

$\because$ Mean service level is 100%

6.6 INVENTORY CONTROL

ABC Analysis [Pareto (80 – 20) rule]: (Always better control):

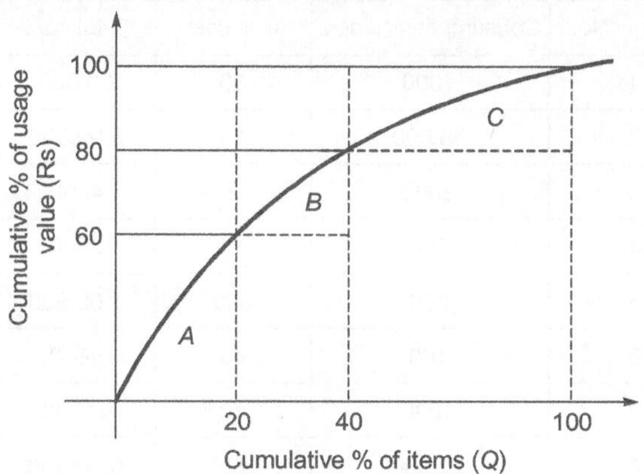

Fig: 6.9

In this analysis, the inventory items in an organization are classified on the basis of their usage in monetary terms. It is very common to observe that usually a small number of items account for a large share of the total cost of materials and a comparatively large number of items involve an insignificant share. Based on this criterion, the items are divided into three categories as follows:

A – high consumption value items;

B – moderate consumption value items and

C – low consumption value item.

The division of the items into various categories is accomplished by plotting the usage value of the items to obtain the *ABC* distribution curve.

Example: 6.16

Classify the given products according to *ABC* analysis?

Product No.	Consumption Value	Unit cost
1	1000	50
2	50,000	10
3	2000	2
4	5000	5
5	200	500
6	100	40
7	1000	10
8	10,000	60

Solution:

We calculate the total cost of each product and as shown in the above graph we segregate the products into '*A*', '*B*' and '*C*' groups. As 20% of items will be in '*A*', 20% will be in '*B*' remaining items in '*C*'.

So, 20% of total items $= \frac{20 \times 8}{100} = 1.6$

So, first two highest value cost products will be in '*A*' (products 2 and 8) next two highest value cost products in '*B*' (products 1 and 5) and the remaining products in '*C*'.

Product No.	Consumption Annual	Unit cost	Total cost	Category
1	1000	50	50,000	*B*
2	50,000	10	5,00,000	*A*
3	2000	2	4000	
4	500	5	2500	
5	200	500	1,00,000	*B*
6	100	40	4000	
7	1000	10	10000	
8	10,000	60	6,00,000	*A*

1. VED Analysis [*V* – vital, *E* – Essential, *D* – desirable]
   Inventories are classified according to the criticality of item and it is used in controlling the level of inventory of spare parts.
2. *XYZ*:
   X – Highest inventory;
   Y – Medium inventory value,
   Z – Lowest inventory value
   In this the inventories are classified according to its value in stores and it is primarily used in reviewing the inventory.
3. FNSD (*F* – Fast; *N* – Normal; *S* – slow; *D* - dead)
   Inventories are classified according to the movement of items from stores.
4. SDE (*S* – Scarce; *D* – Difficult; *E* – Easy) (availability)
   Inventories are classified according to the availability of items.
5. HML (*H* – high; *M* – Medium; *L* – Low)
   Categorization – according to cost (unit cost)

PRACTICE QUESTIONS

1. Classifying items in *A*, *B* and *C* categories for selective control in inventory management is done by arranging items in the decreasing order of
   (a) total inventory costs
   (b) item value
   (c) annual usage value
   (d) item demand

2. In manufacturing management, the term "Dispatching" is used to describe.
   (a) Dispatch of sales order
   (b) Dispatch of factory mail
   (c) Dispatch of finished product to the user
   (d) Dispatch of finished product to the user dispatch of work orders through shop floor.

3. Which of the following factors are to be considered for production scheduling?
   1. Sales forecast
   2. Component design
   3. Route Sheet
   4. Time standards

   Select the correct answer using the codes given below:
   (a) 1, 2 and 3
   (b) 1, 2 and 4
   (c) 1, 3 and 4
   (d) 2, 3 and 4

4. Consider the following statements:
   1. ABC analysis is based on Pareto's principal.
   2. FIFO and LIFO policies can be used for material valuation in materials management.
   3. Simulation can be used for inventory control.
   4. EOQ (Economic Order Quantity) formula ignores variations in demand pattern.

   Which of these statements is/are correct?
   (a) 1 only
   (b) 1 and 3
   (c) 2, 3 and 4
   (d) 1, 2, 3 and 4

5. A device for lifting or lowering objects suspended from a hook at the end of a retractable chain or cable is called
   (a) Hoist
   (b) Jib crane
   (c) Chain conveyor
   (d) Elevator

6. In inventory control theory, the Economic order Quantity (EOQ) is
   (a) average level of inventory
   (b) optimum lot size
   (c) size corresponding to break- even analysis
   (d) capacity of a warehouse

7. **Assertion (A):** Product layout is more amenable to automation than process layout.
   Reason (R): The work to be performed on the product is the determining factor in the positioning of the manufacturing equipment in product layout.
   (a) Both A and R are true and R is the correct explanation of A.
   (b) Both A and R are true but R is not a correct explanation of A.
   (c) A is true but R is false.
   (d) A is false but R is true.

8. Given that, θ = procurement cost per order, D = number of units demanded per year, H = holding cost per unit year, i = rate of interest, P = purchase price per unit. The procurement quantity per order (Q) is given by

(a) $Q = \frac{2 \cdot \theta \cdot D}{H + iP}$
(b) $Q = \sqrt{\frac{2 \cdot \theta \cdot D}{iH + P}}$
(c) $Q = \sqrt{\frac{2 \cdot \theta \cdot D}{H + iP}}$
(d) $Q = \sqrt{\frac{2.\theta}{D(H + iP)}}$

9. Which of the following are the principles of material handling?
1. Keep all handling to the minimum.
2. Move as few pieces as possible in one unit.
3. Move the heaviest weight to the least distance.
4. Select only efficient handling equipment.

Select the correct answer using the codes given below:
(a) 1, 2, 3 and 4
(b) 1, 3 and 4
(c) 1, 2 and 3
(d) 2 and 4

10. Consider the data given in the following table:

		Production Plan		
Period	Demand	Regular	Overtime	Others
		Prod.	Prod.	
1	500	500	–	–
2	650	650	–	–
3	800	650	150	–
4	900	650	150	?

Give the fact that production in regular and overtime is limited to 650 and 150 respectively, the balance demand of 100 units in the 4th period can be met by:
(a) Using overtime in period 2
(b) Using regular productions in period 1
(c) Subcontracting
(d) Using any of the steps in (A), (B) and (C)

11. Annual demand for a product costing ₹ 100 per piece is ₹ 900. Ordering cost per order is ₹ 100 and inventory holding cost is ₹ 2 per unit per year. The economic lot size is
(a) 200
(b) 300
(c) 400
(d) 500

12. Which of the following cost elements are considered while determining the Economic Lot Size for purchase?
1. Inventory carrying cost
2. Procurement cost
3. Set up cost

Select the correct answer using the codes given below:
(a) 1, 2 and 3
(b) 1 and 2
(c) 2 and 3
(d) 1 and 3

13. Which of the following input data are needed for MRP?
1. Master production schedule
2. Inventory position
3. Machine capacity
4. Bill of materials

Select the correct answer using the codes given below:
(a) 1, 2 and 3
(b) 2, 3 and 4
(c) 1, 2 and 4
(d) 1, 3 and 4

14. A manufacturer's master product schedule of product is given below:

Period Planned	Week-1	Week-2	Week-3	Week-4	Week-5	Week-6
Period Production	50	100	100	100	150	50

Each product requires a purchased component A in its sub-assembly. Before the start of week -1, there 400 components of type A in stock. The lead time to procure this component is 2 weeks and the order quantity is 400. Number of components A per product is only one. The manufacturer should place the order for:
(a) 400 components in week-1
(b) 400 components in week-3
(c) 200 components in week-1 and 200 components in week-3
(d) 400 components in week-5

15. Consider the following costs:
1. Cost of inspection and return of goods
2. Cost of obsolescence
3. Cost of scrap
4. Cost of insurance
5. Cost of negotiation with suppliers

Which of these costs are related to inventory carrying cost?
(a) 1, 2 and 3
(b) 1, 3 and 4
(c) 2, 3 and 4
(d) 2, 4 and 5

16. Match **List-I (Files in MRP)** with **List-II (Inputs require(d)** and select the correct answer using the codes given below the lists:

List-I
A. Master production Schedule
B. Bills of materials
C. Inventory records

List-II
1. Scheduled receipts
2. Unit costs and discounts
3. Production capacity
4. Product structure

Codes:

	A	B	C
(a)	4	1	3
(b)	3	4	2
(c)	3	4	1
(d)	4	3	1

17. Economic Order Quantity is the quantity at which the cost of carrying is:
(a) Minimum
(b) Equal to the cost of ordering
(c) Less than the cost of ordering
(d) Cost of overstocking

18. A shop owner with an annual constant demand of 'A' units has ordering costs of ₹ 'P' per order and carrying costs ₹ 'I' per unit per year. The economic order quantity for a purchasing model having no shortage may be determined from

(a) $\sqrt{\frac{24P}{AI}}$ (b) $\sqrt{\frac{24AP}{I}}$

(c) $\sqrt{\frac{2AP}{I}}$ (d) $\sqrt{\frac{2AI}{P}}$

19. A furniture company is maintaining a constant work force which can produce 3000 tables per quarter. The annual demand is 12000 units and is distributed seasonally in accordance with the quarterly indexes $Q_1 = 0.80$, $Q_2 = 1.40$, $Q_3 = 1.00$ and $Q_4 = 0.80$. Inventories are accumulated when demand is less than the capacity and are used up during periods of strong demand to supply the total demand. To take into account any seasonal demand the inventories on hand at the beginning of the first quarter should be at least:
(a) 0 (b) 600
(c) 1200 (d) 2400

20. ABC analysis in materials management is a method of classifying the inventories based on
(a) the value of annual usage of the items (b) economic order quantity
(c) volume of material consumption (d) quantity of materials used

21. In ABC analysis, A items require:
(a) No safety stock (b) Low safety stock
(c) Moderate safety stock (d) High safety stock

22. Which of the following are needed as the input data for materials requirement planning?
1. Weekly production schedule 2. Bill of material
3. Supplier lead time 4. Market forecast
Select the correct answer using the codes given below:
(a) 1, 2 and 3 (c) 1 and 4
(b) 2, 3 and 4 (d) 1, 2, 3 and 4

23. Match **List-I (Production Control Function)** with **List-II (Explanation)** and select the correct answer using the code given below the lists:

List-I
A. Bill of material (BOM)
B. Capacity Resource
C. Material Requirement Planning (MRP)
D. Master Production Schedule (MPS)

List-II
1. A technique for determining the quantity and timing of dependent demand items
2. A technique for determining personnel and equipment capacities needed to reject the production objective
3. Specifies what end items are to be produced and when
4. The part numbers and quantity required per assembly

Codes:

	A	B	C	D
(a)	4	1	2	3
(b)	3	2	1	4
(c)	4	2	1	3
(d)	3	1	2	4

24. Which one of the following is an inventory system that keeps a running record of the amount in storage and replenishes the stock when it drops to a certain level by ordering a fixed quantity?
(a) EOO (b) Periodic
(c) Peripheral (d) ABC

25. In the ABC method of inventory control, Group A constitutes costly items, What is the usual percentage of such items of the total items?
(a) 10 to 20% (b) 20 to 30%
(c) 30 to 40% (d) 40 to 50%

26. If the annual demand of an item becomes half, ordering cost double, holding cost one fourth and the unit cost twice, then what is the ratio of the new EOQ and the earlier EOQ?
(a) $\frac{1}{2}$ (b) $\frac{1}{\sqrt{2}}$
(c) $\sqrt{2}$ (d) 2

27. Which one of the following is not a necessary information input to Material Requirements Planning?
(a) Inventory on hand (b) Bill of materials
(c) Sequence of operations on a job (d) Master production schedule (MPS)

28. Which of the following are the benefits of inventory control?
1. Improvement in customer's relationship
2. Economy in purchasing
3. Elimination of the possibility of duplicate ordering
Select the correct answer using the code given below:
(a) 1, 2 and 3 (b) 1 and 2 only
(c) 2 and 3 only (d) 1 and 3 only

29. Match **List-I** with **List-II** and select the correct answer using the code given below the lists:

List-I	List-II
A. Procurement cost	1. Cost of holding materials
B. Carrying cost	2. Cost of receiving order
C. Economic order quantity	3. Procurement lead time
D. Reorder point	4. Break-even analysis

Codes:

	A	B	C	D
(a)	3	1	4	2
(b)	3	4	1	2
(c)	2	1	4	3
(d)	2	4	1	3

30. In the EOO model, if the unit ordering cost is doubled, the EOQ
(a) is halved (b) is doubled
(c) increases 1.414 times (d) decreases 1 .414 times

31. In the basic EOQ model, if demand is ₹ 60 per month, ordering cost is ₹ 12 per order, holding cost is ₹ 10 per unit per month, what is the EOQ?
(a) 12 (b) 144
(c) 24 (d) 28

32. Which one of the following is correct?
In the basic EOQ model, if lead time increases from 5 to 10 days, the EOQ will
(a) double
(b) decrease by a factor of two
(c) remain the same
(d) the data is insufficient to find EOQ

33. Consider the following steps in production planning and control:
1. Capacity planning
2. Material requirement planning
3. Purchasing
4. Design decisions
Which one of the following is the correct sequence of the above steps in operations management?
(a) 2-3-4-1
(b) 2-4-3-1
(c) 4-1-2-3
(d) 1-2-4-3

34. Which one of the following is correct? Production, planning and control functions are extremely complex in
(a) job-production shop producing small number of pieces only once.
(b) job-production shop producing small number of pieces intermittently.
(c) batch production shop producing a batch only once.
(d) batch production shop producing a batch at irregular intervals.

35. In the production of a product the fixed costs are ₹ 6,000/- and the variable cost is ₹ 10/- per product. If the sale price of the products is ₹ 12/-, the break even volume of product to be made will be
(a) 2000
(b) 3000
(c) 4000
(d) 6000

36. If demand is doubled and inventory carrying cost are halved, then that will be the EOQ?
(a) Half
(b) Same
(c) Twice
(d) Four times

37. Consider the following statements:
The MRP inventory status file contains
1. material on hand
2. planned order
3. planned order release
Which of these statements is/are correct?
(a) 1, 2 and 3
(b) 1 and 2 only
(c) 2 and 3 only
(d) 3 only

38. Consider the following:
1. A master production schedule
2. An inventory status file
3. Bill of material
Which of the above are the inputs to MRP systems?
(a) 1, 2 and 3
(b) 1 and 2 only
(c) 2 and 3 only
(d) 1 and 3 only

39. The lead time in material requirements planning is the time between
(a) floating the tender and receiving the quotations from the vendor.
(b) floating the tender and placing the purchase order to the vendor.
(c) floating the tender and receiving the material from the vendor.
(d) issuing purchase order and receiving the material from the vendor.

40. The following information is added updating the inventory status file in MRP.
(a) Disbursement of inventory (b) Scrap reported for material
(c) Order release (d) Material received

41. EOQ is taken at the point where the cost of carrying equals the cost of
(a) ordering the materials (b) the material
(c) the safety stock (d) both the material and the safety stock

42. The following system is the general policy for A class items in ABC analysis:
1. Very strict control
2. Frequent review of their consumption
3. Safety stock kept
Which of these statements is/are correct?
(a) 1 only (b) 1 and 2 only
(c) 2 only (d) 1, 2 and 3

43. Value engineering is necessary to be used when following symptoms are indicated:
1. New product designs are to be introduced.
2. The firm is unable to meet delivery date.
3. Rate of return on investment goes down.
Which of these statements is/are correct?
(a) 1, 2 and 3 (b) 2 only
(c) 1 and 3 only (d) 2 and 3 only

44. In relation to product flexibility and production volume achieved in computer controlled manufacturing systems, the flexible manufacturing system has
(a) high flexibility in types of product but low volume of production.
(b) moderate product flexibility and moderate production volume.
(c) low product flexibility but high production volume.
(d) extremely low product flexibility but low production volume.

45. Consider the following statements:
MRP constitutes a set of techniques that use
1. Bill of material
2. Inventory data
3. Master production schedule
Which of these statements is/are correct?
(a) 1, 2 and 3 (b) 1 and 3 only
(c) 2 and 3 only (d) 1 only

46. In the inventory control, if the yearly demand for a certain material is fixed, the economic order quantity gives minimum
(a) Inventory carrying cost per year (b) Acquisition cost per year
(c) Total cost per year (d) Number of orders per year

47. If D = annual demand for a material (units per year).
Q = quantity of material ordered at each order point (unit per order)
C = cost of carrying one unit in inventory for one year (rupees per unit per year)
S = average cost of completing an order for a material (rupees per order)
TSC = total annual stocking costs for a material (rupees per year)

Then, the Economic Order Quantity (EOQ) is

(a) $\sqrt{\frac{2DS}{C}}$ (b) $\frac{2DC}{S}$

(c) $\sqrt{\frac{2DC}{S}}$ (d) $\frac{2DS}{C}$

48. Market demand for springs is 8,00,000 per annum. A company purchases these spring in lots and sells them. The cost of making a purchase order is ₹ 1,200. The cost of storage of springs is ₹ 120 per stored piece per annum. The economic order quantity is

(a) 400 (b) 2,828

(c) 4,000 (d) 8,000

49. There are two products *P* and *Q* with the following characteristics.

Product	Demand (units)	Order cost (Rs/order)	Holding Cost (Rs Unit/year)
P	100	50	4
Q	400	50	1

The economic order quantity (EOQ) of products *P* and *Q* will be in the ratio.

(a) 1 : 1 (b) 1 : 2

(c) 1 : 4 (d) 1 : 8

50. A company has an annual demand of 1000 units, ordering cost of ₹ 100 per order and carrying cost of ₹ 100 per unit-year. If the stock-out costs are estimated to be nearly ₹ 400 each time the company runs out-of-stock, the safety stock justified by the carrying cost will be

(a) 4 (b) 20

(c) 40 (d) 100

51. In an MRP system, component demand is

(a) Forecasted

(b) Established by the master production schedule

(c) Calculated by the MRP system from the master production schedule

(d) Ignored

52. Consider the following data for an item. Annual demand: 2500 units per year Ordering cost: ₹ 100 per order inventory holding rate: 25% of unit price.

Price quoted by a supplier:

Order quantity (units)	Unit price (₹)
< 500	10
> 500	9

The optimum order quantity (in units) is

(a) 447 (b) 471

(c) 500 (d) ≥ 600

53. Capacities of production of an item over 3 consecutive months in regular time are 100, 100 and 80 and in overtime are 20, 20 and 40. The demands over those 3 months are 90, 130 and 110. The cost of production in regular time and overtime are respectively ₹ 20 per item and ₹ 24 per item. Inventory carrying cost is ₹ 2 per item month. The levels of starting and final inventory are nil. Backorder is not permitted. For minimum cost of plan, the level of planned production in overtime in the third month is

(a) 40 (b) 30

(c) 20 (d) 0

54. The product structure of an assembly *P* is shown in the figure.

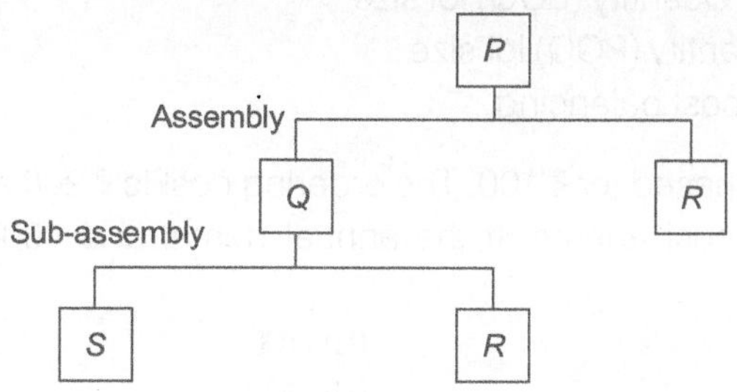

Estimated demand for end product *P* is as follows:

Week	1	2	3	4	5	6
Demand	1000	1000	1000	1000	1200	1200

Ignored lead times for assembly and sub-assembly. Production capacity (per week) for component *R* is the bottleneck operation. Starting with zero inventory, the smallest capacity that will ensure a feasible production plan up to week 6 is

(a) 1000 (b) 1200
(c) 2200 (d) 2400

55. A company uses 2555 units for an item annually. Delivery lead time is 8 days. The reorder point (in number of units) to achieve optimum inventory is

(a) 7 (b) 8
(c) 56 (d) 60

56. If orders are placed once a month to meet an annual demand of 6,000 units, then the average inventory would be:

(a) 200 (b) 250
(c) 300 (d) 500

57. The inventory carrying cost includes

(a) Expenditure incurred for payment of bills
(b) Placing an order
(c) Receiving and inspecting
(d) Obsolescence and depreciation

58. Which of the following correctly represents the average inventory turn over ratio for a raw materials?

(a) Annual sales/Annual Inventory
(b) Average working process volume/total production volume
(c) Annual consumption/annual inventory
(d) Volume of spare parts /total annual sale

59. Setup costs do not include

(a) Labour cost of setting up machines (b) Ordering cost of raw material
(c) Maintenance cost of the machines (d) Cost of processing the work piece

60. In inventory planning, extra inventory is unnecessarily carried tothe end of the planning period when, using one of the following lot size decision policies:

(a) Lot-for-lot production
(b) Economic Order Quantity (EOQ) lot size
(c) Period Order Quantity (POQ) lot size
(d) Part Period total cost balancing

61. An item can be purchased for ₹ 100. The ordering cost is ₹ 200 and the inventory carrying cost is 10% of the item cost annum. If the annual demand is 4000 units, then economic order quantity (in units) is
(a) 50
(b) 100
(c) 200
(d) 400

62. If the demand for an item is doubled and the ordering cost halved, the economic order quantity
(a) remains unchanged
(b) increases by a factor of 2
(c) is doubled
(d) is halved

63. Annual demand for window frames is 10000. Each frame costs ₹ 200 and ordering cost is ₹ 300 per order. Inventory holding cost is ₹ 40 per frame per year. The supplier is willing to offer 2% discount if the order quantity is 1000 or more, and 4% if order quantity is 2000 or more. If the total cost is to be minimized, the retailer should
(a) Order 200 frames every time
(b) Accept 2% discount
(c) Accept 4% discount
(d) Order Economic Order Quantity

64. The maximum level of inventory of an item is 100 and it is 100 and It is achieved with infinite replenishment rate. The inventory becomes zero over one and half month due to consumption at a uniform rate. This cycle continues throughout the year. Ordering cost is ₹ 100 per order and inventory carrying cost is ₹ 10 per item per month. Annual cost (in ₹) of the plan, neglecting material cost, is
(a) 800
(b) 2800
(c) 4800
(d) 6800

65. In a machine shop, pins of 15 mm diameter are produced at a rate of1000 per month and the same is consumed at a rate of 500 per month. The production and consumption continue simultaneously till the maximum inventory is reached. Then inventory is allowed to reduce to zero due to consumption. The lot size of production is1000. If backlog is not allowed, the maximum inventory level is
(a) 400
(b) 500
(c) 600
(d) 700

66. In computing Wilson's economic lot size for an item, by mistake the demand rate estimate used was 40% higher than the tree demand rate. Due to this error in the lot size computation, the total cost of setups plus inventory holding per unit time. Would rise above the true optimum by approximately
(a) 1.4 %
(b) 6.3%
(c) 18.3%
(d) 8.7%

67. The net requirements of an item over 5 consecutive weeks are 50-015-20-20. The inventory carrying costs are ₹ 1 per item per week and ₹ 100 per order respectively. Starting inventory is zero. Use "Least Unit Const. Technique" for developing the plan. The cost of the plan (in ₹) is
(a) 200
(b) 250
(c) 255
(d) 260

OOOO

ANSWERS

INVENTORY

1. (c)	**2.** (d)	**3.** (a)	**4.** (d)	**5.** (a)	**6.** (b)	**7.** (a)
8. (c)	**9.** (b)	**10.** (d)	**11.** (b)	**12.** (a)	**13.** (b)	**14.** (b)
15. (c)	**16.** (b)	**17.** (b)	**18.** (c)	**19.** (a)	**20.** (a)	**21.** (d)
22. (a)	**23.** (a)	**24.** (a)	**25.** (a)	**26.** (d)	**27.** (c)	**28.** (b)
29. (a)	**30.** (c)	**31.** (a)	**32.** (c)	**33.** (c)	**34.** (d)	**35.** (b)
36. (c)	**37.** (a)	**38.** (a)	**39.** (d)	**40.** (a)	**41.** (a)	**42.** (a)
43. (d)	**44.** (a)	**45.** (b)	**46.** (c)	**47.** (a)	**48.** (c)	**49.** (c)
50. (c)	**51.** (b)	**52.** (c)	**53.** (b)	**54.** (d)	**55.** (c)	**56.** (b)
57. (d)	**58.** (b)	**59.** (c)	**60.** (c)	**61.** (d)	**62.** (a)	**63.** (c)
64. (d)	**65.** (b)	**66.** (c)	**67.** (b)			

CHAPTER 7

Project Management

7.1 INTRODUCTION

- Node or event is any point in time space and in between the two nodes there will be an activity which consumes time.

Activity: It is the time consuming effort represented by a line with an arrow head pointing in the direction of progress of completion of work.

Event: An event is a point in time where one or more activities start and/or finish. It is a part of accomplishment and/or decision. A circle is used to represent an event.

- Every project involves some group of activities and some of these activities will be performed parallelly.
- Before starting any activity like construction of a pillar in building, the activities like bringing cement, bricks have to be completed. These activities are called "Predecessor activities".

Node 1 —Activity→ Node 2
12:00 noon   3:00 pm

Fig : 7.1

- The activity which is followed is called "successor activity".
- When all the predecessor and successor activities are arranged in the form of a diagram it is called "precedence diagram".

7.2 RULES FOR CONSTRUCTION OF PRECEDENCE DIAGRAM

1. Project start or project completion is to be considered as only one event in time space and hence cannot be represented by more than one node. So the node at which the project starts can be the 'Burst node' and the node at which the project completes can be the 'Converging Node'. i.e., Many activities can start from one node and can finish at one node only i.e. There should be only one initial and one terminal node.

Burst node   Converging node

Fig: 7.2

2. While constructing the diagram different activities should not cross each other.

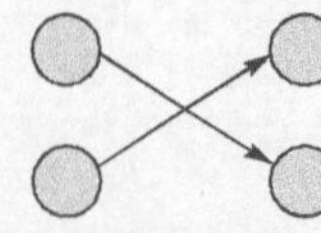

Fig: 7.3

3. More than one activity cannot start at same node and also finish at the same node.

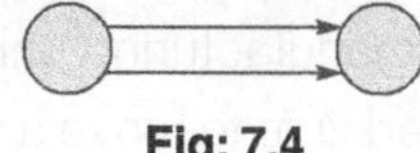

Fig: 7.4

Case (2) and (3) can be avoided by introducing dummy activity.

7.2.1 Dummy Activity

Dummy activities don't consume any time and are used just to complete the precedence diagram. Dummy activities are used only in case of absolute necessity i.e., minimum number of dummy activities must be used.

Dummy activity should be represented by a dotted line.

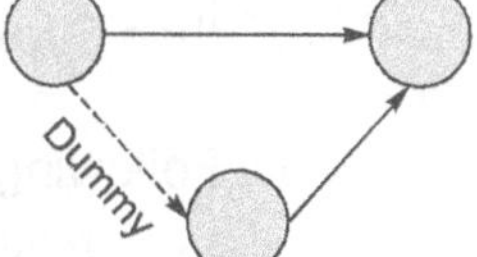

Fig: 7.5

4. Time always flow from left to right.
5. All nodes, with the exception of the terminal node, must have at least one successor.
6. All nodes, except the first, must have at least one predecessor.
7. An arrow specifies only precedence relations; its length has no significance with respect to the time duration accompanying either of the activities that it connects.
8. Cycles or closed-loop paths through the network are not permitted. They imply that an activity is a successor of another activity that depends on it.

Example: 7.1

Draw the precedence diagram for the following data:

Activity	A	B	C	D	E	F	G	H	I
Predecessor	–	–	A	B	C, D	C, D	E	F	G, H

Solution:

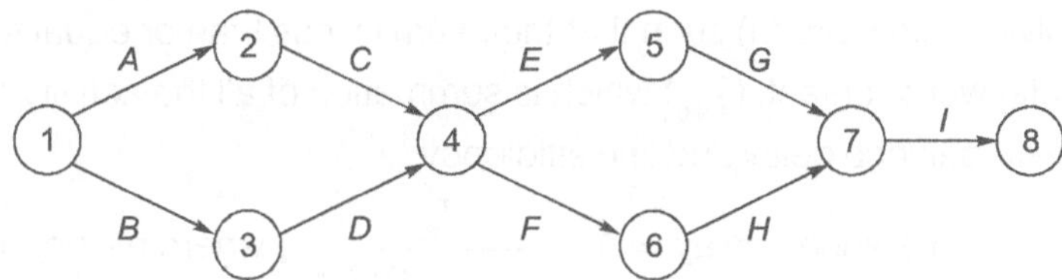

Example: 7.2

Draw the precedence diagram for the following data:

Activity	B	C	E, F	L	G	H	I	M	N	J	P	Q
Predecessor	–	–	B	C	C, F	E, G	H, L	L	H, L	H, L	I, J	M, N

Solution:

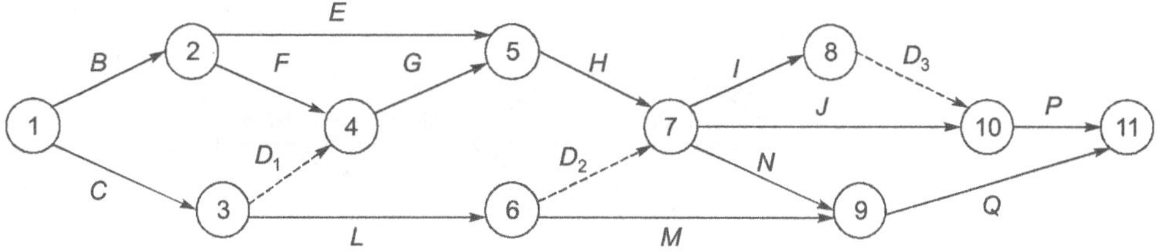

Here D_1, D_2, D_3 are dummy activities.

7.3 LINE BALANCING

- Stations are formed in a typical manufacturing unit by grouping different activities.
- **Cycle Time:** It is the total elapsed time to move a unit of work from the beginning to the end of a process.
- After every cycle time, line advances and whatever was there on the first station comes to the second and then so on.
- Cycle time is calculated by how many units of final products are required within a specified time period.
- E.g., If 1000 products has to be produced in 10 days and if working hours are 20 per day

  then Cycle time is $\frac{1000}{10}$ = 100 per day $\frac{100}{20}$ = 5 per hr $\frac{100}{20}$ = 5 per hr $\frac{5}{60} = \frac{1}{12}$ per min.

- **Following points must be kept in mind while balancing the line:**
  I. Total time of the activities which are assigned to a particular station should be less than or equal to the cycle time.
  II. Before assigning any activity on a particular station all its predecessor activities must be completed on the previous stations.
  III. There will be stations where total activity time is closed to cycle time on such stations, highly skilled workers needs to be employed.
- **Rank position weight method (Helgeson-Birnic)**
  (a) Weight is the summation of times of all the activities which follows that particular activity. It also includes the time of that particular activity.
  (b) In case of alternate paths weight should be taken for the longest path.
  - **Steps in Calculating Line Efficiency**
  1. Calculate the weight of each activity.
  2. Now give number according to their weight and write in descending order.
  3. Now divide into pairs (n) such that their sum is less than or equal to cycle time.
  4. Find total work contact, (T_{wc}) which is summation of all the activity times.
  5. Calculate balance delay and line efficiency.

Note: Balanced delay = $1 - \frac{T_{wc}}{n \times \text{cycletime}}$, where n – no. of pairs

Line efficiency = 1 – delay

Example: 7.3

An assembly of equipment involves the tasks *A* to *N*, the precedence tasks and processing times of these tasks in minute are given in the following precedence diagram. Considering cycle time of 100 minutes at any work station, balance the assembly and calculate the weight of each activity and total work contact, delay and line efficiency.

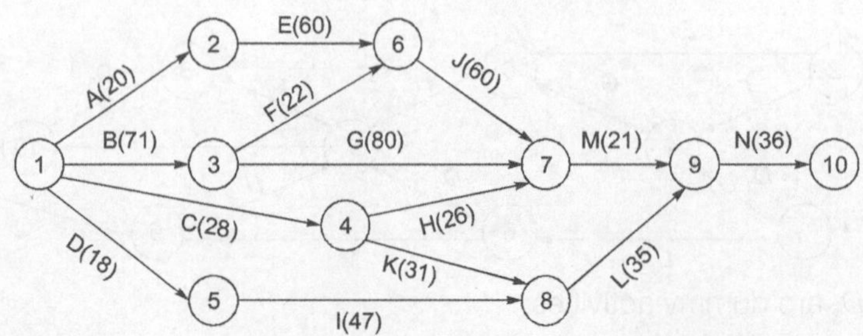

Solution:

Activity	A	B	C	D	E	F	G	H	I	J	K	L	M	N
Weight	197	210	130	136	177	139	137	83	118	117	102	71	57	36
Position	2	1	7	6	3	4	5	11	8	9	10	12	13	14

Work contact time of each station should be less than that of cycle time (here 100).

Stations	Activities according to rank	Station time < Cycle time
1	B A	91
2	E F	82
3	G D	98
4	C I	75
5	J K	91
6	H L M	82
7	N	36

Total work contact (T_{WC}) = 555

$$\text{Balanced delay} = 1 - \frac{T_{WC}}{n \times \text{cycle time}} = 1 - \frac{555}{7 \times 100} = 0.207$$

Line efficiency = 1 – delay

Example: 7.4

An assembly of equipment involves the tasks *A* to *N*, the precedence tasks and processing times of these tasks in minute are given in the following table. Considering cycle time of 20 minutes at any work station, balance the assembly and find optimum number of work stations. Also find the idle time at each work station.

Task	A	B	C	D	E	F	G	H	I	J	K	L	M	N
Predecessor	–	–	–	A	B	C	D	E	F	G	I	J, H	K	L, M
Duration	6	5	4	8	5	4	7	6	10	10	7	10	6	9

Solution:

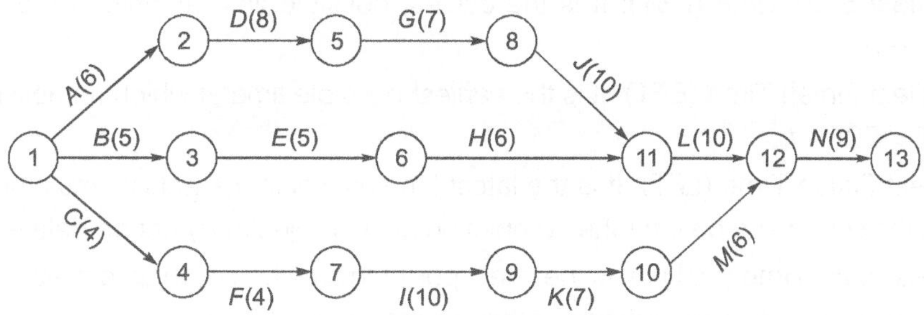

Activity	A	B	C	D	E	F	G	H	I	J	K	L	M	N
Weight	50	35	40	44	30	36	36	25	32	29	22	19	15	9
Position	1	6	3	2	8	4	5	10	7	9	11	12	13	14

Stations	Activities according to rank	Station time < Cycle time
1	ADC	18
2	FBG	16
3	IE	15
4	JHI	16
5	KL	17
6	MN	15

$$\text{Balanced delay} = 1-\frac{97}{120} = 0.192$$

7.4 NETWORK ANALYSIS

The two most commonly used techniques are:

1. CPM (Critical path method)
2. PERT (Programme evaluation and review technique)

PERT and CPM are the scheduling techniques which are used to plan, schedule and control a project consisting of number of inter-related activities. These techniques provide a frame which defines the jobs to be done, integrates them in a logical sequence and provides a system of control over the progress of plan.

CPM and PERT can be applied to production management, particularly for jobbing production and servicing work orders, planning and launching of new products and services, change over to new products or new models etc.

Note: 1. Critical path method (CPM) is deterministic model and activity oriented.
2. Program evaluation review technique (PERT) isprobabilistic model and event oriented.

7.5 TERMINOLOGY USED IN CPM AND PERT

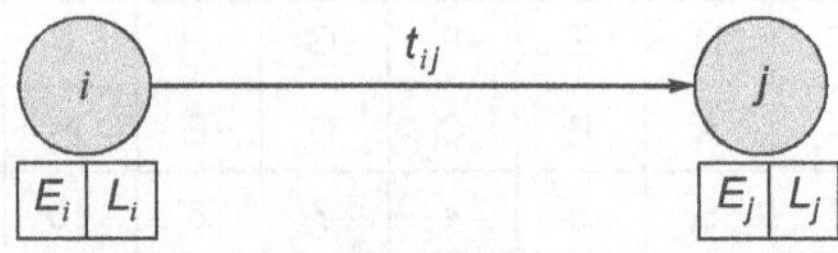

Fig: 7.6

1. **Earliest Start Time (EST):** It is the earliest possible time at which an activity can start. $EST = E_i$
2. **Earliest Finish Time (EFT):** It is the earliest possible time at which an activity can finish. $EFT = EST + t_{ij}$.
3. **Latest Finish Time (LFT):** It is the latest time by which the activity must be completed so that the scheduled date for the completion of the project may not be delayed. $LFT = L_j$.
4. **Latest Start Time (LST) :** It is the latest possible time by which an activity can start without delaying the date of completion of the project $LST = LFT - t_{ij}$
5. **Total Float (TF) (or) Total slack (TS):** Total float is the extra time which is available with any parallel activity without affecting the project completion time.The calculation of slacks or floats is used to determine the critical activities in a project network. Those activities make up the critical path. The critical path is defined as the path with the least slack in the network.

All activities on the critical path are classified as critical activities. These activities can create bottlenecks in the project if they are delayed. The critical path is also the longest path in the network diagram. In large networks, it is possible to have multiple critical paths. In this case, it may be difficult to visually identify all the critical paths. Total float is used in CPM and total slack is used in PERT.Information about slack is important to the project manager, who may have to adjust budgets and resource allocations to stay on schedule. Knowing the amount of slack in an activity is essential if he is to do this without delaying the completion of the project. In a multiproject environment, slack in one project can be used temporarily to free up resources needed for other projects that are behind schedule or overly constrained.

$$TF = LST - EST = LFT - EFT$$

6. **Free Float (FF):** It is the extra time available with the activity without affecting its successor activity. $FF = (E_j - E_i) - t_{ij}$

   E.g.: For a project of Building construction

   Activity is cementing. Successor activity is painting. During cementing if the labour is injured then work has been stopped. If the IT engineer is able to complete cementing in free float days, then the painter doesn't know incident.

7. **Safety Float:** It is extra time available for starting any activity(ij) beyond LST of ith node without affecting the LST of jth node. $SF = (L_j - L_j) - t_{ij}$

8. **Independent Float (IF):** It is surplus time available with any activity without affecting any of the earliest and latest time of any successor activity. Independent floats take a pessimistic view of the situation of an activity. It evaluates the situation assuming that the activity is pressured from both sides, that is, when its predecessors are delayed as late as possible, while its successors are to be started as early as possible. Independent floats are useful for conservative planning purposes. Activities can be buffered with independent floats as a way to handle contingencies. $IF = (E_j - L_i) - t_{ij}$

   Note: $TF + IF = FF + SF$

9. **Critical Activities And Critical Path:** The activities for which total float (TF) is zero are called "Critical activities", any delay on the critical activities will affect the project completion time. Combination of critical activities is called *critical path* and it tells us that "in how much time the project can be completed". It is the longest path. The critical path is represented by double or thick arrow line to distinguish it clearly.

7.6 CRITICAL PATH METHOD (CPM)

The interactive procedure of determining the critical path is as follows:

Step-1: Each activity is indicated by an arrow with the direction of the arrow showing the sequence of activities. Place the activities on the diagram one by one keeping mind what precedes and follows each activity as well as what activity can be done simultaneously.

Step-2: Write zeros in the boxes [|] of the first node.

Step-3: Add duration of first activity to the value written in the box marked [✓|] of the tail node and write the sum in the box marked [✓|] of the head node of the activity. Do this calculation up to last node. If there are parallel activities with same head node value, then choose the maximum value.

Step-4: The value in the box [✓|] of last node should be written in the box marked of last node.

Step-5: Subtract the duration of last activity from the value written in the box marked [✓|] of last node and write that value in the box marked [✓|] of the tile node of the activity. Do this calculation up to first node. If there are parallel activities with same head node value, then choose the minimum value.

Example: 7.5

Draw the network diagram for the given project and show critical path and also calculate total project duration.

Activity	1-2	1-3	2-4	3-4	3-5	4-6	5-6
Weight	2	8	4	1	2	5	6

Solution:

CPM network diagram is:

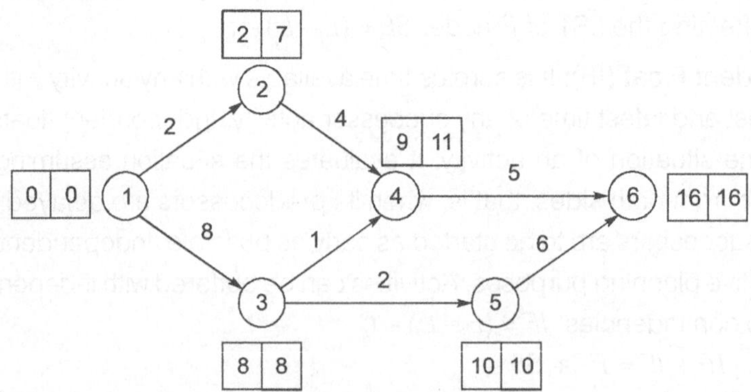

Activity	Duration	EST	EFT	LST	LFT	TF	FF	SF	IF
1-2	2	0	2	5	7	5	0	5	0
1-3	8	0	8	0	8	0	0	0	0
2-4	4	2	6	7	11	5	3	0	–2
3-4	1	8	9	10	11	2	0	2	0
3-5	2	8	10	8	10	0	0	0	0
4-6	5	9	14	11	16	2	2	0	0
5-6	6	10	16	10	16	0	0	0	0

From the above table total float is zero for activities 1-3, 3-5 and 5-6.

So critical path is 1-3-5-6.

So total project duration is = 8 + 2 + 6 = 16.

7.7 CRASHING OF NETWORKS

Crashing: It is a phenomena in the project by which we decrease the duration of the project bygiving more facilities to do the activities [investing more money]. Crashing is the expediting or compression of activity duration. Crashing is done as a trade-off between a shorter task duration and a higher task cost. It must be determined whether the total cost savings realized from reducing the project duration is enough to justify the higher costs associated with reducing individual task durations. If there is a delay penalty associated with a project, it may be possible to reduce the total project cost even though crashing increases individual task costs. If the cost savings on the delay penalty is higher than the incremental cost of reducing the project duration, then crashing is justified. Normal task duration refers to the time required to perform a task under normal circumstances. Crash task duration refers to the reduced time required to perform a task when additional resources are allocated to it. Crashing increases the project cost to decrease the project duration. In case of time over run sometimes project cost may actually decrease by crashing. Only critical activities need to be crashed.Before crashing any critical activity, total float available on the parallel branch must be seen. By crashing that activity we are eating up the total float available on the parallel activity. When the critical activities are crashed equal to the total float on the parallel branch, that branch will also become critical. In the (Q.No. 7.6) when activity (3 – 4) crashed by 3 days, activity (2 – 4) will also become critical. In this situation there will be 2 critical paths. Suppose (3 – 4) is further crashed by 1 day then there will not be any change in project duration because activity (3 – 4) will become uncritical.

So if there are two critical paths then crashing any activity from critical paths has no use, because by such crashing that particular path will become non critical and hence there will not be any change in the project duration.

If there are alternate critical paths, project duration can be decreased by crashing one activity on each path.

The project has the highest cost corresponding to the crash duration and has normal cost corresponding to the normal duration. Thus we have two types of costs and two types of times as defined below.

(i) **Normal Time: Normal** time is the standard time, associated with normal resources of the organization to perform the activity.

(ii) **Crash Time:** Crash time is the minimum possible time in which an activity can be completed by employing extra resources. Crash time is that time, beyond which the activity cannot be shortened by an amount of increase in resources.

(iii) **Normal Cost:** The expenditure incurred on normal resources for completing any activity in normal time is known as normal cost.

(iv) **Crash Cost:** The total expenditure incurred on normal and additional resources for completing the critical activity known as crashed cost.

The time-cost relationship is not linear, but the relationship can be approximated by a straight line, whose slope is called as the "Cost-Slope".

$$\text{Cost slope} = \frac{\text{Crashed cost} - \text{Normal cost}}{\text{Normal time} - \text{Crash time}}$$

Cost slope represents the extra cost of shortening the duration of the activity by one time unit.

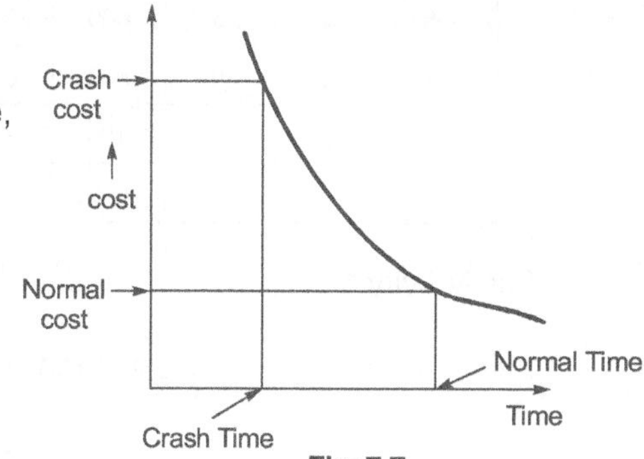

Fig: 7.7

Example: 7.6

In the given project what will be the cost of total project when its duration has to be decreased by 4 days?

Activity	Normal Time	Crash Time	Normal Cost	Crash Cost
1-2	20	17	600	720
1-3	25	25	200	200
2-3	10	8	300	440
2-4	12	6	400	700
3-4	5	2	300	420
4-5	10	5	300	600
4-6	5	3	600	900
5-7	10	5	500	800
6-7	8	3	400	700

Solution:

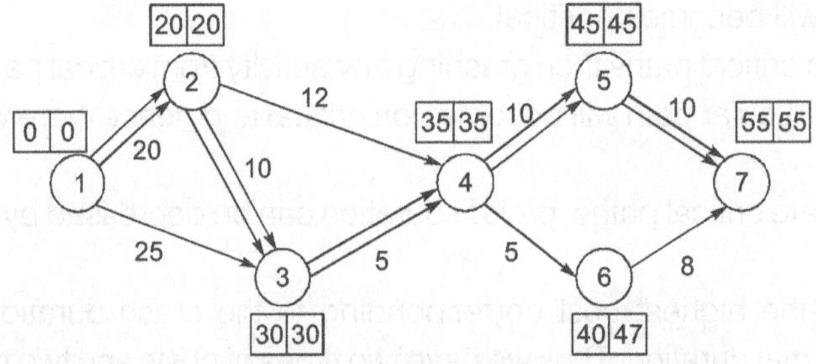

Activity	Normal Time	Crash Time	Normal Cost	Crash Cost	Cost Slope	EST	EFT	LST	LFT	TF	FF	SF	IF
1-2	20	17	600	720	40	0	20	0	20	0	0	0	0
1-3	25	25	200	200	0	0	25	5	30	5	5	5	5
2-3	10	8	300	440	70	20	30	20	30	0	0	0	0
2-4	12	6	400	700	50	20	32	23	35	3	3	3	3
3-4	5	2	300	420	40	30	35	30	35	0	0	0	0
4-5	10	5	300	600	60	35	45	35	45	0	0	0	0
4-6	5	3	600	900	150	35	40	42	47	7	0	7	0
5-7	10	5	500	800	60	45	55	45	55	0	0	0	0
6-7	8	3	400	700	60	40	48	47	55	7	7	0	0
			3600										

For Activity 1-2:

$$\text{Cost slope} = \frac{720-600}{20-17} = 40$$

$$\text{EST} = 0, \text{LFT} = 20$$

$$EFT = EST + t_{1-2} = 0 + 20 = 20$$
$$LST = LFT - t_{1-2} = 20 = 20 = 0$$
$$EST = 0, LFT = 20$$

Therefore 1–2 is critical activity, similarly 2 – 3, 3 – 4, 4 – 5, 5 – 7 have 0 total float.

Total float of 1 – 3 is 5 days and total float of 2 – 4 is 3 days. So we can crash 3 days on activity 3 – 4 and 1 day on activity 1 – 2.

Therefore, Project cost = Total normal cost + 4(40) = 3760

Thus the precedence diagram becomes

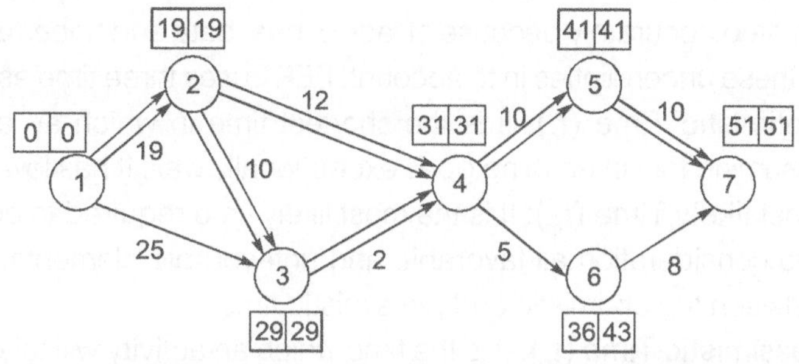

Example: 7.7

Form the above question what will be the cost of the total project when the total project duration decreased by 10 days?

Solution:

If we crash 3, 3, 4 days on activities 1 – 2, 3 – 4, 4 – 5 respectively then the precedence diagram will become

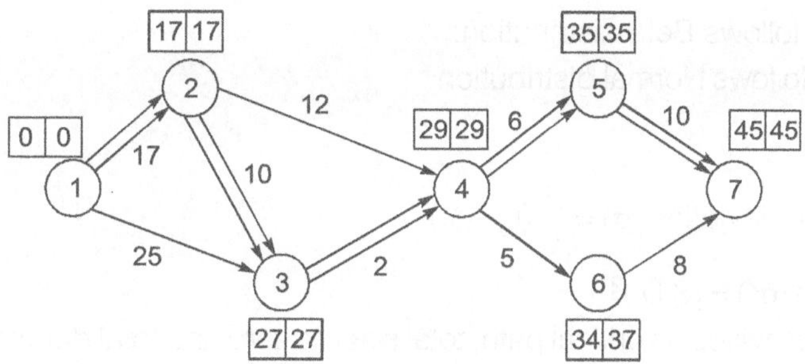

7.8 PERT (PROGRAM EVALUATION REVIEW TECHNIQUE)

The critical path method either assumes that the duration of an activity is known and deterministic or that a point estimate such as the mean or mode can be used in its place. It makes no allowance for activity variance. When fluctuations in performance time are low, this assumption is logically justified and has empirically been shown to produce accurate results.

When high levels of uncertainty exist, however, CPM may not provide a very good estimate of the project completion time. In these situations, there is a need to account explicitly for the effects of uncertainty. PERT is the most common approach that has been developed for this purpose. PERT finds applications in planning and control of complex set of activities, functions and relationships.

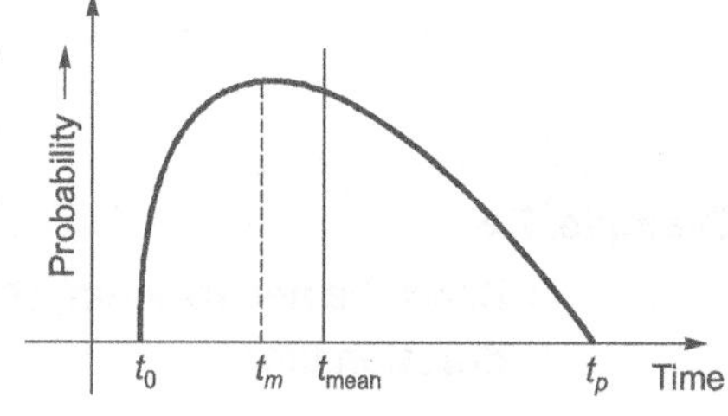

Fig: 7.8

By controlling the critical activities the project can be completed within the scheduled time limit. PERT gives a way of identifying critical activities right at the planning stage so that management is aware of these potentially troublesome areas and exercise proper control over them, so as to complete the project within the schedule time.

(i) Activity time in PERT follows a beta distribution because of following reasons:

1. It is uni-model i.e., shape of the distribution doesn't change by external changes.
2. It cuts two intercepts on the x-axis which can be corresponded to optimistic time and pessimistic time.

(ii) Estimation of Activity Time: PERT is based on the assumption that operation time cannot be estimated accurately because of lack of past data and uncertain ties involved in working. To take these uncertainties in to account, PERT uses three time estimates for each activities.

- **Optimistic Time (t_o):** It is the shortest time in which an activity can be completed assuming that everything goes exceptionally well. It has low probability of occurrence.
- **Most likely Time (t_m):** It is the most likely time required to complete the activity taking into consideration all favorable and unfavorable elements. This estimate of time lies between the optimistic and pessimistic time.
- **Pessimistic Time (t_p):** It is the time which an activity will take to complete if everything turns out to be against expectation. It is also has low probability of occurrence.
- **Mean time** $= \dfrac{t_0 + 4t_m + t_p}{6}$, it is used as the activity time.

Note: Greater the uncertainty, the wider would be the range of the estimated completion times.

7.8.1 In PERT

Activity time follows Beta distribution.
Project time follows Normal distribution

For activity:

1. Standard deviation $(\sigma) = \dfrac{1}{6}(t_p - t_0)$
2. Variance $(\sigma^2) = (\text{S.D.})^2$
3. For the activities on critical path, total slack is zero and total duration time is sum of estimated time on critical path.

For project:

$$Z = \frac{X - \overline{X}}{\sigma} \quad \text{(where } \overline{X}\text{-Project duration time, } \sigma\text{- Variance)}$$

$$\sigma = \sqrt{\sum \text{Variance of critical activities}}$$

$$= \sqrt{\sigma_1^2 + \sigma_2^2 + \ldots}$$

Example: 7.8

(a) Draw the network diagram for given project also show critical path and calculate total duration time.

Activity	1 - 2	1 - 3	1 - 4	2 - 5	3 - 5	4 - 6	5 - 6
t_0	1	1	2	1	2	2	3
t_p	7	7	8	1	14	8	15
t_m	1	4	2	1	5	5	6

(b) What is the probability that the project will be completed in 14 days?

(c) What is the probability that the project will be completed in 21days?

Solution:

(a) PERT network diagram is,

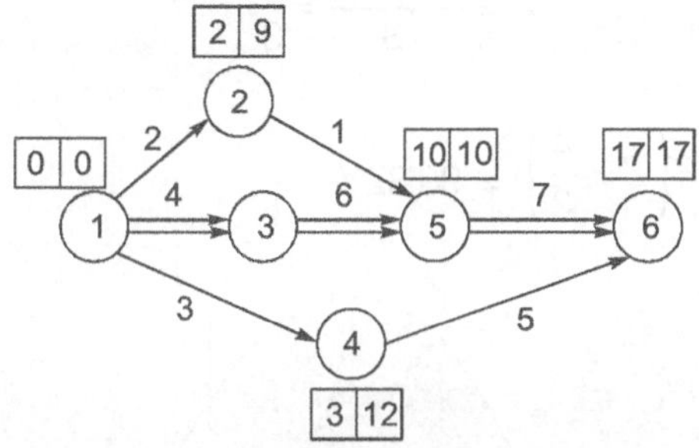

Activity	T_0	T_P	T_m	Mean Time	S.D.	Variance	EST	LST	EFT	LFT	Total Slack
1-2	1	7	1	2	1	1	0	7	2	9	7
1-3	1	7	4	4	1	1	0	0	4	4	0
1-4	2	8	2	3	1	1	0	9	3	12	9
2-5	1	1	1	1	0	0	2	9	3	10	7
3-5	2	14	5	6	2	4	4	4	10	10	0
4-6	2	8	5	5	1	1	3	12	8	17	9
5-6	3	15	6	7	2	4	10	10	17	17	0

Here total slack is minimum for activities 1 - 3, 3 - 5, 5 - 6. So, critical path is 1 - 3 - 5 - 6 and total duration time = 17.

Because PERT is a probabilistic model, there is a 50% probability that project might get completed in 17 days and variance = $\sqrt{1+4+4} = \sqrt{9} = 3$

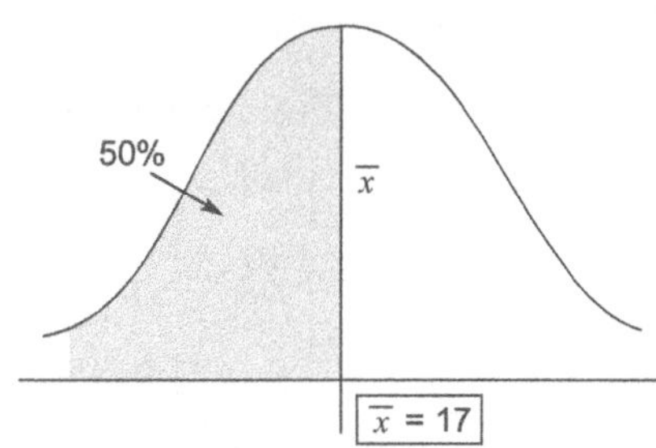

(b)
$$Z = \frac{X-\overline{X}}{a} = \frac{14-17}{3} = -1$$

$$P(Z < -1) = 15.87\%$$

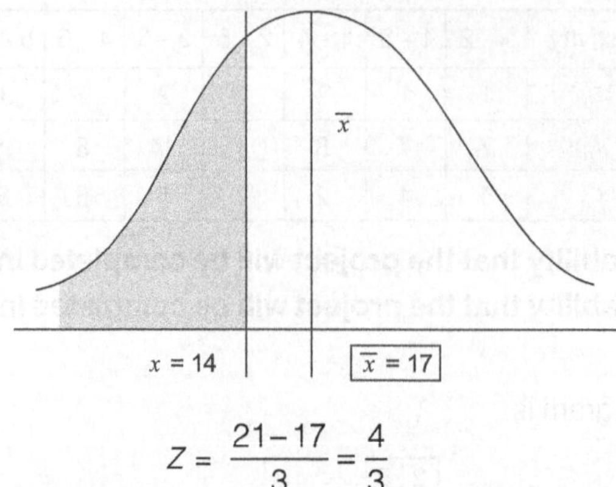

$$Z = \frac{21-17}{3} = \frac{4}{3}$$

$$P\left(Z < \frac{4}{3}\right) = 90.82\%$$

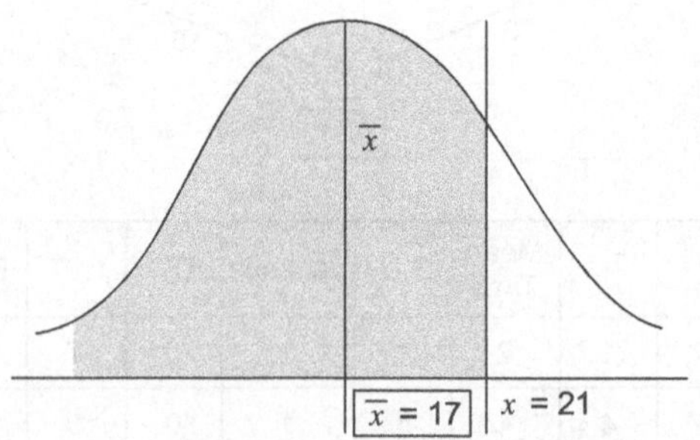

Note:

1. For 50% probability of completion of project total slack of critical activity will be 'zero'.
2. If less than 50% probability of completion of project total slack of critical activity will be negative.
3. If more than 50% probability of completion of project total slack of critical activity will be 'positive'.
4. Total slack for critical activities in PERT will be minimum.

PRACTICE QUESTIONS

1. Which of the following are the guidelines for the construction of a network diagram?
   1. Each activity is represented by one and only one arrow in the network.
   2. Two activities can be identified by the same beginning and end events.
   3. Dangling must be avoided in a network diagram.
   4. Dummy activity consumes no time or resource.

   (a) 1, 2, 3 (b) 1, 3, 4
   (c) 1, 2, 4 (d) 2, 3, 4

2. In the network shown below the critical path is along:

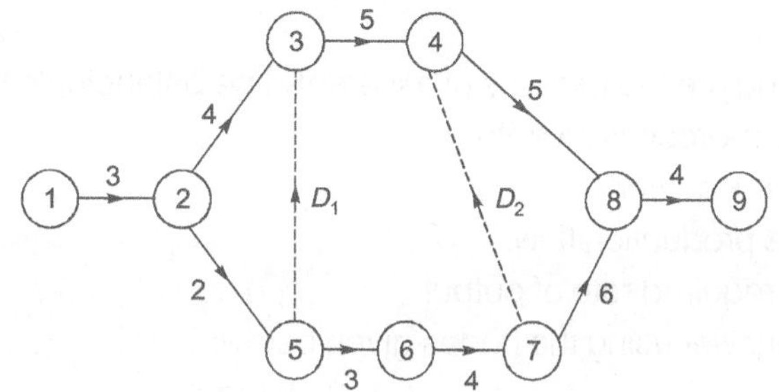

   (a) 1-2-3-4-8-9 (b) 1-2-3-5-6-7-8-9
   (c) 1-2-3-4-7-8-9 (d) 1-2-5-6-7-8-9

3. A production line is said to be balanced when
   (a) There are equal-number of machines at each work station
   (b) There are equal numbers of operators at each work station
   (c) The waiting time for service at each station is the same
   (d) The operation time at each station is the same

4. In a PERT network, expected project duration is found to be 36 days from the start of the project. The variance is four days. The probability that the project will be completed in 36 days is:
   (a) zero (b) 34%.
   (c) 50% (d) 84%

5. The variance ($V1$) for critical path; $a \rightarrow b = 4$ Time units, $b \rightarrow c = 16$ time units, $c \rightarrow d = 4$ time units, $d \rightarrow e = 1$ time unit. The standard deviation of the critical path $a \rightarrow e$ is
   (a) 3 (b) 4
   (c) 5 (d) 6

6. Consider the following sets of tasks to complete the assembly of an engineering component:

Task	a	b	c	d	e	f	g
Time (in sec.)	10	20	15	5	30	15	5
Precedence	–	–	a	b	c	d	e

   The expected production rate is 3000 units per shift of 8 hour duration in 3 shifts. The minimal number workstations that are needed to achieve this production level is:
   (a) 4 (b) 8
   (c) 10 (d) 11

7. Match **List-I (Methods)** with **List-II (Problems)** and select the correct answer using the codes given below the lists:

List-I	List-II
A. Moving average	1. Assembly
B. Line balancing	2. Purchase
C. Economic batch size	3. Forecasting
D. Johnson algorithm	4. Sequencing

Codes:

	A	B	C	D
(a)	1	3	2	4
(b)	1	3	4	2
(c)	3	1	4	2
(d)	3	1	2	4

8. Which of the following are the benefits of assembly line balancing?
   1. It minimizes the in-process inventory.
   2. It reduces the work content.
   3. It smoothens the production flow.
   4. It maintains the required rate of output.

   Select the correct answer using the codes given below:
   (a) 1, 2 and 3 (b) 2, 3 and 4
   (c) 1, 3 and 4 (d) 1, 2 and 4

9. Estimated time T_c and variance of the activities 'V' on the critical path in a PERT network are given in the following table:

Activity	T_c(days)	V (days)
a	17	4
b	15	4
c	8	1

   The probability of completing the project in 43 days is
   (a) 15.6% (b) 50.0%
   (c) 81.4% (d) 90.0 %

10. The earliest occurrence time for event '1' is 8 weeks and the latest occurrence time for event '1' is 26 weeks. The earliest occurrence time for event '2' is 32 weeks and the latest occurrence time for event '2' is 37 weeks. If the activity time is 11 weeks, then the total float will be:
    (a) 11 (b) 13
    (c) 18 (d) 24

11. Time estimates of an activity in a PERT network are:
    Optimistic time t_0 = 9 days; pessimistic time t_p = 21 days and most likely time t_m =15 days. The approximates probability of completion of this activity in 13 days is:
    (a) 16% (b) 34%
    (c) 50% (d) 84%

12. Dummy activities are used in a network to
    (a) Facilitate computation of slacks (b) satisfy precedence requirements
    (c) Determine project completion time (d) avoid use of resources

13. If the earliest starting time for an activity is 8 weeks, the latest finish time is 37 weeks and the duration time of the activity is 11 weeks, then the total float is equal to
    (a) 18 weeks (b) 14 weeks
    (c) 56 weeks (d) 40 weeks

14. For the network shown in the given figure, the earliest expected completion time of the project is

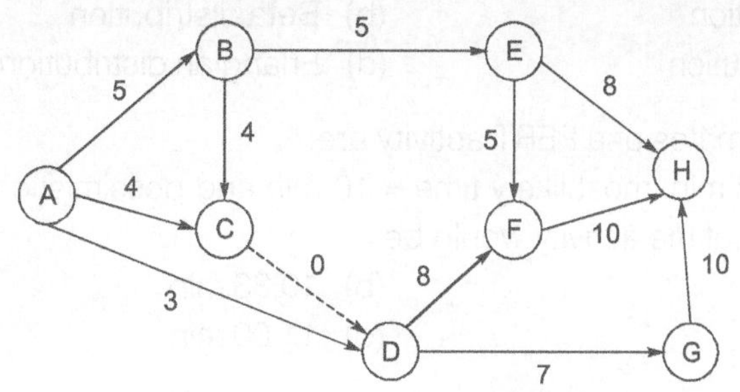

(a) 26 days
(b) 27 days
(c) 30 days
(d) Indeterminable

15. Match **List-I (OR-technique)** with **List-II (Model)** and select the correct answer using the codes given below the lists:

List-I	List-II
A. Branch and Bound technique	1. PERT and CPM
B. Expected Value approach	2. Integer programming
C. Smoothing and Levelling	3. Queuing theory
D. Exponential distribution	4. Decision theory

Codes:

	A	B	C	D
(a)	2	1	4	3
(b)	2	4	1	3
(c)	3	4	1	2
(d)	3	1	4	2

16. A new facility has to be designed to do all the welding for 3 products: *A*, *B* and *C*. Per unit welding time for each product is 20s, 40s and 50s respectively. Daily demand forecast for product *A* is 450, for *B* is 360 and for *C* is 240. A welding line can operate efficiently for 220 minutes a day. Number of welding lines required is

(a) 5
(b) 4
(c) 3
(d) 2

17. Consider the following statements regarding updating of the network:
1. For short duration project, updating is done frequently.
2. For large duration project, frequency of updating is decreased as the project is nearing completion.
3. Updating is caused by over estimated or under estimated times of activities.
4. The outbreak of natural calamity necessitates updating.

Which of these statements are correct?

(a) 1, 2 and 3
(b) 2, 3 and 4
(c) 1, 3 and 4
(d) 1, 2 and 4

18. Which one of the following is true in respect of production control for continuous or assembly line production?

(a) Control is achieved by PERT network.
(b) Johnson algorithm is used for sequencing.
(c) Control is on one work center only.
(d) Control is on flow of identical components through several operations.

19. Which one of the following is assumed for timing the activities in PERT network?
(a) Normal distribution (b) Beta distribution
(c) Binomial distribution (d) Erlangian distribution

20. The three time estimates of a PERT activity are:
Optimistic time = 8 min, most likely time = 10 min and pessimistic time = 14 min.
The expected time of the activity would be
(a) 10.00 min (b) 10.33 min
(c) 10.66 min (d) 11.00 min

21. For the network shown in the figure, the variance along the critical path is 4.

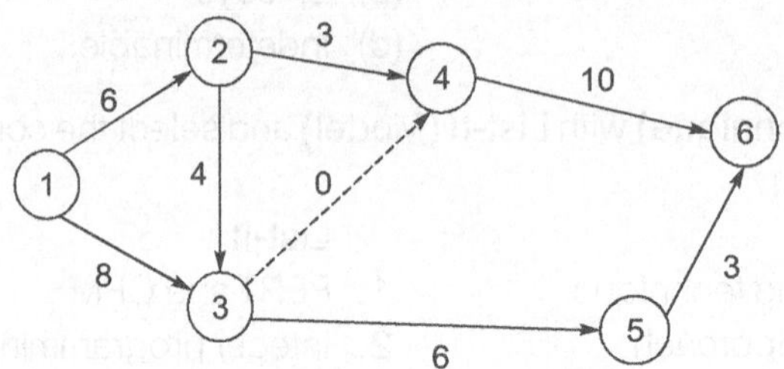

The probability of completion of the project in 24 days is
(a) 68.2% (b) 84.1%
(c) 95.4% (d) 97.7%

22. The variance of the completion time for a project is the sum of variance of
(a) all activity times
(b) non-critical activity times
(c) critical activity times
(d) activity times of first and last activities of the project

23. The earliest time of the completion of the last event in the below network in weeks is

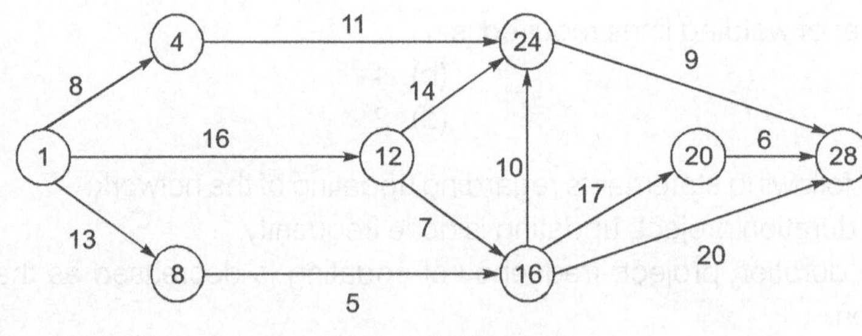

(a) 41 (b) 42
(c) 43 (d) 46

24. Consider the following statements with respect to PERT:
1. It consists of activities with uncertain time phases.
2. This is evolved from Gantt chart.
3. Total slack along the critical path is not zero.
4. There can be more than one critical path in PERT network.
5. It is similar to electrical network.
(a) 1 and 2 (b) 2 and 5
(c) 4 and 1 (d) 3 and 2

25. In a small engineering project, for an activity, the optimistic time is 2 minutes, the most likely time is 5 minutes and the pessimistic time is 8 minutes. What is the expected time of the activity?

(a) 1 minute (b) 5 minutes
(c) 8 minutes (d) 18 minutes

26. The critical path of a network is the path that

(a) takes the shortest time (b) takes the longest time
(c) has the minimum variance (d) has the maximum variance

27. Match **List-I** with **List-II** and select the correct answer using the codes given below the lists:

List-II	List-II
A. Transportation Problem	**1.** Critical path
B. Assignment Problem	**2.** Stage coach
C. Dynamic Problem	**3.** Follows β distribution
D. PERT	**4.** Hungarian method

Code:

	A	B	C	D
(a)	2	1	3	4
(b)	3	4	2	1
(c)	2	4	3	1
(d	3	1	2	4

28. A control chart is established with limits of ±2 standard errors for use in monitoring samples of size $n = 20$. Assume the process to be in control. What is the likelihood of a sample mean falling outside the control limits?

(a) 97.7% (b) 4.5%
(c) 95.5% (d) 2.3%

29. Match **List-I (Parameter)** with **List-II (Definition)** and select the correct answer using the codes given below the lists:

List-I

A. Total work content
B. Workstation process time
C. Cycle time
D. Balance delay

List-II

1. Aggregate of all the work, elements to be done on line.
2. Line inefficiency which results from the idle time due to imperfect allocation or work among stations.
3. Time interval between parts coming off the line.
4. Sum of the times of the work elements done at a station.

Codes:

	A	B	C	D
(a)	1	4	3	2
(b)	1	2	3	4
(c)	3	4	1	2
(d)	3	2	1	4

30. In an assembly line, when the workstation times are unequal, the overall production rate of an assembly line is determined by the
(a) Fastest station time
(b) Slowest station time
(c) Average of all station times
(d) Average of slowest and fastest station times

31. In a network, what is total float equal to?
(a) $LFT_j - EST_i + t_{i-j}$
(b) $EST\, j - LET_i + T_{i-j}$
(c) $EST_j - LFT_i - t_{i-j}$
(d) $LFT_j - EST_i - t_{i-j}$
Where, LFT = latest finish time of an activity; EST = earliest start time of an activity; t_{i-j} = time of activity $i-j$.

32. Consider the following statements in respect of PERT and CPM:
1. PERT is event-oriented while CPM is activity-oriented.
2. PERT is probabilistic while CPM is deterministic.
3. Leveling and smoothing are the techniques related to resource scheduling in CPM.
Which of these statements are correct?
(a) 1, 2 and 3
(b) Only 1 and 2
(c) Only 2 and 3
(d) Only 1 and 3

33. Consider the following statements: Scheduling
1. is a general timetable of manufacturing.
2. is the time phase of loading.
3. is loading all the work in process on machines according to their capacity.
Which of these statements are correct?
(a) 1, 2 and 3
(b) 1 and 2 only
(c) 2 and 3 only
(d) 1 and 3 only

34. In an assembly line, what is the balance delay?
(a) Line efficiency × 100
(b) 100 – Line efficiency (in percentage)
(c) $\frac{\text{Line efficiency}}{100}$
(d) None of the above

35. Match **List-I** with **List-II** and secret the correct answer using the code given below the lists:

List-I	**List-II**
A. Dummy activity	**1.** follows distribution
B. Critical path	**2.** it is built on activity oriented diagram
C. PERT activity	**3.** constructed only to establish sequence
D. Critical path method	**4.** has zero total slack

Codes:

	A	B	C	D
(a)	3	4	1	2
(b)	4	2	3	1
(c)	3	4	2	1
(d)	4	2	1	3

36. Consider the following statements: PERT considers the following time estimates:
1. Optimistic time
2. Pessimistic time
3. Most likely time

Which of these statements are correct?

(a) 1, 2 and 3 (b) 1 and 2 only
(c) 3 only (d) 1 and 3 only

37. Which one of the following statements is not correct?
(a) PERT is probabilistic and CPM is deterministic.
(b) In PERT, events .are used and in CPM activities are used.
(c) In CPM, the probability to complete a project in a given time-duration is calculated.
(d) In CPM crashing is carried out.

38. What is the additional time available for the performance of an activity in PERT and CPM calculated on the basis that all activities will start at their earliest start time, called?
(a) Slack (b) Total float
(c) Free float (d) Independent float

39. If critical path of a project is 20 months with a standard deviation 4 months, what is the probability that the project will be completed in 24 months?
(a) 15.85% (b) 68.3%
(c) 84.2% (d) 95.50%

40. Which one of the following statements is not correct?
(a) PERT is activity oriented and CPM is event oriented.
(b) In PEAT, three time estimates are made, whereas in CPM only one time estimate is made.
(c) In PERT slack is calculated whereas in CPM floats are calculated.
(d) Both PERT and CPM are used for project situations.

41. A PERT activity has an optimistic time estimate of 3 days, a pessimistic time estimate of 8 days, and a most likely time estimate of 10 days. What is the expected time of this activity?
(a) 5.0 days (b) 7.5 days
(c) 8.0 days (d) 8.5 days

42. Consider the below network. Activity times are given in number of day. The earliest expected occurrence time (TE) for event 50 is

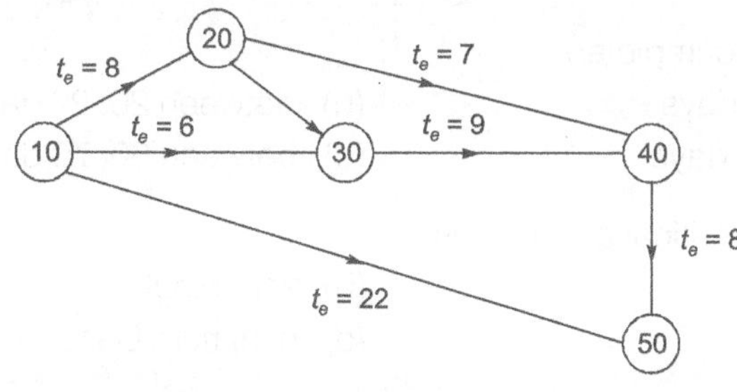

(a) 22 (b) 23
(c) 24 (d) 25

43. Consider the following characteristics of assembly line balancing:
1. Apportionment of sequential work activities into work stations.
2. High utilizations of equipment.
3. Minimization of idle time.

Which of these statements are correct?
(a) 1, 2 and 3 (b) 1 and 2 only
(c) 2 and 3 only (d) 1 and 3 only

44. In CPM, the project duration can be reduced by crashing
(a) one or more non-critical activities (b) one or more critical activities only
(c) one or more dummy activities only (d) activities having independent float

45. Which one of the following statements is not correct?
(a) PERT is probabilistic whereas CPM is deterministic.
(b) In PERT slack on various events in calculation whereas in CPM floats are calculated.
(c) Critical path in network is the path on which events have no slack.
(d) More than four dummy activities cannot be used in a PERT network.

46. In PERT and CPM network the dummy activity
(a) consumes time (b) consumers resources
(c) is used to preserve the logic (d) is a real activity

47. Consider the 3 activities of a CPM network as shown below. Earliest and latest occurrence times of these events are given on the nodes. The total float on activity 20 – 30 is

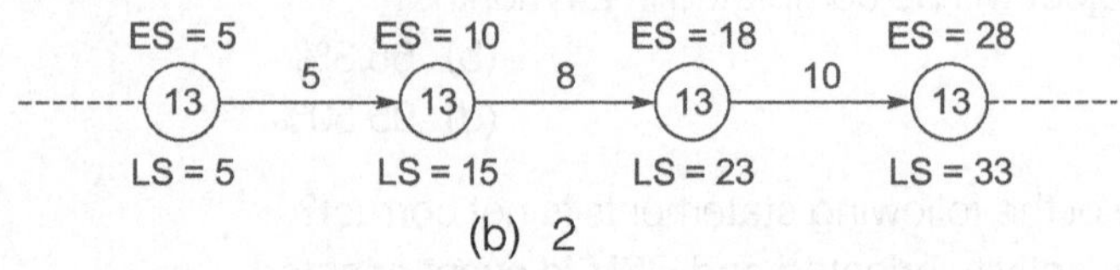

(a) 0 (b) 2
(c) 3 (d) 5

48. A project consist of activities A to M shown in the net in the following figure with the duration of the activities marked in days.

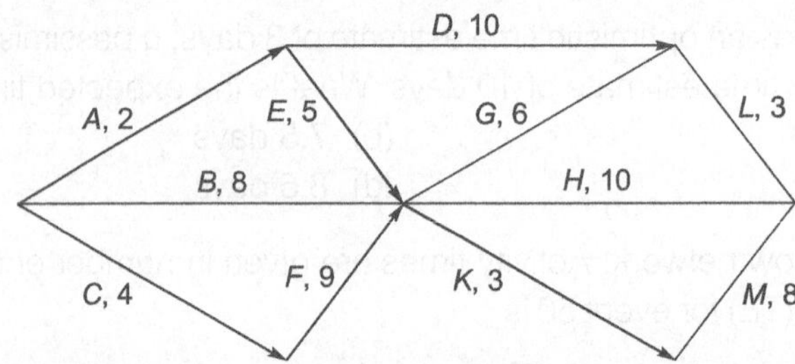

The project can be completed
(a) between 18,19 days (b) between 20, 22 days
(c) between 24, 26 days (d) between 60, 70 days

49. In PERT analysis a critical activity has
(a) maximum Float (b) zero Float
(c) maximum Cost (d) minimum Cost

50. An electronic equipment manufacturer has decided to add a component sub-assembly operation that can produce 80 units during a regular 8-hours shift. This operation consists of three activities as below:

Activity	Standard time (min)
M. Mechanical assembly	12
E. Electric wiring	16
T. Test	3

For line balancing the number of work stations required for the activities *M*, *E* and *T* would respectively be

(a) 2, 3, 1 (b) 3, 2, 1
(c) 2, 4, 2 (d) 2, 1, 3

51. A project has six activities (*A* to *F*) with respective activity durations 7, 5, 6, 6, 8, 4 days. The network has three path *A* – *B*, *C* – *D* and *E* – *F*. All the activities can be crashed with the same crash cost per day. The number of activities that need to be crashed to reduce the project duration by 1 day is
(a) 1 (b) 2
(c) 3 (d) 6

52. The table gives details of an assembly line.

Work station	I	II	III	IV	V	VI
Total task at the workstation (in minutes)	7	9	7	10	9	6

What is the line efficiency of the assembly line?
(a) 70% (b) 75%
(c) 80% (d) 85%

Statement for Linked Answer Questions (53 and 54):
Consider a PERT network for a project involving six tasks (*a* to *f*):

Task	Predecessor	Expected task time (in days)	Variance of the task time (in days^2)
A	–	30	25
B	a	40	64
C	a	60	81
D	b	25	9
E	b, c	45	36
F	d, e	20	9

53. The expected completion time of the project is
(a) 238 days (b) 224 days
(c) 171 days (d) 155 days

54. The standard deviation of the critical path of the project is
(a) $\sqrt{151}$ days (b) $\sqrt{155}$ days
(c) $\sqrt{200}$ days (d) $\sqrt{224}$ days

55. For the network below, the objective is to find the length of the shortest path from node *P* to node *G*. Let be the length of directed arc from node *i* to node *j*.
Let s_j be the length of the shortest path from *P* to node *j*. Which of the following equations can be used to find S_G?

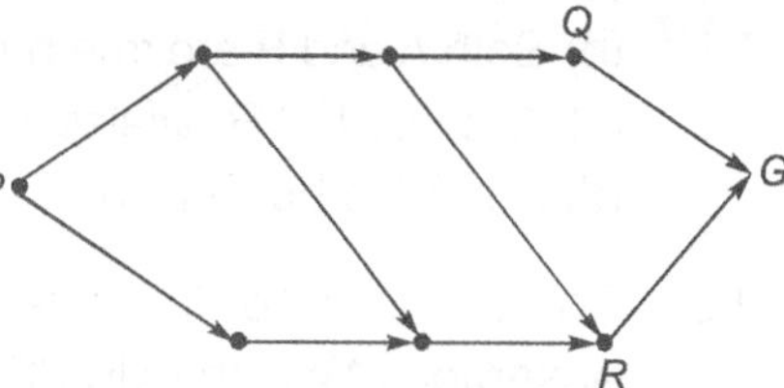

(a) $S_G = \text{Min}\{S_Q, S_R\}$
(b) $S_G = \{S_Q - d_{QG}, S_R - d_{RG}\}$
(c) $S_G = \text{Min}\{S_Q + d_{QG}, S_R + d_{RG}\}$
(d) $S_G = \text{Min}\{d_{QG}, d_{RG}\}$

Common Data for Questions (56 and 57):

Consider the following PERT network:

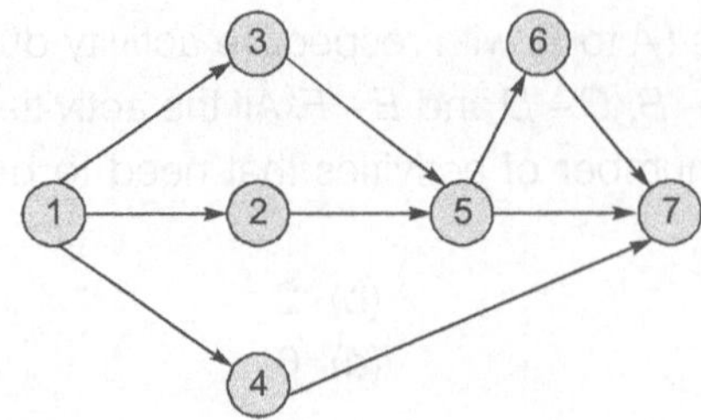

The optimistic time, most likely time and pessimistic time of all the activities are given in the table below:

Activity	Optimistic time (days)	Most likely time (days)	Pessimistic time (days)
1-2	1	2	3
1-3	5	6	7
1-4	3	5	7
2-5	5	7	9
3-5	2	4	6
5-6	4	5	6
4-7	4	6	8
6-7	2	3	4

56. The critical path duration of the network (in days) is
(a) 11
(b) 14
(c) 17
(d) 18

57. The standard deviation of the critical path is
(a) 0.33
(b) 0.55
(c) 0.88
(d) 1.56

DIRECTIONS:

The following items consists of two statements; one labeled as '**Assertion (A)**' and the other as '**Reason (R)**'. You are to examine these two statements carefully and select the answers to these items using the code below:

Codes:
(a) Both A and R are true and R is the correct explanation of A.
(b) Both A and R are true but R is not a correct explanation of A.
(c) A is true but R is false.
(d) A is false but R is true.

58. Consider the following statements:
Assertion (A): Generally PERT is preferred over CPM for the purpose of project evaluation.
Reason (R): PERT is based on the approach of multiple time estimates for each activity.

59. **Assertion (A):** The change in critical path requires rescheduling in a PERT network.
Reason (R): Some of the activities cannot be completed in time due to unexpected breakdown of equipments or non-availability of raw materials.

60. Consider the following statements:
Assertion (A): Assembly line balancing increases productivity.
Reason (R): Assembly line balancing reduces in-process inventory.

61. In CPM network critical path denotes the
(a) Path where maximum resources are used.
(b) Path where minimum resources are used.
(c) Path where delay of one activity prolongs the duration of completion of the project.
(d) Path that gets monitored automatically.

62. Time estimates of a project activity are: *top*,optimistic time = 10 days.*tml*, most likely time = 15 days.*tpcs*, pessimistic time = 22 days.
Variance in days for this activity as per BETA distribution is:
(a) 12 (b) 7
(c) 5 (d) 4

63. The variance (V_1) for critical path $a \rightarrow b$ = 4 time units, $b \rightarrow c$ = 16 time units, $c \rightarrow d$ = 4 time units, $d \rightarrow e$ = 1 time unit.The standard deviation *d* the critical path $a \rightarrow e$ is:
(a) 3 (b) 4
(c) 5 (d) 6

64. In CPM, the cost slope is determined by:
(a) (Crash cost)/(Normal cost) (b) (Crash cost-Normal cost)-(Normal time-Crash time)
(c) Normal cost /Crash cost (d) (Normal cost - Crash cost)/(Normal time -Crash time)

65. Latest start time of an activity in CPM is the
(a) latest occurrence time of the successor event minus the duration of theactivity.
(b) earliest occurrence time for the predecessor event plus the duration ofthe activity.
(c) latest occurrence time of the successor event.
(d) earliest occurrence time for the predecessor event.

66. Match **List-I** with **List-II** and select the correct answer using the codes given below the lists:

List-I	List-II
A. Vogel's approximation method	1. Assignment model
B. Floods technique	2. Transportation model
C. Two phase method	3. PERT and CPM
D. Crashing	4. Linear programming

Codes:

	A	B	C	D
(a)	3	4	1	2
(b)	2	1	4	3
(c)	3	1	4	2
(d)	2	4	1	3

67. Match **List-I** with **List-II** and select the correct answer using thecodes given below the list:

List-I	List-II
A. Control charts forvariables	1. Binomial distribution
B. Control chart for numberof non-conformities	2. Beta distribution
C. Control chart for fractionrejected	3. Normal distribution
D. Activity time distributionin PERT	4. Poisson distribution
	5. Exponential distribution

Codes:

	A	B	C	D
(a)	3	4	1	5
(b)	5	4	3	1
(c)	4	3	1	2
(d)	3	4	1	2

68. The essential condition for the decompression of an activity is
(a) the project time should change due to decompression.
(b) after decompression the time of an activity invariably exceeds its normal time.
(c) an activity could be decompressed to the maximum extent of its normal time.
(d) none of the above.

69. A PERT network has three activities on critical path with meantime 3, 8 and 6, and standard deviation1, 2 and 3 respectively. The probability that the project will be completed in 20 days is:
(a) 0.50 (b) 0.66
(c) 0.84 (d) 0.9

70. Earliest finish time can be regarded as
(a) EST + duration of activity (b) EST – duration of activity
(b) LFT + duration of activity (d) LFT – duration of activity

71. A project consists of three parallel paths with durations and variances of (10, 4), (12, 4) and (12, 9) respectively. According to the standard PERT assumptions, the distribution of the project duration is:
(a) Beta with mean 10 and standard deviation 2
(b) Beta with mean 12 and standard deviation 2
(c) Normal with mean 10 and standard deviation 3
(d) Normal with mean 12 and standard deviation 3

72. A dummy activity is used in PERT network to describe
(a) Precedence relationship (b) Necessary time delay
(c) Resource restriction (d) Resource idleness

73. In PERT, the distribution of activity times is assumed to be:
(a) Normal (b) Gamma
(c) Beta (d) Exponential

74. The expected time (t_e) of a PERT activity in terms of optimistic time (t_o), pessimistic time (t_p) and most likely time (t_m) is given by:
(a) $t_e = \frac{t_o + 4t_m + t_p}{6}$ (b) $t_e = \frac{t_o + 4t_p + t_m}{6}$

(c) $t_e = \frac{t_o + 4t_m + t_p}{3}$ (d) $t_e = \frac{t_o + 4t_p + t_m}{3}$

oooo

ANSWERS

PROJECT MANAGEMENT

1. (b)	**2.** (d)	**3.** (d)	**4.** (c)	**5.** (c)	**6.** (b)	**7.** (d)
8. (c)	**9.** (c)	**10.** (c)	**11.** (a)	**12.** (b)	**13.** (a)	**14.** (c)
15. (a)	**16.** (c)	**17.** (a)	**18.** (b)	**19.** (b)	**20.** (b)	**21.** (d)
22. (c)	**23.** (d)	**24.** (c)	**25.** (b)	**26.** (b)	**27.** (c)	**28.** (b)
29. (a)	**30.** (b)	**31.** (d)	**32.** (b)	**33.** (a)	**34.** (b)	**35.** (a)
36. (a)	**37.** (c)	**38.** (c)	**39.** (c)	**40.** (a)	**41.** (d)	**42.** (d)
43. (a)	**44.** (b)	**45.** (d)	**46.** (c)	**47.** (d)	**48.** (c)	**49.** (d)
50. (a)	**51.** (c)	**52.** (c)	**53.** (d)	**54.** (a)	**55.** (c)	**56.** (d)
57. (c)	**58.** (a)	**59.** (b)	**60.** (b)	**61.** (a)	**62.** (d)	**63.** (c)
64. (b)	**65.** (a)	**66.** (b)	**67.** (d)	**68.** (c)	**69.** (b)	**70.** (a)
71. (d)	**72.** (a)	**73.** (c)	**74.** (a)			

CHAPTER 8

Forecasting & Break Even Analysis

8.1 FIXED COST

Fixed costs are business expenses that are not dependent on the level of goods or service produced by the business. They tend to be time-related, such as salaries or rent being paid per month, and are often referred to as overhead costs. This is in contrast to variable costs, which are volume-related (and are paid per quantity produced). In management accounting, fixed costs are defined as expenses that do not change as a function of the activity of a business, within the relevant period. For example, a retailer must pay rent and utility bills irrespective of sales. Fixed costs are not permanently fixed; they will change over time, but are fixed in relation to the quantity of production for the relevant period. For example, a company may have unexpected and unpredictable expenses unrelated to production; and warehouse costs and the like are fixed only over the time period of the lease.

By definition, there are no fixed costs in the long run. Investment in facilities, equipment, and the basic organization that can't be significantly reduced in a short period of time are referred to as committed fixed costs. Discretionary fixed costs usually arise from annual decisions by management to spend on certain fixed costs items. Examples of discretionary costs are advertising, machine maintenance, and research & development expenditures.

In business planning and management accounting, usage of the terms fixed costs, variable costs and other will often differ from usage in economics, and may depend on the intended use. Some cost accounting practices such as activity-based costing will allocate fixed costs to business activities, in effect treating them as variable costs. This can simplify decision-making, but can be confusing and controversial.

In accounting terminology, fixed costs will broadly include almost all costs (expenses) which are not included in cost of goods sold, and variable costs are those captured in costs of goods sold. The implicit assumption required to make the equivalence between the accounting and economics terminology is that the accounting period is equal to the period in which fixed costs do not vary in relation to production. In practice, this equivalence does not always hold, and depending on the period under consideration by management, some overhead expenses (e.g., sales, general and administrative expenses) can be adjusted by management, and the specific allocation of each expense to each category will be decided under cost accounting.

8.2 VARIABLE COST

Variable costs are expenses that change in proportion to the activity of a business. Variable cost is the sum of marginal costs over all units produced. It can also be considered as normal costs. Fixed costs and variable costs make up the two components of total cost. Direct costs, however, are costs that can easily be associated with a particular cost object. However, not all variable costs are direct costs. For example, variable manufacturing overhead costs are variable costs that and indirect costs, not direct costs. Variable costs are sometimes called unit-level costs as they vary with the number of units produced.

Direct labor and overhead are often called conversion cost, while direct material and direct labor are often referred to as prime cost. For example, a manufacturing firm pays for raw materials. When activity is decreased, less raw material is used, and so the spending for raw materials falls. When activity is increased, more raw material is used and spending therefore rises. Note that the changes in expenses happen with little or no need for managerial intervention. These costs are variable costs. A company will pay for line rental and maintenance fees each period regardless of how much power gets used. And some electrical equipment (air conditioning or lighting) may be kept running even in periods of low activity. These expenses can be regarded as fixed. But beyond this, the company will use electricity to run plant and machinery as required. The busier the company, the more the plant will be run, and so the more electricity gets used. This extra spending can therefore be regarded as variable. In retail the cost of goods is almost entirely a variable cost this is not true of manufacturing where many fixed costs, such as depreciation, are included in the cost of goods. Although taxation usually varies with profit, which in turn varies with sales volume, it is not normally considered a variable cost. For some employees, salary is paid on monthly rates, independent of how many hours the employees work. This is a fixed cost. On the other hand, the hours of hourly employees can often be varied, so this type of labor cost is a variable cost.

There are several cost concepts that influence the economic aspects of managing projects. Within a given scope of analysis, there may be a combination of different types of cost aspects to consider.

Applied direct cost: This represents the amounts recognized in the time period associated with the consumption of labor, material, and other direct resources, without regard to the date of commitment or the date of payment. These amounts are to be charged to work-in-process (WIP) when resources are actually consumed, material resources are withdrawn from inventory for use, or material resources are received and scheduled for use within 60 days.

Direct cost: This is a cost that is directly associated with the actual operations of a project. Typical sources of direct costs are direct material costs and direct labor costs. Direct costs are those that can be reasonably measured and allocated to a specific component of a project.

Estimated cost at completion: This is the sum of the actual direct cost, indirect costs that can be allocated to the contract, and the estimate of costs (direct and indirect) for authorized work remaining.

Fixed cost: This is a cost incurred irrespective of the level of operation of a project. Fixed costs do not vary in proportion to the quantity of output. Examples of costs that make up the fixed cost of a project are administrative expenses, certain types of taxes, insurance cost, depreciation cost, and debt servicing cost. These costs usually do not vary in proportion to the quantity of output.

Incremental cost: This refers to the additional cost of changing the production output from one level to another. Incremental costs are normally variable costs.

Indirect cost: This is a cost that is indirectly associated with project operations. Indirect costs are those that are difficult to assign to specific components of a project. An example of an indirect cost is the cost of computer hardware and software needed to manage project operations. Indirect costs are usually calculated as a percentage of a component of direct costs. For example, the indirect costs in an organization may be computed as 10% of direct labor costs.

Life-cycle cost: This is the sum of all costs, recurring and nonrecurring, associated with a project during its entire life cycle.

Maintenance cost: This is a cost that occurs intermittently or periodically for the purpose of keeping project equipment in good operating condition.

Marginal cost: This is the additional cost of increasing production output by one additional unit. The marginal cost is equal to the slope of the total cost curve or line at the current operating level.

Operating cost: This is a recurring cost needed to keep a project in operation during its life cycle. Operating costs include labor, material, and energy costs.

Opportunity cost: This is the cost of forgoing the opportunity to invest in a venture that would have produced an economic advantage. Opportunity costs are usually incurred owing to limited resources that make it impossible to take advantage of all investment opportunities. They are often defined as the cost of the best rejected opportunity. Opportunity costs can be incurred because of a missed opportunity rather than due to an intentional rejection. In many cases, opportunity costs are hidden or implied because they typically relate to future events that cannot be accurately predicted.

Overhead cost: This is a cost incurred for activities performed in support of the operations of a project. The activities that generate overhead costs support the project efforts rather than contribute directly to the project goal. The handling of overhead costs varies widely from company to company. Typical overhead items are electric power cost, insurance premiums, cost of security, and inventory carrying cost.

Standard cost: This is a cost that represents the normal or expected cost of a unit of the output of an operation. Standard costs are established in advance. They are developed as a composite of several component costs such as direct labor cost per unit, material cost per unit, and allowable overhead charge per unit.

Sunk cost: This is a cost that occurred in the past and cannot be recovered under the present analysis. Sunk costs should have no bearing on the prevailing economic analysis and project decisions.

Total cost: This is the sum of all the variable and fixed costs associated with a project.

8.3 BREAK EVEN ANALYSIS

Break-even charts offer opportunities for several different types of analysis. In addition to the break-even points, other measures of worth or criterion measures may be derived from the charts. A measure, called profit ratio, is presented here for the purpose of obtaining a further comparative basis for competing projects. Profit ratio is defined as the ratio of the profit area to the sum of the profit and loss areas in a break-even chart. The following terms are used in break even analysis.

Profit Ratio = area of the profit region/(area of profit and loss regions)

- Fixed Cost(F.C): it does not vary with production quantity
- Variable cost (V.C):it is proportional to production quantity
- Total cost (T.C) = F.C + V.C
- Total revenue (T.R) = Q × S.P,

where *Q* is quantity of the product .

S.P. is the selling price per unit.

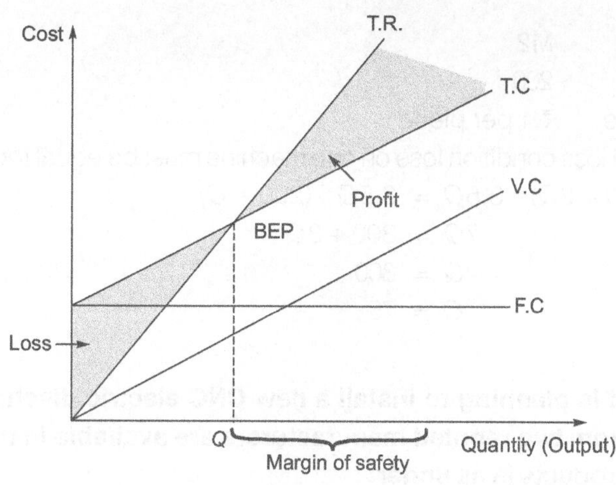

Fig: 8.1

- Profit = T.R – T.C
- The quantity at which there is no profit, no loss this is called **breakeven point (BEP).**
- The number of units sold beyond brake even point, is called **margin of safety.**

Margin of safety = Actual sales – BEP

Example: 8.1

From a manufacturing unit, following data was recorded, total revenue = $100Q - 0.001Q^2$ and the total cost = $0.005Q^2 + 4Q + 20{,}000$. Determine:

1. **What is the output at BEP?**
2. **What is the output for maximum profit?**
3. **What is the output for minimum average unit cost?**

Solution:

(i) At BEP, $T.R = T.C \Rightarrow 0.006Q^2 - 96Q + 20{,}000 = 0$

$\Rightarrow \quad Q_1 = 211.119; \quad Q_2 = 15788.88$

We select minimum value (Q_1) as Q, because beyond Q_2, it is loss

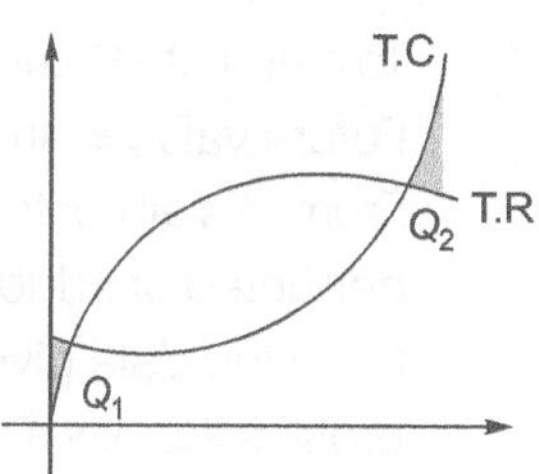

(ii) $\text{Profit }(P) = T.R - T.C$

$$P = 100\,Q - 0.001Q^2 - (0.005Q^2 + 4Q + 20{,}000)$$

$$\frac{dP}{dQ} = 0 \Rightarrow Q = 8000 \text{ unit}$$

(iii) $\text{Average unit cost (Cu)} = \dfrac{T.C}{Q}$

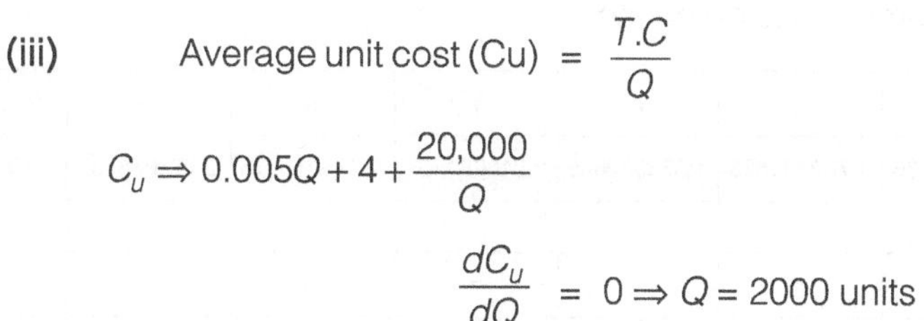

$$C_u \Rightarrow 0.005Q + 4 + \frac{20{,}000}{Q}$$

$$\frac{dC_u}{dQ} = 0 \Rightarrow Q = 2000 \text{ units}$$

Example: 8.2

Two machines of the same production rate are available for use. On machine 1, the fixed cost is ₹ 100 and the variable cost is ₹ 2 per piece produced. The corresponding costs for the machine 2 are ₹ 200 and ₹ 1 respectively. For certain strategic reasons both the machines are to be used concurrently. The sale price of the first 800 units is ₹ 3.50 per unit and subsequently it is only ₹ 3.00. The break even production rate for each machine is

Solution :

	M1	M2
F.C =	100	200
V.C =	₹ 2 per piece	₹ 1 per piece

For no profit and no loss condition loss on one machine must be equal toprofit on another machine

$$1\,(100 + 2Q) - 3.5Q = 3.5Q - (200 + Q)$$
$$7Q = 300 + 3Q$$
$$4Q = 300$$
$$Q = 75$$

Example: 8.3

A die making unit is planning to install a new CNC electric discharge machine in its job shop. Machines from two reputed manufacturers are available in the market. The relevant data about their products is as under:

	Manufacturer A	Manufacturer B
Present cost	1.00 cr	1.50 cr
Annual operating + maintenance cost	0.20 cr	0.12 cr
Salvage value at the end of useful life	0.05 cr	0.02 cr
Estimated useful life	10 yrs.	10 yrs.

Considering rate of return to be 12% per year, what is the best alternative?
P_{wf} – series at 12% for 10 years = 5.65;
P_{wf} single payment at 12% for 10 yrs. = 0.322.

Solution:

To calculate Return on investment following formula is used:

Future value = Amount invested x (1 + Rate of return) $^{\text{number of periods}}$

From this all costs present cost, annual maintenance, operating costs, salvage cost ect. are to be deducted or added to get the net profit made in ordered to make decision.

From the data given choosing manufacturer A gives the net profit of 0.16 cr and B gives the net profit is the basis then manufacturer has to be chose.

S.No.	1	2	3	4	5	6	7	8	9	10
Mfg. A (Profit)	1.12	1.2544	1.404928	1.57351936	1.762341683	1.973822685	2.210681407	2.475963176	2.773078757	3.105848208

S.No.	1	2	3	4	5	6	7	8	9	10
Mfg. B (Profit)	1.68	1.8816	2.107392	2.36027901	2.643512525	2.960734028	3.316022111	3.713944764	40159618136	40658772313

Net profit (A) = 3.11 Cr (revenue generated for 10 years) – 1 Cr (investment)-10*0.2 (maintenance and operating cost for 10 years) + 0.05 Cr (salvage value) = 0.16 Cr. Similarly for B we get net profit = 1.96 Cr.

Example: 8.4

A firm has a fixed cost of ₹ 60,000; selling price per unit is ₹ 60 and variable cost per unit is ₹ 40. Present level of production is 5000 units.

(i) Determine breakeven point in terms of volume and also sales value.

(ii) Calculate the margin of safety.

(iii) What is the change in BEP and margin of safety if fixed costs increase from ₹ 60,000 to ₹ 80,000?

Solution:

(i) Determination of BEP:

$$\text{Break-even point in units} = \frac{\text{Fixed costs}}{\text{Contribution margin per unit}}$$

where, Contribution margin per unit = Selling price per unit – Variable cost per unit

$$= 60 - 40 = ₹\ 20$$

So,

$$\text{BEP in units} = \frac{60{,}000}{20} = 300 \text{ units}$$

BEP in terms of value (in rupees), The formula is

$$\text{BEP in sales value} = \frac{\text{Fixed costs}}{\text{Contribution margin ratio}}$$

where,

$$\text{Contribution margin ratio} = \frac{\text{Seling price-variable cost}}{\text{Selling price}}$$

In the above example, the contribution margin ratio is $\frac{(60-40)}{60} = \frac{20}{60}$

BEP in term's sales value is calculated as below:

$$= \frac{60{,}000}{\left(\frac{20}{60}\right)} = ₹1{,}80{,}000$$

(ii) Determination of margin of safety:

Margin of safety = Number of units sold – Break-even point in units

Margin of safety = 5000 – 3000 = 2000 units

(iii) Determination of BEP with fixed cost of Rs 80,000

where, contribution margin per unit = selling price per unit - variable cost per unit = 60–40 = 20

So,

$$\text{BEP in units} = \frac{80{,}000}{20} = 4000 \text{ units}$$

BEP in terms of value (in rupees), The formula is

$$\text{BEP in sales value} = \frac{\text{Fixed costs}}{\text{Contribution margin ratio}}$$

$$\text{Where contribution margin ratio} = \frac{\text{Selling price} - \text{Variable cost}}{\text{Selling price}}$$

In the above example, the contribution margin ratio is $\frac{(60-40)}{60} = \frac{20}{60}$

BEP in term's sales value is calculated as below:

$$= \frac{80{,}000}{20/60} = ₹\ 2,\ 40{,}000$$

Determination of margin of safety:

Margin of safety = number of units sold – break-even point in units = 5000 – 4000 = 1000 units.

The above calculations show that the firm has to produce 1000 more units in the event of increase in fixed costs by ₹ 20,000. This reduces margin of safety by 1000.

8.4 FORECASTING

Forecasting is process of predicting or estimating the future value of a variable. There are two basic types of forecasting: intrinsic forecasting and extrinsic forecasting. Intrinsic forecasting is based on the assumption that historical data can adequately describe the problem scenario to be forecasted. With intrinsic forecasting, forecasting models based on historical data use extrapolation to generate estimates for the future. Intrinsic forecasting involves the following steps:

- Collecting historical data.
- Developing a quantitative forecasting model based on the data collected.
- Generating forecasts recursively for the future.
- Revising the forecasts as new data elements become available.

Extrinsic forecasting looks outward to external factors and assumes that internal forecasts can be correlated to external factors. For example, an internal forecast of the demand for a new product may be based on external forecasts of household incomes. Good forecasts are predicated on the availability of good data.

Various Methods of Forecasting are as Follows:

1. In **Delphi method**, experts from various departments sit together and chitchat and hence arrive at the expected demand in future. In this method there is no reference made of previous year expected demand. In the standard version, the experts answer questionnaires in two or more rounds. After each round, a facilitator provides an anonymous summary of the experts' forecasts from the previous round as well as the reasons they provided for their judgments. Thus, experts are encouraged to revise their earlier answers in the light of replies of the other members of their panel. It is believed that during this process the range of the answers will decrease and the group will converge towards the correct answer. Finally, the process is stopped after a pre-defined stop criterion and the mean or median scores of the final rounds determine the results.This method is a progressive practice to develop consensus from different experts. The experts are usually selected on the basis of their experience and visibility in the organization.In it, experts are asked to make forecasts anonymously and through an intermediary. Delphi method is implemented as follows:

   (a) **Problem definition:** A decision problem that is considered significant is identified and clearly described.

   (b) **Group selection:** An appropriate group of experts or experienced individuals is formed to address the particular decision problem. Both internal and external experts may be involved in the Delphi process. A leading individual is appointed to serve as the administrator of the decision process. The group may operate through the mail or gather together in a room. In either case, all opinions are expressed anonymously on paper. If the group meets in the same room, care should be taken to provide enough room so that each member does not have the feeling that someone may accidentally or deliberately observe their responses.

(c) **Initial opinion poll:** The technique is initiated by describing the problem to be addressed in unambiguous terms. The group members are requested to submit a list of major areas of concern in their specialty areas as they relate to the decision problem.

(d) **Questionnaire design and distribution:** Questionnaires are prepared to address the areas of concern related to the decision problem. The written responses to the questionnaires are collected and organized by the administrator. The administrator aggregates the responses in a statistical format. For example, the average, mode, and median of the responses may be computed. This analysis is distributed to the decision group. Each member can then see how his or her responses compare with the anonymous views of the other members.

(e) **Iterative balloting:** Additional questionnaires based on the previous responses are passed to the members. The members submit their responses again. They may choose to alter or not to alter their previous responses.

(f) **Silent discussions and consensus:** The iterative balloting may involve anonymous written discussions of why some responses are correct or incorrect. The process is continued until a consensus is reached. A consensus may be declared after five or six iterations of the balloting or when a specified percentage of the group agrees on the questionnaires. If a consensus cannot be declared on a particular point, it may be displayed to the whole group with a note that it does not represent a consensus.

2. **Regression Analysis** is used for long range forecasts. In statistics, regression analysis includes any techniques for modeling and analyzing several variables, when the focus is on the relationship between a dependent variable and one or more independent variables. Regression analysis is widely used for prediction and forecasting, where its use has substantial overlap with the field of machine learning. In this method usually the data is fitted in a ***trend line*** and later on the demand for the future years can be predicted by this trend line. It should be noted that if trend line is used to predict the forecast, correlation coefficient must be calculated before justifying the predicted demand that whether the data fits into the trend line or not. Regression analysis is a mathematical procedure for attributing the variability of one variable to changes in one or more other variables. It is sometimes called line-fitting or curve-fitting. The primary function of regression analysis is to develop a model that expresses the relationship between a dependent variable and one or more independent variables. Time-series analysis is a technique that attempts to predict the future by using historical data. The basic principle of time-series analysis is that the sequence of observations is based on jointly distributed random variables.

8.5 TREND LINE

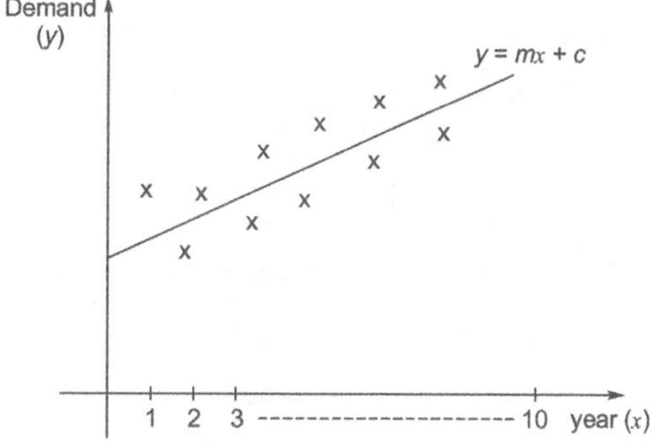

Fig: 8.2

Assume trend line is a straight line of equation,

$$y = mx + c \qquad ...(1)$$

$$\Sigma y = m\Sigma x + c\Sigma 1$$

If n periods,

$$\sum_{1}^{n} y = m\sum_{1}^{n} x + c\sum_{1}^{n} 1$$

$$\Sigma y = m\Sigma x + cn \qquad ...(2)$$

Multiply equation (1) by x

(a)

$$\Sigma(xy = mx^2 + cx)$$

$$\Sigma xy = m\,\Sigma x^2 + c\,\Sigma x \qquad ...(3)$$

(b) Solving equations (2) and (3),

$$\Sigma x \times (\Sigma y = m\,\Sigma x + cn)$$

(c)

$$-n \times (\Sigma xy = m\,\Sigma x^2 + c\Sigma x)$$

$$\Sigma \times \Sigma y - n\,\Sigma\,xy = m\,(\Sigma x)^2 - m\,n\,(\Sigma x^2)$$

$$m = \frac{n\sum xy - \sum x \sum y}{n\sum x^2 - (\sum x)^2}$$

$$c = \frac{1}{n}(\Sigma y - m\Sigma x)$$

Coefficient of Correlation (r):

$$r = \frac{n\Sigma xy - \Sigma x\,\Sigma y}{\sqrt{n\Sigma x^2 - (\Sigma x)^2}\sqrt{n\Sigma y^2 - (\Sigma y)^2}} \qquad (-1 \le r \le +1)$$

- Coefficient of correlation tells us how many % of data points are either on the trend line or in the close proximity?
- If $r = 0.8$, it means 80% data points are in close proximity with the trend line and the line is having upward sloping.
- If $r = -0.6$, it means 60% of data points are on the line but the trend line is having negative sloping. When $r = 0$, no points are falling on the trend line.

Example: 8.5

Following data refers to the demand for a certain product for 5 consecutive years. Using the trend line identify the forecast for 2011 and 2012. And find the coefficient of correlation.

Year	2006	2007	2008	2009	2010
Demand	20,000	25,000	26,000	25,000	30,000

Solution:

Year	X	Demand (y_i)	xy	X	y^2
2006	1	20,000	20,000	1	4×10^8
2007	2	25,000	50,000	2	625×10^6
2008	3	26,000	78,000	3	676×10^6
2009	4	25,000	1,00,000	4	625×10^6
2010	5	30,000	1,50,000	5	900×10^6
	$\Sigma x = 15$	$\Sigma y = 1{,}26{,}000$	$\Sigma xy = 3{,}98{,}000$	$\Sigma x = 15$	$\Sigma y^2 = 3226 \times 10^6$

$$m = \frac{n\Sigma xy - \Sigma x \Sigma y}{n\Sigma x^2 - (\Sigma x)^2} = \frac{5 \times 3,98,000 - 15 \times 1,26,000}{5t55 - 15^2} = 2000$$

$$C = \frac{1}{n}[\Sigma y - m\Sigma x] = \frac{1}{5}[1,26,000 - 2000(15)] = 19,200$$

$\Rightarrow$ The trend line is $y = 2000x + 19200$

forecast for 2011, $y_{x=6} = 2000(6) + 19200$

$= 12000 + 19,200 = 31,200$

forecast for 2012, $y_{x=7} = 2000(7) + 19200 = 33200$

$$r = \frac{5 \times 3,98,000 - (15)(1,26,000)}{\sqrt{5(55) - 15^2} \times \sqrt{5(3226 \times 10^6) - (1,26,000)^2}} = 0.88$$

8.6 FORECASTING ERRORS

1. MAD (Mean absolute deviation)

$$\text{MAD} = \frac{\sum_{i=1}^{i=n} |y_i - F_i|}{n}$$

2. MSE (Mean sum of square errors)

$$\text{MSE} = \frac{\sum_{i=1}^{i=n} (y_i - F_i)^2}{n}$$

3. Average error (Bias)

$$\text{AE} = \frac{\sum_{i=1}^{n} (y_i - F_i)}{n}$$

4. Tracking signal (T_S)

$$T_S = \frac{\sum_{i=1}^{n} (y_i - F_i)}{MAD}$$

Example: 8.6

By using the data given in the above question calculate MAD, MSE, AE & TS.

Solution:

From the above answer $m = 2000$, $c = 19,200$

Year	X	Demand (y_i)	($F_i = mx + c$)
2006	1	20,000	21,200
2007	2	25,000	23,200
2008	3	26,000	25,200
2009	4	25,000	27,200
2010	5	30,000	29,000

$$\Rightarrow \quad \text{MAD} = \frac{\sum_{i=1}^{i=n} |y_i - F_i|}{n} = 1360$$

$$\text{MSE} = \frac{\sum_{i=1}^{i=n} (y_i - F_i)^2}{n} = 2160000$$

$$\text{AE} = \frac{\sum_{i=1}^{n} (y_i - F_i)}{n} = 0$$

Zero average error indicates that sometimes extra components will be produced which goes to stores as inventory and sometimes demand is higher than the forecast. In that situation products are taken from store. So, there is balance of inventory and demand.

$$T_S = \frac{\sum_{i=1}^{n} (y_i - F_i)}{MAD} = 0$$

Example: 8.7

Using the data given in question 8.5 identify that forecasting of this product will be in what range for year 2011 regression with 95% confidence.

Solution:

From normal distribution,

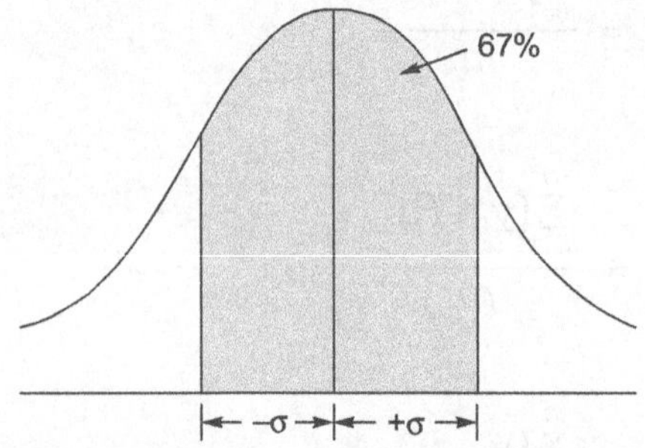

Confidence level,

$$67\ \% = \pm\sigma$$
$$95\ \% = \pm 2\sigma$$
$$99.73\ \% = \pm 3\sigma$$

In regression analysis, $\sigma = \sqrt{\frac{\Sigma (y_i - F_i)^2}{n-2}} = 1897.367$

For year 2011 with 95% confidence level the demand will be in the range of

$$= 31200 \pm 2\sigma$$
$$= (27405.2664, 34994.734)$$

8.7 MOVING AVERAGE METHODS

Moving average methods are being used for medium range forecast and it can be used for maximum forecast up to next quarter. A moving average is commonly used with time series data to smooth out short-term fluctuations and highlight longer-term trends or cycles. The threshold between short-term and long-term depends on the application, and the parameters of the moving average will be set accordingly. In this method, the forecast for the next period is based only on the most recent data values. Whenever a new value is included, the oldest value is dropped. Thus, the average is always computed from a fixed number of values. The weighted average forecast method is based on the assumption that some data points may be more significant than others in generating future forecasts. For example, the most recent data points may weigh more than very old data points in the calculation of future estimates.

Example: 8.8

The following data refers to the demand for a certain product for 12 consecutive years. And 50% weight is given to the recent data and 30%, 20% weights are given to the previous data.

1. **Calculate the forecast for thirteenth year using 3 point moving average**
   (a) **In simple moving average method**
   (b) **In weighted moving average method**
2. **Calculate MAD.**
   (a) **In simple moving average method**
   (b) **In weighted moving average method**

Year	1	2	3	4	5	6	7	8	9	10	11	12
Demand	28	29	28.5	31	34.2	32.7	33.5	31.8	31.9	34.3	35.2	36

Solution:

1. (a) In simple moving average method 3 point forecast for 13th year

$$= \frac{\text{Sum of last three years demand}}{3}$$

$$= \frac{34.3+35.2+36.0}{3} = 35.167$$

(b) In weighted moving average method 3 point forecast for 13th year

$$= \frac{(12^{th}\text{demand})\cdot(12^{th}\text{weightage})+(11^{th}\text{demand})\cdot(11^{th}\text{weightage})+(10^{th}\text{demand})\times(10^{th}\text{weightage})}{12^{th}\text{weightage}+11^{th}\text{weightage}+10^{th}\text{weightage}}$$

$$= \frac{36\times0.5+35.2\times0.3+34.3\times0.2}{0.5+0.3+0.2} = 35.42$$

Period		Demand		Simple Moving Average	Weighted Moving Average
				f_i	F_i
1		28.0		–	–
2		29.0		–	–
3		28.5		–	–
4		31.0		28.50	28.55
5		34.2		29.50	29.85
6		32.7		31.23	32.10
7		33.5		32.63	32.81
8		31.8		33.47	33.40
9		31.9	5 point avg	32.67	32.49
10	4 point avg	34.3		32.40	32.19
11		35.2	3 point avg	32.67	33.08
12		36.0		33.80	34.27
13				35.17	35.42

2. (a) $$\text{MAD} = \frac{\sum_{i=1}^{n}|(y_i - f_i)|}{n}$$

$$= \frac{2.7+4.7+1.47+0.87+1.66+0.87+1.89+2.53+2.2}{9} = 2.067$$

(b) $$\text{MAD} = \frac{\sum_{i=1}^{n}|(y_i - F_i)|}{n}$$

$$= \frac{2.45+4.35+0.6+0.69+1.6+0.59+2.11+2.12+1.73}{9} = 1.8044$$

Short range forecast is meant for forecasting on a daily basis or maximum up to one month. Exponential smoothening techniques are used in short range forecasts. Exponential smoothing is a technique that can be applied to time series data, either to produce smoothed data for presentation, or to make forecasts. **Exponential smoothing** assigns exponentially decreasing weights over time.

8.8 EXPONENTIAL SMOOTHENING

Exponential smoothing is commonly applied to financial market and economic data, but it can be used with any discrete set of repeated measurements. This is a special case of the weighted moving average forecast. The forecast for the next period is computed as the weighted average of the immediate past data point and the forecast of the previous period. In other words, the previous forecast is adjusted based on the deviation (forecast error) of that forecast from the actual data. Forecast for the nth period can be calculated by the formula

$$F_n = F_{n-1} + \alpha(y_{n-1} - F_{n-1})$$

Where, F_n = Forecast for n^{th} period

F_{n-1} = Forecast for $(n-1)^{th}$ period

Y_{n-1} = Actual demand for $(n-1)^{th}$ year

α = Smoothening co-efficient

$$\Rightarrow \quad F_n = \alpha y_{n-1} + (1-\alpha)F_{n-1} \quad \text{(I}^{\text{st}}\text{ order smoothing curve)}$$

$$F_{n-1} = \alpha y_{n-2} + (1-\alpha)F_{n-2}$$

$$F_n = \alpha y_{n-1} + \alpha(1-\alpha)y_{n-2} + (1-\alpha)^2 F_{n-2} \quad \text{(II}^{\text{nd}}\text{ order smoothing curve)}$$

$$F_n = \alpha y_{n-1} + \alpha(1-\alpha)y_{n-2} + \alpha(1-\alpha)^2 y_{n-3} + \ldots + (1-\alpha)^{n-1}F_1$$

Values of α close to 1.0 have less amount of smoothing effect and give greater weight to recent changes in the data, while values of α closer to zero have a greater smoothing effect and are less responsive to recent changes. There is no formally correct procedure for choosing á. Generally α value lies between 0.2 and 0.8.

Example 8.9

Using the 4 point moving average, calculate the quarterly forecast for next year in the following data. This table is given in the solution.

Year	1				2				3			
Quarter	Q_1	Q_2	Q_3	Q_4	Q_1	Q_2	Q_3	Q_4	Q_1	Q_2	Q_3	Q_4
Demand	200	350	370	250	270	410	320	190	300	400	310	205

Solution:

Year	Quarter	Demand	4 period Moving Average	Centered Mov. avg	Seasonal index $\left(\frac{\text{Demand}}{\text{Centered mov. avg}}\right)$
1	Q_1	200		x	x
	Q_2	350	292.5	x	x
	Q_3	370	310.0	301.25	1.228
	Q_4	250	325.0	317.5	0.784
2	Q_1	270	312.0	318.75	0.8471
	Q_2	410	297.5	305	1.3443
	Q_3	320	305.0	301.25	1.062
	Q_4	190	302.5	303.75	0.6255
3	Q_1	300	300.0	301.25	0.9959
	Q_2	400	303.75	301.875	1.3251
	Q_3	310		x	x
	Q_4	205		x	x

Seasonal Index:

Years	Q_1	Q_2	Q_3	Q_4
1	X	X	1.228	0.7874
2	0.8471	1.3443	1.062	0.6255
3	0.9959	1.3251	X	X
Avg :	$IQ_1 = 0.921$	$IQ_2 = 1.3345$	$IQ_3 = 1.145$	$IQ_4 = 0.70645$

I_Q – Avg. seasonal index

$$F_{Q_1} = I_{Q_1} \times \text{most recent value of central moving average of } Q_1$$

So,
$$F_{Q_1} = 0.921 \times 301.25 = 277.45$$
$$F_{Q_2} = 1.3345 \times 301.875 = 402.85$$
$$F_{Q_3} = 1.145 \times 301.25 = 344.93$$
$$F_{Q_4} = 0.70645 \times 303.75 = 214.584$$

Example: 8.10

The following series of 10 observations of sales of a company are given as followed, 390, 390, 320, 370, 340, 330, 340, 390, 310, 350 (All figures in ₹ Lakhs). Given initial forecast is 350 lakhs. Compute the difference between smoothening coefficient α = 0.5 and α = 0.1.

Solution:

Given data:

Forecast for the initial year = 350

Demand for last 10 years is: 390, 390, 320, 370, 340, 330, 340, 390, 310, 350

(i) Smoothening coefficient α = 0.5

$$F_n = F_{n-1} + \alpha(y_{n-1} - F_{n-1})$$
$$F_n = \alpha y_{n-1} + (1-\alpha)F_{n-1}$$
$$F_n = \alpha y_{n-1} + \alpha(1-\alpha)y_{n-2} + \alpha(1-\alpha)^2 y_{n-3} + \ldots + (1-\alpha)^{n-1}F_1$$
$$F_n = 0.5 * 350 + 0.5 * (1-0.5) * 310 + 0.5 * (1-0.5)^2 * 390$$
$$+ 0.5 * (1-0.5)^3 * 340 + 0.5 * (1-0.5)^4 * 330 + 0.5\,(1-0.5)^5 * 340$$
$$+ 0.5 * (1-0.5)^6 * 370 + 0.5 * (1-0.5)^7 * 320 + 0.5 * (1-0.5)^8 * 390$$
$$+ 0.5 * (1-0.5)^9 * 390 + (1-0.5)^{10} * 350$$
$$F_n = 343.75 = 344$$

(ii) Smoothening coefficient $\alpha = 0.1$

$$F_n = 0.1 * 350 + 0.1 * (1-0.1) * 310 + 0.1 * (1-0.1)^2 * 390$$
$$+ 0.1 * (1-0.1)^3 * 340 + 0.1 * (1-0.1)^4 * 330$$
$$+ 0.1 * (1-0.1)^5 * 340 + 0.1 * (1-0.1)^6 * 370$$
$$+ 0.1 * (1-0.1)^7 * 320 + 0.1 * (1-0.1)^8 * 390$$
$$+ 0.1 * (1-0.1)^9 * 390 + (1-0.1)^{10} * 350$$
$$F_n = 349.9 = 350$$

Question: 8.11

The demand for six consecutive periods for a product is as follows:
105, 108, 112, 116, 120, 130

(a) Establish a linear forecaster
(b) Determine the forecasted demand in 11th period
(c) Calculate the coefficient of determination and standard deviation for the line of the best fit.

Solution:

$$y = mx + c$$

$$m = \frac{n\Sigma xy - \Sigma x \Sigma y}{n\Sigma x^2 - (\Sigma x)^2}$$

$$c = \frac{1}{n}\Sigma y - m\Sigma x$$

(a) Year Demand:

x	y	xy	x^2	y^2	F_i	$y_i - F_i$
1	105	105	1	11025	103.392	1.608
2	108	216	4	11664	108.102	– 0.102
3	112	336	9	12544	112.812	– 0.812
4	116	464	16	13456	117.522	– 1.522
5	120	600	25	14400	122.232	– 2.232
6	130	780	36	16900	126.942	– 3.058

$\Sigma x = 21$, $\Sigma y = 691$, $\Sigma xy = 2501$, $\Sigma x^2 = 91$, $\Sigma y^2 = 79989$

$$m = \frac{6 * 2501 - 21 * 691}{6 * 91 - 21^2} = 4.71$$

$$c = \frac{1}{n}(691 - 4.71 * 21) = 98.67$$

Thetrend line is, $y = 4.71 * x + 98.67$

$$y = \frac{33}{7} * x + \frac{296}{3}$$

(b) $$y_{x=11} = \frac{33}{7} * 11 + \frac{296}{3} = 150.49$$

(c)
$$r = \frac{6*2501-21*691}{\sqrt{6*91-21^2}*\sqrt{6*79989-691^2}} = 0.975$$

97.5% data points are in close proximity with the trend line and line is having upward sloping.

$$F_i = y_i = mx_i + c$$

$$F_i = \frac{33}{7}*1+\frac{296}{3} = \frac{2171}{21} = 103.38$$

Standard Deviation (σ):

$$\sigma = \sqrt{\frac{\Sigma(y_i - F_i)^2}{n-2}}$$

$$\sigma = \sqrt{\frac{1.62^2 + (-0.09)^2 + (-0.81)^2 + (-1.52)^2 + (-2.24)^2 + 3.058^2}{4}}$$

$$\sigma = 2.23$$

PRACTICE QUESTIONS

1. Production cost refers to prime cost plus.
   (a) Factory overheads
   (b) Factory and administration overheads
   (c) Factory, administration and sales overheads
   (d) Factory, administration and sales overheads and profit

2. For a small scale industry, the fixed cost per month is ₹ 5000. The variable cost per product is ₹ 20 and sales price is ₹ 30 per price. The break-even production per month will be
   (a) 300 (b) 460
   (c) 500 (d) 10000

3. Which one of the following methods can be used for forecasting the sales potential of a new product?
   (a) Times series analysis (b) Jury of executive opinion method
   (c) Sales force composite method (d) Direct survey method

4. Consider the following aspects:
   1. Speed 2. Decision making
   3. Accuracy 4. Cost savings
   The factors that are considered in forecasting are:
   (a) 1, 2 and 3 (b) 2 and 4
   (c) 1, 3 and 4 (d) 1, 2, 3 and 4

5. Two alternative methods can produce a product first method has a fixed cost of ₹ 2000 and variable cost of ₹ 20 piece. The second method has fixed cost of ₹ 1500 and a variable cost of ₹ 30. The break even quantity between the two alternatives is
   (a) 25 (b) 50
   (c) 75 (d) 100

6. Given:
   T = underlying trend; C = cyclic variations within the trend
   S = seasonal variation within the trend and
   R = residual, remaining or random variation, as per the time series analysis of sales forecasting, the demand will be a function of:
   (a) T and C (b) R and S
   (c) T, C and S (d) T, C, S and R

7. *ABC* and Co. is planning to use the most competitive manufacturing process to produce an ultramodern sports shoe. They can use a fully automatic robot-controlled plant with an investment of ₹ 100 million; alternately they can go in for a cellular manufacturing that has a fixed cost of ₹ 80 million. There is yet another choice of traditional manufacture that needs an investment of ₹ 75 million only. The fully automatic plant can turn out a shoe at a unit variable cost of ₹ 25 per unit, whereas the cellular and the job shop layout would lead to a variable cost of ₹ 40 and ₹ 50 respectively. The break even analysis shows that the break even quantities using automatic plant Vs. traditional plant are in the ratio of 1 : 2. The per unit revenue used in the break even calculation is:

(a) ₹ 75 (b) ₹ 87
(c) ₹ 57 (d) ₹ 55

8. Match **List-I (Topic)** with **List-II (Method of solving)** and select the correct answer using the codes given below the lists:

List-I	List-II
A. Forecasting	1. North-West corner method
B. Linear programming	2. Rowan Plan
C. Wage incentive	3. Method of penalty
D. Work measurement	4. Time series analysis
	5. Work factor system

Codes:

	A	B	C	D
(a)	4	3	1	5
(b)	4	1	5	3
(c)	4	3	2	5
(d)	3	1	2	4

9. Process I requires 20 units of fixed cost and 3 units of variable costs per piece, while process/I required 50 units of fixed costs and 1 unit of variable cost per piece. For a company producing 10 pieces per day:
(a) Process I should be chosen
(b) Process II should be chosen
(c) Either of the two processes should be chosen
(d) A combination of the process I and process should be chosen

10. Based on the given graph, the economic range of batch sizes to be preferred fro general purpose machine (*GP*), *NC* machine (*NC*) and special purpose (*SP*) will be:

Codes:

	GP	*NC*	*SP*
(a)	2	5	4
(b)	1	4	5
(c)	3	2	4
(d)	1	4	2

11. Details of cost for make or buy decision are shown in the below graph. A discount is offered for volume of purchase above '*V*'. Which one of the following ranges would lead to the economic decision?

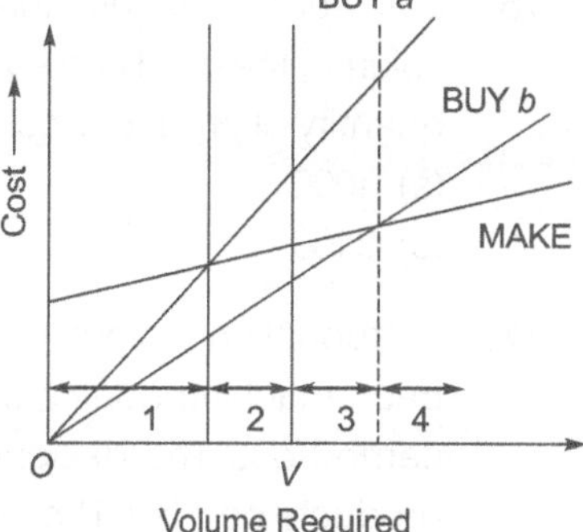

	Buy *a*, *b*	**Make**
(a)	1 and 2	3 and 4
(b)	1 and 3	2 and 4
(c)	2 and 4	1 and 3
(d)	1 and 4	2 and 3

12. Match **List-I (Methods)** with **List-II (Applications)** and select the correct answer using the codes given below the lists:

List-I	List-II
A. Break even analysis	1. To provide different facility at different locations
B. Transportation problem	2. To take action from among the paths with uncertainty
C. Assignment problem	3. To choose between different methods of manufacture
D. Decision tree	4. To determine the location of the additional plant

Codes:

	A	B	C	D
(a)	4	3	1	2
(b)	3	4	1	2
(c)	3	4	2	1
(d)	4	3	2	1

13. A company intends to use exponential smoothing technique for making a forecast for one of its products. The previous year's forecast has been 78 units and the actual demand for the corresponding period turned out to be 73 units. If the value of the smoothening constant α is 0.2, the forecast for the next period will be:

(a) 73 units (b) 75 units
(c) 77 units (d) 78 units

14. A dealer sells a radio set at ₹ 900 and makes 80% profit on his investment. If he can sell it at ₹ 200 more, his profit as percentage of investment will be:

(a) 160 (b) 180
(c) 100 (d) 120

15. Given that:

E = Earning in time T_a,
T_a = Actual time of work,
R = Rate per unit time ,
T_s = Standard time set to complete the task

If $E = R \cdot T_a + \frac{R}{2}(T_s - T_a)$, then the graph between bonus earned and time saved is a:

(a) Straight line a (b) Convex curve
(c) Concave curve (d) Parabola

16. Last year, a manufacture produced 15000 products which were sold for ₹ 300 each. At that volume, the fixed costs were ₹ 15.2 lacs and total variable costs were ₹ 21 lacs. The break even quantity of product would be:

(a) 4000 (b) 5419
(c) 8400 (d) 9500

17. A production system has a product type of layout in which there are four machines laid in series. Each machine does a separate operation. Every product needs all the four operations to be carried out. The designed capacity of each of the four machines is 200, 175, 160 and 210 products per day. The system capacity would be

(a) 210 products per day (b) 200 products per day
(c) 175 products per day (d) 160 products per day

18. Match **List-I** with **List-II** and select the correct answer using the codes given below the lists:

List-I	List-II
A. Decision making under complete certainty	1. Delphi approach
B. Decision making under risk	2. Maximum criterion
C. Decision making under complete uncertainty	3. Transportation model
D. Decision making based on expert opinion	4. Decision tree

Codes:

	A	B	C	D
(a)	3	4	1	2
(b)	4	3	2	1
(c)	3	4	2	1
(d)	4	3	1	2

19. Which one of the following statements is correct?
(a) Time series analysis technique of forecasting is used for very long range forecasting.
(b) Qualitative techniques are used for long range forecasting and quantitative techniques for short and medium range forecasting.
(c) Coefficient of correlation is calculated in case of time series technique.
(d) Market survey and Delphi techniques are used for short range forecasting.

20. The indirect cost of a plant is ₹ 400000 per year. The direct cost is ₹ 20 per product. If the average revenue per product is ₹ 60, the break-even point is:
(a) 10000 products (b) 20000 products
(c) 40000 products (d) 60000 products

21. It is given that the actual demand is 59 units, a previous forecast 64 units and smoothening factor 0.3. What will be the forecast for next period, using exponential smoothing?
(a) 36.9 units (b) 57.5 units
(c) 60.5 units (d) 62.5

22. The demand for a product in the month of March turned out to be 20 units against an earlier made forecast of 20 units. The actual demand for April and May turned to be 25 and 26 units respectively. What will be the forecast for the month of June, using exponential smoothing method and taking smoothing constant a. as 0.27?
(a) 20 units (b) 22 units
(c) 26 units (d) 28 units

23. Process *X* has fixed cost of ₹ 40,000 and variable cost of ₹ 9 per unit whereas process *Y* has fixed cost of As, ₹ 16,000 and variable cost of As. 24 per unit. At what production quantity, the total cost of X and Yare equal?
(a) 1200 units (b) 1600 units
(c) 2000 units (d) 2400 units

24. Which one of the following information combinations has lowest break-even point?

	Fixed Cost (in Rs.)	Variable Cost/unit (in Rs.)	Revenue unit (in Rs.)
(a)	30,000	10	40
(b)	40,000	15	40
(c)	50,000	20	40
(d)	60,000	30	40

25. Which one of the following methods can be used for forecasting when a demand pattern is consistently increasing or decreasing?
(a) Regression analysis (b) Moving average
(c) Variance analysis (d) Weighted moving average

26. For a product, the forecast for the month of January was 500 units. The actual demand turned out to be 450 units. What is the forecast for the month of February using exponential smoothing method with a smoothing coefficient = 0.1?
(a) 455 (b) 495
(c) 500 (d) 545

27. Which one of the following forecasting techniques is most suitable for making long range forecasts?
(a) Time series analysis (b) Regression analysis
(c) Exponential smoothing (d) Market surveys

28. Which one of the following statements is not correct for the exponential smoothing method of demand forecasting?
(a) Demand for the most recent data is given more weightage.
(b) This method requires only the current demand and forecast demand.
(c) This method assigns weight to all the previous data.
(d) This method give equal weightage to all the periods.

29. Which one of the following is a qualitative technique of demand forecasting?
(a) Correlation and regression analysis (b) Moving average method
(c) Delphi technique (d) Exponential smoothing

30. Manufacturing a product requires processing on four machines *A*, *B*, *C*, *D* in the order *A-B-C-D*. The capacities of four machines are $A = 100$, $B = 110$, $C = 120$ and $D = 130$ units per shift. If the expected output is 90% of the system capacity, then what is the expected output?
(a) 90 units (b) 99 units
(c) 108 units (d) 117 units

31. Which one of the following is not a purpose of long-term forecasting?
(a) To plan for the new unit of production
(b) To plan the long-term financial requirement
(c) To make the proper arrangement for training the performer
(d) To decide the purchase program

32. Consider the following statements relating to forecasting:
1. The time horizon to forecast depends upon where the product currently lies in its life cycle.
2. Opinion and judgmental forecasting method sometimes incorporate statistical analysis
3. In exponential smoothing, low values of smoothening constant, alpha result in more smoothing than higher values of alpha.

Which of these statements are correct?
(a) 1, 2 and 3 (b) 1 and 2 only
(c) 1 and 3 only (d) 2 and 3 only

33. Consider the following statements:
Exponential smoothing
1. is a modification of moving average method.
2. is a weighted average of past observations.
3. assigns the highest weightage to the most recent observation.

Which of these statements are correct?
(a) 1, 2 and 3 (b) 1 and 2 only
(c) 2 and 3 only (d) 1 and 3 only

34. If the fixed cost of the assets for a given period doubles, then how much will the break-even quantity becomes?
(a) Half the original value (b) Same as the original value
(c) Twice the original value (d) Four time the original value

35. Which one of the following is not technique of long range forecasting?
(a) Market research and market survey (b) Delphi
(c) Collective Opinion (d) Correlation and Regression

36. Using the exponential smoothing method of forecasting, what will be the forecast for the fourth week if the actual and forecasted demand for the third week is 480 and 500 respectively and $\alpha = 0.2$?
(a) 400 (b) 496
(c) 500 (d) 504

37. A capstan lathe is used to mass-produce, in batches of 200, a particular component. The direct material cost is ₹ 4 per piece, the direct labour cost is ₹ 3 per piece and the overhead costs are 400% of the labour costs. What is the production cost per piece?
(a) ₹ 19 (b) ₹ 23
(c) ₹ 16 (d) ₹ 15

38. Which of the following is the measure of forecast error?
(a) Mean absolute deviation (b) Trend value
(c) Moving average (d) Price fluctuation

39. In a forecasting situation, exponential smoothing with a smoothing constant $\alpha = 0.2$ is to be used. If the demand for n^{th} period is 500 and the actual demand for the corresponding period turned out to be 450, what is the forecast for the $(n + 1)^{th}$ period?
(a) 450 (b) 470
(c) 490 (d) 500

40. Process x has a fixed cost of ₹ 40,000 per month and a variable cost of ₹ 9 per unit. Process Y has a fixed cost of ₹ 16,000 per month and a variable cost of ₹ 24 per unit. At which value, total costs of process X and y will be equal?
(a) 800 (b) 1200
(c) 1600 (d) 2000

41. Consider the following statements:
The break-even point increases
1. if the fixed cost per unit increases.
2. if the variable cost per unit decreases.
3. if the selling price per unit decreases.

Which of these statements is/are correct?
(a) 1 only (b) 1 and 2
(c) 2 and 3 (d) 1 and 3

42. An operations consultant for an automatic car wash wishes to plan for enough capacity to handle 60 cars per hour. Each car will have a wash time of 4 minutes, but there is to be a 25% allowance for setup time, delays and payment transaction. How many car wash stalls should be installed?
(a) 3 (b) 4
(c) 5 (d) 6

43. A product is manufactured by processing on the four work-stations (WS). The capacity of each machine on these work-stations is given in the diagram as shown below. In the diagram M1, M2A, M2B, M3, M4A and M4B are the machines and 500, 275, 275, 560, 200 and 200 are their capacities in number of products made per shift. If the products made in this system are 5% defective, then what will be the output from this system?

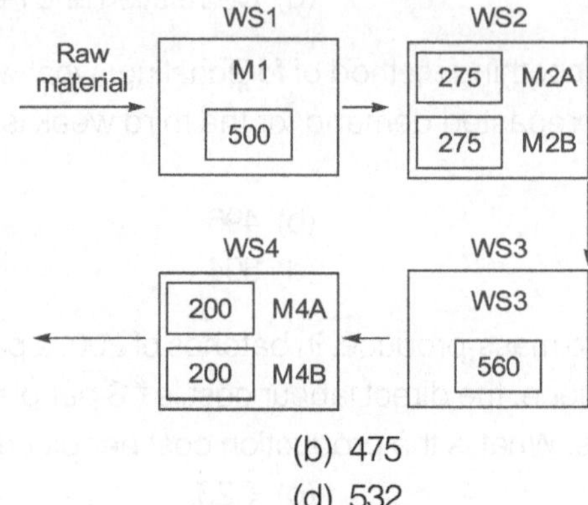

(a) 380 (b) 475
(c) 522 (d) 532

44. Which of the following is not the characteristic of exponential smoothing method of forecasting?
(a) This represents a weighted average of the part observations.
(b) All observations are assigned equal weightage.
(c) If smoothing coefficient is 1 then the latest forecast would be equal to previous period actual demand.
(d) The technique is not simple as compared to moving average method.

45. In exponential smoothing method of forecasting, the forecast for higher values of the smoothing constant
(a) will be more sensitive to forecast of the previous period.
(b) will be more sensitive to changing patterns in demand.
(c) will not be affected by the forecast of the previous period.
(d) will not be affected by the changing patterns in demand.

46. In the moving average method of forecasting, the number of periods (AP) of data is dependent on the
(a) criteria of accuracy only
(b) impulse response only
(c) noise damping only
(d) criteria of accuracy, impulse response and noise damping

47. A dealer for washing machines forecasts the demand at the rate of 600 units per month, for the next four months. The actual demand is found to be 500, 680, 800 and 900 units. The mean absolute deviation (MA(D) and the BIAS are found to be
(a) 170 and –120 (b) –120 and 170
(c) 340 and –240 (d) –240 and 340

48. Two machines of the same production rate are available for use. On machine 1, the fixed cost is ₹ 100 and the variable cost is ₹ 2 per piece produced. The corresponding numbers for the machine are ₹ 200 and ₹ 1 respectively. For certain strategic reasons both the machines are to be used concurrently. The sale price of the first ₹ 800 units is ₹ 3.50 per unit and subsequently it is only ₹ 3.00. The breakeven production rate for each machine is

(a) 75
(b) 100
(c) 150
(d) 600

49. The sale of cycles in a shop in four consecutive moths are given as 70, 68, 82, 95. Exponentially smoothing average method with a smoothing factor of 0.4 is used in forecasting. The expected number of sales in the next month is

(a) 59
(b) 72
(c) 86
(d) 136

50. A manufacturer produces two types of products, 1 and 2, at production levels of x_1 and x_2 respectively. The profit is given is $2x_1 + 5x_2$. The production constraints are:

$$x_1 + 3x_2 \leq 40$$
$$3x_1 + x_2 \leq 24$$
$$x_1 + x_2 \leq 10$$
$$x_1 > 0$$
$$x_2 > 0$$

The maximum profit which can meet the constraints is

(a) 29
(b) 38
(c) 44
(d) 75

51. For product, the forecast and the actual sales for December 2002 were 25 and 20 respectively. If the exponential smoothing constant (α) is taken as 0.2, the forecast sales for January 2003 would be

(a) 21
(b) 23
(c) 24
(d) 27

52. A standard machine tool and an automatic machine tool are being compared for the production of a component. Following data refers to the two machines.

	Standard Machine Tool	Automatic Machine Tool
Setup time	30 min.	2 hours
Machining time per piece	22 min.	5 min
Machine rate	Rs. 200 per hour	Rs. 800 per hours

The breakeven production batch size above which the automatic machine tool will be economical to use, will be

(a) 4
(b) 5
(c) 24
(d) 225

53. The sales of product during the last four years were 860, 880, 870 and 890 units. The forecast for the fourth year was 876 units. If the forecast for the fifth year, using simple exponential smoothing, is equal to the forecast using a three period moving average the value of the exponential smoothing constant α is.

(a) 1/7
(b) 1.5
(c) 2/7
(d) 2/5

54. A component can be product by any of the four process, I, II, III and IV. Process I has fixed cost of ₹ 20 and variable cost of ₹ 3 per piece. Pricess II has a fixed cost of ₹ 50 and variable cost of ₹ 1 per piece. Process III has a fixed cost of ₹ 40.00 and variable cost of ₹ 2 per piece. Process IV has fixed cost of ₹ 10 and variable cost ₹ 4 per piece. If company wishes to produce 100 pieces of the component, from economic point of view it should choose.
(a) Process I
(b) Process II
(c) Process III
(d) Process IV

55. A moving average system is used for forecasting weekly demand $F_1(t)$ and $F_2(t)$ are sequences of forecasts with parameters m_1 and m_2, respectively, where m_1 and m_2 ($m_1 > m_2$)denote the numbers of weeks over which the mobbing averages are taken. The actual demand shows a step increase from d_1 to d_2 at a certain time. Subsequently,
(a) neither $F_1(t)$ nor $F_2(t)$ will catch up with the value d_2
(b) both sequences $F_1(t)$ and $F_2(t)$ will reach d_2 in the same period
(c) $F_1(t)$ will attain the value d_2 before $F_2(t)$
(d) $F_2(t)$ will attain the value d_2 before $F_1(t)$

56. For sales forecasting, pooling of expert opinions is made use of in
(a) Statistical correlation
(b) Delphi technique
(c) Moving average method
(d) Exponential smoothing

57. To meet short range changes in demand of a product, which of the following strategies can be considered?
1. Overtime
2. Subcontracting
3. Building up inventory
4. New investments
Select the correct answer from the codes given below:
(a) 1, 2 and 3
(b) 1, 3 and 4
(c) 2 and 3
(d) 1 and 2

58. Which one of the following is not a technique of Long Range Forecasting?
(a) Market Research and Market Survey
(b) Delphi
(c) Collective Opinion
(d) Correlation and Regression

59. **Assertion (A):** Time series analysis technique of sales-forecasting can be applied to only medium and short-range forecasting.
Reason (R): Qualitative information about the market is necessary for long-range forecasting.
(a) Both A and R are individually true and R is the correct explanation of A.
(b) Both A and R are individually true but R is not the correct explanation of A.
(c) A is true but R is false.
(d) A is false but R is true.

60. Given: T = Underlying trend, C = Cyclic variations within the trend, S = Seasonal variation within the trend and R = Residual, remaining or random variation, as per the time series analysis of sales forecasting, the demand will be a function of:
(a) T and C
(b) R and S
(c) T, C and S
(d) T, C, S and R

61. **Assertion (A):** Moving average method of forecasting demand gives an account of the trends in fluctuations and suppresses day-to-day insignificant fluctuations.
Reason (R): Working out moving averages of the demand data smoothens the random day-to-day fluctuations and represents only significant variations.

(a) Both A and R are true and R is the correct explanation of A.
(b) Both A and R are true but R is NOT the correct explanation of A.
(c) A is true but R is false.
(d) A is false but R is true.

62. It is given that the actual demand is 59 units, a previous forecast 64 units and smoothening factor 0.3. What will be the forecast for next period, using exponential smoothing?
(a) 36.9 units (b) 57.5 units
(c) 60.5 units (d) 62.5 units

63. A company intends to use exponential smoothing technique for making a forecast for one of its products. The previous year's forecast has been 78 units and the actual demand for the corresponding period turned out to be 73 units. If the value of the smoothening constant á is 0.2, the forecast for the next period will be:
(a) 73 units (b) 75 units
(c) 77 units (d) 78 units

64. Match **List-I (Activity)** with **List-II (Technique)** and select the correct answer using the code given below the lists:

List-I	List-II
A. Line balancing	1. Value analysis
B. Product development	2. Exponential smoothing
C. Forecasting	3. Control chart
D. Quality control	4. Selective control
	5. Rank position matrix

Codes:

	A	B	C	D
(a)	2	1	4	3
(b)	5	3	2	1
(c)	2	3	4	1
(d)	5	1	2	3

65. Match **List-I** with **List-II** and select the correct answer using the code given below the lists:

List-I	List-II
A. Moving average	1. Assembly
B. Line balancing	2. Purchase
C. Economic batch size	3. Forecasting
D. Johnson algorithm	4. Sequencing

Codes:

	A	B	C	D
(a)	1	3	2	4
(b)	1	3	4	2
(c)	3	1	4	2
(d)	3	1	2	4

66. A company produces two types of toys : *P* and *Q*. Production time of *Q* is twice that of *P* and the company has a maximum of 2000 time units per day. The supply of raw material is just sufficient to produce 1500 toys (of any type) per day. Toy type *Q* requires an electric switch which is available @ 600 pieces per day only. The company makes a profit of ₹ 3 and ₹ 5 on type *P* and

Q respectively. For maximization of profits, the daily production quantities of *P* and *Q* toys should respectively be

(a) 100, 500 (b) 500, 1000
(c) 800, 600 (d) 1000, 1000

67. A standard machine tool and an automatic machine tool are being compared for the production of a component. Following data refers to the two machine.

	Standard Machine Tool	Automatic Machine Tool
Setup time	30 min.	2 hours
Machining time per piece	22 min.	5 min
Machine rate	Rs. 200 per hour	Rs. 800 per hours

The break-even production batch size above which the automatic machine tool will be economical to use, will be

(a) 4 (b) 5
(c) 24 (d) 225

68. Fixed investments for manufacturing a product in a particular year is Rs. 80,000/- The estimated sales for this period is 2, 00,000/-. The variable cost per unit for this product is Rs. 4/-. If each unit is sold at Rs.20/-, then the break even point would be:

(a) 4,000 (b) 5,000
(c) 10,000 (d) 20,000

69. The fixed costs for a year is ₹ 8 lakhs, variable cost per unit is ₹ 40 and the selling price of each unit is ₹ 200. If the annual estimated sales is ₹ 20,00,000, then the break-even volume is:

(a) 2000 (b) 3000
(c) 3333 (d) 5000

70. A company sells 14,000 units of its product. It has a variable cost of ₹ 15 per unit. Fixed cost is ₹ 47,000 and the required profit is ₹ 23,000 per unit product price (in ₹) will be:

(a) 60 (b) 40
(c) 30 (d) 20

71. Two jigs are under consideration for a drilling operation to make a particular part. Jig *A* costs ₹ 800 and has operating cost of ₹ 0.10 per part. Jig *B* costs ₹ 1200 and has operating cost of ₹ 0.08 per part. The quantity of parts to be manufactured at which either jig will prove equally costly is:

(a) 8000 (b) 15000
(c) 20000 (d) 23000

72. **Assertion (A):** Marginal cost in linear break-even analysis provides the management with useful information for price fixing.

Reason (R): The marginal cost is the maximum value at which the product selling price must be fixed to recover all the costs.

(a) Both A and R are individually true and R is the correct explanation of A.
(b) Both A and R are individually true but R is not the correct explanation of A.
(c) A is true but R is false.
(d) A is false but R is true.

73. The variable cost per unit associated with automated assembly line ($V(A)$, cellular manufacturing ($V(B)$, and job shop production ($V(C)$ will be such that,

(a) $VA > VB > VC$
(b) $VB > VA > VC$
(c) $VC > VB > VA$
(d) $VC > VA > VB$

74. If Break-even point = Total fixed cost ÷ $\left[1 - \frac{\text{variable cost per unit}}{X}\right]$, then X is the

(a) Overheads
(b) Price per unit
(c) Direct cost
(d) Materials cost

75. **Assertion (A):** A larger margin of safety in break-even analysis is helpful for management decision.

Reason (R): If the margin of safety is large, it would indicate that there will be profit even when there is a serious drop in production.

(a) Both A and R are individually true and R is the correct explanation of A.
(b) Both A and R are individually true but R is not the correct explanation of A.
(c) A is true but R is false.
(d) A is false but R is true.

76. Match **List-I (Element of cost)** with **List-II (Nature of cost)** and select the correct answer using the codes given below the lists:

List-I	List-II
A. Interest on capital	1. Variable
B. Direct labour	2. Semi-variable
C. Water and electricity	3. Fixed

Codes:

	A	B	C
(a)	3	1	2
(b)	2	1	3
(c)	3	2	1
(d)	2	3	1

77. **Assertion (A):** It is possible to have more than one break-even point in breakeven charts.

Reason (R): All variable costs are directly variable with production.

(a) Both A and R are individually true and R is the correct explanation of A.
(b) Both A and R are individually true but R is not the correct explanation of A.
(c) A is true but R is false.
(d) A is false but R is true.

78. Process X has a fixed cost of Rs 40,000 per month and a variable cost of ₹ 9 per unit. Process Y has a fixed cost of ₹ 16,000 per month and a variable cost of ₹ 24 per unit. At which value, total costs of processes X and Y will be equal?

(a) 800
(b) 1200
(c) 1600
(d) 2000

79. The indirect cost of a plant is ₹ 4,00,000 per year. The direct cost is ₹ 20 per product. If the average revenue per product is ₹ 60, the break-even point is:

(a) 10000 products
(b) 20000 products
(c) 40000 products
(d) 60000 products

80. In the production of a product the fixed costs are ₹ 6,000 and the variable cost is ₹ 10 per product. If the sale price of the product is ₹ 12, the break even volume of products to be made will be:
(a) 2000 (b) 3000
(c) 4000 (d) 6000

81. On a lathe, the actual machining time required per work piece is 30 minutes. Two types of carbide tools are available, both having a toollife of 60 minutes.
Type I : Brazed type of original cost ₹ 50
Type II : Throwaway tip (square) of original cost ₹ 70
If the overall cost of grinding the cutting edge is ₹ 10 assuming
all the costs are the same for both the types, for break even costs, the appropriate batch size would be:
(a) 2 pieces (b) 4 pieces
(c) 6 pieces (d) 8 pieces

OOOO

ANSWERS

FORECASTING & BREAK EVEN ANALYSIS

1. (a)	**2.** (c)	**3.** (d)	**4.** (b)	**5.** (b)	**6.** (c)	**7.** (a)
8. (c)	**9.** (a)	**10.** (b)	**11.** (a)	**12.** (b)	**13.** (c)	**14.** (d)
15. (a)	**16.** (b)	**17.** (d)	**18.** (c)	**19.** (b)	**20.** (a)	**21.** (d)
22. (b)	**23.** (b)	**24.** (a)	**25.** (a)	**26.** (b)	**27.** (b)	**28.** (d)
29. (c)	**30.** (a)	**31.** (c)	**32.** (b)	**33.** (c)	**34.** (c)	**35.** (d)
36. (b)	**37.** (a)	**38.** (a)	**39.** (c)	**40.** (c)	**41.** (d)	**42.** (c)
43. (a)	**44.** (b)	**45.** (b)	**46.** (d)	**47.** (a)	**48.** (a)	**49.** (b)
50. (a)	**51.** (c)	**52.** (d)	**53.** (c)	**54.** (b)	**55.** (d)	**56.** (b)
57. (b)	**58.** (d)	**59.** (d)	**60.** (c)	**61.** (a)	**62.** (d)	**63.** (c)
64. (d)	**65.** (d)	**66.** (c)	**67.** (d)	**68.** (b)	**69.** (d)	**70.** (d)
71. (c)	**72.** (a)	**73.** (c)	**74.** (b)	**75.** (a)	**76.** (c)	**77.** (d)
78. (c)	**79.** (a)	**80.** (b)	**81.** (a)			

9 CHAPTER

Value Engineering & Work Study

9.1 INTRODUCTION

Value Engineering (VE) is a systematic method to improve the "value" of goods or products and services by using an examination of function. Value, as define, is the ratio of function to cost. Value can therefore be increased by either improving the function or reducing the cost. It is a primary principle of value engineering that basic functions should be preserved and not be reduced as a consequence of pursuing value improvements.

In the United States, value engineering is specifically spelled out in Public Law 104-106, which states "Each executive agency shall establish and maintain cost-effective value engineering procedures and processes". Value engineering is sometimes taught within the project management or industrial engineering body of knowledge as a technique in which the value of a system's outputs is optimized by crafting a mix of performance (function) and costs. In most cases this practice identifies and removes unnecessary expenditures, thereby increasing the value for the manufacturer and/or their customers.

Value Engineering follows structured thought process that is based exclusively on "function", i.e., what something "does" not what it is. For example a screw driver that is being used to stir a can of paint has a "function" of mixing the contents of a point can and not the original connotation of securing a screw into a screw-hole. In value engineering "functions" are always described in a two word abridgment consisting of an active verb and measurable noun (what is being done – the verb – and what is being done to – the noun) and to do so in the most non-prescriptive way possible. In the screw driver and can of paint example, the most basic function would be "blend liquid" which is less prescriptive than 'stir paint" which can be seen to limit the action (by stirring) and to limit the application (only considers paint.) This is the basis of what value engineering refers to as "function analysis".

Value engineering uses rational logic (a unique "how" – "why" questioning technique) and the analysis of function of identify relationships that increases value. It is considered a quantitative method similar to the scientific method, which focuses on hypothesis-conclusion approaches to test relationships, and operations research, which uses model building to identify predictive relationships. Value engineering is also referred to as "value management" and "value methodology" (VM), and 'value analysis" (VA). VE is above all a structured problem solving process based on function analysis – understanding something with such clarity that it can be described in two words, the active verb and measurable noun abridgement. For example, the function of a pencil is to "make marks". This then facilities considering what else can make marks. From a spray can, lipstick, a diamond on glass to astick in the sand, one can then clearly decide upon which alternative solution is most appropriate.

$$\text{Value} = \frac{\text{Function(or)Quality}}{\text{Cost}}$$

9.2 PRODUCT LIFE CYCLE

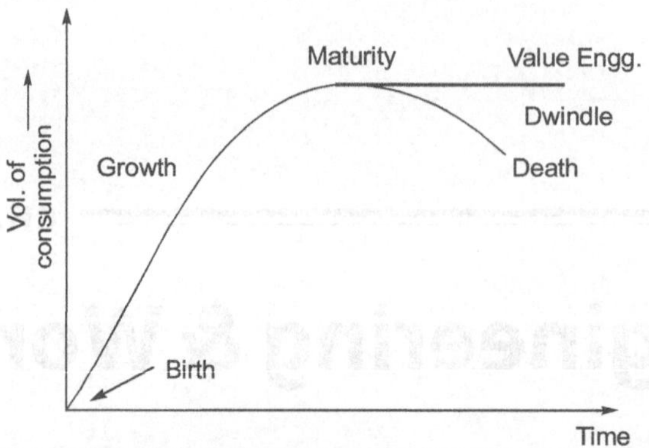

Fig: 9.1

Increasing the value of product means either increasing its functionality by maintaining the same cost or maintaining the same functionality by decreasing the cost. In a competitive market, if the product is not value engineered gradually it will be wiped out from the market.

The four types of values are:

1. **Cost value:** It is the cost of manufacturing one unit.
2. **Use value:** It is the amount of service rendered by the product to the company.
3. **Esteem value:** It is the feature of a product and just by looking at the features, customer develops a desire to have it.
4. **Exchange value:** It is the resale value of the product

   Value Engineering is a special type of cost reduction technique it critically investigates and analyses the different aspects of material, design and production of each and every component of the product.

Following are the different steps in value engineering.

- How to reduce the cost of operation.
- How to reduce the cost of material.
- How to reduce the time of operation.
- How to reduce manpower needed in production.

Procedure of value engineering.

- **Blast:** dismantling all the information about product. (e.g., how it is helpful to costumer)
- **Create:** searching for other alternatives for producing the product.
- **Refine:** choosing the best alternative for the customer's satisfaction.

9.3 WORK STUDY

Work study is used to examine the human work in all its contexts which leads systematically to investigate the factors which affects the efficiency and economy of the situation.

Work study consists of method study and time study.

(i) **Method study**: It involves systematic recording and critical examinations of existing methods and proposing ways to do work and developing easier and more effective methods. It results in production of work content.

(ii) **Time study (Work Contact)**: It is a work measuring method. "Every job is broken down into number of elements. Most scientific methods are being developed to perform each element".

9.4 TIME STUDY

Time study is designed to establish the time for a qualified worker to carry out a specified job at a defined level of performance. Time study is a work measurement technique for recording the times and rates of working for the elements of a specified job carried out under specified conditions and for analyzing the data so as to obtain the time necessary for carrying out the job at a defined level of performance. The objective of time study is to determine reliable time standards for all work, both direct and indirect, with due allowance for fatigue and for personal and unavoidable delays, for the efficient and effective management of operations. The establishment of reliable and accurate time standards makes it possible for companies to define their capacity or output, thus increasing the efficient use of equipment and obtaining optimum utilization of personnel. Because time is a common measure for all jobs, time standards can be used to investigate the difference between actual and standard performance and take appropriate action where necessary. It can also be used to facilitate job design as a basis for comparing various methods of doing the job, purchasing the most productive new equipment, introducing sound production controls, designing an efficient workplace layout, and balancing between work schedules and available manpower. Other benefits of establishing reliable time standards include budgetary control, development of incentive plans, and ensuring that quality specifications are met. Time study reduces the ineffective time.

Purpose of Time Study or Work Measurement

- Evaluate worker's performance.
- Determine the labor input required to perform the task.
- Determine the available capacity.
- Compare work methods.
- To establish wage incentive schemes.

9.5 TECHNIQUES OF WORK MEASUREMENT

- Work sampling
- Predetermined motion time system
- Stop watch time study

9.5.1 Work Sampling

Work sampling is a method of finding the % occurrence of a certain activity by statistical sampling and random observations. Among work measurement techniques, work sampling is one of the simplest available to time study analysts, yet it can be adapted to analyze complex and sophisticated patterns of work. Work sampling is a method of finding the proportions of total time devoted to various activities that constitute a job or work situation by random sampling. It is called by other names, including activity sampling, ratio delay study, random observation method, snap-reading method, and observation ratio study. The results of work sampling are effective for determining machine and personnel utilization, allowances applicable to the job and production standards. They are also particularly useful for analyzing no repetitive or irregularly occurring activities where no complete methods or frequency descriptions are available. Although the same information can be obtained using time study procedures, work sampling often provides this information faster and at considerably less cost. Work sampling studies normally extend over a long period (2-4 week period) to enable a comparatively large number of observations at random intervals to be taken. The percentage of time that a process is in a certain activity is obtained by the ratio of observations of the given activity to the total number of observations. Consider an analyst who takes 100 observations of the shop floor at random intervals over several weeks. It was observed that a certain machine was idle in 30 instances for miscellaneous reasons. The estimated idle time of this machine would then be 30% of the working day. Work sampling is based on the laws of probability and is used to determine the proportions of the total time devoted to the various components of a task. The probability of an event occurring or not occurring is obtained from the statistical binomial distribution. When the number of observations is large, the binomial distribution can be approximated to normal distribution.

Confidence level denotes the long-term probability that the ratio p will be within the accuracy limits. The concept relies on the relative frequency interpretation of probability. Thus, 95% confidence means that if a large number of samples is taken, 95 out of 100 of these will contain the true value of p. The probability value is given by the proportion of the area under the normal curve included for a specified value of standard deviation

Work sampling is most suitable for determining:

- Machine utilization.
- Allowances for unavoidable delays.
- Work standards for direct and indirect work. The technique is particularly suitable for determining standards for indirect and service work.

It follows binomial distribution. So

$$p \times s = k\sigma_p$$

where,

p – probability of occurrence

σ_p – probabilistic standard deviation $\sigma_p = \sqrt{\dfrac{p(1-p)}{n}}$

n – Total number of events

s – accuracy

k – confidence factor

For 99.73% confidence level "k" is 3

95% confidence level "k" is 2

67% confidence level "k" is 1

Example: 9.1

While moving through the workshop, a supervisor finds that 20% of the time operator is not working on a press. This he identifies by making 20 rounds. With 95% confidence and 5% precession how many rounds supervisor should make to justify the 20% idleness of the machine?

Solution:

Given data:

$p = 0.2,$

$k = 2$ (since 95% confidence level)

$s = 5\% = 0.05$

We know, $p.s = k\sigma_p$

but, $\sigma_p = \sqrt{\dfrac{p(1-p)}{n}} = \sqrt{\dfrac{0.2 \times 0.8}{n}}$

So, $0.2 \times 0.05 = 2 \times \sqrt{\dfrac{0.16}{n}} \Rightarrow n = 6400$

Therefore the supervisor should make 6400 rounds to justify 20% idleness of the machine.

9.5.2 Predetermined Motion Time System (PMTS) (PTS)

In PMTS, every activity is divided into no. of elements in such a way that the size of each element is more than 0.04 minute. Stop watch is not used in recording time in PMTS. For ease of measurement, the operation should be divided into groups of motions known as elements. An element is a distinct part of a specified job selected for convenience of observation. It is a division of work that can be easily measured with a stopwatch and that has readily identifiable breakpoints. To divide the operation into individual elements, the analyst should carefully observe the operator over several cycles. A work cycle is the sequence of elements that are required to perform a job or yield a unit of production. The sequence may include elements that do not occur every cycle. It is desirable to determine, prior to conducting the time study, the elements into which the operation is divided. Breaking down the operation into elements improves method description and provides good internal consistency during the time study. Elements also make it possible to reuse the data and permit different ratings for the work cycle. Predetermined time standards (PTS) are techniques that aim at defining the time needed for the performance of various operations by derivation from preset standards of time for various motions and not by direct observation and measurement. PTS is a work measurement technique whereby times established for basic human motions (classified according to the nature of the motion and the conditions under which it is made) are used to build up the time for a job at defined levels of performance. They are derived as a result of studying a large sample of diversified operations. Wink counter is used to record the time.

wink = 1/2000 min = 0.03 sec

PMTS is further divided into 3 categories, according to the way we define element:

(a) **MTM (Method time measurement):** Each motion is having a predetermined time, which is determined by nature of job. Evaluate the economy feasibility of an efficient method of doing a job before using it for production. One has to choose best among the number of different ways to do the job.
In this study time is measured in TMU units.
1 TMU = 0.0006 min

(b) **Basic motion time studies (BMTS):** A single complete movement of body member which starts from rest and end at rest.

(c) **Work factor system (WFS):** A basic motion is defined as, the motion which involves the last amount of difficulty of precision.

9.5.3 Stop Watch Time Study

Stop watch time study is used to develop a time standard based on observations of one experienced worker taken over number of cycle. That is then applied to work of others of the same organization who perform the same work. The basic steps in stop watch time study include.

1. Define the task to be studied and inform the workers who would be studied.
2. Determine the number of cycles to observe.
3. Time the job and rate the workers performance.
4. Compute the standard time also, the number of cycles that must be tied is a function of three things.
   - The variability of observed times
   - The desired accuracy
   - The desired level of confidence interval for the estimated job time

Job is broken into elements (element size should be greater than 0.04 min), for *k*% confidence and *s*% accuracy, the number of observations required to represent the work environment:

$$N = \left[\frac{(k/s)\sqrt{n\Sigma fx^2 - (\Sigma fx)^2}}{\Sigma fx}\right]^2$$

Example: 9.2

In a stopwatch time study, the observations are 10, 9, 10, 9, 10, 10, 11, 10, 10, 11 examine whether there are enough observations for 95% confidence and ±5% precision.

Solution:

x	f	fx	fx^2
9	2	18	162
10	6	60	600
11	2	22	242
		100	1004

$$\Rightarrow \quad N = \left(\frac{\frac{2}{0.05}\sqrt{10(1004)-(10000)}}{100}\right)^2 = \frac{40^3}{100^2} = 6.4$$

6.4 < 10 so sufficient observations has been taken.

Note:

- Observed time = $\frac{\Sigma fx}{n}$
- Normal time = Observed time × Rating factor
- Standard time = Normal time $\left(1 + \frac{\%\text{ Allowance}}{100}\right)$

Allowances

The fundamental purpose of all allowances is to add enough time to normal production time to enable the average worker to meet the standard when performing at standard performance. Even when the most practical, economical, and effective method has been developed, the job will still require the expenditure of human effort, and some allowance must therefore be made for recovery from fatigue and for unavoidable delays. Allowance must also be made to enable a worker to attend to his personal needs. Other special allowances may also have to be added to the basic time in order to arrive at a fair standard. Fatigue and personal needs allowances are in addition to the basic time intended to provide the worker with the opportunity to recover from the physiological and psychological effects of carrying out specified work under specified conditions and to allow attention to personal needs. The amount of allowance will depend on the nature of the job, the work environment, and individual characteristics of the operator. Usually a 5% allowance for personal delays is appropriate in the majority of work environments now-a-days. Special allowances include many different factors related to the process, equipment, materials, and so on and are further classified into unavoidable delays and policy allowances. Unavoidable delays are a small allowance of time that may be included in a standard time to meet legitimate and expected items of work or delays, such as due to power outages, defective materials, waiting lines, late deliveries, and other events beyond the control of the operator. Precise measurement of such occurrences is uneconomical because of their infrequent or irregular occurrence. Policy allowance is an increment, other than bonus increment, applied to standard time to provide a satisfactory level of earnings for a specified level of performance under exceptional circumstances (e.g. new employees, differently abled, workers on light duty, elderly). Special allowances may also be given for any activities that are not normally part of the operation cycle but that are essential to the satisfactory performance of the work. Such allowances may be permanent or temporary and are typically decided by management.

Contingency allowance: It is given to meet legitimate and expected items of work or delays for e.g.: worker has to take care of two different machines and there are some unexpected happenings at different machines.

Fatigue or relaxation allowance: It is given to recover, the worker from psychological and phsiological effects of carrying out specific work.

Example: 9.3

In the above problem, how many more readings are required for 99.7% confidence and 5% accuracy.

Solution:

For 99.7% confidence $k = 3$ and $s = 0.05$

$$N = \left(\frac{\frac{3}{0.05}\sqrt{10(1004)-(10000)}}{100}\right)^2 = 14.4$$

14.4 > 10 so 5 more observations are to be taken.

Example: 9.4

In a stop watch study the observations in Minutes are 0.05, 0.06, 0.05, 0.05, 0.05, 0.06, 0.06, 0.05, 0.06, 0.06, 0.06, 0.06, 0.05, 0.06, 0.05, 0.05.

1. **Have sufficient number of readings being taken for 95% confidence and ±5% accuracy?**
2. **If the operator rating is 120%, what is normal time of an element?**
3. **If personal need allowance, fatigue allowance and contingency allowance are 5%, 6%, 5% respectively what is standard time?**

Solution:

x	f	fx	fx^2
0.05	8	0.40	0.0200
0.06	8	0.48	0.0288
		0.88	**0.0488**

1. $$N = \left(\frac{\frac{2}{0.05}\sqrt{16(0.0488)-(0.88)^2}}{0.88}\right)^2 = 13.223$$

   13.223 <15 so sufficient observations has been taken.

2. Observed time = $\frac{\Sigma fx}{n} = 0.055$

   Normal time = Observed time × Rating factor =0.066

3. Standard time = Normal time $\left(1+\frac{\%\text{ allowance}}{100}\right) = 0.07656$

Example: 9.5

The elemental times (in min.) for 4 cycles of an operation using a time measuring device are presented below:

Elements	Cycle Time (min)			
	C1	C2	C3	C4
1	3.0	3.0	2.6	2.8
2	5.2	5.4	4.8	5.2
3	6.6	6.4	6.8	6.8
4	2.4	2.4	2.2	2.4
5	1.02	1.02	1.04	0.96

Calculate standard time for the operation if :
(i) Elements 2 and 4 are machine dependent.
(ii) For other elements, the operator is rated at 110%.
(iii) Total allowances are 15% of the normal time.

Solution:

Elements	Cycle Time (min)				Observed Time	Normal Time
	C1	C2	C3	C4		
1	3	3	2.6	2.8	2.85	3.135
2	5.2	5.4	4.8	5.2	5.15	5.15
3	6.6	6.4	6.8	6.8	6.65	7.315
4	2.4	2.4	2.2	2.4	2.35	2.35
5	1.02	1.02	1.04	0.96	1.01	1.111

"Normal time = 19.061 min

Standard time = 19.61 x (1+0.15) = 21.92 min

9.6 METHOD STUDY

Objectives of method study:

- Improvement in process and procedures
- Improvement in design of plant and equipment
- Improvement in man, machine and material (process)

Symbols used in Method Study

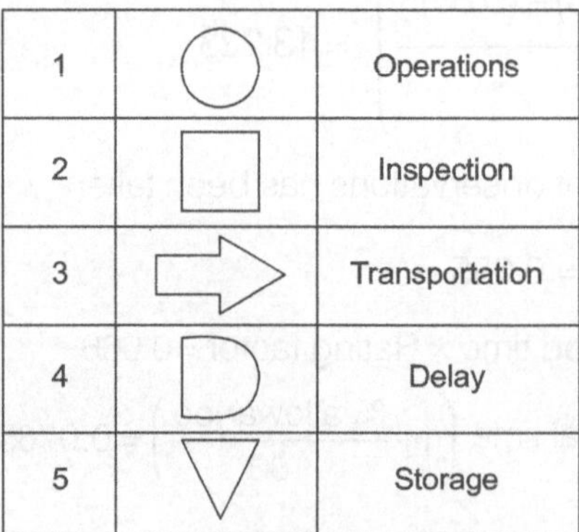

Fig: 9.2

9.6.1. Outline Process Chart

The outline process chart is the foremost technique of recording the process. It records the main activities of the process through the symbols of operation and inspection. Sometimes there activities can be combined. The example is shown in the figure below.

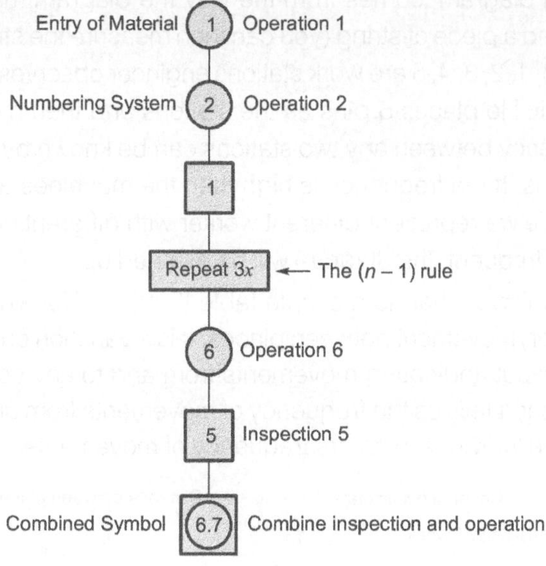

Fig: 9.3

9.6.2. Flow Process Chart

Flow process chart is a sketch or model of the layout of work places, machines, equipment floors and buildings, substantially to scale, showing the location of all activities appearing on a flow process.

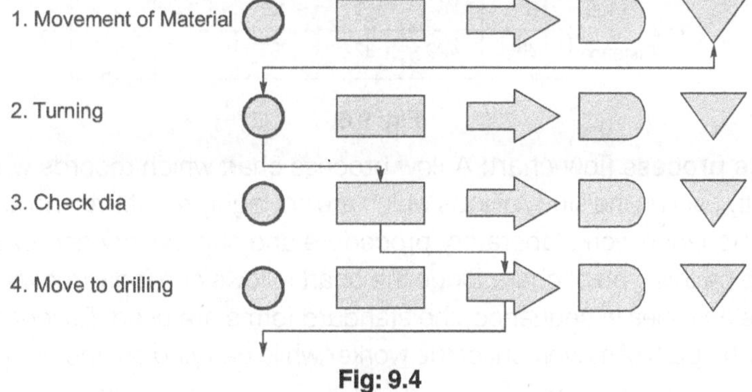

Fig: 9.4

9.6.3. Tools to Record The Movement of a Worker

The workers movement needs to be recorded to ascertain whether wasteful movements exist and to find the most effective way of carrying out the activity. Some of the common tools are:

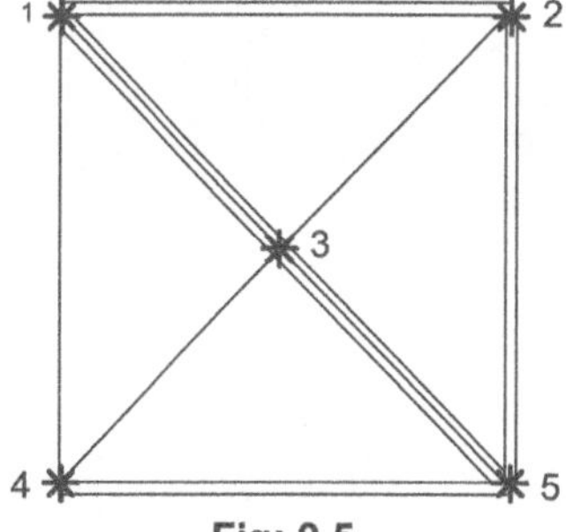

Fig: 9.5

(a) **String diagram:** The placement of equipment and furniture in work areas is often done randomly or sequentially, rather than with any sense of what positioning will make the work easier. The result is that subsequent work requires much more moving about than is necessary. A part of the problem is that when designing a work area, it can be difficult to 'see' what movement will be necessary? The string diagram is a simple tool for analyzing and designing work spaces such that movement can be minimized. The basic diagram simply consists of a map of the work area, with the actual movement drawn from top.

The term 'string diagram' comes from the way the diagram may be created with a scale drawing, pins and a piece of string (you can then measure the string to see how frequent the movements are). 1, 2, 3, 4, 5 are work stations engineer observes the movement of worker by sitting on a chair. He places 5 pins as the stations and then moves the threads along the pins. The frequency between any two stations can be known by counting the no. of threads between two pins. If the frequency is high then the machines are to be closed. If group of workers are there we represent different worker with different colored thread. Butwhen the movements are frequent, the diagram will be meshed up.

(b) Travel chart: A Travel chart is a simple table that is useful where there are multiple (and possibly irregular) movement between places. It is a variation on the check sheet, improving existing plant layout. Indicating movements from and to any combination of a given set of locations. This chart tells us the frequency of movements from one machine to another but it does not give the individual workers frequency of movements.

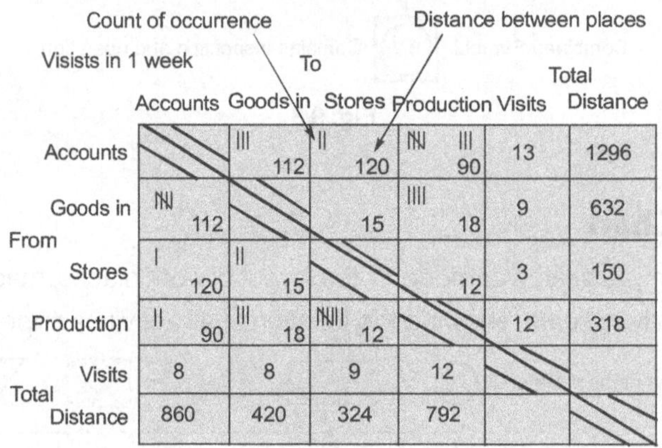

Fig: 9.6

(c) Man type process flow chart: A flow process chart which records what the worker does. Frequently used in the study of jobs which are not highly repetitive and standardized. Service and maintenance work, laboratory procedure and supervisory and executive work can be recorded on this type of chart. Since the chart follows one individual or a group performing the same activities in sequence, the standard forms are used. Essential to attach a sketch showing the path of movement of the worker while carrying out the operation charted.

(d) Multiple activity chart: Where work involves interaction of different subjects, one or more workers arelooking for a group of machines.

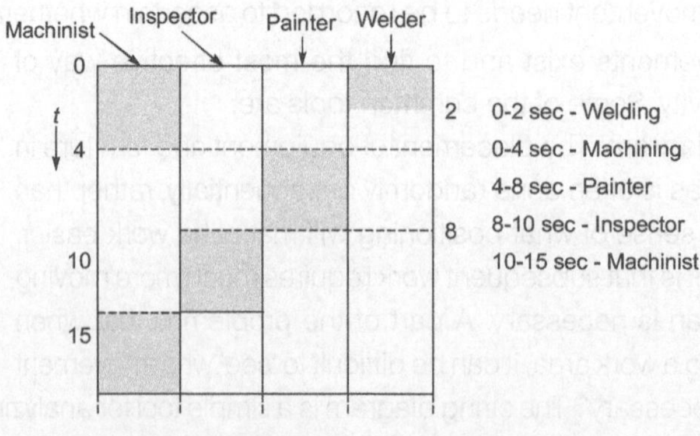

Fig: 9.7

9.7 MICRO MOTION STUDIES

A. Use of The Human Body

1. The two hands should begin and complete their movements at the same time.
2. The two hand not be idle at the same time except during periods of rest.
3. Motions of the arms should be symmetrical and in opposite directions and should be made simultaneously.
4. Hand and body motions should be made at the lowest classification at which it is possible to do the work satisfactorily.
5. Momentum should be employed to help the worker, but should be reduced to a minimum whenever is has to be overcome by muscular effort.
6. Continuous curved movements are to be preferred to straight line motions involving sudden and sharp changes in direction.
7. 'Ballistic' (i.e., free-swinging) movements are faster, easier and more accurate than restricted or controlled movements.
8. Rhythmis essential to the smooth and automatic performance of a repetitive operation. The work should be arranged to permit easy and natural rhythm whenever possible.
9. Work should be arranged so that eye movements are confined to a comfortable area, without the need for frequent change of focus.

B. Arrangement of The Workplace

1. Definite and fixed stations should be provided for all tools and materials to permit habit formation.
2. Tools and materials should be pre-positioned to reduce searching.
3. Gravity feed, bins and containers should be used to deliver the materials as close to the point of use as possible.
4. Tools, materials and controls should be located within the maximum working area and as near to the worker as possible.
5. Materials and tools should be arranged to permit the best sequence of motions.
6. "Drop deliveries" or ejectors should be used wherever possible, so that the operator does not have to use his hands to dispose of the finished work.
7. Provision should be made for adequate lighting, and chair of the type and height to permit good posture should be provided. The height of the workplace and seat should be arranged to allow alternate standing and sitting.
8. The colour of the workplace should contrast with that of the work and thus reduceeye fatigue.

C. Design of Tools and Equipment

1. The hands should be relieved of all work of 'holding' the work piece where this can be done by a jig, fixture or foot-operated device.
2. Two or more tools should be combined wherever possible.
3. Where each finger performs some specific movement, as in typewriting, the load should be distributed in accordance with the inherent capacities of the fingers.
4. Handles such as those on cranks and large screwdrivers should be so designed that as much of the surface of the hand as possible can come into contact with the handle. This is especially necessary when considerable force has to be used on the handle.
5. Levers, crossbars and hand wheels should be placed that the operator can use them with the least change in body position and the greatest "mechanical advantage".

9.8 The Two-Handed Process Chart

The two-handed process chart is a process chart in which the activities of a worker's hands (or limbs) are recorded in their relationship to one another.

9.9 Micro-Motion Study

In certain types of operation and particularly those with very short cycles which are repeated thousands of time (such as the packing of sweets into boxes or food cans into cartons), it is worth while going into much greater detail to determine where movements and efforts can be saved and to develop the best possible pattern of movement, thus enabling the operative to perform the operation repeatedly with a minimum of effort and fatigue. The techniques used for this purpose frequently make use of filming, and are known collectively as micromotion study.

The micromotion group of techniques is based on the idea of dividing human activity into divisions of movements or groups of movements (known as therbligs) according to the purpose for which they are made.

9.9.1 The Simo Chart (Micro Motion form of Operation Process Chart)

A simo chart is chart, often based on firm analysis, used to record simultaneously on a common time scale the therblings or groups of therbligs performed by different parts of the body of one or more workers. To record the movement of operator, a bulb is attached to the hand and the movement of this bulbs are recorded in an ordinary camera such graphs are called cycle graphs. But when the movements of limbs are very complex, *cycle graphs* appears to be mesh, in such cases *chrono cycle graph* is being plotted.

In this case, the bulb attached to the hand of operator blinks and its motions are recorded in a special camera and hence an average graph can be plotted. Simo charts are process chart for micromotion studies.

9.9.2 Therbligs

Symbol	Name	Abbreviation
	Search	Sh
	Find	F
	Select	Si
	Grasp	G
	Hold	H
	Transport Load	TL
	Position	P
	Assemble	A
	Use	U
	Disassemble	DA
	Inspect	I
	Pre-position	PP
	Release load	RL
	Transport empty	TE
	Rest for over-coming fatigue	R
	Unavoidable delay	UD
	Avoidable delay	AD
	Plan	Pn

Fig: 9.8

OOOO

PRACTICE QUESTIONS

1. In the study, the rating factor is applied to determine.
   (a) Standard time of a job
   (b) Merit rating of the worker
   (c) Fixation of incentive rate
   (d) Normal time of job

2. Work study is mainly aimed at
   (a) Determining the most efficient method of performing a job.
   (b) Establishing the minimum time of completion of job.
   (c) Developing the standard method and standard time of a job.
   (d) Economizing the motions involved on the part of the worker while performing a job.

3. Consider the following factors.
   1. Adequate incentive
   2. Ease of administration
   3. Flexibility
   4. Guaranteed basic pay
   5. Higher wages
   6. Simplicity

   Among these, the factors which are to be considered while developing a good wage incentive plan would include.
   (a) 1, 2, 3 and 5
   (b) 2, 3, 4 and 5
   (c) 1, 2, 4 and 6
   (d) 1, 2, 5 and 6

4. Which of the following charts are used for plant layout design?
   1. Operation process chart
   2. Man machine chart
   3. Correlation chart
   4. Travel chart

   Select the correct answer using the codes given below:
   (a) 1, 2, 3 and 4
   (b) 1, 2 and 4
   (c) 1, 3 and 4
   (d) 2 and 3

5. In value engineering important consideration is given to
   (a) Cost reduction
   (b) Profit maximization
   (c) Function concept
   (d) Customer satisfaction

6. Match **List-I (Object)** with **List-II (Tool)** and select the correct answer:

List-I	List-II
A. Improving utilization of supervisory staff	1. Micromotion study
B. Improving plant layout	2. Work sampling
C. Improving work place layout	3. Flow process chamber
D. Improving highly repetitive hand movements	4. Chronocyclegraph

   Codes:

	A	B	C	D
(a)	2	3	1	4
(b)	3	2	1	4
(c)	2	3	4	1
(d)	3	2	4	1

7. Determination of standard time in complex job system is best done through:
   (a) Stop watch time study
   (b) Analysis of micro motions
   (c) Group timing techniques
   (d) Analysis of standard date system

8. Procedure of modifying work content to given more meaning and enjoyment to the job by involving employees in planning, organization and control of their work, is termed as:
(a) Job enlargement (b) Job enrichment
(c) Job rotation (d) Job evaluation

9. Given that: E = Earnings, R = Rate per hour, T = worked in hours, S = Standard time on the basis of date in hours. Rowan wage incentive plan is:
(a) $E = RT + \left(\frac{S-T}{S}\right)$ (b) $E = RT + (S-T)^R$
(c) $E = RT + 0.4\,(S-T)R$ (d) $E = RT + \left(\frac{S-T}{S}\right)RT$

10. Value is usually considered as a relationship between
(a) Utility and Cost (b) Profit and cost
(c) Psychology and Reliability (d) Appearance and Utility

11. Aluminum tie pin and gold tie pin, both serve the purpose of keeping the tie in position. But the gold pin has significance due to:
(a) Exchange value (b) Use value
(c) Esteem value (d) Cost value

12. Consider the following conditions:
1. Minimum wages should be guaranteed.
2. Providing incentive to group efficiency performance.
3. A differential price rate should exist.
4. All standards should be based on optimum standard of production.

Those essential for an incentive plan include
(a) 1 and 4 (b) 1 and 2
(c) 3 and 4 (d) 2 and 3

13. The routing function in a production system design is concerned with:
(a) Manpower utilization (b) Machine unitization
(c) Quality assurance of the product (d) Optimizing material flow through the plan

14. Match **List-I (Type of products)** with **List-II (Type of layout)** and select the correct answer using the codes given below the lists:

List-I	List-II
A. Ball bearings	**1.** Process layout
B. Tools and gauges	**2.** Product layout
C. Large boilers	**3.** Combination of product and process layout
D. Motor cycle assembly	**4.** Fixed position layout

Codes:

	A	B	C	D
(a)	1	3	4	2
(b)	3	1	4	2
(c)	1	2	4	3
(d)	3	1	2	4

15. If one state occurred four times in hundred observations while using 'the work-sampling technique, then the precision of the study using a 95% confidence level will be:
(a) 90% (b) 92%
(c) 95% (d) 98%

16. Consider the following basic steps involved in value analysis:
1. Create 2. Blast 3. Refine
The correct sequence of these steps is
(a) 1, 2, 3 (b) 3, 1, 2
(c) 1, 3, 2 (d) 2, 1, 3

17. Consider the following statements: Dispatching
1. is the action of operations, planning and control.
2. releases work to the operating divisions.
3. conveys instructions to the shop floor.
Which of these statements are correct?
(a) 1, 2 and 3 (b) 1 and 2
(c) 2 and 3 (d) 1 and 3

18. The characteristic life-cycle of a product consists of four periods. The rate of consumption increases rapidly at the beginning of the:
(a) Incubation period (b) Growth period
(c) Maturity period (d) Decline period

19. Match **List-I (Charts)** with **List-II (Details)** and select the correct answer:

List-I	List-II
A. Multiple activity chart	1. Work factor system
B. SIMO chart	2. Movement of material
C. String diagram	3. Motion analysis
D. MTM	4. Working and idle time of two or more men/machines.

Codes:

	A	B	C	D
(a)	4	3	1	2
(b)	3	4	2	1
(c)	4	3	2	1
(d)	3	4	1	2

20. The type of layout suitable for use of the concept, principles and approaches of group technology is:
(a) Product layout (b) Job-shop layout
(c) Fixed position layout (d) Cellular layout

21. The standard time of an operation has been calculated as 10 min. The worker was rated at 80% If the relaxation and other allowance were 25%, then the observed time would be:
(a) 12.5 min (b) 10 min
(c) 8 min (d) 6.5 min

22. MTM is a work measurement technique by
(a) Stopwatch study (b) Work sampling
(c) Predetermined motion time system (d) Past data comparison

23. A process of discovering and identifying the pertinent information relating to the nature of a specific job is called
(a) Job identification
(b) Job description
(c) Job analysis
(d) Job classification

24. Which one of the following statements is correct in relation to production, planning and control?
(a) Expediting initiates the execution of production plans, whereas dispatching maintains them and sees them through to their successful completion.
(b) Dispatching initiates the execution of production plans, whereas expediting maintains them and sees them through to their successful completion.
(c) Both dispatching and expediting initiate the execution of production plans.
(d) Both dispatching and expediting maintain the production plans and see them through to their successful completion.

25. Consider the following statements regarding plant location and plant layout:
1. Qualitative factor analysis is a method of evaluating a potential location without applying quantitative values to the decision criteria.
2. The three determinants of the type of layout are type of product, type of process and the volume of production.
3. An appliance manufacturing plant where products are made on assembly lines would be classified as job shop type of layout.

Which of these statements is/are correct?
(a) 1, 2 and 3
(b) 1 and 2
(c) 2 only
(d) 3 only

26. Routing in production planning and control refers to the
(a) balancing of load on machines.
(b) authorization of work to be performed.
(c) progress of work performed.
(d) sequence of operations to be performed.

27. The management is interested to know the percentage of idle time of an equipment. The trial study showed that percentage of idle time would be 20%. The number of random observations necessary for 95% level of confidence and +5% accuracy is:
(a) 6400
(b) 10,000
(c) 40
(d) 160

28. Which one of the following is NOT a technique of PMTS?
(a) Synthetic data
(b) Stop-watch time study
(c) Work-factor
(d) MTM

29. Which one of the following combinations is valid for product layout?
(a) General purpose machine and skilled labour
(b) General purpose machine and unskilled labour
(c) Special purpose machine and semi-skilled labour
(d) Special purpose machine and skilled labour

30. During manufacture of cement, the handling of limestone is done by
(a) Belt conveyor
(b) Bucket conveyor
(c) Overhead crane
(d) Fork-lift crane

31. In production, planning and control, the document which authorizes the start of an operation on the shop floor is the
(a) Dispatch order
(b) Route plan
(c) Loading chart
(d) Schedule

32. Dispatching function of production, planning and control is
(a) the dispatch of finished goods on order.
(b) the movement of in-process material from shop to shop.
(c) authorizing a production work order to be launched.
(d) the dispatch of bills and Invoice to the customers.

33. Which one of the following is the preferred logical sequence in the development of a new product?
(a) Technical feasibility, Social acceptability and economic viability
(b) Social acceptability, economic viability and technical feasibility
(c) Economic viability, social acceptability and technical feasibility
(d) Technical feasibility, economic viability and social acceptability

34. The reason for diversification is to:
(a) Reduce production cost
(b) Balance low demand high capacity situation
(c) Satisfy more customers
(d) Improve capacity utilization

35. The proper sequence of activities for material requirement planning are:
(a) Master production schedule, capacity planning, MRP and order release
(b) Order release, master production schedule, MRP and capacity planning
(c) Master production schedule, order release, capacity planning and MRP
(d) Capacity planning, master production schedule, MRP and order release·

36. Standard time is:
(a) Normal time + Allowances
(b) (Normal time × Rating) + Allowances
(c) $\left(\frac{\text{Normal time}}{\text{Rating}}\right) + \text{Allowance}$
(d) Normal time + (Allowances x Rating)

37. Which one of the following is not a technique of Predetermined Motion Time Systems?
(a) Work factor system
(b) MTM
(c) Synthetic data
(d) Stopwatch time study

38. Consider the following steps which are involved in constructing a function analysis system technique of value engineering:
1. Find the critical path
2. Prepare a function worksheet
3. Listing of functions
4. Diagram layout

Which of the following gives the correct sequence of steps?
(a) 1-3-2-4
(b) 2-1-3-4
(c) 4-2-3-1
(d) 3-2-4-1

39. Match **List-I** (Study) with **List-II** (Related factors) and select the correct answer using the codes given below the lists:

List-I	**List-II**
A. Job enrichment	**1.** Gilbreth's principles
B. Job evaluation	**2.** Movement of limbs by work factor system
C. Method study	**3.** Herzberg motivators
D. Time study	**4.** Jacques time span of discretion

Codes:

	A	B	C	D
(a)	2	1	4	3
(b)	3	4	1	2
(c)	2	4	1	3
(d)	3	1	4	2

40. Consider the following statements: The objective of value analysis is:
1. To reduce the cost
2. To increase the profit
3. To improve quality

Which of these statements are correct?
(a) only 1 and 2 (b) only 1 and 3
(c) only 2 and 3 (d) 1, 2 and 3

41. Which one of the following is not a technique under Predetermined Motion Time System (PMTS)?
(a) Work factor (b) Synthetic data
(c) Stopwatch time study (d) MTM

42. Which one of the following statements is correct? Standard time is obtained from normal time by adding the policy allowance and
(a) Personal allowances only (b) Fatigue allowances only
(c) Delay allowances only (d) Personal, fatigue and delay allowances

43. Which one of the following statements is not correct?
(a) Work sampling is a technique of work measurement.
(b) Method study is a technique aimed at evolving improved methods.
(c) Synthetic data is not a technique covered under predetermined motion time systems.
(d) 'Select' is the first step of method study.

44. A time standard for a data entry clerk is to be set. A job is rated at 120 percent, it takes 30 seconds to enter each record and the allowances are 15%. What is the normal time?
(a) 25 seconds (b) 30 seconds
(c) 36 seconds (d) 40 seconds

45. Which one of the following statements is not correct?
(a) Schedule chart shows the processing of a job on various work centres against time.
(b) Load chart shows the processing of various jobs on a work centre against time.
(c) Dispatching is the activity related with dispatching of goods to the customers.
(d) Routing is the activity related with the operations and their sequence to the performed on the job.

46. Weekly production requirements of a product are 1000 items. The cycle time of producing one product on a machine is 10 minutes. The factory works on two shift basis in which total available time is 16 hours. Out of the available time about 25% is expected to be wasted on break downs, material unavailability and quality related problems. The factory works for 5 days in a week. How many machines are required to fulfill the production requirements?
(a) 2 (b) 3
(c) 4 (d) 6

47. Consider the following aspects:
1. Functional
2. Operational
3. Aesthetic

Which of the above aspects is/are to be analyzed in connection with the product development?
(a) 1, 2 and 3 (b) 1 and 2 only
(c) 2 and 3 only (d) 3 only

48. Consider the following statements:
The immediate objective of a product is
1. to simulate sales functions.
2. to utilize the existing equipment and power.
3. to monopolize the market.

Which of these statements is/are correct?
(a) 1, 2 and 3 (b) 1 and 2 only
(c) 2 and 3 only (d) 3 only

49. Which one of the following is not a work measurement technique?
(a) Time study (b) Work sampling
(c) Motion time data (d) Micromotion study

50. If in a time study, the observed time is 0.75 min, rating factor = 110% and allowances are 20% of normal time, then what is the standard time?
(a) 0.82 min (b) 0.975 min
(c) 0.99 min (d) 1.03

51. For a confidence level of 95% and accuracy ±5%, the number of cycles to be timed in a time study is equal to

$$\left[K\sqrt{\frac{N\Sigma X^2 - (\Sigma X)^2}{\Sigma X}}\right]^2$$

Where N = number of observation taken; $X\,X = X_1, X_2, \ldots\ldots X_N$ are individual observations. What is the value of K?
(a) 10 (b) 20
(c) 30 (d) 40

52. Consider the following statements:
1. A system-oriented approach
2. A multidiscipline team approach
3. A function-oriented approach.

Which of the above refer to value engineering?
(a) 1, 2 and 3 (b) 1 and 2 only
(c) 2 and 3 only (d) 1 and 3 only

53. During the time study on a job, the representative time, the rating and allowances are observed to be 0.4 minutes, 120% and 10 % of standard time respectively. The normal time and standard time, in minutes, are respectively.
(a) 0.48 and 0.533 (b) 0.533 and 0.48
(c) 0.6 and 0.066 (d) 0.7 and 0.8

54. The symbol used for Transport in work study is
(a) ⇒ (b) T
(c) □ (d) ∇

55. A residential school stipulates the study hours as 8.00 pm to 10.30 pm. Warden makes random checks on a certain student 11 occasions a day during the study hours over a period of 10 days and observes that he is studying on 71 occasions. Using 98% confidence interval, the estimated minimum hours of his study during that 10 day period is
(a) 8.5 hours (b) 13.9 hours
(c) 16.1 hours (d) 18.4 hours

56. A soldering operation was work-sampled over two days (16 hours during which an employee soldered 108 joints. Actual working time was 90% of the total time and the performance rating was estimated to be 120 percent. If the contract provides allowance of 20 percent of the total time available, the standard time for the operation would be
(a) 8 min (b) 8.9 min
(c) 10 min (d) 12 min

57. An assembly activity is represented on an operation process chart by the symbol
(a) □ (b) A
(c) D (d) O

58. A welding operation is time-studied during which an operator was pace-rated as 120%. The operator took, on an average, 8 minutes for producing the weld-joint. If a total of 10% allowances are allowed for this operation .The expected standard production rate of the weld-joint (in units per 8 hour day) is
(a) 45 (b) 50
(c) 55 (d) 60

59. Consider the following phases:
1. Information phase 2. Evaluation phase
3. Creative phase 4. Investigation phase
The correct sequence of these phases in value engineering is
(a) 1, 3, 4, 2 (b) 1, 3, 2, 4
(c) 3, 1, 4, 2 (d) 3, 1, 2, 4

60. In value engineering the term 'value' refers to
(a) Market value (b) Relation between cost and efficiency
(c) Relation between function and cost (d) Relation between predictability and cost

61. Value analysis is particularly of interest when
(a) Jobbing work economics are involved
(b) Production is one large scale
(c) Only few components are involved
(d) Costly equipment is used.

62. The principles of motion economy are mostly used while conducting
(a) a method study on an operation.
(b) a time study on an operation.
(c) a financial appraisal of an operation.
(d) a feasibility study of the proposed manufacturing plant.

63. The individual human variability in time studies to determine theproduction standards is taken care of by:
(a) Personal allowances (b) Work allowances
(c) Rating factor (d) None of the above

64. The standard time of an operation while conducting a time study is:
(a) Mean observed time + Allowances
(b) Normal time × Allowances
(c) Mean observed time × Rating factor + Allowances
(d) Normal time × Rating factor + Allowances

65. Fifty observations of a production operation revealed a mean cycletime of 10 min. The worker was evaluated to be performing at 90%efficiency. Assuming the allowances to be 10% of, the normal time,the standard time (in seconds) for the job is:
(a) 0.198 (b) 7.3
(c) 9.0 (d) 9.9

66. In a time study exercise, the time observed for an activity was 54 seconds. The operator had a performance rating of 120. A personaltime allowance of 10% is given. The standard time for the activity, in seconds, is:
(a) 54 (b) 60.8
(c) 72 (d) 58.32

67. A stop watch time study on an operator with a performance ratingof 120 yielded a time of 2 minute. If allowances of 10% of the totalavailable time are to be given, the standard time of the operation is:
(a) 2 minutes (b) 2.4 minutes
(c) 2.64 minutes (d) 2.67 minutes

68. The actual observed time for an operation was 1 minute per piece. Ifthe performance rating of the operator was 120 and a 5 per centpersonal time is to be provided, the standard time in minute perpiece is:
(a) 1.000 (b) 1.200
(c) 1.250 (d) 1.263

69. Which of the following hand-motion belongs to 'Therblig' in motion study.
1. Unavoidable delay 2. Pre-position
3. Select 4. Reach
Select the correct answer from the codes given below:
(a) 1 and 4 (b) 1 and 2
(c) 1, 2 and 3 (d) 2, 3 and 4

70. Repetitive fast speed activities can be effectively analyzed by takingphotograph at
(a) Low speed and screening at low speed
(b) High speed and screening at high speed
(c) High speed and screening at low speed
(d) Low speed and screening at high speed

71. Match **List-I (Charts)** with **List-II (Operations/Information)** using the codes given below the lists:

List-I
A. Standard process sheet
B. Multiple activity chart
C. Right and left hand operation chart
D. SIMO chart

List-II
1. Operations involving assembly
2. Operations involving the combination of men and machines
3. Work measurement
4. Basic information for routing
5. Therblig

Codes:

	A	B	C	D
(a)	4	3	1	2
(b)	1	2	4	5
(c)	1	3	4	2
(d)	4	2	1	5

72. Consider the following objectives:
1. To train the individual regarding motion economy.
2. To assist in research projects in the field of work study.
3. To help in the collection of Motion Time data.

The objectives of Micromotion Study would include
(a) 1, 2 and 3 (b) 1 and 2
(c) 2 and 3 (d) 1 and 3

73. Consider the following steps:
1. Method time measurement
2. Work sampling
3. Work factor system.

PMTS (Predetermined motion time systems) in work study wouldinclude:
(a) 1, 2 and 3 (b) 1 and 2
(c) 2 and 3 (d) 1 and 3

74. Work study involves
(a) only method study (b) only work measurement
(c) method study and work measurement (d) only motion study

75. Match **List-I** with **List-II** and select the correct answer using the codes given below the lists:

List-I	List-II
A. Time study	1. Stop watch
B. Work factor system	2. Clinograph
C. Micromotion study	3. Body member
D. Cycle graph	4. High speed film
	5. Small electric bulb

Codes:

	A	B	C	D
(a)	4	3	2	1
(b)	5	3	4	2
(c)	1	4	3	5
(d)	1	3	4	5

76. Motions of limbs are through

1. Elbow
2. Finger
3. Hip
4. Shoulder
5. Wrist

What is the correct sequence in descending order of motion in terms of time of fatigue involved?

(a) 3 - 4 - 1 - 5 - 2
(b) 2 - 5 - 1 - 4 - 3
(c) 5 - 2 - 3 - 1 - 4
(d) 4 - 3 - 2 - 1 - 5

77. Match **List-I (Type of Chart)** with **List-II (Definition)** and select the correct answer using the codes given below the lists:

List-I

A. Outline process chart
B. Multiple Activity chart
C. SIMO chart
D. Non-machining chart

List-II

1. It is used to record the activities ofone subject in relation.
2. It is a chart in which activities of themachine or machines are recorded inrelation to that of the operator to one or moreothers.
3. It records the main activities of theprocess through the symbols ofoperation and inspection.
4. It is used to record the activities ofthe hands of an operator.
5. It makes use of Therblig for chartingminute elements of an operation.

Codes:

	A	B	C	D
(a)	3	2	5	1
(b)	5	1	4	2
(c)	3	1	5	2
(d)	5	2	4	1

78. A SIMO chart should be used with

(a) Process charts
(b) Flow diagrams
(c) Man-machine operation charts
(d) Therbligs

79. A graphical representation of the coordinated activities (i.e. fundamental motions) of anoperator's body members, on a commontime scale is known as:

(a) SIMO chart
(b) Man-Machine chart
(c) Two-handed process chart
(d) Gantt chart

80. Consider the following charts:

1. Man-machine chart
2. SIMO chart
3. Load chart

Those used in method study would include:

(a) 1, 2 and 3
(b) 1 and 2
(c) 2 and 3
(d) 1 and 3

81. Consider the following statements:

Method study is carried out to achieve

1. The most effective use of plant and equipment.

2. The most effective use of human efforts.
3. Evaluation of human work.

Which of the statements given above are correct?

(a) 1 and 3 only (b) 2 and 3 only
(c) 1 and 2 only (d) 1, 2 and 3

82. Consider the following activities:

1. Body movement
2. Work capability of individuals
3. Movement of materials

Which of these activities is observed in method study?

(a) 1, 2 and 3 (b) 2 and 3
(c) 1 and 3 (d) 1 and 2

83. Match **List-I (Therbligs symbols)** with **List-II (Motions)** and selectthe correct answer using the codes given below the lists:

List-I	List-II
A. 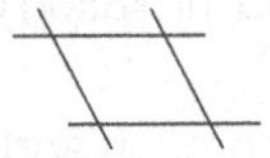	1. Stop watch
B. 	2. Clinograph
C. 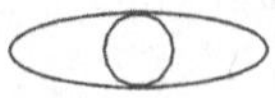	3. Body member
D. 	4. High speed film
	5. Small electric bulb

Codes:

	A	B	C	D
(a)	1	2	3	4
(b)	4	3	2	1
(c)	3	4	1	2
(d)	4	3	1	2

84. Therbligs are essential in

(a) Flow process chart (b) Motion economy
(c) Method-analysis chart (d) Suggestion system

85. Simo charts are used for

(a) Inspection of parts (b) Operator movements
(c) Work done at one place (d) Simulation of models

86. In which of the following operations, micro motion study technique is used?

1. Short cycle operations lasting two minutes or less.
2. Long cycle operations lasting more than five minutes.
3. Medium cycle operations lasting between two and five minutes.

Select the correct answer using the codes given below:

(a) 1 only (b) 1 and 2
(c) 2 and 3 (d) 1, 2 and 3

87. Standard time is:
(a) Average time + Allowances (b) Average time – Allowances
(c) Normal time – Allowances (d) Normal time + Allowances

88. Standard times (ST) and labour rates are as in the table. Labour overheads are 20% of labour cost.

Activity	ST.min	Labour Rate ₹/hr.
Cutting	2	550
Inspection	0.5	400
Packaging	0.5	400

If the material cost is ₹ 25/unit, what will be the total cost ofproduction in ₹ per unit?
(a) 25 (b) 55
(c) 45 (d) 35

89. For a manual operation to study the total processing standard timeusing a chronometer, following observations were made:
Processing time : 16 minutes
Rating of the worker : 120%
Personal allowance : 0.6 minutes
Basic fatigue allowance : 1.92 minutes
Unavoidable delay allowance : 1.08 minutes
What is the standard operating time for the operation?
(a) 16 minutes (b) 17.92 minutes
(c) 22.8 minutes (d) None of the above

90. In a stop-watch time study, the observed time was 0.16 minute; the performance rating factor was 125 on the 100 normal (percentage scale). What is the standard time in minutes if 10% allowances are permitted?
(a) 0.180 (b) 0.200
(c) 0.220 (d) 0.240

91. There is 8 hours duty and a job should take 30 minutes to complete it. But after 8 hours, an operator is able to complete only 14 such jobs. The operator's performance is:
(a) 77.5% (b) 78.5%
(c) 87.5% (d) 97.5%

92. Match **List-I (Techniques of work measurement)** with **List-II (Usages in Indian industry)** and select the correct answer using the codes given below the lists:

List-I	List-II
A. Stop-watch study	1. 5%
B. Standard based study	2. 10%
C. Work sampling	3. 80%
D. Historical data based	

Codes:

	A	B	C	D
(a)	3	1	1	2
(b)	2	1	3	1
(c)	3	2	1	2
(d)	2	3	1	1

93. Match **List-I** with **List-II** and select the correct answer using thecodes given below the lists:

List-I	List-II
A. Statistic	1. Performance Rating
B. MTM	2. Motion Study
C. Stop Watch	3. Work Measurement
D. Man Machine Chart	4. Work Sampling
E. Standard Time	

Codes:

	A	B	C	D	E
(a)	4	3	3	2	1
(b)	4	2	3	2	1
(c)	2	3	4	1	2
(d)	3	1	4	2	1

94. Which one of the following techniques is used for determiningallowances in time study?
(a) Acceptance sampling (b) Linear regression
(c) Performance rating (d) work sampling

95. Consider the following statements:
The principle of motion economy related to the use of human bodyis that the two hands should
1. Begin as well as complete their motions at the same time.
2. Not be idle at the same time except during rest.
3. Be relieved of all work that can be done more advantageously bya jig, fixture or foot- operated device.

Which of these statements are correct?
(a) 1, 2 and 3 (b) 1 and 2
(c) 2 and 3 (d) 1 and 3

96. Consider the following principles:
1. Trying to avoid the use of hands for holding.
2. Relieving the hands of work whenever possible.
3. Keeping the work in the normal work area.
4. Avoiding having both hands doing the same thing at the sametime.

Principles of motion economy would include:
(a) 1, 2 and 3 (b) 1, 3 and 4
(c) 1, 3, and 4 (d) 1, 2 and 3

97. From the point of motion economy it is preferable to move
(a) Both hands in the same direction (b) Right hand first and then left hand
(c) Only one hand at a time (d) Both hands in opposite directions

98. The number of cycles to be timed in a stopwatch time study dependsupon the
(a) discretion of the time study engineer.
(b) time of each cycle and the accuracy of results desired.
(c) time available to the time study engineer.
(d) nature of the operation and as well as the operator.

99. In respect of time study, match **List-I (Situations)** with **List-II (Allowance)** and select the correct answer using the codes givenbelow the lists:

List-I	List-II
A. To allow for personal needs	1. Contingency allowance
B. To meet legitimate delay in work	2. Policy allowance
C. Offered under special circumstances	3. Injury allowanceto add to the earnings
	4. Relaxation allowance

Codes:

	A	B	C
(a)	4	1	2
(b)	3	2	4
(c)	4	2	3
(d)	3	1	2

100. Which one of the following statements regarding time study is correct?
   (a) While conducting time study, it is important to get historical records of preceding times.
   (b) It is based on a procedure originally proposed by Frederick W. Taylor.
   (c) It is necessary to multiply the measured time by the reciprocal oflearning curve.
   (d) One should be careful to collect data under just-in-time conditions.

DIRECTION:
The following items consists of two statements; one labeled as **'Assertion (A)'** and the other as **"Reason (R)'**. You are to examine these two statements carefully and select the answer to these items using the code given below:

Codes:
   (a) Both A and R are true and R is the correct explanation of A.
   (b) Both A and R are true but R is not a correct explanation of A.
   (c) A is true but R is false.
   (d) A is false but R is true.

101. **Assertion (A):** Value analysis is superior to other conventional cost reduction techniques.
   Reason (R): In conventional cost reduction techniques, value is increased by widening tolerance bands.

102. **Assertion (A):** Value Engineering is concerned with increasing the quality of the product even at enhanced cost to fulfill the customer requirements .
   Reason (A): Customer requirements are changing very rapidly and survival of a manufacturing industry is linked with fulfilling the customers requirements.

103. **Assertion(A):** Value engineering is a technique applied to compete in the market only at the time of introduction of a product orservice.
   Reason(R): Increasing the functional worth of a product appreciably, keeping the cost almost constant, is the real objective of value engineering.

104. **Assertion (A):** SIMO chart reveals the deficiencies in the motion pattern of the process chart.
   Reason (R): SIMO chart and operator processes chart yield the same results.

105. **Assertion (A):** Split hand type stopwatch is preferred in time study by stop watch method.
   Reason (R): Split hand type stopwatch eliminates possibilities of delay in nothing the reading.

○○○○

ANSWERS

VALUE ENGINEERING & WORK STUDY

1. (d)	**2.** (c)	**3.** (c)	**4.** (b)	**5.** (a)	**6.** (c)	**7.** (d)
8. (a)	**9.** (d)	**10.** (a)	**11.** (c)	**12.** (a)	**13.** (d)	**14.** (c)
15. (d)	**16.** (d)	**17.** (a)	**18.** (b)	**19.** (c)	**20.** (d)	**21.** (b)
22. (c)	**23.** (a)	**24.** (b)	**25.** (c)	**26.** (d)	**27.** (a)	**28.** (b)
29. (d)	**30.** (a)	**31.** (a)	**32.** (c)	**33.** (b)	**34.** (c)	**35.** (d)
36. (a)	**37.** (d)	**38.** (d)	**39.** (b)	**40.** (b)	**41.** (c)	**42.** (d)
43. (c)	**44.** (c)	**45.** (c)	**46.** (b)	**47.** (a)	**48.** (a)	**49.** (d)
50. (c)	**51.** (d)	**52.** (a)	**53.** (a)	**54.** (a)	**55.** (c)	**56.** (d)
57. (d)	**58.** (a)	**59.** (d)	**60.** (c)	**61.** (a)	**62.** (a)	**63.** (c)
64. (c)	**65.** (d)	**66.** (c)	**67.** (c)	**68.** (c)	**69.** (c)	**70.** (c)
71. (d)	**72.** (d)	**73.** (d)	**74.** (c)	**75.** (d)	**76.** (a)	**77.** (a)
78. (d)	**79.** (a)	**80.** (b)	**81.** (d)	**82.** (a)	**83.** (d)	**84.** (b)
85. (b)	**86.** (b)	**87.** (b)	**88.** (d)	**89.** (c)	**90.** (c)	**91.** (a)
92. (d)	**93.** (a)	**94.** (d)	**95.** (d)	**96.** (b)	**97.** (d)	**98.** (b)
99. (a)	**100.** (b)	**101.** (b)	**102.** (d)	**103.** (d)	**104.** (c)	**105.** (a)

CHAPTER 10

Robots

10.1 INTRODUCTION

Robot is an automatically controlled material handling unit that is widely used in the manufacturing industry. It is generally used for high volume production and better quality. Implementation of robot technology with integration of automatic system can contribute to increase in productivity of the company and enhances its profitability.

Another definition from Robot Institute of America is that the robot is a programmable multi function manipulator designed to move and manipulate material, parts, tools or specialized devices through variable programmed motions for the performance of a variety of specified tasks.

There are a number of successful examples of robot applications such as the following:

Robots perform more than 98 percent of the spot welding on Ford's Taurus and Sable cars in USA. A robot drills holes in the vertical tail fins at general dynamics compared to man when the job was done manually. Robots insert disk drives into personal computers and snap keys onto electronic type writer keyboards.

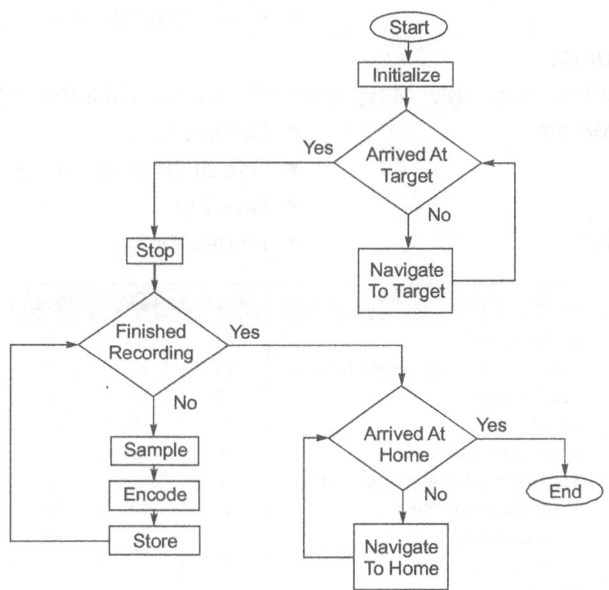

Fig: 10.1 The simple robotic flow chart

All the Robots have Following Basic Components:

1. **Manipulators:** This is the mechanical unit often called as the arm, that manipulate the end effectors and does the actual work of the robot. The manipulators are composed of mechanical linkages and joints with actuators to drive the mechanism directly or indirectly through gears, chains, or ball screws.
2. **Feedback devices:** They consist of the various transducers that sense the actual position/ orientation of various linkages and joints and send this information to the controllers.
3. **End effectors:** The grippers or tools are attached to the end of the arm and perform the actual operations.
4. **Controller:** It is the brains of the robot that control all the movements of the manipulator and the end effectors.
5. Power supply.

10.2 ROBOT APPLICATIONS

Industrial Robots are automatic machines, which are observed to perform the following tasks in manufacturing:

(a) **Parts handling:**

This may involve tasks like the following:

- Recognising, sorting/separating the parts.
- Picking and placing the parts at desired locations.
- Palletising and de-palletising.
- Loading and unloading the parts on required machines etc.

(b) **Parts processing:**

This may involve operations like:

- Routing
- Riveting
- Grinding
- Polishing
- Drilling
- Arc welding
- Coating
- Heat treatment etc.

(c) **Product Building:**

This may involve assembly of typical parts/products like the following:

- Electrical Motors
- Solenoids
- Bolting
- Spot welding
- Car bodies
- Circuit boards and operations like
- Riveting
- Inspection etc.

	1985	1990	1995
Machine tending	16%	15%	15%
Material Transfer (Machine Tending)	16	15	15
Spot Welding	26	15	10
Arc Welding	10	10	9
Spray painting/coating	10	10	7
Processing (Drilling, Grinding etc.)	5	7	7
Electronics assembly	6	12	14
Other assembly	5	8	12
Inspection	5	7	10
Others	1	1	1

Table: 10.1 Applications of robots in industries

Robots are being applied in industries because of the following reasons:

- Hazardous or uncomfortable working conditions
- Difficult handling
- Multi shift operation
- Repetitive tasks
- Higher accuracy

Advantages of Robots

- Robots have high accuracy and repeatability much more accurate than human being.
- Robots can perform multiple operations or tasks at the same time.
- Robots work continuously without any humanity needs and illnesses.
- Robots and their sensors can have capabilities beyond that of humans.
- The use of Robot increase productivity, efficiency, quality reproducibility and safety of products.
- Robots can work in hazardous environments, handling of unhygienic material, rescue operations, bomb disposal etc.
- Robotics and automation in industries may cause social problems like unemployment and may affect economy.

10.3 ROBOT TYPES

10.3.1 Types of Robots by Applications

Now-a-days, robots do a lot of different tasks in different fields and the number of jobs entrusted to robots is growing steadily. That's why one of the best ways to classify robots is by their applications:

- **Industrial robots:** Industrial robots are robots used in an industrial manufacturing environment. Usually these are articulated arms specifically developed for such applications as welding, material handling, painting and others. If we judge purely by application this type could also include some automated guided vehicles and other robots.
- **Domestic or household robots:** These are the robots used at home or for domestic purposes. This type of robots includes several different devices such as robotic vacuum cleaners, robotic pool cleaners, sweepers, gutter cleaners and other robots that can do different chores. Also, some surveillance and telepresence robots could be regarded as household robots if used in that environment.
- **Medical robots:** Robots used in medicine and medical institutions. First and fore most-surgery robots. Also, some automated guided vehicles and may be lifting aides.
- **Military robots:** Robots used in military. This type of robots includes bomb disposal robots, different transportation robots, reconnaissance drones. Often robots initially created for military purposes can be used in law enforcement, search and rescue operations.
- **Service robots:** Robots that don't fall into other types by usage. These could be different data gathering robots, robots made to show off technologies, robots used for research, etc.

10.3.2 Types of Robots by Locomotion and Kinematics

As you can understand, robot's application alone does not provide enough information when talking about a specific robot. So they can also be classified as:

1. Stationary robots (Including robotic arms with a global axis of movement)

- Cartesian/Gantry robots
- Cylindrical robots
- Spherical robots
- SCARA robots
- Articulated robots (robotic arms)
- Parallel robots

2. Wheeled robots

- Single wheel (ball) robots
- Two-wheel robots
- Three and more wheel robots

3. Legged robots

- Bipedal robots (humanoid robots)
- Tripedal robots
- Quadrupedal robots
- Hexapod robots
- Robot with other number of legs

4. Swimming robots

5. Flying robots

6. Mobile spherical robots (robotic balls)

7. Swarm robots

10.3.3 Cartesian co-ordinates Robots

A cartesian coordinate robot (also called linear robot) is an industrial robot whose three principal axis of control are linear (i.e. they move in a straight line rather than rotate) and are at right angles to each other. The three sliding joints correspond to moving the wrist up-down, in-out, back-forth. Among other advantages, this mechanical arrangement simplifies the robot control arm solution. Cartesian coordinate robots with the horizontal member supported at both ends are sometimes called Gantry robots. They are often quite large.

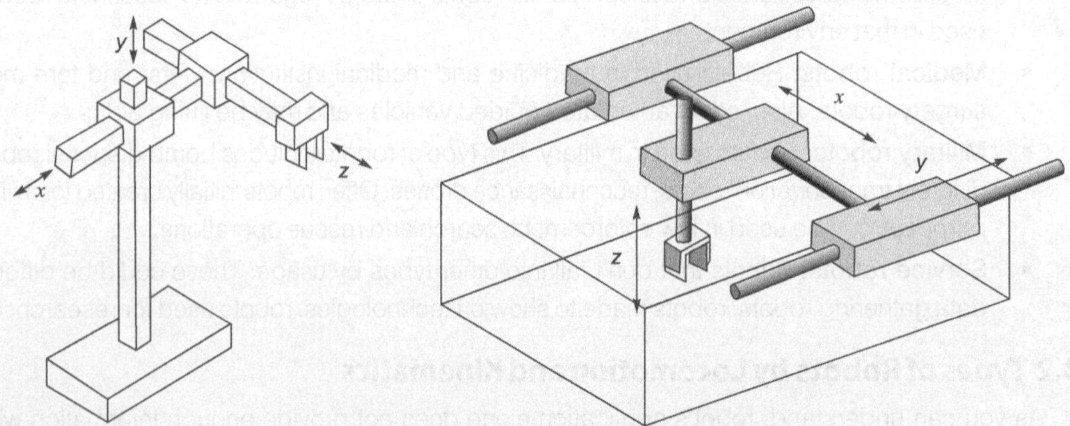

Fig. 10.2 Cartesian Robot Cofigurations

Positioning may be done by linear motion along three principal axes: left and right, in and out and up and down. These axes are known, respectively, as the Cartesian axes *X*, *Y* and *Z* shows a typical manipulator arm for a Cartesian co-ordinates robots. This is one of the simplest types of robots.

10.3.4 Spherical or Polar Coordinate Robots

In this type of robot there are mostly rotational axes. The axes for the spherical co-ordinates are θ, the rotational axis, *R*, the reach axis and β, the bend-up and down axis. The work area serviced by a polar co-ordinate robot is the space between two concentric hemispheres. The reach of the arm is de-concentric hemispheres. The reach of the arm defines the inner hemisphere when it is fully retracted along the *R*-axis.

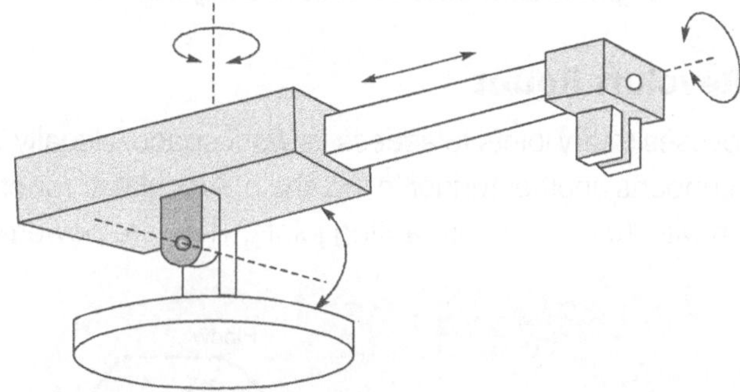

Fig. 10.3 Spherical or polar coordinate Robot

10.3.5 Cylindrical Coordinate Robots

A cylindrical robot has two linear axes and one rotary axis. The robot derives its name from the operating envelope (the space in which a robot operates that is created by moving the axes from limit to limit).

The *Z*-axis is located inside the base, resulting in a compact end-of-arm design that allows the robot to "reach" into tight work envelopes without sacrificing speed or repeatability.

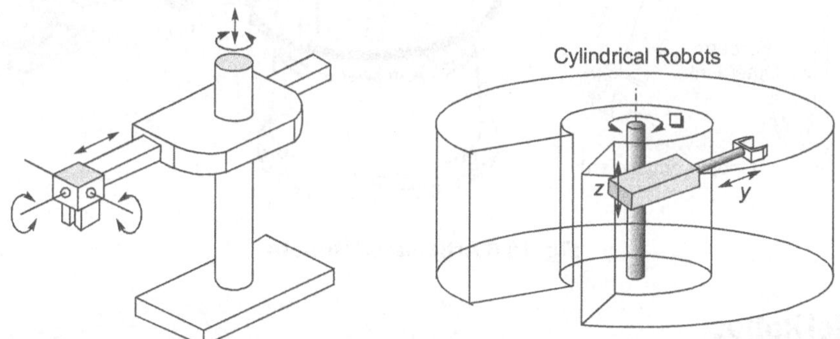

Fig. 10.4 Cylindrical Robot configurations

10.3.6 Jointed Arm Robot

It consists of three straight members connected by two rotational joints and mounted on rotary base. This type of configuration is similar to the human arm. The three members connected by rotational joints are analogous to the human shoulder, elbow and wrist. Here the arm can rotate about all three axes, hence the robot is called a revolute Co-ordinates, articulate or jointed arm robot. This type of configuration has low resolution which depends upon arm length however it can move at high speeds.

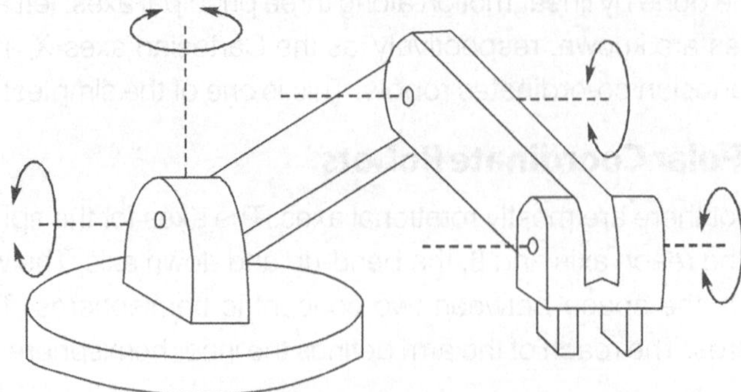

Fig. 10.5 Jointed Arm Robot Configuration

10.3.7 Articulate or Revolute Robot

An articulated robot uses rotary joints to access its work space. Usually the joints are arranged in a "chain", so that one joint supports another further in the chain. Articulated robots range from simple two-jointed structures to robots with 10 or more interacting joints. They are powered by a variety of means, like electric motors etc.

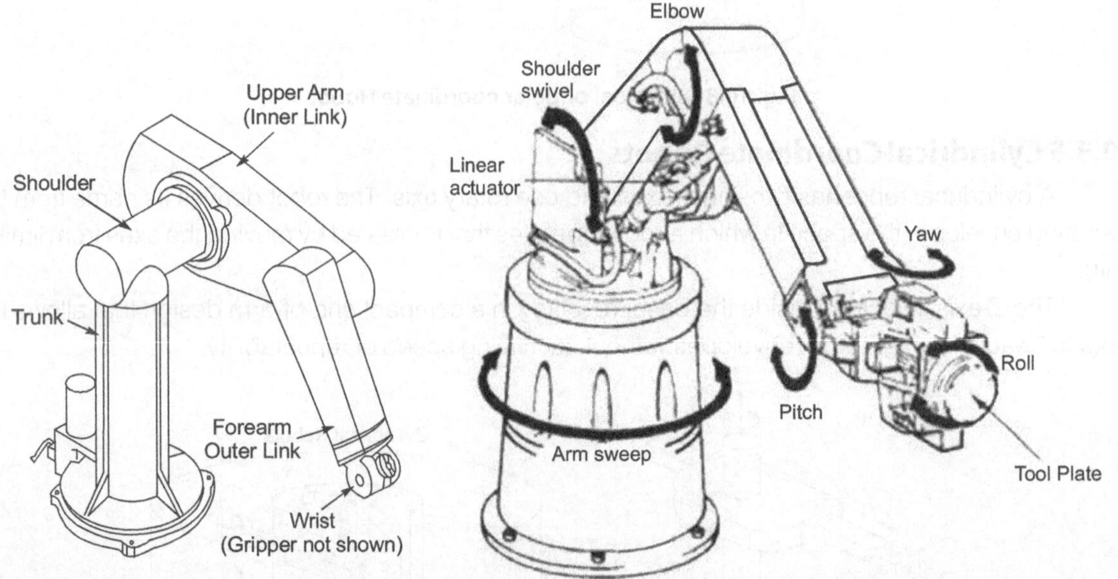

Fig. 10.6 Articulated Robots

10.3.8 Parallel Robot

The robot manipulators can be either serial or parallel. In a parallel robot, the end-effector is connected to the base through several chains of interconnected links. Therefore, a parallel robot has at least two legs or arms. Most of its joints are not actuated, and many of these passive joints have several degrees-of-freedom (DOFs) (e.g. spherical, universal and planar joints).

Two of the most popular parallel robots are the telescoping-leg hexapod used in most motion simulators (often called "motion platforms") and the "Delta robot", generally used for rapid pick-and-place. While there are fewer parallel robots than serial robots in use, the variety of parallel robots is larger.

A typical application of parallel robot is a mobile platform handling cockpit flight simulators. It is a robot whose arms have concurrent prismatic or rotary joints.

Fig. 10.7: Parallel Robot

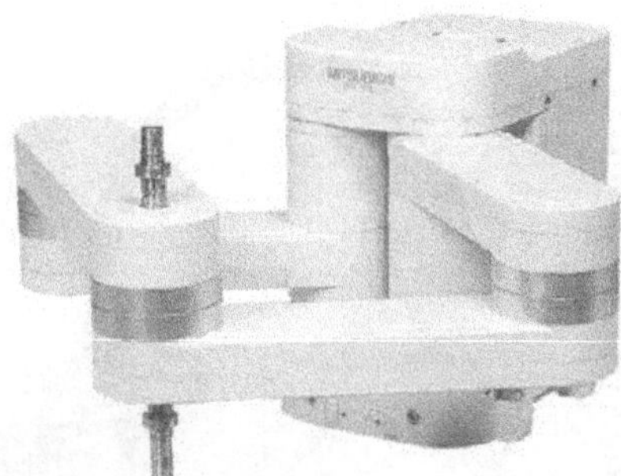

Fig. 10.8: A typical parallel robot from Mitsubishi Electric

10.3.9 SCARA Robot

The SCARA acronym stands for Selective Compliance Assembly Robot Arm or Selective Compliance Articulated Robot Arm. The robot was developed under the guidance of Hiroshi Makino, a professor at the University of Yamanashi. Its arm was rigid in the Z-axis and flexible in the XY-axes, which allowed it to adjust to holes in the XY-axes. The second characteristic of the SCARA is the jointed two-link arm arrangement similar to our human arms, hence the often-used term, expressed. This feature allows the arm to extend into confined areas and then retract or "fold up" out of the way. This is beneficial for transferring parts from one cell to another or for loading/ unloading process stations that are enclosed. Most SCARA robots are based on serial architectures, which means that the first motor should carry all other motors

The SCARA robot is based on a 4-axis design. Four axis robots are configured in a slightly dissimilar mode than the ordinary 6-axis robot models. In its place of three axes in the wrist area, four axis robots have one. Their simplified design allows them to provide maximum stability and strength for applications such as material handling and palletizing. Some four axis robot models have reinforcement bars along the upper and lower arms. These bars make the robot sturdier.

The 4 axis SCARA robots are ideal for high-speed assembly, kitting, packaging, and other material-handling applications. Innovations have lead the industry for over twenty-five years. SCARAs are generally faster and cleaner than comparable Cartesian robot systems. Their single pedestal mount requires a small footprint and provides an easy, unhindered form of mounting. On the other hand, SCARAs can be more expensive than comparable Cartesian systems and the controlling software requires inverse kinematics for linear interpolated movements.

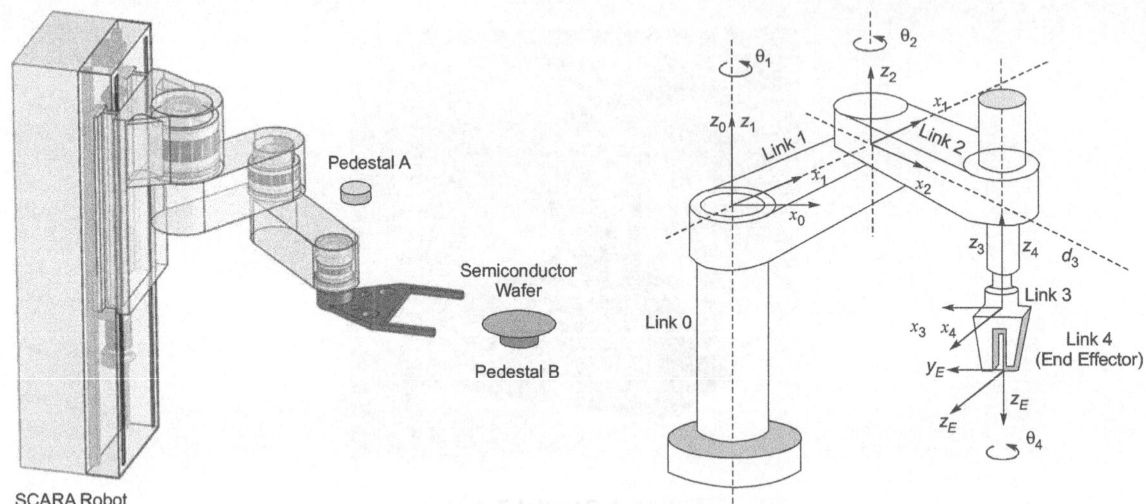

Fig. 10.9: SCARA Robot Configurations

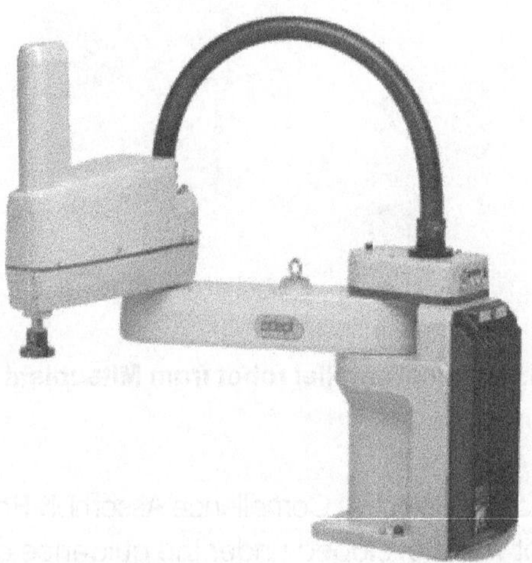

Fig. 10.10: A typical four axis SCARA Robot

Adept's high speed SCARA robot (4-axis robot) innovations have lead the industry for over twenty-five years. In 1984, Adept introduced the Adept One SCARA robot, the world's first direct-drive robot. The Adept One SCARA robot changed the face of robotics with its innovative, cutting-edge design. The four axises are designated as:

J1 Axis: The base axis allows the four axis robot to pivot from left to right.

J2 Axis: This axis is attached to the base configuration. It manoeuvres the robot forward and backwards.

J3 Axis: This critical axis joins the upper and lower arms.

J4 Axis: The wrist axis rotates the EOAT.

Equation of SCARA Robot Positioning

To designate how the two main motion actuators, the shoulder joint and the elbow joint position the end effectors, we need to calculate the 'forward kinematics' of the arm, i.e. equations that translate the combined shoulder and elbow rotations into the X and Y co-ordinates of the load point.

The equations, which denote the shoulder-connected segment as length Ls, the elbow-connected segment as Length Le, the shoulder angle as phi (Φ), and the elbow angle as theta (Θ), are given by the following equations 1 and 2.

$$x = L_s \cos\phi + L_e \cos(\phi + \theta) \quad ...(1)$$
$$y = L_s \sin\phi + L_e \sin(\phi + \theta) \quad ...(2)$$

This is basic trigonometry. If we know the lengths of the upper and lower arm parts and the angles of the two joints, we can calculate the *X* and *Y* axis co-ordinates of the end effector.

However there is a problem over here that the mathematical procedure is the reverse of the practical situation. What we actually know is the desired *XY* co-ordinates; what we want to calculate is the two joint angles. Therefore here we need to use the inverse kinematics, which is more complicated.

$$d = \sqrt{x^2 + y^2} \quad ...(3)$$

$$\phi = \sin^{-1}\left(\frac{x}{d}\right) - \cos^{-1}\left(\frac{d^2 + L_s^2 - L_e^2}{2L_s d}\right) \quad ...(4)$$

$$\theta = 90° - \sin^{-1}\left(\frac{x}{d}\right) + \cos^{-1}\left(\frac{L_e^2 + d^2 - L_s^2}{2L_s d}\right) \quad ...(5)$$

To begin with, there are always two ways to get to every location in the motion plane: with the arm cranked to the left or with the arm cranked to the right. Nevertheless, still using basic trigonometry we can derive the equations for the two joint angles (phi and theta) given *X* and *Y*. They are given by the following equations 3, 4 and 5.

Applications of SCARA Robots

1. Screw tightening work using robot vision
2. Process-to-process transfer using inverse specifications
3. Process-to-process transfer of heavy workpieces
4. Finished product inspection, touch-panel type evaluation machine
5. Conveying masks for wafers
6. Tall work pieces conveying and stacking machine
7. Assembly cell (independent cell)
8. Assembly cell (line cell)
9. Assembly cell (Handling unit for special purpose tester)

10.4 ROBOT ANATOMY AND RELATED ATTRIBUTES

10.4.1 Joints and Links

The manipulator of industrial automation consists of a series of joints and links. Automation anatomy deals with the study of various joints and links and alternative aspects of the manipulator's physical construction. An automation joint provides relative motion between 2 links of the robot. Each joint, or axis, provides a particular degree-of-freedom (dof) of motion. In most of the cases, just one degree-of-freedom is related to each joint. Thus the robots will be classified in according to the overall variety of degree of freedom they posses.

Each joint is connected to 2 links, they are input link and output link. Joint provides controlled relative movement between the input link and output link. An automation link is the rigid part of the robot manipulator. Most of the robots area unit mounted upon a stationary base, like the ground. From this base, a joint-link listing theme could also be recognized as shown in Figure. The robotic base and its association to the primary joint area unit termed as link-0. The primary joint within the sequence is joint-1. Link-0 is that the input link for joint-1, whereas the output link from joint-1 is link-1-which ends up in joint-2. Therefore link one is, at the same time, the output link for joint-1 and also the input link for joint-2. This joint-link-numbering theme is followed for all joints and links within the robotic systems.

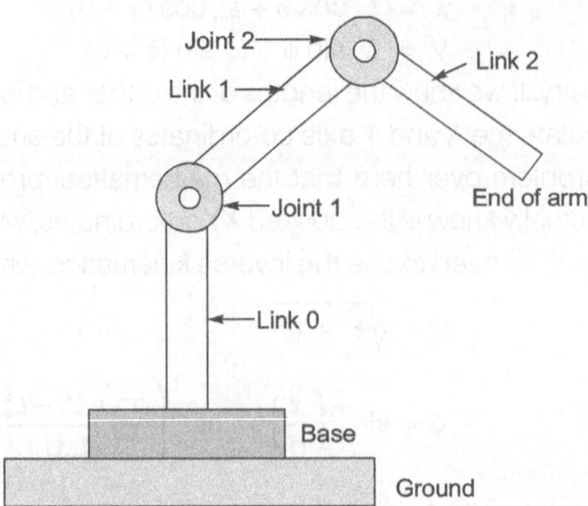

Fig. 10.11: Diagram of Robot Construction showing how a robot is made up of a series of Join-link Combinations

(a) **Linear joint (type L joint):** The relative movement between the input link and the output link is a translational sliding motion, with the axes of the two links being parallel.

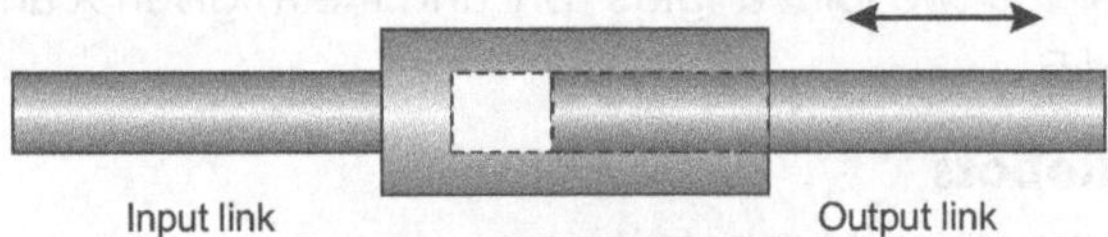

Fig 10.12: Linear Joint

(b) **Orthogonal joint (type U joint):** This type of joint also have translational sliding motion, but the input and output links are perpendicular to each other during the move.

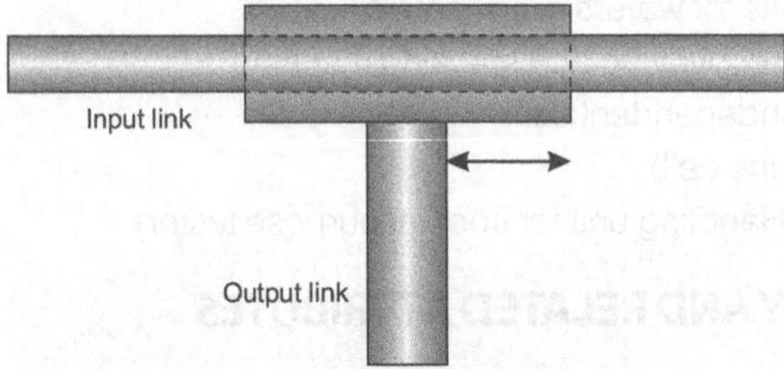

Fig. 10.13: Orthogonal Joint

(c) **Rotational joint (type R joint):** This type of joint provides rotational relative motion, with the axis of rotation perpendicular to the axes of the input and output links.

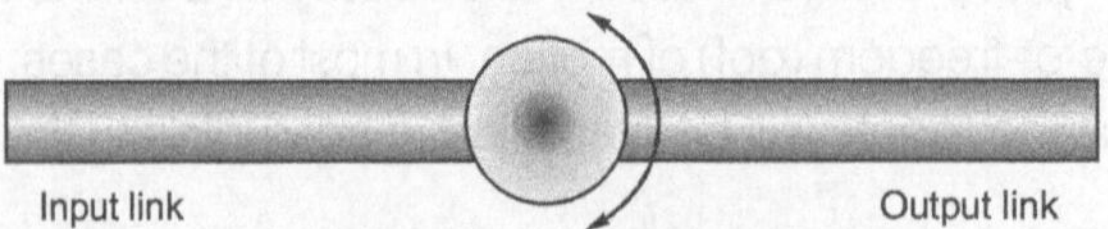

Fig. 10.14: Rotational Joint

(d) **Twisting joint (type T joint):** This joint also involves rotary motion, but the axis or rotation is parallel to the axes of the two links.

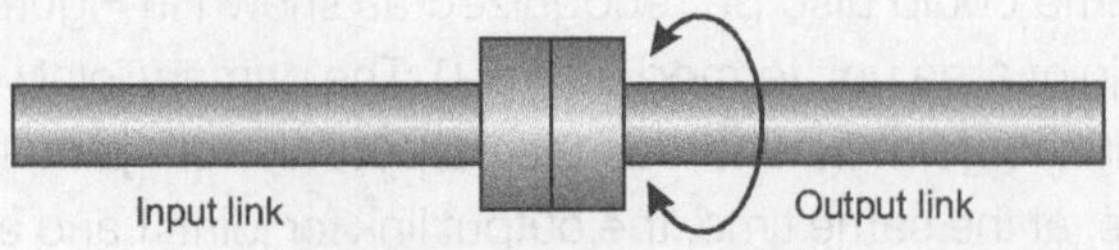

Fig. 10.15: Twisting Joint

(e) Revolving joint (type V-joint, V from the "v" in revolving): In this type, axis of input link is parallel to the axis of rotation of the joint. However the axis of the output link is perpendicular to the axis of rotation.

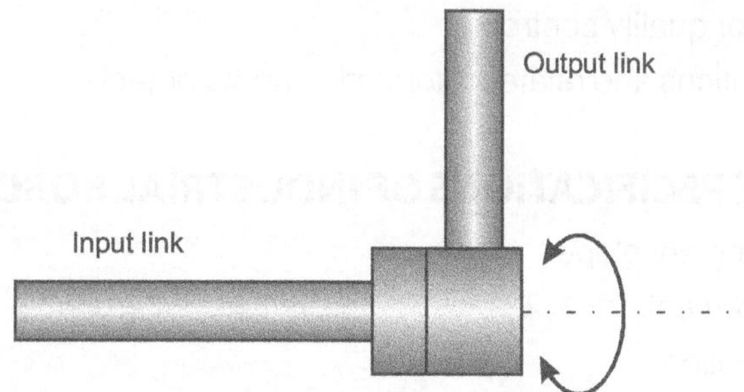

Fig. 10.16: Revolving Joint

10.4.2 End Effectors

End effectors are the devices attached to the robot's wrist to perform a specific task. The end effectors are two types: Gripers and Tools.

Grippers

- Mechanical Grippers
- Magnetized grippers
- Scoops (to carry fluids)
- Suction cups or vacuum cups
- Hooks

10.4.3 Tools

Tools are used when the robot is required to perform some processing operation on the work piece. Here the robot manipulate the tool relative to the work piece. The tools used as end effectors by robot to perform processing operations like

- Arc welding tool
- Spot welding gun
- Rotating spindle for drilling, grinding etc.
- Spray painting gun
- Assembly tool like automatic screwdriver

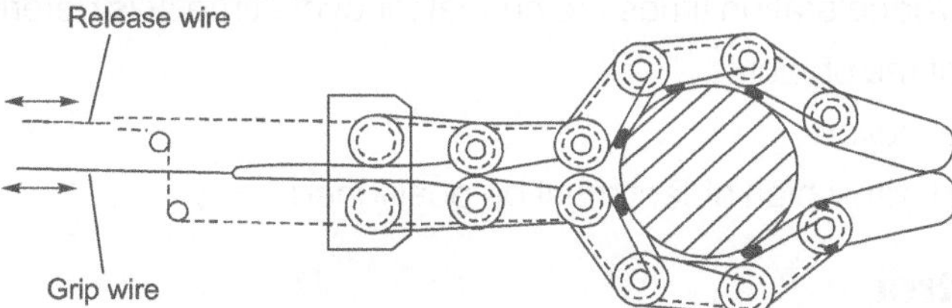

Fig. 10.17: Robot Gripper

10.4.4 Sensors in Robotics

Types of Sensors

- Tactile sensors (touch sensors, force sensors, tactile array sensors).
- Proximity and range sensors (optical sensors, acoustical sensors, electromagnetic sensors).
- Miscellaneous sensors (transducers and sensors which sense variables such temperature, pressure, fluid flow, thermocouples, voice sensors).
- Machine vision systems.

Uses of Sensors

- Safety monitoring
- Interlocks in work cell control
- Part inspection for quality control
- Determining positions and related information about objects

10.5 PERFORMANCE SPECIFICATIONS OF INDUSTRIAL ROBOTS

- Size of the working envelope
- Precision of movement
  - Control resolution
  - Accuracy
  - Repeatability
- Lifting capability
- Number of robot axes
- Speed of movement
  - maximum speed
  - acceleration/deceleration time
- Motion control
  - path control
  - velocity control
- Types of drive motors
  - hydraulic
  - electric
  - pneumatic

10.5.1 Weight Carrying Capacity

- The lifting capability provided by manufacturer doesn't include the weight of the end effector
- Usual Range 2.5lb -2000lb (About 1.1 to 900 Kg)
- Condition to be satisfied:

  Load Capability > Total weight of work piece + weight of end effector + Safety range

10.5.2 Speed of Movement

Speed with which the robot can manipulate the end effector

- Acceleration/deceleration times are crucial for cycle time. It is determined by:
  - Weight of the object
  - Distance moved
  - Precision with which object must be positioned

10.5.3 Motion Control

- Path control - how accurately a robot traces a given path (critical for gluing, painting, welding applications);
- Velocity control-how well the velocity is controlled (critical for gluing, painting applications)
- Types of control path:
  - Point to point control (used in assembly, palletizing, machine loading); - continuous path control/walk through (paint spraying, welding).
  - Controlled path (paint spraying, welding).

Important Parameters of Robots:

(A) axes of motion (B) arm movement (C) wrist movement (D) end of arm speed (E) Weight carrying capacity (F) control (G) memory (H) programming method (I) positioning accuracy and repeatability (J) end of arm tooling (K) interfacing (L) Maximum ambient operating temperature.

10.5.4 Type of Drive System

- Hydraulic
  - High strength and high speed
  - Mechanical simplicity
  - Large robots, Takes floor space
  - Used usually for heavy payloads
- Electric Motor (Servo/Stepper)
  - High accuracy and repeatability
  - Less floor space
  - Low cost
  - Easy maintenance
- Pneumatic
- Smaller units, quick assembly
- High cycle rate
- Easy maintenance

10.5.5 Direct and Inverse Kinematics

Kinematics

Kinematics is the study of motion of a body without considering the cause (Force) of that motion. Within this Kinematics one will study the Configuration, Velocity, Acceleration and all higher order derivatives of the Position Variable.

Formulating the correct kinematic models for a robot mechanism is very important for analyzing the behavior of manipulators.

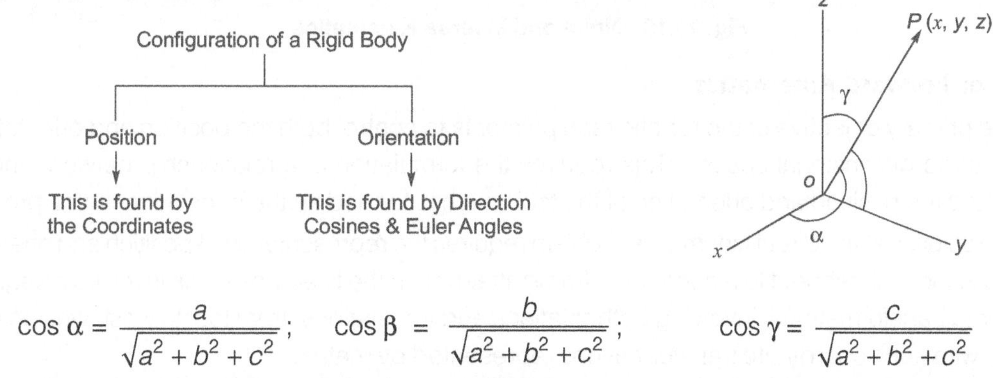

$$\cos\alpha = \frac{a}{\sqrt{a^2+b^2+c^2}}; \quad \cos\beta = \frac{b}{\sqrt{a^2+b^2+c^2}}; \quad \cos\gamma = \frac{c}{\sqrt{a^2+b^2+c^2}}$$

The behavior of the Robot Mechanism mainly depends on the Interconnection. This interconnection technically called as Kinematic pair. For understanding of the Kinematics a good understanding of the Kinematic pair is necessary.

Kinematic Pairs are Mainly Classified into Three types:

(a) Lower Pair (Area Contact)

(b) Higher Pair (Point Contact)

(c) Wrapping Pair (One completely wrapped over other)

Degrees of Freedom

The number of Co-ordinates that are needed to describe the relative motion permitted in a Kinematic pair is called as degrees of freedom.

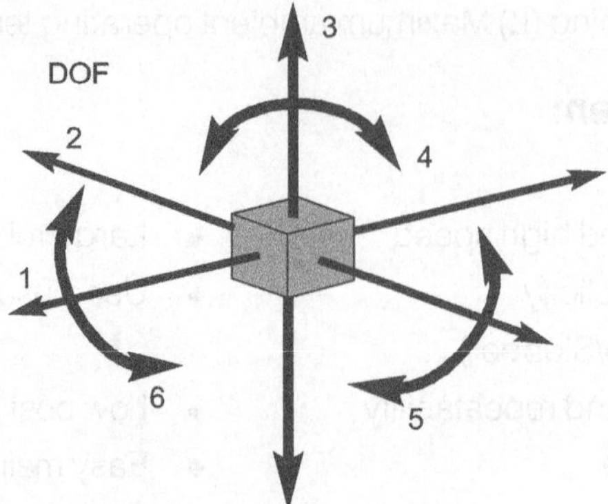

Fig. 10.18: Degree of Freedom

Pair Variable

The Co-ordinates that are used to describe the relative movement is called Pair variable.

In Robotics we deal with the two types of Kinematics. They are:

1. Direct or Forward Kinematics
2. Inverse Kinematics

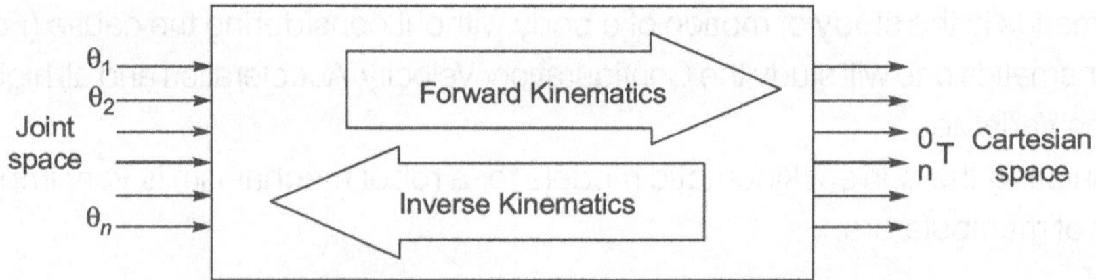

Fig. 10.19: Direct and Inverse Kinematics

1. Direct or Forward Kinematics

The primary objective of the robotic manipulator is to control both the position and orientation of the tool in three dimensional spaces. This requires the formulation of a relationship between the joint variables and the position and orientation of the tool which is termed as the direct kinematics problem.

The solution to the direct kinematics problem requires the representation of position and orientation of the mobile tool with respect to a coordinate frame attached to the fixed base, this involves a sequence of coordinate transformations, involving both rotations and translations, from tool to wrist, wrist to elbow and so on; with each coordinate transformations represented by matrix.

Denavit-Hartenberg Notation:

- Any robot can be described kinematically by 4 quantities of each link
  - ♦ Two for the link
  - ♦ Two to describe the link's connection
- For revolute joints θ_1 is called joint variable (the other there quantities are fixed).
- For Prismatic joints, *di* is the joint variable (the other three quantities are fixed).
- The definition of mechanisms by means of these quantities is called as Denavit - Hartenberg notation.

In Forward or Direct Kinematics

Given information: The values of the joint variables.

Required information: The Position and orientation of the end effector.

2. Inverse Kinematics

The Inverse Kinematics problem of a Robot is stated as "given the desired end-effector position, what must be the angles at all of the robots joints?"

Humans solve this problem all the time without even thinking about it. When we are lifting something from floor we just reach out and lift it. We don't think, "my shoulder needs to do this, my elbow needs to do that, etc.

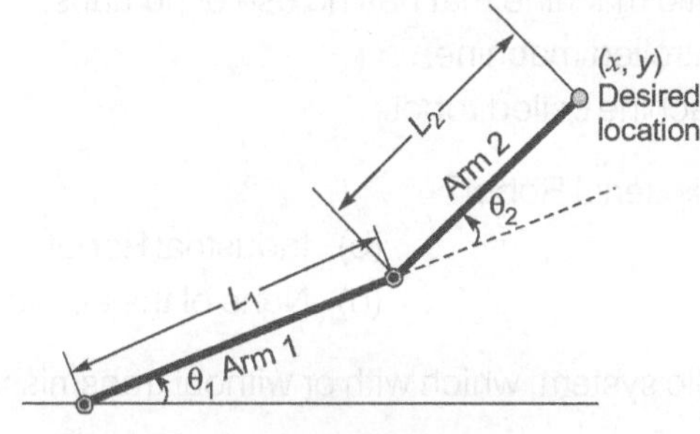

Fig. 10.20

To lift the object present at the desired location (x, y) the Arm 1 has to make an angle of θ_1 with the horizontal and the Arm 2 has to make the angle of θ_2 with the Arm 1 as shown above. This kind of analysis is done in the Inverse Kinematics problem.

In Inverse Kinematics

Given data: The position and the orientation of the end effector.

Required data: The values of the joint Variables.

PRACTICE QUESTIONS

1. Which of the following is not the functionality of Robot?
   (a) Reprogramability (b) Multifuctionality
   (c) Responsibility (d) Efficient Performance

2. Which of the following is not the categorization of Robot?
   (a) Robot is a manipulator which controlled by computer program.
   (b) Robot is an automatic machine that has no use of humans.
   (c) Robots is a self controlled machine.
   (d) Semi automated machine called robot.

3. Which of the following is serial Robot?
   (a) Commercial Robot (b) Industrial Robot
   (c) In House Robot (d) None of the above

4. Pneumatic and Hydraulic system, which with or without transmission elements provides motion to robot links is called?
   (a) Motor (b) Sensor
   (c) Actuator (d) None of the above

5. Which is not the classification of robot?
   (a) Cylindrical Robot (b) Revolute Robot
   (c) Spherical Robot (d) None of the above

6. According to motion of arm which of following is a type of robot?
   (a) Physical manipulator (b) Continuous path robot
   (c) Fixed sequence robot (d) Intelligent robot

7. According to technique used which of the following is not a type of robot?
   (a) Trouble-free robots (b) Average technique robot
   (c) Complicated industrial robot (d) Point to point robot

8. The configuration of a robot using a telescoping arm that can be raised or lowered on a horizontal pivot mounted on a rotating base is called
   (a) Polar (b) Cylindrical
   (c) Cartesian coordinate (d) Jointed arm

9. Trajectory of a robot means:
   (a) Path traced by the end effectors (b) Kinematics of Robot
   (c) Robot joints (d) Robot programming

10. Which part of a robot provides motion to the manipulator and end-effectors?
    (a) Controller (b) Sensor
    (c) Actuator (d) All of the above

11. Which of the following is not the type of actuator?
    (a) Digital Actuator (b) Pneumatic Actuator
    (c) Hydraulic and eclectic actuator (d) None of the above

12. The physical structure of Robot which moves around is called?
(a) Manipulator (b) End-effectors
(c) Joints (d) Links

13. The kinematic part of the robot or manipulator is called.
(a) Links (b) Joints
(c) End-effectors (d) None of the above

14. In a robot or manipulator comprises part is called.
(a) Links (b) Joints
(c) End-effectors (d) None of the above

15. What is the full form of SCARA?
(a) Sliding Compliance Assembly Robot Arm
(b) Selective Compliance Accumulated Robot Arm
(c) Selective Compliance Assembly Robot Arm
(d) Selective Compliance Assembly Robot ambient

16. SCARA robot works on the principle of which type of axis?
(a) 3-axis robot (b) 2-axis robot
(c) 4-axis robot (d) None of the above

17. SCARA arm is rigid in which direction?
(a) X-direction (b) Y-direction
(c) XY-direction (d) Z-direction

18. In a robot the 'Rotary Joints' are known as
(a) Revolute (b) Prismatic
(c) Cylindrical (d) Spherical

19. In a robot the 'Translatory Joints' is known as
(a) Revolute (b) Prismatic
(c) Cylindrical (d) Spherical

20. SCARA robot is very suitable in which kind of operations?
(a) Single operation (b) Rotary operation
(c) Assembly operation (d) Translatory operation

21. Which of the following is the type of joints in Robot?
(a) Rotary Joints (b) Translatory Joints
(c) Revaluate Joints (d) (a) and (b) only

22. Which one of the following is the third basic component of robots besides power supply and control (memory) console?
(a) Software (b) Coaxial cable
(c) Mechanical unit arm (d) Microcomputer

23. Which of the following is not a important parameters of robot?
(a) Axes of motion (b) Arm movement
(c) Wrist movement (d) Physical manipulator

24. Consider the following statements:
Good dynamic performance is usually difficult to achieve in robots which contain a rotary base because
1. Position, speed and acceleration of the other joints cause variations in the reflected torque and moment of inertia.
2. The moment of inertia reflected at the base depends upon the weight of the object being carried.
3. The moment of inertia reflected at the base also depends upon the distance between the base axis and the manipulated object.

Which of the above statements is/are correct?
(a) 1, 2 and 3 b) 2 and 3 only
(c) 1 only d) 1 and 3 only

25. Consider the following characteristics of a robot:
1. The tip of the robot arm moves from one point to another with its in-between path not being defined.
2. It can be used for drilling holes at difference points in a workpiece.
3. It can be used for *V* butt joint welding between two points.
4. The memory capacity required for its control unit is low.

Which of these are the characteristics associated with a point to point robot?
(a) 1 and 2 (b) 1, 3 and 4
(c) 1, 2 and 4 (d) 2, 3 and 4

26. What is the full form of AGV?
(a) Automated Grouped Vehicles (b) Alternative Guided Vehicles
(c) Automatic Guided Vehicles (d) All time Guided Vehicles

27. In which of the following categories of Robot AGV placed?
(a) A saturated robot (b) A mobile robot
(c) A uncontrolled robot (d) A natural robot

28. A cylindrical robot has how many types of linear axes?
(a) One (b) Two
(c) Three (d) Four

29. If the arm can rotate about all three axes, the robot is called
(a) Jointed arm (b) Polar coordinates
(c) Cartesian coordinate (d) None of the above

30. Single wheel robots are called as
(a) Legged robots (b) Arm robots
(c) Ball robots (d) 4-axis robots

31. Maximum possible number of degrees of freedom for a rigid body in a plane motion is
(a) 6 (b) 3
(c) 2 (d) 5

32. An android takes the form of:
(a) An insect
(b) A human body
(c) A simple robot with human appearance
(d) Binocular vision

33. An automotive robot might best keep itself traveling down a specific lane of traffic by using:
(a) Binaural hearing (b) Epi-polar navigation
(c) Edge detection (d) A second-generation end effector

34. A rule-based system is also known as:
(a) Artificial intelligence (b) An expert system
(c) An analytical engine (d) An automated guided vehicle

35. According to motion of the arms which of following is a type of robot?
(a) Physical manipulator (b) Continuous path robot
(c) Fixed sequence robot (d) Intelligent robot

36. In which year, one of the first humanoid robots was exhibited at the annual exhibition of the model engineers society in London?
(a) 1930 (b) 1920
(c) 1928 (d) 1924

37. Who invented first humanoid robots?
(a) Czech (b) Josef capek
(c) W.H.Richards (d) None of the above

38. Who created the first electronic autonomous robots with complex behaviour?
(a) Gakutensoku (b) Archibald Low
(c) William Grey Walter (d) Rodon Brooks

39. The first palletizing robot was introduced in which year?
(a) 1947 (b) 1940
(c) 1936 (d) 1963

40. The figure below represents a triangle *PQR* with initial coordinates of the vertices as *P*(1,3) *Q*(4,5) and *R*(5,3.5). The triangle is rotated in the X-Y plane about the vertex *P* by angle θ in clockwise direction. If $\sin\theta = 0.6$ and $\cos\theta = 0.8$, the new coordinates of the vertex *Q* are: 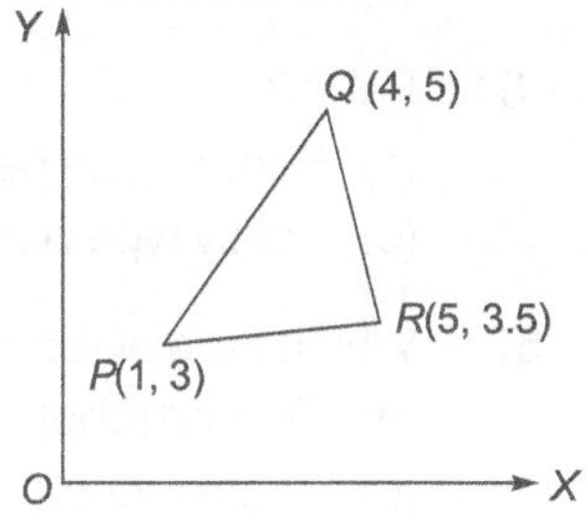
(a) (4.6, 2.8) (b) (3.2, 4.6)
(c) (7.9, 5.5) (d) (5.5, 7.9)

Y
Q (4, 5)
R(5, 3.5)
P(1, 3)
O
X

41. There are two points *P* & *Q* on a planar rigid body. The relative velocity between the two points
(a) should always be along *PQ*.
(b) can be Oriented along any direction.
(c) should always be perpendicular to *PQ*.
(d) should be along *QP* when the body undergoes pure translation.

42. Who invented the first robot in the world?
(a) George Devol (b) Czech
(c) Archibald low (d) None of the above

43. The scara robot was developed under the guidance of
(a) Sankyo Seiki (b) Hiroshi Makino
(c) William Grey Walter (d) None of the above

44. In contrast with expensive big robots which robots are cheap and simple?
(a) Virtual robots (b) Stationary robots
(c) Beam robots (d) Mechanical robots

45. A manipulator is also known as a:
(a) Track drive (b) Robot arm
(c) Vision system (d) Robot controller

46. Spherical coordinates can uniquely define the position of a point in up to:
(a) One dimension (b) Two dimensions
(c) Three dimensions (d) Four dimensions

47. There are two points *P* and *Q* on a planar rigid body. The relative velocity between the two points
(a) should always be along *PQ*.
(b) can be oriented along any direction.
(c) should always be perpendicular to *PQ*.
(d) should be along *QP* when the body undergoes pure translation.

48. The physical structure of Robot which moves around is called?
(a) Manipulator (b) End-effectors
(c) Joints (d) Links

49. The kinematic part of the robot or manipulator is called
(a) Links (b) Joints
(c) End-effectors (d) None of the above

50. The Tripedal Robot is which type of Robot?
(a) Wheeled robot (b) Legged Robot
(c) Stationary Robot (d) None of the above

51. PaPeRo stands for _______.
(a) Partner-type personal robot (b) Partial type personal robot
(c) Policy type partial robot (d) None of the above

52. Which type of robots are fixed in one place and cannot move?
(a) Ground robots (b) Military robots
(c) Scara robots (d) Stationary robots

53. The number of ways in which a robot arm can move is known as:
(a) Degrees of rotation (b) Degrees of freedom
(c) Degrees of arc (d) Coordinate geometry

54. A Robot arm *PQ* with end Coordinates *P*(0, 0) and *Q*(2, 5) rotates counter clockwise about *P* in the *XY* plane by 90 degrees. The new coordinate pair of the end point *Q* is:
(a) (–2, 5) (b) (–5, 2)
(c) (–5, –2) (d) (2, –5)

55. In the Inverse kinematics problem which of the following information about the end effector is known?
(a) Only Position (b) Only orientation
(c) Both Position and Orientation (d) None of the above

56. The region throughout which a robot arm can accomplish tasks is called its:
(a) Coordinate geometry (b) Reference axis
(c) Reference frame (d) Work envelope

57. What is the name for information sent from robot sensors to robot controllers?
(a) Temperature (b) Pressure
(c) Feedback (d) Signal

58. Robots that have been designed to operate in low gravity environment such as
(a) Aerial robots (b) Earth orbit
(c) Underwater vehicles (d) None of the above

59. A Cartesian coordinate robot also called
(a) Linear robot (b) Cylindrical robot
(c) Spherical robot (d) Axis robot

60. In orthogonal joint the input and output links are ________.
(a) Parallel to each other (b) Co-linear to each other
(c) Perpendicular to each other (d) Can rotate at any angle

OOOO

ANSWERS

ROBOTS

1. (c)	**2.** (a)	**3.** (b)	**4.** (c)	**5.** (d)	**6.** (b)	**7.** (d)
8. (b)	**9.** (a)	**10.** (c)	**11.** (a)	**12.** (a)	**13.** (b)	**14.** (a)
15. (c)	**16.** (c)	**17.** (d)	**18.** (a)	**19.** (b)	**20.** (c)	**21.** (d)
22. (c)	**23.** (d)	**24.** (b)	**25.** (c)	**26.** (c)	**27.** (b)	**28.** (b)
29. (a)	**30.** (c)	**31.** (b)	**32.** (b)	**33.** (c)	**34.** (b)	**35.** (b)
36. (c)	**37.** (c)	**38.** (c)	**39.** (d)	**40.** (a)	**41.** (c)	**42.** (a)
43. (a)	**44.** (c)	**45.** (b)	**46.** (c)	**47.** (c)	**48.** (a)	**49.** (b)
50. (b)	**51.** (a)	**52.** (d)	**53.** (b)	**54.** (b)	**55.** (c)	**56.** (d)
57. (c)	**58.** (b)	**59.** (a)	**60.** (c)			

CHAPTER 11

Quality Control

11.1 INTRODUCTION

Quality is having two types of definition.According to the +ve concept it is "Fitness for use". According to Philip B Crossbay "it conformers to requirement and not goodness". Taguchi propounded a negative concept of Quality and according to him "Quality is the loss suffered by the society by using the product". For example a thermosetting plastic manufacturing company, how much damage it incurs to the environment decides, the quality of product.Quality control may generally be defined as a system that maintains a desired level of quality, through feedback on product/service characteristics and implementation of remedial actions, in case of a deviation of such characteristics from a specified standard. This general area may be divided into three main subareas: off-line quality control, statistical process control, and acceptance sampling plans.

11.2 SEVEN QUALITY CONTROL TOOLS

1. Histogram
2. Pareto analysis
3. Cause of effect (Fish-bone diagram)
4. Defect concentration diagram
5. Check sheets
6. Scatter diagram
7. Control chart

11.2.1 Histogram

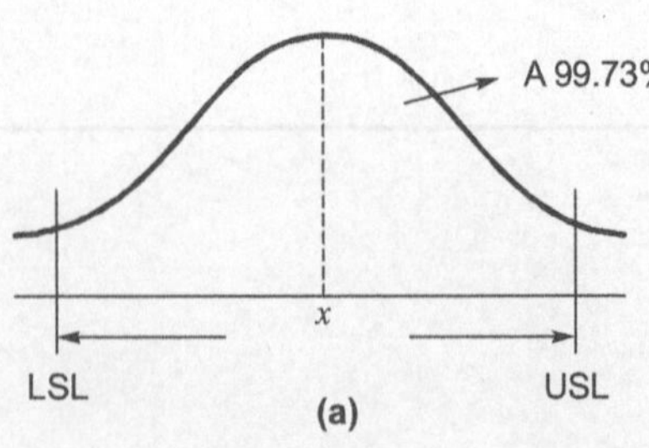

(a)

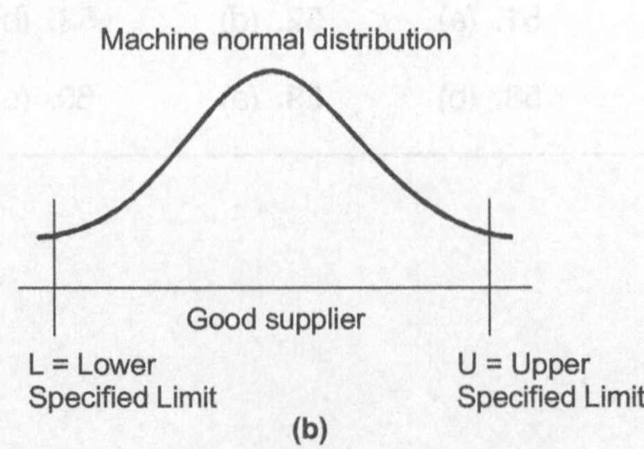

(b)

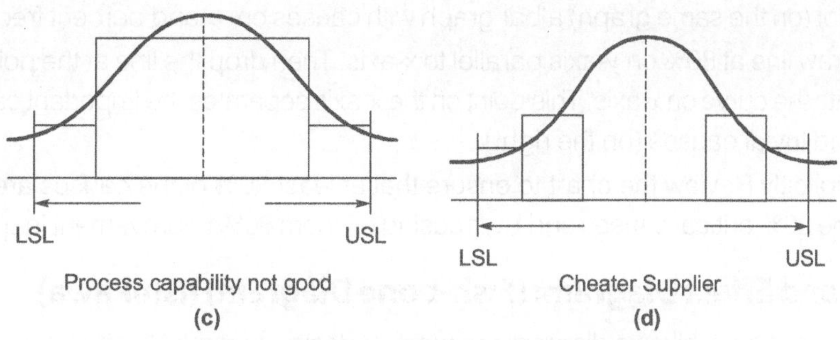

Fig: 11.1 Normal Distribution (Histogram)

Histogram is a tool by which process capability of machine at the suppliers end can be understood by just sitting at receivers end. When a lot of raw material is received, each and every product is checked and Histogram is plotted.

If Histogram appears like Fig. 11.1 (b), it means machine at supplier end are capable to produce component within the specification limits. If histogram appears as shown in Fig. 11.1 (c) it means machines are not capable and after producing the component supplier is inspecting at his end. If sometimes he forgets to inspect the component due to some reason quality of my product at the receiver's end will suffer.

If histogram appears as shown in Fig. 11.1 (d), it means although the machines are capable enough but the best quality product suppliers sending somewhere else. So supplier is not very reliable.

11.2.2 Pareto Analysis (80–20 rule)

Pareto analysis is a statistical technique in decision making that is used for selection of a limited number of tasks that produce significant overall effect. It uses the Pareto principle – the idea that by doing 20% of work, 80% of the advantage of doing the entire job can be generated. Or in terms of quality improvement a large majority of problems (80%) are produced by a few key causes (20%). Pareto analysis is a formal technique useful where many possible courses of action are competing for attention. In essence, the problem-solver estimates the benefit delivered by each action, then selects a number of the most effective actions that deliver a total benefit reasonably close to the maximal possible one.

Pareto analysis is a creative way of looking at causes of problems because it helps stimulate thinking and organize thoughts. However, it can be limited by its exclusion of possibly important problems which may be small initially, but which grow with time. It should be combined with other analytical tools such as failure mode and effects analysis and fault free analysis for example. This technique helps to identify the top 20% of causes that needs to be addressed to resolve the 80% of the problems. Once the top 20% of the causes are identified, then tools like the Ishikawa diagram or Fish-bone analysis can be used to identify the root causes of the problems. The application of the Pareto analysis in risk management allows management to focus on the 20% of the risks that have the most impact on the project.

Steps to Identify the Important Causes using Pareto Analysis:

Step 1: Form an explicit table listing the causes and their frequency as a percentage.

Step 2: Arrange the rows in the decreasing order of importance of the causes (i.e., the most important cause first).

Step 3: Add a cumulative percentage column to the table.

Step 4: Plot with causes on x-and cumulative percentage on *y*-axis.

Step 5: Join the above points to form a curve.

Step 6: Plot (on the same graph) a bar graph with causes on $-x$ and percent frequency on y-axis.

Step 7: Draw line at 80% on y-axis parallel to x-axis. Then drop the line at the point of intersection with the curve on x-axis. This point on the x-axis separates the important causes (on the left) and trivial causes (on the right).

Step 8: Explicitly Review the chart to ensure that at least 80% of the causes are captured.

There will be 20% critical causes and by focusing on them 80% improvement in quality is possible.

11.2.3. Cause and Effect Diagram: (Fish-bone Diagram) (Ishikawa)

Common uses of the Ishikawa diagram are product design and quality effect prevention, to identify potential factors causing an overall effect. Each cause or reason for imperfection is a source of variation. Causes are usually grouped into major categories to identify these sources of variation.

Once a defect comes out by looking at this diagram its origin can be diagnosed and corrective action can be taken.

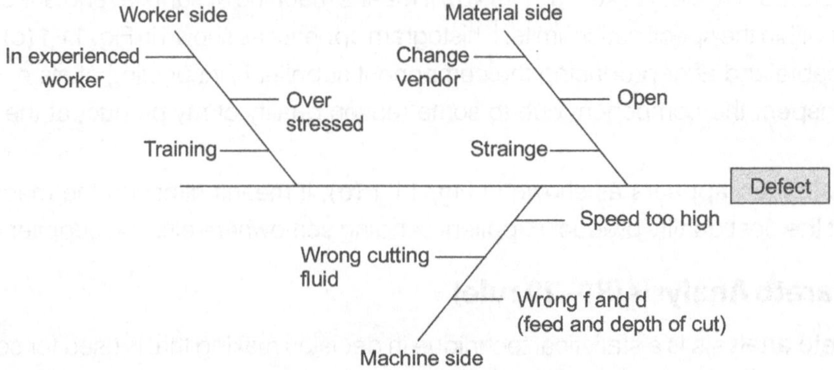

Fig: 11.2 Fish bone diagram

11.2.4 Defect Concentration Diagram (Stratification)

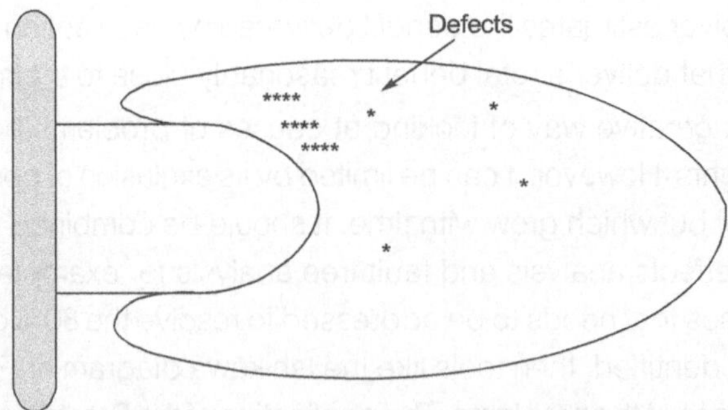

Fig: 11.3 Defect concentration diagram

The diagram of product is plotted over paper and as soon as a defective piece comes out the location of defect is plotted over paper. When certain number of defectives comes out of the machine these diagrams are analyzed and if the concentration is more at a particular point it means there is some problem in die at that location.

11.2.5 Check Sheets

It is the initial stage of plotting the histogram and data is stored in the form of tables. Check sheets are specifically used when there are number of quality characteristics that have to be controlled.

11.2.6 Scatter Diagrams

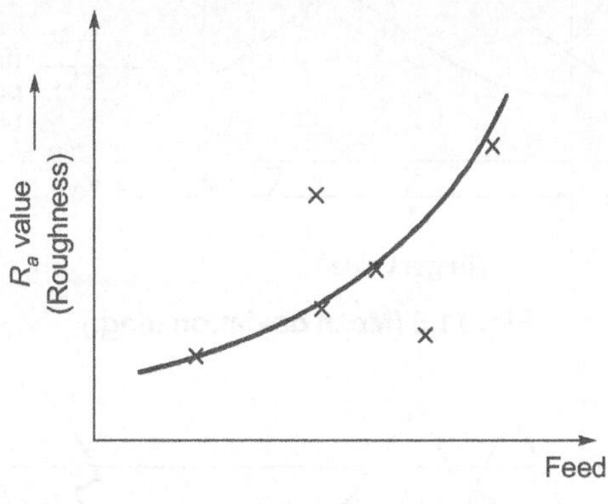

Fig: 11.4

Scatter diagrams are plotted between quality characteristic and one variable e.g. Roughness valued and feed. If roughness appears to be expected than corrective action should not be taken.

11.2.7 Control Charts

Control chart tells us when to allow the process to continue or avoid unnecessary adjustments with machine and when to take the corrective action. On to same problem either on the material side or from the operator side it is quite possible that either targeted value $\bar{x}$ has changed, or σ' (Process dispersion) has changed. These changes must be reflected on the control chart so that the corrective action can be taken. Quality characteristics fall into two broad classes: variables and attributes. Characteristics that are measurable and are expressed on a numerical scale are called variables. The waiting time in a bank before being served, expressed in minutes, is a variable, as are the density of a liquid in grams per cubic centimeter and the resistance of a coil in ohms. Prior to defining an attribute, we should defined a nonconformity and a nonconforming unit. A nonconformity is a quality characteristic that does not meet its stipulated specifications. Let's say that the specification to produce shafts of 25 ± 0.3 mm diameter. If we have a shaft having diameter 45 mm, its geometry is a non-conformity. A non-conforming unit has one or more non-conformities such that the unit is unable to meet the intended standards and is unable to function as required. A quality characteristic is said to be an attribute if it is classified as either conforming or non-conforming to a stipulated specification. A quality characteristic that cannot be measured on a numerical scale is expressed as an attribute. For example, the color of a fabric is either acceptable or not. However, there are some variables that are treated as attributes because it is simpler to measure them this way or because it is difficult to obtain data on them. For example, the diameter of a shaft is a variable. But if we measure the diameter using a GO/NOGO gage and classify it as either conforming or nonconforming (with respect to some established specifications), the characteristic is expressed as an attribute. The reasons for using a GO/NOGO gage, as opposed to a micrometer, could be economic; that is, the time needed to obtain a measurement using a GO/NOGO gage may be much shorter and hence less expensive.

Variable control charts are used for those quality characteristics which follow normal distribution. e.g.: Length, diameter etc. Attributes refers to those characteristics when cannot be measured directly like. Appearance, % defective, number of missing rivets etc. e.g. *C* charts, *p* and 100 *p* charts.

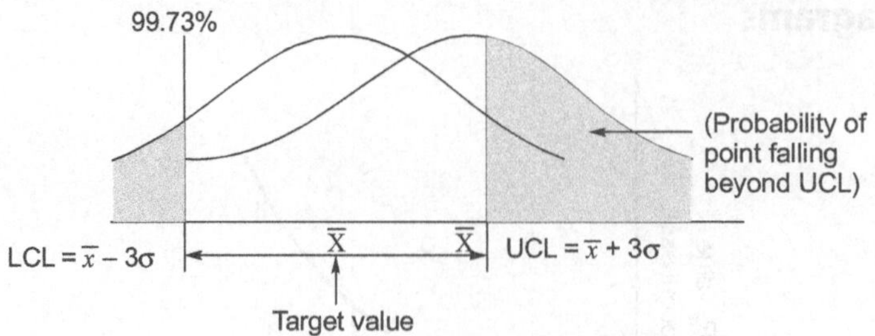

Fig: 11.5 (Mean deviation diag.)

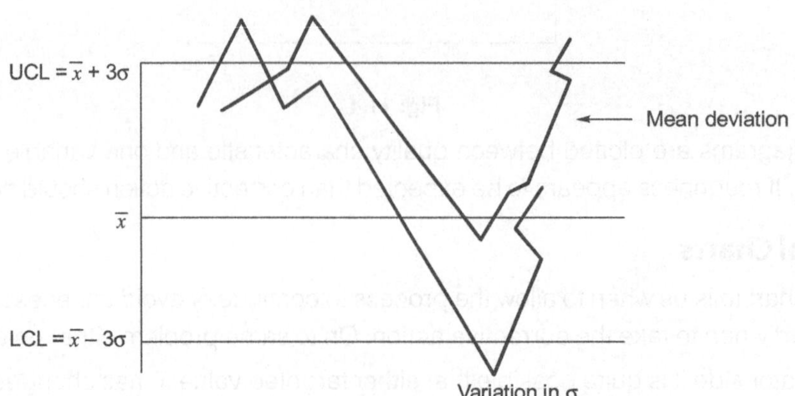

Fig: 11.6 $\bar{X}$ chart with shift in the process mean

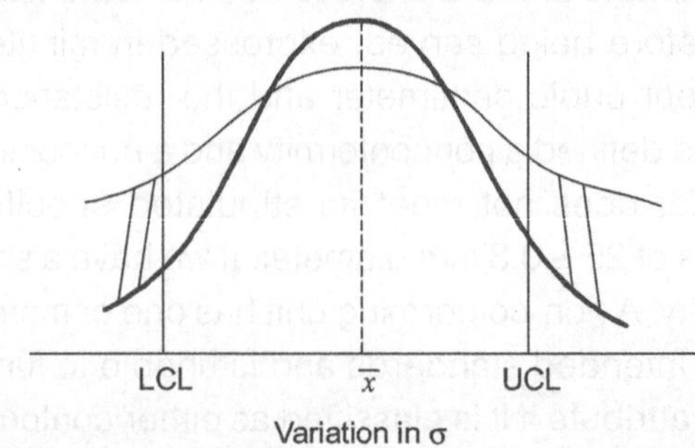

Fig: 11.7 Normal distribution with variation in standard deviation

Following are the factors that change the mean of the process.

1. Tool and Die wear
2. m/c vibrations
3. Wear or minor failureof machine parts change of machine or process
4. Change of m/c or process

Following are the factors that changes the process dispersion

1. Deviation of depression
2. Carelessness of operator
3. New or inexperienced work
4. Frequent resetting of m/c
5. Deterioration in condition of m/c

Control chart tells us when to allow the process to continue and not taking corrective actions and when the process is actually shifted and hence the corrective act on should be taken.When the process mean has shifted in forward direction as shown in Fig. 11.5 it can be seen that area of the normal distribution above the UCL increases. And over the control charts 11.6 points start falling over the control limit between mean and UCL. If the process dispersion has changed as shown Fig. 11.7. Points on the control charts Fig. 11.6 starts falling simultaneously above the UCL and below the LCL.

11.3 TYPES OF ERRORS IN CONTROL CHARTS

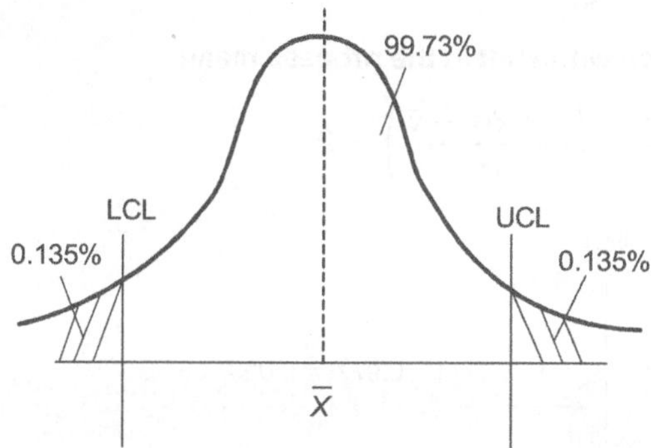

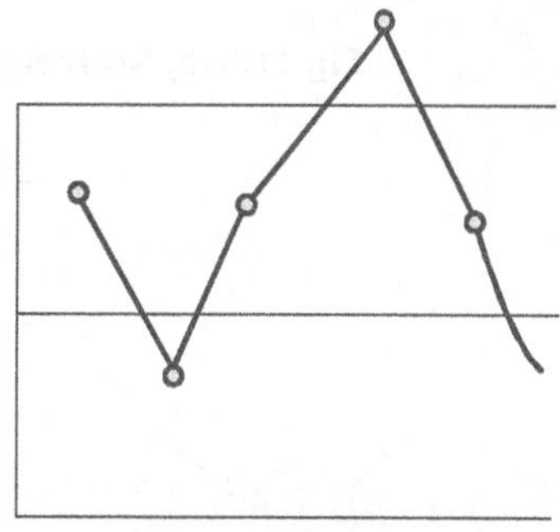

Fig: 11.8

11.3.1 Type-1 Error or α-error

In any production process, regardless of how well designed or carefully maintained certain amount of inherent or natural variability will always exist. This natural variability or "background noise" is the cumulative effect of many small, essentially unavoidable causes. In the framework of statistical quality control, this natural variability is often called a "stable system of change causes." A process that is operating with only **change causes of variation** present is said to be **in statistical control.** In other words, the chance causes are an inherent part of the process.

Other kinds of variability may occasionally be present in the output of a process. This variability in key quality characteristic usually arises from three sources: Improperly adjusted or controlled machines, operator errors, or defective raw material. Such variability is generally large when compared to be background noise, and it usually represents an unacceptable level of process performance. We refer to these sources of variability that are not part of the chance cause pattern as **assignable causes of variation.** A process that is operating in the presence of assignable cause is said to be an **out-of-control process.**

A major objective of statistical process control is to quickly detect the occurrence of assignable causes of process shifts so that investigation of the process and corrective action may be undertaken before many nonconforming units are manufactured. The **control chart** is an on-line process-monitoring technique widely used for the purpose. Although the process is within the statistical control i.e., Neither mean nor standard deviation has changed but still there is some are under the normal distribution beyond the control limits Fig. 11.8 due to which points will fall beyond the control limits. These are called chance causes and no corrective action should be taken. Total area beyond the control limits is called probability of type-1 error or α-error.

11.3.2 Type-2 – Error (β-error) (Assignable causes)

Suppose the process mean has shifted by "σ′"

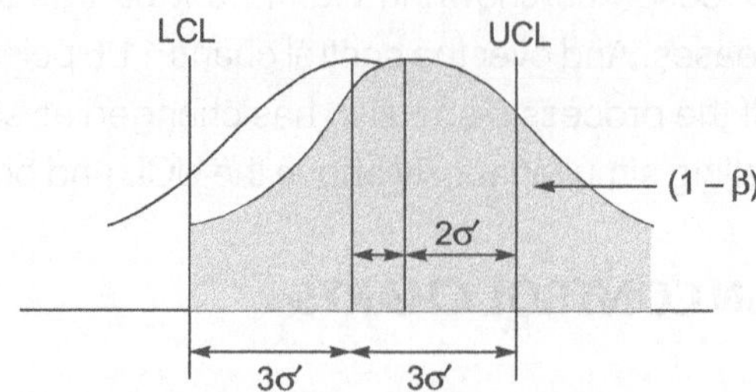

Fig 11.9 (a) Normal distribution with shift in the process mean

$$Z = \frac{x - \bar{x}}{\sigma'} = \left(\frac{\bar{x} + 2\sigma' - \bar{x}}{\sigma'}\right) = 2$$

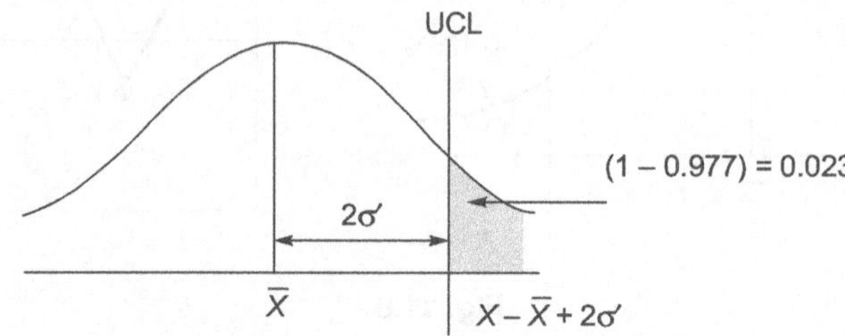

Fig 11.9 (b) Distribution area falling beyond UCL

$$\beta = 0.9773$$

$$\text{Average run length (ARL)} = \frac{1}{1-\beta} = \frac{1}{0.023} = 44$$

If the process mean has shifted by σ′ but still a major portion of area will show under control points. This probability is called type-2 – error or β- error.

It can be seen in the above analysis that if the mean has been shifted by σ′ than 1 out of 44 observation will show a point out of UCL. So sensitivity of X chart is very poor

11.4 $\bar{X}$ - CHARTS

To improve the sensitivity of x-chart, $\bar{x}$- charts are used. Here rather than individual sample, select group and calculate mean and range within the subgroup.

N	Group of 4					
1	X_1	X_2	X_3	X_4	$\bar{X}$	$R = X_{max} - X_{min}$
1	—	—	—	—	—	—
2	—	—	—	—	—	—
1	—	—	—	—	—	—
1	—	—	—	—	—	—
1	—	—	—	—	—	—
N	$\bar{X} = \frac{X_1 + X_2 + X_3 + X_4}{n}$				n = Number of sub groups	
	$\bar{R} = \frac{\Sigma R}{N}$				N = Number of groups	

Control Limit for $\bar{X}$-Charts

$$\bar{x} \pm 3\sigma_{\bar{x}} = \bar{x} \pm 3\frac{\sigma'}{\sqrt{n}} \left\{\sigma_{\bar{x}} = \frac{\sigma'}{\sqrt{n}}\right\}$$

Where n is sub group size.

Also control limits can be represented by

$$C.L. = \bar{x} \pm A_2\bar{R}$$

$$\sigma' = \frac{\bar{R}}{d_2},$$

Where A_2 and d_2 are constants depends up on the subgroup size.

Control Limits for *R*-Chart

R-Charts are used when $n \le 9$

$$UCL = D_4\bar{R} = D_2\sigma'$$

$$LCL = D_3\bar{R} = D_1\sigma'$$

$$D_2, D_1 = 0 \text{ for } n \le 6$$

Control Limits for σ-Chart

σ-charts are used when $n \ge 9$

$UCL = B_4\,\bar{\sigma} = B_2\,\sigma'$

$LCL = B_3\,\bar{\sigma} = B_1\,\sigma'$

$\sigma_{\bar{x}}$ = Std., deviation of $\bar{x}$-chart

σ' = Std., deviation of the process

Effect of '*n*' on the sensitivity of $\bar{x}$-chart

Suppose, $n = 4$

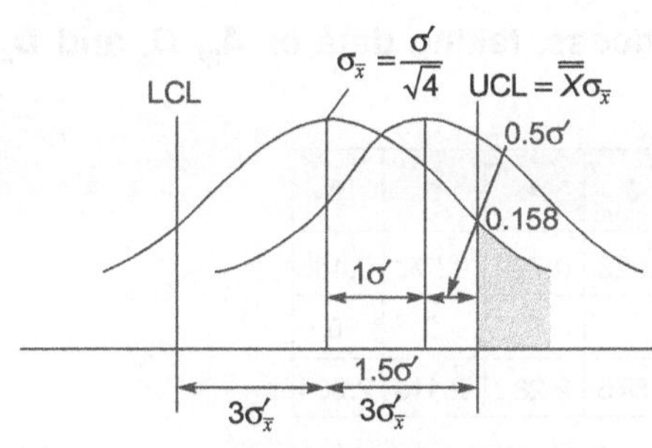

Fig: 11.10 (a)

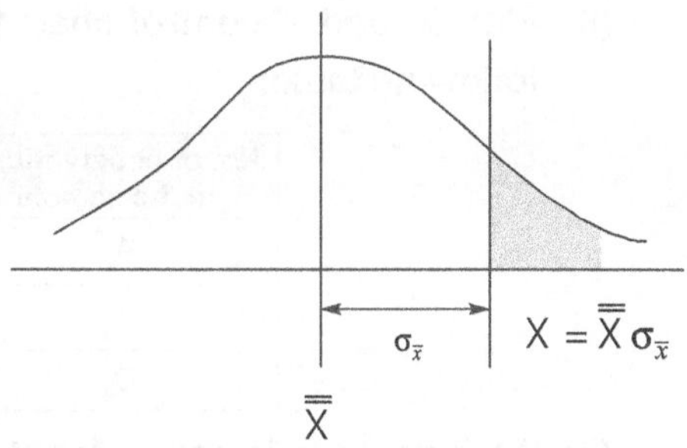

Fig: 11.10 (b)

$$\sigma\bar{x} = \frac{\sigma'}{\sqrt{n}} = \frac{\sigma'}{2}$$

So, $$\sigma' = 2\sigma_{\bar{x}}$$

$$z = \frac{x - \bar{x}}{\sigma_{\bar{x}}} = \frac{(\bar{x} + 0.5\sigma') - \bar{x}}{\sigma_{\bar{x}}} = 1$$

From normal distributions table are corresponding to $z = 1$ is 0.842

Average run length (ARL) samples $= \frac{1}{1-\beta} = 6.3$

So total observation taken before a point falls outside UCL = 6.3 × 4 = 25.2

It can be seen in the above analysis that for a subgroup size 4 when then process mean shifts by σ′ control chat will show a point out of upper control limit in approximately 6.3 samples or 25 observations. This means that $\bar{x}$ charts are more sensitive than x–charts. This sensitively will improve by increasing the sample size.

For $n = 9$

$$\sigma_{\bar{x}} = \frac{\sigma'}{\sqrt{9}} = \frac{\sigma'}{3}$$

$$x = x = \bar{x} \pm 3\sigma_{\bar{x}} = \bar{x} \pm \sigma'$$

$$z = \frac{x - \bar{x}}{\sigma_{\bar{x}}} = 0$$

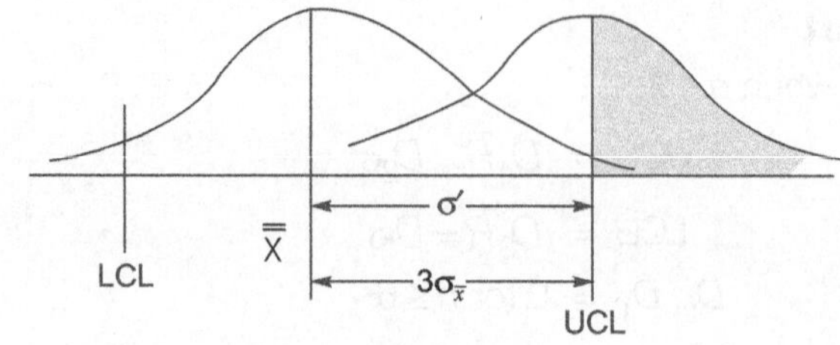

Fig: 11.11

Since 50% are is falling beyond UCL so every second point will show out of control.

Example: 11.1

A process was set to produce rivets of 10 mm length. The first 32 pieces made by the process were found to have the following lengths (in mm):

9.9,	10.0,	10.0,	9.9,	9.9,	9.9,	10.0,	10.0,
10.1,	10.1	10.0,	10.0,	9.9,	10.1,	10.1,	9.9,
9.9,	10.1,	10.0,	10.1,	10.0,	9.9,	9.9,	9.9,
10.1,	10.0,	10.0,	10.1,	10.0,	10.0,	10.0,	10.1,

(i) Plot $\bar{X}$ and R control chart for the process, taking data or A_2, D_3 and D_4 from the following table:

No. of observations in the sample	2	3	4	5	6
A_2	1.88	1.023	0.729	0.577	0.483
D_3	0	0	0	0	0
D_4	3.276	2.575	2.282	2.115	2.004

(ii) If the process is not under statistical control, discuss what steps should be taken to make the control chart viable?

Solution:

Let us take subgroup size '4'

S. No	X_1	X_2	X_3	X_4	$\bar{X}$	$\bar{R}$
1	9.9	10.0	10.0	9.99	9.95	0.1
2	9.9	9.9	10.0	10.0	9.95	0.1
3	10.1	10.1	10.0	10.0	10.05	0.1
4	9.9	10.1	10.1	9.99	10	0.2
5	9.9	10.1	10	10.1	10.025	0.2
6	10	9.9	9.9	9.9	9.925	0.1
7	10.1	10	10	10.1	10.05	0.1
8	10	10	10	10.1	10.025	0.1
						R = 0.125

For $n = 4$

$A_2 = 0.729$

$D_3 = 0, D_4 = 2.282$

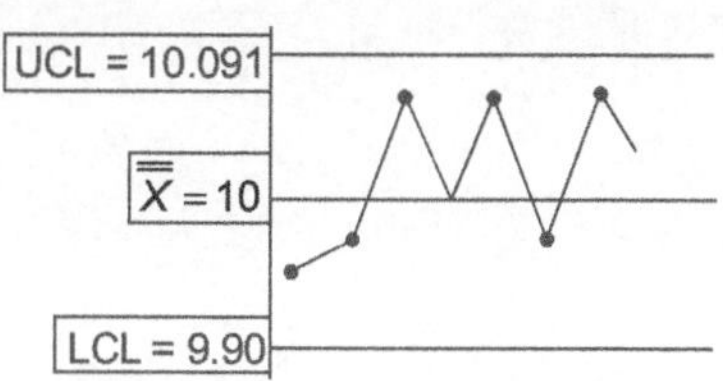

(i) $\bar{x}$- Chart:

$$UCL = \bar{x} + A_2\bar{R} = 10 + 0.729 \times 0.125 = 10.091$$

$$LCL = \bar{\bar{x}} - A_2\bar{R} = 9.90$$

On $\bar{x}$ chart it can be seen that 3 out of 6 consecutive points are falling in between $\bar{\bar{x}}$ and UCL and the probability of this event according to the chance is very low. It is also observed from $\bar{R}$ chart that all the points are falling with in control limits so that is no change in σ. So it is quite possible that due to wear on tool, machine vibration etc the process mean might have shifted in upward direction. So the corrective action can be taken.

(ii) *R*-Chart

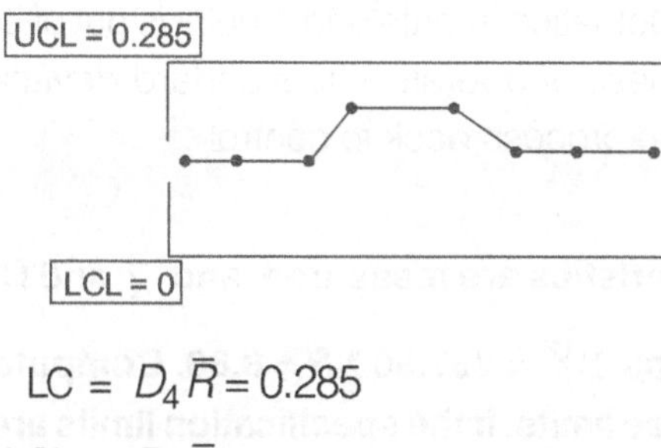

$$LC = D_4\bar{R} = 0.285$$

$$LCL = D_3\bar{R} = 0$$

Example: 11.2

What is the different between control charts for variables and attributes? Where do you need a larger sample size in the above and why? 4 batches of products are inspected at 90 minute intervals and their percentage differences in weigh from the nominal are given below. Assume that normal process average variation is 0.9% and process standard deviation is 0.5%, range UCL is 5 times 5D, plot $\bar{X}$ - R chart indicating various control limits. Is the process under control?

Solution:

First 2 sections of the problem are answered in sections 11.1.7 and 11.3 respectively. As given in the problem subgroups of 5 items each are taken from a manufacturing process at regular intervals.

B-I	B-2	B-3	B-4
1.2	0.6	0.6	2.1
1.8	0.3	1.5	0.6
1.5	0.3	1.0	0.6
0.9	0.0	0.0	2.7
0.3	0.3	1.9	2.7
X→1.14	0.3	1.0	1.74
R→1.5	0.6	1.9	2.1

Here, $n = 5$

$\bar{x} = 0.9$

$\sigma' = 0.5$

(i) $\bar{x}$- Chart:

$$C.L. = \bar{x} \pm \frac{3\sigma'}{\sqrt{n}} = 0.9 \pm 3 \times \frac{0.5}{\sqrt{5}}$$

$$UCL = 1.570$$

$$LCL = 0.229$$

(ii) *R*-Chart:

$$UCL_{\bar{R}} = 5\sigma' = 5 \times 0.5 = 2.5$$

$$LCL_{\bar{R}} = 0$$

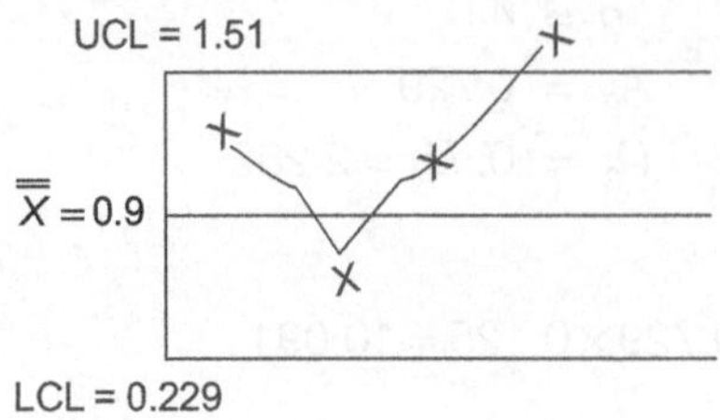

(iii) *R*-Chart:

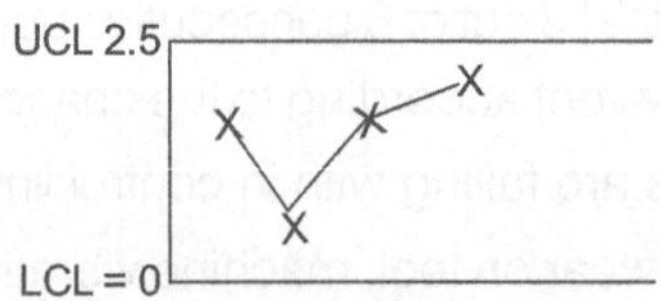

R-chart indicates the variation in the process dispersion and it can be seen in the *R*-chart that there is an upward trend and two consecutive points are falling very close to UCL. Same thing is reflected over $\bar{x}$ chart that there is heavy fluctuation in data and 1 point is out of UCL. This indicate that either due to frequent resetting or carelessness of operator the standard deviation has increased so corrective action should be taken to bring the process back to control.

Example: 11.3

A certain quality characteristics are measured, and $\bar{X}$ and R values are computed for each subgroup. After 25 groups $\Sigma\bar{X}$ = 357.50 ΣR = 8.80. Compute control chart limits. All point both charts fall within these limits. If the specification limits are 14.40 ± 0.40 what conclusions can you draw about the ability of the existing process to produce items within these specifications? Suggest possible ways in which the situation could be improved.

$A_2 = 0.58, D_3 = 0, D_4 = 2.11, d_2 = 2.326$

Solution:

$$\Sigma\bar{X} = 357.5$$

$$\Sigma\bar{R} = 8.8$$

$$A_2 = 0.58,\ D_3 = 0,\ D_4 = 2.11,\ d_2 = 2.326$$

$$\bar{\bar{x}} = \frac{357.5}{25} = 14.3$$

$$\bar{R} = \frac{\Sigma R}{N} = \frac{8.8}{25} = 0.352$$

Control Limits for $\bar{x}$-chart

$$\bar{\bar{x}} \pm A_2\bar{R}$$

$$\text{UCL} = 14.50$$

$$\text{LCL} = 14.09$$

Control Limit for *R*-chart

$$\text{UCL} = D_4\bar{R} = 0.742$$

$$\text{LCL} = 0$$

Specification limits = 14.4 ± 0.4 (It can be plotted only on x - chart)

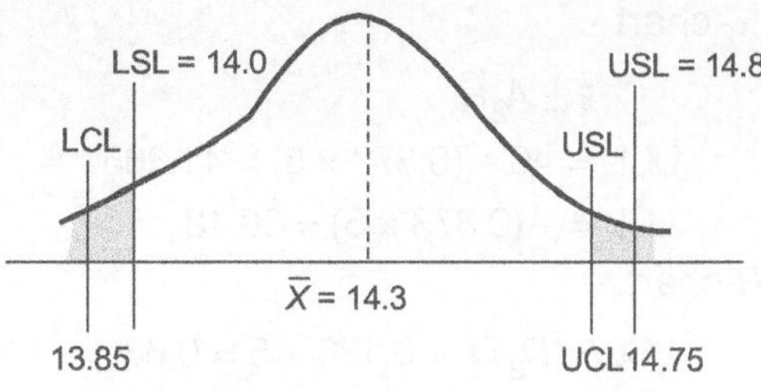

But, $$\sigma' = \frac{\overline{R}}{d_2} = \frac{0.352}{2.326} = 0.15$$

Control Limits for x-chart,

$$UCL = 14.3 + 3(0.15) = 14.75$$

$$LCL = 14.3 - 3(0.15) = 13.85$$

Process capability index,

$$Cp = \frac{U - L}{6\sigma'}$$

$Cp < 1$ = not capable = 1 just capable

$Cp > 1$ very much capable

Specification limits can only be plotted on x-chart and it can be seen in the normal distribution chart that in existing situation lot of defectives will be produce above the LCL. Since the process capability index in the given situation is less than 1 so the process is not capable to produce component within specification limits. Situation can be improved by targeting the process mean at center of specification limits.

Example: 11.4

Samples of $n = 8$ items each are taken from a manufacturing process at regular intervals. A quality characteristic is measured, and $\bar{x}$ and R values are calculated for each sample.

After 50 samples, we have $\sum_{i=1}^{50} \bar{x}_i = 2000$ **and** $\sum_{i=1}^{50} \overline{R}_i = 250$

Assume that the quality characteristic is normally distributed.

(i) Compute control limits for the $\bar{x}$ and R control charts.

(ii) All points on both control charts fall between the control limits computed in part (i). What are the natural tolerance limits of the process?

(iii) If the specification limits are 41 ± 5.0, what are your conclusions regarding the ability of the process to produce items within these specifications?

(iv) Assuming that if an item exceeds the upper specification limit it can be reworked, and if it is below the lower specification limit it must be scrapped, what percent scrap and rework is the process producing?

(v) Make suggestions as to how the process performance can be improved?

Solution:

$n = 8$; $N = 50$; $\Sigma\overline{X} = 2000$; $\Sigma R = 250$; $A_2 = 0.373$; $d_2 = 2.847$; $D_3 = 0.136$

$D_4 = 1.864$; $\bar{\bar{x}} = \frac{\Sigma\overline{X}}{N} = 40$; $\overline{R} = \frac{\Sigma R}{N} = \frac{250}{50} = 5$

Control Limits for $\bar{x}$-chart

$$\bar{x} \pm A_2\bar{R}$$

$$UCL = 40 + (0.373 \times 5) = 41.865$$

$$LCL = -(0.373 \times 5) = 38.13$$

Control Limits for R-chart

$$LCL = D_3\bar{R} = 0.136 \times 5 = 0.68$$

$$UCL = D_4\bar{R} = 1.864 \times 5 = 9.32$$

Control Limits for x-Chart

$$\sigma' = \frac{\bar{R}}{d_2} = 1.75$$

$$= \bar{x} \pm 3\sigma'$$

Specification limits 41 ± 5 (given)

$$U - L = 10$$

$$6\sigma' = 6 \times 1.75 = 10.5$$

$$C_p = 0.95 = \frac{U-L}{6\sigma'} = 0.95$$

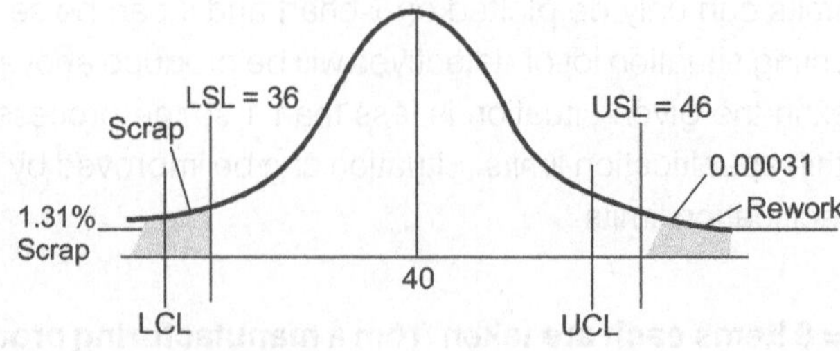

Re-work calculation:

$$Z = \frac{\bar{x} - \bar{x}}{\sigma'} = \frac{46 - 40}{1.75} = 3.42$$

Area corresponding to this Z value from the normal distribution table is $\int_{-\infty}^{46} P(x)dx = 0.9996$

So rework as shown in figure is = 1 – 0.9996 = 0.00031 = 0.031%

Corrective action: Shift the process mean at the target value of specification i.e., 41.

$$Z = \frac{36 - 40}{1.75} = -2.28$$

$$= 0.0113 = 1.13\%$$

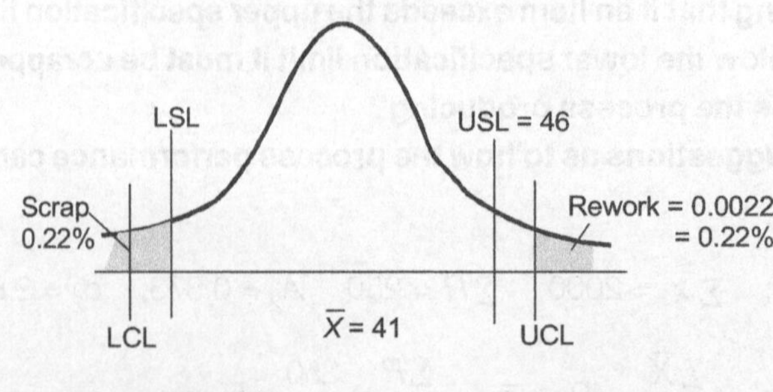

$$Z = \frac{46 - 41}{1.75} = 2.85$$

The corresponding area from the normal distribution table

$$\int_{-\infty}^{46} P(x)dx = 0.9978$$

So % is $1 - 0.9978 = 0.0022$ i.e., 0.22% in the present situation since normal distribution is symmetrically placed between specification limits, so rework and scrap will be same.

11.5 ATTRIBUTES CHARTS

$\bar{x}$ and *R* (or $\bar{x}$ and *s*) charts:

Consider using variables control charts in these situations:

1. A new process is coming on stream, or a new product is being manufactured by an existing process.
2. The process has been in operation for some time, but it is chronically in trouble or unable to hold the specified tolerances.
3. The process is in trouble, and the control chart can be useful for diagnostic purposes (troubleshooting).
4. Destructive testing (or other expensive testing procedures) is required.
5. It is desirable to reduce acceptance-sampling or other downstream testing to a minimum when the process can be operated in control.
6. Attributes control charts have been used, but the process is either out of control or in control but the yield is unacceptable.
7. There are very tight specifications, overlapping assembly tolerances, or other difficult manufacturing problems.
8. The operator must decide whether or not to adjust the process, or when a setup must be evaluated.
9. A change in product specification is desired.
10. Process stability and capability must be continuously demonstrated, such as in regulated industries.

(P charts, c charts, and u charts):

Consider using attributes control charts in these situations:

1. Operators control the assignable causes, and it is necessary to reduce process fallout.
2. The process is a complex assembly operation and product quality is measured in terms of the occurrence of nonconformities, successful or unsuccessful product function, and so forth. (Examples include computers, office automation equipment, automobiles, and the major subsystem of these products.)
3. Process control is necessary, but measurement data cannot be obtained.
4. A historical summary of process performance is necessary. Attributes control charts, such as p charts, c charts, and u charts, are very effective for summarizing information about the process for management review.
5. Remember that attributes charts are generally inferior to charts for variables. Always use $\bar{x}$ and *R* or $\bar{x}$ and s charts whenever possible.

Probability of Binomial distribution,

$$P_r = {}^nC_r(p)^r(1-p)^{n-r}$$

p = Average fraction defective

n = Number of samples

r = Number of defectives

1. P-chart (Fraction deviation)

$$CL = p \pm 3\sigma_{pb} \rightarrow \text{Standard deviation of } p \text{ chart } = p \pm 3\sqrt{\frac{p(1-p)}{n}}$$

2. Number of defective (np – chart) = $np \pm 3\sqrt{np(1-p)}$

3. 100 – p chart (%defective) $CL = 100 \pm 3\sqrt{\frac{100p(100-100p)}{n}}$

4. When 'n' is very high and 'p' is very less, Binomial distribution reduces to Poisons distribution Number of defects (C-chart)

$$CL = \bar{C} \pm 3\sqrt{\bar{C}}$$
$$C = \text{Avg. defects}$$

Characteristics of Attributes Charts

1. Same chart can be maintained for no. of quality characteristics.
2. Cost of collecting the data is low.
3. Whole quality history can be presented to the management in very precise form
4. But it is very difficult to diagnose to attributes charts for taking corrective action.

Example: 11.5

If in a lot 10 percent components are found defective, find, the probability, that in a random sample of 5 components not more than one is defective.

Solution:

$$p = 0.1$$
$$n = 5$$

For

$$p(d \le 1) = p(d = 0) + p(d = 1) = 0.91$$
$$p(d = 0) = {}^5C_0(p)^0(1-p)^5 = 0.59$$
$$p(d = 1) = {}^5C_1(p)^1(1-p)^4 = 0.32$$
$$p(d > 1) = 1 - p(d \le 1) = 1 - \{p(d = 0) + p(d = 1)\}$$
$$= 0.09$$

(Probability that there will be more than one defective)

Example: 11.6

A person operates a machine and makes capacitors. He has been advised to keep track of the percentage defectives at his work center. He knows that with this type of process, they expect about 4% defectives plus or minus some chance variation. He wishes to initially construct a control chart for defectives. He has prepared ten daily samples of hundred capacitors each.

Sample No.	1	2	3	4	5	6	7	8	9	10
% Defective	4	3	3	6	1	9	5	12	4	3

(i) Construct the relevant control charts what are the upper and lower control limits?

(ii) Plot the data points on the proposed control chart. Is the process under control? What follow up steps should be undertaken it any?

Solution:

We will construct 100-p chart or percentage defective chart in this case

$$n = 100$$

$$100p = 4$$

$$CL = 4 \pm 3\sqrt{\frac{4\times(100-4)}{100}}$$

$$UCL = 9.878$$

$$LCL = -1.87 = (LCL = 0 \text{ since it is } -ve)$$

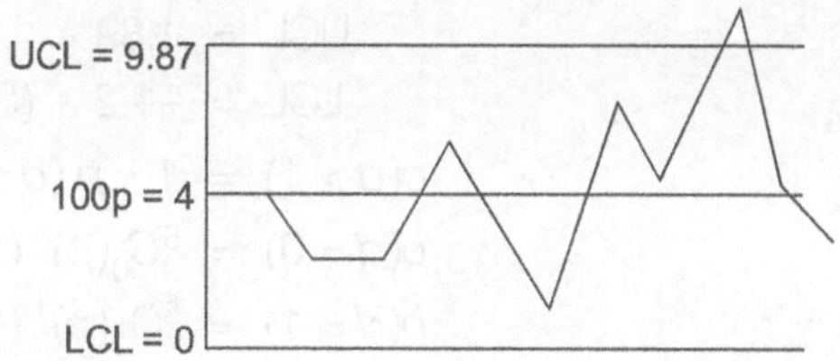

UCL = 9.87

100p = 4

LCL = 0

It can be seen in the 100 p chart that 4-consecutive points are falling above process mean 4%. And one out of these 4 points is falling above UCL so the process is not under statistical control because these points are not due to chance causes. May be the average fraction defectives have increased due to change in vendor. So incoming material quality should be checked.

Example: 11.7

A set of data obtained from inspection of castings, with a sample size of 20 castings are shown in the table:

Group No.	1	2	3	4	5	6	7	8	9	10
No. of defects	76	68	76	89	47	69	83	93	70	79

Compute:

(i) The process average and control limits.

(ii) The process average for future production and,

(iii) Revised control limits.

Solution:

Since number of defects one given in the problem. So we will construct C-chart

$$\bar{C} = \frac{\Sigma C}{10} = \frac{750}{10} = 75$$

$$\text{C.L.} = \bar{C} \pm 3\sqrt{\bar{C}} = 75 \pm 3\sqrt{75}$$

$$UCL = 100.98 \text{ and } LCL = 49.02$$

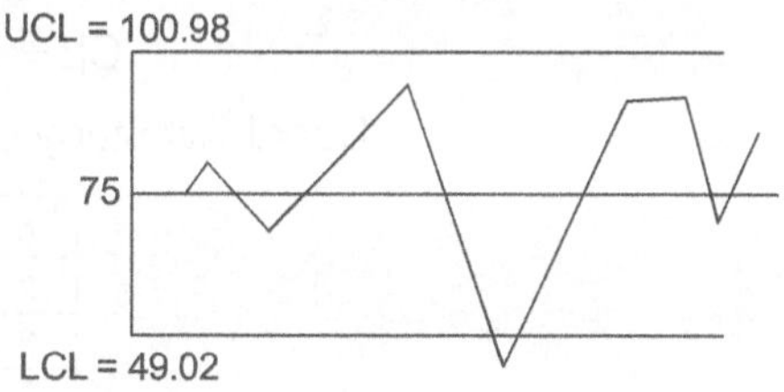

UCL = 100.98

75

LCL = 49.02

Note: To calculate the modified control limits the points which are falling beyond the control limits has to be removed from the data and by calculating the process avg., control limits are modified

Now,
$$\bar{C} = 78.11$$

$$CL = 78.11 \pm 3\sqrt{78.11}$$

$$UCL = 104.624$$

$$LCL = 51.6$$

It can be observed that all the data points are falling within these control limits. So these control limits can be used to control the future quality control.

Example: 11.8

In a lot there are 6% defectives when the sample size is 5 find the probability of the type 1 error in np chart.

Solution:

$$p = 0.06, n = 5$$

$$CL = np \pm 3\sqrt{np(1-p)}$$

$$= 5\,(0.06) \pm 3\sqrt{(5\times 0.06)\,(1-0.06)}$$

$$= 0.3 \pm 1.59$$

$$\text{UCL} = 1.89$$

$$\text{LCL} = -1.2 \quad \text{(So it will be 0)}$$

$$p(d > 1) = 1 - p(d \le 1)$$

$$p(d = 0) = {}^5C_0(p)^0(1 - 0.06)^5 = 0.73$$

$$p(d = 1) = {}^5C_1(p)^1(1 - 0.06)^4 = 0.23$$

$$p(d > 1) = 1 - (0.73 + 0.23) = 0.04$$

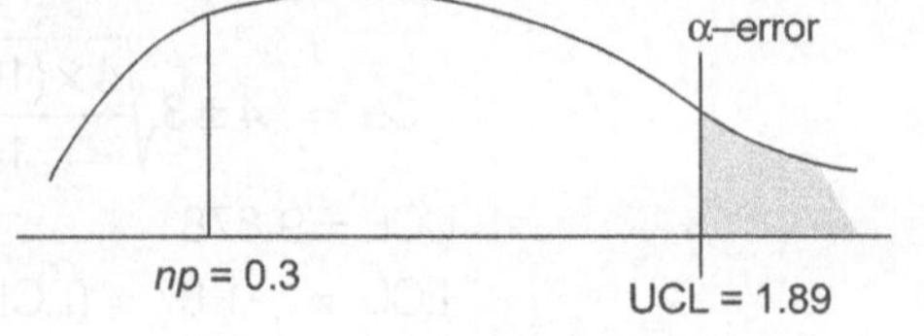

Probability of type-I error is 0.04.

SUMMARY

Notation:

UCL-Upper Control Limit

LCL-Lower Control Limit

CL – Centre Line

n – Sample size

PCR-Process Capability Ratio

σ' – Process standard deviation

$\bar{x}$ – Average of Measurements

$\bar{\bar{x}}$ – Average of Averages

R – Range

$\bar{R}$ – Average of Ranges

USL–Upper Specification Limit

LSL–Lower Specification Limit

Variables data ($\bar{x}$ and R Control Charts)

$\bar{x}$ Control Chart	R Control Chart
$\text{UCL} = \bar{\bar{x}} + A_2\bar{R}$	$\text{UCL} = \bar{R}\,D_4$
$\text{LCL} = \bar{\bar{x}} - A_2\bar{R}$	$\text{LCL} = \bar{R}\,D_3$
$\text{CL} = \bar{\bar{x}}$	$\text{CL} = \bar{R}$

Capability Study Cp = (USL – LSL/($6\sigma'$); where $\sigma' = \bar{R}/d_2$

n	A_2	D_3	D_4	d_2
2	1.880	0.000	3.267	1.128
3	1.023	0.000	2.575	1.693
4	0.729	0.000	2.282	2.059
5	0.577	0.000	2.114	2.326
6	0.483	0.000	2.004	2.534
7	0.419	0.076	1.924	2.704
8	0.373	01.36	1.864	2.847
9	0.337	0.184	1.816	2.970
10	0.308	0.223	1.777	3.078

Attribute Data (*p*, *np*, *c* and *u* Control Charts)

	p(Fraction)	*np* (number of non-conforming)	*c* (count of non conformances)	*u* (count of non conformances/unit)
CL	$\bar{p}$	$n\bar{p}$	$\bar{c}$	$\bar{u}$
UCL	$p+3\sqrt{\frac{\bar{p}(1-\bar{p})}{n}}$	$n\bar{p}+3\sqrt{np(1-\bar{p})}$	$\bar{c}+3\sqrt{c}$	$\bar{u}+3\sqrt{\frac{\bar{u}}{n}}$
LCL	$\bar{p}-3\sqrt{\frac{\bar{p}(1-\bar{p})}{n}}$	$n\bar{p}-3\sqrt{n\bar{p}(1-\bar{p})}$	$\bar{c}-3\sqrt{c}$	$\bar{u}-3\sqrt{\frac{\bar{u}}{n}}$
Notes	If n varies use $\bar{n}$ or individual n_i	n must be a constant	n must be a constant	If n varies, use $\bar{n}$ or individual n_i

Table 11.1: Control Chart Formulas

11.6 SAMPLING INSPECTIONS

A sample is taken from the lot, and some quality characteristic of the units in the sample is inspected. On the basis of the information in this sample, a decision is made regarding lot disposition. Usually, this decision is either to accept or to reject the lot.Lot that is accepted is sent forward for further processing, and rejected lots may be reworked or scrapped. Acceptance sampling plans involve inspection of a product or service. When 100% inspection of all items is not feasible, a decision has to be made as to how many items should be sampled or whether the batch should be sampled at all. The information obtained from the sample is used to decide whether to accept or reject the entire batch or lot. In the case of attributes, one parameter is the acceptable number of non-conforming items in the sample. If the number of non-conforming items observed is less than or equal to this number, the batch is accepted. This is known as the acceptance number. In the case of variables, one parameter may be the proportion of items in the sample that are outside the specifications. This proportion would have to be less than or equal to a standard for the lot to be accepted. A plan that determines the number of items to sample and the acceptance criteria of the lot, based on meeting certain stipulated conditions (such as the risk of rejecting a good lot or accepting a bad lot), is known as an acceptance sampling plan.

Three aspects of Sampling are Important:

1. It is the purpose of acceptance sampling to sentence lots, not to estimate the lot quality. Most acceptance – sampling plans are not designed for estimation purposes.
2. Acceptance-sampling plans do not provide any direction form of quality control. Acceptance sampling simply accepts and rejects lots. Even if all lots are of the same quality, sampling will accept some lots and reject others, the accepted lots being no better than the rejected ones. Process controls are used to control and systematically improve quality, but acceptance sampling is not.
3. The most effective use of acceptance sampling is not to "inspect quality into the production", but rather as an audit tool to ensure that the output of process conforms to requirements.

Acceptance sampling is most likely to be useful in the following situations:

1. When testing is destructive?
2. When the cost of 100% inspection is extremely high?
3. When 100% inspection is not technologically feasible or would require so much calendar time that production scheduling would be seriously impacted?
4. When there are many items to be inspected and the inspection error rate is sufficiently high that 100% inspection might cause a higher percentage of defective units to be passed than would occur with the use of a sampling plan?
5. When the supplier has an excellent quality history, and some reduction in inspection from 100% is desired, but the supplier's process capability is sufficiently low as to make no inspection an unsatisfactory alternative?
6. When there are potentially serious product liability risks, and although the supplier's process is satisfactory, a program for continuously monitoring the product is necessary?

Advantages and Disadvantages of Sampling

When acceptance sampling is contrasted with 100% inspection, it has the following advantages:

1. It is usually less expensive because there is less inspection.
2. There is less handling of the product, hence reduced damage.

3. Fewer personnel are involved in inspection activities.
4. It often greatly reduces the amount of inspection error.
5. It is applicable to destructive testing.
6. The rejection of entire lots as opposed to the simple return of defectives often provides a stronger motivation to the supplier for quality improvements.

Acceptance sampling also has several disadvantages, however. These include the following:

1. There are risks of accepting "bad" lots and rejecting 'good" lots.
2. Less information is usually generated about the product or about the process that manufactured the product.
3. Acceptance sampling requires planning and documentation of the acceptance-sampling procedure whereas 100% inspection does not required documentation.

11.6.1 Types of Sampling Plans:

(i) A single-sampling plane:

A single-sampling plane is a lot-sentencing procedure in which one sample of *'n'* units is selected at random from the lot, and the disposition of the lot is determined based on the information contained in that sample.

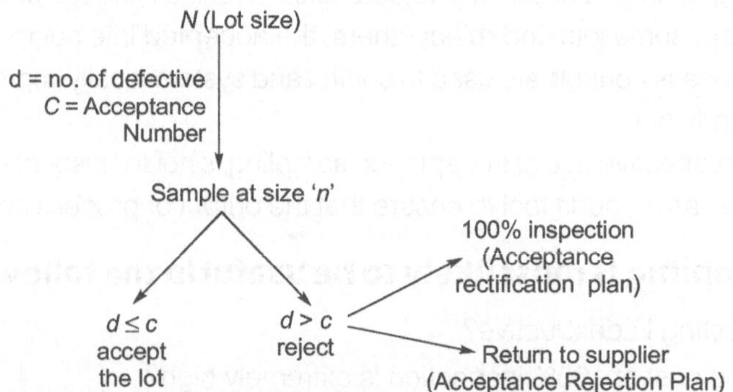

Fig: 11.12 Representation of single sampling plan

(ii) Doubling-sampling plans:

Doubling-sampling plans are somewhat more complicated. Following an initial sample, a decision based on the information in that sample is made either to (1) accept the lot, (2) reject the lot, or (3) take a second sample. If the second sample is taken, the information from both the first and second sample is combined in order to reach a decision whether to accept or reject the lot.

⇒ Pa = Probability of acceptance

Pr = Probability of rejection

$$Pa + Pr = 1$$

p = Avg. fraction defective in incoming lot

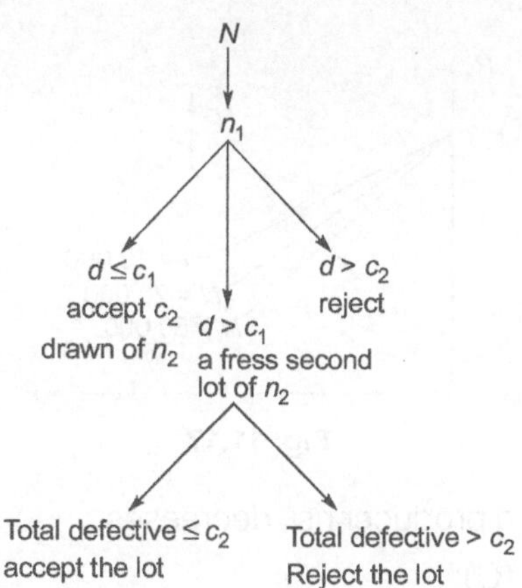

Fig: 11.13 Representation of double sampling plan

As the incoming quality deteriorates outgoing quality also suffers. But when incoming quality decreases beyond a certain value outgoing quality starts improving because most of the lots will pass through 100% inspection root.

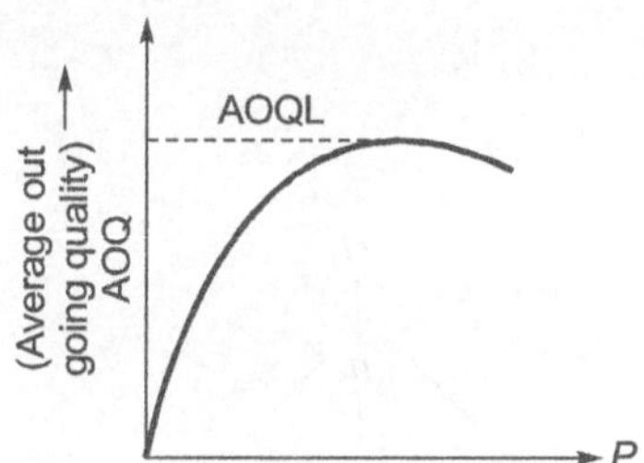

Fig: 11.14 Average outgoing quality

11.7 O.C. CURVE (Operating Characteristic curve)

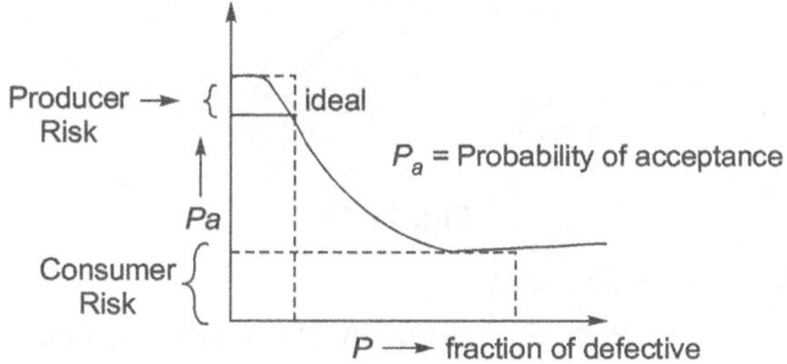

Fig: 11.15 OC Curve

Effect of n(sample size):

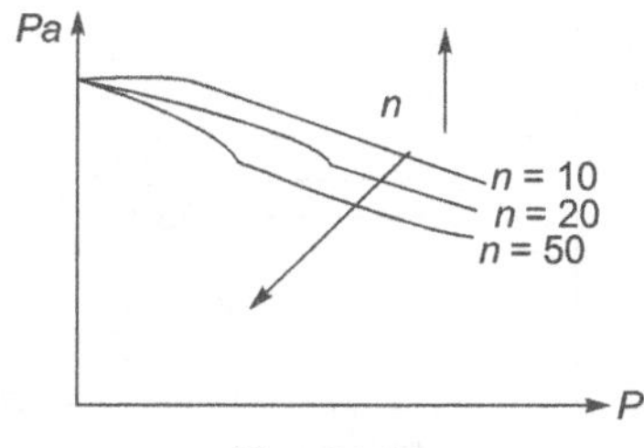

Fig: 11.16

By increasing value of 'n' consumer risk decreases and producer's risk increases.

Effect of lot size (*N*):

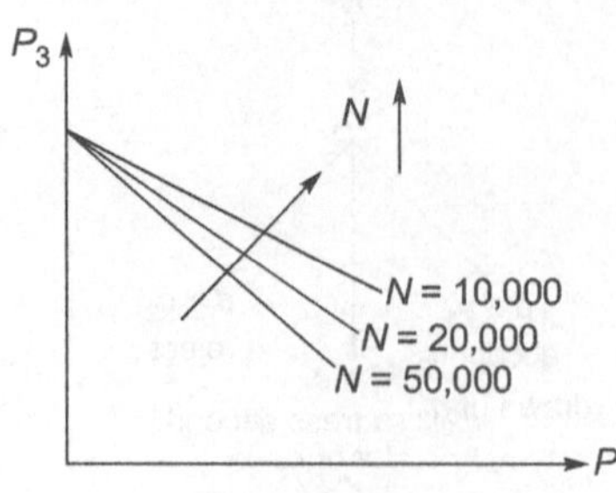

Fig: 11.17

Consumer risk increases and producer risk decreases

Effect of acceptance No. (C):

Both consumer and producer's risk decreases

Avg. Total inspection (ATI) in single sampling plane

ATI = $n + (N - n)Pr$

N – Lot size

N – Samples

Pr – Probability of rejection

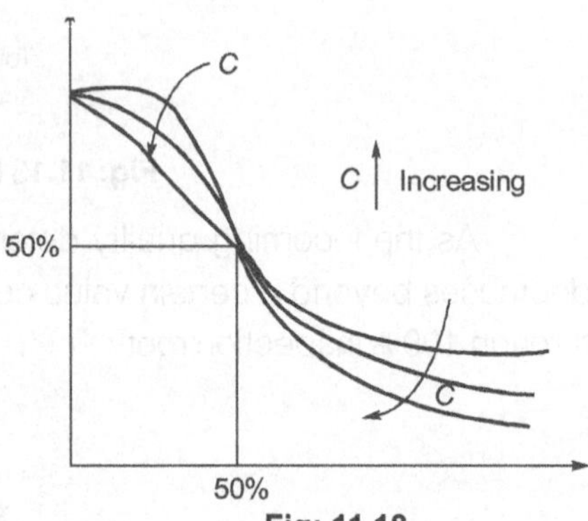

Fig: 11.18

Double sampling plan (DSP)

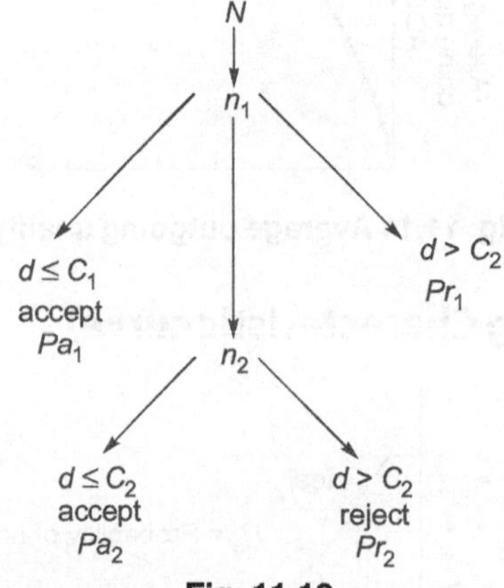

Fig: 11.19

$$Pa_1 + Pa_2 + Pr_1 + Pr_2 = 1$$

Pcs = Probability of continuation sample

Pcs = $1 - (Pa_1 + Pr_1)$ or $(Pa_2 + Pr_2)$

Characteristics of DSP

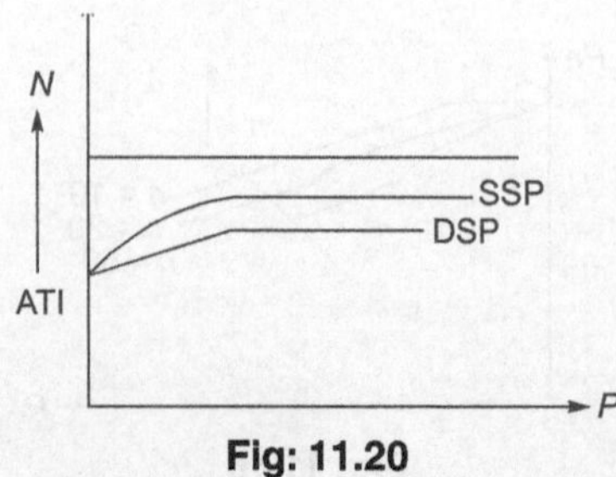

Fig: 11.20

1. Average total inspection of DSP is smaller than single sampling plan.

2. It is more convincing that the lot was rejected based on two samples.
3. It requires greater administrative efforts to executes DSP.

Average sample No (ASN) On an average number of samples drawn from the lot.

S.S.P = n

D.S.P = $n_1 + n_2$Pcs

Example: 11.9

In a lot size of 10,000 following data is given for DSP (double sampling plan) $n_1 = 100$, $n_2 = 50$, $C_1 = 0$, $C_2 = 2$

If the avg. fraction defectives in lot are 1% determine the total probability of acceptance AOQ and ATI.

Solution:

$$p = 1\% = 0.01$$

$P^{b \to \text{Sample number}}_{a \to \text{number of defectives}}$

P_2^1 = Probability of having 2 defectives in the first sample.

P_1^2 Probability at having 1 defective in the second sample.

$$Pa_1 = P(d=0) = {}^{100}C_0\,(p)^0\,(1-p)^{100} = 0.366$$

$$Pr_1 = P(d>2) = 1 - \left[P_0^1 + P_1^1 + P_2^1\right] = 0.081$$

$$P_1^1 = C_1(0.01)^1\,(0.99)^{99} = 0.369$$

$$P_2^1 = {}^{100}C_2(0.01)^2\,(0.99)^{98} = 0.184$$

Probability of acceptance based on the second sample

$$Pa_2 = P_{a=1}^1 \times P_{d\le 1}^2 + P_{d=2}^1 P_{d=0}^2 = 0.447$$

$$P_{d=0}^2 = {}^{50}C_0(p)^0(1-p)^{50} = {}^{50}C_0(0.01)^0(0.99)^{50} = 0.605$$

$$P_{d=1}^2 = {}^{50}C_1(p)^1(1-p)^{49} = 0.305$$

$$P_{d\le 1}^2 = P_0^2 + P_1^2 = 0.91$$

$$Pr_2 = 1 - (Pa_1 + Pr_1 + Pa_2) = 0.105$$

or, $$Pr_2 = P_{a=1}^1 \times P_{d>1}^2 + P_{a=2}^2 \times P_{d>0}^2 = 0.105$$

Total probability of acceptance,

$$P_a = Pa_1 + Pa_2 = 0.813$$

$$P_{cs} = 1 - (Pa_1 + Pr_1) = Pa_2 + Pr_2$$

$$AOQ = P \times P_a = P \times (Pa_1 + Pa_2) = 0.00813$$

$$ATI = n_1 + n_2 P_{cs} + (N - n_1)\,Pr_1 + (N - n_1 - n_2)\,Pr_2 = 1953$$

11.8 TOTAL QUALITY CONTROL (TQC)

1. Quality development:
   - Design
2. Quality Maintenance:
   - Manufacturing Department
3. Quality Improvement:
   - Marketing Department

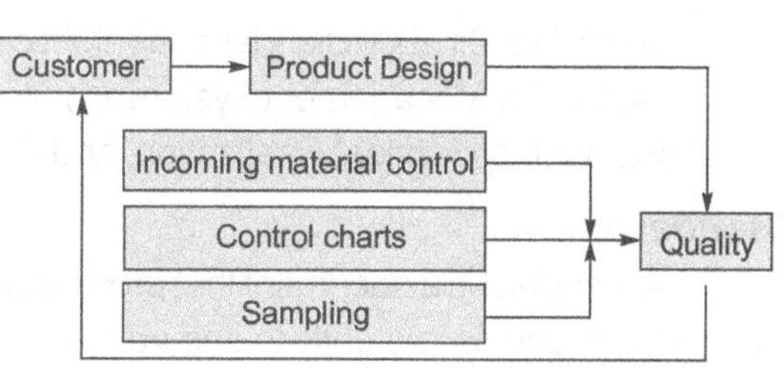

Fig. 11.21

TQC is continuous process of quality development (function of Design department).

Quality maintenance (Function of Mfg. Department) Quality improvement (Function of Marketing department) which takes places by taking feedback from customer and trying to improve design further.

11.9 EDWARDS DEMING'S AWARD

1. Create a constancy of purpose focused on the improvement of products and services.
2. Adopt a new philosophy that recognizes we are in a different economic era.
3. Do not rely on mass inspection to "control" quality.
4. Do not award business to suppliers on the basis of price alone, but also consider quality.
5. Focus on continuous improvement.
6. Practice modern training methods and invest in on-the-job training for all employees.
7. Improve leadership, and practice modern supervision methods.
8. Drive out fear.
9. Break down the barriers between functional areas of the business.
10. Eliminate targets, slogans, and numerical goals for the workforce.
11. Eliminate numerical quotas and work standards.
12. Remove the barriers that discourage employees from doing their jobs.
13. Institute an ongoing program of education for all employees.
14. Create a structure in top management that will vigorously advocate the first 13 points.

11.10 TOTAL QUALITY MANAGEMENT

Total quality management (TQM) is a strategy for implementing and managing quality improvement activities on an organization wide basis. TQM began in the early 1980s, with the philosophies of Deming and Juran as the focal point. It evolved into a broader spectrum of concepts and ideas, involving participative organizations and work culture, customers focus, supplier's quality improvement, integration of the quality system with business goals, and many other activities to focus all elements of the organization around the quality improvement goal.

11.11 QUALITY SYSTEMS AND STANDARDS

The International Standards Organization (Founded in 1946 in Geneva, Switzerland), known as ISO, has developed a series of standard for quality systems. The first standards were issued in 1987. The current version of the standard is known as the ISO 9000 series.

ISO 9000:2000 Quality Management System – Fundamental and Vocabulary

ISO 9001:2000 Quality Management System – Requirements

ISO 9004:2000 Quality Management System – Guidelines for Performance Improvement

ISO 9000 is also an American National Standards Institute and an ASQ standard

The ISO 9001:2000 Standard has eight clauses: (1) Scope, (2) Normative References (3) Definitions, (4) Quality Management System, (5) Management Responsibility, (6) Resource Management, (7) Product (or Service) Realization, and (8) Measurement, Analysis and Improvement.

Standard

A standard is a document that provides requirements, specifications, guidelines or characteristics that can be used consistently to ensure that materials, products, processes and services are fit for their purpose.

ISO

It is a non-governmental, independent international organization developed for the purpose of publishing international standards (called ISO standards) to ensure quality, safety and efficiency of products, services and systems. In English language, it is an International Organization for Standardization (IOS) but the term 'ISO' was derived from a Greek word called 'isos', meaning equal.

Initially, delegates from 25 countries met in Institute of Civil Engineers in London 'to facilitate the international coordination and unification of industrial standards'. Officially, on 23 February 1947, they declared the society as "ISO". Now, 161 countries are members in the ISO. The 161 countries and 3368 technical bodies take care of the developments of the standards. There are three types of members in ISO, full members (or member bodies), correspondent members and subscriber members. The first two members can sell and adopt international standards and participate in meetings regarding ISO, but, third type can only be up to date with the standards, they cannot sell and adopt standards. No individual or company or organization can be a member, only a country can be one types of the members. Since 1947, till now the ISO has published 21000 international standards and each standard has its own number for example ISO 9000-Quality management, ISO 14000-Environmental management, ISO 45001-Occupational Health and Safety etc,.

ISO 9000 : Quality Management

It provides guidance and tools to companies and organizations which help their products and services consistently meet customer requirements and consistently improvement in quality. The ISO 9000 is a family of four standards as given below.

1. **ISO 9000:2015** – It covers fundamental concepts and vocabulary required for quality management.
2. **ISO 9001 : 2015** – It sets out the requirements of quality managements.
3. **ISO 9004 : 2009** – It focuses on how to make a quality management system more effective and efficiently (in other words, managing for the sustained success of an organization a quality management approach).
4. **ISO 19011 : 2011** – It gives guidelines for auditing quality management systems.

ISO 9000 : 2015

This International Standard gives the fundamental vocabulary, concepts and principles of quality management systems(SQM) and it is the foundation for other SQM standards. It is developed by ISO/TC 176 (TC refers to technical committee that developed the standard). It helps the user effectively and efficiently in implementing a SQM. It assists organizations to realize their objectives. It applicable to all organizations without considering their size and complexity involved. It increases the awareness of duties, commitment in achieving goals, customer satisfaction.

It contains fundamental concepts, the seven quality management principles:

(i) Customer focus
(ii) Leadership
(iii) Engagement of people
(iv) Process approach
(v) Improvement
(vi) Evidence based decision making
(vii) Relationship management)

Explaining each and every principle with their " statement", "rationale" - describing the reason to use the principle, "key benefits" and "possible actions" that the organization takes in applying the principles. In the standard, the vocabulary, definitions and terms related to people , organization, activity, process requirement, data, information, documentation, determination, action and audit, and also concept relationship and their graphical representation are arranged conceptual wise.

For example: Under terms related to people, 'top management' is defined "a person or group of people who directs and controls an organization at the highest level".

ISO 9001 : 2015 (is an improve version of ISO 9001 : 2008)

This International Standard specifies requirements for a quality management system. These requirements are complementary to the requirements for products and services. This standard works based on the 4th principle of quality management, process approach, which enables an organization to plan its processes and control the interrelationships and interdependencies among the processes of the system, so that the overall performance of the organization can be enhanced. It is done by systematic definition of processes and their interactions.

The process approach is implemented by Plan-Do-Check-Act (PDCA) cycle and risk based thinking. PDCA cycle can be applied for all the processes to the QMS. The PDCA in relation to this standard is graphically presented in Fig. 11.22.

Plan: Objectives of system and processes, means to deliver results according to customer requirements, organization's policies, identification of risks and opportunities are to be planed.

Do: Implement whatever was planed.

Check: Measure and monitor, wherever applicable, the processes, services and resulting products against whatever planed.

Act: Take actions as necessary to improve performance.

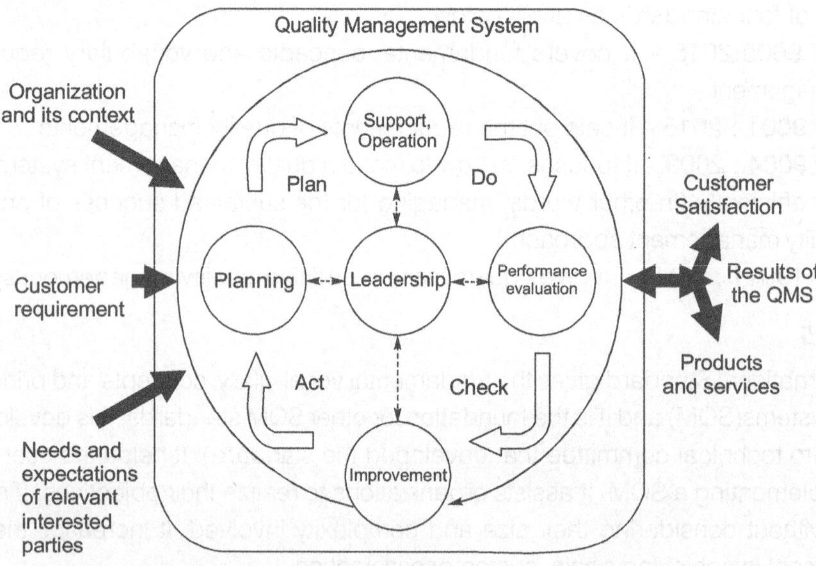

Fig 11.22: ISO 9001:2015 is graphically represented in PDCA cycle

Risk-based thinking is nothing but identifying the factors that could cause its processes and its quality management system to move away from the planned results, and then, the factors are placed in preventive controls to minimize negative effects and to make maximum use of opportunities as they arise. In other words, an organization needs to plan and implement actions to address risks and opportunities. Identifying both risks and opportunities are important to increase effectiveness of quality management system and improved results. The risk is the uncertainty and it may positive or negative. The opportunities are certain circumstances that attract customer attention, development of new products and services, reduction of wastage etc.

ISO 9004 : 2009

In a complex, demanding and ever-changing environment, the ISO 9004 : 2009 by a quality management approach act as guidance to support the achievement of sustained success of any organization. Sustained success of an organization depends on the ability of the organization in meeting the needs and expectations of customers and interested parties, over a long time and in a balanced manner. It is possible by effective management of the organization through knowledge of the organizations environment.

It act as self- assist tool for the review of maturity level of organization, including its leadership, strategy, management system, resources and processes, to identify areas strengths, weaknesses and opportunities for improvements or innovation or both.

This standard is nothing but an extended mode of ISO 9001 addressing expectations and needs of all parties and providing systematic guidance for continual improvement of the organization. It is show graphically in the following Fig. 11.23.

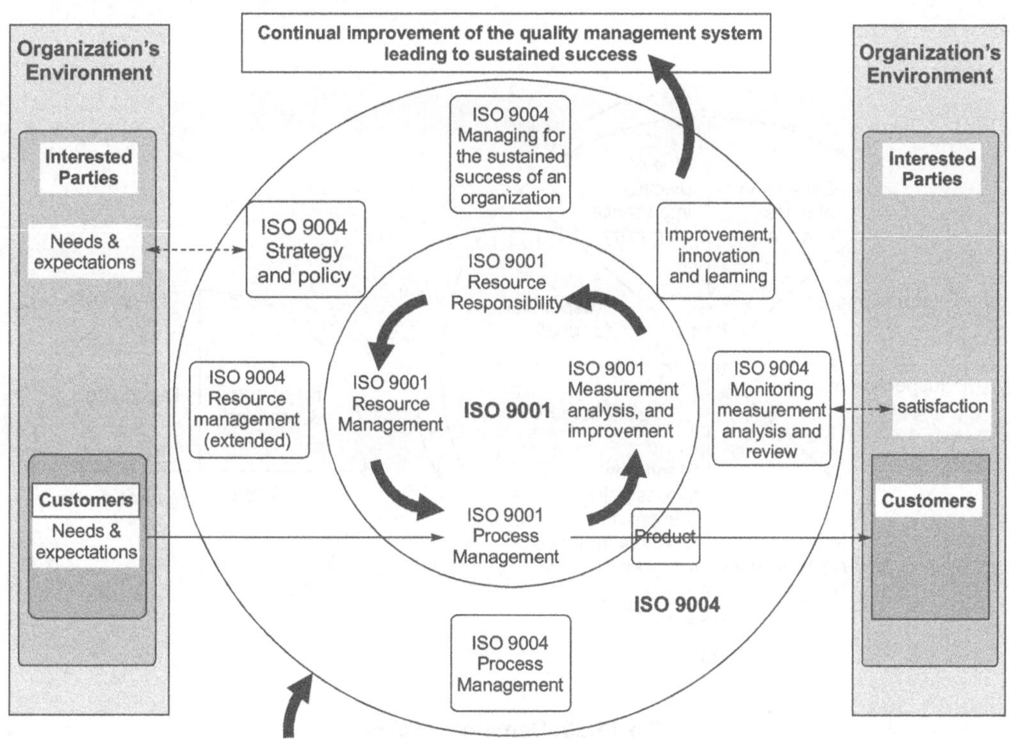

Fig 11.23: Extended model of a process-based quality management system

ISO 19011 : 2011

ISO 19011 : 2011 gives guidance on auditing management systems, including the principles of auditing, developing management system audits, balancing an audit, as well as guidance on the evaluation of competence of individuals involved in the audit process, including the person managing the audit programme, auditors and audit groups.

Organizations that need to conduct external and internal audits of management systems has to use ISO 19011 : 2011 for better conformity. Sometimes special considerations are given to other types of audits for the application of ISO ISO 19011 : 2011.

11.12 QUALITY WHEEL OR CYCLES

At the time of world war II, to improve productivity, Shewhart in U.S came up with a 'new' idea of continuous improvement in productivity by spiraling 'specification, production and inspection as shown in Fig.11.24. Deming, in 1950, extended the Shewhart's idia into two different quality controle modules in two different conferences as shown in Fig. 11.24. The first (Fig. 11.25(a)) was presented to JUSE engineers and the second (Fig. 11.25(b)) to executive officers. The Japanese use to call the first one as eight-bladed rotating fan and the other, Deming cycle. These are the basis for all the complex model present now a days.

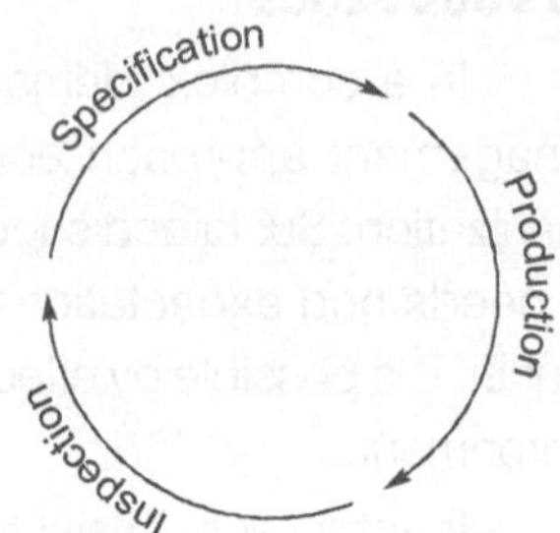

Fig 11.24: Shewhart's idia for improving productivity

In 1959, "PDCA cycle" meaning 'planning, doing, checking results and action'. It was more popular because it was more general, beyond manufacturing, it has been adopted in business areas. Thereafter, more complex terms were introduced within the PDCA and named as a standardize, deploy, verify, act (SDYA).

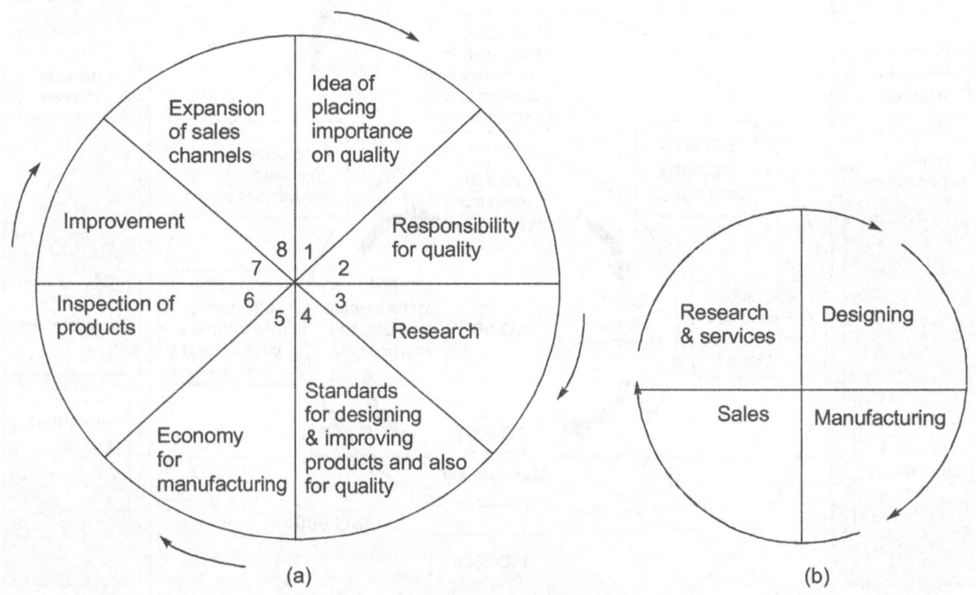

Fig 11.25: Deming's cycles

Last, but far from least, is "quality loop". It appears in the ANSI/ ASQC Standard 9004 (ISO 9004) manuals. The standard is designed to give guidance for developing internal quality systems and manuals.

These entire simple graphic pictures (quality cycles), are interested to emphasize that the quality improvement process is a continuous ongoing process and it is act as a reminder to a initiator and helps him focus on improvement in quality.

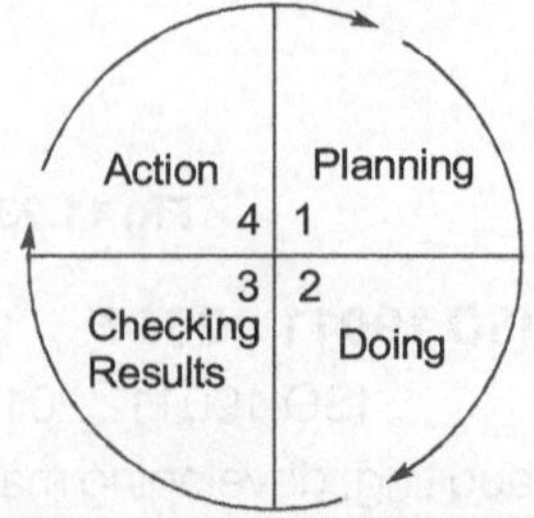

Fig 11.26: PDCA Cycle

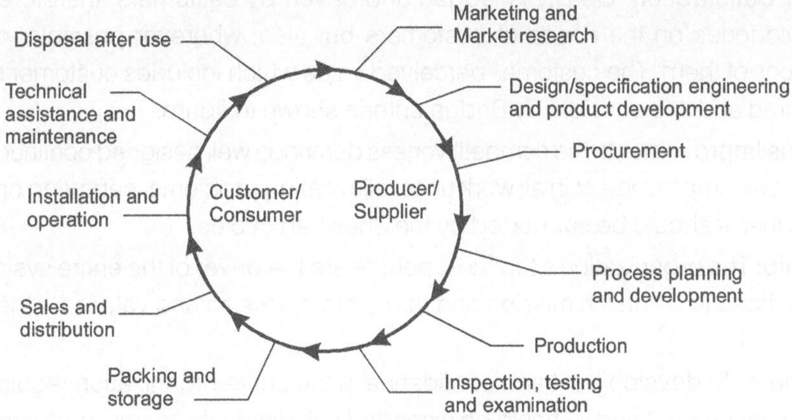

Fig. 11.27: Quality Loop

Total Quality Management (TQM)

Total quality management (TQM) is a philosophy and system that focuses on customer satisfaction in terms of continuous improvement of the quality of products and services. It involves 'leadership' and 'commitment' of top management, 'team building', 'employee involvement and empowerment', 'decisions based on facts, data and analysis', providing 'superior quality', 'shortening response time', 'quantitative performance indicators' and also 'cycles of improvement'. All these factors are explained in the following discussion.

Philosophy: It is nothing but a participative management. It calls teams from top level (horizontal cross functional teams and vertical functional interdepartmental teams) to the lowest possible, what we call works or " natural work teams" for decision makings for the establishment of partnerships with employees, suppliers, educational institutions, customers etc.

System: Japanese have more emphasis on 'System'. It integrate number of elements which set quality, response time, productivity, constant measurement and analysis, and open channels of co-operation, communication, feedback. The system is in four parts, namely, information and analysis, strategic quality planning, human resource development and management, management of process quality.

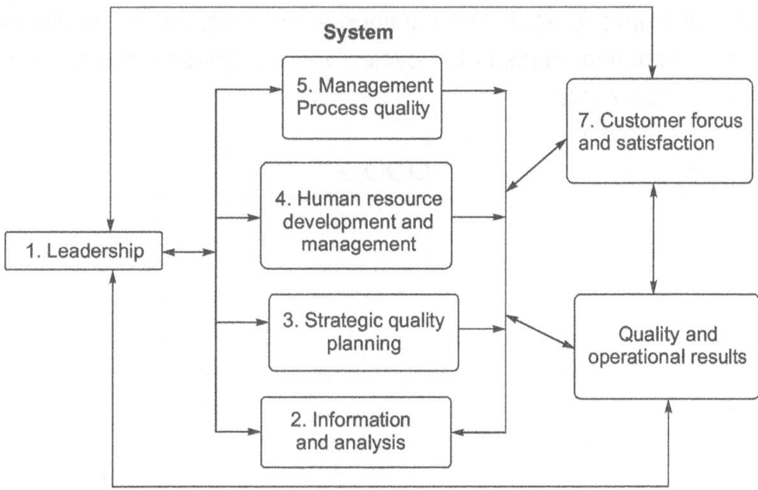

Fig 11.28: Bridge criteria (Dynamic Relationships)

Customer Satisfaction: Quality is judged and driven by customers, therefore, the system not only should focus on the needs of customers but also, wherever possible, must exceed the expectations of them. The customer-perceived value which includes customer satisfaction must be measured and it is possible by Bridge criteria shown in figure.

Continuous Improvement: The competitiveness demands well designed continuous improvement. It requires daily improvement in all work units, eliminating problems, capturing opportunities to do better. Further, it should be supported by the Shewhart cycles.

Leadership: The organization's top most people are the driver of the entire system and therefore it is in their hand to establish mission and formulate the vision and values for the improvement of quality.

Commitment: To develop trust and confidence in the entire organization require commitment of top most management and it should be extended to individuals, teams, partnership relationships with customers etc.

Teambuilding: It is a criterion for full participation, cultural transformation and for reward systems individually as well as team achievements in organization.

Employee Involvement and Empowerment: The criterion 4 in the system points out how to utilize human resources. Motivation of the work force is the heart of improvement in performance which also include educating different skills and supplying new equipments and tools.

Decisions Based on Facts, Data, and Analysis: The second element of the system focuses on selection of data points, measurement methods and analysis for better decisions to improve quality. The fact is, "if you don't measure it you can't improve it".

Provide Superior Quality: The quality of product begins with its design stage and it is stage at which the error cost is much lower than that in downstream of manufacturing method.

Shortening Response Time: How quickly the product comes into the market in response with the demands impact the market share. Now, it is being achieved by cycle time reduction and error prevention.

Quantitative Performance Indicators

Statistical tools like statistical quality control (SQC), quality charts etc,. are called the quantitative performance indicators and these needs to be condensed rather than giving detailed information to the top most management people.

Future Cycles of Improvement: The continuous improvement in quality requires use of the quality cycles and improvements in the cycles and it requires long range out-look and strong commitment to stake holders.

PRACTICE QUESTIONS

1. Which of the following correctly explains process capability?
   (a Maximum capacity of the machine
   (b) Mean value of the measured variable
   (c) Lead time of the process
   (d) Maximum deviation of the measured variables of the components

Direction: Each of the next consists of two statements, one labelled as the **'Assertion (A)'** and the other as **'Reason (R)'**. You are to examine these two statements carefully and select the answers to these items using the codes given below:

Codes:
(a) Both A and R are individually true and R is the correct explanation of A.
(b) Both A and R are individually true but R is not the correct explanation of A.
(c) A is true but R is false.
(d) A is false but R is true.

2. **Assertion (A):** In case of control charts for variables, if some points fall outside the control limits, it is concluded that the process is not under control.
   Reason (R): It was experimentally proved by Stewart that averages of four or more consecutive readings from a universe (population) or from a process, when plotted, will form a normal distribution curve.

3. **Assertion (A):** Double sampling is preferred over single sampling when the quality of incoming lots is expected to be either very good or very bad.
   Reason (R): With double sampling, the amount of inspection required will be lesser than that in the case of single sampling.

4. **Assertion (A):** While plotting control charts for variables, averages of sub-groups of readings are used rather than the individual readings.
   Reason (R): If control charts are plotted with the individual readings, the labor of plotting the chart will increase.

5. **Assertion (A):** In Dodge Roaming sampling tables, the screening inspection of rejected lots is also included.
   Reason (R): Dodge Roaming plans are indexed at an LTPD of 10 percent.

6. **Assertion (A):** Job enrichment increases the job satisfaction of the employee.
   Reason (R): The jobs of wireman and lineman doing indoor and outdoor works respectively can be integrated for better results.

7. **Assertion (A):** In case of control charts for variables, the average of readings of a subgroup of four and more is plotted rather than the individual readings.
   Reason (R): Plotting of individual readings needs a lot of time and effort.

8. Match **List-I** with **List-II** and select the correct answer using the codes given below the lists:

List-I	List-II
A. Control charts for variables	1. Binomial distribution
B. Control chart for number of non-conformities	2. Beta distribution
C. Control chart for fraction rejected	3. Normal distribution
D. Activity time distribution in PERT	4. Poisson distribution
	5. Exponential distribution

Codes:

	A	B	C	D
(a)	3	4	1	5
(b)	5	4	3	1
(c)	4	3	1	2
(d)	3	4	1	2

9. Match **List-I** with **List-II** and select the correct answer using the codes given below the lists:

List-I	List-II
A. OC curve	1. Acceptance sampling
B. AOQL	2. Dodge Roaming table
C. Binomial distribution	3. p-charts
D. Normal curve	4. Control charts for variables

Codes:

	A	B	C	D
(a)	1	2	3	4
(b)	1	3	2	4
(c)	4	2	3	1
(d)	4	3	2	1

10. Match **List-I (Charts)** with **List-II (Operations/Information's)** and select the correct answer using the codes given below the lists:

List-I

A. Standard process sheet
B. Multiple activity chart
C. Right and left hand operation chart
D. SIMO chart

List-II

1. Operations involving assembly and inspection without machine
2. Operations involving the combination of men and machines
3. Work measurement
4. Basic information for routing
5. Therbligs

Codes:

	A	B	C	D
(a)	4	3	1	2
(b)	1	2	4	5
(c)	1	3	4	2
(d)	4	2	1	5

11. Which of the following hand-motion belongs to 'Therbligs' in motion study?

1. Unavoidable delay
2. Preposition
3. Select
4. Reach

Select the correct answer from the codes given below:

(a) 1 and 4
(b) 1 and 2
(c) 2 and 3
(d) 1 and 3

12. In a study to estimate the idle time of a machine, out of 100 random observations the machine is found idle on 40 observations. The total random observations required for 95% confidence level and ±5% accuracy are

(a) 384
(b) 600
(c) 2400
(d) 9600

13. Consider the following statements:

Control chart for variables provides the

1. basic variability of the quality characteristic.
2. consistency of performance.
3. number of products falling outside the tolerance limits.

Which of these statements are correct?

(a) 1, 2 and 3
(b) 1 and 2
(c) 2 and 3
(d) 1 and 3

14. Match **List-I (Scientist)** with **List-II (Research work)** and select the correct answer using the codes given below the lists:

List-I	List-II
A. Schewart	**1.** Less function in quality
B. Taguchi	**2.** Queuing model
C. Erland	**3.** Zero defect
	4. Control charts

Codes:

	A	B	C
(a)	3	1	2
(b)	4	3	1
(c)	4	1	2
(d)	3	4	1

15. Match **List-I (Wage payment plans)** with **List-II (Method of payment)** and select the correct answer using the codes given below the lists:

List-I	List-II
A. Time based	**1.** Stock distribution
B. Price rate	**2.** 100% bonus
C. Gain sharing	**3.** Taylor differential price rate
D. Indirect payments	**4.** Straight salary

Codes:

	A	B	C	D
(a)	4	3	2	1
(b)	2	1	4	3
(c)	4	1	2	3
(d)	2	3	4	1

16. Match **List-I (Limits in normal distribution)** with **List-II (Population covered)** and select the correct answer using the codes given below the lists:

List-I	List-II
A. $\pm 3\sigma$	1. 0.3413
B. $\pm 2\sigma$	2. 0.6826
C. $\pm 1\sigma$	3. 0.9973
	4. 0.9545

Codes:

	A	B	C
(a)	3	4	2
(b)	3	2	4
(c)	4	2	3
(d)	4	3	2

17. Match **List-I (Persons with whom the models are associated)** with **List-II (Models)** and select the correct answer using the codes given below the lists:

List-I	List-II
A. J. Von Newmann	1. Waiting lines
B. G. Dantzig	2. Simulation
C. A Erlang	3. Dynamic programming
D. Richard Bellman	4. Competitive strategies
	5. Allocation by simplex method

Codes:

	A	B	C	D
(a)	2	1	5	4
(b)	4	5	1	3
(c)	2	5	1	4
(d)	4	1	5	3

18. The graph shows the results of various quality levels for a component. Consider the following statements:

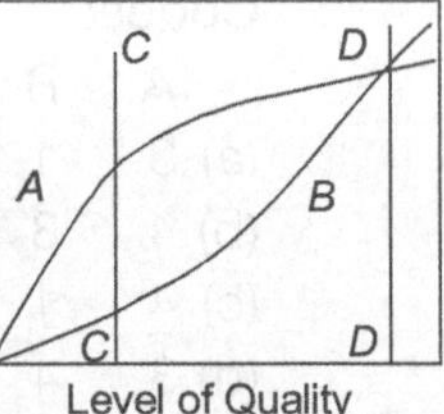

1. Curve A shows the variation of value of components.
2. Curve B shows the variation of cost of the component.
3. Graph is called as fish bone diagram.
4. The preferred level of, quality is given by line CC.
5. The preferred level of quality is given by line DO.

Which of these statements are correct?

(a) 1, 2 and 5 (b) 1, 3 and 4
(c) 2, 3 and 4 (d) 1, 2 and 4

19. Which one of the following types of layout is used for the manufacture of huge aircrafts?

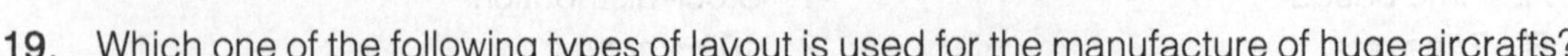

(a) Product layout (b) Process layout
(c) Fixed position layout (d) Combination layout

20. Which of the following statements correctly defines the term 'dispatching'?

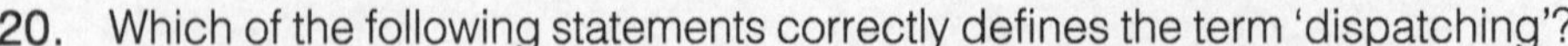

(a) Maintaining the record of time of starting and completion of each operation.
(b) The appraisal and evaluation of human work in terms of time.
(c) Taking all such steps which are meant to affect and implement the programs of production according to plans.
(d) Moving the work after completion to the next process or machine on the route.

21. Match **List-I (Trend/Defect)** with **List-II (Chart)** and select the correct answer:

List-I	List-II
A. Trend	1. R-Chart
B. Dispersion	2. C-Chart
C. Number of defects	3. X-Chart
D. Number of defective	4. Np-Chart
	5. U-Chart

Codes:

	A	B	C	D		A	B	C	D
(a)	5	3	2	4	(b)	3	1	4	2
(c)	3	1	2	4	(d)	3	4	5	2

22. Consider the following statements in respect of double sampling plan:
   1. Average number of pieces inspected is double that of single sampling.
   2. Average number of pieces inspected is less than that for single sampling.
   3. Decision to accept or reject the lot is taken only after the inspection of both samples.
   4. Decision to accept or reject the lot is reached sometime after one sample and sometimes after two samples.

   Which of these statements are correct?
   (a) 1, 2 and 3 (b) 2 and 4
   (c) 1 and 4 (d) 2 and 3

23. Consider the following statements:
   1. Preparation of master production schedule is an iterative process.
   2. Schedule charts are made with respect to jobs while load charts are made with respect to machines.
   3. MRP is done before master production scheduling.

   Which of these statements are correct?
   (a) 1, 2 and 3 (b) 1 and 2
   (c) 2 and 3 (d) 1 and 3

24. Match **List-I (PPC Functions)** with **List-II (Activity)** and select the correct answer using the codes given below the lists:

   List-I
   A. Capacity planning
   B. Shop floor control
   C. Master production schedule
   D. Material requirement planning

   List-II
   1. Listing products to be assembled and when to be delivered
   2. Rescheduling orders based on production priorities
   3. Closure tolerances
   4. Monitor progress of orders and report their status
   5. Planning of labor and equipment

Codes:

	A	B	C	D		A	B	C	D
(a)	1	4	3	2	(b)	5	2	1	4
(c)	1	2	3	4	(d)	5	4	1	2

25. A company has four work centers *A*, *S*, *C* and *D*, with per day capacities of 450 units, 390 units, 360 units and 400 units respectively. The machines are laid down in order *A*, *S*, *C* and *D* and product has to be operated on all these machines for getting converted into finished product. The actual output turns out to be 306 units per day. What is the system efficiency?
(a) 68% (b) 78%
(c) 80% (d) 85%

26. Match **List-I (Quality control concepts)** with **List-II (Quality control techniques)** and select the correct answer using the codes given below the lists:

List-I	List-II
A. Tightened and reduced inspection	1. Dodge Roaming tables
B. Lot tolerance percent defective	2. Control chart for variables.
C. Poisson distribution	3. MIL standards
D. Normal distribution	4. Control chart for number of non-conformities

Codes:

	A	B	C	D		A	B	C	D
(a)	2	1	4	3	(b)	3	4	1	2
(c)	3	1	4	2	(d)	2	4	1	3

27. Quality control chart for average was maintained for a dimension of the product. After the control was established, it was found that the standard deviation (cr) of the process was 1.00 mm. The dimension of the part is 70 ± 2.5 mm. Parts above 72.5 mm can be reworked but parts below 67.5 mm have to be scrapped. What should be the setting of the process to ensure production of no scrap and to minimize the rework?
(a) 68.5 mm (b) 70 mm
(c) 70.5 mm (d) 72.5 mm

28. Consider the following statements with respect to control charts for attributes:
1. The lower control-limit is non-negative.
2. Normal distribution is the order for this data.
3. The lower control limit is not significant.
4. These charts give the average quality characteristics.

Which of these statements are correct?
(a) 1, 2 and 3 (b) 2, 3 and 4
(c) 1, 3 and 4 (d) 1, 2 and 4

29. Match **List-I (Symbols in Flowcharts)** with **List-II (Actions)** and select the correct answer using the codes given below the lists:

List-I	List-II
A. Parallelogram	1. Decision
B. Diamond shaped box	2. Stop
C. Ellipse	3. Processing
D. Rectangle	4. Input/output

Codes:

	A	B	C	D		A	B	C	D
(a)	4	3	2	1	(b)	2	1	4	3
(c)	4	1	2	3	(d)	2	3	4	1

30. Match **List-I (Activity)** with **List-II (Technique)** and select the correct answer using the codes given below the lists:

List-I	List-II
A. Line Balancing	1. Value analysis
B. Product Development	2. Exponential smoothing
C. Forecasting	3. Control chart
D. Quality Control	4. Selective control
	5. Rank position matrix

Codes:

	A	B	C	D
(a)	2	1	4	3
(b)	5	3	2	1
(c)	2	3	4	1
(d)	5	1	2	3

31. What are the key functions of a master schedule?
   1. To generate material and capacity requirements.
   2. To maintain valid priorities.
   3. An effective capacity utilization.
   4. Planning the quantity and timing of output over the intermediate time horizons.

   Select the correct answer using the codes given below:
   (a) 1, 2 and 3 (b) 2, 3 and 4
   (c) 1, 3 and 4 (d) 1, 2 and 4

32. Which one of the following is not the characteristics of acceptance sampling?
   (a) This is widely suitable in mass production.
   (b) It causes less fatigue to inspectors.
   (c) This is much economical.
   (d) It gives definite assurance for the conformation of the specifications for all the pieces.

33. Which one of the following statements is not correct?
   (a) The operating characteristics curve of an acceptance sampling plan shows the ability of the plan to distinguish between good and bad lots.
   (b) No sampling plan can give complete protection against the acceptance of defective products.
   (c) C-chart has straight line limits and U chart has zig-zag limits.
   (d) Double sampling results it} more inspection than single sampling if the incoming quality is very bad.

Direction: Each of the next consists of two statements, one labelled as the **'Assertion (A)'** and the other as **'Reason (R)'**. You are to examine these two statements carefully and select the answers to these items using the codes given below:

Codes:
(a) Both A and R are individually true and R is the correct explanation of A.
(b) Both A and R are individually true but R is not the correct explanation of A.
(c) A is true but R is false.
(d) A is false but R is true.

34. **Assertion (A):** In case of Control Chart for fraction rejected (p-chart), binomial distribution is used.
   Reason (R): In binomial distribution probability of the event varies with each draw.

35. **Assertion (A):** In case of Control Chart for variables, the averages of Sub-groups of readings are plotted instead of plotting individual readings.
Reason (R): It has been proved through experiments that averages will form normal distribution curve.

36. If in a process on the shop floor, the specifications are not met, but the charts for variables show control, then which of the following actions should be taken?
(a) Changes the process
(b) Change the method measurement
(c) Change the worker or provide him training
(d) Change the specification or upgrade the process

37. An operating characteristic curve (OC curve) is a plot between
(a) consumers risk and producer risk.
(b) probability of acceptance and probability of rejection.
(c) percentage of defective and probability of acceptance.
(d) average outgoing quality and probability of acceptance.

38. Which one of the following statements is not correct for the TQC?
(a) It is about the product quality and quality of the business processes.
(b) It is restricted to product quality.
(c) It utilizes quality circles.
(d) It utilizes zero defect programs.

39. The probability law that determines the fluctuations of fraction defective is
(a) Poisson (b) Normal
(c) Binomial (d) Exponential

40. In the probability of an acceptance of a 1% defective lot is 0.95 then AOQ is
(a) 0.01 (b) 0.10
(c) 0.0095 (d) 0.095

OOOO

ANSWERS

QUALITY CONTROL

1. (d)	**2.** (b)	**3.** (d)	**4.** (b)	**5.** (b)	**6.** (d)	**7.** (a)
8. (d)	**9.** (a)	**10.** (b)	**11.** (a)	**12.** (c)	**13.** (a)	**14.** (a)
15. (b)	**16.** (a)	**17.** (c)	**18.** (c)	**19.** (c)	**20.** (c)	**21.** (b)
22. (b)	**23.** (b)	**24.** (b)	**25.** (b)	**26.** (c)	**27.** (c)	**28.** (c)
29. (c)	**30.** (d)	**31.** (b)	**32.** (a)	**33.** (d)	**34.** (d)	**35.** (c)
36. (b)	**37.** (c)	**38.** (c)	**39.** (c)	**40.** (c)		

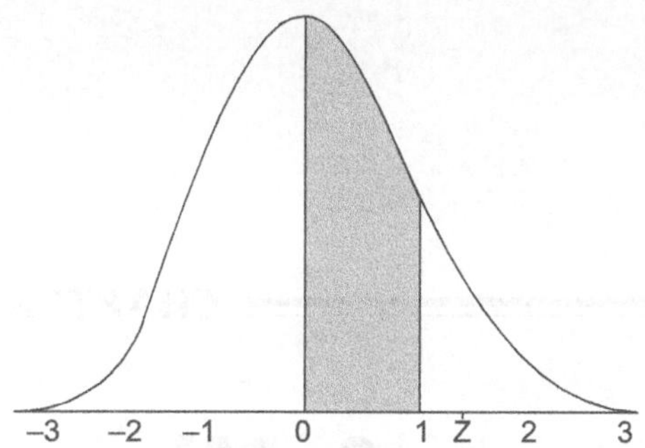

Normal Distribution Table
(Table shows total area under distribution up to "X")

Z	0.00	0.01	0.02	0.03	0.04	0.05	0.06	0.07	0.08	0.09
0.0	D.5O00	0.5040	0.5080	0.5120	0.5160	0.5199	0.5239	0.5279	0.5319	0.5359
0.1	0.5398	0.5438	0.5478	0.5517	0.5557	0.5596	0.5636	0.5675	0.5714	0.5753
0.2	0.5793	0.5832	0.5871	0.5910	0.5948	0.5987	0.6026	0.6064	0.6103	0.6141
0.3	0.6179	0.6217	0.6255	0.6293	0.6331	0.6368	0.6406	0.6443	0.6480	0.6517
0.4	0.6554	0.6591	0.6628	0.6664	0.6700	0.6736	0.6772	0.6808	0.6844	0.6879
0.5	0.6915	0.6950	0.6985	0.7019	0.7054	0.7088	0.7123	0.7157	0.7190	0.7224
0.6	0.7257	0.7291	0.7324	0.7357	0.7389	0.7422	0.7454	0.7486	0.7517	0.7549
0.7	0.7580	0.7611	0.7642	0.7673	0.7704	0.7734	0.7764	0.7794	0.7823	0.7852
0.8	0.7881	0.7910	0.7939	0.7967	0.7995	0.8023	0.8051	0.8078	0.8106	0.8133
0.9	0.8159	0.8186	0.8212	0.3238	0.8264	0.8289	0.8315	0.8340	08365	0.8389
1.0	0.8413	0.8438	0.8461	0.8485	0.8508	0.8531	0.85S4	0.8577	0.8599	0.8621
1.1	0.8643	0.8685	0.8686	0.8708	0.8729	0.8749	0.8770	0.8790	0.8810	0.8830
1.2	0.8849	0.8869	0.8888	0.8907	0.8925	0.8944	0.8962	0.8960	0.8997	0.9015
1.3	0.9032	0.9049	0.9066	0.9082	0.9099	09115	0.9131	0.9147	0.9162	0.9177
1.4	0.9192	0.9207	0.9222	0.9236	0.9251	0.9265	0.9279	0.9292	0.9306	0.9319
1.5	0.9332	0.9345	0.9357	0.9370	0.9382	0.9394	0.9406	0.9418	0.9429	0.9441
1.6	0.9452	0.9463	0.9474	0.9464	0.9495	0.9505	0.9515	0.9525	0.9535	0.9545
1.7	0.9554	0.9564	0.9573	0.9582	0.9591	0.9599	0.9608	0.9616	0.9625	0.9633
1.8	0.S641	0.9649	0.9656	0.9664	0.9671	0.9678	0.9686	0.9693	0.9699	0.9706
1.9	0.9713	0.9719	0.9726	0.9732	0.9738	0.9744	0.9750	0.9756	0.9761	0.9767
2.0	0.9772	0.9778	0.9783	0.9788	0.9793	0.9798	0.9803	0.9808	0.9812	0.9817
2.1	0.9821	0.9826	0.9830	0.9834	0.9838	0.9642	0.9846	0.9650	0.9854	0.9857
2.2	0.9861	0.9864	0.9868	0.9871	0.9875	0.9878	0.9881	0.9884	0.9587	0.9890
2.3	0.9893	0.9896	0.9898	0.9901	0.9904	0.9906	0.9909	0.9911	0.9913	0.9916
2.4	0.9918	0.9920	0.9922	0.9925	0.9927	0.9929	0.9931	0.9932	0.9934	0.9936
2.5	0.9938	0.9940	0.9941	0.9943	0.9945	09946	0.9948	0.9949	0.9951	0.9952
2.6	0.9953	0.9955	0.9956	0.9957	0.9959	0.9960	0.9961	0.9962	0.9963	0.9964
2.7	0.9965	0.9966	0.9967	0.9968	0.9969	0.9970	0.9971	0.9972	0.9973	0.9974
2.8	09974	0.9975	0.9976	0.9977	0.9977	0.9978	0.9979	0.9979	0.9980	0.9981
2.9	0.9981	0.9962	0.9982	0.9983	0.9984	0.9984	0.9985	0.9985	0.9986	0.9986
3.0	0.9987	0.9987	0.9987	0.9988	0.9988	0.9989	0.9989	0.9989	0.9990	0.9990
3.1	0.9990	0.9991	0.9991	0.9991	0.9992	0.9992	0.9992	0.9992	0.9993	0.9993
3.2	0.9993	0.9993	0.9994	0.9994	0.9994	0.9994	0.9994	0.9995	0.9995	0.9995
3.3	0.9995	0.9995	0.9995	0.9996	0.9996	0.9996	0.9996	0.9996	0.9996	0.9997
3.4	0.9997	0.9997	0.9997	0.9997	0.9997	0.9997	0.9997	0.9997	0.9997	0.9998
3.5	0.9998	0.9998	0.9998	0.9998	0.9998	0.9996	0.9998	0.9998	0.9998	0.9998
3.6	0.9996	0.9998	0.9999	0.9999	0.9999	0.9999	0.9999	0.9999	0.9999	0.9999
3.7	0.9999	0.9999	0.9999	0.9999	0.9999	0.9999	0.9999	0.9999	0.9999	0.9999
3.8	0.9999	0.9999	0.9999	0.9999	0.9999	0.9999	0.9999	0.9999	0.9999	0.9999
3.9	1.0000	1.0000	1.0000	1.0000	1.0000	1.0000	1.0000	1.0000	1.0000	1.0000

CHAPTER 12

Microprocessor & Microcontroller

12.1 MICROPROCESSOR

A Microprocessor, known as computer processor with general purpose central processing unit (CPU) fabricated on a single integrated circuit (IC). Microprocessor is an IC which has only the CPU inside them i.e. only the processing powers such as Intel's Pentium 1, 2, 3, 4, core 2 duo, i3, i5 etc. The integration of a whole CPU onto a single chip or on a few chips greatly reduced the cost of processing power. Single-chip processors increase reliability as there are very few electrical connections to fail. These microprocessors don't have RAM, ROM, and other peripheral on the chip. A system designer has to add them externally to make them functional. Application of microprocessor includes Desktop PC's, Laptops, notepads etc.

The microprocessor is a small but very powerful electronic brain that operates at a high speed and is often used to carry out instructions of a computer program in order to perform arithmetic and logical operations, storing the data, system control, input / output operations etc. as per the instructions. The important characteristics of a microprocessor are the widths of its internal and external address bus and data bus (and instruction), its clock rate and its instruction set.

The main task of a microprocessor is to accept data as input from input devices then process this data according to the instructions and provide the results of these instructions as output through output devices. The first commercial Microprocessor was released by Intel in November 1971, named as 4004. It was 4-bit microprocessor since it processed only 4 bits of data at a time. This was the CPU member of a set of four LSI integrated circuits called the MCS-4, which was originally designed for use in a calculator but was marketed as "programmable controller for logic replacement". This very short word size is mainly the limitations imposed by the limited maximum integrated circuit density.

As integrated circuit densities increased with the rapid development of integrated circuit manufacturing technology, the power and performance of the microprocessors also increased. This is reflected in the increase in the CPU word size to 4, 8, 16, and by mid-1980s, 32 bits. The Intel 4004 was followed by the 4040, 8008, 8080, 8086, 80186, 80286, 80386, 486 and Pentium and others. Other families include the Motorola 6800 and 680x0 families, National Semiconductor 16000 and National Semiconductor 32000, SPARC, ARM, MIPS, Zilog Z8000, Power PC and the Inmos Transputer family.

The larger, more recent microprocessor families have gradually acquired most of the features of large computers. As the microprocessor industry has developed, several families of microprocessors with numerous "support" chips including RAM, ROM, I/O controllers etc. have come into the market. A single chip microprocessor may include other components such as memory (RAM, ROM, PROM), memory management, caches, floating-point unit, input/output ports and timers. Such devices are also known as microcontrollers.

Microcomputers have given rise to a new class of general-purpose machines called personal computers. These are small low cost computers that are designed to sit on an ordinary office desk or to be portable.

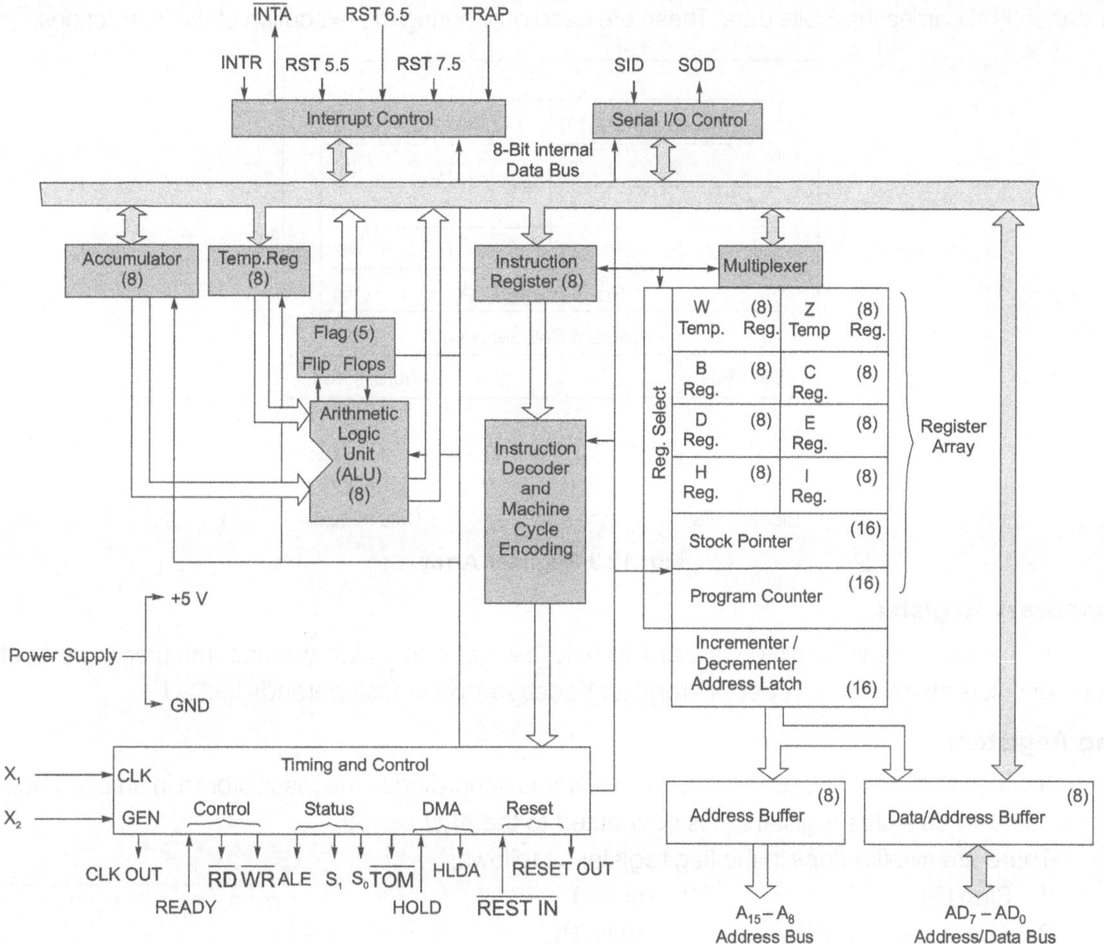

Fig: 12.1 Block diagram of 8085 microprocessor

Fig: 12.2 The Intel core i7 and Pentium Microprocessors

Accumulator

It is an 8-bit register which is used to perform arithmetical and logical operation. It stores the output of any operation. It also works as registers for I/O accesses.

Arithmetic Logic Unit (ALU)

The arithmetic logic unit (ALU) is a digital electronic circuit that performs the arithmetic and logical operations. An ALU is a fundamental building block of several computing devices, including the central processing unit (CPU) of computers, floating point units (FPUs) etc.

Registers

These are general purposes registers. Microprocessor consist 6 general purpose registers of 8biteach named as B, C, D, E, H and L. Generally theses registers are not used for storing the data permanently. It carries the 8 bits data. These are used only during the execution of the instructions.

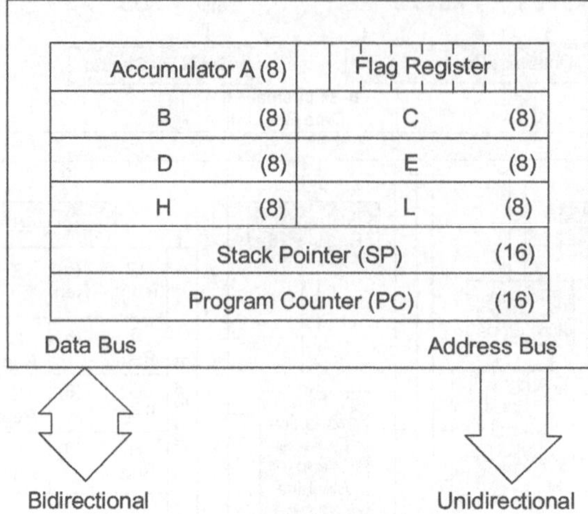

Fig: 12.3 Register Array

Temporary Register

It is an 8-bit register which is used to hold the data on which the accumulator is computing operations. It is also called as operand register because it provides operands to ALU.

Flag Registers

It consists of 5 flip flop which changes its status according to the result stored in an accumulator. It is also known as status registers. It is connected to the ALU.

There are five flip-flops in the flag register as follows:

1. Sign (S),
2. zero (z),
3. Auxiliary Carry (AC),
4. Parity (P),
5. Carry (C)

D_7	D_6	D_5	D_4	D_3	D_2	D_1	D_0
S	Z		AC		P		CY

The bit position of the flip-flop in flag register is:

All of the three flip-flop set and reset according to the stored result in the accumulator.

1. **Sign (S):** If D_7 of the result is 1 then sign flag is set otherwise reset. As we know that a number on the D_7 always decides the sign of the number. If D_7 is 1, the number is negative. If D_7 is 0, the number is positive.
2. **Zeros (Z):** If the result stored in an accumulator is zero then this flip flop is set otherwise it is reset.
3. **Auxiliary Carry (AC):** If any carry goes from D_3 to D_4 in the output then it is set otherwise it is reset.
4. **Parity (P):** If the no of 1's is even in the output stored in the accumulator then it is set otherwise it is reset for the odd.
5. **Carry (C):** If the result stored in an accumulator generates a carry in its final output then it is set otherwise it is reset.

Instruction Registers (IR): It is an 8-bit register. When an instruction is fetched from memory then it is stored in this register.

Instruction Decoder: Instruction decoder identifies the instructions. It takes the information's from instruction register and decodes the instruction to be performed.

Program Counter: It is a 16-bit register used as memory pointer. It stores the memory address of the next instruction to be executed. So we can say that this register is used for sequencing the program. Generally the memory has16 bit addresses so that it has 16-bit memory. The program counter is set to 0000H.

Stack Pointer: It is also a 16-bit register used as memory pointer. It points to the memory location called stack. Generally stack is a reserved portion of memory where information can be stores or taken back together.

Timing and Control Unit: It provides timing and control signal to the microprocessor to perform the various operation. It has three control signals. It controls all external and internal circuits. It operates with reference to clock signal and synchronizes all the data transfers.

There are three control signals:

1. **ALE (Arithmetic Latch Enable):** It provides control signal to synchronize the components of microprocessor.
2. **RD:** This is active low used for reading operation.
3. **WR:** This is active low used for writing operation.

There are three status signal used in microprocessor S0, S1 and IO/M. It changes its status according the provided input to these pins.

Serial Input Output Control:

IO/M (Active Low)	S1	S2	Data Bus Status (Ouput)
0	0	0	Halt
0	0	1	Memory WRITE
0	1	0	Memory READ
1	0	1	IO WRITE
1	1	0	IO READ
0	1	1	Opcode fetch
1	1	1	Interrupt acknowledge

Table: 12.1: Active low flag, sign flag and data bus

There are two pins in this unit. This unit is used for serial data communications.

Interrupt Unit:

There are 6 interrupt pins in this unit. Generally an external hardware is connected to these pins. These pins provide interrupt signal sent by external hardware to microprocessor and microprocessor sends acknowledgement for receiving the interrupt signal. Generally INTA is used for acknowledgement.

12.2 INTERNAL STRUCTURE OF A MICROPROCESSOR

Microprocessor includes an arithmetic logic unit (ALU) and a control logic section. The ALU performs different operations such as addition, subtraction, and operations such as AND or OR. Each operation of the ALU sets one or more flags in a status register, which indicate the results of the last operation (zero value, negative number, overflow, or others). The control logic carry out many tasks such as decoding, fetching, handling the execution and finally storing the results. It check/guide the flow of data through the different parts of the computer. Function of control unit is also to regulate the time controls of the processor.

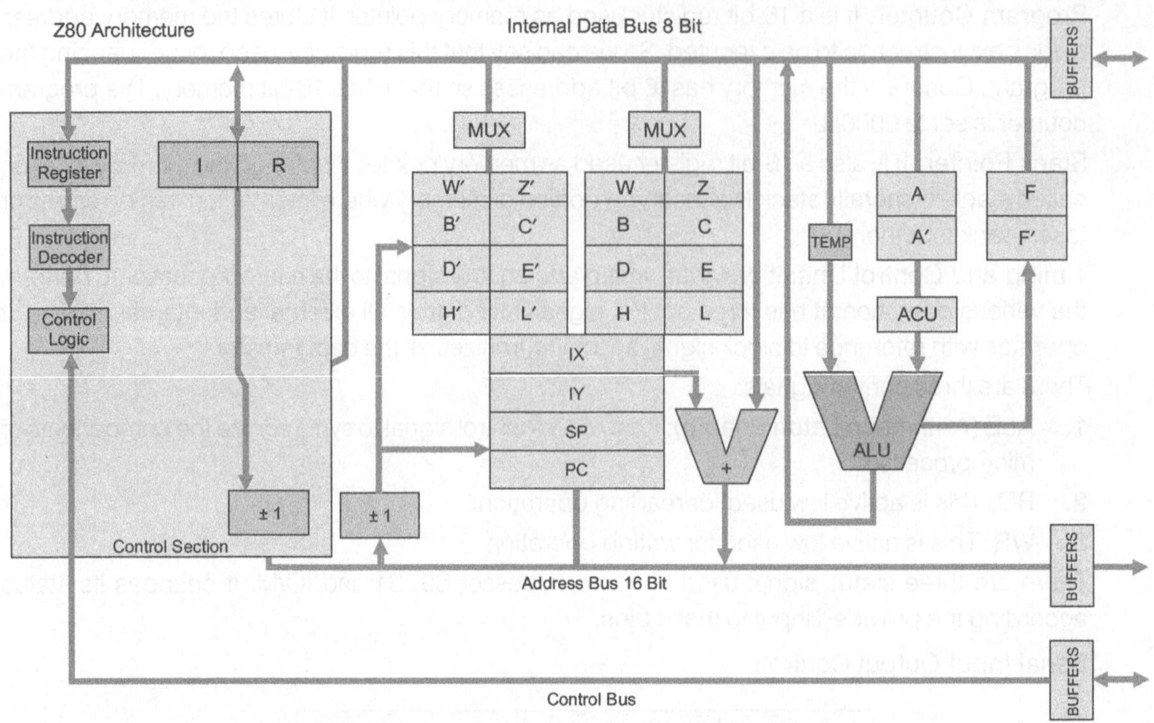

Fig: 12.4 Internal structure of a microprocessor

12.3 CLOCK SPEED

Clock speed is the speed that the microprocessor executes each instruction or each vibration of the clock. The CPU requires a fixed number of clock ticks, or cycles, to execute each instruction. If the clock rate is fast the speed of CPU also become faster, which also affect the execution speed. Clock Speeds are usually determined in MHz, 1 MHz representing 1 million cycles per second, or in GHz, 1 GHz representing 1 thousand million cycles per second. Higher the CPU speed, better the computer will perform, in a general sense. Other components can improve a computer's performance as well, like memory (RAM) and the motherboard, as well as the number of cores that a processor has, like dual core or quad core. The speed of dual core is less than the speed of quad core. The quad core processor can perform more calculations than dual core.

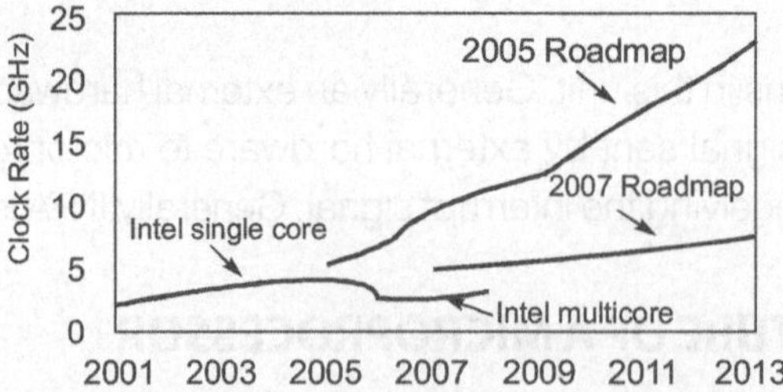

Fig: 12.5 The improvement in Clock Speed of processors in 21 century

12.4 INPUT/OUTPUT PORTS (I/O PORTS)

In all the 8051 microcontrollers there is 4 I/O ports, each comprising of 8-bits which can be configured as inputs or outputs. Accordingly, in total of 32 input/output pins, enabling the microcontroller to be connected to peripheral devices that are available for use.

Pin configuration, i.e. whether it is to be configured as an input (1) or an output (0), which depends on its logic state. To configure a microcontroller pin as an output, it is necessary to apply a logic zero (0) to appropriate I/O port bit. In this case, voltage level on appropriate pin will be 0 V.

To configure a microcontroller pin as an input, it is necessary to apply a logic one (1) to appropriate port. In this case, voltage level on appropriate pin will be 5 V (as is the case with any TTL input). This may seem confusing but don't lose your patience. It all becomes clear after studying simple electronic circuits connected to an I/O pin.

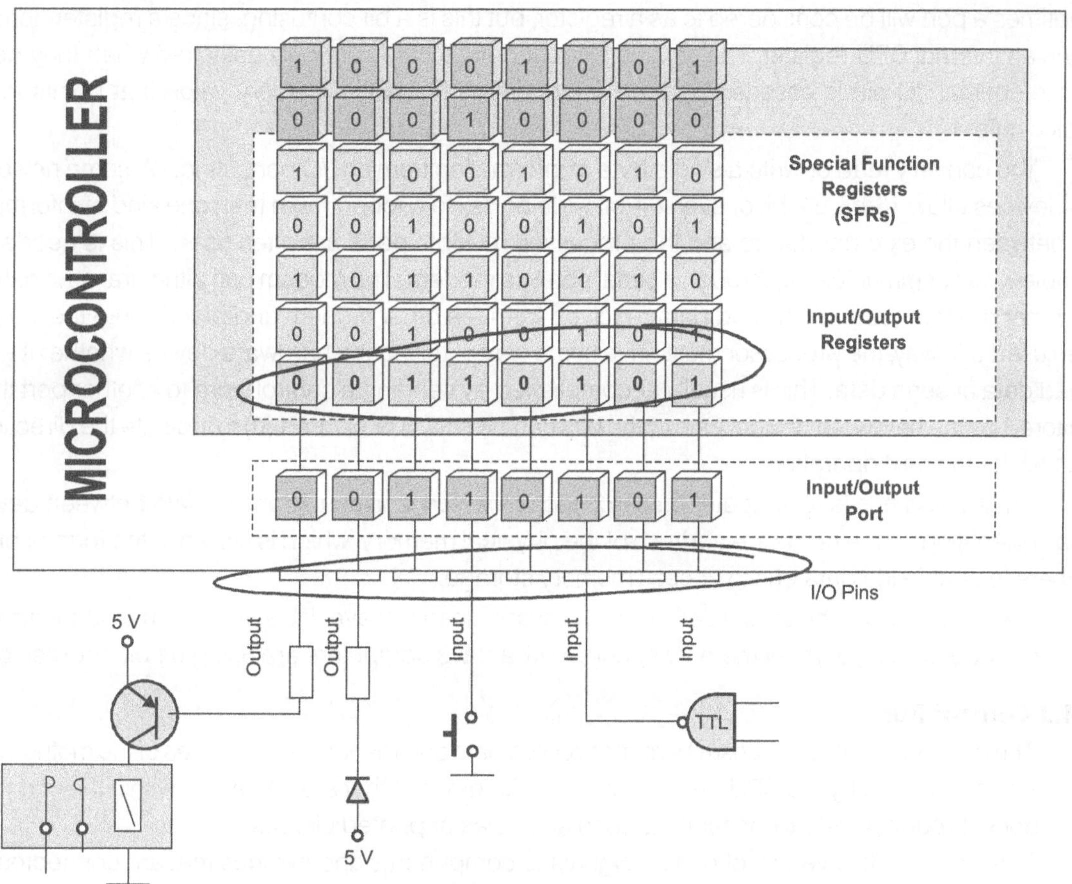

Fig: 12.6 Input/ Output Ports (I/O Ports)

Figure above illustrates a simplified schematic of all circuits within the microcontroller connected to one of its pins. It refers to all the pins except those of the P0 port which do not have pull-up resistors built-in.

12.4.1 Data Bus

The data bus is a series of pins on the processor that are used to get data into, or out of, the processor chip itself. All memory and input and output devices are connected to the data bus, but depending on the current state of the address of bus and other control pins on the processor, only one chip can actually be connected to the data bus at any given moment.

The data bus may be 4-bit, 8-bit, 16-bit, 32-bit or perhaps 64-bits wide. A wider data bus allows the processor to read and write more bits of data in a single operation. This technique is used with PCI-based cards on PC-compatibles to achieve faster input and output operations for certain devices. In other cases however, using more bits is a waste of time, because the device connected at the other end of the data bus only supports 4 or 8-bit transfers at a time. In this case it is very important to ignore the unused bits. I/O works on a microprocessor at a low-level.

12.4.2 Address Bus

Every CPU has a number of pins, which work together, called an address bus. The address bus is used to read or write to memory, most often RAM chips. However most modern microprocessors use the address bus for more than just reading and writing to memory.

By toggling a special pin, the CPU can switch from using the address bus for accessing RAM, to using the address bus to talk to other semi-intelligent chips that are also connected to the address bus. When used in this way, we are said to be using I/O port addressing, instead of normal memory addresses. Sometimes a port will be considered to as a register, but this is a bit confusing, since a register normally means an internal CPU register. The semi-intelligent device chips are only activated when they detect that the special I/O pin is asserted and the address bus holds the memory value that points to that specific chip.

You can only read or write a single byte of information from an I/O port, although some newer I/O chip devices allow 16-bit, 32-bit or even 64-bit wide ports. To support more than one kind of information flow between the external device and the processor, multiple ports are often used. This is needed for example when communicating through a serial port to a modem. The modem can either transmit data out to another modem (output), or read data received from the other modem and place it into the I/O port. When used this way, the processor must have some way of telling the hardware device whether it wants to read data or send data. This is usually accomplished by sending a control word to another port that is monitored by the hardware device. One of the bits can be set (1) or cleared (0) to indicate the direction of data flow for the next operation.

An address bus is a computer bus architecture which is used to transfer data between devices that are identified by the hardware address of the physical memory, which is stored in the form of binary numbers to enable the data bus to access memory storage.

It is measured by the amount of memory a system can retrieve. If a system with a 32-bit address bus can address 4 Gigabyte of memory space. Now a days computers are using 64 bit address bus.

12.4.3 Control Bus

The control bus used to transmit signals to coordinate and manage the activities of the motherboard components. It is used by the CPU to communicate with devices that are contained within the computer. This is done through physical connections such as cables or printed circuits.

The CPU sends a variety of control signals to components and devices that are connected to it using the control bus. One of the main objectives of a bus is to minimize the lines that are needed for communication. An individual bus permits communication between devices using one data channel. The control bus is bidirectional and assists the CPU in synchronizing control signals to internal devices and external components. It is comprised of interrupt lines, byte enable lines, read/write signals and status lines.

12.5 MICROCONTROLLER

To overcome the drawback of the microprocessor, microcontroller was developed. Microcontroller has a CPU, in addition with a fixed amount of RAM (random access memory), ROM (read only memory) and other peripherals all embedded on a single chip. Now a day different manufacturers develop microcontrollers with a wide range of features available in different versions. Some manufacturers are ATMEL, Microchip, TI, Freescale, Philips, Motorola etc.

Microcontrollers are used in automatically controlled products and various devices, such as automobile engine control systems, implantable medical devices, remote controls, office machines, appliances, power tools, toys and other embedded systems.

Microprocessor is an IC which has only the CPU inside them i.e. only the processing powers such as Intel's Pentium 1, 2, 3, 4, core 2 duo, i3, i5 etc. These microprocessors don't have RAM, ROM and other peripheral on the chip. A system designer has to add them externally to make them functional. Application of microprocessor includes Desktop PC's, Laptops, notepads etc.

But this is not the case with Microcontrollers. Microcontroller has a CPU, in addition with a fixed amount of RAM, ROM and other peripherals all embedded on a single chip. At times it is also termed as a mini computer or a computer on a single chip. Today different manufacturers produce microcontrollers with a wide range of features available in different versions. Some manufacturers are ATMEL, Microchip, TI, Freescale, Philips, Motorola etc.

Microcontrollers are designed to perform specific tasks. Specific means applications where the relationship of input and output is defined. Depending on the input, some processing needs to be done and output is delivered. For example, keyboards, mouse, washing machine, digicam, pendrive, remote, microwave, cars, bikes, telephone, mobiles, watches, etc. Since the applications are very specific, they need small resources like RAM, ROM, I/O ports etc. and hence can be embedded on a single chip. This in turn reduces the size and the cost.

Microprocessor find applications where tasks are unspecific like developing software, games, websites, photo editing, creating documents etc. In such cases the relationship between input and output is not defined. They need high amount of resources like RAM, ROM, I/O ports etc.

The clock speed of the Microprocessor is quite high as compared to the microcontroller. Whereas the microcontrollers operate from a few MHz to 30 to 50 MHz, today's microprocessor operate above 1 GHz as they perform complex tasks.

Comparing microcontroller and microprocessor in terms of cost is not justified. Undoubtedly a microcontroller is far cheaper than a microprocessor. However microcontroller cannot be used in place of microprocessor and using a microprocessor is not advised in place of a microcontroller as it makes the application quite costly. Microprocessor cannot be used stand alone. They need other peripherals like RAM, ROM, buffer, I/O ports etc and hence a system designed around a microprocessor is quite costly.

12.6 HOW TO WRITE A SIMPLE LCD PROGRAM

If we want to send a command or a character to the LCD, we must first check to see if the LCD is busy or not. If not, then it is OK to send the command or character. Let us take a look at the sequence of instructions we need to use to check the busy status.

1. Set the microcontroller port data direction to input. Let us call this DDR port as Data Dir.
2. Set the pin connected to the LCD RW to ON (read mode).
3. Set the pin connected to the LCD RS to OFF (command mode).
4. Turn the enable on, and then off after a tiny delay.
5. Read the D_7 pin to determine if it is a 1 or a 0.
6. Do numbers 4 and 5 until the D_7 is 0 (meaning that it is not busy).

A Typical Program:

```
#include <avr/io.h>
#include <util/delay.h>
#define MrLCDsCrib PORTB
#define DataDir_MrLCDsCrib DDRB
#define MrLCDsControl PORTD
#define DataDir_MrLCDsControl DDRD
```

```
#define Light Switch 5
#define Read Write 7
#define BiPolar Mood 2
void Check_IF_MrLCD_isBusy(void);
void Peek_A_Boo(void);
void Send_A_Command (unsigned char command);
void Send_A_Character (unsigned char character);
void Send_A_String (char *string);
int main(void)
{
DataDir_MrLCDsControl |= 1<<LightSwitch | 1<<ReadWrite | 1<<BiPolarMood;
_delay_ms(15);
Send_A_Command(0x01); //Clear Screen 0x01 = 00000001
_delay_ms(2);
Send_A_Command(0x38);
_delay_us(50);
Send_A_Command(0b00001110);
_delay_us(50);

Send_A_Character(0x4E); //N
Send_A_Character(0x65); //e
Send_A_Character(0x77); //w
Send_A_Character(0x62); //b
Send_A_Character(0x69); //i
Send_A_Character(0x65); //e
Send_A_Character(0x48); //H
Send_A_Character(0x61); //a
Send_A_Character(0x63); //c
Send_A_Character(0x6B); //k
Send_A_Character(0x2E); //.
Send_A_Character(0x63); //c
Send_A_Character(0x6F); //o
Send_A_Character(0x6D); //m
Send_A_String("Patrick");
while(1)
{
}
}
void Check_IF_MrLCD_isBusy()
{
DataDir_MrLCDsCrib = 0;
MrLCDsControl |= 1<<ReadWrite;
MrLCDsControl&= ~1<<BiPolarMood;
```

```
while (MrLCDsCrib>= 0x80)
{
Peek_A_Boo();
}
DataDir_MrLCDsCrib = 0xFF; //0xFF means 0b11111111
}
void Peek_A_Boo()
{
MrLCDsControl |= 1<<LightSwitch;
asm volatile ("nop");
asm volatile ("nop");
MrLCDsControl&= ~1<<LightSwitch;
}
void Send_A_Command(unsigned char command)
{
Check_IF_MrLCD_isBusy();
MrLCDsCrib = command;
MrLCDsControl&= ~ ((1<<ReadWrite)|(1<<BiPolarMood));
Peek_A_Boo();
MrLCDsCrib = 0;
}
void Send_A_Character(unsigned char character)
{
Check_IF_MrLCD_isBusy();
MrLCDsCrib = character;
MrLCDsControl&= ~ (1<<ReadWrite);
MrLCDsControl |= 1<<BiPolarMood;
Peek_A_Boo();
MrLCDsCrib = 0;
}
```

12.7 THE PROGRAMMABLE LOGIC CONTROLLER (PLC)

Programmable logic controller also known as PLC is a specialized computer used to control machines and processes. The PLC uses a programmable memory to store/save instructions and specific functions that include ON/OFF control, counting, arithmetic, timing, sequencing and also data handling.

There are several advantages of PLC control system as follows:

- It is flexible.
- It has faster response time.
- It has no moving parts- Solid state.
- Plc control systems are less expensive.
- It is easy to trouble shoot.
- It is easy to repair and expand-Modular-design.

12.7.1 The History of PLC

The Programmable Logic Controllers were designed and developed by Modicon as a relay replace for GM and Landis.

- These controllers eliminated the need for rewiring and adding additional hardware for each new configuration of logic.
- The new system rapidly increased the functionality of the controls while reducing the cabinet space that housed the logic.
- The first PLC, model 084, was invented by Dick Morley in 1969.
- The first successful PLC, the 184, was introduced in 1973 and was designed.

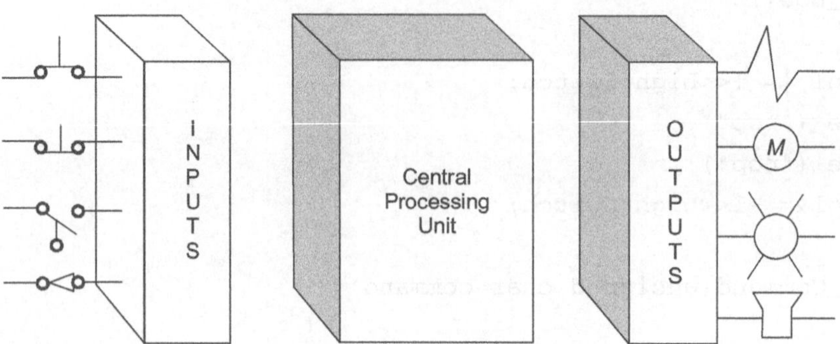

Fig: 12.7 The structure of a PLC

12.7.2 Steps of PLC Operations

There are four basic steps in the operation of all PLCs; Input Scan, Program Scan, Output Scan, and Housekeeping. These steps continually take place in a repeating loop.

Step 1: Input Scan: In this step the state of all input devices that are connected to the PLC system are detected.

Step 2: Program Scan: This step executes the user created program logic.

Step 3: Output Scan: This step energizes or de-energize all output devices that are connected to the PLC.

Step 4: Housekeeping: This step includes communications with programming terminals, internal diagnostics, etc.

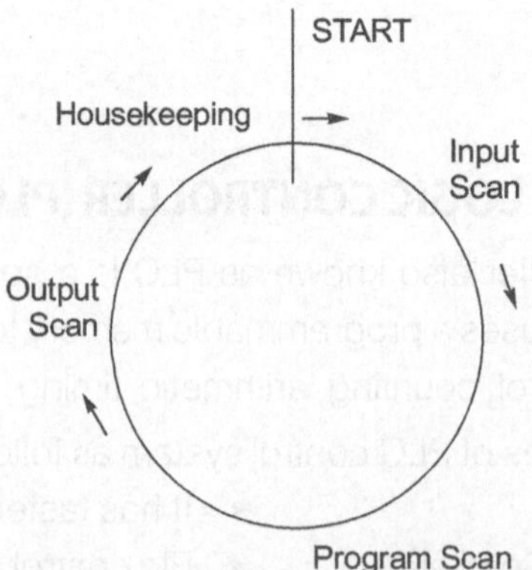

Fig: 12.8 Step of PLC operation

INPUTS

- Switches and Pushbuttons
- Sensing Devices
  - o Limit Switches
  - o Photoelectric Sensors
  - o Proximity Sensors
- Condition Sensors
- Encoders
  - o Pressure Switches
  - o Level Switches
  - o Temperature Switches
  - o Vacuum Switches

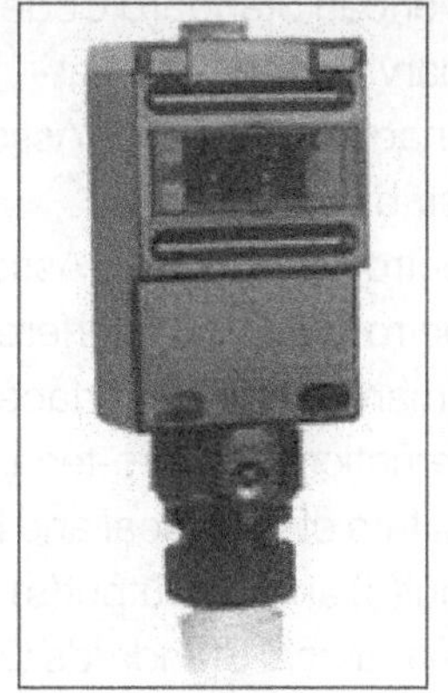

OUTPUTS

- Valves
- Motor Starters
- Solenoids
- Actuators
- Horns and Alarms
- Stacklights
- Control Relays
- Counter/Totalizer
- Pumps
- Printers
- Fans

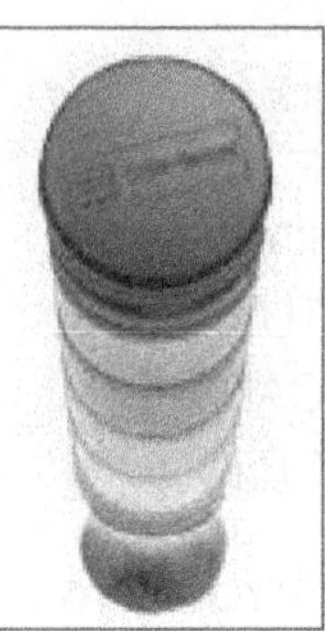

Fig: 12.9 Different types of Input/output Devices

12.7.3 Factors to be Considered while Selection of a PLC System

There are many PLC systems available in the market today. Other than cost, following factors need to beconsidered for selection of best suitable PLC system for the given application.

- Will the system be powered by AC or DC voltage?
- Does the PLC have enough memory to run the user program?
- Does the system run fast enough to meet the given application's requirements?
- What type of software is used to program the PLC?
- If the PLC is able to manage the number of inputs and outputs that the given application requires?
- If required for the given application, can the PLC handle analog inputs and outputs, or a combination of both analog and discrete inputs and outputs?
- Will the system be located in one place or spread out over a large area?
- How you are going to communicate with the PLC?
- Do you need network connectivity and can it be added to the PLC?

Table: 2 Terms and their abbreviations used in Mechatronics

ASCII	:	American Standard Code for Information Interchange
BCD	:	Binary Coded Decimal
CSA	:	Canadian Standards Association
DIO	:	Distributed I/O
EIA	:	Electronic Industries Association
EMI	:	Electro Magnetic Interference
HMI	:	Human Machine Interface
IEC	:	International Electro-technical Commission
IEEE	:	Institute of Electrical and Electronic Engineers
I/O	:	Input(s) and/or Output(s)
ISO	:	International Standards Organization
LL	:	Ladder Logic
LSB	:	Least Significant Bit
MMI	:	Man Machine Interface
MODICON	:	Modular Digital Controller
MSB	:	Most Significant Bit
PID	:	Proportional Integral Derivative (feedback control)
RF	:	Radio Frequency
RIO	:	Remote I/O
RTU	:	Remote Terminal Unit
SCADA	:	Supervisory Control And Data Acquisition
TCP/IP	:	Transmission Control Protocol / Internet Protocol

Solved Problems:

Q.1 What are the various criteria to choose the microcontroller?

Ans: Following are the important criteria to choose the microprocessor:

1. Availability of software development tools like compilers, debuggers, assemblers
2. Meeting the computing needs of the task at hand efficiently at low-cost.
3. Reliable sources/manufacturers
4. Wide availability
5. The amount of RAM and ROM on chip
6. The number of I/O pins and the timer on the chip
7. Power consumption
8. Packaging speed of the device
9. Cost per unit.

Q.2 What do you understand by Flip-flop?

Ans: A Flip-flop is a basic electronic circuit used for storing information in a digital machine. It is a bi-stable device. It means it has two stable states.
It consists of one or more inputs and two complement outputs.

Q.3 Write the memory size of 8085 microprocessor?

Ans: 8085 microprocessor has 8 data lines and 16 address lines. The memory size of any microprocessor depends on the number of address lines. The general formula is 2^n, where n= number of address lines. For 8085 there are 2^16= 64 K bytes memory size.

Q.4 How many bits is 8085 microprocessor?

Ans: Microprocessor is named on the basis of number of data lines in it. 8085 is an 8-bit microprocessor as it has 8-bit data lines.

Q.5 What are the various interrupts in 8085 microprocessor? Which is the highest priority interrupt?

Ans: There are 6 types of interrupts in 8085. They are

(a) TRAP (b) RST 7.5
(c) RST 6.5 (d) RST 5.5
(e) INTR

Q.6 Which cycle is used to fetch and execute the instructions?

Ans: Instruction cycle is used to fetch and execute the instructions. In this cycle the instruction is fetched, decoded and executed to produce the required output.

Q.7 How many address lines are there in 8085 microprocessor?

Ans: There are 16 address lines in 8085. They are multiplexed address and data lines. Address bus of 8085 is of 16 bits. During the first machine cycle these address lines are used as data lines and in the next machine cycle all the 16 lines act as address lines.

Q.8 Why crystal is being preferred as a clock source?

Ans: Reasons-high stability, large Q (Quality Factor) & the frequency that doesn't drift with aging. Therefore crystal is used as a clock source most of the times.

Q.9 Name High order or Low order Register in 8085 microprocessor?

Ans: Flag is known as Low order register & Accumulator is known as High order Register in 8085 microprocessor.

Q.10 Where does CPU Enhanced mode originate from?

Ans: Intel's 80386 was the first 32-bit processor, and so the company had to backward-support the 8086. All the modern Intel-based processors run in the enhanced mode which are capable to switch in between real mode and protected mode, which is the current mode of operation.

Q.11 What are the different types of buses?

Ans: Three types of buses are there:

Address bus: It carries the Address to the memory to fetch either instruction.

Data bus: It carries data from the memory.

Control bus: It carries the control signals like RD/WR, Select etc.

Unsolved Subjective Problems:

Q.1 Describe the register set of microprocessor in details.

Q.2 Draw block diagram of microprocessor and give the functioning of ALU, Accumulator, and temporary register.

Q.3 Write a note on address bus and data bus.

Q.4 Differentiate between microprocessor and microcontroller.

Q.5 Write a note on input/output interface of microprocessor.

Q.6 Write a note on timing and control unit of microprocessor.

Q.7 Define following terms:

(i) DMA controller (ii) stack pointer
(iii) Program counter (iv) Register array
(v) multiplexer (vi) Address buffer/Data buffer

OOOO

PRACTICE QUESTIONS

1. The devices that provide the means for a computer to communicate with the user or other computers are referred to as:
(a) CPU (b) ALU
(c) I/O (d) none of the above

2. The software used to drive microprocessor-based systems is called:
(a) Assembly language (b) Firmware
(c) Machine language code (d) BASIC interpreter instructions

3. The circuits in the 8085A that provide the arithmetic and logic functions are called the:
(a) CPU (b) ALU
(c) I/O (d) none of the above

4. How many buses are connected as part of the 8085A microprocessor?
(a) 2 (b) 3
(c) 5 (d) 8

5. The ______ ensures that only one IC is active at a time to avoid a bus conflict caused by two ICs writing different data to the same bus.
(a) control bus (c) control instructions
(c) address decoder (d) CPU

6. How many bits are used in the data bus?
(a) 7 (b) 8
(c) 9 (d) 16

7. The items that you can physically touch in a computer system are called:
(a) software (b) firmware
(c) hardware (d) none of the above

8. Single-bit indicators that may be set or cleared to show the results of logical or arithmetic operations are the:
(a) flags (b) registers
(c) monitors (d) decisions

9. When referring to instruction words, a mnemonic is
(a) a short abbreviation for the operand address.
(c) a short abbreviation for the operation to be performed.
(c) a short abbreviation for the data word stored at the operand address.
(d) shorthand for machine language.

10. The technique of assigning a memory address to each I/O device in the computer system is called:
(a) memory-mapped I/O (b) ported I/O
(c) dedicated I/O (d) wired I/O

11. When was the first 8-bit microprocessor introduced?
(a) 1969 (b) 1974
(c) 1979 (d) 1985

12. What type of circuit is used at the interface point of an output port?
(a) Decoder
(b) Latch
(c) Tristate buffer
(d) None of the above

13. I/O mapped systems identify their input/output devices by giving them a(n) _______.
(a) 8-bit port number
(b) 16-bit port number
(c) 8-bit buffer number
(d) 8-bit instruction

14. What type of circuit is used at the interface point of an input port?
(a) Decoder
(b) Latch
(c) Tristate buffer
(d) None of the above

15. The register in the 8085 A that is used to keep track of the memory address of the next op-code to be run in the program is the:
(a) stack pointer
(b) program counter
(c) instruction pointer
(d) accumulator

16. The control bus and memories share a bidirectional bus in a typical microprocessor system.
(a) True
(b) False

17. All computer programs for a machine are called:
(a) Software
(b) Firmware
(c) Hardware
(d) None of the above

18. The 8085A is a(n):
(a) 16-bit parallel CPU
(b) 8-bit serial CPU
(c) 8-bit parallel CPU
(d) none of the above

19. Since microprocessor CPUs does not understand mnemonics therefore, they have to be converted to _____.
(a) hexadecimal machine code
(b) binary machine code
(c) assembly language
(d) all of the above

20. A register in the microprocessor that keeps track of the answer or results of any arithmetic or logic operation is the:
(a) stack pointer
(b) program counter
(c) instruction pointer
(d) accumulator

21. What is the difference between a mnemonic code and machine code?
(a) There is no difference.
(b) Machine codes are in binary, mnemonic codes are in shorthand English.
(c) Machine codes are in shorthand English, mnemonic codes are in binary.
(d) Machine codes are in shorthand English, mnemonic code are in special character.

22. Which bus is a bidirectional bus?
(a) Address bus
(b) Data bus
(c) Address bus and data bus
(d) None of the above

23. Which of the following buses are primarily used to carry signals that direct other ICs to find out what type of operation is being performed?
(a) Data bus
(b) Control bus
(c) Address bus
(d) Address decoder bus

24. What kind of computer program is used to convert mnemonic code to machine code?
(a) Debug (b) Assembler
(c) C++ (d) Fortran

25. Which of the following are the three basic sections of a microprocessor unit?
(a) Operand, register, and arithmetic/logic unit (ALU)
(b) Control and timing, register, and arithmetic/logic unit (ALU)
(c) Control and timing, register, and memory
(d) Arithmetic/logic unit (ALU), memory, and input/output

26. Which of the following companies have made the 8051 series of microcontrollers?
(a) Atmel (b) Philips
(c) None of above (d) Both a and b

27. AT89C2051 (ATMEL) microcontroller has RAM of:
(a) 128 bytes (b) 256 bytes
(c) 64 bytes (d) 512 bytes

28. 8051 series microcontroller has how many 16-bit registers?
(a) 2 (b) 3
(c) 1 (d) 0

29. What happen if we push data onto the stack then the stack pointer?
(a) Increases with every push (b) Decreases with every push
(c) None of above (d) Both a and b

30. The SF stands for ______.
(a) Service flag (b) Sign flag
(c) Single flag (d) Condition flag

31. The OF is called as ______.
(a) Overflow flag (b) Overdue flag
(c) One flag (d) Over flag

32. The IF is called as ______.
(a) Initial flag (b) Indicate flag
(c) Interrupt flag (d) Inter flag

33. The SP is indicated by ______.
(a) Single pointer (b) Stack pointer
(c) Source pointer (d) System pointer

34. The BP is indicated by ______.
(a) Base pointer (b) Binary pointer
(c) Bit pointer (d) Byte pointer

35. The SS is called as ______.
(a) Single stack (b) Stack segment
(c) Sequence stack (d) Source stack

36. The index register is used to hold ______.
(a) Memory register (b) Offset address
(c) Segment memory (d) Offset memory

37. The BIU prefetches the instruction from memory and store them in
(a) Queue (b) Register
(c) Memory (d) Stack

38. The DS is called as ________.
(a) Data segment (b) Digital segment
(c) Divide segment (d) Decode segment

39. The CS register store________ in code segment
(a) Instruction Stream (b) Instruction path
(c) Instruction codes (d) Instruction stream line

40. The push source copies a word from source to
(a) Stack (b) Memory
(c) Register (d) Destination

41. INC destination increments the content of destination by
(a) 1 (b) 2
(c) 30 (d) 41

42. The IMUL source is a signed ________.
(a) Multiplication (b) Addition
(c) Subtraction (d) Division

43. The JS is called as ________.
(a) Jump the signed bit (b) Jump single bit
(c) Jump simple bit (d) Jump signal bit

44. Instruction providing both segment base and offset address is called
(a) Below type (b) Far type
(c) Low type (d) High type

45. The conditional branch instruction specifies for branching
(a) Conditions (b) Instruction
(c) Address (d) Memory

46. Which flag is used by microprocessor to determine whether the specified condition exists or not?
(a) Carry flag (b) Conditional flag
(c) Common flag (d) Sign flag

47. Which of the following is used to translate a byte from one code to another code?
(a) XLAT (b) XCHNG
(c) POP (d) PUSH

48. Which of the following contains an offset instead of the actual address?
(a) SP (b) IP
(c) ES (d) SS

49. The 8086 fetches instructions one after another from ________.
(a) Code segment of memory (b) IP of memory
(c) ES of memory (d) SS of memory

50. The address bits are sent out on lines through
(a) A16-19 (b) A0-17
(c) D0-D17 (d) C0-C17

51. Which of the following is used to write into memory?
(a) RD (b) WR
(c) RD / WR (d) CLK

52. The 1 MB byte of memory can be divided into _____ segment.
(a) 1 Kbyte (b) 64 Kbyte
(c) 33 Kbyte (d) 34 Kbyte

53. The RD, WR, M/IO is the heart of control for a mode of
(a) Minimum (b) Maximum
(c) Compatibility mode (d) Control mode

54. Which instruction at the end of the interrupt service program takes the execution back to the interrupted program?
(a) Forward (b) Return
(c) Data (d) Line

55. To perform any operations, the microprocessor should identify the _______.
(a) Register (b) Memory
(c) Interface (d) System

56. The Microprocessor places _________ address on the address bus
(a) 4 bit (b) 8 bit
(c) 16 bit (d) 32 bit

57. Which decoder of memory chip will identify and select the register for the EPROM?
(a) Internal decoder (b) External decoder
(c) Address decoder (d) Data decoder

58. Which signal is provided by a microprocessor to indicate the read operation?
(a) LOW (b) MCMW
(c) MCMR (d) MCMWR

59. Which signal is generated by combining RD and WR signals with IO/M?
(a) Control (b) Memory
(c) Register (d) System

60. Memory is an integral part of _________.
(a) Supercomputer (b) Microcomputer
(c) Mini computer (d) Mainframe computer

61. The primary function of ________ is to accept data from I/P devices.
(a) Multiprocessor (b) Microprocessor
(c) Peripherals (d) Interfaces

62. Which signal prevents the microprocessor from reading the same data more than one?
(a) Pipelining (b) Handshaking
(c) Controlling (d) Signaling

63. Which is used to connect more microprocessors?
(a) Peripheral device (b) Cascade
(c) I/O devices (d) Control unit

64. In which year, 8086 was introduced?
(a) 1978
(b) 1979
(c) 1977
(d) 1981

65. 8086 and 8088 contain transistors
(a) 29000
(b) 24000
(c) 34000
(d) 54000

66. The register or memory location that is pushed into the stack at the end must be
(a) popped off last
(b) pushed off first
(c) popped off first
(d) pushed off last

67. What is DEN?
(a) Direct enable
(b) Data entered
(c) Data enable
(d) Data encoding

68. In 8086, example for Non maskable interrupts are _______.
(a) TRAP
(b) RST6.5
(c) INTR
(d) RST6.6

69. In 8086 microprocessor which of the following statement is not true?
(a) A coprocessor is interfaced in max. mode.
(b) A coprocessor is interfaced in min. mode.
(c) I/O can be interfaced in max. / min. mode.
(d) Supports pipelining

70. The stack segment register contains
(a) address of the stack segment.
(b) the base address of the stack segment.
(c) the pointer address of the stack segment.
(d) data in the stack segment.

OOOO

ANSWERS

MICROPROCESSOR AND MICROCONTROLLERS

1. (c)	**2.** (a)	**3.** (b)	**4.** (b)	**5.** (c)	**6.** (b)	**7.** (c)
8. (a)	**9.** (b)	**10.** (a)	**11.** (b)	**12.** (b)	**13.** (a)	**14.** (c)
15. (b)	**16.** (b)	**17.** (a)	**18.** (c)	**19.** (b)	**20.** (d)	**21.** (b)
22. (b)	**23.** (b)	**24.** (b)	**25.** (b)	**26.** (d)	**27.** (a)	**28.** (a)
29. (a)	**30.** (b)	**31.** (a)	**32.** (c)	**33.** (b)	**34.** (a)	**35.** (b)
36. (a)	**37.** (a)	**38.** (a)	**39.** (c)	**40.** (a)	**41.** (a)	**42.** (a)
43. (a)	**44.** (b)	**45.** (a)	**46.** (b)	**47.** (a)	**48.** (b)	**49.** (a)
50. (a)	**51.** (b)	**52.** (b)	**53.** (a)	**54.** (b)	**55.** (a)	**56.** (c)
57. (a)	**58.** (c)	**59.** (a)	**60.** (b)	**61.** (b)	**62.** (b)	**63.** (b)
64. (a)	**65.** (a)	**66.** (c)	**67.** (c)	**68.** (a)	**69.** (b)	**70.** (b)

CHAPTER 13

Mechatronics Devices

13.1 PIEZOELECTRIC ACCELEROMETERS

Vibration and shock are big challenge of our daily life which causes lots of problems in life, like overheating, wearing, looseness, misalignment and many more problems, which must be reduced to increase the efficiency and life comfort. Vibration can be generated and transmitted by turbines, motor, bridges, towers and also can be by human body. Vibrations are desirable in some condition and in some condition they are undesirable and destructive in nature. Consequently, there is a need to understand the root cause of vibration and find the way to reduce or end these vibrations. So we developed a sensor name piezoelectric accelerometer who serves as a link between vibrating structures and electronic measurement equipment.

13.1.1 Accelerometers

It is a device which is designed to measure rate of change of speed due to motion, Vibration , impact events. Accelerometers are mechanically attached to structure for which acceleration or vibration is to be measured.

Different types of accelerometer are available which uses different types of technology; some of them uses piezoelectric effect. They contain microscopic crystal structures which get stressed by applied forces and causes generate voltage. It can also be done by sensing changes in capacitance. For this we have two microscopic crystal structure next to each other and certain capacitance between them. When an accelerative force moves one of the structure then it cause to change capacitance. We can add some circuitry to convert capacitance to voltage and we get accelerometer. There are more methods including piezo resistive effect, light and hot air bubble.

13.1.2 Piezoelectric Accelerometer

It is an accelerometer that works on the piezoelectric effect of certain material to find out dynamic changes in mechanical variables like mechanical shock, vibration, acceleration etc.

Just like all transducers piezoelectric accelerometer convert energy from one form to another and give electrical signals in response to a quantity or property that is being measured. Using the general sensing method upon which all accelerometers are based, acceleration act upon seismic mass that is restrained

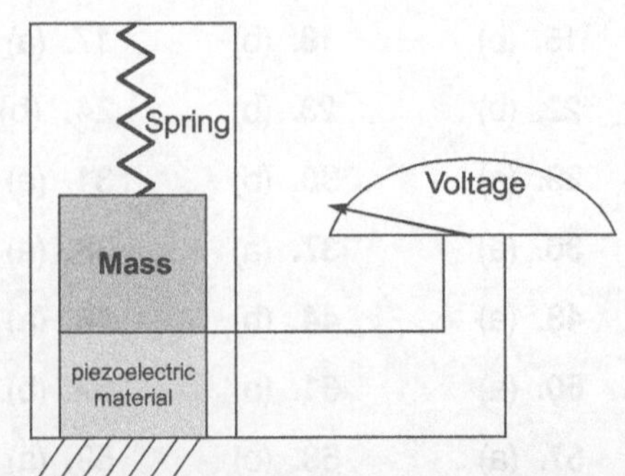

Fig. 13.1 An illustration about working of a piezoelectric accelerometer

by a spring or suspended cantilever beam and converts a physical force into an electrical signal. Before the acceleration is converted into an electric quantity, it must be converted into a displacement or force. This conversion is shown below in figure 1 by spring system.

The accelerometers Metra is manufacturing accelerometersfor over 40 years and it's working is based on the phenomenon of piezoelectricity. "Piezo" is the Greek word (piezein) whose meaning is to squeeze. Whenever a piezoelectric material is stressed it causes to generate electrical charge. If combined with a seismic mass then it can generate an electric charge signal which is proportional to vibration acceleration.

In Metra's accelerometers active element consists of a carefully selected ceramic material with good piezoelectric properties called Lead-Zirconate Titanate (PZT). Specially formulated Lead-Zirconate Titanate provides stable performance and long-term stability. High stability similar to quartz accelerometers can be achieved by an artificial aging process of the piezoceramic sensing element. The sensitivity of ceramics is 100 times higher than quartz materials. Therefore piezoceramic accelerometers are the better option at low frequencies and low acceleration conditions.

13.1.3 Piezoelectric Accelerometers Advantages

- Wide dynamic range, free of noise or negligible-Best fit for shock measurement and also for almost imperceptible vibration.
- Excellent linearity over their dynamic range.
- Wide frequency range and very high frequencies can also be measured.
- Compact and highly sensitive.
- No moving parts so there is no wear.
- Self-generating so no external power required.
- Great variety of models available for nearly any purpose.
- Integration of the output signal provides velocity and displacement.

Sensor Type	Advantage	Disadvantage
Piezoresistive	It can Measure static acceleration	Resolution is limited because of resistive noise, only for low and medium frequencies and it requires Supply voltage
Electrodynamic/ Geophone	Manufacturing cost is less	Work only at low frequencies
Capacitive	It can also measure static acceleration and cheap manufacturing	Low resolution, Fragile

Table 13.1 Comparison of piezoelectric accelerometer with other common sensors

13.1.4 Piezoelectric Transducer Model

A piezoceremic accelerometer can be represented in a electric model as the capacitance C with charge Q and voltage $V = Q/C$ and in a mechanical model as a mass-damper-spring (m-b-k), with acceleration a as input and $\Delta T/T$ strain as output.

These two models are linked by the piezoelectric effect of the transducer with stress $E\Delta T/T$ as input and charge electric field $V/T = Q/(CT)$ as output. Here we take a diagram model of the piezoceramic accelerometer, linking these three sub-models will be developed.

The strain rate is ΔT/T, along the same axis 3 and produces the electric field V/T as defined in the numerator:

$$g_{33} = \frac{V/T}{\sigma_3} = \frac{\text{Electric field produced in direction 3 V/m}}{\text{Mechanical stress applied in direction 3 N/ m}^3}$$

where, $\sigma_3 = E_3 = E\,\Delta T/T$

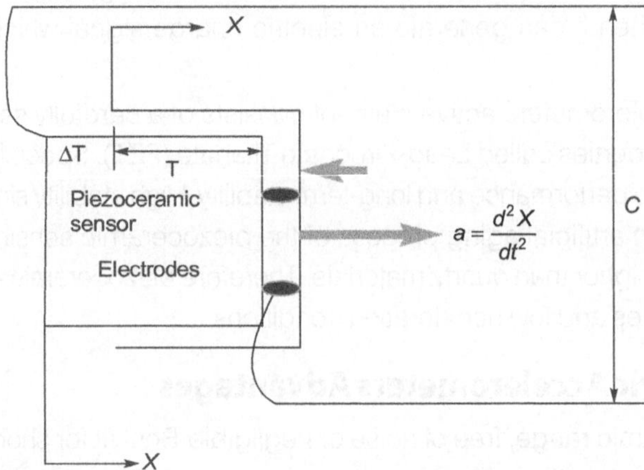

Fig: 13.2 Schematic diagram of a Piezoceramic accelerometer

$$V = g_{33}\,\sigma_3 T = g_{33}\,E\Delta T$$

Given the relationship,

$$Q = CV \text{ or } Q = C\,g_{33}\ E\Delta T \text{ and the capacitance}$$

$$C = cWL/T$$

The charge due to the strain ΔT/T is

$$Q = cWL\,g_{33}\,E\Delta T/T$$

This gives the transfer function,

$$\frac{Q(s)}{\Delta T(s)/T} = cWLg_{33}E$$

Example: 13.1

If a Lower Limiting Frequency (LLF) of 1 Hz is required, what value for R_t (Total resistance of accelerometer, cable and preamplifier input) is required?

(Assuming that A is approximately 10^5 and C_f (Feedback capacitance) is about 1 nf)

Solution:

$$R_t = \frac{1}{2\pi Cf} = \frac{1}{2\pi\times 1\times 10^5\times 10^{-9}} = 1.6\,\text{k}\Omega$$

This example illustrates the immunity of the lower limiting frequencies of a charge amplifier to changes in the input load condition. It would be very difficult to make the combined resistance of the accelerometer, connectors and preamplifier input drop to the magnitude indicated in this example. Even complete immersion of the accelerometer in water would not cause this.

Charge Sensitivity

The output voltage of a charge amplifier is proportional to the input charge and therefore to the acceleration of the accelerometer. The gain is controlled by the feedback capacitance across the operational amplifier.

Input and output volatage V_i and V_0 are related by the equation:

$$V_0 = -AV_i$$

A = Gain of operational amplifier

Lower Limiting Frequency (LLF)

The low frequency response of a charge amplifier is determined by the time constant set by the feedback circuit around the operational amplifier and is unaffected by changes in the input load conditions. The lower limiting frequency (LLF) is changed by varying the feedback resistance. Here A is the factor which show the reduction in load.

Example:13.2

Electric charge of a Piezoelectric sensor produced be a strain along axis 3.

Assume a piezoceramic sensor BM400 Type I, with dimension 0.5" × 1.5" × 0.020" (12.7 mm × 38.1 mm × 0.5 mm) and with the same parameters as

$E = 8 \times 10^{10}$ (N/m²); $T = 0.5 \times 10^{-3}$ (m); $L = 38.1 \times 10^{-3}$ (m); $C = 11.95 \times 10^{-9}$ (F/m)

Calculate the charge for a sensor strain $\Delta T/T = 10^{-6}$ (m/m).

Solution:

In this case, the charge and the strain are both along axis, and the piezoelectric coefficient is given as:

$$g_{33} = 25 \times 10^{-3} \text{ (Vm/N)}$$

such that the transfer function, from figure below is equivalent to the conversion gain

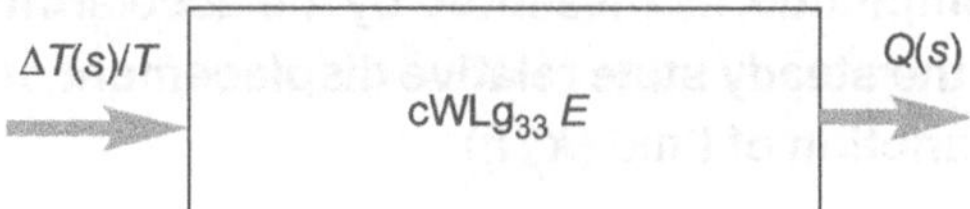

Block diagram model of piezoceramic transducing effect

$$cWLg_{33}E = (11.95 \times 10^{-9})(12.7 \times 10^{-3})(38.1 \times 10^{-3})(25 \times 10^{-3})$$
$$(25 \times 10^{-3})(8 \times 10^{10})$$

If the sensor is subjected to a 10^{-6} (m/m) strain , the charge Q is

$$Q = cWLg_{33}E\Delta T/T = 1.16 \times 10^{-2}(10^{-6})$$
$$= 1.16 \times 10^{-8}\ (C)$$

From a given static deflection ΔT, a change Q is generated. Given the capacitance C of the piezoelectric transducer, the corresponding voltage is $V = Q/C$. the determination of Q and ΔT from the measurement of V poses some problems. Due to leakage resistance Rleak of the piezoceramic transducer and the input resistance of the voltmeter R_m, the voltage V across the capacitance C decrease in time as the initial charge $Q(0)$ is discharged by these resistances.

R is the equivalent of the two resistances given by:

$$R = \frac{1}{\left(\frac{1}{R_{leak}} + \frac{1}{R_m}\right)}$$

The current, $\quad i(t) = -\frac{dQ(t)}{dt}$ is the same as the current in R.

The voltage, $\quad V(t) = \frac{Q(t)}{C}$ gives

$$i(t) = \frac{V(t)}{R}$$

and
$$\frac{dQ(t)}{dt} + \frac{Q(t)}{RC} = 0$$

for initial condition $Q(0)$, the solution of this differential equation is

$$Q(t) = Q(0)\, e^{(-t/RC)}$$
$$V(t) = (Q(0)/C)\, e^{(-t/RC)}$$

The charge $Q(t)$ decrease in time with a time constant RC. It is important to measure $Q(0)$ accurately, given its dependences on the static deflection ΔT of interest. The indirect measurement by $V(t)$ of $Q(0)$ for the duration of the measurement . Alternatively, a charge amplifier has to be connected between the piezoceramic transducer and the voltmeter to convert the charge input into a proportional voltage output.

Unsolved Problem:

An accelerometer is designed and has the following data,
Seismic mass = 100g; Spring constant = 4000 N/m; Damping constant = 40 Ns/m.
When accelerometer is mounted on object then
Displacement is $x_{in}(t) = 5\sin(100t)$ mm.
Find the following data:

(a) Actual acceleration amplitude of the object.
(b) The amplitude of steady state relative displacement between the seismic mass and the housing of the accelerometer.
(c) The acceleration amplitude, as measured by the accelerometer.
(d) An expression for the steady state relative displacement of the seismic mass relative to the housing as a function of time ($X_r(t)$).

13.2 OPTICAL ENCODER

Optical encoder is an electromechanical device which is used to monitor the motion, velocity and position of operating mechanism like shaft and axle with the help of light source and some sort of photo sensors. The information obtained from the photo sensors is further translated into some useful electronic waveform. The analog and digital signals can be used to determine position, direction and velocity of shaft and axle. It is usually used with a motor, so the motor provides rotary motion and encoder gives the feedback about the location/orientation of the axis and/or amount of angle turned by the shaft.

13.2.1 Construction of Optical Encoder

The optical encoder mainly consists of two units:

(i) Moving Unit

The moving unit is attached to and moves with the device (shaft) being monitored. The moving unit contains the information to be sensed by the stationary unit. Moving unit consists of a scale or a disk. These disk or scale consists of alternative areas of transparency and opaqucity to the passing light. The shape, size, frequency of these areas are the basis of the output information supplied by the encoder.

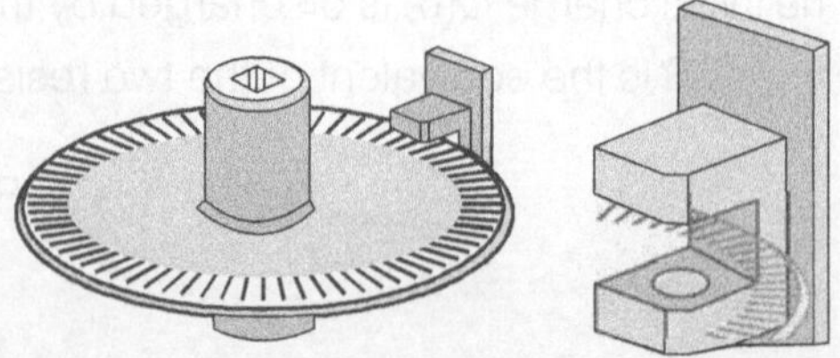

Fig: 13.3 Optical Shaft Encoder Disc

These scales are made up of glass in rotary optical encoders and in linear optical encoders scale may be of both type glass or metal. The reflective coating on the metal scales can be done with the help of gold.

(ii) Stationary Unit

The stationary unit consists of a light emitting diode and a photo sensing unit like solar cell (as shown in Fig. 13.4) on the opposite side of a disc or a scale through which the light passes. As the light passes through the moving disc or the scale, the voltage pulses are generated.

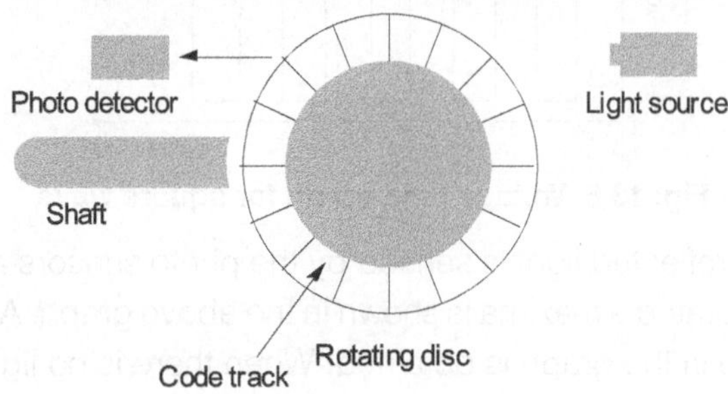

Fig: 13.4 Rotating Disc

13.2.2 Types of Optical Encoders and their Working Principle

(i) Rotary Optical Encoder:

Rotary encoders are used to determine the direction of rotation and value of rotation of a controlled shaft by means of continuous light and photo receptors. As shown in the figure below the two light emitting diode mostly the laser diode send two parallel continuous light through a chopping wheel which is a disc with alternate opaque and transparent radio bans. The controlled shaft is connected to the center of the disc. So when the shaft turns some angle results in the rotation of chopping wheel hence there will be interruption in the light pass. If wheel rotates in clockwise sense then firstly there will be interruption in first light beam after that in second light beam. If the sense of rotation is counter clockwise then the sequence of interruption of light beam will also be reversed. These interruptions in light beams are sensed by the photo receptors and transmit the data to a microprocessor.

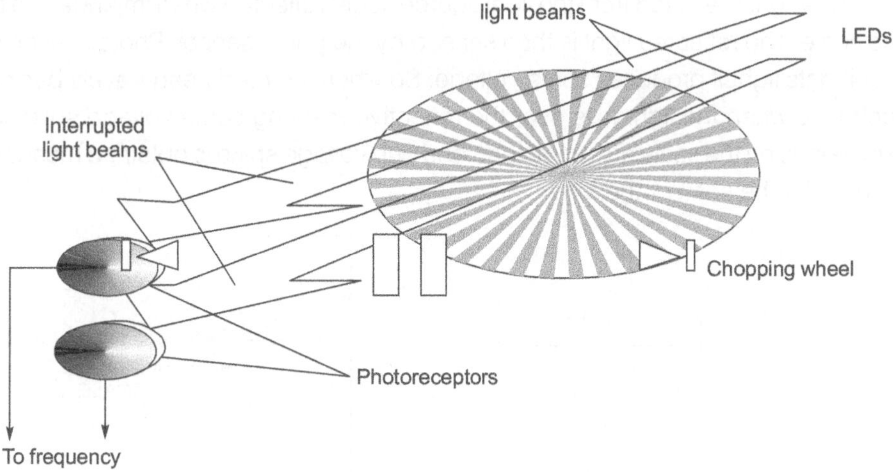

Fig: 13.5 Rotary optical encoder

Voltage Time Graph:

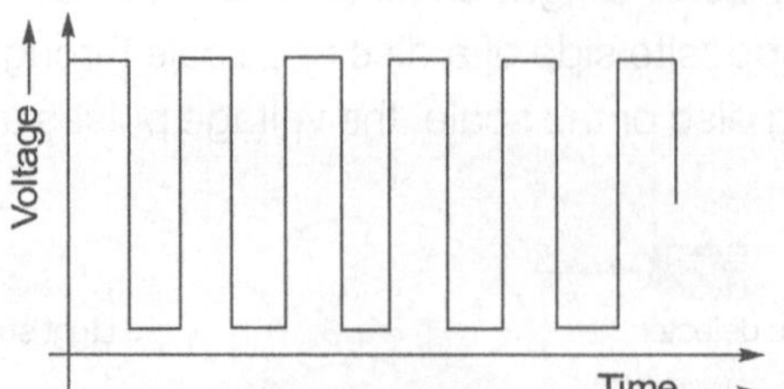

Fig: 13.6 Voltage time graph for square wave

As the interrupted or reflected light is sensed by the photo sensors a voltage pulse is obtained. When a voltage pulse is generated a maxima is shown in the above graph. As long as the photo sensors receive light maximum value in the graph is obtained. When there is no light which is received by the photo sensors then there will not be any voltage pulse generated. Hence it shows minima in the above shown graph.

Instead of square wave as shown in the above diagram we can also use a sinusoidal wave to represent voltage time graph.

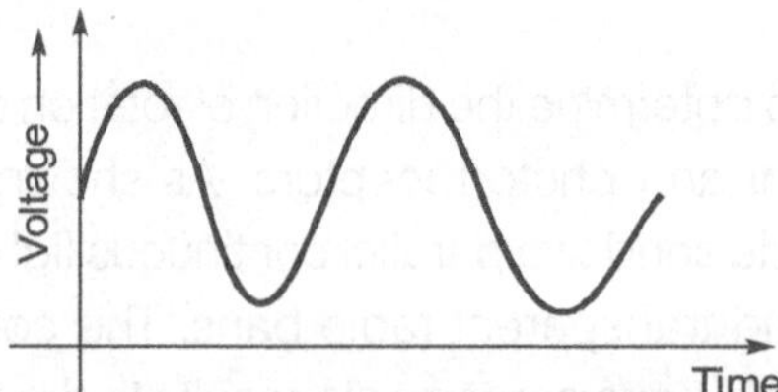

Fig: 13.7 Voltage Time Graph for Sinusoidal wave

(ii) Linear Optical Encoder:

The Fig. 13.8 shows the representation of a linear optical encoder. The reed head moves with the axis, while the scale is stationary in case of linear scale optical encoder. The scale can be made up of glass or metal as the light is emitted from the light source. It get reflected when impinges on the reflective marking of the scale. The reflected light is then sensed by the photo sensor. Photo sensor is like a solar cell. Whenever it gets light it produces some voltage. So when the reed head travels back and forth on the scale, each time when the light falls over the reflective marking some voltage spike is produced. Suppose the markings on the scale are 1mm apart and one voltage spike is obtained means the distance of 1mm is covered by the shaft or the axle.

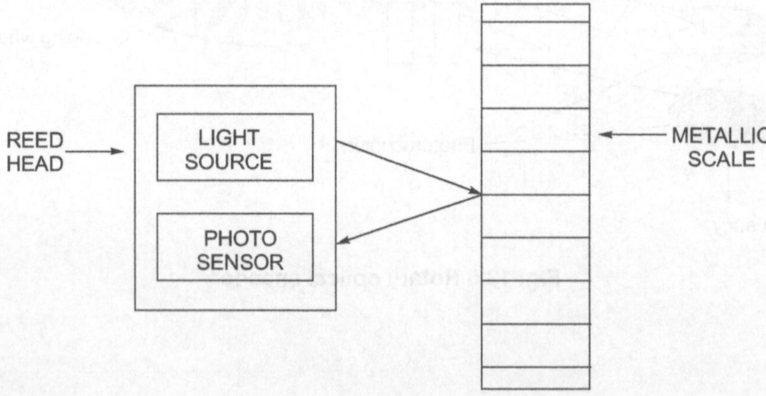

Fig: 13.8 Linear Optical Encoder

Determination of the Direction of Displacement

To determine the direction of movement two light sources are used. Two light sources are called as light souce-1 and light source-2 and the emitted light beams are called as signal-1 and signal-2. Suppose that the reed head is moving in downward direction so the light source 1 will be first to get reflected from the reflective markings on the scale. Hence signal-1 will show a peak before the signal-2. As shown in the Fig. 13.9 it is clear that the reed head is moving in downward direction.

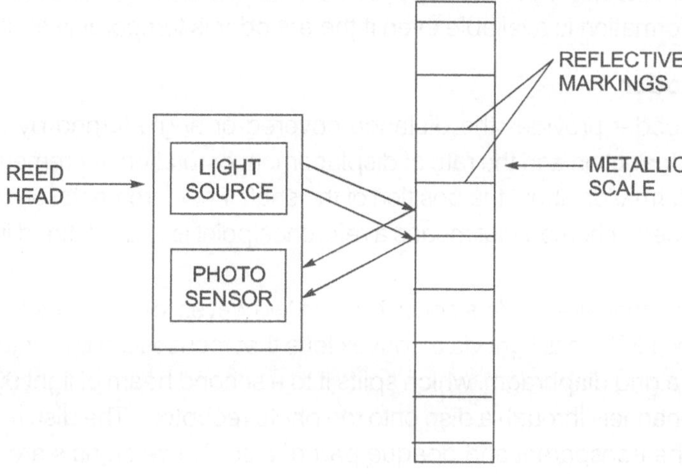

Fig: 13.9

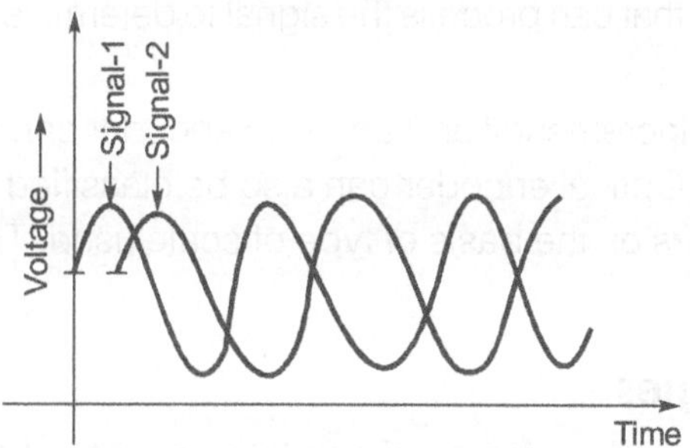

Fig: 13.10 Determination of the Direction of Displacement

(iii) Glass Scale Optical Encoders:

In glass scale optical encoders as the reed head travels the light get travelled through the glass. As in the diagram shown below some portion of the glass scale is blackened to prevent the light coming from the light emitting diode.

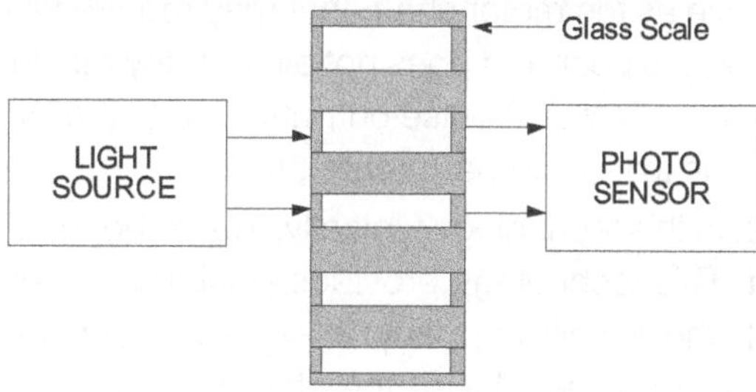

Fig: 13.11 Glass Scale Optical Encoder

Further the encoders are also classified as absolute and incremental encoders as follows:

(iv) Absolute Encoder:

Absolute encoder provides the specific information about the location of axle or the shaft. The absolute encoder provides the exact co-ordinates of the position of the shaft. An absolute encoder has multiple detectors and a disc with multiple, unique tracks. The disc produces Gray code output, (named after Bell Labs physicist Frank Gray) a binary numeral system for which (unlike straight binary) successive values differ by one bit. Therefore, if the encoder stops in the transition the maximum possible error can be only 0.5 bit. This information is available even if the encoder is temporarily shut down.

(v) Incremental Encoder

Incremental encoder provides the distance covered or angle turned by the shaft. It also tells about the directional information and the rate of displacement or rotation. Incremental encoder does not provide the specific information about the position of the shaft. For incremental encoder the machine set up needs to be referenced or homed that means a reference point is to be defined in case of incremental encoder.

The output of incremental encoders consists of the two waves, each corresponding to an increment of rotation. Typically, the LED emits light via a convex lens that focuses the light into a parallel beam; the beam passes through a grid diaphragm, which splits it to a second beam of light 90° out of phase. Light passes from A and B channels through a disc onto the photo receptors. The disc rotation creates a light-dark pattern through the transparent and opaque part of disc. These signals are analyzed by a photo receptors array and decoding circuitry; beams A and B are each received by two different diodes and converted into two square-wave signals ... 90° out of phase, commonly known as quadrature output. It's then send to the microprocessor that can process the signal to determine the number of pulses, direction, speed, and other information.

The combination of both incremental and absolute encoder can also be used like incremental in x, y-axis and absolute in z-axis. Optical encoder can also be classified as linear scale optical encoder and rotary scale optical encoders on the basis of type of scale used. The scale may be transparent or made up of metal.

13.2.3 Encoder Technologies

- **Conductive:** Here a series of circumferential copper tracks etched on a PCB is used. The contact brushes distinguish the conductive areas. This form of encoder is now rarely seen except as a user input in digital multi-meters.
- **Optical:** Optical encoders uses light rays falling onto a photodiode through slits in a metal or glass disc. Reflective versions also exist. This is one of the most common technologies. However they are very sensitive to dust.
- **On Axis Magnetic:** This technology typically uses a specially magnetized two pole neodymium magnet the same size as the motor shaft, that may requires a custom motor shaft be used. However the accuracy is poor and does not allow many resolution options. This technology does not typically offer UVW or Z pulse outputs. Due to the two pole magnet there is lots of jitter on the output due to the internal interpolation.
- **Off Axis Magnetic:** In this technology typically, rubber bonded ferrite magnets attached to a metal hub is used. This technology provides flexibility in design and low cost for custom applications. Due to the flexibility in many off axis encoder chips they can be programmed to accept any number of pole widths so the chip can be placed in any position as per the requirement. Magnetic encoders operate in harsh environments where optical encoders cannot work.

13.2.4 Benefits of Optical Encoders:

The optical shaft encoder can be used to improve a robot. The encoder can calculate distance traveled and speed, which can be used to monitor, for example, the speed of a robot and angular position. These parameters can help you with performing various tasks with robot.

13.2.5 Applications of Optical Encoders:

The optical shaft encoder can be used to track distance traveled, direction of motion, or position of any rotary component, such as a gripper arm. The encoder can also be used to detect movement, which could make good interaction between the robot and its environment (e.g., human-robot interaction). If a human moves a robot arm that is attached to an encoder (e.g., during a handshake), the robot detects the arm movement and the direction(s) and distance(s) traveled, helping the robot classify the interaction as a handshake.

Fig: 13.12 Optical shaft encoder mounting system

13.2.6 Range, Limits, Resolution and Accuracy

The diameter of the disk does not matter but the diameter of the wheel or gear whose shaft passes through the encoder does matter. The periphery of the wheel is equal to diameter multiplied by pi (approx. 3.14). Which when multiplied by the number of revolutions becomes the distance traveled.

The optical shaft encoder can detect up to 1,700 pulses per second, which corresponds to 18.9 revolutions per second and 1,133 rpm (revolutions per minute).

Rotary encoders are specified for form factor, level of ruggedness, and resolution. For incremental encoders, resolution is defined as counts per turn. For absolute single-turn encoders, it is defined as positions per turn, expressed as a multi-bit word.

If a machine must measure the travel of a 25-in. lead screw in increments of 0.001 in., for example, then it requires an absolute encoder with a resolution of 25,000 points. That said, resolution here is usually defined in terms of bits: A 12-bit encoder, for example, refers to the binary number 212 that is 4,096 decimal. Thus, a 12-bit encoder has a resolution of 4,096 points.

Accuracy (unlike resolution) depends in whole-system interactions with the application, and is traceable to the encoding disc and the deviation between actual and theoretical position. A good 12 or 13-bit encoder, for example, is accurate to within half a count on the least significant bit.

Repeatability, the encoder's ability to read the same point each time the shaft is in a particular position, is defined as the deviation of actual encoder position between subsequent identical code readings. Although it has no relation to accuracy, it is usually four to ten times better.

13.2.7 Precautions to be taken care while using Optical Encoders

- Encoder should be clean because the light going to be sensed by the sensor will not be properly transmitted if the encoder is dirty and hence there will be a fluctuation in voltage pulse. So encoder will not give a correct reading.
- The reed head should be parallel to the scale because if it is not parallel then there will be a voltage difference between the two voltage pulses obtained by the reflected light.

13.3 RESOLVERS

Resolvers and Encoders are the most prevalent feedback devices for motion control systems. Thus include consideration of, response time, accuracy and resolution limitations. Digital "a-quad-b" encoders and sine encoders are explained. Resolvers and resolver-to-digital converters (RDC), the processing of resolver signals into position feedback, both hardware and software resolver-to-digital converters are explained. The 1/T interpolation or "Clock pulse counting" is explained.

Resolvers are primarily known as motion sensor. It is a part of mechatronic systems. Resolvers are used to measure the angular displacement. It's a type of rotary electrical transformer which is used to measure degrees of rotation. It's also considered an analog device and has digitalized counterparts act as the digital resolver, encoder.

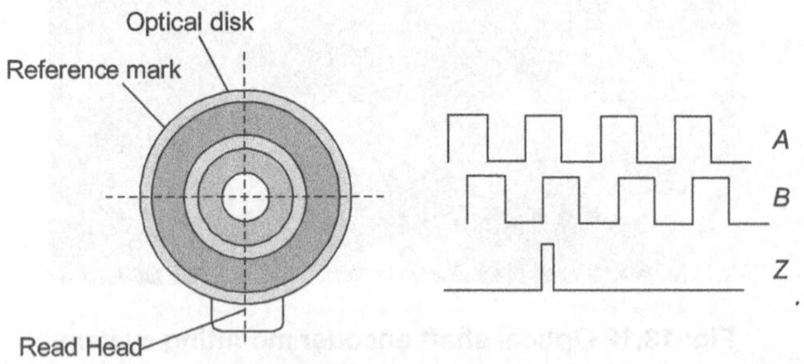

Fig: 13.13 Resolver Sensor

The accurate servo system and rotor are used to measure angular displacement in resolvers. Their transmission can be differentiated to attain velocity.

The rotor consists of single coil and attached to a cylindrical rotating object to produce an alternating source current which is indicating by V_{ref} (as shown in Fig. 13.14).

While stator is attached with two windings and mutually perpendicular, with the induced voltages (as shown in Fig. 13.14.)

Fig: 13.14 Winding Arrangement

$$V_{01} = K\,V_{ref}\sin\theta$$

$$V_{02} = K\,V_{ref}\cos\theta$$

Where, K = Transform ratio (maximum output voltage/input voltage)

V_{ref} = Excitation voltage ($V_{ref} = V_0 \sin\omega t$)

θ = Rotor angle with respect to the stator

13.3.1 Description of Resolvers:

The most popular type of resolver is the brushless transmitter resolver. On the outer manifestation, this type of resolver may look like a small electrical motor having a rotor and stator. On the inner side, the configuration of the wire form windings makes it different.

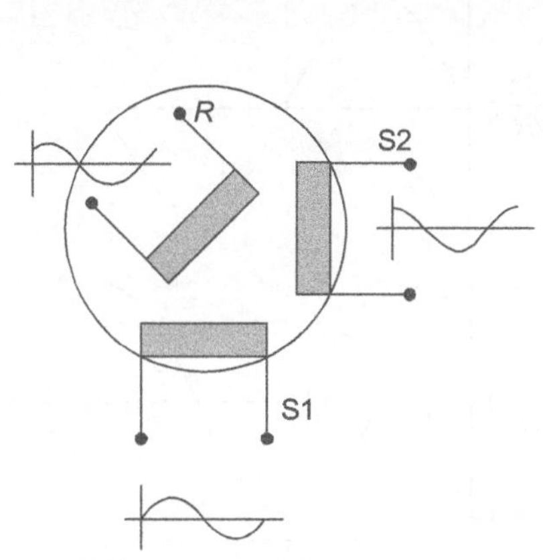

Fig: 13.15 Concept of rotor excited resolver

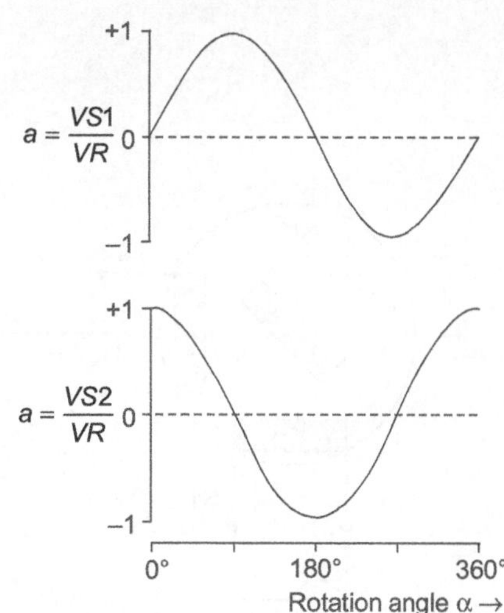

Fig: 13.16 Rotor Excitation and Response

The stator portion of the resolver houses three windings:

An exciter winding and two two-phase windings (usually labeled "x" and "y") (case of a brushless resolver). The exciter winding is positioned on the top; it is in fact a coil of a turning (rotary) transformer. The current is induced in this transformer without electrical connection, thus there are no wires to the rotor limiting its rotation and no need for brushes. The two other windings are on the bottom, wound on a lamination. They are configured perpendicular to each other. The rotor houses a coil, which is the secondary winding of the turning transformer, and a separate primary winding in a lamination, exciting the two-phase windings on the stator.

The stator is fixed on the primary winding of the transformer and is excited by a sinusoidal electric current, which by electromagnetic induction induces current in the rotor. The windings are mounted on the axis of the resolver.In each and every position the same current is induced. This current then flows through the other winding on the rotor, in turn inducing current in its secondary windings, the two-phase windings back on the stator. The two two-phase windings, fixed at right (90°) angles to each other on the stator, produce a sine and cosine feedback current. The relative magnitudes of the two-phase voltages are measured and used to find out the angle of the rotor relative to the stator. The feedback signals repeat their waveforms in the lead of one full revolution, This device may also appear in non-brushless type resolvers, i.e., only consisting in two lamination stacks, rotor and stator.

Resolvers have very precise analog conversion from polar to rectangular coordinates. Excitation voltage is the magnitude and Shaft angle is the polar angle.The [x] and [y] are output components. Resolvers with four-lead rotors can rotate [x] and [y] coordinates, with the shaft position giving the desired rotation angle.

Resolvers with four output leads are general sine/cosine computational devices. The feedback windings are tightly attached to the input windings, and their accuracy can be increased, when it is used with electronic driver amplifiers and they can be tumble ("resolver chains") to evaluate functions with numerous terms, perhaps of a number of angles. For the position calculation, Resolver-to-Digital Converters are generally used. Sine and cosine signal converted into binary signal (10 to 16 bit wide) that can more comfortably be used by the controller.

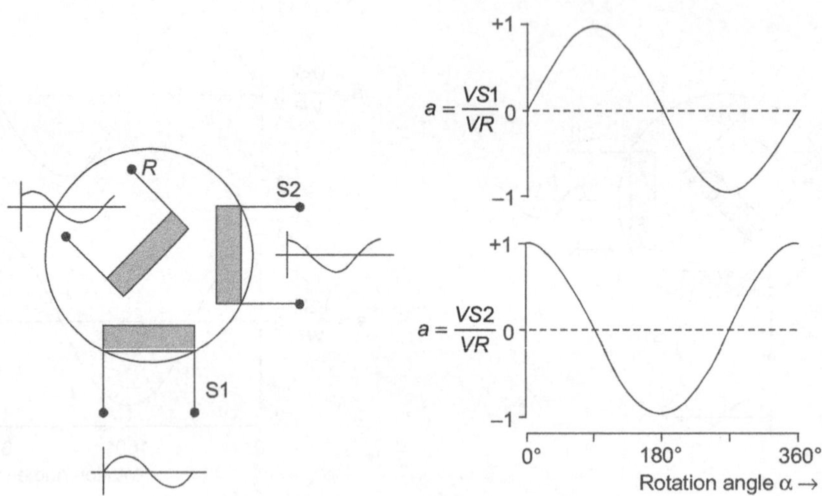

R = ROTOR, S1 = STATOR1, S2 = STATOR2

Fig: 13.17 Rotor Excited Response

13.3.2 Types of Resolvers

The basic resolvers are two-pole resolvers, meaning that the angular information is the mechanical angle of the stator. These devices can deliver the absolute angular position. Other types of resolver are multi-pole resolvers. They have 2p poles (p pole pairs), and thus can deliver p cycles in one rotation of the rotor: the electrical angle is p times the mechanical angle. Some types of resolvers include both types, with the 2-pole windings used for absolute position and the multi-pole windings for accurate position. Two-pole resolvers can usually reach angular accuracy up to about ±5′ (minutes of arc), whereas a multi-pole resolver can provide better accuracy, up to 10″ (arc-seconds) for 16-pole resolvers, to even 1″ for 128-pole resolvers.

Multi-pole resolvers may also be used for monitoring multi-pole electrical motors. This device can be used in any application in which the exact rotation of an object relative to another object is needed, such as in a rotary antenna platform or a robot. In actual practice, the resolver is usually directly mounted to an electric motor. The resolver feedback signals are usually monitored for multiple revolutions by another device. This allows for geared reduction of assemblies being rotated and improved accuracy from the resolver system.

Resolvers designed for terrestrial use tend to be driven at 50-60 Hz (utility frequency), while those for marine or aviation use tend to operate at 400 Hz (the frequency of the on-board generator driven by the engines).In aerospace applications utilize 2930 Hz to 10 kHz at voltages ranging from $4 V_{rms}$ to $10 V_{rms}$. Many of the aerospace applications are used to determine the position of an actuator or torque motor position. Control systems tend to use higher frequencies (5 kHz).

On the basis of winding types of resolver include:

(i) Receiver Resolvers

These types of resolvers are used in the opposite way to transmitter resolvers (the type described above). The two di-phased windings are energized, the ratio between the sine and cosine representing the electrical angle. The system turns the rotor to obtain a zero voltage in the rotor winding. At this position, the mechanical angle of the rotor equals the electrical angle applied to the stator.

(ii) Differential Resolvers

These types combine two di-phased primary windings in one of the stacks of sheets, as with the receiver, and two di-phased secondary windings in the other. The relationship of the electrical angle given by the two secondary windings and the other angles are secondary electrical angle, primary electrical angle and mechanical angle. These types were used, for instance, as analog trigonometric-function calculators.

A related type is also the transolver, mixing a two-phase winding like the resolver and a tri-phased winding like the synchro.Less then 24 Volt AC voltage is eventually used for all resolvers.

13.3.3 Applications of Resolver

The resolvers find wide applications in:

- Servo Motors
- Steel and Papermills
- Fuel Systems of Jet Engine
- Communication Position Systems
- Land Based Military Vehicles
- Factory Automation
- Oil and Gas Production
- Aircraft Flight Surface Actuators
- Missile Fin Actuators

13.3.4 Advantages of Resolver

The resolvers have following advantages/features:

- Wide operating temperature range
- Capability of rotatable at high speeds
- Absolute position detection
- Highly resistant to noise
- Excellent environmental resistance
- High reliability
- Long distance transmission available
- Compact assembly

13.4 INDUCTOSYN

Inductosyn is a basic analog sensor, for high precision measurement of position. The Inductosyn is similar to a resolver or synchro. That is, the physical quantity that is sensitive to the position of the machine element is Inductive coupling between two sets of conductors. The basic principle is that when the scale winding is excited with an AC voltage, it magnetically couples to the slider windings, inducing voltages that are functions of the slider's position with respect to the scale.

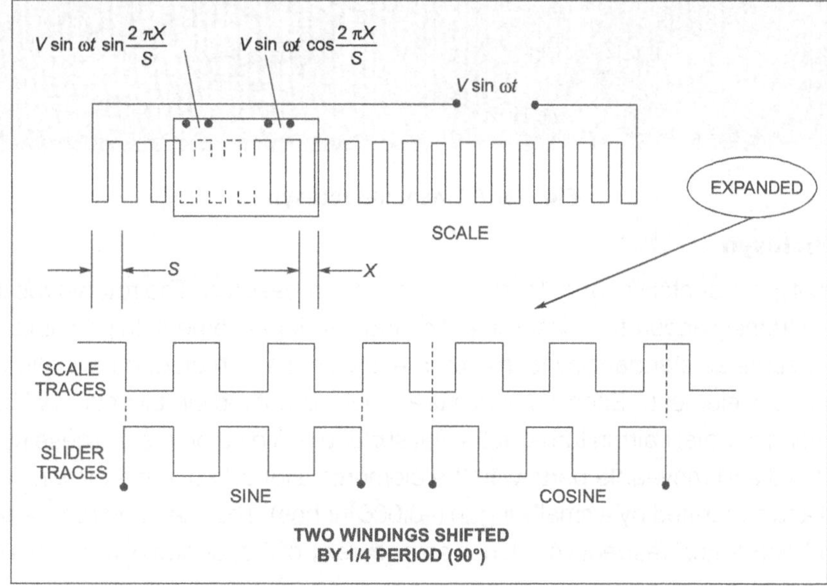

Fig: 13.18 Schematics of an Inductosyn position measurement system.

The induced voltage is proportional to the sine and cosine of the slider's spacing within the cyclic pitch of the scale. Let S be the distance between the two pitches, and X is the displacement of the slider, then:

$$V(\text{sine input}) = V\sin\omega t \quad \ldots(1)$$

$$V(\text{sine output}) = V\sin\omega t \sin[2\pi X/S] \quad \ldots(2)$$

$$V(\text{cosine output}) = V\sin\omega t \cos[2\pi X/S] \quad \ldots(3)$$

13.4.1 Types of Inductosyn

The two types of inductosyn transducers are namely, linear inductosyn and Rotary inductosyn.

(i) Linear Inductosyn:

In a linear inductosyn, linear position is measured. The linear Inductosyn consists of two magnetically coupled parts:

1. **Scale:** This part is fixed to one axis such as machine tool bed. The base material of steel, stainless steel, or aluminum is covered by an insulating layer. There is a printed-circuit trace in the form of a digital signal.
2. **Slider:** It moves along the scale in conjunction to the device to be positioned. The slider is 2 inches long and has two separate but identical printed circuit traces bonded to the surface that faces the scale. These two traces have patternd similar to the waveform on the scale with exactly the same cyclic pitch, but traces are shifted by some part of the pitch.

Since each scale is attached to the machine structure, the gross temperature expansion effect is same as the body of the machine. A slight deviation due to differential expansion between the glass and the machine bed can exist over the distance from the center of the scale to near its end. This error amounts to about 35 microinches for a change in temperature of 10° F. Generally its accuracy is more than 0.00254 mm. with a repeatability of 0.0635 mm.

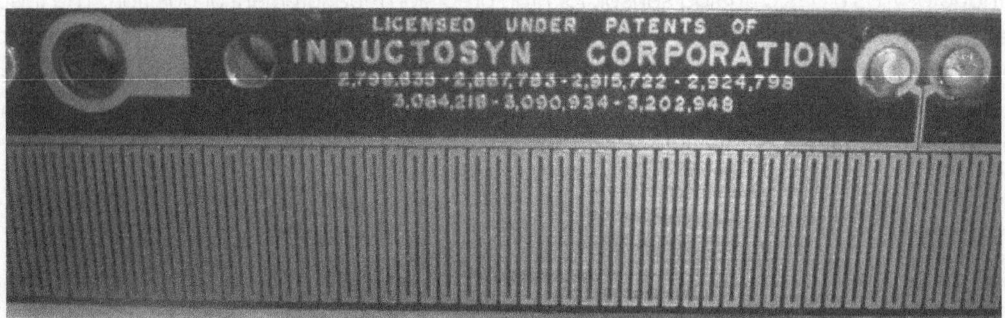

Fig: 13.19 Linear Inductosyn

(ii) Rotary Inductosyn

The rotary-type inductosyn, angular displacement is measured. The rotary-type inductosyn is a device used for extremely accurate measurement of angular displacement. In principle, the rotary-type inductosyn is the same as standard synchros and resolvers, i.e., an electromagnetic coupling effect between two conductor elements. Each element has a precision printed circuit pattern with parallel hairpin turns repeated along a radial hairpin turns on the flat surface of a disc or plate. These two elements are attached to the fixed and moveable parts with the elements aligned so that their winding patterns are mutually parallel and separated by a small air gap (–0.006 inches). The fixed and moveable elements are called the "stator" and "rotor" respectively. It has an accuracy of 5 seconds of arc with a repeatability of 1 second of arc.

Fig. 13.20 Rotary Inductosyn

The errors, how small they are, can be either random errors due to readout electronics or systematic errors due to inductosyn itself. The two systematic errors are cyclic errors and once per revolution error (in the case of a rotary inductosyn). The once per revolution error has a cycle 360 degrees. The cyclic errors have three major components: the fundamental error, the second harmonic error, and the fourth harmonic error.

The advantages of using Inductosyn transducer are that it produces very low error. The operation of the Inductosyn is not affected by oils and coolants or by dirt on the plates. It is low in impedance and can be easily operated.

13.4.2 Applications of Inductosyn

Inductosyn transducers are used in automation, scientific applications, military and aerospace applications.

Automation and Scientific Applications

Inductosyn is being used in every type of machine tool e.g. a Rotary Jig Boring machine incorporates rotary and linear Inductosyn transducers to achieve positioning accuracies of ±3 arc seconds and ±0.0002 inch. It is common to find a rebuilt machine tool with a new digital readout or Numerical Control Systems that utilizes the original linear and rotary inductosyn scales installed even a 20 or 30 years ago. Other automation applications includes an automatic gauge control system for rolling mills, precision robotics, special test for robotic systems and calibration and test standards.

Military and Aerospace Applications

Inductosyn are widely used as a position transducer in military and aerospace industry. Three important characteristics for military and aerospace applications are insenstivity to temperature effects, the ability to be mounted in a variety of substrate materials and high reliability. Other characteristics are resistance to shock and vibrations, temperature extremes, high pressure & hard vacuum, plus continuous operations after exposure to contaminants such as oil, liquids, dust, dirt and salt spray. Typical military applications include airborne infrared scanner, airborne side locking radar antenna, space flight qualified satellite Gimbal system, space flight qualified robotic arms, cryogenic chambers, ground surveillance radar antenna, large celestial telescopes, motion simulators, inertial navigation system for submarine and surface vessels, Land mobile target acquisition and tracking systems, ship borne target acquisition and tracking systems etc.

Fig: 13.21 The Rapier uses Inductosyn transducer to transmit target tracking and missile launch angles

13.4.3 Linear Micro-Inductosyn Sensor

Based on the "Inductosyn" principle and fabrication using thin-film technology, micro inductosyn sensors have also been developed. The use of thin-film technology in inductive measuring systems result in large degree of integration, miniaturization, and Low-manufacturing costs. In order to utilize an Inductosyn sensor in long-lasting and higher accuracy in various applications like positioning during microassembly, position measurement for microactuators etc., sensor miniaturization is essential. The accuracy of a standard Inductosyn sensor with a period of 2 mm is ±2.5 μm. However use of thin film technology can reduce the period size to as small as 50 μm and we can attain an accuracy of 500 nm or below. The major difficulty in such a miniaturization is the loss of sensor signals. Even though, such a reduction of the sensor signals due to the miniaturization can be recompensed by the integration of soft magnetic poles and flux guides around the meander sensing coils of Inductosyn sensor. Therefore, the coupling between excitation and sensing coils grows considerably.

Description of Linear Micro Inductosyn Sensor:

Fig. 13.22 shows a Inductosyn sensor. It comprises of three coil systems. One contains the magnetic scale that is placed on the stationary part of the system (stator) and is provided with a planar meander coil. The sensing part of the system (traveler) is placed on a slider. It consists of two planar meander coils which are situated opposite and parallel to the stationary coil of the scale. If the excitation coil is placed consistently with the sensing coil, an optimum coupling between the coils outcomes in maximum induced voltage. With a set off of a quarter of the period between the two sensing coils, a phase shift of 90 between the two output signals can be accomplished, a prerequisite for detecting the direction of motion in incremental systems. One period is formed by a basic S-shaped element of the meander coil.

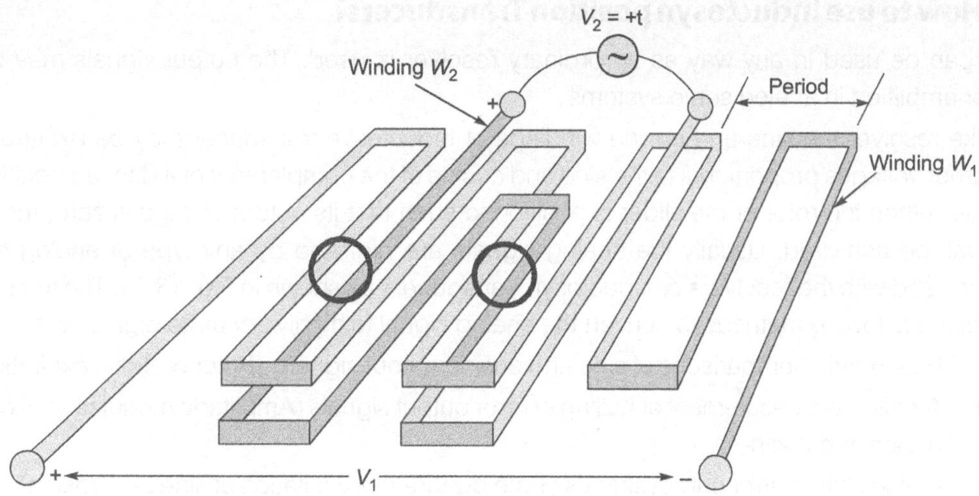

Fig: 13.22 Representation of Micro inductosyn position measuring system

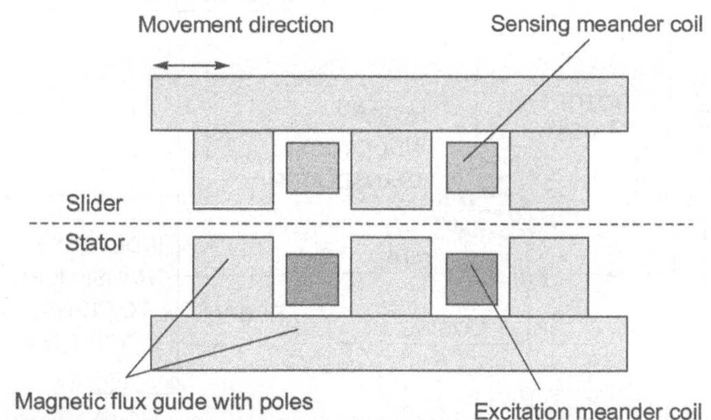

Fig: 13.23 Schematic representation of one segment of a linear micro Inductosyn sensor

To enhance the coupling between excitation and sensing coils of the micro device, a soft magnetic flux guide not available in a macroscopic Inductosyn has been provided. Fig. 13.23 shows a typical representation of one portion of the linear micro Inductosyn positioning sensor.

13.4.4 Criteria for Selection of Inductosyn

Accuracy: Choose rotary diameter or linear scale type or width to satisfy accuracy needed or mounting restrictions. Specially selected units can provide greater than standard accuracy. The highest accuracy can be possible with Adjustable Linear scales.

Cycle length: Select cycle length to suit your system requirements. Accuracy is not strictly a function of cyclic pitch. Standard linear cyclic pitches measure 0.1 inch, 0.2 inch and 2 mm. Standard rotary inductosyn incorporates from 2 to 2048 poles.

Travel and Overall length: Before inductosyn selection, determine overall length and travel required. For Tape units allow for over travel to clear tape tension supports. For bar scales, this is not a consideration, as they are free of mechanical interference at their ends.

Standard Materials: Bar scale, sliders and rotary unit substrates are precision ground plates of hot rolled steel or Aluminium, closely matching thermal coefficients of most machine parts. Almost any other substrate material may also be specially manufactured on demand. Tape scale substrates are used in spring steel, stainless steel or Aluminium.

13.4.5 How to use Inductosyn position Transducers?

It can be used in any way as an ordinary resolver is used. The output signals may be used directly or amplified in analog servo systems.

Like resolver the sine and cosine windings of Inductosyn transducer may be excited with in-phase carrier voltages proportional to the sine and cosine of the complement of a desired position in the pitch cycle. When the rotor or the slider is positioned such that its output voltage is zero, the desired position will be achieved. Usually the analog signals are digitized by any type of analog to digital converters used with the resolvers or inductosyn transducers as shown in Fig. 13.24. These converters use one of the following methods to convert the analog signal to highly accurate digital data:

- Ratiometric comparisons of sine and cosine output signals. (Rotor or Scale excitation)
- Amplitude measurement or nulling of error output signals (Amplitude modulation of excitation of sine and cosine).
- Phase shift of error output signals (Time quadrature excitation of sine and cosine).

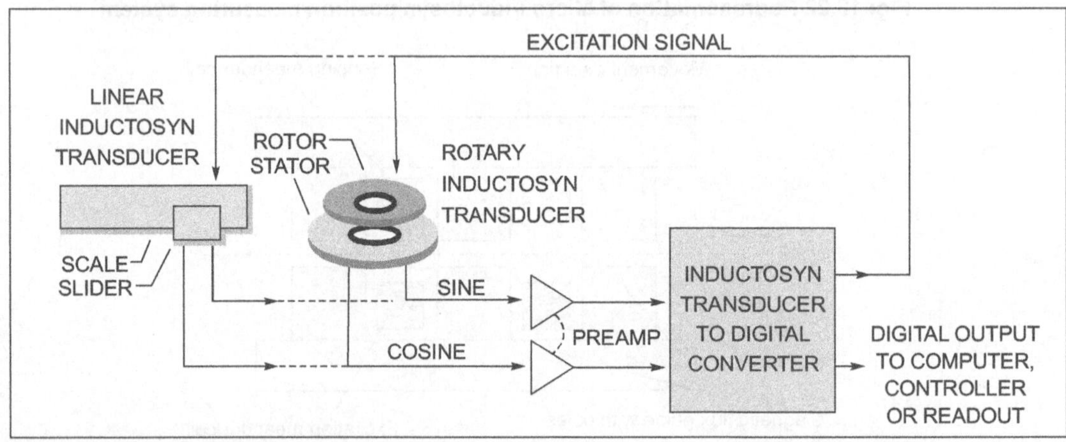

Fig: 13.24 Typical inductosyn transducer to digital output subsystem

13.4.6 Electrical Characteristics

Winding impedance is approximately inversely proportional to cycle length, and varies directly with scale length or diameter. Voltage transformation ratio (VTR) is independent of scale length when the slider is excited. Direct, slip ring or rotary transformer coupling may be specified for rotary units. Transformers will change the VTR and impedance for otherwise similar units.

Specified at a frequency of 10 kHz, Inductosyn units have been operated at frequencies in the range of 200 Hz to 200 kHz. Recommended operating range for most of them is 2.5 kHz to 100 kHz.

Output or error signal voltage signal is directly proportional to the carrier frequency. Maximum error signals range from1 to 100 mV, 2 V excitation at 10 kHz.

Electrical Sources of Error

No coupling can be allowed between rotor and stator (scale and slider) circuits except for the inductive coupling provided by the inductosyn windings. To minimize extraneous coupling, stators and sliders have an electrostatic shield applied over the windings. This shield must not be removed, and should be grounded directly through the mounting bolts.

13.4.7 Accessories used with Inductosyn:

Several items are used to simplify the integration of Inductosyn position transducers into the system. These include:

Analog to Digital Converters

These converters include the necessary reference oscillators. When combined with a pre-amplifier and power supplies this provides digital position data to computers, numerical control systems, position display systems and motion control systems.

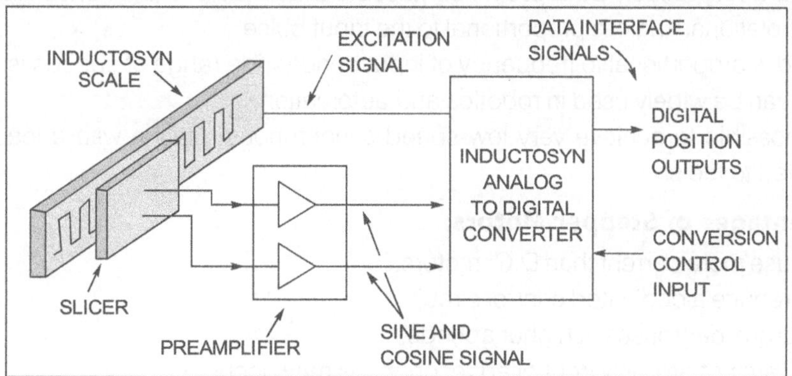

Fig: 13.25 Analog to Digital Converters

Preamplifiers

The inductosyn transducers output signal amplitude requires that an appropriate gain amplifier be added.

Other accessories are Digital Readout Assemblies, Special and custom Products, Correction Logic Assemblies.

13.5 STEPPER MOTORS

Stepper motors are very versatile and important member among the machines designed till today. With the help of stepper motors it has been possible to create a kind of revolution in the areas of robotics which is meant to carry parts, machines, materials etc. Stepper motors also proved like a pole backbone not only in robotics areas but also in electromedical fields, basically in radiation therapy.

A stepper motor is basically a brushless DC motor whose rotor rotates in discrete angular movements when its stator winding is energised in a programmed manner. In stepper motor a full rotation is divided into a number of equal steps. The position of rotor can be precisely controlled to move and hold at any one of these steps without any feedback system (an open-loop control). In a broad way the magnetic interaction which occurs between rotor poles and poles of the sequentially energised stator windings causes the rotor to move. Each of this rotation is called a step and the angle of each step is called step angle. With the help of this definition it can be said that stepper motor is actually a digital actuator whose input supply is in the form of programmed energization of the stator winding and whose output is in the form of discrete angular rotation.

13.5.1 Advantages and Disadvantages of Stepper Motors

Some of the advantages of stepper motors are:

- They can be driven in open loop configuration hence no feedback is necessary and therefore they are less costly.
- They have high torque at start-up and low speeds.
- They are free from contamination and no accumulative position error is there.
- They respond directly to digital signals and hence they are natural choice for digital computers.
- They are less likely to stall or slip.
- They have high repeatability of step size, due to which they are widely used in positioning.

- They can be repeatedly stalled without damage.
- They are rugged and durable so they can work in any environment.
- They are very simple mechanically hence no such maintenance is required.
- Their response is excellent during starting, stopping and reversing.
- They are very reliable because no contact brushes are there and hence life is more.
- Their rotational angle is proportional to the input pulse.
- Speed is proportional to frequency of input hence wide range of speeds is possible.
- They can be widely used in robotics and automation.
- It is possible to achieve very low-speed synchronous rotation with a load that is directly coupled to the shaft.

Disadvantages of Stepper Motors:

- They use more current than D.C. motors.
- They require a dedicated control circuit.
- The torque decreases at higher speeds.
- If they are not properly controlled resonances may occur.
- They are difficult to operate at extremely high speeds.

13.5.2 Types of Stepper Motors

The stepper motors are mainly classified into three types which are variable reluctance, permanent magnet and hybrid stepper motors respectively.

(i) Variable Reluctance (VR) Stepper Motors

The variable reluctance stepper motors are characterized by the fact that they do not have any permanent magnet either on stator or rotor. These motors consist of salient pole stator with concentrated three or four phase winding and a salient pole rotor. The rotor is made from ferromagnetic laminations, carries no winding. The stator produces flux which causes the rotor movement through a single step so that reluctance seen by the stator field is minimum and the stator flux linkages are maximized for given stator currents.

In a 3-phase 6/2 pole variable reluctance motor there are six salient poles with concentrated series (or parallel) windings, so that stator has effectively three phase winding. The stator winding is excited from a dc source through a suitable electronic switching device. Suppose AA′, BB′ and CC′ represent the respective coils of stator. Therefore when coils AA′ are excited the rotor is at a position say $\theta = 0°$. When coils AA′ are de-energized and coils BB′ are excited, the rotor moves through a step angle of 60° clockwise (CW). Further when current is withdrawn from coils BB' and coils CC′ are excited, the rotor further moves through a step of 60° CW so that $\theta = 120°$. In this manner rotor will complete one revolution trough six steps. The step angle in this case is 60°.

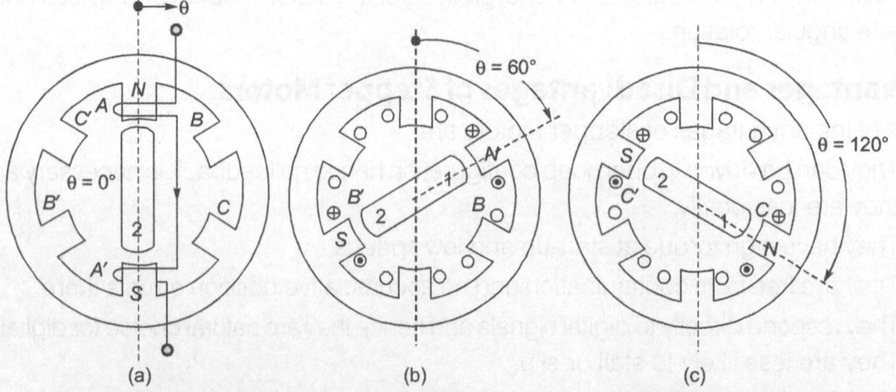

Fig: 13.26 Internal structure of Variable Reluctance (VR) Stepper Motors

Generally the magnitude of step angle is given by:

$$\text{Step angle} = \frac{360°}{mP}$$

where,

m = number of phase windings on the stator

P = number of rotor teeth or poles

In the above case if phase windings A and B are excited simultaneously, then rotor would move through a step angle of 30° CW so that $\theta = 30°$. The rotor would now occupy a position midway between stator poles carrying phase windings A and B. This technique of reducing step angle is called as micro-stepping.

Lower values of step angle can be achieved by using a stepper motor with more number of poles on stator and teeth on rotor. For example in a 4 phase 8/6 pole VRSM, the concentrated windings on diametrically opposite poles are connected in series (or parallel) so as to obtain an effective 4 phase winding on stator. In this case the step angle is 15°.

Example: 13.3

Find the step angle for stepper motor having 4-phases and 6 poles. Also find the angular rotation when 30 digital pulses are supplied.

Solution:

Given: $m = 4$; $p = 6$

Hence, $$\text{Step angle} = \frac{360°}{4 * 6} = 15°$$

Angular displacement with 30 digital pulses:

$$\Phi = 30 * 15° = 450°$$

(ii) Permanent Magnet (PM) Stepper Motor

The stator of permanent magnet stepper motor consists of salient poles with concentrated windings, just like the stator of a VRSM. The rotor as the name of this motor suggest, consists of permanent magnet poles. For the illustration of the working principle of PMSM an elementary form of 2-phase 4/2 pole stepper motor is considered here. The concentrated winding on diametrically opposite poles are connected in series so as to result in 2-phase winding on the stator. The rotor is magnetized to give two permanent magnets.

The working of this motor is like.

Two coils AA' connected in series constitute phase A winding. When this winding is excited with current ia, the stator produced poles attract the rotor permanent magnet poles so that their magnetic axis coincides. Let this exciting of phase A winding be denoted by $+A$.

Now the current in phase A winding is reduced to zero while phase B winding is excited with current I_b. Stator produced poles now attract the rotor poles, causing a CW step rotation through $\theta = 90°$. Let the exciting of phase B winding be denoted by $+B$.

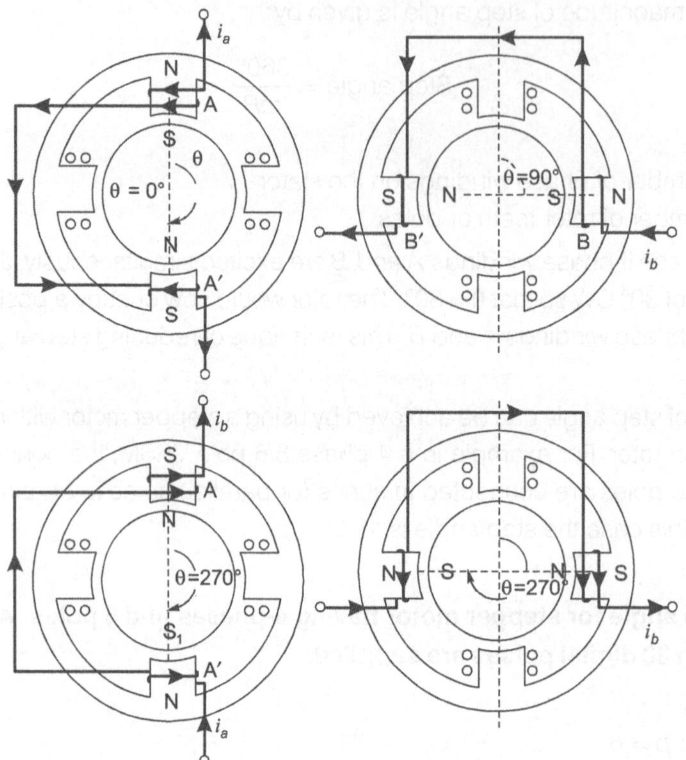

Fig: 13.27 Internal structure of Permanent Magnet (PM) Stepper Motor

Now the phase winding *A* is again excited but with current opposite to i_a that is $-i_a$ this time. Now rotor poles further move through a step of 90° CW so that θ =180°. This step of exciting phase winding be denoted by –*A*.

Now the phase winding *B* is made to carry exciting current opposite to that of i_b that is $-i_b$ this time. The rotor again executes further step of 90° CW so that θ = 270°. This method of exciting phase *B* winding be designated as –*B*.

For further 90° CW step phase winding *B* is de-energized and phase winding *A* is energized. This shows that four steps complete one revolution of the rotor movement.

So here by the application of each current pulse to the stator winding in proper sequence, the rotor can be made to execute discrete angular steps of 90°. Sequence of exciting the stator phase winding is +*A*, +*B*, –*A*, –*B*, +*A* for CW rotor movement. For CCW rotor rotation, sequence of exciting stator phase winding is +*A*, –*B*, –*A*, +*B*, –*B*.

If both the stator windings are excited in the sequence +*A* together with +*B*, then the resultant stator field is along the interpolar axis, the rotor therefore moves a step of 45° CW. This shows for obtaining the angular step of 45° CW the switching sequence should be as +*A*, (+*A* +*B*), +*B*, (+*B* –*A*), –*A*, (–*A* – *B*), –*B*, (–*B* +*A*), +*A*.

This method of reducing step angle to half the normal step is called half step mode of excitation. This is achieved by exciting in proper sequence, one phase winding, one and two phase winding together, one phase winding and so on as described above.

In PMSM even with zero exciting currents, some torque is produced tending to align the permanent magnet poles with the stator teeth; this however is not the case in VRSM. PMSM therefore have the advantage of developing some torque to maintain if the drive circuitry fails. PMSM have the disadvantage that smaller steps are not feasible because of the difficulties encountered in their construction.

(iii) Hybrid Stepper Motor (HSM)

A hybrid stepper motor combines the feature of both PM and VR stepper motor. It consists of an axial permanent magnet at the two ends of which are attached two identical ferromagnetic stacks. These two stacks consist of equal number of teeth. At one end stack attains north magnetic polarity and at the other end, stack gets south magnetic polarity. The two stacks have an angular displacement of one half of the rotor tooth pitch. The stator has salient pole structure which is continuous from one end to other end of the stator pole structure. The stator poles carry concentrated winding like other types of stepper motors.

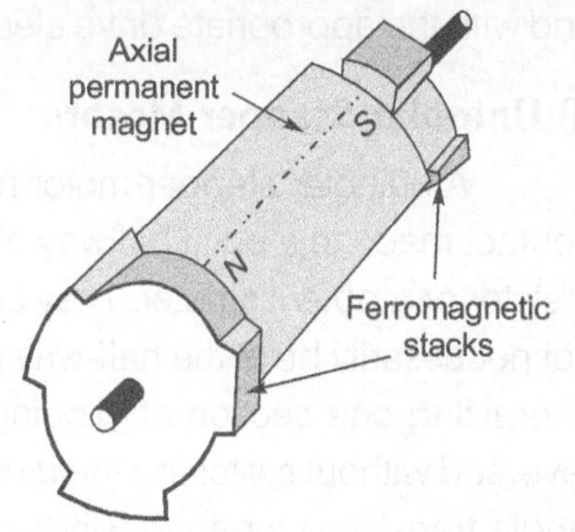

Fig: 13.28 Hybrid Stepper Motor (HSM)

For understanding the hybrid stepper motors an illustration is given here:

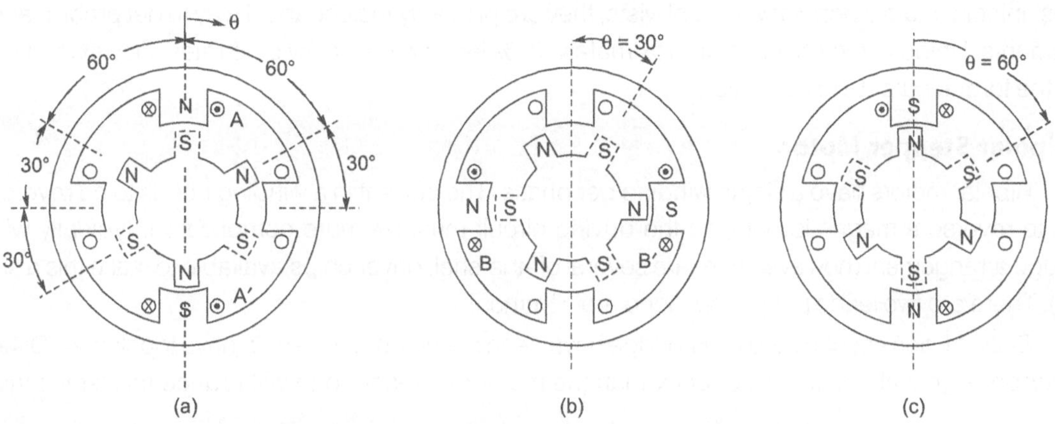

Fig: 13.29 Internal Structure of Hybrid Stepper Motor (HSM)

Let north poles are at the front end while south poles are at the far end. When phase winding *A* is energized with current ia, *N* pole at *A* and *S* pole at *A′* are created on the stator. Pole at *A* attracts *S* pole of far end and pole at *A′* attracts *N* pole of the front end. This equilibrium position of rotor structure results in maximizing the flux linkages with phase winding *A*. For turning the rotor clockwise through a step, de-energizing of the phase winding *A* and exciting of phase winding *B* is done so that *N* pole at *B* and *S* pole at *B′* are created on stator. Pole at *B* attracts *S* pole of rear end and pole at *B′* attracts the *N* pole of the front end, so a step angular rotation of 30° CW is achieved. In the next equilibrium position, maximum flux linkages are now linked with phase winding *B*. If the excitation is removed from phase winding *A*, pole on *A* attracts front N pole and pole at *A′* attracts rear *S* pole. This gives rise to a further step angle movement of 30° CW. In this manner 12 steps will complete one revolution. Sequence of exciting the phase winding for clockwise rotation is *ABA'B'A* and therefore for CCW rotation, the sequence will be *AB'A'BA*. As in PMSM, the rotor poles in HSM also tend to align themselves with the stator teeth when stator exciting current is absent.

13.5.3 Classification of Stepper Motors on the Basis of Phases and Winding

Further the stepper motors can also be classified as two phase stepper motors and multiphase stepper motors. The two phase stepper motors have two basic types of winding arrangements for the electromagnetic coils i.e. bipolar and unipolar. The Multi-phase stepper motors have more than two phases and they tend to have much lower vibration.

The multi-phase stepper motors are although more expensive, they do have a higher power density and with the appropriate drive electronics are often better suited for several application.

(i) Unipolar Stepper Motors

A unipolar stepper motor has one winding with a center tap per phase. (A center tap (CT) is a contact made to a point halfway along a winding of a transformer or inductor, or along the element of a resistor or a potentiometer. They are sometimes used on inductors for the coupling of signals, and may not necessarily be at the half-way point, but rather, closer to one end). The magnetic flux is reversed by energizing one section of windings or the other. Since in this arrangement a magnetic pole can be reversed without switching the direction of current, the commutation circuit become very simple (e.g., a single transistor) for each winding. Typically, given a phase, the center tap of each winding is made common: giving three leads per phase and six leads for a typical two phase motor. Often, these two phase commons are internally joined, so the motor has only five leads. A micro controller or stepper motor controller can be used to activate the drive transistors in the right order, and this ease of operation makes unipolar motors popular with hobbyists; they are probably the cheapest way to get precise angular movements. Unipolar motors have approximately 30 % less torque at low step rates. However at higher rates the torque output are equivalent.

(ii) Bipolar Stepper Motor

Bipolar motors have a single winding per phase. The current in a winding needs to be reversed in order to reverse a magnetic pole, so the driving circuit must be more complicated, typically with an H-bridge arrangement (however there are several off-the-shelf driver chips available to make this a simple affair). There are two leads per phase, none are common.

Static friction effects using an H-bridge have been observed with certain drive topologies. Dithering the stepper signal at a higher frequency than the motor can respond to will reduce this "static friction" effect.

Because windings are better utilized, they are more powerful than a unipolar motor of the same weight. This is due to the physical space occupied by the windings. A unipolar motor has twice the amount of wire in the same space, but only half used at any point in time, hence is 50% efficient (or approximately 70% of the torque output available). Though a bipolar stepper motor is more complicated to drive, the abundance of driver chips means this is much less difficult to achieve.

13.5.4 The Terminology used for Stepper Motors

Holding Torque

The maximum steady torque that can be applied to the shaft of an energized motor without causing rotation.

Detent Torque

The maximum torque that can be applied to the shaft of a non-energized motor without causing rotation.

Torque-Speed Curve

The speed-torque characteristics of a stepping motor are a function of the drive circuit, excitation method and load inertia. Torque/speed curve have torque on the Y-axis and speed on the X-axis, measured in PPS (pulses per seconds) or Hz.

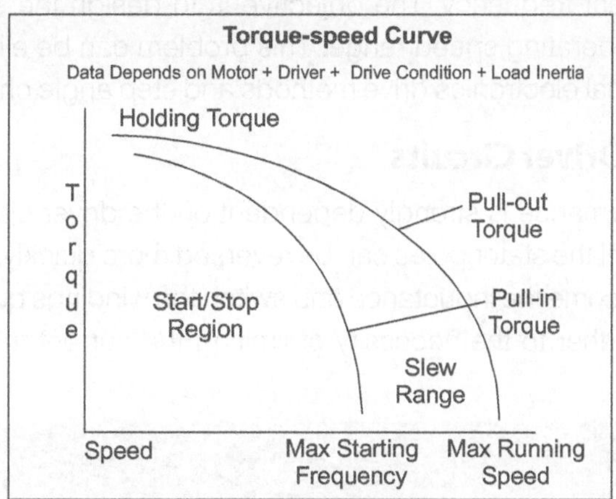

Fig: 13.30 Torque-Speed Curve

Maximum Slew Frequency

The maximum rate at which the step motor will run and remain in synchronism.

Maximum Starting Frequency

The maximum pulse rate (frequency) at which an unloaded step motor can start and run without missing steps or stop without missing steps.

Pull-out Torque

The maximum torque that can be applied to the shaft of a step motor (running at constant speed) and not cause it to lose step.

Pull-in Torque

The maximum torque at which a step motor can start, stop and reverse the direction of rotation without losing step. The maximum torque at which an energized step motor will start and run in synchronism, without losing steps, at constant speed.

Slewing Range

This is the area between the pull-in and pull-out torque curves where a step motor can run without losing step, when the speed is increased or decreased gradually. Motor must be brought up to the slew range with acceleration and deceleration technique known as ramping.

Start-Stop Range

This is the range where a stepping motor can start, stop and reverse the direction of rotation without losing step.

Accuracy

This is defined as the difference between the theoretical and actual rotor position expressed as a percentage of the step angle. The standard accuracy is ±5%. This position error is non-cumulative.

Hysteresis Error

This is the maximum accumulated error from theoretical position for both forward and backward direction of rotation.

Resonance

A step motor operates on a series of input pulses, each pulse causing the rotor to advance one step. In this time the motor's rotor must accelerate and then decelerate to a stop. This causes oscillation, overshoot and vibration. There are some speeds at which the motor will not run.

This is called resonant frequency. The objective is to design the system so that no resonant frequencies appear in the operating speed range. This problem can be eliminated by means of using mechanical dampers, external electronics drive methods and step angle changes.

13.5.5 Stepper motor Driver Circuits

Stepper motor performance is strongly dependent on the driver circuit. Torque curves may be extended to greater speeds if the stator poles can be reversed more quickly, the limiting factor being the winding inductance. To overcome the inductance and switch the windings quickly, one must increase the drive voltage. This leads further to the necessity of limiting the current that these high voltages may otherwise induce.

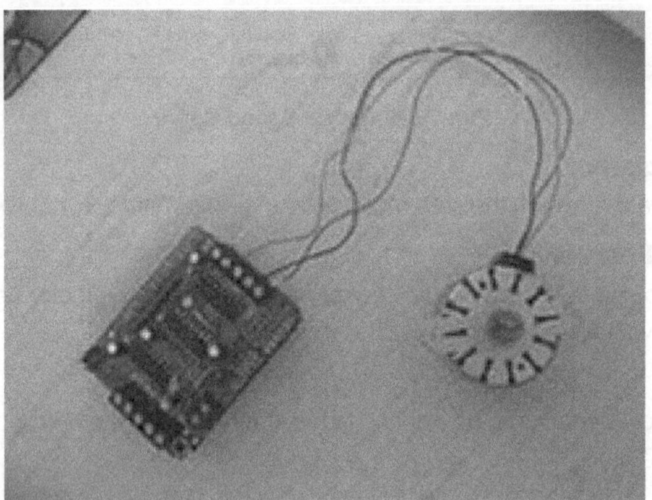

Fig: 13.31 Stepper motor with Adafruit Motor Shield drive circuit for use with Arduino card

(i) *L/R* Driver Circuits

L/R driver circuits are also called constant voltage drives because a constant positive or negative voltage is applied to each winding to set the step positions. Here the winding current, (not the voltage) applies torque to the stepper motor shaft. The current I in each winding is related to the applied voltage V by the winding inductance L and the winding resistance R. The resistance R determines the maximum current according to Ohm's law $I = V/R$. The inductance L determines the maximum rate of change of the current in the winding according to the formula for an inductor $dI/dt = V/L$. Thus when the stepper motor is controlled by an *L/R* drive, the maximum speed is limited by its inductance since at some speed, the voltage V will be changing faster than the current I can keep up. In simple terms the rate of change of current is *L/R* (e.g. a 10 mH inductance with 2 ohms resistance will take 5 ms to reach approx 2/3 of maximum torque or around 24 ms to reach 99% of maximum torque). To obtain high torque at high speeds requires a large drive voltage with a low resistance and low inductance.

(ii) Chopper Drive Circuits

Chopper drive circuits are also called constant current drives because they apply a somewhat constant current in each winding rather than a constant voltage. In each step, a very high voltage is applied to the winding initially. This causes the current in the winding to rise quickly since $dI/dt = V/L$ where V is very large. The current in each winding is monitored by the controller, usually by measuring the voltage across a small sense resistor in series with each winding. When the current exceeds a specified value, the voltage is switched off or "chopped", typically by a power transistors.

When the winding current falls below a specified value, the voltage is switched on again. In this way, the current is maintained relatively constant for a particular step position. This requires additional electronics to measure the winding current, and control the switching. The chopper drive circuit allows stepper motors to run with higher torque at higher speeds than *L/R* drives.

(iii) Wave Drive (One phase on):

In this drive method only a single phase is activated at a time. It has the same number of steps as the full step drive, but the motor will have significantly less than rated torque. However it is rarely used in stepper motors.

(iv) Full Step Drive (Two phases on)

This is the usual method for full step driving the stepper motor. Two phases are always on therefore the motor provides its maximum rated torque. As soon as one phase is turned off, another one is turned on. Wave drive and single phase full step are both one and the same, with same number of steps but difference in torque.

(v) Half stepping

In half stepping, the drive alternates between two phases on and a single phase on. This increases the angular resolution and the motor also has less torque (about 70%) at the full step position (when only a single phase is on). This may be compensated by increasing the current in the active winding. The advantage of half stepping is that the drive electronics need not change to support it.

(vi) Microstepping

In microstepping, commonly referred to as "sine cosine microstepping" the winding current approximates a sinusoidal AC waveform. Sine cosine microstepping is the most common form, but other waveforms can also be used. As the microsteps become smaller, motor operation becomes more smooth, which greatly reduce resonance in the stepper motor and the components connected to the motor, as well as the itself. Gear reducers may be used to increase resolution of positioning.

For example many contemporary hybrid steper motors are rated such that the travel of every full step (e.g.: 1.8 degrees per full step or 200 full steps per revolution) will be within 3% or 5% of the travel of every other full step, as long as the motor is operated within its specified operating ranges. Several manufacturers show that their motors can easily maintain the 3% or 5% equality of step travel size as step size is reduced from full stepping down to 1/10 stepping. Therefore, as the microstepping divisor number grows, step size repeatability degrades. At large step size reductions it may require to release many microstep commands before the motion start at all and then the motion can be a "jump" to a new position.

13.5.6 Stepper Motor Load Calculations and Selection

To select the proper stepper motor, the following must be determined.

1. Load Conditions
   (a) Friction Load
   (b) Load Inertia
2. Dynamic Load Conditions
   (a) Drive Circuit
   (b) Maximum Speed (PPS/Frequency)
   (c) Acceleration/Deacceleration Pattern

With the above load information, the proper stepper motor can be selected.

(i) Load Inertia

The following is an example for calculating the inertia of a hollow cylinder.

$$J = (1/8) \cdot M \cdot (D_1^2 + D_2^2) \text{ (kg-cm}^2\text{)}$$

Where, M = mass of pulley (kg)

D_1 = outside diameter (cm)

D_2 = inside diameter (cm)

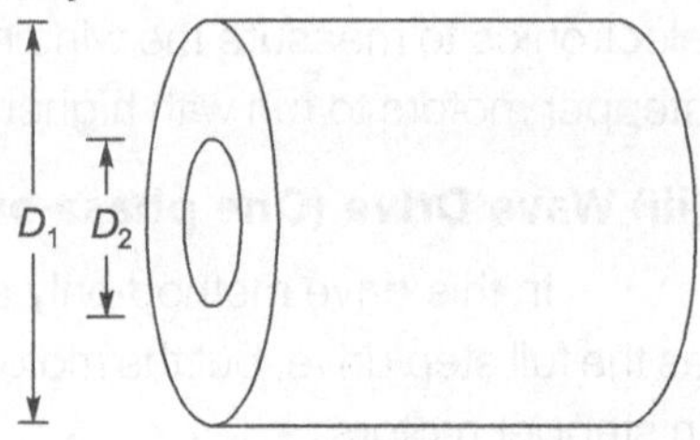

Fig: 13.32 Hollow Cylinder

Linear systems can be related to rotational systems by utilizing the kinetic energy equations for the two systems.

For Linear Translations:

$$\text{Energy} = 1/2\, mv^2 = 1/2\, J\omega^2$$

where, M = mass

v = velocity

J = inertia

ω = angular velocity

1. **Gear Drive System:**

   When gears are used to drive a load, the inertia reflected to the motor is expressed by the following equation:

   $$J = (Z_1/Z_2)^2 \cdot (J_2 + J_3) + J_1$$

   where, Z_1, Z_2 = Number of gear teeth

   J_1, J_2, J_3 = Inertia (kg-cm²)

   J = Reflected inertia (kg-cm²)

2. **Pulley and Belt system:**

   A motor and a belt drive arrangement is used for linear load translation.

   $$J = 2J_1 + 1/4\, M \cdot D^2$$

   where, J = Total inertia reflected to motor (kg-cm²)

   J_1 = Inertia of pulley (kg-cm²)

   D = diameter of pulley (cm)

   M = weight of load (kg)

(ii) Determination of Load Acceleration/Deacceleration Pattern

Load Calculation:

To determine the torque required to drive the load the following equation is to be satisfied.

$$T_m = T_f + T_j$$

where, T_m = Pull-out torque (kgf-cm)

T_f = Friction torque (kgf-cm)

T_j = Inertia load (kgf-cm)

$$T_J = (J_R + J_L)/g \cdot (p \cdot q \cdot s)/180\ .\ df/dt$$

where, J_R = Rotor inertia (kg-cm²)

J_L = Load inertia (kg-cm²)

q = Step angle (deg)

g = Acceleration due to gravity= 980 (cm/sec²)

f = Drive frequency (PPS)

Example: 13.4

A 1.8 degree step motor is to be accelerated from 100 to 1000 pulses per second (PPS) in 50 ms, J_R = 100 g-cm^2, J_1 = 1 kg-cm^2. The necessary pull-out torque is:

Solution:

$$T_J = (0.1 + 1)/980 \cdot (p \cdot 1.8)/180 \cdot (1000\text{-}100)/0.05$$
$$= 0.635 \text{ (kgf-cm)}$$

Linear Acceleration

For linear acceleration as shown in the Fig.13.33, frequency $f(t)$, inertial system frequency $fj(t)$ and inertia load T_J are expressed as follows:

$$f(t) = (f_1 - f_0)/t_1 \cdot t + f_0$$
$$T_J = (J_R + J_L)/g \cdot (p \cdot q \cdot s)/180 \cdot (f_1 - f_0)/t_1$$

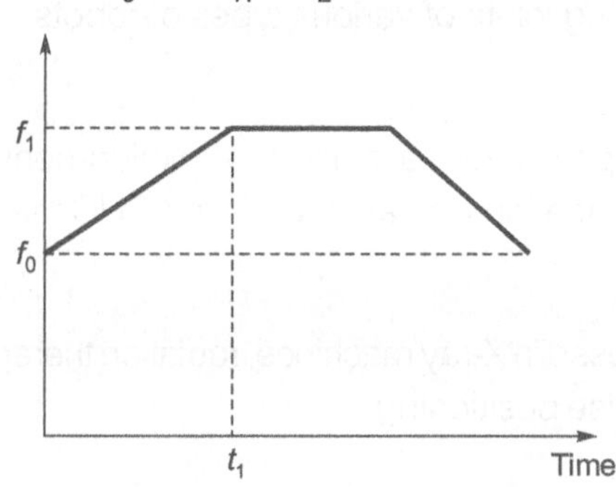

Fig: 13.33 Linear Acceleration

Exponential Acceleration

For exponential acceleration as shown in figure 13.34, drive frequency $f(t)$, inertial system frequency $f_j(t)$ and inertia load T_J are expressed as follows:

$$f(t) = f_1 \cdot (1 - e^{-(t/t1)}) + f_0$$
$$T_J = (J_R + J_L)/g \cdot (p \cdot q \cdot s)/180 \cdot f_1/t \cdot e^{-(t/t1)}$$

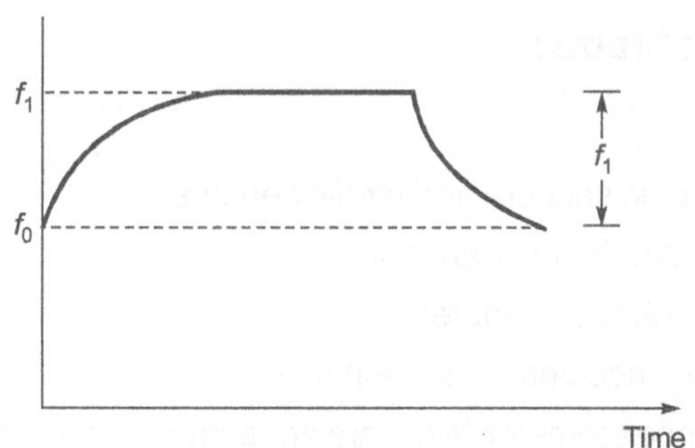

Fig: 13.34 Exponential Acceleration

13.5.7 Applications of Stepper Motors

Stepper motors find applications in many fields some of them are:

Instrumentation Applications

There are essentially low torque applications in which the torque ranges from a few gm-cm to a maximum of 1 kg-cm. Typical examples of such applications are quartz watches, remote camera shutter operations, clocks on railway platforms, mechanical D/A converter etc.

Applications in Computer Peripherals

This important class of application of stepper motors is characterized by the phrase "High performance high volume". The motors employed in these applications have medium torque rating that is 1-2 kg-cm. Typical examples are computer printers, image scanner, floppy and compact disc disk drive, image scanners, digital X-Y plotter, magnetic tape transport, paper tape drive etc.

Applications in Office Equipments

Typical examples of stepper motor applications in this field are electronic typewriter, facsimile (Xerox) machine.

Robotics

Stepper motors are very popular for the reason of its applications in robotics. Stepper motors are popular as an actuator for activating joints of various types of robots.

CNC Machines

Computer controlled stepper motors are used for motion-control positioning system. They are used in holding or positioning applications in various NC and CNC machines with open loop control.

Electro-Medical Applications

Stepper motors are widely used in X-ray machines, radiation therapy units, CAT-scanners, ultrasound scanners etc., which require precise positioning.

Lasers and Optics

In the field of lasers and optics stepper motors are often used in precision positioning equipment such as linear actuators, linear stages, rotation stages, mirror mounts and goniometers, intelligent lighting etc. Other uses are in packaging machinery, and positioning of valve pilot stages for fluid control systems.

Miscellaneous Applications

These include slot machines, 3-D printers, nuclear reactor, aerospace and various industrial applications.

Unsolved Subjective Problems:

Piezoelectric Sensor:

Q.1 Describe the piezoelectric sensors and tactile sensors.

Q.2 Write short notes on piezoelectric transducer.

Q.3 Write short notes on the Accelerometer.

Q.4 Explain the Piezoelectric accelerometer principle.

Q.5 Define Piezoelectric accelerometer. What are advantages of piezoelectric accelerometer?

Q.6 Write the short note on Piezoelectric transducer model.

Q.7 Compare Piezoelectric accelerometer advantages and disadvantages with piezoresistive, Geophone, capacitive sensor type.

Optical Encoders:

Q.1 Explain the principle and operation of optical encoders.

Q.2 Write short notes on Incremental encoder.

Q.3 What is meant by incremental and absolute encoder?

Q.4 Write down the detail classification of encoders.

Q.5 Define encoder with suitable diagram and its advantages.
Q.6 What is encoder, explain with neat sketch?
Q.7 Write the differences between optical and incremental encoder.
Q.8 Write down the different industrial applications of optical encoder.
Q.9 Write down the short note on rotary optical encoder with suitable diagram.
Q.10 Discuss the term range, limits, resolution and accuracy of encoders.
Q.11 Write down the important precautions to be taken care while using Optical Encoders.
Q.12 What is Glass scale optical encoders?
Q.13 Explain the different encoder technologies.
Q.14 Explain the construction of optical encoder.
Q.15 How will you determine the direction of displacement using optical encoder?

Resolvers:

Q.1 What is resolver? Explain with neat sketch.
Q.2 Define resolver and write down its classification.
Q.3 Write down the working principle of resolver with suitable diagram.
Q.4 Write down the industrial applications of resolver.
Q.5 Explain the difference between Receiver resolvers and Differential resolvers.
Q.6 Write brief description about Resolver vs encoder.
Q.7 Explain the design of resolver and its applications.
Q.8 Classify the different categories of resolver.
Q.9 Write different type of brushless resolver. Explain any one.
Q.10 Write short note on Rotary Variable Differential Transformers (RVDT).
Q.11 Explain the conversion process of resolver to digital converter.
Q.12 Explain angular measurement devices of resolver to digital conversion.
Q.13 Discuss different parameters of synchro and resolver.
Q.14 Explain transolver and differential resolver.
Q.15 Explain the term SMARTSYN and SINGLSYN in resolver.

Inductosyn:

Q.1 Describe the inductosysn position transducers with their benefits and features.
Q.2 What is the principle involved behind the operation of inductosysn? Explain briefly with the help of diagram.
Q.3 Write a short note on voltage output as a function of position.
Q.4 Write difference between rotary and linear inductosyn transducers.
Q.5 Name the selection tradeoffs for inductosysn transducers. What is the cycle length?
Q.6 What are the standard materials used for the transducers?
Q.7 Explain briefly the types of rotary transducers.
Q.8 What are the accessories required for the transducers?
Q.9 What are the mounting requirements and the mechanical errors involved?
Q.10 What are capacitively coupled units?
Q.11 Explain thermal stability in transducers.

Q.12 What are the benefits of non-contacting elements in rotary and linear transducers?
Q.13 How to use inductosyn transducers? Write the detail procedure.
Q.14 What are special inductosyn packaging?
Q.15 Name the common forms of linear scales used in linear transducers. Explain any two with diagram.
Q.16 What are preamplifiers?

Stepper Motor:

Q.1 Write short note on stepper motor. What is step single in stepper motor?
Q.2 Specify the types of stepper motor and differentiate any two types in details.
Q.3 Write a short note on stepper motor driver boards.
Q.4 Discuss the role of following terms in control of stepper motor:
(i) Micro-steps (ii) Stepper motor speed
(iii) Acceleration (iv) Position feedback
(v) Initial position (vi) Arduino library
(vii) Demonstration of Arduino code (viii) Arduino pulse width modulation (PWM)
Q.5 How does a stepper motor work?
Q.6 Differentiate between unipolar motor and bipolar motor in two phase stepper motor.
Q.7 Write short note on phase current waveforms in stepper motor.
Q.8 Define following terms?
(i) Pull-in torque
(ii) Pull- out torque
(iii) Detent torque
Q.9 What are the applications of stepper motors?
Q.10 Write advantages and disadvantages of stepper motor.
Q.11 Write a short note on basic construction of stepper motor.
Q.12 What is the difference between stepper motors and servomotors?
Q.13 What is the basic step of the program to run a stepper motor?
Q.14 What is a stepper motor? Explain the working principle of stepper motor in half step mode?
Q.15 Derive the differential equation governing the mechanical system of an electric motor.

Bibliography:

D. Dinulovic, D. Hermann, J. Fluegge, and H. H. Gatzen, "Development of a Linear Micro-Inductosyn Sensor", IEEE Transactions on Magnetics, Vol. 42, No. 10, October 2006.

PRACTICE QUESTIONS

Piezoelectric Accelerometer:

1. Piezoelectric accelerometer work on which of the following phenomenon?
   (a) Microscopic crystal structures get stressed when force applied and which cause to generation of voltage.
   (b) In this Microscopic crystal vibrate with applied force which cause calibration of accelerometer.
   (c) It sense a change in electrical capacitance, with respect to acceleration.
   (d) It work on Archimedes principle.

2. Piezoelectric accelerometer advantages are:
   (i) It can measure static current.
   (ii) Manufacturing cost is less
   (iii) High resolution fragile.
   Which of the following is correct?
   (a) All of above (b) (i) and (ii)
   (c) (i) and (iii) (d) (ii) and (iii)

3. Which of the following is false about piezoelectric accelerometer?
   (a) It can measure temperature of the system.
   (b) Resolution is limited because of resistive noise, only for low and medium frequencies and it required supply voltage.
   (c) It can also measure static acceleration and cheap manufacturing.
   (d) It is a device which is designed to measure rate of change of speed due to motion, vibration, impact events.

4. Power input in Piezoelectric accelerometer can be
   (a) Self-generating so no external power required
   (b) AC type
   (c) DC type
   (d) All of above

5. Which of the following accelerometer work on piezoelectric effect?
   (a) Piezoelectric accelerometer (b) Piezoresistive accelerometer
   (c) Capacitive accelerometer (d) Geophone/Elecrodynamic accelerometer

6. Which of the following is true about wear in piezoelectric accelerometer?
   (a) No moving parts so there is no wear.
   (b) High wear rate but can be decrease with proper maintenance and lubrication.
   (c) Wear rate can't control because lubrication can decrease efficiency.
   (d) None of above

7. Which of following is false? Where term has usual meaning.

   (a) $g_{33} = \frac{VT}{\sigma_3} \frac{\text{Electrical field produced in direction 3 V/m}}{\text{Mechanical stress applied in direction 3 N/m}^3}$

(b) $V = g_{33}\,\sigma_3 T = g_{33}\,E\Delta T$
(c) $Q = cWLg_{33}\,E\Delta T/T$
(d) $R_t = \dfrac{1}{2\pi cf}$

8. Vibration produces deflection in the beam, which is maximum at the free end, to measure this deflection device used is?
(a) Rotameter (b) Doppler VIbrometer
(c) ORP meter (d) Tension gauge

9. Principle used for manufacturing of piezoelectric accelerometer
(a) Piezoresistance (b) Piezoelectricity
(c) Both of above (d) None of above

10. Two types of piezoelectric material that are used for PCB accelerometers are
(a) Quartz (b) Polycrystalline ceramics
(c) Both of above (d) None of above

11. ICP stand for
(a) Internal circuit-piezo electric (b) Integrated circuit-piezo accelerometer
(c) Internal circuit-piezo accelerometer (d) Integrated circuit-piezo electric

12. Dynamic range is the
(a) it is the range between the smallest acceleration detectable by the accelerometer to the largest.
(b) largest detectable range of accelerometer.
(c) smallest detectable range of accelerometer.
(d) none of above.

13. For higher output sensitivity, we use:
(a) Ceramic crystal (b) Quartz crystal
(c) Both have same result (d) Does not hav any effect

14. For higher temperature operation, we use:
(a) Ceramic crystal (b) Quartz crystal
(c) Both have same result (d) Does not have any effect

15. For an accelerometer to be useful the output needs to be
(a) parallel to the acceleration that it is measuring.
(b) perpendicular to the acceleration that it is measuring.
(c) inversely proportional to the acceleration that it is measuring.
(d) directly proportional to the acceleration that it is measuring.

16. IEPE stand for
(a) Internal Electronics Piezo Electric (b) Integrated ElectricalPiezo Electronics
(c) Integrated Electronics Piezo Electric (d) Internal Electronics Piezo Electronics

17. Amplitude linearity is the
(a) degree of accuracy for accelerometer report to output.
(b) use to provde value to input.
(c) degree of accuracy maintain by changing input.
(d) aintain linear relation between input and output.

18. Accelerometer is the transducer for:
(a) Vibration (b) Shock
(c) Absolute motion (d) All the above

19. Input range of accelerometer specify that
(a) maximum allowable acceleration that can be measured.
(b) minimum allowable acceleration that can be measured.
(c) range of allowable acceleration that can be measured.
(d) none of above

20. The PE accelerometer uses an internal PE element coupled with a loading mass to form a
(a) single degree of freedom "mass-spring" system
(b) two degree system
(c) highly sensitive device
(d) none of above

Optical Encoders:

21. If an absolute encoder stops in transition, then what can be the maximum possible error in the reading?
(a) 2 bit (b) 0.5 bit
(c) 4 bit (d) 1 bit

22. An optical shaft encoder is having a disc of 25 mm radius and is able to detect up to 1700 pulses/sec., which is corresponding to 1133 rpm. If we assume that it is rotating at its maximum speed, then the distance travelled by encoder wheel in one minute is (take pi = 3.14)
(a) 150 M (b) 178 M
(c) 128 M (d) 198 M

23. The function of photo detector in optical encoder is
(a) to emit light (b) to absorb light
(c) to increase voltage (d) to detect light and convert into voltage signal

24. The optical shaft encoder can detect up to the range of
(a) 1200 pulses/sec. (b) 1000 pulses/sec
(c) 1700 pulses/sec. (d) 1500 pulses/sec

25. What is the material used to make reflective markings on an optical encoder Scale?
(a) Glass (b) Gold
(c) Copper (d) Diamond

26. Optical encoder is used to
(a) monitor the motion (b) frequency modeling
(c) voltage transformation (d) none of the above

27. Which of the following is not a part of an optical encoder?
(a) photo diode (b) reed head
(c) optical microscope (d) coded disk

28. The output information supplied by the optical encoder does not depend upon:
(a) size and shape of radio bans (b) size of the coded disc
(c) frequency of radio bans (d) all above

29. What does a minima shows in voltage time graph obtained from optical encoder?
(a) Optical encoder is faulty (b) A voltage pulse is generated
(c) No voltage pulse due to radio ban (d) Photo sensors receiving light

30. Exact position coordinates of a shaft can be obtained with the help of:
(a) increamental encoder (b) shaft encoder
(c) encoder disc (d) absolute encoder

31. The phase difference between the two light waves split by the grid diaphragm in incremental encoder is (in degrees):
(a) 180 (b) 90
(c) 60 (d) 120

32. An optical encoder measures a travel of 25 inch lead screw in increaments of 0.001 inch then the resolution of encoder required is:
(a) 20000 (b) 25000
(c) 12500 (d) 2500

33. In a rotary optical encoder diameter of coded disc is 60 mm and the encoder generates 5000 pulses per revolution, then the resolution of the encoder in mm is (approx.):
(a) 0.004 (b) 0.4
(c) 0.04 (d) 400

34. A circuit that converts n inputs to 2 ^ *n* outputs is called
(a) encoder (b) decoder
(c) comparator (d) carry look ahead

35. Encoders are made by three
(a) AND gate (b) OR gate
(c) NAND gate (d) XOR gate

36. Decoder is a
(a) combinational circuit (b) sequential circuit
(c) complex circuit (d) gate

37. IC decoders are made with
(a) AND gate (b) OR gate
(c) NAND gate (d) XOR gate

38. BCD to seven segment is a
(a) Encoder (b) Decoder
(c) Comparator (d) Carry look ahead

39. Which of the following is a digital transducer?
(a) Strain gauge (b) Encoder
(c) Thermistor (d) LVDT

40. Control sequence's state is indicated by
(a) state box (b) decision box
(c) data box (d) conditional box

41. The transducer that converts the input signal into the output signal, which is a discrete function of time is known as:
(a) Active transducer (b) Analog transducer
(c) Digital transducer (d) Pulse transducer

42. A transducer that converts the measurand into the form of pulse is a
(a) active transducer (b) analog transducer
(c) digital transducer (d) pulse transducer

43. Sequential operations in digital system are described by:
(a) Map (b) ASM chart
(c) Flowchart (d) Graph

44. Will any code disc work with any encoder module?
(a) YES (b) NO

45. Can an encoder module be used to detect the presence or absence of an object?
(a) YES (b) NO

46. For a received sequence of 6 bits, which decoding mechanism deals with the selection of best correlated sequence, especially by correlating the received sequence and all permissible sequences?
(a) Soft Decision Decoding (b) Hard Decision Decoding
(c) Both (a) and (b) (d) None of the above

47. Which decoding method involves the evaluation by means of Fano Algorithm?
(a) Maximum Likelihood Decoding (b) Sequential Decoding
(c) Both (a) and (b) (d) None of the above

48. For the 4 states of an encoder on the vertical axis of Trellis diagram, what do/does the solid line indicates?
(a) '0' input (b) '1' input
(c) Both (a) and (b) (d) None of the above

49. During the shifting of bits in an encoder, how are the transitions in the states represented?
(a) By lines (b) By circles
(c) By summers (d) By squares

50. While representing the convolutional code by (n, k, m), what does 'm' signify or represent in it?
(a) Coded bits (b) Message bits
(c) Memory order (d) All of the above

51. At any given time, the output of an encoder depends on ______.
(a) Past input (b) Present input
(c) Both (a) and (b) (d) None of the above

52. The sensor generally used in incremental optical encoder is
(a) LED (b) LCD
(c) photodiode (d) either (a) or (b)

Resolvers:

53. What is the required voltage for all resolvers?
(a) < 24 V ac (b) > 24 V ac
(c) < 24 V dc (d) None of the above

54. In resolver the rotor is attached with how many number of coils?
(a) Single coil (b) Double coil
(c) Multiple (d) (a) and (b)

55. For what purpose resolvers are used?
(a) Angular displacement (b) Linear
(c) Rotary (d) None of these

56. Stator is attached with number of coils:
(a) Single coil (b) Double coil
(c) Multiple (d) None of these

57. The popular application of resolvers is in ....
(a) military, (b) aerospace
(c) ac servo motors (d) all of the above

58. Which type of signal resolvers transmit?
(a) Analog (b) Digital
(c) Both Analog and Digital (d) None of the above

59. On increasing the speed of a resolver, the absolute information is ....
(a) lost (b) gain
(c) neither lost nor gain (d) either lost either gain

60. Multiple speed resolvers are achieved by increasing the number of magnetic poles in
(a) rotor and stator equally (b) rotor
(c) stator (d) rotor and stator unequally

61. The lack of optics and precision alignment in resolver increases ....
(a) shock and vibration capabilities (b) shocking capabilities
(c) damping capabilities (d) absorbing capabilities

62. Which of the following devices are commonly used as error detectors in instruments?
(a) Vernistats (b) Microsyns
(c) Resolvers (d) Any of the above

63. A controller, essentially, is ....
(a) sensor (b) clipper
(c) comparator (d) amplifier

64. Which of the following devices is used for conversion of co-ordinates?
(a) Microsyn (b) Selsyn
(c) Synchro-resolver (d) Synchro-transformer

65. The resolver is like a small transformer with ....
(a) 1 Primary and 2 secondary winding (b) 1 Primary
(c) 2 secondary winding (d) none of the above

66. The_______ will vary as the shaft of the resolver rotates.
(a) Peak voltage (b) Displacement
(c) velocity (d) none of the above

67. The important characteristic of the resolver is the ______ of each secondary winding.
(a) Peak voltage (amplitude) (b) Angular displacement
(c) linear displacement (d) any of the above

68. The_______ is located on the shaft of the resolver is called the rotor.
(a) Secondary winding (b) Primary winding
(c) Both (a) and (b) (d) Primary and secondary

69. A typical resolver has three windings
(a) a primary winding and two secondary windings
(b) two primary windings and a secondary winding
(c) both (a) and (b)
(d) all of the above

70. In resolver the primary winding is used as the input for an ....
(a) AC and DC drive signal (b) DC drive signal
(c) AC drive signal (d) None of the above

71. The rotor of resolver is made from a material such as ....
(a) stainless steel (b) Iron or steel
(c) cast steel (d) any of the above

72. In resolver the output from the secondary will be in the form of a ....
(a) sinusoid and cosinuoid (b) only sinusoid
(c) only cosinuoid (d) none of the above

73. The strengths of resolver are
(a) Reliable, Robust and Accurate (b) Bulky, heavy
(c) Long life, Skilful and Expensive (d) All of the above

74. The weakness of the resolver are
(a) Reliable, Robust and Accurate
(b) Long life, Skilful and Expensive
(c) Bulky, heavy, expensive, needs skilled worker
(d) None of the above

75. The applications of resolver are
(a) permanent magnet motor commutation and speed control
(b) both (a) and (c)
(c) ac and dc servo motor commutation and speed control
(d) none of the above

76. The resolver provide two voltages whose ratio represents the absolute position of the input shaft. (where θ = shaft angle)
(a) $\frac{\sin\theta}{\cos\theta = \tan\theta}$ (b) $\frac{\cos\theta}{\sin\theta} = \cot\theta$
(c) Both (a) and (b) (d) None of the above

77. The resolvers are excited by
(a) DC Sine wave (b) AC Sine wave
(c) Pulsed square wave (d) AC Cosine wave

Inductosyn:

78. An inductosyn can provide Absolute position data and Incremental position data as ____.
(a) Either of these (b) Both of them together
(c) None of them (d) Either or Both of them

79. An inductosyn do generally have_____.
(a) High wear (b) Little wear
(c) Zero wear (d) None of the above

80. For linear inductosyn, the printed circuit comprises of______
(a) Radial hairpin turns (b) Parallel hairpin turns
(c) Both of them (d) None of the above

81. For rotary inductosyn, the printed circuit comprises of______.
(a) Radial hairpin turns (b) Parallel hairpin turns
(c) Both of above (d) None of the above

82. Accessories used in inductosyn
(a) Analog to digital converters (b) Preamplifiers
(c) Digital Readout Assemblies (d) All of the above

83. In automation applications inductosyn transducers are used for
(a) Machine tools (b) Rolling Mills
(c) Precision robotics (d) All of the above

84. In inductosyn ______.
(a) the slider is moving (b) the slider is fixed
(c) the scale is moving (d) none of the above

85. The linear Inductosyn transducers are made by______
(a) Thick film technology (b) Thin film technology
(c) Laser micro machining (d) None of them

86. Inductosyn position Transducers can be used as:
(a) Ratiometric comparisons of sine and cosine output signals
(b) Amplitude measurement or nulling of error output signals
(c) Phase shift of error output signals
(d) All of the above

87. Recommended operating range for the Inductosyn transducer is
(a) 1 kHz to 50 kHz (b) 5 kHz to 50 kHz
(c) 2.5 kHz to 100 kHz (d) 10 kHz to 100 kHz

88. What does an inductosyn resembles to in terms of operation?
(a) Multipole resolver (b) Synchros
(c) LVDT (d) Hall Effect sensors

89. At what transformation ratio does an inductosyn operate on?
(a) 1 : 100 (b) 1000 : 1
(c) 100 : 1 (d) 1 : 1000

90. What is the sine output of an inductosyn if S is the distance between pitches, and X is the slider displacement within a pitch, and the scale is energized with a voltage $V \sin t$?
(a) $V \sin\omega t \cos[2\pi X/S]$ (b) $V \sin\omega t \sin[2\pi X/S]$
(c) $V \cos\omega t \sin[2\pi X/S]$ (d) $V \cos\omega t \cos[2\pi X/S]$

91. How is orientation of an inductosyn decided?
(a) By calculating distance between pitches.
(b) By calculating slider displacement within a pitch.
(c) By counting successive pitches in either direction.
(d) By calculating voltage coupling between the two slider windings.

92. What is true about inductosyn?
(a) Requires ohmic contact (b) Do not require amplification
(c) Has highly efficient transformation (d) Contains large number of cycles

93. How can be an inductosyn used?
(a) In a Transmitter and Receiver mode (b) As a linear transducer
(c) As a single unit with a resolver (d) All of the above

94. The slider and the scale in an inductosyn are separated by a gap with
(a) Electromagnetic Screen (b) Electrostatic Screen
(c) CRT Screen (d) None of the Above

95. What is the accuracy of an inductosyn?
(a) ±0.5 arc second (b) 0.0001 inches
(c) Both (a) and (b) (d) None of the above

Stepper Motor:

96. A salient pole synchronous motor is running at no load. Its field current is switched-off. V the motor will
(a) come to stop.
(b) continue to run at synchronous speed.
(c) continue to run at a speed slightly more than the synchronous speed.
(d) continue to run at a speed slightly less than the synchronous speed.

97. The frequency of the rotor current in a 3-phase 50 Hz, 4 pole induction motor at full v load speed is about
(a) 50 Hz (b) 20 Hz
(c) 2 Hz (d) Zero

98. In a stepper motor the angular displacement
(a) can be precisely controlled.
(b) it cannot be readily interfaced with micro computer based controller.
(c) the angular displacement cannot be precisely controlled.
(d) it cannot be used for positioning of work tables and tools in NC machines.

99. A stepper motor is
(a) a dc motor (b) a single-phase ac motor
(c) a multi-phase motor (d) a two phase motor

100. The 'sheath' is used in cable to
(a) provide strength to the cable
(b) provide proper insulation
(c) prevent the moisture from entering the cable
(d) avoid chances of rust on strands

101. The drive motor used in a mixer-grinder is a
(a) dc motor (b) induction motor
(c) synchronous motor (d) universal motor

102. In a capacitor start single-phase induction motor, the capacitor is connected
(a) in series with main winding (b) in series with auxiliary winding
(c) in series with both the windings (d) in parallel with auxiliary winding

103. A 3 stack stepper motor with 12 numbers of rotor teeth has a step angle of ______.
(a) 12° (b) 8°
(c) 24° (d) 10°

104. In case of a universal motor, torque pulsation is minimized by ______.
(a) load inertia (b) rotor inertia
(c) both rotor and load inertia (d) none of the above

105. The speed-torque characteristics of a DC series motor are approximately similar to those of the ______ motor.
(a) universal (b) synchronous
(c) DC shunt (d) two-phase

106. The torque-speed characteristics of an a.c. operated universal motor has a _____ characteristic and it _____ be started under no-load condition.
(a) inverse, can (b) nearly inverse, can
(c) inverse, cannot (d) nearly inverse, cannot

107. The direction of rotation of hysteresis motor is reversed by
(a) shift shaded pole with respect to main pole
(b) reversing supply lead
(c) either (a) or (b)
(d) neither (a) nor (b)

108. A 1.8° step, 4-phase stepper motor has a total of 40 teeth on 8 pole of stator. The number of rotor teeth for their rotor will be
(a) 40 (b) 50
(c) 100 (d) 80

109. Reduction in the capacitance of a capacitor-start motor, results in reduced
(a) noise (b) speed
(c) starting torque (d) armature reaction

110. Regenerative braking
(a) can be used for stopping a motor.
(b) cannot be easily applied to DC series motors.
(c) can be easily applied to DC shunt motors.
(d) cannot be used when motor load has overhauling characteristics.

111. If the field circuits of an unloaded salient pole synchronous motor gets suddenly open circuited, then
(a) the motor stops.
(b) It continues to run at the same speed.
(c) its runs at the slower speed.
(d) It runs at a very high speed.

112. A single phase Hysteresis motor
(a) can run at synchronous speed only.
(b) can run at sub synchronous speed only.
(c) can run at synchronous and super synchronous speed.
(d) can run at synchronous and sub synchronous speed.

113. A three-stack VR stepper motor has a step angle of 10°. What is the number of rotor teeth in each stack?
(a) 36 (b) 24
(c) 18 (d) 12

114. If a hybrid stepper motor has a rotor pitch of 36° and a step angle of 9°, the number of its phases must be:
(a) 4 (b) 2
(c) 3 (d) 6

115. What is the step angle of a permanent-magnet stepper motor having 8 stator poles and 4 rotor poles?
(a) 60° (b) 45°
(c) 30° (d) 15°

116. A stepping motor is a .... device.
(a) mechanical (b) electrical
(c) analogue (d) incremental

117. Operation of stepping motors at high speeds is referred to as:
(a fast forward (b) slewing
(c) inching (d) jogging

118. Which of the following phase switching sequence represents half-step operation of a VR stepper motor?
(a) A, B, C, A........... (b) A, C, B, A...........
(c) AB, BC, CA, AB.............. (d) A, AB, B, BC..............

119. The rotational speed of a given stepper motor is determined solely by the
(a) shaft load (b) step pulse frequency
(c) polarity of stator current (d) magnitude of stator current

120. A stepper motor may be considered as a .... converter.
(a) dc to dc (b) ac to ac
(c) dc to ac (d) digital-to-analogue

121. The rotor of a stepper motor has no
(a) windings (b) commutator
(c) brushes (d) all of the above

122. Wave excitation of a stepper motor results in
(a) microstepping (b) half-stepping
(c) increased step angle (d) reduced resolution

123. A stepper motor having a resolution of 300 steps/rev and running at 2400 rpm has a pulse rate of, pps.
(a) 4000 (b) 8000
(c) 6000 (d) 10,000

124. The torque sexerted by the rotor magnetic field of a PM stepping motor with unexcited stator is called .... torque.
(a) reluctance (b) detent
(c) holding (d) either (b) or (c)

125. A variable reluctance stepper motor is constructed of .... material with salient poles.
(a) paramagnetic (b) ferromagnetic
(c) diamagnetic (d) non-magnetic

126. Which of the following motor would suit applications where constant speed is absolutelyessential to ensure a consistent product?
(a) Brushless dc motor
(b) Disk motor
(c) Permanent-magnet synchronous motor
(d) Stepper motor

127. A switched reluctance motor differs from a VR stepper motor in the sense that it
(a) has rotor poles of ferromagnetic material.
(b) rotates continuously.
(c) is designed for open-loop operation only.
(d) has lower efficiency.

128. The most common two-phase ac servomotor differs from the standard ac induction motor because it has
(a) higher rotor resistance (b) higher power rating
(c) motor stator windings (d) greater inertia

OOOO

ANSWERS

MECHATRONICS DEVICES

Piezoelectric Accelerometer

1. (a)	**2.** (a)	**3.** (a)	**4.** (a)	**5.** (a)	**6.** (a)	**7.** (a)
8. (b)	**9.** (c)	**10.** (c)	**11.** (d)	**12.** (a)	**13.** (a)	**14.** (b)
15. (d)	**16.** (c)	**17.** (a)	**18.** (d)	**19.** (a)	**20.** (a)	

Optical Encoders

21. (b)	**22.** (b)	**23.** (d)	**24.** (c)	**25.** (b)	**26.** (a)	**27.** (c)
28. (b)	**29.** (c)	**30.** (d)	**31.** (b)	**32.** (b)	**33.** (c)	**34.** (b)
35. (b)	**36.** (a)	**37.** (c)	**38.** (b)	**39.** (b)	**40.** (a)	**41.** (c)
42. (d)	**43.** (c)	**44.** (b)	**45.** (b)	**46.** (a)	**47.** (b)	**48.** (a)
49. (a)	**50.** (c)	**51.** (c)	**52.** (c)			

Resolvers

53. (b)	**54.** (a)	**55.** (a)	**56.** (b)	**57.** (d)	**58.** (a)	**59.** (a)
60. (a)	**61.** (a)	**62.** (d)	**63.** (c)	**64.** (c)	**65.** (a)	**66.** (a)
67. (a)	**68.** (b)	**69.** (a)	**70.** (c)	**71.** (b)	**72.** (a)	**73.** (a)
74. (c)	**75.** (b)	**76.** (a)	**77.** (b)			

Inductosyn

78. (a)	**79.** (c)	**80.** (b)	**81.** (a)	**82.** (d)	**83.** (d)	**84.** (a)
85. (b)	**86.** (d)	**87.** (c)	**88.** (a)	**89.** (c)	**90.** (b)	**91.** (c)
92. (d)	**93.** (d)	**94.** (b)	**95.** (c)			

Stepper Motor

96. (b)	**97.** (c)	**98.** (a)	**99.** (d)	**100.** (a)	**101.** (d)	**102.** (b)
103. (d)	**104.** (c)	**105.** (a)	**106.** (c)	**107.** (a)	**108.** (b)	**109.** (c)
110.(b)	**111.** (b)	**112.** (a)	**113.** (d)	**114.** (a)	**115.** (b)	**116.** (d)
117.(b)	**118.** (d)	**119.** (b)	**120.** (d)	**121.** (d)	**122.** (b)	**123.** (c)
124.(d)	**125.** (b)	**126.** (c)	**127.** (b)	**128.** (a)		

CHAPTER 14

Sensors and Actuators

14.1 SENSORS

A sensor is an electronic element in mechatronic or measurement system that acquires a physical parameter and change it into a signal that can be processed by the system. Often the active element of a sensor is referred as a transducer. The monitoring and control systems require sensors to measure physical quantities such as position, distance, force, strain, temperature, vibration and acceleration.

Design of Sensors and transducer always involves the application of some principles of chemistry and physics. Sensors in manufacturing are used for automation of production processes as well as process monitoring activities.

14.1.1 Definition of Sensor

Sensor is defined as an element which produces a signal corresponding to the quantity under measurement. According to the Instrument Society of America, sensor can be defined as "A device which provides a usable output in response to a specified measurand." Here, the output is usually an 'electrical quantity' and measurand is a 'physical quantity, property or condition which is to be measured'. Thus in the case of, say, a thermister, the quantity being measured is temperature and the sensor transforms an input of temperature into a change in resistance.

14.1.2 Advantages of Sensors

Sensor technology has the important advantages in manufacturing automation as follows:

- Sensors alarm the system operators about the failure of any of the subunits of manufacturing systems. It helps to reduce the downtime of complete manufacturing system by taking preventative measures.
- By employing sensor technology requirement of skilled and experienced labor decreases.
- High quality products with ultra-precision can be achieved.

14.1.3 Transducer

It is defined as an element which, when subjected to a physical change experiences a related change or an element which converts a specified measurand into a usable output by using a transducing principal. It can also be defined as a device that converts a signal from one form of energy to another form.

When a transducer converts a measurable quantity (sound pressure level, optical intensity, magnetic field, etc.) into an electrical voltage or an electrical current then it is called a sensor. When the transducer converts an electrical signal into another form of energy such as sound (which, incidentally, is a pressure field), light, mechanical movement, etc. then it is called as an actuator. A wire of constantan alloy (copper-nickel 55-45% alloy) can be called as a sensor because variation in mechanical displacement (tension or compression) can be sensed as a change in electrical resistance. This wire becomes a transducer with appropriate electrodes and input-output mechanism attached to it. Thus we can say that 'sensors are transducers'.

14.1.4 Sensor Specifications

Sensors or measurement systems are not perfect systems. One should know the capability and shortcoming of a sensors or measurement system to properly assess its performance before using it. Sensor specifications tell the user about variations from the ideal behavior of the sensors. Following are the various specifications of a sensor/transducer system. The sensor or transducer specifications include range, span, error, accuracy, nonlinearity, sensitivity, hysteresis, dead band/time, resolution, stability, Repeatability and response time.

(i) Range

The range of a sensor indicates the limits between which the input can vary. Thus, for example, a pressure sensor for the measurement of pressure might have a range of 1 to 10,000 psi.

(ii) Span

The span is the difference between the maximum and minimum values of the input. Thus, the above-mentioned pressure sensor will have a span of 9,999 psi.

(iii) Error

Error is the difference between the result of the measurement and the true value of the input or the quantity under measurement. For example A thermocouple giving a temperature reading of 38.6 °C, while the actual temperature is 40 °C, then the error is –0.4 °C.

(iv) Accuracy

The accuracy is the closeness of the agreement between the result of the measurement and the actual value of the measurand. It may also be defined as the proximity of measurement results to the true value. It is often expressed as a percentage of the full range output or full-scale deflection. For example a piezoelectric transducer is capable to detect pressures between 1 KPa to 70 MPa. If it is specified with the accuracy of about ±0.5 % full scale, then the reading given can be expected to be within ± 0.35 MPa.

(v) Sensitivity

Sensitivity of a sensor is defined as the ratio of change in the output value of a sensor to the change in input value that causes the output change. For example, a hall effect sensor may have a sensitivity of –10 mV/mT (milli volt/ milli tesla; 1 mT = 10 Gauss (G)).

(vi) Nonlinearity

The nonlinearity indicates the maximum deviation of the actual measured curve of a sensor from the ideal curve. Fig. 14.1 shows a somewhat exaggerated relationship between the ideal, or least squares fit, line and the actual measured or calibration line. Linearity is often specified in terms of percentage of nonlinearity, which is defined as:

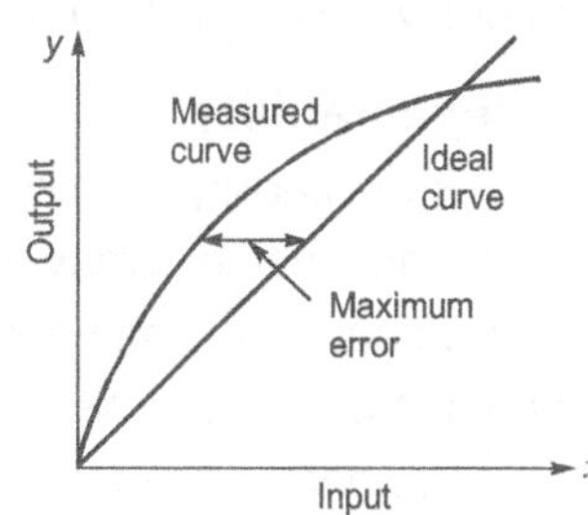

Fig: 14.1 Non-linearity error

$$\text{Non-linearity (\%)} = \frac{\text{Maximum deviation in input}}{\text{Maximum full scale input}} \quad ...(1)$$

The static nonlinearity defined by equation (1) is dependent upon environmental factors, including temperature, humidity, vibration and acoustic noise level. Therefore it is important to know under what conditions the specification is valid.

(vii) Hysteresis

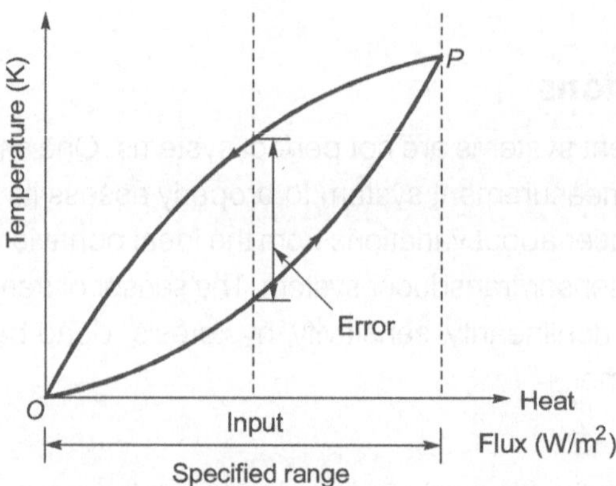

Fig: 14.2 Hysteresis error curve

The hysteresis is an error of a sensor, which is defined as the maximum difference in output at any measurement value within the sensor's specified range when approaching the point first with increasing and then with decreasing the input parameter. Fig. 14.2 shows the hysteresis error (shown exaggerated for clarity) might have occurred during the measurement of temperature using a thermocouple. The hysteresis error is normally specified as a positive or negative percentage of the specified input range.

(viii) Resolution

Resolution is the smallest detectable incremental change of input parameter that can be noticed in the output signal. Resolution is expressed either as a fraction of the full-scale reading or in absolute terms. For example, if an LVDT sensor measures a displacement up to 50 mm and it provides an output as a number between 1 and 200 then the resolution of the sensor device is 0.25 mm.

(ix) Stability

Stability is the ability of a sensor device to give the same output when used to measure a constant input continuously over a period of time. The term 'drift' is used to indicate the change in output that occurs over a period of time. It is expressed as the percentage of full range output.

(x) Dead Band/Time

The dead band or dead space of a transducer is the range of input values for which there is no output. The dead time of a sensor device is the time interval between the application of an input and the moment when output begins to respond or change.

(xi) Repeatability

Repeatability is specified as the ability of a sensor to give the same output for repeated applications of same input value. It may also be defined as the variation in measurements taken by the same person or instrument on the same item, under the same conditions, and in a short period of time. It is usually expressed as a percentage of the full range output:

$$\text{Repeatability} = (\text{maximum} - \text{minimum values given}) \times 100/\text{full range} \quad ...(2)$$

(xii) Response Time

Response time describes the speed of change in the output on a step-wise change in the input or the measurand. It is always specified along with the input step and the output range for which the response time is defined.

14.1.5 Classification of Sensors

The classification of sensors in view of their applications in manufacturing is as follows:

A. **Velocity and Motion Sensors:**
- Incremental encoder
- Tacho-generator
- Pyroelectric sensors

B. **Force Sensors:**
- Strain gauge load cell

C. **Fluid Pressure Sensors:**
- Diaphragm pressure gauge
- Capsules, bellows, pressure tubes
- Piezoelectric sensors
- Tactile sensor

D. **Displacement, Position and Proximity Sensors**
- Potentiometer
- Strain-gauged element
- Pneumatic sensors
- Proximity switches (magnetic)
- Hall effect sensors
- Capacitive element
- Eddy current proximity sensors
- Differential transformers

E. **Liquid flow Sensors:**
- Orifice plate
- Turbine meter

F. **Liquid level Sensor:**
- Differential pressure
- Floats

G. **Temperature Sensors:**
- Thermo-diodes and transistors
- Thermocouples
- Light sensors
- Resistance temperature detectors
- Thermistors
- Photo resistors
- Photo transistor
- Bimetallic strip

14.1.6 Displacement and Position Sensors

Displacement sensors are basically used for the measurement of movement of an object. Position sensors are used to find the position of an object in relation to some reference point. Proximity sensors are a sort of position sensor and are used to trace when an object has moved within particular critical distance of a transducer.

(i) Potentiometer Sensors

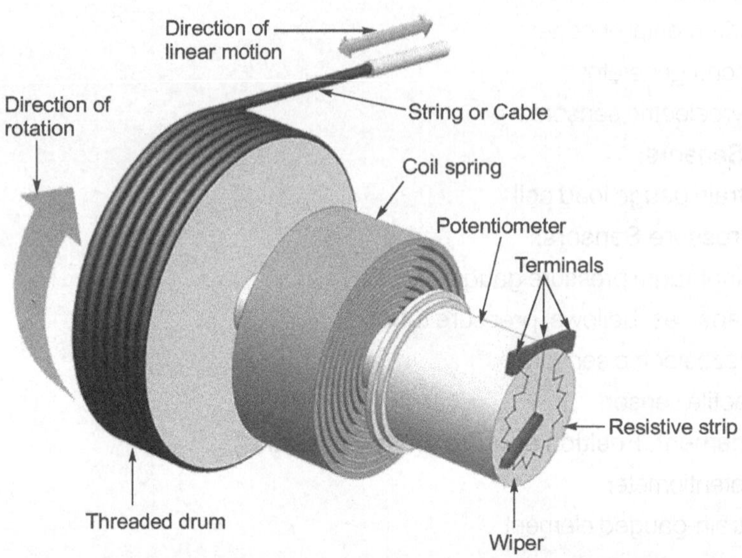

Fig: 14.3 Schematic of a potentiometer sensor for measurement of linear displacement

Fig. 14.3 shows the internal structure of a rotary type potentiometer sensor used for measurement of the linear displacement. The potentiometer can be linear or angular type. It is based on the principle of conversion of mechanical displacement into an electrical signal. It has a resistive element and a sliding contact (wiper). The slider moves along this conductive body, acting as a movable electric contact.

The object, whose displacement is to be measured, is connected to the slider using:

- a moving rod (for linear displacement)
- a rotating shaft (for angular displacement)
- a cable that is kept stretched during operation

The resistive element is a wire wound track or conductive plastic. The track consists of a closely packed resistive coil. Conductive plastic is made up of plastic resin embedded with the carbon powder. Wire wound track has a resolution of the order of ±0.01%, while the conductive plastic may have the resolution of about 0.1 μm.

During the operation of potentiometer, a voltage VS is applied across the resistive element. When the slider comes into contact with the wire, the resistive element is divided into two parts, and hence a voltage divider circuit is formed. The output voltage (VA) is measured as shown in the Fig. 14.3. The output voltage is proportional to the displacement of the slider over the wire. Then the displacement as an output parameter that is to be measured is calibrated against the output voltage VA.

Applications of Potentiometer

These sensors are primarily used in the control systems with a loop of feedback to ensure that the moving member or component reaches its commanded position.

These sensors are used on machine-tool controls, elevators, liquid-level assemblies, forklift trucks, automobile throttle controls etc. In manufacturing process, these sensors are employed in control of injection molding machines, wood working machinery, printing, spraying, robotics, etc.

(ii) Strain Gauges

The strain developed is defined as a ratio of change in length in the same direction in which the load is applied to the original length of the element. The produced strain causes a change in the element's resistance. Therefore, we can say that,

$$\frac{\Delta R}{R} \propto \varepsilon \quad \text{...(3)}$$

$$\frac{\Delta R}{R} = G\varepsilon \quad \text{...(4)}$$

where G is the proportionality constant and it is also called gauge factor. G value is considered in between 2 to 4 and the resistances are taken of the order of 100 Ω.

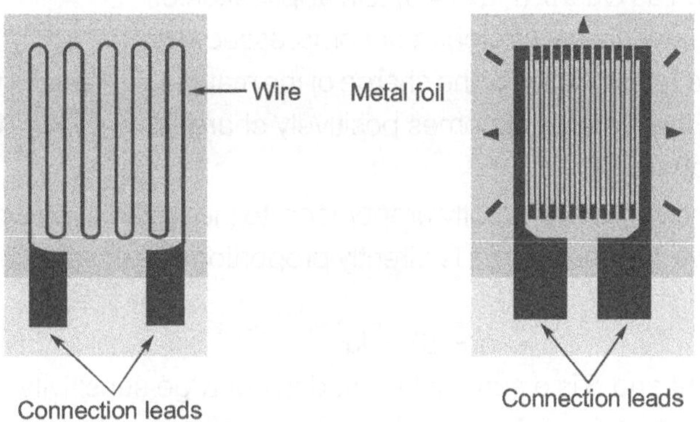

Fig: 14.4 A pattern of resistive foils

Wheatstone's Bridge

Resistance strain gauge follows the principle of change in resistance as per the equation (4). It comprises of resistive foil shown in Fig. 14.4. These foils are made of Constantan alloy (copper-nickel 55-45% alloy) and the foils are stick to a backing material plastic (ployimide), epoxy or glass fiber reinforced epoxy. The strain gauges are fixed to the work material using epoxy or Cyanoacrylate cement Eastman 910 SL. As the shape of the work piece changes due to external loading, the resistance of strain gauge element changes. This resistance change can be sensed using a Wheatstone's resistance bridge principle as shown in Fig. 14.5. In the balanced bridge we can have a relation:

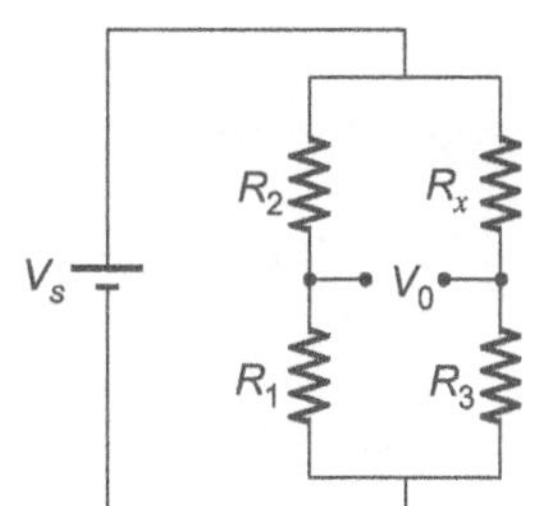

Fig: 14.5 Wheatstone's bridge

$$\frac{R_2}{R_1} = \frac{Rx}{R_2} \quad \text{... (5)}$$

where R_x is the resistance of strain gauge element, R_2 is balancing/adjustable resistor, R_1 and R_3 are resistors which have constant value. The measured deformation or displacement by the stain gauge is calibrated against change in resistance of adjustable resistor R_2 which makes the voltage across nodes A and B equal to zero.

Applications of strain gauges

Strain gauges are broadly employed in stress analysis and diagnosis of machines and failure analysis. Basically, they are employed for multi-axial stress fatigue testing, proof testing, residual stress and vibration measurement, torque measurement, bending and deflection measurement, compression and tension measurement and strain measurement.

Primarily the strain gauges are used as sensors for machine tools and safety in automobiles. In particular, they are used in the force calculation of machine tools, hydraulic or pneumatic press and as impact sensors in aerospace vehicles.

14.1.7 Velocity, Motion, Force and Pressure Sensors:

(i) Piezoelectric Sensor

Piezoelectric sensors are used for the quantification of pressure, acceleration and dynamic-forces like oscillation, impact forces, or high speed compression or tension. It contains piezoelectric ionic crystal materials such as Quartz (Fig. 14.6). On application of force or pressure these materials get stretched or compressed. As a result of compression the redistribution of the charge of the material takes place. One face of the material becomes positively charged and the other negatively charged.

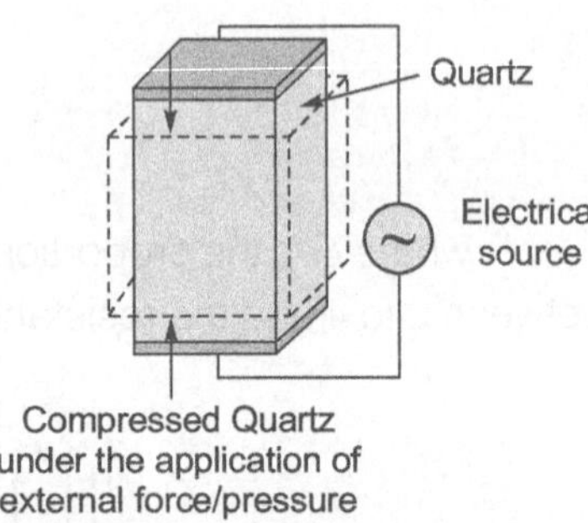

Fig: 14.6 Working principle of Piezoelectric sensor

The charge q on the surface is directly proportional to the distance by which the charge has been moved. The distance moved by the charge is directly proportional to the applied force. Therefore, it can be written,

$$q = SF = kx \qquad ...(6)$$

where, k is constant and S is a constant termed the charge sensitivity.

(ii) Tachogenerator

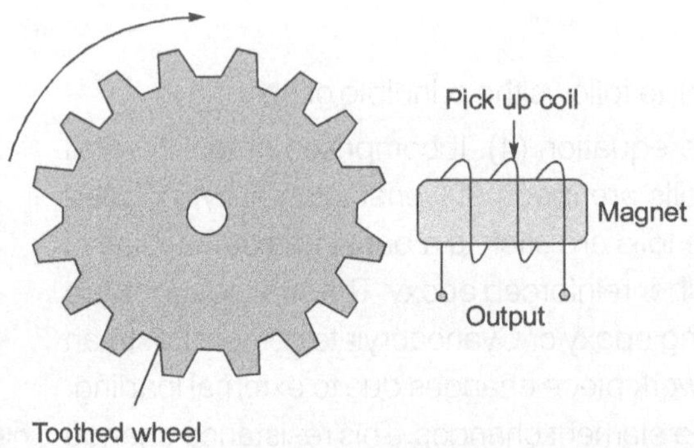

Fig: 14.7 The working principle of Techogenerator

Tachogenerator works on the principle of variable reluctance. It consists of an assembly of a toothed wheel and a magnetic circuit as shown in Fig. 14.7. A toothed wheel is mounted on the shaft or the element of which angular motion is to be measured. The magnetic circuit comprising of an electromagnetic coil wound on a ferromagnetic material. The air gap between the tooth of the wheel and magnetic core changes with the rotation of the wheel, which results in a cyclic change in magnetic flux associated with the coil. The alternating emf is generated which is the measure of angular motion. Finally a pulse shaping signal conditioner is used to transform the output into a number of pulses which are counted by a counter.

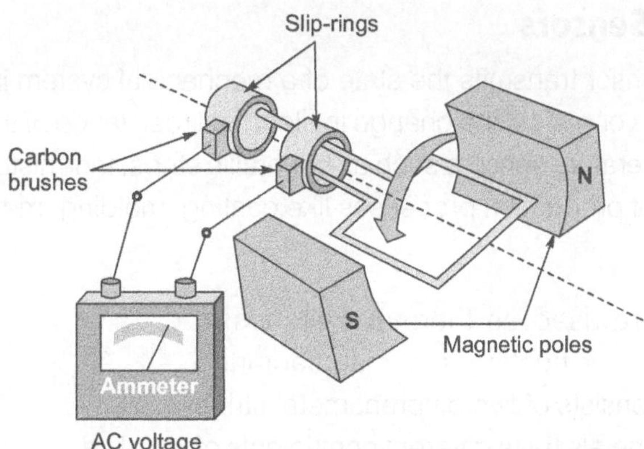

Fig: 14.8 Construction and working of AC generator

An alternating current (AC) generator can also be used as a tachognerator. It consists of rotor coil which rotates with the shaft. Fig. 14.8 shows the schematic of an AC generator. The rotor rotates in the magnetic field produced by a stationary permanent magnet or an electromagnet. During this process, an alternating emf is generated which is the measure of the angular velocity of the rotor. In general, these sensors have a nonlinearity error of about ± 0.15% and they can be used for maximum speed up to about 10000 RPM.

14.1.8 Light Sensors

A light sensor is a device that is used to identify the light. Todays many types of light sensors such as photocell/photo-resistor and photo diodes are being employed in industrial and other manufacturing applications.

Photoresistor, also called as a light dependent resistor (LDR) has a resistor whose resistance decreases with increasing incident light intensity. It is made of a high resistance semiconductor material, cadmium sulfide (CdS). As per the principle of photoconductivity, the resistance of cadmium sulfide photoresistor decreases with the amount of light incident upon it. This is due to the generation of mobile carriers when photons are absorbed by the semiconductor material.

Fig. 14.9 shows the construction of a photoresistor.

The CdS resistor coil is mounted on a ceramic substrate. This assembly is surrounded by a resin material. The sensitive coil electrodes are connected to the control system through lead wires. When the high intensity light fall on the electrodes, the resistance of resistor coil decreases, which is further converted into the appropriate signals with the help of microprocessor.

Photoresistors are employed in scientific applications and almost any branch of industry for safety, inspection, enjoyment, sound reproduction, and control, measurement.

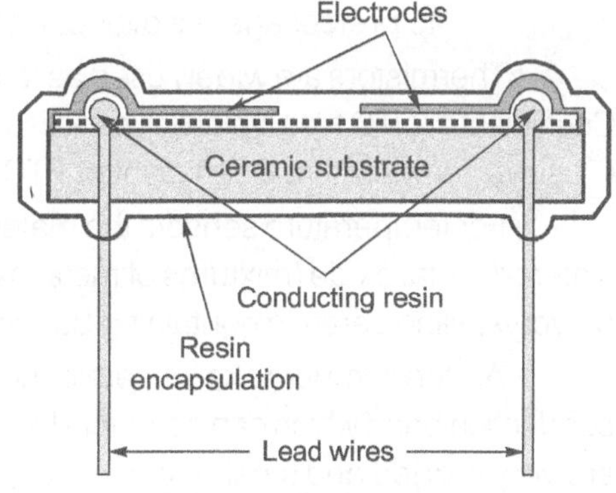

Fig: 14.9 Construction of a photoresistor

Photo resistor applications:

- Computers, televisions, wireless phones employ ambient light sensors to auto control the brightness of screen.
- Barcode scanners
- In space and robotics
- Auto flash for camera
- Industrial process control

14.1.9 Temperature Sensors

The temperature sensor transmits the state of a mechanical system in the form of expansion or contraction of liquids, solids or gases, the change in electrical resistance of thermoelectric, conductors, semiconductors emf. Temperature sensors such as bimetallic strips, thermistors, thermocouples etc. are widely used in inspection of production processes like casting, molding, metal cutting etc.

(i) Bimetallic Strips

Bimetallic strips are used as thermal switches in controlling the temperature or heating in a manufacturing processes or systems. It consists of two different metal strips bonded together. The two metals have different coefficients of expansion. When the temperature rises the strips bend into a curve and the metal with a higher coefficient of expansion on outer side of the curve. Figure 14.10 shows the schematic diagram of a bimetallic strip type temperature sensor. As the temperature increases strips bends and the soft iron comes in closer proximity of the small magnet and further touches it. Then the electric circuit completes and generates an alarm. In this way bimetallic strips help in controlling the temperature of the desired application or process.

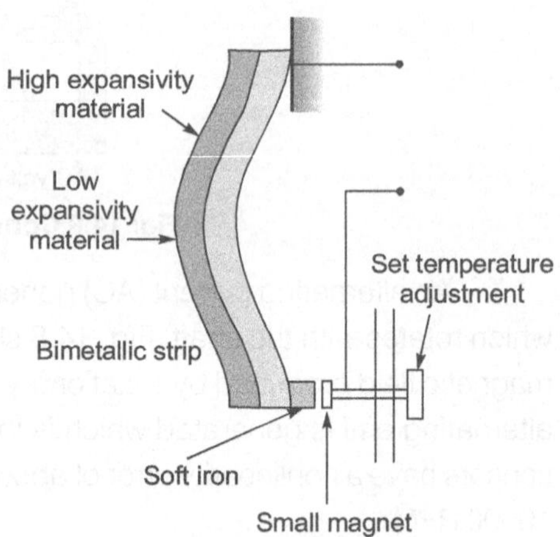

Fig: 14.10 Construction and working of Bi-metallic strip

(ii) Thermistors

A thermistor is a type of resister whose resistance is much more dependent on temperature than a standard resistor. The word thermistor is made by combining words thermal and resistor. Thermistors are of two types:

- Negative Temperature Coefficient or NTC type, in which the resistance decreases with temperature to protect against inrush overvoltage conditions. They are installed parallel in a circuit.
- Positive Temperature Coefficient or PTC type, in which the resistance increases with temperature to protect against over current conditions. They are installed in series in a circuit.

Thermistors are widely used as temperature sensors, inrush current limiter, (Negative Temperature Coefficient or NTC type typically), self-resetting over current protectors, and self-regulating heating elements. (Positive Temperature Coefficient or PTC type typically).

For temperature sensors the material used in thermistor is generally a semiconductor material like sintered metal oxide (mixtures of metal oxides, cobalt, chromium, iron, manganese and nickel) or doped polycrystalline ceramic containing barium titanate (BaTiO3) and other compounds.

As the temperature of semiconductor material increases, more number of electrons come in conduction band which can conduct electricity and hence the resistance of material decreases. Thermistors are very rugged and small in dimensions. They exhibit nonlinear response characteristics.

Thermistors are available in the form of pressed disc, rod, plate, bead or cast chip of semiconducting material. Fig. 14.11 shows the construction of a bead type thermistor. It has a small bead of dimension from 0.5 mm to 5 mm coated with ceramic or glass material. The bead is connected to the electric circuit through two leads.

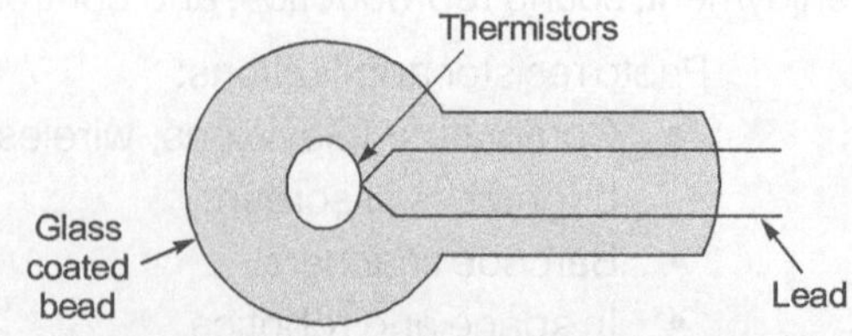

Fig: 14.11 Schematic of a thermistor

The leads are contained in a stainless steel tube for protection from the environment.

Applications of Thermistors:

- To monitor the coolant temperature and/or oil temperature inside the engine.
- To monitor the temperature of an incubator.
- Thermistors are used in modern digital thermostats.
- To monitor the temperature of battery packs while charging.
- To monitor temperature of hot ends of 3D printers. The thermistors monitor the heat produced and allow the printer's control circuitry to maintain a constant temperature for melting the plastic wire.
- To maintain the correct temperature in the food Handling and processing industry equipments
- To control the operations of consumer appliances such as toasters, coffee makers, refrigerators, freezers, hair dryers, etc.

14.1.10 Applications of Sensors in Automobiles

In automobiles sensors are widely used for engine management systems and electro-mechanical accelerometers in airbag deployment applications. The sensor inputs are used for better performance, safety and control. Automobile sensors are also available for pressure and position sensing, electronic stability control, air bag, tire pressure monitoring systems etc. With increasing electronic content in vehicles, automotive sensor applications continue to grow. Some of the general automobile sensors are detailed below:

S. No.	Name of the Sensor	Purpose
1.	Air-fuel Ratio Meter	To monitor the correct air-fuel ratio for an engine
2.	Engine speed sensor	To monitor engine speed
3.	Throttle Position Sensor	To monitor the position of the throttle in an engine
4.	Crank Position Sensor	To monitor piston's TDC position in engine.
5.	Cam Position Sensor	To monitor piston valves in engine
6.	Knock Sensor	To detect engine knocking because of timing advance
7.	Engine Coolant Temperature sensor	To measure the engine temperature
8.	Engine Coolant Temperature sensor	To measure the engine temperature
9.	Mass Air Flow or MAF Sensor	To notify the mass of air entering the engine to the ECU
10.	Oxygen/Lamda Sensor	To monitor the amount of oxygen in the exhaust
11.	Fuel Pressure Sensor	To measure Fuel Pressure in the system
12.	Vehicle Speed Sensor (VSS)	To measure the speed of a vehicle

Table 14.1

(i) Coolant Temperature Sensor

The coolant temperature sensor is used to measure the temperature of the engine coolant of an internal combustion engine. The readings from this sensor are then fed back to the Engine control unit (ECU), which uses this data to adjust the fuel injection and ignition timing. On some vehicles the sensor may also be used to switch on the electric cooling fan. The data may also be used to provide readings for a coolant temperature gauge on the dashboard.

Fig: 14.12 Coolant temperature sensor

(ii) Throttle Position Sensor (TPS)

The TPS is a potentiometer attached to the throttle shaft. A voltage signal is supplied to the sensor, and a variable voltage is returned. The voltage increases as the throttle is opened. This signal and the manifold absolute pressure (MAP) output determines how much air goes into the engine so the computer can respond quickly to changes, increasing or decreasing the fuel rate as necessary.

(iii) Knock Sensor

Engine knock is characteristic of an uncontrolled combustion process and can cause engine damage. That is prevented by a knock sensor, a noise sensor near the engine. The Knock Sensor is a Piezoelectric device that when you stress it, a voltage is produced. It senses knock and transmits information to the electronic engine management control unit. This influences process control in the engine, for example timing and fuel injection until knock is eliminated. Knock is frequently caused by fuel that does not comply with the required minimum quality.

14.1.11 Data Conversion Devices

Data Conversion Devices are very important parts of a Machine Control Unit (MCU). MCU is controlled by various computers or microcontrollers which are accepting signals only in the form of 0s and 1s, while the signals received from sensors are generally in analog form. Therefore a system is essentially required to convert analog signals into digital signals or vis-à-vies. Analog to Digital Converter is abbreviated as ADC. Fig. 14.13 shows a standard control system along with data conversion circuits. On the basis of signals received from sensors, MCU induces actuating signals in digital form.

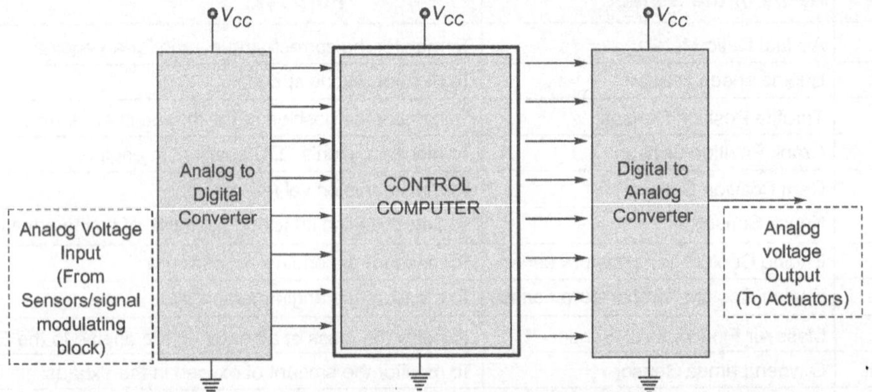

Fig: 14.13 A control system with DAC and ADC devices

(i) Basic Parts of ADCs and DACs

(a) **Encoders:** Though the output obtained from comparators is in the form of 0s and 1s, still not be called binary output. A sequence of 0s and 1s will be converted into binary code by using Encoder. A simple encoder converts $2n$ input lines into 'n' output lines. These 'n' output lines pursue binary algebra.

(b) **Comparators:** In general ADCs and DACs comprise of comparators. This is a combination of diodes and Operational Amplifiers. A comparator is a device which compares the current input or voltage inputs at its two terminal ends and provide output in the form of digital signal i.e. if $V+$ and $V-$ be input voltages at two terminals of comparator then output of comparator will be as:

$$V+ > V- \rightarrow \text{Output } 1$$
$$V+ < V- \rightarrow \text{Output } 0$$

(c) **Analog to Digital Converter (ADC):** ADCs are employed to convert analog to digital signals. There are so many techniques used for ADC conversion, some of them are:

1. Direct conversion ADC or Flash ADC
2. Integrating ADC
3. Successive Approximation ADC
4. A ramp-compare ADC
5. Delta-encoded ADC or counter-ramp
6. Time-interleaved ADC
7. Pipeline ADC (also called subranging quantizer)
8. Wilkinson ADC
9. Sigma-delta ADC (also known as a delta-sigma ADC)

(d) **Digital to Analog Converters:** DACs are used to convert digital signals into analog signals. Here we discuss a few techniques:

1. Over sampling DACs or interpolating DACs
2. The binary-weighted DAC
3. The R-2R ladder
4. Switched resistor DAC
5. Switched current source DAC
6. Switched capacitor DAC
7. Pulse-width modulator
8. The thermometer-coded DAC
9. The Successive-Approximation or Cyclic DAC,

14.2 HALL EFFECT SENSOR

Hall Effect is an ideal sensing technology. A hall element is made by using a thin conducting sheet where its output terminals are kept perpendicular to the direction of current.

The block diagram of a Hall Effect sensing device is shown in Figure 14.14. A Hall Effect based sensing element is often called a Hall device. A Hall Effect sensor senses the magnetic field and measures the physical quantity (like current, temperature, position and pressure, etc.) through the change in the magnetic field around the medium in which the physical quantity is to be measured through the input interface. The electrical signal from the Hall Effect sensor is converted into a desired signal according to the application requirements of the output interface.

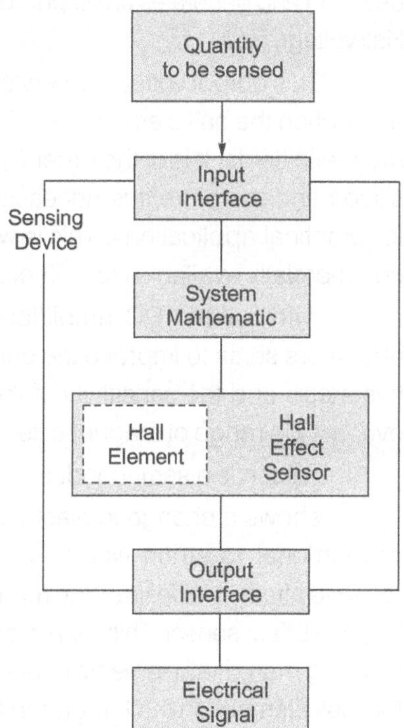

Fig: 14.14 General Sensor based on Hall Effect

14.2.1 Theory of Hall Effect

The Hall Effect was discovered by the physicist Edwin H. Hall in the year 1879. The Hall Effect was named after him. The theory of Hall Effect states that a voltage potential is developed across a conductor when a magnetic field is applied at right angles to the direction of an electric current in the conductor.

This voltage potential is known as Hall voltage. The Hall Effect has been used to develop sensing elements which measure the polarity and intensity of a magnetic field. These magnetic field sensors have been further developed into position transducers, where a change in the position of a magnet attached to a target leads to a change in the magnetic flux density at the location of the Hall device.

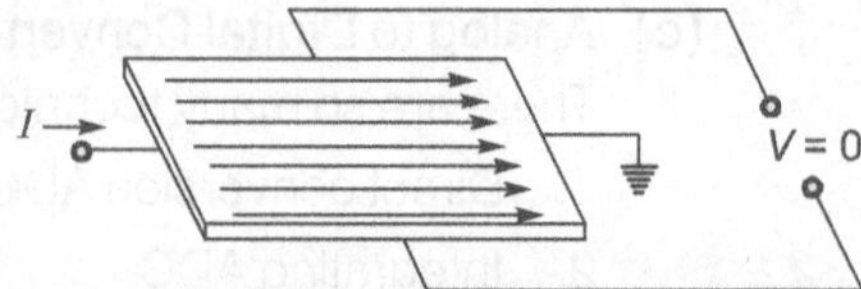

Fig: 14.15 Hall effect principle (with no magnetic field)

Fig. 14.15 illustrates the basic principle of Hall Effect, which shows a Hall element through which electricity is passed. The output terminals are placed perpendicular to the direction of the current. It can be observed from Fig. 14.15 that when a magnetic field is absent, current distribution is uniform and no potential difference is developed across the output terminals.

When a magnetic field is present perpendicular to the direction of current, as shown in Fig. 14.16 a Lorentz force is generated which disturbs the current distribution and thus a potential difference (voltage) is developed across the output. This voltage is known as Hall voltage (V_H).

Fig: 14.16 Hall effect principle (with magnetic field)

$$V_H \alpha I \times B \quad ...(1)$$

The relation of the Hall voltage with a magnetic field and current is shown in equation (1). The magnitudeof the Hall voltage depends on the current and the magnetic field.

Hall Voltage, V_H is directly proportional to magnetic field, B for a defined value of current. Hence, the magnetic field can be determined by measuring the Hall voltage. When the magnetic flux density changes, the sensor detects it and generates an output voltage called the Hall voltage (V_H).

This output voltage is very small (a few μV) even when the hall element is subjected to strong magnetic fields. It is of the order 7 μv/Vs/Gauss in silicon and therefore it is necessary to amplify it for practical applications. This is why most of the commercially available Hall Effect devices come with built-in DC amplifiers and voltage regulators so as to improve the output voltage, hysteresis and the sensitivity of the sensors which eventually allow the Hall Effect sensors to operate over a wide range of magnetic field conditions and power supplies.

Fig: 14.17 Principle of Hall effect

Silicon is a semi-conducting material that shows a change in electrical resistance proportional to strain which is called piezo-resistive effect. It is desirable to reduce this effect in a Hall Effect sensor. This can be accomplished by using many Hall elements or/and by orienting the Hall element on the Integrated Chip (IC).

Two Hall elements that are located in close proximity are shown in Fig 11.18.

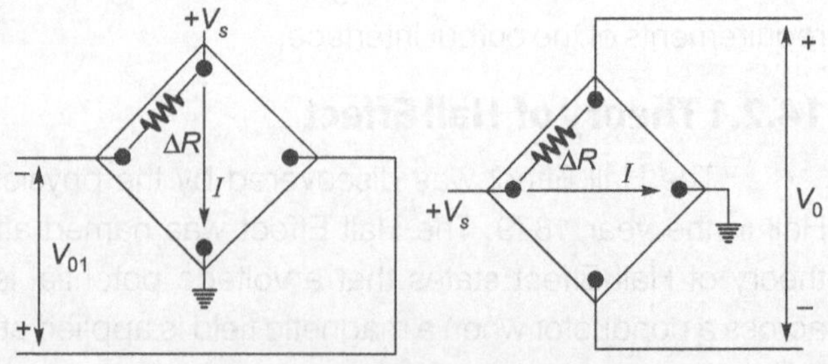

Fig: 14.18 Hall element orientation

They are positioned in such a manner that they both experience an equal packaging stress, denoted by ΔR. The excitations of the first and second Hall elements are along the vertical and horizontal axes respectively. The signal due to stress is eliminated by adding the two outputs.

14.2.2 Basic Hall Effect Sensors

A Hall effect sensor is a transducer that varies its output voltage in response to a magnetic field.

The principle of working of a Hall Effect sensor is shown in Fig. 14.19. Hall effect sensors basically work on the principle that when a beam of charged particles passes through a magnetic field, forces are exerted on the particles and the current beam is deflected from its straight line path. And thus one side of the disc will be negatively charged and the other side will be positively charged. This charge separation is responsible for the generation of potential difference which is the measure of distance of the magnetic field from the disc carrying current.

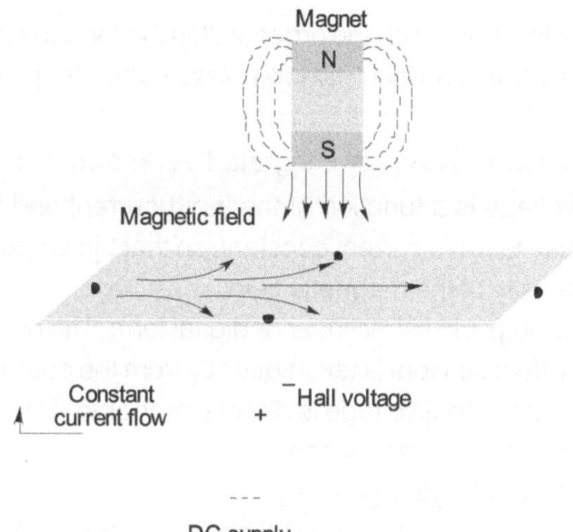

Fig: 14.19 Principle of working of Hall effect sensor

The typical application of Hall Effect sensor is to measure the fluid level in a container. The container contains a float with a permanent magnet attached at its top. An electric circuit with a current carrying disc is mounted in the casing. When the fluid level rises, the magnet comes close to the disc and a potential difference is generated. This voltage then triggers a switch to prevent the fluid to come inside the container.

Hall Effect sensors need necessary signal conditioning circuitry. They can generally be operated at 100 kHz. Amplifier stage and temperature compensation constitute the needed signal conditioning electronics. Voltage regulation is necessary when operating from an unregulated supply. Fig. 14.20 illustrates a basic Hall Effect sensor. If the output voltage or Hall voltage is measured when a magnetic field is absent, the output shown will be zero as shown in Fig. 14.15.

However, if the voltage at each output connection is measured with respect to the ground, a non-zero voltage will be developed. This voltage is called common mode voltage (CMV) that is equal in magnitude at each output terminal. It is the potential difference that is zero. The amplifier shown in Fig. 13.20 must be a differential amplifier so as to amplify only the potential difference-the Hall voltage.

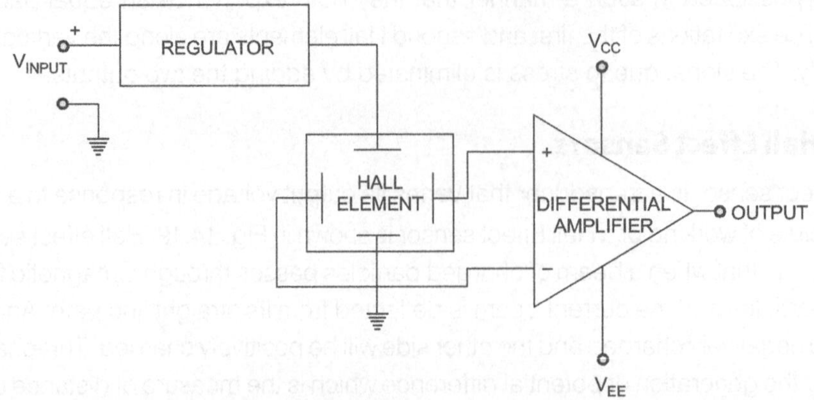

Fig: 14.20 Basic Hall effect sensor

The Hall voltage is a low-level signal on the order of 30 μV in the presence of one Gauss magnetic field. This low-level output requires an amplifier with low noise, moderate gain and high input impedance. A differential amplifier with these characteristics can be readily integrated with the Hall element.

Temperature compensation is also easily integrated. As known from the equation (1) that Hall voltage is a function of the input current and the purpose of the regulator is to maintain this current constant, so that the output of the sensor only reflects the intensity of the magnetic field.

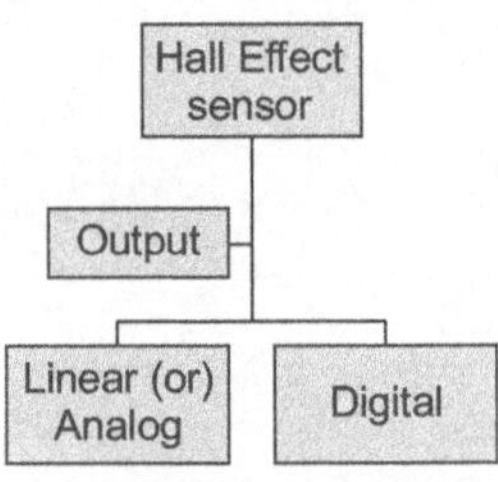

Fig: 14.21

Hall Effect sensor has its output in either linear or digital form. The output signal for linear or analog Hall Effect sensors is taken directly from the output of the operational amplifier where the output voltage is directly proportional to the magnetic field passing through the Hall Effect sensor.

This Output voltage or Hall voltage is given by:

$$V_H = R_H\left\{\frac{I \times B}{t}\right\}$$

Where,

V_H = Hall Voltage (V)

R_H = Hall Effect co-efficient

I = Current flowing through the sensor (Ampere)

B = Magnetic flux density (Tesla)

t = Thickness of the sensor (mm)

14.2.3 Analog Output Sensors

Fig. 14.23 shows a basic analog output device. The output of the Analog output sensor is directly proportional to the magnetic field to which it is subjected to. The sensed magnetic field can be either positive or negative. As a result, both positive and negative power supplies are required as the output of the amplifier will be driven either positive or negative.

To avoid the need for two power supplies, a fixed offset or bias can be introduced into the differential amplifier. The bias value appears on the output when no magnetic field is present and this bias value is referred to as a Null voltage. When a positive magnetic field is sensed, the output increases above the null voltage. On the contrary, when a negative magnetic field is sensed, the output decreases below the null voltage, but remains positive. This concept is shown in Fig. 14.22.

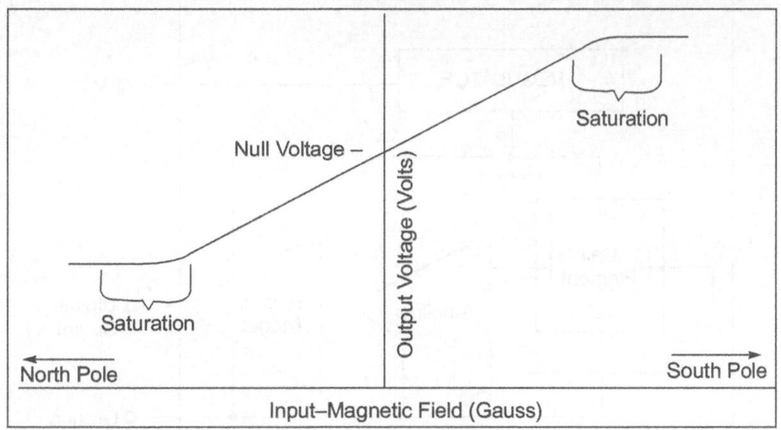

Fig:14.22 Null voltage concept

The output of the amplifier cannot go beyond the point set by the power supply. In fact, the amplifier tends to saturate before the output reaches this point. This saturation is illustrated in Fig. 14.21. It is to be noted that this saturation takes place in the amplifier and not in the Hall element. Thus, large magnetic fields are not going to damage the Hall Effect sensors, but rather push them into saturation.

To further increase the interface flexibility of the device, it is desirable to add an open emitter, open collector, or push-pull transistor to the output of the differential amplifier. Fig. 14.23 shows a complete analog output Hall Effect sensor.

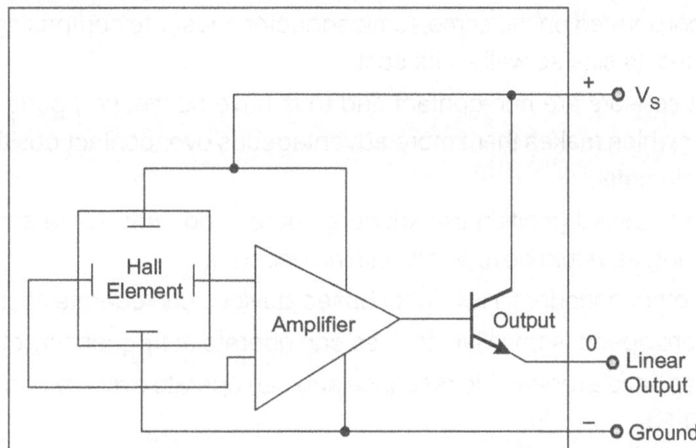

Fig: 14.23 Simple Analog Output Sensor (SS49/ SS19 types)

14.2.4 Digital Output Sensors

By adding Schmitt trigger circuit, the basic analog output device illustrated in Fig. 14.23 can be converted into a digital output sensor. The output of a digital output sensor can be seen in the form of either ON or OFF. Fig. 14.24 shows an internally regulated digital output Hall Effect sensor.

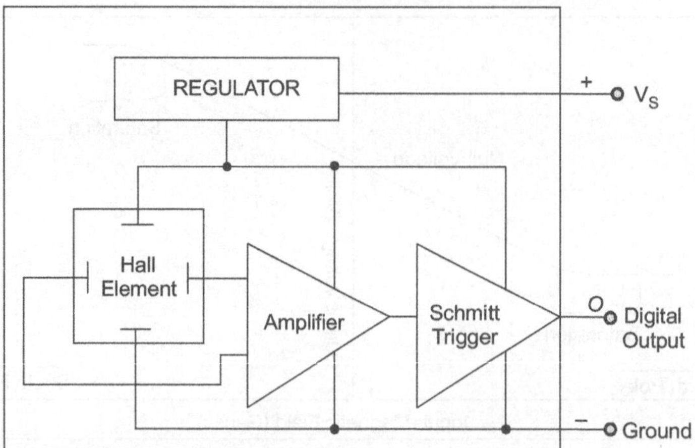

Fig: 14.24 Digital Output Hall Effect sensor

Schmitt trigger is used to compare the output of the differential amplifier with a preset reference limit as shown in Fig. 14.24. When this output of the differential amplifier crosses the reference point, the Schmitt trigger turns on. Conversely, when the output of the differential amplifier lies below the reference point, the Schmitt trigger turns off.

14.2.5 Advantages of Hall Effect Sensors

- Most of the Hall Effect sensors are made from a semiconductor material which gives an advantage to be constructed so that some or the entire signal conditioning circuitry needed can be incorporated on the same semiconductor substrate comprising the sensor element. This reduces its size as well as its cost.
- Hall Effect sensors are non-contact and thus have no wearing parts to limit the life of the transducer which makes them more advantageous over contact position transducers such as a potentiometer.
- In Hall Effect based position transducers, there is no need for re-zeroing after a glitch or power cycling as would be required with an encoder.
- Unlike the other encoders, Hall Effect based devices can operate at zero speed.
- Besides zero speed, some Hall devices can operate at frequencies of over 100 kHz.
- Hall devices have a repeatable response and can operate over a broad range of temperature (–40 to 150°C).
- A Hall Effect sensor, however, has an essentially infinite resolution and indicates even small changes in position with good linearity and monotonic characteristic.

14.2.6 Applications of Hall Effect Sensors

Hall Effect sensors are being used in various applications. Some of them are as follows:

- Measurement of displacement, detection of position of an object.
- To determine whether a semiconductor is a p-type or n-type.
- To measure the mobility of charge carriers.
- To measure the carrier concentration of semiconductor materials.
- To measure the strength of magnetic flux density.
- To determine the conductivity of a material.

- Can be used as proximity probes in instrumentation applications.
- To measure the speed of a turbo-generator in power plants.
- To lock and unlock keyboard operations of computers through keyboard switches.
- To measure the level in a fuel tank (used with a float having the position magnet).
- To measure pedal position in a car.
- Used in non-contact joysticks, keyboards, flow meters, voltage regulators, speed detectors and other industrial and commercial products.
- Used as a magnetic switch for an electric transducer.
- Used for proximity switching.
- Can be used as a component of a position transducer or as a position sensing component of another type of transducer.
- Used in the design of instruments such as magnetic field meter, Hall-effect multiplier, etc.
- To measure the liquid level over several meters using a linear array of Hall devices.
- They are used for the measurement of current and power.
- Their non-contact nature of operation, good immunity to environmental contaminants and ability to sustain in severe conditions make them quite popular in industrial automation.
- They can replace optical and light sensors where the surrounding environment contains water, vibration, dirt or oil such as in automotive applications.

14.3 ACTUATORS

Actuators are output devices which convert the energy from pressurized hydraulic oil or compressed air into the required type of mechanical action or motion. In general, hydraulic or pneumatic systems are used for gripping and/or moving operations in the industry. These operations are carried out by the use of actuators.

Actuators are the final control elements in a control system. They receive a low power command signal and energy input to amplify the command signal as appropriate to produce the required output. Applications of the actuators range from simple low power switches to high power hydraulic devices operating flaps and control surfaces on aircraft; valves, car steering, etc.

1. **Linear actuators:** These devices convert hydraulic/pneumatic energy into linear motion.
2. **Rotary actuators:** These devices convert hydraulic/pneumatic energy into rotary motion.
3. **Actuators to operate flow control valves:** These are used to control the flow and pressure of fluids such as gases, steam or liquids.

14.3.1 TYPES OF ACTUATORS

(i) Mechanical Actuators:

In mechanical actuators normally a rotary motion is converted into linear motion to perform an operation. The operation of mechanical actuators is based on combinations of structural components, such as gears and rails, or pulleys and chains etc. Basic example of mechanical actuator is chain block hoisting weight in which mechanical motion of chain over the sprocket is utilized to lift a rated load.

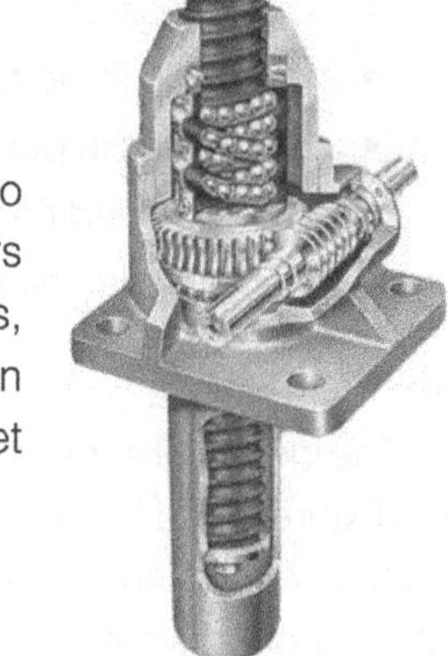

Fig: 14.25 Mechanical Actuator

Advantages:

- They are easier to specify and design than pneumatic or hydraulic actuators.

- Mechanical actuators also do not require hydraulic fluid or compressed gas (pneumatic) to operate and therefore are a lower cost solution.

Disadvantages:

- Mechanical linear actuators require lubrication for long life and reliability.
- These types of actuators operate at temperatures ranging from –30°F to 160°F (–35°C to 70 °C).

Applications

- Screw jack- Screw Jacks are also used for raising and lowering maintenance platforms, opening and closing air dampers, oven doors and sluice gates, and adjusting tooling machine beds, cable tension and workplace tables.
- Comb drive- Comb-drives are often used as linear actuators. The electrostatic forces act between two electrically conductive combs. Comb drive actuators typically operate at the micro- or nanometer scale and are generally manufactured by bulk micromachining or surface micro-machining on a silicon wafer substrate.

(ii) Pneumatic Actuators

Pneumatic energy is most commonly used for actuators used for main engine controls. In this type, compressed air at high pressure is used which converts this energy into either linear or rotary motion. It derives mechanical power from compressed air and converts it into kinetic energy. Pneumatic actuators enable large forces to be produced from relatively small pressure changes. These forces are often used with valves to move diaphragms to affect the flow of liquid through the valve. The most common example is "Main engine pneumatic actuator" used for changing of roller position over cam shaft for reversing.

Advantages:

- Ecological purity
- Sophisticated transfer mechanisms are not required
- Low cost
- High speed operation
- Ease in reversal of movements
- Tolerance to overloads, up to a full stop
- Explosion and fire safety
- Ability to accumulation and transportation

Disadvantages:

- Compressibility of the air
- Impossibility to receive uniform and constant speed of the working bodies movement
- Difficulties in performance at slow speed
- Limited conditions use of compressed air is beneficial up to the definite values of pressure
- Compressed air requires good preparation.

Applications

The industrial applications of pneumatic actuators include automation, logic and sequence control, holding fixtures, and high-power motion control. Automotive applications include power steering, power brakes and ventilation controls. Aerospace applications include flight-control systems, steering control systems, air conditioning and brake control systems. Some typical applications are discussed below.

Pneumatic Processing Center

The scheme of the pneumatic processing center with a rotary table is shown in Fig. 14.25. The pneumatic processing center carries out the following functions: step-by-step rotation with the help of a rotary table - parts cutting with the help of tools 2-7 (drilling, grinding, milling); reception, positioning and fixing a detail with the help of the block 1; delivery of a detail with the help of the block 8. On the rotary table various processes of serial part cutting can be carried out.

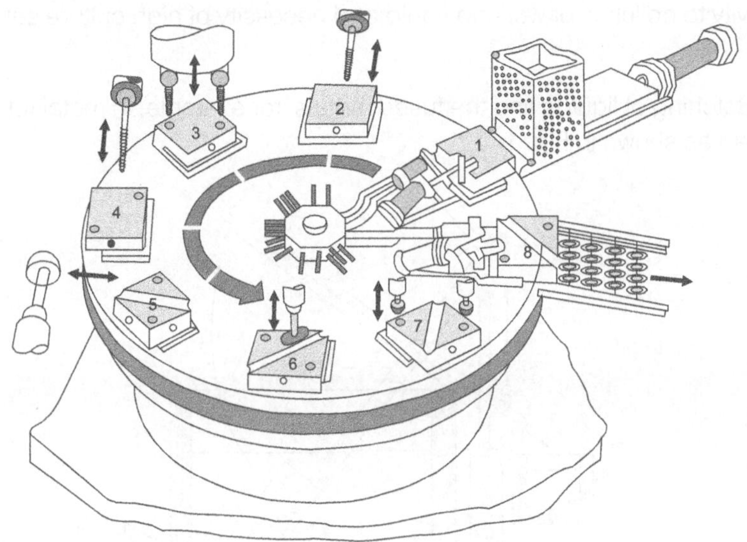

Fig: 14.26 Pneumatic processing centre

(iii) Hydraulic Actuators

Unlike air, liquid cannot be compressed and hence hydraulics generates higher energy than any other system. All systems involving high loads are operated by hydraulic actuators in which oil pressure is applied on mechanical actuator to give an output in terms of rotary or linear motion. Basic example of hydraulic actuator is steering gear of ship in which hydraulic pressure is used to move the rudder actuator. It converts hydraulic power into useful mechanical work. It is based on principle of Pascal's Law.

(a) It is used where very high speed and large forces are required.
(b) It requires lesser work (compression) than pneumatic actuator.
(c) It has higher load capacity.
(d) It has high efficiency and power according to the size ratio.

Advantages:

- Infinitely variable control of gear-ratio in a wide range and an opportunity to create the big reduction ratio.
- Small specific weight, i.e. the weight of a hydro-actuator is in a ratio of transmitted capacity (0.2, 0.3 kg /kWt).
- Opportunity of simple and reliable protection of the engine from overloads.
- Lesser sluggishness of the rotating parts, providing faster change of operating modes (start-up, dispersal, reverser and stop).
- Simplicity of transformation of rotary movement into reciprocating one.
- Opportunity of positioning a hydraulic engine at a distance from an energy source and freedom in making configuration.

Disadvantages:

- The efficiency of a volumetric hydraulic actuator is a little bit lower, than efficiency of mechanical and electric actuators, and during regulation it is reduced.
- Temperature conditions of operation of a hydraulic actuator influence its characteristics.
- The efficiency of a hydraulic actuator is a little reduced in the process of exhaustion of its resource owing to the increase in backlashes and the increase of outflow of liquid (falling of volumetric efficiency).
- Sensitivity to pollution of working liquid and necessity of high culture service.

Applications

Batching: Batching of liquids and the fused metals, for example, in metal foundry can be made by the system as shown in Fig. 14.27.

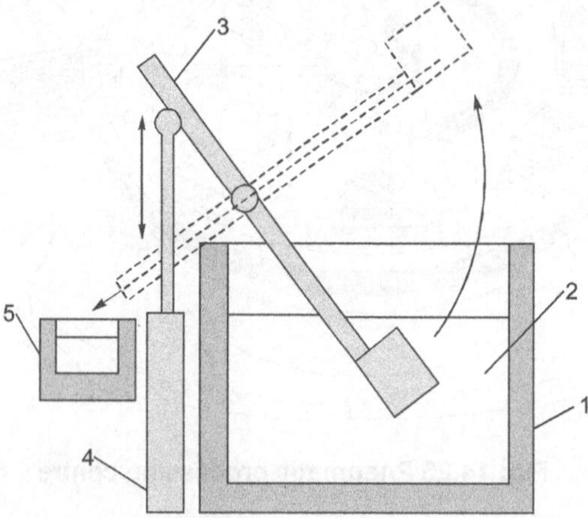

Fig: 14.27 Automated batching of liquids or molten metals

The lever with a ladle is actuated by the power cylinder. The volume of a ladle corresponds to a required dose of liquid which gets in the top position of a rod of the power cylinder. With the rod moving to the bottom position the liquid from the ladle is automatically poured in accepting chamber.

Hydraulic cylinder: A hydraulic cylinder (also called a linear hydraulic motor) is a mechanical actuator that is used to give a unidirectional force through a unidirectional stroke. It has many applications, notably in construction equipment (engineering vehicles), manufacturing machinery, and civil engineering.

They are primarily of two types:

- Tie rod style cylinders and
- welded body style cylinders

Tie rod cylinder: Tie rod style hydraulic cylinders use high strength threaded steel rods to hold the two end caps to the cylinder barrel. This method of construction is most often seen in industrial factory applications. Small bore cylinders usually have 4 tie rods, while large bore cylinders may require as many as 16 or 20 tie rods in order to retain the end caps under the tremendous forces produced. Tie rod style cylinders can be completely disassembled for service and repair, and they are not always customizable.

The National Fluid Power Association (NFPA) has standardized the dimensions of hydraulic tie rod cylinders. This enables cylinders from different manufacturers to interchange within the same mountings.

Welded body cylinder: Welded body cylinders have no tie rods. The barrel is welded directly to the end caps. The ports are welded to the barrel. The front rod gland is usually threaded into or bolted to the cylinder barrel. This allows the piston rod assembly and the rod seals to be removed for service.

(iv) Electrical Actuators

It is one of the cleanest and readily available forms of actuating system as it does not involve oil? as there is no need to compress air, hence no extra machinery is required. Electrical energy is always available on ship. The electrical energy is used to actuate a mechanical system using magnetic field i.e. EMF. The basic examples are electrical motor operated valve and magnetic valve actuator or solenoid valve.

In solenoid valve the electrical signal magnetizes the upper portion of the valve, which will then attract the valve seat and open the system. When electrical supply is removed, the valve gets closed by spring action.

Advantages:

- Widespread availability of power supply.
- Basic drive element and components are lighter than fluid power.
- High power conversion efficiency.
- No pollution so environmental friendly operation.
- Accuracy and repeatability compared to cost.
- Quiet and clean operation.
- Easily maintained and repaired.
- Drive system is suitable to electronic control.
- A wide range of control options for the specific motion profile.
- Better adaptability for machines that involve flexible processes and low operational costs.
- Greater economy in moderate scale deployments that leverage their performance advantages.
- Reduced replacement costs, particularly in applications in which the electronics are separate from the actuator.
- More flexible drive options, such as using a more economical stepper motor for accurate positioning at lower speeds, or a more costly servomotor for superior performance at high speeds.
- Greater accuracy through the use of high-precision screws and anti-backlash mechanisms, which can provide accuracies to ten-thousandths of an inch.

Disadvantages:

- Requires mechanical transmission system.
- Requires additional electrical power which adds to the cost.
- Not safe in explosive atmospheres.
- High component costs.

Applications:

Servomechanism: A powered mechanism producing motion or forces at a higher level of energy than the input level, e.g. in the brakes and steering of large motor vehicles, especially where feedback is employed to make the control automatic. Other applications include Electric motor, Electroactive polymer etc.

(v) Hybrid Actuators:

These are combinations of some of the above systems which control the mechanical part of the system. A common example is the Thermo hydraulic electronic actuator used in operating valves in hot water system, wherein hot water liquid is used along with electronic system acting as a control for the valve.

The hybrid actuator has certainly some advantages and drawbacks which may be summarized below:

- A hybrid actuator may save a considerable amount of energy when the mass moment of inertia of the hybrid actuator is reduced to the required degree, because, an important amount of energy will be converted into heat energy in direct-drive servomotor applications.
- The initial cost of the actuator depends on the power requirement of the machine. The need for higher power requirement will reduce the relative cost of the hybrid actuator when compared with the direct servo drive systems, because the cost of the servomotor is directly proportional to its size.

Applications

Cut to length machine: Cut To Length Lines can do uncoiling, leveling, measuring, cross-cutting to length and stacking work. It mainly includes uncoiler, leveler, measuring encoder, shearer, conveyor, stacker, hydraulic system, pneumatic system and electrical system, etc., the line can make sure of accurate feeding and shearing.

Other applications are Web printing machine, Injection molding machine etc.

Bibliography

1. Ramsden, E., Hall Effect Sensors-Theory and Applications, 2nd edition; Elsevier: Amsterdam, The Netherlands, 2006.
2. K.P. Ramachandran, G.K. Vijayaraghavan, Mechatronics: Integrated Mechanical Electronic Systems, John Wiley & Sons, 2008.
3. B. Visvesvara Rao, K. Raja Rajeswari, P. Chalam Raju Pantulu, K. Bhaskara Rama Murty, Electronic Circuit Analysis, Pearson, 2012.
4. Anil K. Maini, Varsha Agrawal, Electronic Devices and Circuits, Wiley- India, 2009.
5. David S. Nyce: Linear Position Sensors: Theory and Application, New Jersey, John Wiley & Sons, Inc. 2004.

Solved Subjective PROBLEMS

Q.1 What advantage does a mechanical linear actuator have vs. a hydraulic actuator or a pneumatic actuator?

Ans: Mechanical linear actuators reduce the complexity of the design process because they are easier to specify and design than pneumatic or hydraulic actuators. Mechanical linear actuators also do not require hydraulic fluid or compressed gas (pneumatic) to operate and therefore are a lower cost solutions.

Q.2 How precise *actuator can be* in terms of positional accuracy?

Ans: Positional accuracy can be expressed as both positioning time how exact in terms of time is the load delivered to a specific position and actual position how close the load is delivered to the intended location or spot. Mechanical linear actuators can deliver positioning times of 30 millis econds and positioning accuracy of less than 0.25 mm (0.01 inches).

Q.3 How fast can a mechanical actuator actually travel in terms of inches per second?

Ans: The actual speed of a mechanical actuator is highly dependent on the size and weight of the load that it moves. For practical purposes, the maximum speed of a mechanical actuator is 50 inches per minute.

Q.4 What is the operational temperature range for a mechanical actuator?

Ans: Mechanical actuators operate at temperatures ranging from -30° F to 160° F (-35°C to 75°C).

Unsolved Subjective PROBLEMS

Q.1 Define hall effect sensor? Write its advantages and disadvantages.

Q.2 Explain design procedure of hall effect sensors.

Q.3 What is hall effect sensor? Describe in brief with neat sketch.

Q.4 Classify hall effect sensor.

Q.5 How to select hall effect sensors for brushless dc motors?

Q.6 What are the characteristics of hall effect sensors and also write down its application?

Q.7 What are the advantage of a shunt resistor vs. a hall effect sensor?

Q.8 Differentiate the reed sensors vs. hall effect sensors.

Q.9 Describe the working principle of hall effect sensor with neat sketch.

Q.10 What are the pin configurations and functions of hall effect sensor.

Q.11 Write different industrial application and implementation process of hall effect sensor.

Q.12 Describe signal processing and interface of hall effect sensor.

Q.13 Explain materials for hall effect sensor.

Q.14 Explain the arduino hall effect sensor working.

Q.15 What is an actuator? Briefly explain different types of actuators.

Q.16 Write advantage and disadvantage of actuators and their applications.

Q.17 Write short note on sensors.

Q.18 Briefly explain advantages and applications of sensors.

Q.19 Give detail classification of sensors.

Q.20 Write detail description of displacement and position sensors.

Q.21 Briefly explain temperature and light sensors.

Q.22 Write the applications of thermistors.

Q.23 Write the sensor/transducers specifications.

Q.24 Write in brief about a potentiometer sensor for measurement of linear displacement with schematic diagram.

Q.25 What is tachogenerator? Explain its working principle.

PRACTICE QUESTIONS

1. Which of the following is/are characteristic/s of mechatronic products and systems?
   (a) Functional interaction between mechanical, electronic and information technologies.
   (b) Spatial interaction of subsystems in one physical unit.
   (c) Intelligence related to the control functions of the mechatronics system.
   (d) All of the above.

2. The mechatronics is an interdisciplinary field in which the disciplines those act together are:
   (a) Mechanical systems and Electronic systems
   (b) Mechanical systems and Information technology
   (c) Electronic systems and Information technology
   (d) Mechanical systems, Electronic systems and Information technology

3. Group the followings into Mechanical systems, Electronic systems and Information technology.
   1. Automation
   2. Mechanical elements
   3. Software engineering
   4. Precision mechanics
   5. Microelectronics
   6. Artificial intelligence
   7. Sensors and actuators

   (a) Mechanical Systems: 2, 4
   Electronic System: 5, 7
   Information Technology: 1, 3, 6

   (b) Mechanical Systems: 2, 7
   Electronic System: 4, 5, 6
   Information Technology: 1, 3

   (c) Mechanical Systems: 2, 4
   Electronic System: 5, 6, 7
   Information Technology: 1, 3

   (d) Mechanical Systems: 2, 7
   Electronic System: 4, 5
   Information Technology: 1, 3, 6

4. What is used to make considerable simplification in the devices such as watches and cameras, etc. as compared to pure mechanical designs?
   (a) Actuators with electrical auxiliary energy
   (b) Amplifiers with electrical auxiliary energy
   (c) Both (a) and (b)
   (d) None of the above

5. In which stage the measurement system comes in contact with the measurand or the quantity to be measured?
   (a) Transducer Stage
   (b) Signal Processor Stage
   (c) Output Stage
   (d) None of the above

6. Arrange the following components of temperature measurement system according to measurement systems.
   Hot body, Display system, Thermocouple, Amplifier and converter
   (a) Hot body----Display system-----Thermocouple-----Amplifier and converter
   (b) Hot body----Amplifier and converter-----Thermocouple-----Display system
   (c) Hot body----Thermocouple-----Amplifier and converter-----Display system
   (d) Display system-----Hot body----Thermocouple-----Amplifier and converter

7. The characteristic that provides an output with respect to the input is called as _______.
   (a) Calibration of a system (b) Response of a system
   (c) Characteristic relation of a system (d) Instrumentation of a system

8. The study of relationship between the input and output, when the input is invariant with respect to time is called as _______.
   (a) Static characteristics of instruments (b) Dynamic characteristics of instruments
   (c) Variable characteristics of instruments (d) None of the above

9. The process of establishment of a relationship between the input to the instrument and output from the instrument is called as _____.
   (a) Static sensitivity (b) Static characterization
   (c) Static accuracy (d) Static calibration

10. _______ is the curve plotted between input and output by giving known inputs to an instrument and obtaining corresponding outputs.
    (a) Characteristic curve (b) Accuracy curve
    (c) Calibration curve (d) Sensitivity curve

11. Which type of actuators have more power output?
    (a) Hydraulic Actuators (b) Pneumatic Actuators
    (c) Stepper motors (d) all of these

12. Which actuator has more precise motion?
    (a) Hydraulic Actuator (b) Pneumatic Actuator
    (c) Stepper motor (d) All of these

13. Paddle shifters are used for?
    (a) Acceleration (b) Changing gears
    (c) Braking (d) Clutch

14. Paddle shifter is a kind of ______ gear shifting assembly.
    (a) Clutch (b) Stick
    (c) Clutch less (d) none of these

15. Generally _____ actuator is used in paddle shifters.
    (a) Hydraulic Actuator (b) Pneumatic Actuator
    (c) Stepper motor (d) All of above

16. What is the best choice for temperature measurement according temp range, accuracy, sensitivity, cost?
    (a) RTD (b) Thermistor
    (c) Thermocouple (d) Pyrometer

17. DC tachogenerator are sometime preferred over AC tachogenerator because
    (a) they do not need maintenance
    (b) it is possible to know the direction of rotation
    (c) it is possible to know the direction of rotation and magnitude of speed
    (d) all of the above

18. A sensor that convert speed of rotaion directly into electrical signal is called
    (a) tachogenerators (b) tachometer
    (c) venture meter (d) orifice meter

19. In transducer with Doppler effect, the type of input used is ______.
(a) X-rays
(b) ultraviolet rays
(c) electronic beam
(d) an ultrasonic or radio beam

20. The best device for measuring temperature of hot body radiating energy in visible spectrum is using.
(a) Thermistor
(b) Optical pyrometer
(c) Thermocouple
(d) RTD

21. Capacitive pressure transducer have the advantage of
(a) large temp range
(b) good thermal conductivity
(c) good frequency response
(d) high input impedance

22. Pressductor is a device of
(a) velocity transducer
(b) pressure transducer
(c) magneto elastic type force transducer
(d) flow transducer

23. What type of displacement sensors are shown here?

(a) Absolute position encoders
(b) Inductive proximity sensors
(c) Opto-switches
(d) Potentiometers

24. Hall voltage is directly proportional to ______.
(a) current
(b) electric field
(c) magnetic flux density
(d) all of above

25. What does a Hall Effect measurement measure?
(a) The mobility
(b) The Hall mobility
(c) The carrier density and carrier type
(d) The Hall carrier density and the carrier type
(e) The effective mass

26. Hall Effect may be used to
(a) Determine whether semiconductor is p-type or n-type
(b) Determine the carrier concentration
(c) Calculate the mobility
(d) All the above

27. Electric field strength related to hall voltage is given by
(a) VHd
(b) VH/d
(c) VHE
(d) Ed

28. Measurement of Hall coefficient enables the determination of
(a) mobility of charge carriers
(b) type of conductivity and concentration of charge carriers
(c) temperature coefficient and thermal conductivity
(d) none of the above

29. Hall probe is made up of
(a) Metals (b) Non metals
(c) Semiconductor (d) Radioactive material

30. In Hall Effect, voltage across probe is known as
(a) Hall voltage (b) Electro motive force
(c) Potential difference (d) None of the above

31. A Hall effect device is sensitive to
(a) Magnetic field (b) Moisture
(c) Infrared (d) Ultrasound

32. Measurement of the Hall coefficient in a semiconductor provides information on the
(a) Sign and mass of charge carriers
(b) Mass and concentration of charge carriers
(c) Sign of charge carriers alone
(d) Sign and concentration of charge carriers

33. Hall Effect is observed in a specimen when it (metal or a semi conductor) is carrying current and placed in a magnetic field. The resultant electric field inside the specimen will be in
(a) a direction normal to both current and magnetic field.
(b) the direction of current.
(c) a direction anti parallel to the magnetic field.
(d) none of the above.

34. What does a Hall Effect sensor sense?
(a) Temperature (b) Magnetic field
(c) Moisture (d) Pressure

35. The Hall Effect voltage in intrinsic silicon is
(a) Positive (b) Negative
(c) Zero (d) None of the above

36. Which are the output sensor applications?
(a) Door interlocks (b) Valve position sensors
(c) Joy stick applications (d) All of the above

37. The Hall Effect is _____.
(a) a phenomenon with no practical applications
(b) used in various sensor applications
(c) used to develop potentials of thousands of volts
(d) the basis of solar cell operation

38. According to Hall effect, the Hall voltage is proportional to
(a) The product of B and I (b) Inverse of the product of B and I
(c) I only (d) B only

39. A Hall Effect sensor
(a) exists only in theory .
(b) is a non-contacting magnetic sensor.
(c) can operate only a few times before failure.
(d) produces very large voltages.

40. The Hall coefficient of an intrinsic semiconductor is
(a) Positive under all conditions
(b) Negative under all conditions
(c) Zero under all conditions
(d) None of the above

41. Which are the Linear output sensor applications
(a) Disk drives (b) Flow meters
(c) Both (a) and (b) (d) None of the above

42. A sensor is _____.
(a) an element which acquires a physical parameter and changes it into a signal
(b) a device that converts a physical parameter into mechanical signal
(c) an instrument that acquires input signal and changes it into many output signals
(d) a device that senses the speed of a car

OOOO

ANSWERS

SENSORS AND ACTUATORS

1. (d)	2. (d)	3. (a)	4. (c)	5. (a)	6. (c)	7. (b)
8. (a)	9. (d)	10. (c)	11. (a)	12. (c)	13. (b)	14. (c)
15. (b)	16. (a)	17. (c)	18. (a)	19. (d)	20. (b)	21. (c)
22. (c)	23. (b)	24. (c)	25. (d)	26. (d)	27. (b)	28. (b)
29. (c)	30. (a)	31. (a)	32. (d)	33. (a)	34. (b)	35. (b)
36. (d)	37. (b)	38. (a)	39. (b)	40. (b)	41. (c)	42. (b)

CHAPTER 15

Control Systems

15.1 INTRODUCTION

Control systems in an interdisciplinary field covering many areas of engineering and sciences. It is a device that controls the behavior of other devices. It is working as an interconnection between connected components or related in such a manner as to give commands, or regulate other component or itself. It is found in abundance in all sectors of industry, such as quality control of manufactured products, automatic assembly lines, machine-tool control, space technology, computer control, transportation systems, power systems, robotics, Micro-Electro-Mechanical Systems (MEMS), nanotechnology, and many others.

The study and design of automatic control system is also a field known as control engineering. In the modern era, it has become a part of everyday life. From device simple as a toaster to complex systems like space shuttle control engineering plays a crucial role. The control system is a component that is added to other components to increase system functionality and also to get the desired output from the system.

The basic ingredients of a control system can be described by:

1. Objectives of control.
2. Control-system components.
3. Results or outputs.

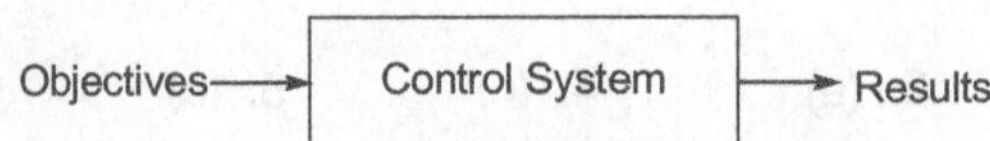

Fig: 15.1 Basic components of Control System

The basic relationship among these three components is illustrated in Fig. 15.1. In more technical terms, the objectives can be identified with inputs, or actuating signals, and the results are also called outputs, or controlled variables. In general, the objective of the control system is to control the outputs in some prescribed manner by the inputs through the elements of the control system.

15.2 CHARACTERISTICS OF CONTROL SYSTEMS

A good control system must have the following characteristics:

Accuracy: It is the measurement tolerance of any instrument and it defines the limit of error that instrument can make in working condition. It can be improved by feedback element and the detector must be present in the control system.

Sensitivity: Control system parameter always varies with the surrounding conditions, internal disturbance or because of any other reason. Any good control system should be insensitive to such parameter and sensitive to input signals only. This change can be called as sensitivity.

Noise: An undesirable input signal is known as noise, a good control system should ignore these noise effects for better performance.

Stability: It is one of the most desirable characteristics of control system, for any bounded input the output must also be bounded. If the input is zero the output must also be zero and it is known as the stable system.

Bandwidth: Bandwidth should be as large as possible for better frequency response of a control system.

Speed: It is the time which system takes to reach stable condition. For a good control system, speed should be higher and have minimum transient period.

Oscillation: For stability of the control system, it must have a minimum or constant oscillation.

15.3 EXAMPLES OF CONTROL SYSTEMS

Control systems find numerous and widespread applications from everyday life to extraordinary applications in science, industry, and society. Here are a few examples:

(a) Residential heating and air-conditioning systems controlled by a thermostat.
(b) The speed control of an automobile.
(c) Automatic traffic signal system at roadway intersections.
(d) Control system which automatically turns on a room lamp at dusk, and turns it off in daylight.
(e) Automatic hot water heater.
(f) Environmental test chamber temperature control system.
(g) An automatic positioning system for a missile launcher.
(h) An automatic speed control for a field controlled DC motor.
(i) The alttitude control system of a typical space vehicle.
(j) Automatic position control system of a high speed automated train system.
(k) Human heart using a pacemaker.
(l) An elevator position control system used in high rise multi-level buildings.

15.4 CONTROLLER

It is a system which can control the behavior of other devices or systems. There are a number of different standard types of control systems such as P, PD, PI, and PID controllers. They are very common in the production of physical systems, however they have several drawbacks.

15.5 COMPENSATOR

It is a control system that regulates another system, this is done by conditioning the input or output to that system. Compensators are typically employed to correct a single design flaw, with the intention of applying effect on other aspects of the design in a minimal manner. There are a number of different compensator units that can be employed to help fix certain system that are outside of a proper operating range.

The phase characteristics are necessary for compensation system, especially if the magnitude response is to remain constant. Occasionally, it is necessary to alter the phase characteristics of a given system, without altering the magnitude characteristics. To do this, we need to alter the frequency response in such a way that the phase response is altered, but the magnitude response is not altered. To do this, we implement a special variety of controllers known as phase compensators. They are called compensators because they help to improve the phase response of the system. There are two general types of compensators: Lead Compensators and Lag Compensators. If we combine the two types, we can get a special Lead-Lag Compensator system.

15.6 CONTROL SYSTEM CONFIGURATION

There are two types of control system configurations:

1. Open loop control systems or non-feedback control systems.
2. Closed loop control systems or feedback control systems.

15.6.1 Open loop Systems

An open loop control system utilizes an actuating device to control the process directly without using feedback channel. A component or process to be controlled can be represented by a block diagram as shown in Fig. 15.2. The block can be investigated one at a time, the output of one block will be input to another block and we can use cause and effect reasoning. This will become complicated when it is connected in a close loop system because of interaction between different blocks.

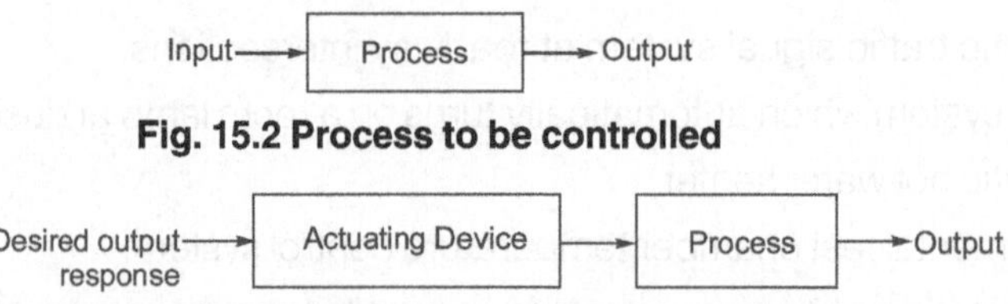

Fig. 15.2 Process to be controlled

Fig. 15.3 Open loop control system (Non feedback)

Example: Electronic fan switch.

Reference input: When the fan switches on, a 230 V is applied. So reference input is 230 V signal.

Controller: The electronic voltage controller when turning the knob to the desired position, the voltage will increase or decrease to an appropriate value. It can have a value like 230 V which is at maximum speed and 115 V at half speed and so on. Once we set the speed nothing need to be done, let there are three fans and you turn the knob at same amount but the speed is slightly different for every fan. This happens because of inappropriate settings, inconsistency in ball bearing performance, imperfect blade design which causes different amount of drag forces. So, an open loop system is one where we cannot correct the error of desired output and the actual output.

Advantages:

1. Simple construction
2. Low cost
3. Maintenance is easy
4. Stability is good

Disadvantages

1 Less Accuracy
2. Reliability is less
3. The change in output cannot be modified

Other Examples: Electric hand dryer, Automatic washing machine, Bread toaster, Automatic tea or coffee maker, Light switches etc.

15.6.2 Close Loop System

A closed loop control system uses a measurement of the output and feedback of this signal to compare it with the desired output. The system can be easily spotted by seeing its block relation, it does not always maintain only relation from one block head to another block tail, it also has relation from different blocks as shown in Fig. 15.4 of closed loop feedback control system. Since the increasing complexity of the system is under control and the optimum performance of feedback system has grown it in past few decades.

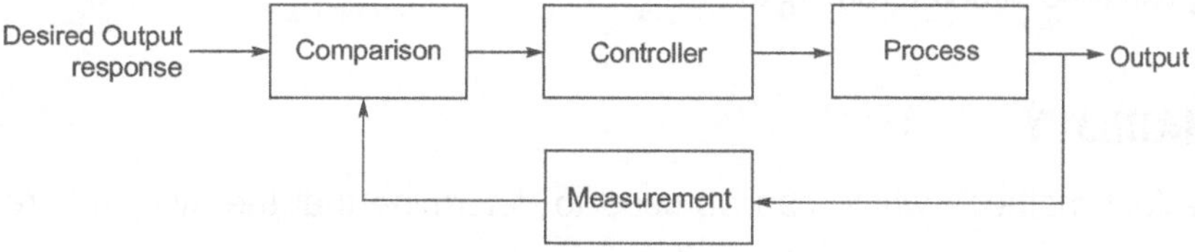

Fig. 15.4 Close loop control system (feedback system)

Advantages:

1. Close loop control is more accurate, even in the case of non-linearity.
2. Highly accurate because the error of output can be modified by feedback signal.
3. Range of Bandwidth is large.
4. Lesser sensitive to disturbance and noise.
5. Lesser sensitive to the characteristics and parameter variations.

Disadvantages:

1. The cost is high.
2. Design is complicated.
3. More maintenance required, which further increases the cost.
4. Overall gain reduces due to feedback.

15.7 CONTROLLABILITY

It can be defined as the ability of taking input from any external source to make changes in the internal state of any device from one state to another state in a given time interval. A system is at a state of vector X can be called as controllable if the state of system is changed when input is changed.

15.7.1 Controllability Matrix

For linear time-invariant system, ζ has full row rank of p.

(P is the dimension of the matrix also called order of the system)

$$\zeta = [B \cdot AB \cdot A^2B \,..... \, A^{p-1}\, B] \in R^{p \times pq}$$

A system can be called as controllable when a state X_1 can be transferred to the zero state $X = 0$ in a given number of steps.

A system can be called as controllable when the rank of the system matrix A is p, and the rank of the controllability matrix is,

$$\text{Rank}\,(\zeta) = \text{Rank}\,(A^{-1}\zeta) = p$$

If the second equation is not satisfied, the system can't be treated as controllable.

In MATLAB controllability matrix can be easily created with the ctrb command. For controllability matrix (ζ) simply type.

$$\zeta = \text{ctrb}\,(A, B)$$

Where A and B are already shown in the equation above. If we want to find out that the system is controllable or not we have to use the command rank to find out if it has full rank. If

$$\text{Rank } (A) < p$$

Then this is a case in which reachability does not followed by controllability. But controllability is always followed by reachability. Controllability only have reachability when the state transition matrix is nonsingular.

Any state example X_1 can be called as reachable if input is applied and it changed the state from X_0 to X_1 in the given time interval from T_0 to T_1.

15.8 REACHABILITY

We have four methods which can be used to determine that the system is reachable or not reachable.

1. If the p rows of $\phi(t, \tau)$, $B(t)$ are linearly independent over the field of complex numbers. That is, if the rank of the product of those two matrices is equal to p for all values of t and π.
2. If the rank of the controllability matrix is the same as the rank of the system matrix A.
3. If the rank of rank $[\lambda I - A, B] = p$ for all eigenvalues λ of the matrix A.
4. If the rank of the reachability gramian (described below) is equal to the rank of the system matrix A.

Each one of these conditions is both necessary and sufficient for a system to be reachable. If any one test fails, all the tests will fail, and the system will not be reachable. If any test is positive, then all the tests will be positive, and the system will be reachable.

15.9 GRAMIANS

It is a mathematical function which can be used to find out specific things about a system. Here we can use gramians to find out that system is reachable or controllable. It is one of the most complicated methods, so only used when analyzing method are failed.

Gramians that are presented here are all matrices with dimension $p \times p$. The size is the same as that of system matrix A.

Gramians presented here can be explained using a general case of time-variant system. To convert this into time-invariant equation, we can do substitution like this:

$$\phi\,(t, \tau) \rightarrow e^{A(t-\tau)}$$

$$\phi'\,(t, \tau) \rightarrow e^{A'(t-\tau)}$$

Here we used notation X' to represent the transpose of matrix X, and it is opposed to the conventional notation (X^T).

15.9.1 Reachability Gramian

We can explain the reachability gramian in the following way

$$W_r(t_0, t_1) = \int_{t_0}^{t_1} \phi(t_1, \tau) B(\tau)\, B'(\tau)\, \phi'(t_1, \tau) d\tau$$

This system can be reachable if the rank of the reachability gramian is equal to the rank of the system matrix:

$$\text{Rank } (W_r) = p$$

15.9.2 Controllability Gramian

It can be explained for a system (A, B) as

$$W_c(t_0, t_1) = \int_{t_0}^{t_1} \phi(t_0, \tau)B(\tau)\, B'(\tau)\, \phi'(t_0, \tau)d\tau$$

The system is controllable in the case, if the rank of the controllability gramian is equal to the rank of the system matrix:

$$\text{Rank}\,(Wc) = p$$

If the system is time-invariant, there will be two important points that can be made. Firstly, we have to reduce to the same equation of the reachability gramian and the controllability gramian. So, for LTI (Linear time-invariant)systems, if we can be able to find one gramian, then we have automatically known both gramians. Secondly, the controllability gramian can also be used as the answer to the following Lyapunov equation:

$$AWc + Wc\,A' = -BB'$$

MATLAB and other few software's have functions that can solve the Lyapunov equation. With last relation, we can also find out the controllability gramian using these existing functions.

15.10 OBSERVABILITY

The state-variables of a system may fail to be measured for any of the reasons listed below.

1. The particular state variable location might not be physically accessible.
2. It may also not able to be measured because of absence of appropriate measuring instrument or the state-variable is measured in units for which there is no availability of any measurement device.
3. The state-variables may be derived as dummy variables that do not have any physical meaning.

If things cannot be directly observed, for any of the reasons above, it may be necessary to calculate or estimate the values of the internal state variables, using only the input/output relation of the system, and the output history of the system from the starting. In other words, we must ask whether or not it is possible to determine what the inside of the system (the internal system states) is like, by only observing the outside performance of the system (input and output). We can provide the following formal definition of mathematical observability:

"A system with an initial state, $x(t_0)$ is observable if and only if the value of the initial state can be determined from the system output $y(t)$ that has been observed through the time interval $t_0 < t < t_f$. If the initial state cannot be so determined, the system is unobservable."

Complete Observability

A system is said to be completely observable if all the possible initial states of the system can be observed. The system that fails this criteria are said to be unobservable.

15.10.1 Observability Matrix

The observability of the system is dependant only on the system states and the system output, so we can simplify our state equations to remove the input terms.

Matrix Dimensions:

$$A: p \times p$$
$$B: p \times q$$
$$C: r \times p$$

$$D: r \times q$$
$$x'(t) = Ax(t)$$
$$y(t) = Cx(t)$$

Therefore, we can show that the observability of the system is dependant only on the coefficient matrices A and C. We can show precisely how to determine whether a system is observable, using only these two matrices. If we have the observability matrix Q:

$$Q = \begin{bmatrix} C \\ CA \\ CA^2 \\ \vdots \\ CA^{p-1} \end{bmatrix}$$

we can show that the system is observable if and only if the Q matrix has a rank of p. Notice that the Q matrix has the dimensions $pr \times p$.

MATLAB allows one to easily create the observability matrix with the obsv command. To create the observabilty matrix Q simply type

$$Q = \text{obsv}(A, C)$$

Where A and C are mentioned above. Then in order to determine if the system is observable or not one can use the rank command to determine if it has full rank.

15.10.2 Observability Gramian

We can define an observability gramian as:

$$W_0(t_0, t_1) = \int_{t_0}^{t_1} \phi'(\tau, t_0)C'(\tau)\, C(\tau)\, \phi(\tau, t_0)d\tau$$

A system is completely state observable at time $t_0 < t < t_1$ if and only if the rank of the observability gramian is equal to the size p of the system matrix A.

If the system (A, B, C, D) is time-invariant, we can construct the observability gramian as the solution to the Lyapunov equation:

$$A'W_o + W_oA = -C'C$$

15.10.3 Constructability Gramian

We can define a constructability gramian as:

$$W_{cn}(t_0, t_1) = \int_{t_0}^{t_1} \phi'(\tau, t_1)C'(\tau)\, C(\tau)\, \phi(\tau, t_1)d\tau$$

A system is completely state observable at an initial time t_0 if and only if there exists a finite t_1 such that:

$$\text{rank}(W_o) = \text{rank}(W_{cn}) = p$$

We have to remember that the constructability and observability gramians both are very similar, and typically they can both be calculated at the same time, only substituting in different values into the state-transition matrix.

15.11 DETECTABILITY

A system is detectable if all states that cannot be observed decay to zero asymptotically.

15.12 CONSTRUCTABILITY

A system is constructable if the present state of the system can be determined from the present and past outputs and inputs to the system. If a system is observable, then it is also constructable. The relationship does not work the other way around.

15.13 DUALITY PRINCIPLE

Controllability and observability concepts are very similar. There is a strong relationship between these two terms. A system (*A*, *B*) is controllable in the case of only that the system (*A′*, *C*, *B′*, *D*) is observable. It can be proven by plugging *A′* in for *A*, and *B′* in for *C* into the observability Gramian. Finally our equation will exactly show mirror of the formula for the controllability gramian, implying that the two results are the same.

Example: 15.1

A system has a transfer function of $G(s)=\dfrac{s+2}{(s+1)(s+3)(s+4)}$**. Find its poles and zeros, its gain at d.c and its response to a unit step input.**

Solution:

The dc gain is obtained by putting $s = 0$ so that,

$$G(0) = \frac{2}{(1\times 3\times 4)}=\frac{1}{6}$$

The poles are −1, −3 and −4 and there is a single zero at −2. The output, $Y(s)$, for a unit step input into $G(s)$ is given by

$$Y(s) = \frac{s+2}{s(s+1)(s+3)(s+4)}$$

which needs to be put into partial fractions to find the output time function.

The partial fractions are $\dfrac{A}{s}+\dfrac{B}{s+1}+\dfrac{c}{s+3}+\dfrac{D}{s+4}$ and for this to be equal to $Y(s)$ then

$$\frac{s+2}{s(s+1)(s+3)(s+4)} = \frac{A}{s}+\frac{B}{s+1}+\frac{C}{s+3}+\frac{D}{s+4}$$

Because of the input step function $Y(s)$ has four poles, one at $s = 0$, in addition to the three of $G(s)$. Thus the right hand side (RHS) of the equation has four terms with a coefficient, known as the residue at the pole, over each pole. The long way to solve for the residues *A*, *B*, *C* and *D* is first to work out the RHS with the common denominator, that is

$$\frac{A(s+1)(s+3)(s+4)+Bs(s+3)(s+4)+Cs(s+1)(s+4)+Ds(s+1)(s+3)}{s(s+1)(s+3)(s+4)}$$

Then expand the numerator and compare the coefficients in the powers of s, thus, for example, these cubed term which is zero on the left hand side (LHS) and the constant term which is 2 on the LHS give $A + B + C + D = 0$ and $12\,A = 2$, respectively. Similarly the s squared and s terms yield two more linear equations involving, and which can then be solved for, *A*, *B*, *C* and *D*. However, the quick approach is to recognize that above equation is valid for all values of s, so that if both sides of the equation are multiplied by *s* and *s* is taken equal to zero then

$$\frac{s+2}{(s+1)(s+3)(s+4)} = A \text{ It will give } A = \frac{1}{6}$$

$$\frac{s+2}{s(s+3)(s+4)} = B \text{ It will give } B = -\frac{1}{6}$$

$$\frac{s+2}{s(s+1)(s+4)} = C \text{ It will give } C = -\frac{1}{6}$$

$$\frac{s+2}{s(s+1)(s+3)} = D \text{ It will give } D = \frac{1}{6}$$

This procedure is often known as the cover up rule as to work out a residue one multiplies the expression by its denominator and then equates s to the pole value.

The solution for the output by inverting the rhs of equation is

$$y(t) = \left(\frac{1}{6}\right)(1 - e^{-t} - e^{-3t} + e^{-4t})$$

The first term in the brackets may also be written as $u(t)$ as the solution for $y(t)$ is only valid for $t > 0$. Note that the final value of the step response, which can be obtained from either $\lim_{t\to\infty} y(t)$ is A which is equal to 1/6. Also the initial value, which can be obtained from $\lim_{t\to 0} y(t)$ is zero. When asked to sketch a step response it is useful to have the initial slope which can be obtained from differentiating $y(t)$ or in the s domain from $\lim_{s\to\infty} s^2Y(s)$ as in the s domain the slope of y(t) in Matlab can be used to check partial fractions using the instruction [r,p,k] = residue (num,den) here r is the residue at the pole p, and k is only finite when the number of zeros is equal to the number of poles, i.e. when the transfer function is not strictly proper and is D in a state space representation. Thus for this example one has

```
>> num = [1 2]; den = [1 8 19 12 0];
>> [r, p, k] = residue(num,den)
         r = 0.1667
            -0.1667
            -0.1667
             0.1667
         p = -4.0000
            -3.0000
            -1.00000
         k = [ ]
```

The step response which is obtained from the commands

```
>> G = tf([1 2],[1 8 19 12]);
>> step(G)
```

is given in Fig. 15.5 and obviously confirms the final value of 1/6 = 0.167.

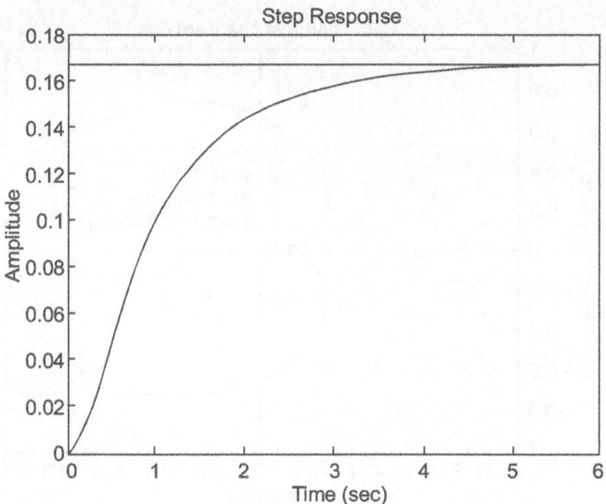

Fig: 15.5 Step response of transfer function

Example: 15.2

A network has a transfer function of $G(s) = 1/(1 + sT)^n$. Calculate the frequency at which it will have a phase shift of –180° and the corresponding gain. What are the values for $n = 3$ and 6. Check the result for $n = 3$ using Matlab and explain how you have obtained the result.

Solution:

This example is chosen to illustrate a situation where the best approach is to work in the polar form (i.e.gain and phase).

$$\text{Here } |G(j\omega)| = \frac{1}{(1+\omega^2T^2)^{n/2}} \quad \text{and} \quad ArgG(j\omega) = n\tan^{-1}(\omega T)$$

Thus the phase is –180° when $n\tan^{-1}(\omega T) = \pi$, which gives $\omega T = \tan\left(\frac{\pi}{n}\right)$ and a corresponding gain

$$\text{of } |G(j\omega)| = \frac{1}{\left(1+\tan^2\left(\frac{\pi}{n}\right)\right)^{n/2}}$$

In particular for $n = 3$, $\omega T = \tan(\pi/3) = 3$ and $|G(j\omega)| = \frac{1}{(1+3)^{3/2}} = 1/8 = 0.125$; and for $n = 6$,

$$\omega T = \tan\left(\frac{\pi}{6}\right) = \frac{1}{\sqrt{3}} \text{ and } |G(j\omega)| = \frac{1}{\left(1+\frac{1}{3}\right)^{\frac{3}{2}}} = \frac{3\sqrt{3}}{8} = 0.650$$

The commands to get the Nyquist plot in Matlab for $n = 3$ are

```
>> G = tf(1,[1 3 3 1]);
    >> Nyquist (G)
```

The plot is shown in Figure 15.6 and is drawn for both positive and negative frequencies, ω. The arrows mark the direction of increasing ω and the plot for negative ω is the mirror image in the real axis of that for positive ω. Or stated alternatively, the expression for a Nyquist plot has a real part which is an even function of ω and an imaginary part which is an odd function of ω.

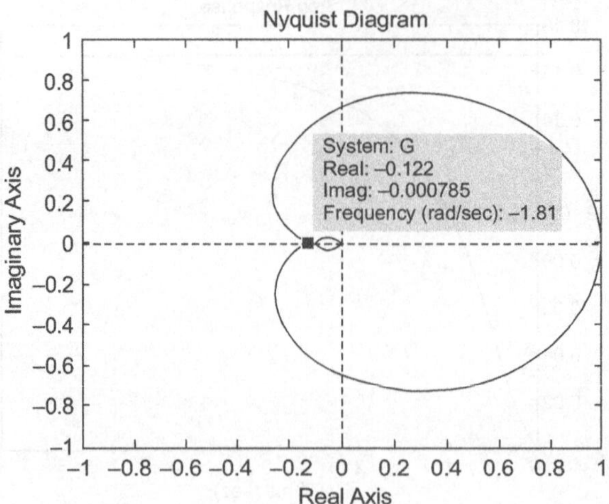

Fig: 15.6 Nyquist plot

To find the gain and frequency when the phase is –180° the cursor can be used as shown in Fig. 15.6 to obtain an approximate result on the command margin (G), which gives 18.1 dB (this corresponds to –0.125) at a frequency of 1.73 rads/s.

Unsolved Numerical Problems:

Q.1 Find the unit step response of the transfer function $G(s) = \dfrac{s^2+6s+8}{s^2+4s+3}$.

Ans. $\dfrac{8}{3} - \dfrac{3}{2}e^{-t} - \dfrac{1}{6}e^{-3t}$

Q.2 Find the unit impulse response of the transfer function $G(s) = \dfrac{s+1}{(s+2)^2(s+3)}$.

Ans. $2e^{-2t} - 2e^{-3t} - te^{-2t}$

Q.3 Find the unit step response of the transfer function $G(s) = \dfrac{5}{s^2+2s+5}$. What is the final value of the output? Check this result by using the final value theorem.

Ans. $1 - e^{-t}\cos(2t) - 0.5e^{-t}\sin(2t)$; 1

Q.4 Prove that the frequency response of a transfer function G(s) has a real part which is even in ω and an imaginary part which is odd in ω.

Q.5 Show that the phase lead network $G(s)\dfrac{1+sT}{1+s\alpha T}$ where $\alpha < 1$ has a maximum phase lead of $\sin^{-1}\dfrac{1-\alpha}{1+\alpha}$ at the angular frequency of $\omega_m = \dfrac{1}{T\sqrt{\alpha}}$ and that the corresponding gain in dB is $-10\log_{10}\alpha$.

Q.6 A unit negative feedback system has an open loop transfer function $Gs(s) = \frac{K(1+s+s^2)}{s(1+s)^3}$.

Determine the maximum value of K if the close loop frequency response should never exceed 0dB. Check the result using Matlab.

15.14 MATH MODELING AND SIMULATION

15.14.1 Scientific Approach to Engineering Reality

Since very early days of existence; man has been urged to interact with his environment to fulfill his essential needs. With time the "modes" of interaction, he has relied upon have become more varied and more sophisticated. More specifically, his scientific and engineering endeavor is one of the more mature forms of interaction with the real world.

Mathematical modeling plays a very important role in the entire process as it helps to analyze various variables and parameters of the system/subsystem under consideration, both in quantitative and qualitative terms. The corresponding mathematical model predicts the future behavior of the system under consideration. Recent developments in mathematical sciences and computers have led to improved modeling and understanding of situations in all areas of human activity, including not only engineering, medicine, biology, ecology, environment, geology, oceanography but in economics and a variety of other social sciences. Modeling and computer simulation have become valuable tools for example, in design of engineering Systems and manufacturing industry for improving the development process; in ecological and environmental sciences for analysis of biodiversity and prediction of weather, ocean circulation, effects of deforestation, global warming, climatic change, storm surges etc. This whole range of scientific activity can be fostered through a forum where scientists from different disciplines, such as Mathematics, Biology, Medicine, Environment, Ecology and various branches of Engineering as well as Social Sciences can meet and discuss various relevant problems that human society faces today. The stimulating effect that produced by remarkable results by the approach is the subject of systematic search to improve methodological skills.

15.14.2 Simulation

A simulation generally refers to a computerized version of the model which is run over time to study the implications of the defined interactions. Simulations are generally iterative in there development. One develops a model, simulates it, learns from the simulation, revises the model, and continues the iterations until an adequate level of understanding is developed.

15.14.3 Techniques of Simulation

Discrete hybrid system: (Standardization and interoperability): As the CAD and simulation are mandatory for design and result forecasting, this is the technique that focuses on modeling as a tool for prototype design, virtually and interactively refine the solution. Diversified but simple and advanced tools with feedback system can lead to a greater level of high end applications with competence. Multilevel of applications and systems works for modeling and simulation.

15.14.4 Simulation Method

From the days of bacon-father of scientific philosophy to present days, people scientifically said the four steps in simulation as- observation of physical system, formulation of methodology, or modeling, system process study and finally performance.

In current age of scientific research two steps are considered. In this, 1st Step is always a model building or formalization steps-clearly scientifically - In the sense that one tries to gain sufficient understanding of phenomenon by constructing an abstract representation.

In 2nd step the formal model is analyzed and utilized in order to learn how the real system can be manipulated for man's own purposes: clearly this has an engineering flavour -the role of computer becomes more apparent.

A human being is apt in making abstractions, he is skillful in recognizing patterns and making associations. He can perform calculations, he has a memory, etc; so it is to be expected that the modeling approach, he uses is the result of the his scientific capabilities. The model builder himself relies on an abstract model in order to "function" adequately. One could view all computing that supports model-building and model analysis as simulation activities- It can be differentiated from the classical as called "Simulation in the Large".

Simulation to the rescue: Almost simulation is misunderstood by all to be the act of running a program, which represents an abstract model in order to study the real system's behaviour.

Simulation is used as a means to overcome the existing imbalance between the major interaction stages.

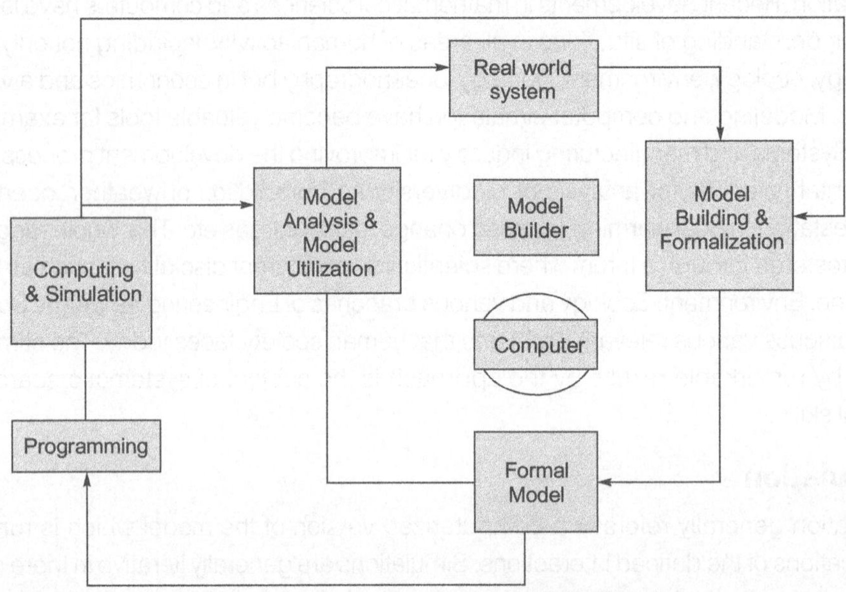

Fig:15.7 Interaction between Man Machine & Reality

The model builder as in Fig. 15.7 here, who previously stood in the center of the overall process, now has the computer as a partner to support him. By analogy it is easy to understand that the computer needs a proper "language" in order to operate. Basically the machine works on the program, and it is the model builder who chooses and implements these programs with the help of suitable software tools. The program relates to the formal model and the computing and simulation activity of the machine directly influences and supports the basic activities: model building and model analysis.

In recent years research in methodology has intensified for different reasons. Mathematical language as formalization tool specifies the issue in methodology. One of the most striking relationship between a model and the real world process is abstraction. The abstraction process is fundamental to the modeling process. For example: when considering the trajectories of objects; such as spacecrafts and planets in space, the laws of motion can be applied. In this process the related nature of the object is not important. After abstraction, they are essentially thought of as a mass quantity at the center of gravity.

For proper interaction it is essential that the model building step and the model analysis step can be properly carried through. To a large extent mathematical skills for analyzing the equations, except for very easy equations, are inadequate. The final model should be selected after creating and analyzing the sufficient number valid models.

15.14.5 Formation of the Mathematical Model

The formulation of Mathematical model consists of three steps:

1. Specification of components.
2. Specification of variables and parameters.
3. Specification of functional relationships.

A complete knowledge of the system, which is being considered, as well as proficiency in mathematics are necessary conditions for construction of valid mathematical model. Model building depends in part on-(1) the analyst's experience (2) trial and error procedures (3) a considerable amount of luck.

The suggestions from the knowledgeable are: (1) suggest some desirable characteristics of mathematical models used in computer simulation experiments, (2) Outline some of the major difficulties in model building and (3) Specify some of the basic elements of which mathematical models are composed.

A system may conceptually be defined as a set structure:

$$S = (T, X, \Omega, Q, Y, \delta, \lambda)$$

Where,

T is the time base.

X is the input set.

Ω is the input segment set.

Q is the internal state set.

Y is the output set.

δ is the state transition function.

λ is the output function.

What are the interpretations and restrictions put on these elements?

Time Base:

T is a set, which represents clock time and serves to order events. Common choices for T are I the integers or R the reals; S is said to be a discrete time respectively, the continuous time system accordingly.

Input Set:

X is a set representing that part of the interface through which the environment affects the system, e.g. through the inflow of information or material. Thus the system is viewed as being subjected at any time to inputs from the set X, over which it has no direct control.

Input Segment Set:

An input segment describes a pattern of inputs to the system over some time period. When embedded in a large system such a pattern is determined by the system's environment. When the system is isolated, by cutting its input wires, so to speak, these wires are free and the environment is replaced by a set of segments, which for reconstitutability should include all the patterns receivable by S as a component in the large system.

Internal State Set:

The set Q of internal states represents the memory of the system, i.e. the residue of its past history, which will affect its present and future response. This is the heart of modeling of internal structure, which was referred to earlier.

State Transition Function:

The state transition function is a map $\delta : Q \times \Omega \rightarrow Q$

Its representation is that when the system is in state q at time t_0 and an input segment $\varpi:(t_0, t_1) X$ is applied, then $\delta(q, \varpi)$ is the state of system at time t_1. Thus the internal state at any time and the input segment from that time on, uniquely determine the state of the end of the segment.

Output Set:

Y is a set representing that part of the interface through which the system affects the environment. The interpretation is the same as that for the input value set except for direction. Embedded in a large system the input (output) of its environment.

Output Function:

In its simplest form the output function is a map $\lambda: Q \rightarrow Y$, which relates the hypothetical internal state of the system to the effect of the system on its environment. Such an Output map, however, does not permit direct influence from the inputs on the outputs.

Some Principles Useful in Simulation:

Very frequently used are the Newton's Laws of motion, D-Alembert's principle, Laplace Transformation Laws and Lagrange's Equations.

D-Alembert's principle states that the addition of inertia forces to a real force system allowed a solution to be obtained from the equations of equilibrium.

Equations below states the principle

Below are D-Alembert's equations:

Equations (1) and (2) shows linear and angular accelerations:

$$\Sigma F = mA_G \quad \text{...(1)}$$

$$\Sigma T_G = I_a \quad \text{...(2)}$$

Algebraic rearrangement of the above equations give:

$$\Sigma F + (-mA_G) = 0 \quad \text{...(3)}$$

$$\Sigma T_G + (-I_a) = 0 \quad \text{...(4)}$$

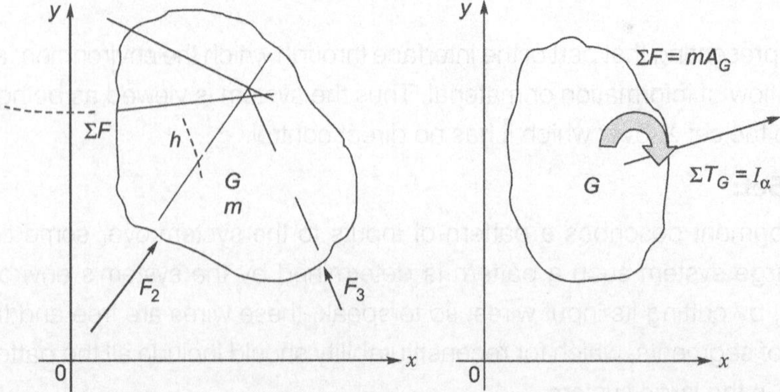

Fig: 15.8

Laplace Transformation: is the device for converting a differential equation into an algebraic equation so that it can be manipulated by the ordinary rules of algebra.

One of the advantages of the Laplace Transform approach to the solution of differential equations is that tables of inverse transforms are provided to reduce the labour involved.

Lagrange's equations: For a system having several degrees of freedom and described by the generalized coordinates $q_1, q_2, \ldots, q_n$ the Lagrange's equation for the ith co-ordinate is written as:

$$\frac{d}{d_t}\frac{\delta T}{\delta q_i} - \frac{\delta T}{\delta q_i} + \frac{\delta V}{\delta q_i} = Q_i$$

(Where T and V are the Total kinetic and potential energies, respectively, of the entire system, and Q_i is the generalized force, including damping and friction forces, associated with the q_i coordinate.

15.14.6 Computer Application

Computer simulation has become a useful part of modeling many natural systems in physics, chemistry and biology, human systems in economics and social science (the computational sociology) as well as in engineering to gain insight into the operation of those systems. A good example of the usefulness of using computers to simulate can be found in the field of network traffic simulation. In such simulations the model behaviour will change each simulation according to the set of initial parameters assumed for the environment. Computer simulations are often considered to be human out of the loop simulations.

Traditionally, the formal modeling of systems has been via a mathematical models, which attempts to find analytical solutions to problems which enables the prediction of the behaviour of the system from a set of parameters and initial conditions. Computer simulation is often used as an adjunct to, or substitution for, modeling systems for which simple closed form analytic solutions are not possible. There are many different types of computer simulation, the common feature they all share is the attempt to generate a sample of representative scenarios for a model in which a complete enumeration of all possible states of the model would be prohibitive or impossible.

In using the Analog computer, voltage is used to represent physical quantities, such as displacements, velocities, forces etc. For example 1 in/sec of velocity is represented by 44 volts so $Sx = 44$ volts/(in./sec). The electric circuit, amplifier, ramp functions, amplitude and time scaling etc. are some terms used with computer simulation.

e.g: Summing amplifier in this the grid and output voltages are related by the equation $e_0 = Ae_g$, where e_g is the grid voltage and e_0 is the output voltage and A is the gain of the amplifier. This (A) is of the order 10^4 to 10^8 depending on the amplifier gain and frequency.

Earlier simulation methods need large mainframe system. Nowadays digital devices are replacing this and there are handfuls of tactics driven packages as discussed below in details.

15.14.7 Digital Solutions

Some packages for simulation are described briefly here:

Monte Carlo algorithm

A numerical Monte Carlo method is used to find solutions to mathematical problems (which may have many variables) that cannot easily be solved, for example, by integral calculus, or other numerical methods. Its efficiency relative to other numerical methods increases when the dimension of the problem increases.

Monte Carlo methods are very important in computational physics and related applied fields, and have diverse applications from esoteric quantum chromodynamics calculations to designing heat shields and aerodynamic forms.

These methods have proven efficient in solving the integro-differential equations defining the radiance field, and thus these methods have been used in global illumination computations which produce photorealistic images of virtual 3D models, with applications in video games, architecture, design, computer generated films, special effects in cinema, business, economics and other fields.

MATLAB/Simulink Software

MATLAB: MATLAB is a high-level language and interactive environment that enables us to perform computationally intensive tasks faster than with traditional programming languages such as C, C++, and Fortran.

Simulink: Simulink is a platform for multi domain simulation and Model-Based Design of dynamic systems. It provides an interactive graphical environment.

A: A is a list of software (common purpose) packages for modeling and simulation of dynamic systems is given here.

ADAMS: (MSC Software, Inc.): Simulation of 3-dimensional mechanical systems. Many professional users in the automotive industry.

ITI-SIM (ITI): Mechatronics and Hydraulics Simulation Software.

DYNAST (Czech Technical University): General purpose simulation tool, mainly used for mechatronics and hydraulics.

MATHMODELICA (MathCore Engineering AB): Object-oriented modeling, simulation, integration and visualization of physical systems based on the Modelica language.

SIMPACK (INTEC): Analysis and design of general mechanical systems. Many users in automotive and railway industry (special modules to handle wheel/track contact of trains).

20-SIM (Twente University; Control lab Products): A general purpose bond-graph modeling and simulation tool. VISSIM (Visual Solutions): "Modeling, simulation and control system design software for end users".

15.14.8 Modeling Equations

Here is simulink example for understanding of how to model equations?

e.g.: Model the equation that converts Celsius temperature to Fahrenheit. Obtain a display of Fahrenheit-Celsius temperature graph over a range of 0 to 100°C.

$$T_F = 9/5\, T_C + 32$$

First, consider the blocks needed to build the model. These are:

- A ramp block to input the temperature signal, from the source library.
- A constant block, to define the constant of 32, also from the source library.
- A gain block, to multiply the input signal by 9/5, from the Linear library.
- A sum block, to add the two quantities, also from the Linear library.
- A scope block to display the output, from the sink library.

To create a SIMULINK block diagram presentation select new from the file menu.

This provides an untitled blank window for designing and simulating a dynamic system.

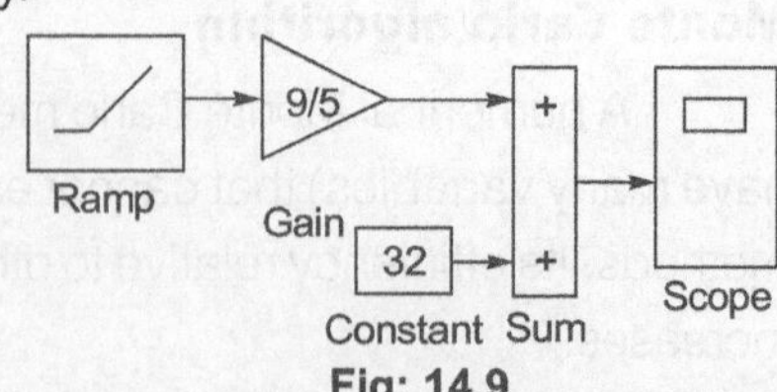

Fig: 14.9

Copy the above blocks from the block libraries into the new window by depressing the mouse button and dragging. Assign the parameter values to the Gain and Constant blocks by opening (double clicking on) each block and entering the appropriate value.

Then click on the **close** button to apply the value and close the dialog box. The next step is to connect these icons together by drawing lines connecting the icons using the left mouse button (hold the button down and drag the mouse to draw a line). You should now have the SIMULINK block diagram as shown in figure 15.9.

Subjective Questions:

Q.1 Discuss the method of finding transient response of a control system from their root locus.

Q.2 Draw a sketch of the close loop control system and explain the basic elements of the above system.

Q.3 Explain shaft control system with neat sketch.

Q.4 List the various modes of control system.

Q.5 What are the basic elements of feedback system?

Q.6 Explain the difference between open loop and close loop control systems.

Q.7 Explain path control loops for position and velocity control in axis controlling system for constant frequency and constant velocity commands.

Q.8 Explain adaptive control system with a diagram.

Q.9 What are the advantages and disadvantages of open loop system?

Q.10 Explain the control system for the domestic central heating system involving a bimetallic thermostat and that involving a microprocessor.

Bibliography

Derek P. Atherton, "Control Engineering Problems with Solution", Bookboon.com

Karl Johan Astrom, "Feedback systems, An Introduction for scientists and Engineers", E-Book.

Jan Willem Polderman, Jan C. Willems, "Introduction to the Mathematical Theory of systems and control", E-book

Control Systems, wikibooks.org

Control Systems and Control Systems Engineering with Classical and Modern Techniques and Advanced Concepts, wikibooks.org

PRACTICE QUESTIONS

1. As a result of introduction of negative feedback which of the following will not decrease?
(a) Bandwidth (b) Overall gain
(c) Distortion (d) Instability

2. Which of the following should be done to make an unstable system stable?
(a) The gain of the system should be decreased.
(b) The gain of the system should be increased.
(c) The number of poles to the loop transfer function should be increased.
(d) The number of zeros to the loop transfer function should be increased.

3. Regenerative feedback implies feedback with
(a) oscillations (b) step input
(c) negative sign (d) positive sign

4. The output of a feedback control system must be a function of
(a) Reference and output (b) reference and input
(e) input and feedback signal (d) output and feedback signal

5. ______ is an open loop control system.
(a) Ward Leonard control (b) Field controlled D.C. motor
(c) Stroboscope (d) Metadyne

6. Band width of a control system for better frequency response should be
(a) High (b) Low
(c) Medium (d) Does not depend on bandwidth

7. The band width, in a feedback amplifier:
(a) remains unaffected
(b) decreases by the same amount as the gain increase
(c) increases by the same amount as the gain decrease
(d) decreases by the same amount as the gain decrease

8. The system output can be delayed by a finite, predetermined amount of time is known as
(a) Delay (b) Idle delay
(c) Time shift (d) Delay margin

9. On which of the following factors does the sensitivity of a closed loop system to gainc hanges and load disturbances depend?
(a) Frequency (b) Loop gain
(c) Forward gain (d) All of the above

10. The transient response, with feedback system,
(a) rises slowly (b) rises quickly
(c) decays slowly (d) decays quickly

11. For stability oscillation of the control system should be:
(a) Minimum (b) Constant
(c) Both of above (d) Either (a) or (b)

12. Which of the following statements is correct for any closed loop system?
    (a) All the coefficients can have zero value.
    (b) All the coefficients are always non-zero.
    (c) Only one of the static error coefficients has a finite non-zero value.
    (d) None of the above.

13. Which of the following is an open loop control system?
    (a) Field controlled D.C. motor (b) Ward leonard control
    (c) Metadyne (d) Stroboscope

14. _____ is a closed loop system.
    (a) Autopilot for an aircraft (b) Direct current generator
    (c) Car starter (d) Electric switch

15. Due to which of the following reasons excessive band width in control systems should be avoided?
    (a) It leads to slow speed of response (b) It leads to low relative stability
    (c) Noise is proportional to band width (d) None of the above

16. In a control system the output of the controller is given to
    (a) final control element (b) amplifier
    (c) comparator (d) sensor
    (e) none of the above

17. A controller, essentially, is a
    (a) sensor (b) clipper
    (c) comparator (d) amplifier

18. By which of the following the control action is determined when a man walks along a path?
    (a) Brain (b) Hands
    (c) Legs (d) Eyes

19. Which of the following are correct about the close loop control system?
    (i) Close loop is more accurate, even in the case of non-linearity .
    (ii) Range of Bandwidth is large.
    (iii) Higher sensitive to disturbance and noise.
    (a) (i) only (b) (ii) only
    (c) (i) and (ii) (d) (i), (ii) and (iii)

20. _____ is a part of the human temperature control system.
    (a) Digestive system (b) Perspiration system
    (c) Ear (d) Leg movement

21. A closed loop system is distinguished from open loop system by which of the following?
    (a) Servomechanism (b) Feedback
    (c) Output pattern (d) Input pattern

22. _____ is not a final control element.
    (a) Control valve (b) Potentiometer
    (c) Electro-pneumatic converter (d) Servomotor

23. Which of the following are correct?
    (i) Open loop are less accurate than close loop.

(ii) In an open loop change in output can't be modified.
(iii) Stability in close loop is more than an open loop control system.
(a) (i) only (b) (ii) only
(c) (i) and (ii) (d) (i), (ii) and (iii)

24. In pneumatic control systems the control valve used as final control element which converts
(a) pressure signal to electric signal (b) pressure signal to position change
(c) electric signal to pressure signal (d) position change to pressure signal
(e) none of the above

25. A differentiator is usually not a part of a control system because it
(a) reduces damping (b) reduces the gain margin
(c) increases input noise (d) increases error

26. Any externally introduced signal affecting the controlled output is called a
(a) feedback (b) stimulus
(c) signal (d) gain control

27. In a control system integral error compensation _____ steady state error
(a) increases (b) minimizes
(c) does not have any effect on (d) any of the above

28. With feedback _____ reduces.
(a) system stability (b) system gain
(c) system stability and gain (d) none of the above

29. An electric hand drier is a ______ loop control system.
(a) open (b) closed
(c) partially closed (d) any of the above

30. In MATLAB to create controllability matrix we need command name is
(a) ctrb (b) corb
(c) ctlb (d) ctby

31. A control system working under unknown random actions is called
(a) computer control system (b) digital data system
(c) stochastic control system (d) adaptive control system

32. A car is running at a constant speed of 50 km/h, which of the following is the feedback element for the driver?
(a) Clutch (b) Eyes
(c) Needle of the speedometer (d) Steering wheel
(e) None of the above

33. What is correct about detectability?
(a) A system is detectable if all states that cannot be observed decay to zero asymptotically.
(b) A system is detectable if all states that cannot be observed decay to maximum asymptotically.
(c) A system is detectable if all states that cannot be observed decay to minimum asymptotically.
(d) None of the above.

34. The initial response when the output is not equal to the input is called:
(a) Transient response (b) Error response
(c) Dynamic response (d) Either of the above

35. A good control system has all the following features except
(a) good stability
(b) slow response
(c) good accuracy
(d) sufficient power handling capacity

36. In closed loop control system, with positive value of feedback gain the overall gain of the system will
(a) decrease
(b) increase
(c) be unaffected
(d) any of the above

37. _____ has tendency to oscillate.
(a) Open loop system
(b) Closed loop system
(c) Both (a) and (b)
(d) Neither (a) nor (b)

38. In open loop system
(a) the control action depends on the size of the system.
(b) the control action depends on system variables.
(c) the control action depends on the input signal.
(d) the control action is independent of the output.

39. Which of the following statements is not necessarily correct for open loop control system?
(a) Input command is the sole factor responsible for providing the control action.
(b) Presence of non-linearity's cause malfunctioning.
(c) Less expensive.
(d) Generally free from problems of non-linearity's.

40. A control system in which the control action is somehow dependent on the output is known as:
(a) Close loop system
(b) Semi-closed loop system
(c) Open loop system
(d) None of the above

41. In an open loop control system
(a) output is independent of control input.
(b) output is dependent on control input.
(c) only system parameters have an effect on the control output.
(d) none of the above.

42. For an open loop control system which of the following statements is incorrect?
(a) Less expensive
(b) Recalibration is not required for maintaining the required quality of the output
(c) Construction is simple and maintenance easy
(d) Errors are caused by disturbances

43. Which is the correct relation between observable and constructable?
(a) If a system is constructable, then it is also observable.
(b) If a system is observable, then it is also constructable.
(c) Observable and constructable must be together, if one come another must be there.
(d) It depends on other parameters also.

44. What is Simulation of math model meant for
(a) development of a math model, simulate and run it
(b) gets feedback and improve/revise the model
(c) undergoes iterations until adequate findings
(d) all the above together

45. Find out false statement:
(a) A math model builder can perform calculations.
(b) The math model has a memory and scientific blend of capabilities etc.
(c) The math model uses available data only.
(d) Simulation using math model is called "Simulation in the Large".

46. The abstraction process is fundamental to the modeling process
(a) True (b) Probably
(c) False (d) Can't be said

47. Computer simulation has become a useful part of modeling natural systems to gain insight into the operation of below mentioned systems:
(a) Physics, Chemistry and Biology,
(b) Human systems in Economics and Social Science (the Computational Sociology)
(c) Engineering
(d) All of above

48. In below mentioned software (common purpose) packages which is used for modeling and simulation of systems:
(a) ADAMS (b) DYNAST
(c) SIMPACK (d) All the above

49. After reading following statements in math modeling by software, answer the correct option below:
"After selecting the file option from menu the block is drawn by lines and then process is specified."
(a) First and second both steps are correct.
(b First is correct second is incorrect.
(c) First step is incorrect second step is correct.
(d) Both options are incorrect, as program does all.

50. To Model the equation that converts Celsius temperature to Fahrenheit Following is correct:
(a) $T_F = 9/5\ T_C + 32$ (b) $T_F = 9/5 T_C - 32$
(c) $T_F = 5/9\ T_C + 32$ (d) $T_F = 5/9\ T_C - 32$

51. One of the real benefits of modeling and simulation is its ability to accomplish a time and space compression between the interrelationships within a system.
(a) True (b) Probably
(c) False (d) Can't be said

52. Modeling and simulation can provide a way of understanding dynamic complexity.
(a) True (b) Probably
(c) False (d) Can't be said

OOOO

ANSWERS

CONTROL SYSTEMS

1. (a)	2. (b)	3. (d)	4. (a)	5. (b)	6. (a)	7. (c)
8. (b)	9. (d)	10. (d)	11. (d)	12. (c)	13. (a)	14. (a)
15. (c)	16. (a)	17. (c)	18. (d)	19. (c)	20. (b)	21. (b)
22. (b)	23. (c)	24. (b)	25. (c)	26. (b)	27. (b)	28. (b)
29. (a)	30. (a)	31. (c)	32. (c)	33. (a)	34. (a)	35. (b)
36. (a)	37. (b)	38. (d)	39. (b)	40. (a)	41. (a)	42. (b)
43. (b)	44. (d)	45. (c)	46. (a)	47. (d)	48. (d)	49. (a)
50.(a)	51. (a)	52. (a)				